LATINOS IN THE UNITED STATES

History, Law and Perspective

Series Editor

ANTOINETTE SEDILLO LÓPEZ
University of New Mexico
School of Law

Advisory Panel

Tobias Duran, Ph.D.
Cecelia M. Espenoza, J.D.
Paul Finkelman, Ph.D.
Christian Fritz, J.D., Ph.D.
F. Chris Garcia, Ph.D.
Placido Gomez, J.D., LL.M.
Richard Gonzales, J.D.
Emlen Hall, J.D.
Berta Hernandez, J.D.
Eduardo Hernandez-Chavez, Ph.D.
Victor Lopez, J.D.
Jose Martinez, J.D.
Margaret Montoya, J.D.
Michael Olivas, Ph.D., J.D.
Leo Romero, J.D., LL.M.
Christine M. Sierra, Ph.D.
Gloria Valencia-Weber, J.D.

A GARLAND SERIES

SERIES CONTENTS

HISTORICAL THEMES AND IDENTITY
Mestizaje and Labels

LATINA ISSUES
Fragments of Historia(ella)
(Herstory)

CRIMINAL JUSTICE AND
LATINO COMMUNITIES

LATINO EMPLOYMENT, LABOR
ORGANIZATIONS AND IMMIGRATION

LATINO LANGUAGE AND EDUCATION
Communication and the Dream Deferred

LAND GRANTS, HOUSING
AND POLITICAL POWER

VOLUME

5

LATINO LANGUAGE AND EDUCATION

COMMUNICATION AND THE DREAM DEFERRED

Edited with an introduction by
ANTOINETTE SEDILLO LÓPEZ

GARLAND PUBLISHING, INC.
New York & London
1995

Library of Congress Cataloging-in-Publication Data

Latino language and education : communication and the dream
deferred / edited with an introduction by Antoinette Sedillo
López.
    p.   cm. — (Latinos in the United States ; v. 5)
Includes bibliographical references.
ISBN 0–8153–1774–3 (alk. paper)
    1. Hispanic Americans—Education. 2. Language policy—
United States. 3. Education, Bilingual—United States.
I. López, Antoinette Sedillo. II. Series.
LC2669.L38 1995
371.97'68'073—dc20   94–36776
                                               CIP

Printed on acid-free, 250-year-life paper
Manufactured in the United States of America

To my children, Victor Francisco and Graciela Raquel.
Esta colección es tu historia y tu herencia.

CONTENTS

INTRODUCTION

Latinos have lost their language twice. Their ancestors lost their native tongues under the tutelage of Spanish priests and in necessity of interacting in a Spanish public sphere. The first generations to be colonized were probably bilingual, but gradually Spanish became the mother tongue of Latino peoples. Today in the United States, Latinos are experiencing the same demoralizing linguistic process. To participate in the public life of the United States, a command of English is required. Some groups hope to hasten the demise of other languages by participating in the English-only movement. In other nations it is a mark of education and culture to be able to speak another language. In the United States it often seems a badge of shame.

Language and education are related. A child's language is affected by his home and community. His education is influenced by his language, his home and his community. His ability to succeed educationally depends on the school's ability to communicate with the child. Language and education are thus vehicles for Latinos to achieve the American dream. Bilingual education offers hope to children whose primary language is Spanish. Most Latino parents want their children to learn English. Many of them also want their children to retain proficiency in Spanish and to develop intellectually in math, reading and writing while learning English. Because language represents a cultural identity, bilingual education also tends to raise political as well as pedagogical issues. The articles by leading linguists, law professors, historians and education specialists address a broad range of language rights and education issues, including bilingual education.

The tragedy is that Latinos, no matter what the method of instruction, are not faring well in the U.S. educational system. In all educational settings, Latinos trail their Anglo and other minority peers. The articles in this volume demonstrate that Latinos suffer the highest high school dropout rate, tend to do less well on standardized achievement tests, are underrepresented in higher education both as students and as professors and face unique problems in law school and other professional and doctoral programs.

Language

Bill Piatt outlines case law that implies a constitutional right to language. However, the "right" has proven to be illusory. For example, the Supreme Court has upheld "English only" rules in the workplace. Courts have permitted the court process to proceed in a civil case without an interpreter. They have not required that notice of the termination or reduction of welfare benefits be in Spanish. However, default judgments have been set aside for language barriers, and schools may not deny an education to children because of a language barrier. Piatt develops arguments in favor of recognizing a human right to language and proposes a framework for protecting language rights.

Eduardo Hernández-Chávez explores the linguistic implications of native language loss for a community and a culture, specifically among Chicanos. He demonstrates that loss of native language skills is a regular, predictable process and gives examples of common language errors and borrowing as well as other language change patterns. The loss of the language can lead to a loss of identity, self-esteem and sense of community. He proposes revitalization strategies to counteract the devastating effects of language loss. His proposal involves valuing the ethnic language, ensuring sufficient native language interactions so that full language acquisition takes place and actively involving the parents and the community.

Juan Perea discusses the apparent conflict between the Supreme Court's description of a "fundamental right" to language as described in *Meyer v. Nebraska*[1] with the Court's failure to protect language rights in the workplace. He describes the cases on English-only workplace rules and argues that primary language should be protected under Title VII of the Civil Rights Act.

Education

This section of the anthology provides an overview of important educational data and issues. Vilma Ortiz provides statistics concerning the educational attainment of Hispanic youths as compared to non-Hispanic white youth. She reviews literature concerning the intergenerational transmission of socioeconomic status. She compares the educational attainment of first-, second- and third-generation Hispanic youths to that of non-Hispanic white youth. Controlling for family socioeconomic background, she finds that Hispanic youth are educationally disadvantaged compared to non-Hispanic white youth. She draws comparisons between Mexican origin, Puerto Ricans and other Hispanic groups and finds some interesting differences. Generational status and family background proved to be very important in understanding the achievements of Hispanic youth. First-generation Hispanic youth are educationally disadvantaged when controlling for family educational background. However, second-generation Hispanic youth have significantly higher educational achievements than their white peers after controlling for family background. Third-generation educational attainment for Hispanic and non-Hispanic youth did not differ significantly. Thus, education policy should take family background and generational status into account in reaching out to Latino youths.

Rachel Moran's article describes various bilingual educational programs. She uses status conflict analysis to describe how bilingual education supporters and opponents have used language education as a proxy for seeking deference and respect for the status of their culture, customs and values. She outlines the history of bilingual education policy-making at the federal level as well as bilingual education litigation and the "English only" movement. She suggests that bilingual education proponents seek to alter the status order by enhancing respect for their way of life. English only proponents are seeking to defend their traditional place in the status order. This conflict makes bilingual education a cultural battleground and educational needs of the Spanish-speaking children may be neglected.

Guadalupe Salinas examines the results of desegregation efforts on behalf of Mexican-American students in the Southwest. In *Cisneros v. Corpus Christi Independent School District* [2] the court found that Mexican Americans are an identifiable ethnic minority group for desegregation purposes. Salinas elaborates on the reasons for finding that Mexican Americans are an identifiable ethnic minority group and analyzes cases that have sought education remedies for Mexican-American school children. He describes, for example, school districts attempting to satisfy federal laws by integrating Blacks and Mexican Americans in one school and retaining all Anglo students in a separate school. He identifies ability grouping as a concept that segregates children in classrooms within a school.

Guadalupe San Miguel discusses the effect of Mexican-American organizing and the politics of school desegregation in Texas from 1945 to 1980. He describes the role of organizations such as the League of United Latin American Citizens (LULAC), the American G.I. Forum and the Mexican American Legal Defense Fund (MALDEF) in seeking to affect educational policy. He concludes that old Mexican-American organizations have been replaced by new, more aggressive interest groups focused more heavily on litigation. However, while tactics changed, the ideological basis remained constant. Mexican Americans sought solutions to problems and reform rather than challenges to the structure and institution.

Joe Ortega and Peter Roos detail the problems facing Chicanos in the public schools. They discuss segregation of Mexican children, testing and ability grouping, tracking, lack of understanding of Chicano culture and the small numbers of Chicano teachers. They mention textbooks that ignore Chicano contributions and culture and cite studies that show that minority students are subject to more disciplinary action. They outline the needs of non-English-speaking children and the role that bilingual programs should play as well as the need to educate the children of undocumented workers.

Jorge Rangel and Carlos Alcala in 1972 presented a project report on de jure segregation of Chicanos in Texas schools. They report the findings of a ten-month study of Mexican-American educational discrimination in Texas. The study demonstrates that segregation resulted from state action and intent to segregate. The Texas state constitution in 1876 explicitly provided for separate schools for white and "colored" children. Districts thus established "Mexican schools" as early as 1902 and created a pattern of Black, white and Mexican schools. This early pattern of separating children continued through the time of the report. Further, the distribution of Chicano professional staff reveals that Chicano teachers were underrepresented and even more segregated within Chicano schools than the students. The report evaluates the judicial and the administrative response to the segregated system. The article outlines possible strategies for pushing school districts to remedy the segregation while balancing the need for bilingual-bicultural education imbalances in Texas.

Joaquin Avila, in an early speech, describes the Mexican American Legal Defense and Education Fund efforts to address the needs of language minority children. He reviews the major litigation and legislation in which MALDEF has been involved. He also reviews state laws that make bilingual education available for students who need the program. MALDEF has been an active and vigorous proponent of meeting the needs of Latino children.

Anthony J. Cortese presents data on enrollment, persistence and achievement of Mexican Americans in higher education. He compares this data with similar data on other minorities and whites. He finds an acute underrepresentation of Hispanics and blacks enrolled in Carnegie I land grant institutions. They had more erratic persistence patterns and withdrew at high rates. He considers the social context and cultural factors that indicate obstacles to Mexican Americans' success in educational attainment. He calls for curricular changes recognizing the diversity of the minority experience, teacher training on appreciation for diversity and empowerment of the Mexican-American community in the education of their children as well as aggressive affirmative action programs to remedy the situation.

Melba J.T. Vasquez writes of the barriers facing Mexican-American women in higher education. Chicano men tend to receive more support for their educational aspirations than Chicanas. She evaluates how structural barriers such as "ability-grouping" in the public schools, standardized testing and the low socioeconomic status of Chicano parents affect Mexican-American women's pursuit of higher education. She finds that encouragement by their mothers to do well in school is important for Chicanas to succeed in pursuing higher education.

Michael A. Olivas outlines the history of traditionally Indian, Chicano and Puerto Rican colleges, which are in jeopardy and whose identity is at issue. Financial support has consistently been a problem. He calls for a Hispanic initiative and an Indian initiative along the lines of the Black college initiative to value these institutions' role in educating their communities.

Leo Romero, Richard Delgado and Cruz Reynoso describe the unique problems facing Chicano students in law school. They outline the history of law schools beginning to admit and recruit Chicano students. They point out that these schools have an obligation to ensure that these students receive a quality education that will enable them to succeed on the bar examination and as lawyers. They describe programs, such as the Council on Legal Education Opportunity (CLEO) summer program and stipend, which help Chicano law students with the educational and financial demands of law school. They also describe generally shared cultural values that affect Chicanos' law school experiences. From their combined experience in law teaching they identify patterns of Chicanos' responses to law school. They suggest curricular changes and teaching methods and attitudes that can more fully address the needs of Chicano law students.

NOTES

1. 262 U.S. 390 (1923).
2. Civil Action No. 68-C-95 (S.D. Tex., June 4, 1970).

FURTHER READING

Carter, Thomas P., *Mexican Americans in School: A History of Educational Neglect.* New York: College Entrance Examination Board, 1970.

Chapa, Jorge, "The Myth of Hispanic Progress: Trends in the Educational and Economic Attainment of Mexican Americans," 14 *Harvard Journal of Hispanic Policy* 17 (1989–90)

Chused, Richard H., "The Hiring and Retention of Minorities and Women on American Law School Faculties," 137 *University of Pennsylvania Law Review* 537 (1988).

Fishman, James J., and Lawrence Strause, "Case Note, Endless Journey: Integration and the Provision of Equal Educational Opportunity in Denver's Public Schools: A Study of Keyes v. School District No. 1," 32 *Howard Law Journal* 627 (1989).

Gandara, Patricia, "Passing Through the Eye of the Needle: High Achieving Chicanas," 4 *Hispanic Journal of Behavioral Sciences* 167 (1982).

Hernández-Chávez, Eduardo, "Language Policy in the United States: A History of Cultural Genocide." (Forthcoming.)

Keller, Gary D., Rafael Magallan and James R. Deneen, *Assessment and Access: Hispanics in Higher Education.* Albany: State University of New York Press, 1991.

Moran, Rachel F., "The Politics of Discretion: Federal Intervention in Bilingual Education," 76 *California Law Review* 1248 (1988).

Olivas, Michael A., *The Dilemma of Access: Minorities in the Colleges.* Washington: Howard University Press, 1979.

———, *Latino College Students.* New York: Teachers College Press, 1986.

Padilla, Raymond V., *Bilingual Education Technology*. Ypsilanti: Department of Foreign Languages and Bilingual Studies, Bilingual Programs, Eastern Michigan University, 1981.

————,*Theory in Bilingual Education*. Ypsilanti: Department of Foreign Languages and Bilingual Studies, Bilingual Programs, Eastern Michigan University, 1983.

————,*Theory, Technology, and Public Policy on Bilingual Education*. Rosslyn, Va.: National Clearinghouse for Bilingual Education, 1983.

Perea, Juan F., "Demography and Distrust: An Essay on American Languages, Cultural Pluralism, and Official English," 77 *Minnesota Law Review* 269 (1992).

Piatt, Bill, *Only English?: Law and Language Policy in the United States*. Albuquerque: University of New Mexico Press, 1990.

Reynoso, Cruz, Jose Alvarez, Albert F. Moreno, Mario Olmos, Anthony Quintero, and William Soria, "La Raza, The Law and the Law Schools," 1970 *University of Toledo Law Review* 809.

TOWARD DOMESTIC RECOGNITION OF A HUMAN RIGHT TO LANGUAGE

Bill Piatt *

I. INTRODUCTION

To what extent do we have the right, in this country, to express ourselves or receive communications in a language other than English? While there are threads of authority running through our law that appear to provide some answers to this question in several contexts, there is no clearly defined "right to language" in the United States. It is as though the threads have not been woven into the fabric of the law, but rather surface as bothersome loose ends to be plucked off when inconvenient. This Article will examine the existing sources of a right to language, consider why we should be willing to accommodate more than one language, and suggest an analytical framework for the recognition in this country of the human right to language.

II. THE CONFUSING STATE OF DOMESTIC LAW

The notion that there is a constitutionally protected right to express oneself or receive communications in a language other than English is supported by federal court decisions in several contexts.

In *Meyer v. Nebraska,*[1] the United States Supreme Court reversed a conviction of a Nebraska schoolteacher who had been convicted of violating a state statute which prohibited the teaching of any language other than English in any school to a child who had not passed the eighth grade.[2] The Court determined that the right to teach a language and the right of parents to engage a teacher to so instruct their children are among the liberties protected against infringement by the due process clause of the fourteenth amend-

---

* Associate Professor of Law, Washburn University; B.A., 1972, Eastern New Mexico University; J.D., 1975, University of New Mexico. The author gratefully acknowledges the assistance and advice of his colleagues, Myrl L. Duncan and Liaquat Ali Khan.
    1.   262 U.S. 390 (1923).
    2.   *Id.* at 403.

ment.[3] On the same day, and relying upon the *Meyer* decision, the Supreme Court struck down similar statutes in Ohio and Iowa.[4]

Three years later, the Supreme Court again relied on *Meyer* in declaring unconstitutional a Philippine statute which required Chinese merchants to keep their books in English, Spanish, or in a local dialect, thereby prohibiting them from utilizing the only language they understood.[5] The Court found the law invalid "because it deprives Chinese persons—situated as they are, with their extensive and important business long established—of their liberty and property without due process of law, and denies them the equal protection of the laws."[6]

In 1970, it was determined that the sixth amendment's confrontation clause, made applicable to the states through the fourteenth amendment, requires that non English-speaking defendants be informed of their right to simultaneous interpretation of proceedings at the government's expense.[7] The Court determined that

---

3. Mere knowledge of the German language cannot reasonably be regarded as harmful. Heretofore it has been commonly looked upon as helpful and desirable. Plaintiff in error taught this language in school as part of his occupation. His right thus to teach and the right of parents to engage him so to instruct their children, we think, are within the liberty of the Amendment.

Id. at 400.

The Court went on to note:

It is said the purpose of the legislation was to promote civic development by inhibiting training and education of the immature in foreign tongues and ideals before they could learn English and acquire American ideals; and "that the English language should be and become the mother tongue of all children reared in this State." It is also affirmed that the foreign born population is very large, that certain communities commonly use foreign words, follow foreign leaders, move in a foreign atmosphere, and that the children are thereby hindered from becoming citizens of the most useful type and the public safety is imperiled.

That the State may do much, go very far, indeed, in order to improve the quality of its citizens, physically, mentally and morally, is clear; but the individual has certain fundamental rights which must be respected. The protection of the Constitution extends to all, to those who speak other languages as well as to those born with English on the tongue. Perhaps it would be highly advantageous if all had ready understanding of our ordinary speech, but this cannot be coerced by methods which conflict with the Constitution—a desirable end cannot be promoted by prohibited means.

Id. at 401.

4. Bartels v. Iowa, 262 U.S. 404, 409 (1923) (consolidation of *Bartels* with Bohning v. Ohio and Pohl v. Ohio).

5. Yu Cong Eng v. Trinidad, 271 U.S. 500, 528 (1926).

6. *Id.* at 524-25.

7. United States *ex rel* Negron v. New York, 434 F.2d 386, 390-91 (2nd Cir. 1970). The decision served as the impetus for federal statutes requiring interpreters in the federal courts. H.R. REP. No. 95-1687, 95th Cong., 2d Sess. 4, *reprinted in* 1978 U.S. CODE CONG. &

otherwise the trial would be a "babble of voices"[8] with the defendant unable to understand the precise nature of the testimony against him[9] and hampering the capacity of his counsel to conduct effective cross-examination.[10] The Court noted:

> Not only for the sake of effective cross-examination, however, but as a matter of simple humaneness, Negron deserved more than to sit in total incomprehension as the trial proceeded. Particularly inappropriate in this nation where many languages are spoken is a callousness to the crippling language handicap of a newcomer to its shores, whose life and freedom the state by its criminal processes chooses to put in jeopardy.[11]

At least one United States District Court has recognized a constitutional right to bilingual education. In the case of *Serna v. Portales Municipal Schools*,[12] the plaintiffs were Spanish-surnamed minors represented by their parents. They claimed that unlawful discrimination against them resulted from the defendant's educational program tailored to educate a middle-class child from an English-speaking family without regard for the educational needs of the child from an environment where Spanish is the predominant language.[13] The trial court found defendant to have violated the equal protection rights of plaintiffs[14] and ordered, among other remedies, that defendant provide bilingual instruction and seek funding under the federal and state bilingual education acts for that instructional program.[15] On appeal, the Tenth Circuit found that the district court had reached the correct result and affirmed the remedial steps ordered by that court, but it did not reach the equal protection issue. Rather, the court chose to follow the approach adopted by the United States Supreme Court in *Lau v. Nichols*.[16] In *Lau*, Chinese-speaking plaintiffs alleged the public school system denied them an education because the only classes

---

Ad. News 4652-53. *See* 28 U.S.C.S. § 1827a-k (Law. Co-op. Supp. 1985). *See also* the "discretionary" provisions of 18 U.S.C. § 3006A(e) (1982), Fed. R. Civ. P. 43(f), Fed. R. Crim. P. 28(b), and Fed. R. Evid. 604.

8. *Negron*, 434 F.2d at 388.
9. *Id.* at 389.
10. *Id.* at 390.
11. *Id.*
12. 351 F. Supp. 1279 (D.N.M. 1972), *aff'd*, 499 F.2d 1147 (10th Cir. 1974).
13. *Id.* at 1281.
14. *Id.* at 1283.
15. *Id.* at 1283.
16. 414 U.S. 563 (1974).

offered were in the English language.[17] The *Lau* decision found a deprivation of statutory rights under 42 U.S.C. section 2000d (section 601 of Title VI of the Civil Rights Act of 1964) and the regulations of the Health Education and Welfare Department[18] requiring school systems to take remedial steps to rectify language deficiency problems.[19] In *Serna*, the Tenth Circuit adopted the *Lau* approach and affirmed the court-ordered bilingual education plan on statutory grounds,[20] noting the damage suffered by children whose language rights are not respected. This damage included feelings of inadequacy and lowered self-esteem which developed when Spanish-surnamed children came to school and found that their language and culture were totally rejected and that only English was acceptable. The child who goes to a school where he finds no evidence of his language, culture and ethnic group withdraws and does not participate. Such children often demonstrate both academic and emotional disorders, feel frustrated, and express their frustration through lack of attendance, school or community involvement. Their frustrations are further reflected in hostile behavior, discipline problems and eventually dropping out of school.[21]

A tavern's policy against the speaking of "foreign" languages at the bar was held to be unlawful racial discrimination against

---

17. *Id.* at 566.

18. *Id.*

19. *See* Office for Civil Rights Notice, 35 Fed. Reg. 11595 (1970)(stating, "[w]here inability to speak and understand the English language excludes national origin minority group children from effective participation in the educational program offered by a school district, the district must take affirmative steps to rectify the language deficiency in order to open its instructional program to these students.") (clarifying HEW policy on the responsibility of school districts to provide equal educational opportunities to national origin/minority group children deficient in English language skills under Title VI of HEW regulations). Current version at 35 Fed. Reg. 11595 (1970); 45 C.F.R. § 80 (1986). The U.S. Department of Education assumed the responsibility for these matters in 1979. *See* Department of Education Organization Act, 20 U.S.C. § 3401 (1982).

20. *Serna*, 499 F.2d at 1153. Four years after *Lau*, the Supreme Court held that Title VI embodied certain constitutional principles in University of Cal. Regents v. Bakke, 438 U.S. 265, 286 (1978). Whether a constitutional right to bilingual education might be inferred is open to debate. *See* Note, *Proposal: Bilingual Education Guidelines for the Courts and the Schools*, 33 EMORY L.J. 588 (1984). *But cf.* San Antonio Ind. School Dist. v. Rodriguez, 411 U.S. 1, 2 (1973)(education is not a "fundamental" right).

21. *Serna*, 499 F.2d at 1150. Teaching the Spanish-speaking child exclusively in English communicates a powerful message to the child that he or she is a second-class citizen. *See* United States v. Texas, 506 F. Supp. 405, 420 (E.D. Tex. 1981), *rev'd on other grounds*, 680 F.2d 356, 372 (5th Cir. 1982).

Mexican-Americans in *Hernandez v. Erlenbusch*.[22] In disposing of the argument that the English-only rule was justified because non-Spanish-speaking customers were "irritated" by the speaking of the Spanish language, the Court stated:

> Just as the Constitution forbids banishing blacks to the back of the bus so as not to arouse the racial animosity of the preferred white passengers, it also forbids ordering Spanish-speaking patrons to the "back booth or out" to avoid antagonizing English-speaking beer drinkers.
>
> The lame justification that a discriminatory policy helps preserve the peace is as unacceptable in barrooms as it was in buses. Catering to prejudice out of fear of provoking greater prejudice only perpetuates racism. Courts faithful to the fourteenth amendment will not permit, either by camouflage or cavalier treatment, equal protection so to be profaned.[23]

In addition to the recognition of a constitutional "right to language" in the contexts noted above, there may be a first amendment right to receive broadcast programming in languages other than English.[24]

Federal statutes (and accompanying regulations) also provide a guarantee of the exercise of language rights in a number of contexts, including education,[25] court interpreters,[26] employment,[27] and voting rights.[28] Various state constitutional provisions[29] and

---

22. 368 F. Supp. 752 (D.C. Cir. 1973). The court provides this background:
    The events in August 1972 which produced this case took place in a nondescript little tavern in Forest Grove. They involved nothing more—nor less—lofty than the right of some American citizens to enjoy a bottle of beer at the tavern bar and to speak in Spanish while doing so. The fact that the case was brought is indicative that our society has made significant progress in casting off the more overt forms of racial discrimination. The actions in the tavern—and immediately outside—are, however, a sad reminder that significant racially discriminatory attitudes still remain.
    These events furnish a fresh illustration of the truth uttered by President Kennedy a decade ago that ". . . this nation, for all its hopes and all its boasts, will not be fully free until all its citizens are free."
    Id. at 753-54.
23. *Hernandez,* 368 F. Supp. at 755-56.
24. Piatt, *Linguistic Diversity on the Airwaves: Spanish Language Broadcasting and the FCC,* 2 LA RAZA L.J. 101 (1984).
25. Civil Rights Act of 1964, 42 U.S.C. § 2000d (1982); Equal Educational Opportunity Act, 20 U.S.C. § 1703(f)(1982); Bilingual Education Act, 20 U.S.C.S. § 3222 (Law. Co-op. Supp. 1985).
26. Refer to note 7 *supra* and accompanying text.
27. 42 U.S.C. § 2000e-2(a) (1982).
28. Voting Rights Act, 42 U.S.C.S. § 1973b(f) (Law. Co-op. Supp. 1985).
29. *E.g.,* N.M. CONST. art. XX, § 12 (publication of laws in English and Spanish); art.

statutes[30] also afford recognition of language rights.

State courts have invalidated default judgments taken against non-English-speaking litigants[31] and have declared contract provisions unconscionable where a person's lack of English fluency precluded equality of bargaining power.[32]

Numerous scholarly articles have discussed, in differing contexts, aspects of a right to use or receive communications in a "foreign" language.[33]

While the reader, at this point, might conclude that the contours of a generic "language right" emerge from the authorities cited to this point, it is important to recognize contradicting lines

---

XII, § 8 (teachers to learn English and Spanish); art. XIX, § 1 (publication of proposed constitutional amendments).

Some state constitutions prohibit "national origin" discrimination. See ALASKA CONST. art. 1, § 3, and CONN. CONST. art. I, § 20. Protection of language rights under a "national origin" theory is discussed and critiqued *infra*.

LA. CONST. art. I, § 3 provides that no law shall discriminate against a person because of that person's "culture." See the discussion below of the interrelation of language and culture.

But see NEB. CONST. of 1875, art. 1, § 27 (1920)(English declared to be the official language of the state).

30. The statutes are numerous. Many states provide for bilingual education by statute. *E.g.*, ALASKA STAT. §§ 14.30.400-410 (1982); CAL. EDUC. CODE §§ 52160-52186 (West 1978 & Supp. 1986); CONN. GEN. STAT. ANN. §§ 10-17 to 10-17g (West 1977 & Supp. 1985); ILL. ANN. STAT. ch. 122, §§ 14C-1 to -12 (Smith-Hurd Supp. 1985); KAN. STAT. ANN. §§ 72-9501 to 9510 (1985); LA. REV. STAT. ANN. § 17:273 (West 1982); MASS. GEN. LAWS ANN. ch. 71A, §§ 1-9 1978 (West 1985); MICH. COMP. LAWS ANN. §§ 380.1153-.1157 (West Supp. 1985); N.J. STAT. ANN. §§ 18A:35-15 to 26 (West Supp. 1985); TEX. EDUC. CODE ANN. §§ 21.451-.459, .461-.463 (Vernon Supp. 1986); WASH. REV. CODE ANN. §§ 28A.58.800-.810 (West Supp. 1986); WIS. STAT. ANN. §§ 115.95-.996 (West Supp. 1985).

Many states provide for bilingual voting assistance. *E.g.*, N.M. STAT. ANN. ch. 1, art. 1-2-3 (1985); ILL. ANN. STAT. ch. 46, § 24-9 (Smith-Hurd Supp. 1985); D.C. CODE ANN. § 1-1309 (1985).

Court interpreters are required in many states. *See, e.g.*, MD. CTS. & JUD. PROC. CODE ANN. § 9-114 (1984); KAN. STAT. ANN. § 75-4351 (1984).

New Mexico even requires pesticide labels to be printed in Spanish as well as English. N.M. STAT. ANN. § 76-4-4k (1978).

Louisiana requires the teaching of the French language and the culture and history of French populations in its public schools. LA. REV. STAT. ANN. § 17:272 (West 1982).

31. *E.g.*, Cota v. Southern Arizona Bank & Trust Co., 17 Ariz. App. 326, 497 P.2d 833 (1972).

32. *E.g.*, Frostifresh Corp. v. Reynoso, 52 Misc. 2d 26, 274 N.Y.S. 2d 757 (Dist. Ct. 1966), *rev'd as to damages*, 54 Misc. 2d 119, 281 N.Y.S. 2d 964 (N.Y. App. Term 1967).

33. The articles are numerous. *See, e.g.*, in addition to other articles cited herein: Groisser, *A Right to Translation Assistance in Administrative Proceedings*, 16 COLUM. J.L. & SOC. PROBS. 469 (1981); Avila, *Equal Educational Opportunities for Language Minority Children*, 55 U. COLO. L. REV. 559 (1984).

of authority and the illusiveness of this right to language in a number of contexts where litigants have sought to assert it. One such area is the "right" of a bilingual worker to speak a language other than English on the job.

First, let us consider a bit of background. The Equal Employment Opportunity Act prohibits employment discrimination on the basis of race, color, religion, sex, or national origin.[34] Early decisions by the Equal Employment Opportunity Commission (E.E.O.C.) protected language rights at the workplace under the "national origin" pigeonhole,[35] and courts agreed that this category affords such protection.[36] Early cases found in violation of the Act, for example, involved situations where an employer fired a Spanish-surnamed American for supposedly poor work attributed to language difficulties[37] and for company rules prohibiting Spanish language communications among employees.[38] Courts accepted and continue to accept the proposition that employment discrimination based upon language[39] or accent[40] is unlawful discrimination based upon national origin. Courts have also recognized that 42 U.S.C. section 1981 may provide a parallel remedy to the Equal Employment Opportunity Act on this issue.[41]

However, the scope of the right to language on the job is questionable after the decision in *Garcia v. Gloor*.[42] In 1975 Garcia was hired as a salesman by a lumber store in Brownsville, Texas. More than three-fourths of the population in the business area was Hispanic. Many of the store's customers expressed the desire to be waited on by Spanish-speaking salespeople. Garcia was hired precisely because he was bilingual. He was instructed to use English with English-speaking customers and Spanish with Spanish-speaking customers. However, the owner imposed another language rule on Garcia: even though three-fourths of the store's workers and

---

34. 42 U.S.C. § 2000e-2(a) (1982).

35. *See* 29 C.F.R. § 1606 (1985).

36. Jones v. United Gas Imp. Corp., 68 F.R.D. 1 (E.D. Pa. 1975). The Equal Education Opportunity Act, 20 U.S.C. § 1703(f) (1982), explicitly protects language rights under a "national origin" theory. See the critique of this approach in section IV *infra*.

37. 2 FAIR EMPL. PRAC. CAS. (BNA) No. YAU 9-048, at 78 (June 30, 1969).

38. 1973 EEOC Decisions (CCH) No. 71-446 ¶ 6173 (Nov. 5, 1970).

39. Saucedo v. Brothers Well Serv. Inc., 464 F. Supp. 919, 920 (S.D. Tex. 1979).

40. Carino v. University of Okla. Bd. of Regents, 750 F.2d 815, 819 (10th Cir. 1984).

41. Vasquez v. McAllen Bag & Supply Co., 660 F.2d 686, 688 (5th Cir. 1981), *cert. denied*, 458 U.S. 1122 (1982).

42. Garcia v. Gloor, 618 F.2d 264 (5th Cir. 1980), *cert. denied*, 449 U.S. 1113 (1981).

customers spoke Spanish, Garcia and all other Spanish-speaking employees were forbidden from speaking Spanish on the job, unless communicating with a Spanish-speaking customer.[43] Among the reasons given by the owner for this rule was that the English-speaking customers (only one-fourth of the total population in the area), objected to the Spanish-speaking employees communicating in a language which they did not understand.[44] One day Garcia was asked a question by another Spanish-speaking clerk about an item requested by a customer. Garcia responded, in Spanish, that the article was not available. The owner overheard this exchange and fired Garcia. In rejecting Garcia's claim for relief under 42 U.S.C. setion 2000e-2(a), the district court found there were "valid business reasons" for the rule.[45] On appeal, the Fifth Circuit Court upheld the district court, refusing to critically examine either the validity of the "business reasons" offered or whether the business needs could be met in a less restrictive manner than the imposition of an "English-only" rule.[46] The court found Garcia's conduct to be a deliberate violation of the rule, concluding that a language which a bilingual person elects to speak at a particular time is a matter of choice.[47]

The "right to language" has proved illusory in other areas as well. Courts have concluded that the refusal to appoint an interpreter in a civil proceeding does not violate due process,[48] and that Spanish-speaking welfare recipients have no constitutional right to be notified in Spanish of the termination or reduction of their benefits.[49]

---

43. *Id.* at 266.
44. *Id.* at 267.
45. *Id.*
46. *Id.* at 271.
47. *Id.* at 270, 272.
48. Jara v. Municipal Ct., 21 Cal. 3d 181, 578 P.2d 94, 145 Cal. Rptr. 847 (1978), *cert. denied,* 439 U.S. 1067 (1979). The court felt the inquiry should be whether the party had alternative means to secure the relief sought—means other than resort to the trial court itself for aid. The existence of such "alternate means" precludes a claim of a due process or equal protection violation if the court fails to appoint an interpreter at court expense. The harshness of this ruling may be ameliorated in states which, by statute or court rule, appoint interpreters in civil proceedings. *See, e.g.,* KAN. STAT. ANN. §§ 75-4351 to 75-4355 (1984)(providing for interpreters in civil and administrative hearings, as well as in criminal matters).
49. Guerrero v. Carleson, 9 Cal. 3d 808, 512 P.2d 833, 109 Cal. Rptr. 201 (1973), *cert. denied,* 414 U.S. 1137 (1974). The Court relied, in part, on a determination that because English is required for naturalization, English is the national language. There are several problems with this approach. First, it ignores the fact that outside of the context of natural-

The confusing state of our domestic law regarding the right to language might well be illustrated by considering the curious results which follow from applying the principles elicited thus far to the situation of a hypothetical Ms. Martinez. Ms. Martinez is a United States citizen. She works part-time and also receives public assistance for her children. She is bilingual, but her primary language, and that of her school-aged children, is Spanish.

Ms. Martinez is fired from her job one day because some customers complain to her boss that she spoke Spanish to a co-worker in their presence, contrary to the store's "English only" rule. On the way home she stops in the tavern to drink a beer. The same customers are seated in the bar. When Ms. Martinez begins to tell another patron of her problems, in Spanish, the same customers object, this time to the tavern manager. The manager orders Ms. Martinez from the bar.

As it turns out, this just has not been her day. At home she learns of the status of two lawsuits filed against her several months previously by different department stores for failure to pay debts allegedly owed to them. In the first suit, Ms. Martinez had not fully understood the complaint and summons due to her language situation and had thrown them away. Now, the store notifies her it has taken a default judgment against her. Ms. Martinez did not really understand the second complaint and summons either, but tried to answer. Now, she finds, it has been set for trial in a few days. She is very worried because she knows her English is not good enough for her to understand what is going on in court and explain her side of the story to the judge.

Poor Ms. Martinez' troubles are not finished for the day. Her children tell her they have been thrown out of school because their English is so bad they are flunking all their subjects. The day's

---

ization there is no "official" language of this country. Refer to note 100 *infra* and accompanying text. Second, persons seeking naturalization are held to much stricter standards than native born citizens. For example, people who are mentally insane, retarded, or people who are chronic alcoholics or paupers are all excluded from admission into the United States by the immigration laws. 8 U.S.C. § 1182 (1982). Using the immigration laws to infer a national language would make no more sense than using them to infer this country has a national policy opposed to the mentally retarded. Third, even within the naturalization laws themselves, the standards vary. Those immigrants who are at least 50 years old and who have resided in this country for at least 20 years may take the citizenship examination in the language of their choice. 8 U.S.C. § 1423 (1982). Congressman Manuel Lujan, Jr., R-N.M., has recently introduced legislation which would reduce the 20 year residency requirement to five years for persons over 65 years of age. Martinez, *Oportunidad del Congreso Para Hacer Algo Notable,* El Visitante Dominical, Dec. 8, 1985, at 3.

mail also brings word that the welfare assistance she receives for them has been terminated because she failed to provide information required last month by the welfare agency. Ms. Martinez understood neither the request nor the termination notice because they are written in English.

Consider the curious results which obtain from an application of our domestic laws to Ms. Martinez' situation. She would have a cause of action under 42 U.S.C. section 1981 against the bar owner and its customers,[50] and yet her employment termination for exactly the same conduct would be upheld.[51] (Is the right to speak Spanish more sacred in a bar than on the job?)

Regarding her consumer problems, it may be better for her to have ignored the summons and complaint rather than try to answer and appear to defend herself. Courts have set aside default judgments for a language barrier[52] but may not afford her an interpreter at the trial if she attempts to defend.[53]

Ms. Martinez would find, considering her children's situation, that the state could not deny her children an education based upon their language situation.[54] It could, however, because of the language barrier, effectively deny them the food, shelter and medical care necessary to sustain their lives while they try to study.[55]

These are admittedly dramatic, oversimplified applications. They illustrate, however, that we have not thought through whether and why we might choose to respect language differences in this country.

III.   WHY SHOULD WE RECOGNIZE A "RIGHT" TO ANY LANGUAGE OTHER THAN ENGLISH?

It appears to be an unfortunate reality that many monolingual persons in this country feel threatened by the use of a language they do not understand,[56] and exhibit hostility to the concept of

---

50. *Hernandez*, 368 F. Supp. at 755-56.
51. *Garcia*, 618 F.2d at 272.
52. *Cota*, 17 Ariz. App. at 327-28, 497 P.2d at 834-35.
53. *Jara*, 21 Cal. 3d at 186, 578 P.2d at 97, 145 Cal. Rptr. at 850.
54. Refer to notes 12-21 *supra* and accompanying text.
55. Refer to note 49 *supra* and accompanying text.
56. Consider the following:
   A proposed amendment to the Constitution would declare "the English language shall be the official language of the United States" and "neither the United States nor any state shall require . . . the use in the United States of any language other than English." It would prohibit governments from mandating multilingual publi-

legal recognition of the right to use any language other than English.[57] Perhaps part of the explanation for the inconsistent recognition of language rights in this country which we saw in part II of this Article is that monolingual legislators, judges, and attorneys carry, at least subconsciously, some of these same feelings into the decision-making process. Even those courts and legislatures which have taken a more enlightened approach to the recognition of language rights may have never completely expressed or perhaps even understood why the right to maintain their native language would be viewed by people as important, useful, beneficial, and even beautiful. Perhaps an examination at this point, of the sociological and anthropological views of language and culture would be an important digression.

In our day-to-day existence we take language for granted. If we do think about it at all, particularly if we are monolingual, we assume that "it is a vehicle equally fitted to convey any beliefs."[58] Such a view is inconsistent with the studies of Edward Sapir. Sapir, an American linguist, maintained that:

The relation between language and experience is often misunder-

---

cations and from establishing bilingual education as a general entitlement. It would end the pernicious practice of providing bilingual ballots, a practice that denies the link between citizenship and shared culture . . . .

Teddy Roosevelt's life was one long Fourth of July, a symphony of fireworks and flamboyant rhetoric. He embodied the vigor of the nation during the flood tide of immigration. He said: "We have room for but one language here and that is the English language, for we intend to see that the crucible turns our people out as Americans, of American nationality, and not as dwellers in a polyglot boarding house." American life, with its atomizing emphasis on individualism, increasingly resembles life in a centrifuge. Bilingualism is a gratuitous intensification of disintegrative forces. It imprisons immigrants in their origins and encourages what Jacques Barzun, a supporter of the constitutional amendment, calls "cultural solipsism."

Will, *In Defense of the Mother Tongue*, NEWSWEEK, July 8, 1985, at 78.

Several local governments have adopted "English-only" statutes or resolutions. *See* El Hispano (Albuquerque, N.M.), June 28, 1985, at 6. Rio Arriba County, New Mexico, on the other hand, is considering alternating the language used at its County Commission meetings between English and Spanish. *See* Rio Grande Sun (Espanola, N.M.), Jan. 30, 1986, at A10.

57. "[W]ere significant Mexican-American groups to advocate irredentist-like positions, such as open borders or state-recognized official bilingualism, one should expect to see the growth of nativist sentiments on the part of many Americans, who would question the loyalty of Mexican-Americans." Weiner, *Transborder Peoples*, in MEXICAN-AMERICANS IN COMPARATIVE PERSPECTIVE 130, 155 (W. Connor ed. 1985). Note that this country already acknowledges some degree of "official bilingualism" in the circumstances described in part II *supra* of this Article.

58. P. HENLE, LANGUAGE, THOUGHT AND CULTURE 1 (1966).

11

stood. Language is not merely a more or less systematic inventory of the various items of experience which seem relevant to the individual, as is so often naively assumed, but is also a self-contained, creative symbolic organization, which not only refers to experience largely acquired without its help but actually defines experience for us by reason of its formal completeness and because of our unconscious projection of its implicit expectations into the field of experience.[59]

Benjamin Lee Whorf, a student of Sapir, developed Sapir's claim, maintaining that language constitutes a sort of logic, a general frame of reference, and as a result, molds the thoughts of its users. He claimed that significant relationships exist between the general aspects of a language and the characteristics of the culture wherein it developed. Whorf substantiated this thesis by comparing American Indian languages, notably Hopi, with European languages. Whorf found the differences among the European languages so insignificant in comparison to the differences between them and Hopi, that he grouped the European languages together under the title "Standard Average European" (SAE).[60]

The causal relation between language and culture has been documented in many other studies.[61] "Ethnolinguistics" has emerged as a field of study of the role of language in the transmission of culture from one generation to another ("enculturation") and from one culture to another ("acculturation").[62] "Sociolinguistics" is an even more recently emerging field. It considers the differential social roles of various languages co-existing in the same society, the development and spread of auxiliary languages in multilingual situations, the role of language as ethnic identification, and problems of language policy in education.[63] Identifying and studying the causal relationship between language and culture is not to say which influences the other. "Either may be the causal agent, both may be the joint effects of a common cause, or there may be mutual causal action."[64] Nonetheless, it is clear that language and culture are inseparably interrelated. Perhaps the most

---

59. *Id.*

60. *Id.* at 2.

61. R. BURLING, MAN'S MANY VOICES—LANGUAGE IN ITS CULTURAL CONTEXT (1970); BLOUNT & SANCHES, SOCIOCULTURAL DIMENSIONS OF LANGUAGE CHANGE (1977).

62. Greenberg, *The Science of Linguistics, reprinted in,* P. HAMMOND, CULTURAL AND SOCIAL ANTHROPOLOGY 388-97 (1975).

63. *Id.*

64. P. HENLE, *supra* note 58, at 5.

succinct expression of this relationship is that "[t]he world appears different to a person using one vocabulary than it would to a person using another."[65]

People, particularly children, who are denied the right to view the world through their language and culture are made to feel inferior, and they react negatively.[66] Nonetheless, even if there is a

---

65. *Id.* at 7. Henle borrowed a definition of culture as "all those historically created designs for living, explicit and implicit, rational, irrational and nonrational, which exist at any given time as potential guides for the behavior of men." *Id.* at 3, *referring to*, Kluckhohn & Kelly, *The Concept of Culture*, in THE SCIENCE OF MAN IN THE WORLD CRISES 97 (1945). Henle illustrated his conclusion that "world view" is influenced by vocabulary and vice-versa, as follows:

> The Navaho, for example, possess color terms corresponding roughly to our "white," "red," and "yellow" but none which are equivalent to our "black," "grey," "brown," "blue," and "green."
>
> They have two terms corresponding to "black," one denoting the black of darkness, the other the black of such objects as coal. Our "grey" and "brown," however, correspond to a single term in their language and likewise our "blue" and "green." As far as vocabulary is concerned, they divide the spectrum into segments different from ours. It would seem probable that on many occasions of casual perception they would not bother to notice whether an object were brown or grey, and that they would [not] merely avoid discussions as to whether a shade of color in a trying light was blue or green, but they would not even make the distinction.
>
> This example must not be taken as showing that the Navahos are incapable of making color distinctions which are familiar to us. They do not suffer from a peculiar form of color-blindness any more than we do since we lack words for the two sorts of black which they distinguish. The point is rather that their vocabulary tends to let them leave other distinctions unnoticed which we habitually make.
>
> If we are right in claiming an influence of vocabulary on perception, it might be expected that vocabulary would influence other aspects of thought as well. The divisions we make in our experience depend on how we perceive and so would be subject to the same linguistic influence as perception. Once again, one would expect the influence to run in both directions. If, in thinking about the world, one has occasion to use certain ideas, one would expect them to be added to the vocabulary, either directly or through metaphor; this is probably the primary influence. Once the term is in the vocabulary, however, it would constitute an influence both on perception and conception.

Id. at 7-8.

66. Refer to note 21 *supra*. *See also* REYNOSO, COMMUNITY DISPUTE RESOLUTION: HISPANIC CONCERNS, THE ELEMENTS OF GOOD PRACTICE IN DISPUTE RESOLUTION 215 (1985):

> High on the agenda of most Hispanic groups are the issues of bilingualism or multilingualism and biculturalism or multiculturalism. They believe that in a country as great as ours all people have a right to their own ethnicity, their own language. These rights are based in the Constitution of this country. So when there is an effort by others to take away that right there is resentment. The resentment doesn't always rise to the level of a conflict.

Id.

See also Piatt, *Linguistic Diversity on the Airwaves: Spanish Language Broadcasting and the FCC*, 1 LA RAZA L.J. at 112-13 (1984)(rejection of culture and language at school

link between language and culture and even if people feel bad or inferior if we force them to set their language and culture aside to join the "melting pot," the United States is a predominantly English-speaking country. For their own good, should not all people in this country be required to adopt the majority language and set any other aside in order to be successful here?

No one would seriously challenge the fact that English is the predominant language in this country; that social and economic pressures require one to acquire a good command of the language in order to become successful.[67] It does not follow, though, as a matter of logic and as demonstrated by empirical research, that the native speaker of a language other than English should be officially stripped of his or her tongue in order to obtain English proficiency[68] and resultant socio-economic success.[69] Human beings ap-

---

results in serious academic and emotional problems for Hispanics, particularly children).

67. Cultural and societal forces in the United Kingdom and the United States, in particular, have pushed nonnative English speakers who have come to these countries as immigrants, refugees, or migrant workers to learn English so that they might move into the work force and achieve acceptance in the society beyond their own communities. In modern times, no official national-level policies mandate English; the status of English has been achieved in these countries without official declaration or the help of an official language academy. For speakers of other languages, the primary mandate for English has come from societal forces working on an individual's desire to secure education and employment, move into English-speaking social circles, and negotiate daily interactions with the bureaucratic and commercial mainstream.

Heath, *Language Policies: Patterns of Retention and Maintenance*, in MEXICAN-AMERICANS IN COMPARATIVE PERSPECTIVE 259 (W. Connor ed. 1985).

68. These research findings [in second language acquisition] also bear on the advocacy of maintenance bilingual programs. Such goals for bilingual education are not in conflict with so-called "mainstream" American ideals, since fully functional bilingualism can be attained at no expense to English. Research shows that it is wrong to think of the two languages of the bilingual in competition for limited mental space (an old view deriving from empiricist notions about language). Rather, they are interdependent and build upon each other. Recent research on the effects of a developed bilingualism in children shows that they enjoy not only the benefits of knowing two languages and literatures, but added cognitive skills and awareness about language as well. We have successfully debunked the long-held belief, rooted in work at the turn of the century on the intelligence of immigrants, that bilingualism results in the mental confusion. Should we choose to value the resources of the non-English languages with which the language minority students come to school, we need only to continue providing these students instruction in their native language even as they progress in English.

Hakuta & Campbell, *The Future of Bilingual Education*, COSSA Washington Update, Consortium of Social Science Associations (Mar. 22, 1985).

69. While the acquisition of English proficiency clearly facilitates the process of socioeconomic achievement among Hispanic men, there is no basis for assuming that bilingual education programs which encourage retention of Spanish among

parently have the capacity and the desire to alternatively view the world through different languages and cultures.

In addition to these philosophical responses, there are some very practical reasons why this country should choose to recognize some degree of "official bilingualism,"[70] at least as regards the Spanish language. While studies in this country have shown that during the first half of this century most European immigrant groups did not pass on their language intergenerationally, Spanish is an exception.[71] One study estimates that in 1985 there were 13,191,300 Spanish speakers in this country, representing almost a fourfold increase from the 3.3 million Spanish speakers in 1960.[72] A number of factors suggest that Spanish will be maintained as an important second language in this country.[73]

Hispanics will necessarily retard their socioeconomic success. Our results suggest that foreign-born workers could improve their occupational status by participating in bilingual education programs, although it is unclear how much emphasis must be placed on improving English language skills and how much should be devoted to teaching basic skills in reading, arithmetic, and communication in order to produce desired outcomes. We hasten to add that participation in bilingual education programs should not be geared to eliminate the use of Spanish, for among the native-born who tend to have a better command of English, Spanish bilingualism does not depress socioeconomic achievement. Thus, the persistent dilemma for policy analysts is assuring that ethnic populations acquire sufficient proficiency in English to equip them for successful labor market experiences while not forcing the loss of native languages. In other words, the ultimate challenge for bilingual education programs is one of balancing the pressures of assimilation and ethnic pluralism.

M. Tienda & L. Neidert, *Language, Education, and the Socioeconomic Achievement of Hispanic Origin Men,* in THE MEXICAN AMERICAN EXPERIENCE 374 (1985).

70. The extent of this recognition will be discussed in part IV *infra.*

71. Macias, *National Language Profile of the Mexican-Origin Population in the United States,* in MEXICAN-AMERICANS IN COMPARATIVE PERSPECTIVE 285, 306 (W. Connor ed. 1985).

72. *Id.* at 287.

73. Gaarder presents nine variables, or characteristics, of Spanish speakers that he feels will support Spanish-language maintenance in the United States: (1) the length of time Spanish speakers, as indigenous groups, have been in the United States prior to Anglos and other Euro-Americans, (2) the large size of the Spanish-speaking population, (3) the relative homogeneity of the Spanish speakers, (4) constant in-migration of other Spanish speakers to reinforce the domestic population, (5) cultural access to and renewal from the hinterland (Mexico, Puerto Rico, Latin America), (6) intergenerational stability of the extended family of Spanish speakers, (7) religio-societal isolation among Spanish speakers, (8) present-day tolerance of cultural diversity in the United States, and (9) the relative isolation and hence linguistic solidarity of the Spanish-speaking group.

Gaarder argues from the previous experiences of language groups in the United States and elsewhere, but others suggest that some of the variables he has identified as supporting language maintenance actually have not done so. For example, Kloss, in his discussion of German in the United States, classifies the large

Another very practical reason to encourage maintenance of "foreign" language is that our ignorance of them is a "crippling factor" in dealing with other nations.[74] Our schools are failing to produce functional bilinguals through their foreign language programs.[75] Encouraging our bilingual citizens to maintain their linguistic diversity may produce the very beneficial result that the majority population will acquire some second-language skills, as well as a multicultural outlook from the bilingual population.[76]

---

size of a language group, in and of itself, as an ambivalent (rather than supporting) factor for language maintenance.

One way of exploring this question is to compare Spanish speakers with other language groups in the United States in order to identify similarities and differences. The configuration or simultaneous occurrences of variables also may be important. In addition to the factors just listed, I suggest the following for consideration:

First, Spanish speakers in the United States are the northern-most segment of more than 200 million Spanish speakers in Latin America. This is an additional factor in the historical contiguity between the domestic Spanish speakers and their "country of origin."

Second, unlike the situation among turn-of-the-century immigrants, the linguistic diversity among present-day immigrants is low. As the number of persons from Spanish-speaking countries increases and they swell the barrios of U.S.-born Spanish speakers, the linguistic diversity continues to be low but the numbers of bilingual and monolingual Spanish speakers are increasing.

Third, the historical continuity of Spanish speakers in their primary settlement areas continues (the southwestern United States and Puerto Rico), but their spread or migration to other parts of the United States has given the Spanish-speaking population a national character.

Fourth, there is an intergenerational commingling, partly from the continuing inmigration and partly from internal migration.

Fifth, the development of an institutional language infrastructure has continued. For example, in the schools, bilingual schooling has increased and Spanish continues to be the most popular "foreign language" in high schools and colleges. Language issues have forced the strict enforcement of voting rights and judicial due process (court interpreters are now required) for persons who speak little or no English. The Spanish-language mass media—particularly broadcast media—continue to grow; they have been characterized as the "fifth network." Chicano literature is experiencing a resurgence in Spanish.

Id. at 307-308.

74. "The failure to communicate with foreigners in their own language prevents them from understanding us as we really are. It makes it difficult for us to project our real purposes to other people." Vernon Walters, U.S. Ambassador to the United Nations, U.S. NEWS & WORLD REP., June 15, 1985, at 31.

75. Refer to Hakuta & Campbell, *supra* note 68.

76. According to a 1985 survey by the Strategy Research Corporation, 41% of non-Hispanics living in the Miami, Florida, area now believe that for their children to succeed, it is essential for them to read and write Spanish. Sixty percent said they enjoy socializing with Latino friends. Ericksen, *Assimilation is Working in Miami—In Reverse*, El Perico (Kansas City, Mo.), Aug. 1985, at 10.

This in turn could only help us in our international relations, particularly with our Latin American neighbors to the south.

IV. Toward Recognition of a Right to Language

Assuming that we wish to recognize some legal protection and recognition of a right to language, the problem is to develop an analytical framework that fairly takes into account legitimate societal needs and the rights of the individual who speaks a language other than English.

As a first step, this writer would abandon the concept which forces protection of language rights into the "national origin" pigeonhole.[77] The real interests we seek to protect when we afford some language protection appear to be the individual's rights to: 1) view the world through his or her own language and culture, and 2) not be shut off from the exercise of some fundamental legal right or the satisfaction of some basic human need because of a language barrier.[78] Many of those individuals whose language rights we would protect are native-born United States citizens. Using a "national origin" fiction is thus analytically unsound, and may perpetuate the fear of some monolingual persons that the use of a language other than English is "foreign."[79] Also, this writer would urge abandonment of limiting language protection under the theory that because language is "mutable", the right to its exercise should inherently be limited, at least as regards bilinguals.[80] The exercise of the choice of a "world view" through the eyes of a religion is protected, although clearly such a choice is mutable.[81]

---

77. Refer to notes 35, 36 *supra* and accompanying text. *See also* Note, *A Trait-Based Approach to National Origin Claims Under Title VII*, 94 Yale L.J. 1164 (1985).

78. Refer to text *supra*, parts II and III.

79. Throughout this Article, the writer has consciously avoided referring to languages other than English as "foreign languages." While it may be easier to refer to any language other than English as "foreign," any language in use in this country cannot be "foreign" to its native speakers. This is particularly true in the case of the Spanish language which was in use in what is now the southwest United States long before English was spoken there. For an historical summary, *see* Harvard Encyclopedia of American Ethnic Groups 700-19 (Thernstrom ed. 1980). On a personal level, the author cannot bring himself to classify the Spanish language, which he learned in this country through family, social contacts, and in the school systems, as a "foreign" language.

80. *Garcia*, 618 F.2d at 270. *See* Note, *Garcia v. Gloor: Mutable Characteristics Rationale Extended to National Origin Discrimination*, 32 Mercer L. Rev. 1275 (1981). The author of that article would allow an employer to restrict bilingual language choices but under a "job relatedness" standard rather than under a "mutable-immutable" rationale.

81. *Garcia*, 618 F.2d at 269. The United Nations Charter, to which the United States

The existing, patchwork protection of language rights should be replaced with an analysis that can be summarized as follows:

1. Where, because of a language barrier, an individual is denied the exercise of a fundamental legal right or denied access to a basic human need, society would recognize "limited official bilingualism" in order to allow access to the right or the need;

2. Where circumstances require communications in one standard language understood by the majority, for the immediate safety of persons or property, society would recognize "limited official monolingualism";

3. In the vast majority of other communications, individuals would be free to utilize any language of choice, and society would provide a remedy for infringement of that right.

Having sketched the outline, let us turn to filling it in.

A. Limited Official Bilingualism

Courts have demonstrated proficiency in identifying Bill of Rights guarantees so fundamental to the American scheme of justice so as to apply to the states via the due process clause of the fourteenth amendment.[82] They have also been able to identify, among others, the right to travel,[83] the right to vote,[84] and the right to properly defend oneself in criminal proceedings,[85] as fundamental interests for equal protection purposes. Where the exercise of such a right is prohibited by one's poverty, courts have determined that the right or interest is so fundamental that society should provide assistance so that the right can be exercised.[86] Similarly, courts and legislatures have implicitly recognized that there are some fundamental rights, such as the right to confront wit-

---

is a party, identifies one of the purposes of the U.N. to be that of "promoting and encouraging respect for human rights and for fundamental freedoms for all without distinction as to race, sex, language, or religion." 59 Stat. 1033, 1037 (1945).

82. Benton v. Maryland, 395 U.S. 784 (1969).

83. Shapiro v. Thompson, 394 U.S. 618 (1969).

84. Harper v. Virginia Bd. of Elections, 383 U.S. 663 (1966).

85. *E.g.*, Tate v. Short, 401 U.S. 395 (1971)(indigent convicted of offenses punishable by fine only cannot be incarcerated to satisfy fines); Douglas v. California, 372 U.S. 353 (1963) (indigents entitled to state-provided appellate counsel); Griffin v. Illinois, 351 U.S. 12 (1956)(indigents entitled to state-provided trial transcript for use on appeal).

86. *E.g.*, Argersinger v. Hamlin, 407 U.S. 25 (1972); Gideon v. Wainwright, 372 U.S. 335 (1963)(indigent has right to state-provided counsel in criminal matters, and, absent a knowing waiver, may not be imprisoned for any offense unless represented by counsel).

nesses at a criminal trial[87] or the right to vote,[88] which cannot effectively be exercised by a person who does not understand the process due to a language barrier. In such cases, society provides interpreters or bilingual materials to allow the exercise of the right.

Courts and legislatures should continue the process of identifying the fundamental legal rights which should not be foreclosed to persons with a language barrier. Where such a right is identified, society should provide bilingual assistance where the right would otherwise be foreclosed to persons with limited English proficiency.

One area where the right should be extended immediately is in the civil courts and before administrative bodies. The relative financial interests at stake (for example, tenant eviction proceedings or hearings to terminate public assistance) may be greater than in relatively minor criminal proceedings. We choose not to allow our criminal courts to be a "babble of voices."[89] We may have the right to maintain business records in an understandable language.[90] Why should not litigants in civil and administrative proceedings be afforded more than the facade of justice that may now exist for those not completely proficient in English?[91]

There are needs which, although not categorized by our system of jurisprudence as "fundamental rights," would nonetheless be recognized by us as basic to our survival and advancement as a species. Among these would be the need for food and shelter, and a basic education.[92] Where a human being in our society would oth-

---

87. Refer to notes 7-10 *supra* and accompanying text.

88. Refer to Voting Rights Act, *supra* note 28.

89. *Negron*, 434 F.2d at 390-91.

90. *Yu Cong Eng.*, 271 U.S. at 500-01.

91. A study conducted on behalf of the Director of the Administrative Office of the United States Courts pursuant to the Court Interpreters Act of 1978, 28 U.S.C. § 1827 (1982), found that because of the sophisticated language level used in the courts, it is necessary to have a minimum of fourteen years of education to understand the proceedings of a criminal trial and still more to understand a civil trial. *See* Seltzer v. Foley, 502 F. Supp. 600, 604 (S.D.N.Y. 1980).

92. *See* MASLOW, TOWARD A PSYCHOLOGY OF BEING 199-200 (1962).

Basic need gratification is too often taken to mean objects, things, possessions, money, clothes, automobiles and the like. But these do not in themselves gratify the basic needs which, after the bodily needs are taken care of, are for (1) protection, safety, security, (2) belongingness, as in a family, a community, a clan, a gang, friendship, affection, love, (3) respect, esteem, approval, dignity, self-respect and (4) freedom for the fullest development of one's talents and capacities, actualization of the self. This seems simple enough and yet few people anywhere in the world seem able to assimilate its meaning. Because the lowest and most urgent needs are material, for example food, shelter, clothes, etc., they tend to generalize this to a chiefly materialistic psychology of motivation, forgetting that

erwise be entitled to have these needs met by means of public assistance or public education, society should allow the person with a language barrier access to them. In the case of public assistance, we should provide interpreters to assist with the application process and through any administrative hearings that are otherwise available. In the case of public education, given the profound negative impact upon children whose language and culture are rejected by monolingual institutions,[93] we should recognize a right to bilingual education.

Acknowledging a "right" to bilingual education would undoubtedly be controversial. The United States Secretary of Education has recently made bitter attacks upon the concept.[94] Yet, the self-image and future success of our children is profoundly affected by the majority's acceptance or non-acceptance of their language and culture. We should utilize their language skills and thought processes to foster intellectual development while simultaneously assisting them in obtaining English language proficiency. It should not be necessary for them to sacrifice their rich native language, culture, and self-esteem in order to participate in the educational system and in society.[95] We cannot afford, at this late date, to return to punishing our children for viewing the world through their language and culture.[96]

Implementing this move to "limited official bilingualism" would require overhaul of legislative enactments and judicial precedents. Undoubtedly, it would be costly.[97] The same things

---

there are higher, non-material needs as well which are also "basic."

93. Refer to note 21 *supra* and accompanying text.

94. Address by William J. Bennett to Association for a Better New York (Sept. 26, 1985). *See also* BARKER, *Bennett's Be Initiative: A Deceitful Step in the Wrong Direction,* LA VOZ DEL LLANO, KAN. ADV. COMM. ON MEX. AM. AFF., Jan. 1986, at 1.

95. Excerpt from New York State Regents Position Paper on Bilingual Education, *reprinted in, Position Paper on the Role of English as a Second Language in Bilingual Education,* Georgetown University. *See also* UNESCO, *The Use of Vernacular Languages in Education* (1953), *reprinted in,* Baral, *Second Language Acquisition Theories Relevant to Bilingual Education,* in THEORY, TECHNOLOGY, AND PUBLIC POLICY ON BILINGUAL EDUCATION (1983).

96. Many Hispanics recall days when they were punished, often physically, for speaking Spanish at school. *See* Guzman, *Dando Fin a las Angustias del Pasado,* El Visitante Dominical, Nov. 10, 1985, at 8. *See also* Reynoso, *supra* note 66, at 215. Instatement of "English-only" in the schools would implicitly mean some discipline would be imposed upon those children who could not or would not comply.

97. *See* Carmona v. Sheffield, 325 F. Supp. 1341 (N.D. Cal. 1971). Since *Carmona,* the United States court system has adopted and implemented guidelines for the certification and use of interpreters. Refer to note 6 *supra.* The wheel would not have to be reinvented:

can be said, however, of the recognition of a right to state-provided transcripts or attorneys for indigents facing the criminal process. In those cases courts identified the right as fundamental, knowing that additional economic burdens would be placed on the state. The duty to alleviate the deprivation of rights which cannot be exercised because of a language barrier has been held to be clear and compelling, notwithstanding that there may be practical problems to overcome in providing complete and effective relief.[98]

B. Limited Official Monolingualism

There are circumstances where communication in English in this country should be required. Allowing airplane pilots, for example, to communicate with each other and the ground in any language of choice could be inherently dangerous to person and property. There are other communications, such as traffic signs or emergency communications which society should require to be made in the majority language to protect persons and property from the immediate risk of harm. Similarly, although not on the "emergency" level, employers should be free to require their employees to communicate with potential customers in the language of the customer's choice to facilitate commerce and protect the employer's property interest in the business. In recognizing "limited official monolingualism," society should place the burden on the proponent of the enforced monolingualism to demonstrate that the danger to person or property outweighs the individual right to expression before imposing the use of the language. "Irritation" by monolingual customers or other third parties would be insufficient justification for the imposition of the majority language.[99]

C. Language of Choice in Other Circumstances

In the vast range of remaining communications, government would adhere to its tradition of adopting no official language nor

---

interpreters certified in federal courts could be utilized in administrative proceedings without the cost of training and certification. Libraries across the country now have access to information regarding educational materials in languages other than English. *See* Valentine, *Minority Language Selection: Helping Ourselves to Help Others*, WILSON LIBR. BULL. at 26-29 (Jan. 1986).

98. United States v. Texas, 506 F. Supp. at 437-438.

99. *Hernandez*, 368 F. Supp. at 752. *Cf.* Diaz v. Pan American World Airways, Inc., 442 F.2d 385 (5th Cir. 1971)(customer preference for female stewardesses insufficient justification for refusal to hire men for same jobs).

denying personal liberties in language selection.[100] Courts would provide a remedy for private interference with language use, consistent with *Hernandez.*[101]

V. Conclusion

It is time to recognize a human right to language in this country. The analysis presented in this article could serve as a starting point. We should reject attempts to adopt an "English-only" constitutional amendment.[102] Such an amendment, if adopted, would immediately return our criminal courts, for many people, to a "babble of voices," would disenfranchise many of our voters, would impose second-class status and feelings of inferiority upon many of our children, and would signal the other nations of the world that we are not yet ready to join them in an attempt to appreciate any world view other than our own.

---

100. Following the Anglo-Saxon tradition of considering language choice the responsibility of the individual, the United States has maintained the English custom of not regulating language officially or of denying personal liberties in language through federal policies. In spite of several efforts in the colonial and early national periods to establish an academy of language to formulate policies and standards of language use, the United States consistently turned down such proposals from both political officials and citizens. Since the nineteenth century some states and local communities have tried to promote a monolingual tradition and to emphasize standard English as the mark of reason, ethics, and aesthetics, but the federal government has formulated no official language policy.

Heath, *Language Policies: Patterns of Retention and Maintenance, supra* note 67 at 266.

Attempts to establish a national language academy are traced in Heath, *A National Language Academy: Debate in the New Nation,* 11 INT'L J. OF THE SOC. LANGUAGE 9-44 (1976).

101. Refer to note 22 *supra* and accompanying text.

102. Refer to note 56 *supra.*

Chapter 4

Native Language Loss and Its Implications for Revitalization of Spanish in Chicano Communities

Eduardo Hernández-Chávez

The loss of first language skills by native speakers of Spanish is a problem that, until recently, has received scant attention either in the linguistics literature or among educators of language minority students. Large numbers of Chicano children and young people from Spanish-speaking families either no longer learn the language or acquire but a limited facility in it. As a result, patterns of communication are disrupted, cultural and social structures break down, and youth become alienated from their communities. The institutional processes that lead to native language loss are well established, and the shift to English is very far along in many Chicano communities. Responsible for these conditions are the truly rapid changes in American society in recent decades involving urbanization, technological growth, and the spread of mass culture. Additionally, many educational and governmental policies are driven directly by social and political philosophies whose ultimate aims are the linguistic and cultural assimilation of ethnic minorities.

In this chapter, I will first provide an overview of language loss processes and will then discuss the linguistic manifestations of loss among Chicanos, the relationship of loss to language acquisition and use, the sociocultural mechanisms that give it shape, and its effects on individuals and society. In the final section I will discuss some of the implications of these concepts for educators, especially bilingual educators and teachers of Spanish for native speakers.

The Loss of Language

Much existing research on language loss has been concerned with the attrition of language skills by learners of a foreign or second language after varying periods away from formal study. Considerable work has also been done among aphasics, persons who have undergone partial or complete loss of linguistic functioning due to some physical trauma. (Studies on second language loss in Spanish include Pratella, 1970, and Cohen, 1974. For a sampling of relevant research on bilingual aphasia, see Paradis, 1977; Albert and Obler, 1978; and Galloway, 1978.) Among normal populations, loss of first or native language has, until fairly recently, been studied largely in sociolinguistic contexts in which the language varieties themselves are dying. This research on 'language death' includes studies on Irish (Breatnach, 1964), Biloxi (Haas, 1968), Scots Gaelic (Dorian, 1978, 1981), Tlaxcalan Náhuatl (Hill and Hill, 1977), and Aravanitka Albanian (Trudgill, 1976–77), among others. Recently, a number of researchers have investigated native language loss in different ethnic group contexts in the United States, such as Saltrelli, 1975a; and Henzl, 1977. A few studies have begun to focus on the progressive decrease in Spanish proficiency by Chicano speakers (Saltarelli, 1975b; Ostyn, 1972; Merino, 1983; Silva-Corvalán, 1983a, 1983b, 1986, 1988; Gutiérrez, 1990; Ocampo, 1990; and Hernández-Chávez, 1990a, 1990b, 1990c). For a compendium of studies on language loss see Williamson (1982).

The loss processes described by these investigators have been observed in mostly cross-generational studies. In general, they find that the first, or immigrant generation, is monolingual or highly dominant in Spanish and evinces a proficiency fully comparable to that of native speakers in any other Spanish-speaking region. As subsequent generations become increasingly proficient in English, they tend also to become progressively less proficient in Spanish, a situation described by Silva-Corvalán (1988) as the 'bilingual continuum.'

It should be noted that it is not generation of residence in the US *per se* that is the key variable in explaining language loss. Silva-Corvalán, for example, has conducted a number of studies investigating the effects of bilingualism among three different generations of Mexican Americans in Los Angeles. In a recent report on this project (Silva-Corvalán, 1988), she notes that some of her Generation III speakers, who have been in the US the longest, retained more Spanish than some Generation II speakers. Also, there exist numerous communities, especially in New Mexico but also throughout the Southwest, where Chicanos have lived for many generations, not just three or four. Until fairly recent times, most of these communities have maintained a stable bilingualism, and loss has been minimal. We need to look for other factors — rapid social change comes to mind — that, together with patterns of inter-generational transmission of language, account for language loss.

In the decline of native language proficiency from one generation to the next, the more complex linguistic structures, which are learned late in normal acquisition, *fail to be learned* and are thus lost. It is also entirely possible that, at lower levels of proficiency, previously acquired structures might *actually be forgotten* by particular individuals. However, in cross-generational studies, the forgetting of structures, once they are learned, would be extremely difficult to ascertain.

The direct investigation of language forgetting requires the study of loss in the same individuals over time. One of the studies reviewed for this paper, Merino (1983), was conducted in this way with a group of kindergarten to fourth grade children in a bilingual education program. In a longitudinal portion of the study, Merino retested the children after a two-year lapse. She found that not only did most of the children fail to progress, but some 50 per cent actually *forgot* some of the structures they had learned previously.

As with the cross-generational studies, the lost structures are those, such as the subjunctive and relative clauses, that are normally acquired late. This gives some support to the notion that forgetting involves processes that are a 'mirror image' of those of acquisition (Bailey, 1973; cited in Merino, 1983; Silva-Corvalán, 1990). However, in Merino's data, not all of the structures lost, such as the past tense, are late-acquired forms, so at least some other processes are operating as

59

well. Preliminary results from one of my own studies among Spanish speakers in New Mexico (Hernández-Chávez, 1990a) are suggestive in this regard. Such strategies may be involved as the elimination of redundancy (for example, the indirect object marker *a* in *Mi abuela le daba un ataque de corazón*) or the restructuring of certain semantic contrasts like the use of *estar* instead of *ser* with predicate nouns to indicate change of status (for example, *Cuando ya yo nací, yo creo que [él] ya estaba panadero*). Additionally, this study shows that the borrowing of structures from English may also violate the mirror image hypothesis. Thus, *Yo fui nacida en Las Vegas, Nuevo México* seems clearly to be a calque on the English passive of 'I was born in Las Vegas, New Mexico.' And *Muy limpiecita viejita* uses the English word order of 'A very clean little old lady.' In all these cases, the changed structures demonstrate a pattern of loss, yet they involve less advanced structures than some which are retained. Thus, the linguistic processes of loss, though clearly related to acquisition processes, are seen to be fairly complex.

Language loss exhibits important differences between speaking and comprehension proficiencies, also observed by Merino (1983). Speaking performance in Spanish dropped sharply, especially by grade four, but comprehension showed no change across the grades. She suggests that comprehension may be more resistant to loss. This is consistent with language acquisition research which has shown that comprehension normally precedes and is superior to speaking performance (see Fraser, Bellugi, and Brown, 1963). Merino's findings also receive confirmation from the experience and common knowledge within Chicano communities that, even where speaking skills are almost entirely lost, comprehension may be quite active.

Although the studies reviewed focus mainly on the grammatical system, loss may occur differentially in any of the various linguistic skills. Beside the differences just noted in comprehension and production, loss may occur in discourse skills, the lexicon, and presumably phonology as well. Silva-Corvalán (1988), observes that preferential use of particular grammatical structures correlates with certain parts of narratives. Thus, only the most proficient speakers used direct quotations or the historical present as evaluative devices (that is, certain constructions or types of expressions that create or maintain a high level of interest as, for example '*Ven a la casa*', *me dice*. 'Come over to the house', she tells me.) Speakers in the second and third generations will also tend to produce narratives that are much less fluent in their delivery than first generation speakers.

Silva-Corvalán (1983a and b) also observes, along with Koike (1987), that where fully developed evaluative devices are not available in narratives because of loss, speakers will often code-switch to English when using Spanish. On the other hand, in a recently completed study of the role of New Mexican Spanish (Hernández-Chávez, 1990c), I found that, while gaps in vocabulary do trigger some switches among English-dominant speakers, a more common occasion for lexical and phrasal switching was cultural content. Words and phrases referring to activities or events most generally experienced in English and in the dominant culture (for example, school, work, commerical transactions) would tend to trigger switches to English — even though the relevant vocabulary is familiar to the speaker. The more a speaker had contact with Anglo-American activities, the greater the reliance on code-switching in speaking of those contexts. Nevertheless, lexical skills are most certainly an important aspect of language loss, either through failure to acquire certain vocabulary or through forgetting.

60

We have little evidence of loss in phonological systems, though much of what has been called interference may, in fact, be loss in relation to monolingual community norms. Indeed, experience by members of the Chicano community indicates that certain distinctions such as *r:rr* tend to accompany other forms of loss and are interpreted by community members as indicating diminished proficiency.[1]

As suggested above, any of these forms of loss implies a fully developed norm. This norm cannot be some idealized standard described in handbooks nor even a widely accepted spoken standard. Were this the case, monolingual speakers of regional or social class varieties of the language might be deemed to have undergone language loss if, in their variety, certain distinctions were no longer made. Thus, it cannot be considered loss if a Spanish speaker fails to use the future subjunctive (e.g., *viniere* 'will perhaps come') or the preterite perfect, (e.g., *hubo llegado* 'had once arrived') found only in certain frozen expressions and as archaic literary forms. Similarly, speakers of non-standard varieties are not necessarily losing Spanish if they use periphrastic constructions in the place of the tense functions of the inflected future or conditional, (*voy a volver* 'I am going to return' instead of *volveré* 'I will return') or if they use the imperfect for the past subjunctive in certain constructions (e.g., *Le ofreciera trabajo si podía* [<*si pudiera*.].

Such differences from other forms of Spanish may represent autonomous changes or changes due to cultural or social factors rather than to loss (Sánchez, 1983). At the same time, for Chicanos, it is striking that such forms are found mainly in native-born speakers who demonstrate other characteristics of loss, so it is not a straightforward matter to distinguish loss from dialectal variation or from change across generations. The principal criterion must be the language proficiency of monolingual or Spanish dominant speakers within the community in question. The assumption is that such speakers are fully proficient in the language and that differences from other varieties are dialectal in nature. Changes among English-dominant speakers not shared by the Spanish-dominant speakers in the same community would then be considered strong indications of language loss.

Linguistic Processes in Loss

The research on language loss uniformly demonstrates that loss of native language skills, far from being random or idiosyncratic, is a highly regular process. Indeed, it can be seen as obeying certain general principles found in other dynamic systems of language such as language acquisition, sociolinguistic variation, and historical change. Thus, for example, Henzl (1977, cited in Merino, 1983), in her study of four generations of Czech-Americans undergoing loss will *regularize* certain case endings where alternate forms are normally used with different classes of nouns. In language acquistion, children use similar processes of regularization, not only with case systems but also with irregular tense or number markings. For example, at certain stages in the acquisition of English, children will use forms like *goed* for *went* and *mans* for *men*. At other stages they will simplify redundant marking, as where gender is marked on both articles and nouns. Henzl notes a similar elimination of redundancies in the Czech case system as does Hernández-Chávez (1990a) for Spanish indirect objects.

61

Another common acquisition process is what is often referred to as *overmarking*, as when child learners of English say 'Nobody don't like me', or 'I didn't broke it', doubly marking the negative and the past tense. Merino (1983) provides a clear example of this process in loss. In her longitudinal study, subjects who earlier used the conditional conjunction *a menos* 'unless' as well as *si* 'if', later used the overmarked form *a menos si* to express the notion 'unless.'

Both Merino and Henzl observe the *'overextension'* or generalization to forms of one class from those of other, minor, classes as in the use of the -*ar* conjugation endings in Spanish for verbs from the -*er* and -*ir* conjugations. This is most certainly related to general word formation processes in Spanish by which new words and borrowings are overwhelmingly assigned to the -*ar* conjugation.

Other language change patterns are seen to be recapitulated in language loss through the *simplification* and *neutralization* of grammatical structures reported by several investigators. Henzl (1977) shows that, in the later stages of loss, the case system in Czech is replaced by word order. Similarly, loss of a variety of verbal inflections is noted for Chicano Spanish by Merino (1983) and Silva-Corvalán (1988). Among these are the future, conditional, past and present subjunctives, and the perfect tenses which tend to be substituted by less complex forms. Thus, the inflected future is replaced by the *ir a* construction; the conditional and the past subjunctive by the imperfect; the present subjunctive by the indicative; and the perfect tenses by the simple past. In certain narrative contexts, the imperfect and preterite verb forms become neutralized. That is, there is a tendency for only the imperfect to be used with stative verbs such as *ser*, *tener*, and *haber* and for the preterite to be used with event verbs. Similarly, the distinction between *ser* and *estar* becomes blurred in certain pragmatic contexts (Silva-Corvalán, 1988, 1990; Hernández-Chávez, 1990a).

An important characteristic of loss processes observed by most of these investigators is that until loss is quite well advanced, the substitutions, simplifications, neutralizations, etc. are variable rather than categorial. Loss first appears as a decrease in frequency of use, in appropriate contexts, of the more complex forms. For example, Pousada and Poplack (1979), in a study of Spanish- and English-dominant Puerto Ricans in New York, found a decrease among English-dominant speakers in the use of the future, conditional, and plusperfect tenses. They also showed a reduction in occurrence of the subjunctive as did Ocampo (1990). As noted above, Silva-Corvalán (1988) reports a diminished preference for certain constructions like the historical present and rhetorical questions within evaluative structures of narratives where those constructions are normally prevalent. Gutiérrez (1990) shows similar patterns in the decreasing use of various subordination structures.

Language Acquisition, Language Use, and Language Loss

Child language acquisition studies demonstrate that the basic structures of the native language are normally learned by the age of five or six. Yet, we also know that language learning continues well into adulthood. Several studies have shown, for example, that the mastery of complex syntax and semantics continues throughout the elementary school years. (General introductions to child language acquisition are found in Clark and Clark, 1977, and in Moskowitz, 1978; for more comprehensive, cross-cultural studies, see Ferguson, 1973. For work on older children, refer to Chomsky, 1968, and Kessel, 1970). Research on sociolinguistic variation among pre-teens and teens reveals that there is considerable development of phonological, lexical, and grammatical variables related to style and social groupings (Fischer, 1958; Labov, 1964; Wolfram, 1969). Moreover, in literate, technological societies, many individuals strive throughout their careers to elaborate their vocabulary and grammatical structure and to fine tune their writing and speaking styles.

All of this amounts to normal language development, and the normal range of proficiencies attained is delimited by such factors as social and cultural interactions, formal schooling and individual aptitude. For all but perhaps the most standardized and specialized forms of speech and writing, which depend on explicit tuition, full natural language learning depends principally on what Krashen (1981), writing about second language acquisition, has called 'comprehensible input'. In a first language context, we interpret this to mean interactions through language in ways that are cognitively, socially, and culturally significant for the learner. They must include sufficient and continual linguistic communication with family members, peers, and other members of the community over the crucial periods of natural language learning. Anything short of this kind and amount of sufficient meaningful interaction will result in a curtailed or otherwise incomplete development of language, i.e. language loss.

In a monolingual community or in a bilingual community with a clear separation of functions for each language by societal domain ('bilingualism with diglossia', Fishman, 1972), the most likely learning conditions will include availability of the full range of interactions necessary for completely normal language acquisition. However, in bilingual communities where the language of a dominant society encroaches on domains that are critical for the acquisition of a subordinate, ethnic language, conditions strongly disfavor the full development of the latter.

Diminished language use, then, goes hand in glove with language loss. As the social functions of an ethnic language become more restricted, so do the opportunities for the broad variety of meaningful interactions that are necessary for successful transmission of the language to the next generation. Imperfect learning is the result. The mainstream language then becomes dominant, and a steep downward spiral in the use and acquisition of the ethnic language is set in motion. A shift in language use, in this analysis, is seen as the social-functional precursor of loss, which reflects incomplete learning by individuals. Similarly, the maintenance of language use patterns is the social-functional concomitant of natural language acquisition.

Sociocultural Mechanisms of Loss

Fifteen years ago Spanish speakers in the United States numbered 10.6 million and today are estimated at 19.4 million persons (US Bureau of the Census, 1990). A large percentage of these are recent immigrants, and with the proximity of Mexico and other areas of Latin America, their numbers will undoubtedly continue to grow for the forseeable future. And, although Spanish speakers are found in all of the states, they are concentrated in just a few. Most are poor.

Given these demographic facts — numbers, recency of arrival, continued immigration, concentration of population, low socio-economic status — all favoring the native language, the prospects for the maintenance of Spanish would seem extremely bright: large size and geographic concentration provide the ethnic community the resources to develop cultural maintenance institutions, and in their daily lives, members of the community have greater opportunities for interaction with each other; new immigration is generally drawn to areas of ethnic concentration, increasing the size of the group and regenerating the pool of dominant speakers of the language; and the relative lack of social mobility reinforces the geographic concentration at the same time that it enhances a sense of group solidarity.

These plus other factors such as relationship to the homeland, attitudes toward language and ethnicity, discrimination, etc., are generally considered to favor maintenance (Grosjean, 1982). Indeed, many earlier studies concluded, mostly on the basis of language use patterns, that Spanish in the US was being maintained. (See, for example, Patella and Kuvlesky, 1963; Fishman and Hofman, 1966; Hayden, 1966; and Skrabanek, 1970). Yet, it is becoming increasingly clear that such factors are not sufficient to staunch the linguistic hemorrhage. A review of several of these studies by Hernández-Chávez (1978) reveals that the presumed maintenance was largely an artifact of the growth of population through immigration. In recent years, study after study shows a progressive shift to English in the second and third generations and even in younger first generation immigrants, mirroring the language loss studies cited above. (See Gaarder, n.d.; Thompson, 1970; Laosa, 1975; Ortiz, 1975; Faltis, 1976; López, 1978; Gutiérrez, 1980; Hudson-Edwards and Bills, 1982; and Floyd, 1982. Floyd, 1985, reviews several of these works).

An important sociolinguistic question, then, especially for educators and other language planners dedicated to linguistic and cultural pluralism, is what processes — powerful enough to override the maintenance factors noted above — operate within and outside the Chicano community that lead so forcefully and, perhaps, inexorably toward shift and loss.

Although English is not the official language of the United States, there are strong Anglo-Saxon traditions and a multitude of federal and state laws that make English the *de facto* national language. Since at least the middle of the nineteenth century, conflicts between Mexicans and Anglos in the Southwest and anti-foreigner bias generated by Southern European immigration in the East led to a series of repressive laws mandating schooling, official publications, and court proceedings to be in English. In the latter half of the 1800s, English was mandated in the Territories for government business. During that same time, several of the states passed legislation with similar provisions as well as laws requiring English literacy for voting. By the end of the century, no fewer than thirty-nine states had enacted statutes restricting non-English schools. (See Liebowitz, 1969; Kloss, 1977; Hernández-Chávez, 1990b; and Piatt, 1990, for extended historical treatments of language policies).

In this century the Mexican Revolution, two World Wars, the Great Depression, the Cold War, and the Oil Crisis have all fed xenophobic attitudes which have been reflected in further discriminatory legislation and practices that have generally been upheld by the courts. For example, the Nationality Act of 1940 required English for the first time for naturalization of citizenship; the Internal Security Act of 1950 added reading and writing to those requirements. Lassiter v. Northhampton Election Board (360 US 45, 1959), upheld those provisions in a

North Carolina case. Later, Castro v. California (2 Cal. 3d 223, 1970) ruled that the state interest in a common language was such that election materials in Spanish could not be required. There have been similar decisions in various areas of language law.

Such statutory and judicial mandates follow from and comprise an integral part of Anglo-American principles of cultural hegemony. Non-English speaking peoples are to be subjected to the 'great melting pot', not so much to create a new and hardened alloy, but to be recast, as English-speaking replicas conforming to Anglo cultural molds. Non-Europeans have generally been considered inferior, and according to the influential educator Elwood Cubberly early this century, society must instill in them, 'so far as can be done, the Anglo-Saxon conception of righteousness, law and order, and our popular government. . . .' (Cubberly, 1909, pp. 15–16). Also in the same period, Theodore Roosevelt insisted that we 'have room for but one language here and that is the English language, for we intend to see that the crucible turns our people out as Americans, of American nationality. . . .' (US English, 1987).

These notions continue to modern times. Heller (1966) decries the kind of socialization by Mexican-American families that promotes 'family ties, honor, and masculinity', neglecting the values conducive to a dynamic, industrialized society — 'achievement, independence, and deferred gratification'. More recently, the official English movement has launched an all-out campaign against linguistic pluralism. It is expressly opposed to multilingual ballots and bilingual education, though its underlying impetus seems to be fear of Hispanic political power and the desire to control Mexican immigration. Giving voice to these feelings in a statement under an *English First* letterhead, Representative Jim Horn of Texas warns that if bilingual balloting is allowed to continue, 'the next American President could well be elected by people who can't read or speak English!' (Californians United, 1987, p. 80). In a similar vein, reporter Harold Gilliam, who covers the environment for *This World*, states 'The time has come to risk being politically incorrect. . . . There are too many people in California. Immigration must stop'. (Gilliam, 1993). Columnist George Wills expresses clearly the underlying philosophy:

> [The government] should not be bashful about affirming the virtues of 'Anglo culture' — including the political arrangements bequeathed by the men of July 4, 1776, a distinctly Anglo group. The promise of America is bound up with the virtues and achievements of 'Anglo culture', which is bound up with English. (*Newsweek*, July 8, 1985).

It is this political context in which local and state governments have passed English-only legislation, educators have imposed Spanish sanctions and sought English immersion curriculums, and employers have dismissed employees for using Spanish in the workplace.

The effect on Spanish speakers is chilling. Not only does English come to be seen by Chicanos as the highly valued language of education and commerce, Spanish is viewed as a hindrance, a language that blocks advancement and acceptance by the broader society. Many schoolchildren, experiencing embarrassment and shame in their desire to be accepted, reject the use of their native language and even deny their ethnicity. Parents attribute their own socioeconomic conditions, not to a history of poverty, lack of education, and political powerlessness, but to a lack of English skills. Understandably, they fear for their children's future without English. They easily accede to the insistence of teachers and other authority figures that they discourage the use of Spanish in the home while they encourage the use of English. There is little awareness that, under such conditions, their children's knowledge of Spanish will inevitably deteriorate or what the social and cultural consequences might be.

We must add to these attitudinal factors the ubiquitousness of English: at school both in and out of the classroom, in the popular entertainment media, in the workplace, in commerce, in social services and government, etc. Under these circumstances, the acquisition and use of English is inevitable. The fears of parents and the English-only advocates alike in this regard are quite unfounded.

What is not inevitable is the retention of Spanish. English becomes the usual and preferred mode of communication, not only in ethnically mixed domains, but soon for intra-ethnic communication in Chicano barrios themselves. From there it is a short leap into the home, the final refuge of the ethnic language. Older children begin to use it with younger siblings. Parents, most of whom have no explicit ideology concerning language and culture, begin to accept English from their children, even if they barely comprehend it themselves. Reasons for the young people to use Spanish are reduced to communication with monolingual family members and to stylistic codeswitching for re-affirming group identity (Gumperz and Hernández-Chávez, 1970). There are no longer 'sufficient meaningful interactions', and the native language begins to slip away.

Revitalization Strategies in Education and Society

A shared language embodies peoplehood — and in this we can agree with the proponents of official English. It encodes the customs and traditions of ethnicity; it is the means of social interaction in the family and community; it carries with it the emotional attachments of upbringing and the values that give meaning to a shared existence; in short, it is crucial to the notion of culture.

Language loss threatens to destroy these relationships. Communication between different-language community members is weakened; the sense of a shared destiny is lost; intra-ethnic conflicts arise; historical knowledge fails to be passed on; and individuals suffer feelings of alienation from their historical ethnicity. These are some of the consequences, at least in part, of language loss. There are possibly others. Cultural alienation can have as its products poor educational performance, socioeconomic marginalization, and a host of other ills. (See Hernández-Chávez, 1978, 1985, 1990b for further discussion of these points).

It would seem to follow, then, that contrary to the wisdom of the advocates of forced assimilation, a healthy society demands an enlightened cultural pluralism. Such a society is one in which the cultures of ethnic groups, far from being prohibited or even merely tolerated, are actively encouraged by the majority institutions. It is a society in which ethnic communities, and thereby their individual members, are strengthened in their own institutions and ways of life and in which powerful ways are found for interethnic collaboration and cooperation. Forced assimilation weakens the assimilated and, thus, the whole; pluralism provides variety, liberates the ethnic group, and strengthens the entire society.

It is not the intent of this chapter to explore in depth all the ramifications of this model except to provide a number of comments about education as it relates to the development of Spanish for Chicanos. We cannot, however, limit our discussion to methodological questions since the revitalization of Spanish in communities where the language is being lost is not just a technical issue. Rather, it is a fundamentally philosophical one and one of setting goals and defining principles from which flow the educational approaches to be taken. We will briefly discuss these issues and their sociopolitical setting as a context for our discussion of education.

The goals for Spanish revitalization cannot be separated from those for cultural pluralism in the sense discussed above. While language is seen as a critical aspect of pluralism, it is not the only component (and perhaps not even the central one). The important goal is the development of the community — educationally, economically, socially, politically — through Spanish, through English, or bilingually. For the individual, we must add a strong sense of self, grounded in the native culture, and the full development of cognitive capabilities. The native language is a critical ingredient in all of this precisely because it can contribute to these goals, and without it, individuals are uprooted, and the community tends to fragment. (See Hernández-Chávez, 1978 and 1985).

We have emphasized the importance of language to the development, participation in, and transmission of culture and we have seen that both the language and the ethnic culture in many Chicano communities is stigmatized. Few people will regularly choose to use a stigmatized language without a strong ideological commitment. These realities give rise to a first principle in language revitalization efforts, namely that *ways must be found to infuse the ethnic language and culture with a positive image and value*, both within and outside the ethnic community. In many Chicano communities, there exist a variety of cultural activities and organizations which serve to promote ethnic solidarity and pride. Such communities must be encouraged to develop these kinds of activities as a way to bolster community pride and ethnic identity.

In addition to such efforts within the community itself, a crucial requisite of social value for a minority language is official standing. Although Spanish enjoys some legal status through such measures as bilingual ballots under the Voting Rights Act, federal and state bilingual education statutes, the Court Interpreters Act, and a few favorable court rulings, it must be pointed out that most of this is grudging and limited support, at best, or else it is for the benefit of the state (see Hernández-Chávez, 1989). Legal recognition that the language minority has the right to use and to maintain its own language for a wide variety of public and private purposes would best serve revitalization efforts. Such recognition would have far-ranging implications for public policy and for the use and prestige of the ethnic language.

Weinreich (1953) defines prestige as 'the value of a language in social advance' (p. 79). An obvious measure of this value is the usefulness of the language for employment. Currently, there exist positions for interpreters, bilingual educators, secretaries, clerks, etc. Most of these, however, have a sort of negative prestige in that they generally involve more responsibilities, yet they pay no more than their monolingual counterparts. Moreover, they are generally created for the convenience and purposes of the employer, not to enhance linguistic pluralism. There exist other positions, as in the foreign service or in international commerce, but Chicanos have either not entered these in great numbers or their native language

67

skills are not sufficiently developed to be a source of personal or professional pride. Similarly, the linguistic preparation of persons in the service professions is entirely left to chance. Revitalization movements, therefore, need to ally themselves with efforts to achieve language rights both in the public and private sectors. Researchers, educators, and other persons interested in language revitalization must, at the very least, become informed about the needs in these areas.

A critical source of prestige is the incorporation of the ethnic language and culture into public school curricula. It is believed by many that cultural values have no place in the curriculum, yet this belief is wholly contrary to long-established educational practice. Though they are often considered to be neutral, the history, arts, social studies, and literature taught in American schools are patently English and Anglo-American. This is certainly legitimate and necessary, but for minority children the failure to teach through their own culture is alienating and is a major contributor to language and cultural loss.

Many people call for the establishment of private after-school ethnic classes to maintain the language and culture. This position is taken not only by official-English advocates, but by ethnic group spokepersons as well, such as Armas (1990). There is no question that ethnic communities can and should engage in a variety of this kind of activity on their own behalf. But we can accept them as strategies for language retention only with reservations. First, that kind of effort is often too late and it is certainly too little, especially given the resources available to most Chicano communities. Retention and/or revitalization of language requires a much more massive effort. The public schools and other majority group institutions are to be held largely responsible for the negative attitudes of students toward the native language and culture and for the failure to develop skills and knowledge in them. Therefore, they have an obligation to attempt to undo that damage. Moreover, ethnic groups themselves, as taxpayers and as citizens or residents, have the right to expect the schools to meet their children's needs in such a vital area.

Nor is the undertaking to teach the minority culture to be taken lightly. Periodically focusing on Mexican national holidays and heroes, for example, only reinforces the idea that culture is an academic exercise and incidental to real life. The culture to be taught needs to be integral to the curriculum, a regular and systematic part of the everyday subjects. Equally as important, cultural instruction must be relevant to students' lives and those of members of their community. Its goal must be to establish a strong sense of cultural identity (as it does for Anglo students), a goal that implies the development of an awareness of the social, economic and political conditions that define the community.

Thus the language of the community must also permeate the curriculum. This follows both from the first principle, enunciated above, and from a second principle of language revitalization: *steps must be taken to insure sufficient native language interactions for full acquisition to take place.* Bilingual education programs, as currently structured, are totally inadequate for this purpose. The principal (and irremediable) difficulty with these programs is that they follow an openly assimilationist philosophy that is codified into law by all the relevant federal and state statutes (see Hernández-Chávez, 1978, 1979, 1985, for discussion). Daily classes in Spanish language arts can certainly be of help, but unless these are supported by important use of the language as a medium of instruction, the criterion of sufficient meaningful interactions cannot be met.

Compare English instruction for Anglo students. Were all their subjects except English given in a foreign language, there would likely develop important gaps in their English knowledge of terms in mathematics, social studies, science, etc. — not just technical terms, but terms in these fields that are necessary for any educated discourse — even though the rest of their world is surrounded by English. For most language minority students, the rest of their world *is* surrounded by English, which they will learn fluently in due course. Development and maintenance of their native language skills demands the use of that language in significant and useful ways as part of their normal scholastic activities, not just in structured language lessons, which are necessarily restricted in their linguistic input to the student. Full language acquisition must have available to it the total range of communicative possibilities by which the learner may selectively recreate the language in a natural order (Chomsky, 1965).

It follows that other opportunities need to be sought outside the curriculum for students to use the language. Many suggestions come to mind. In schools, the active use of Spanish by students, teachers and other staff can be encouraged outside the classroom. Library and other reading materials in Spanish can be given high visibility and use, and increasing use can be made of Spanish-language films, videos, audiotapes and other educational materials. Students and staff can be encouraged to use Spanish in extracurricular and enrichment activities.

Depending upon the commitment of students, faculty, administrators, and the community at large, more intense and creative efforts can be made to raise the prestige of the language and to provide ample meaningful interactions in it. An example might be a native language immersion program on the model of one in Woodland, California. Essential features of this program are that it includes among its students dominant speakers of both Spanish and English, but the language use and curriculum are geared to meet the characteristics and needs of the Spanish-dominant children. (For the English speakers, the methodology applied is similar to that in immersion programs that have many demonstrated successes). Parents are closely involved in all aspects of the program (See Trueba, *et al.*, 1993).

Another example is a proposal for a high school program in Española, New Mexico. This program will use Spanish as a medium of instruction for several hours a day using the local variety[2] as a basis while expanding students' comprehension and use of other varieties for academic purposes. Central to this model is the involvement of students in summer camps, where Spanish will be the medium of interaction and exchange programs for teachers and students with counterparts in Mexico and other Spanish-speaking countries (Davis, 1990).

These two programs have in common *the active involvement of parents and other segments of the community*, a third principle of a revitalization program. The schools are clearly a central institution in this effort because of their tremendous influence on children. But, ultimately, the language and culture must have enough vitality within families and communities to continue to develop across generations. For this, the participation of many different parts of the community is essential. Members of the community must become aware of all aspects of language and cultural loss and must become active partners with their children and with a variety of societal institutions in their revitalization.

The principles of native language revitalization efforts and the modes of implementation suggested above impose heavy burdens on parents, students, educators and language planners concerned with language and culture loss. There

69

are surely other principles and other ways of putting them into effect. But we are convinced that they are no less difficult. Language loss is very far advanced in many Chicano communities, to the point that it may involve heroic efforts to make Spanish viable again. We need to ask whether such efforts are possible and, if so, whether they are feasible or even desirable. The position taken here is that much harm has accrued due to the breakneck pace of change and that it is imperative that communities work, at the very least, to slow it down and make it more manageable and less destructive.

Notes

1 'r:rr' means that some persons tend to substitute the rr (double r sound, as in *perro* = dog) for the r (single r sound, as in *pero* = but). The reason is that the rr is a difficult sound that must be mastered.
2 'Variety' is used in order to rank-order different dialects or to distinguish them from the 'standard' form which some people believe does not exist in real life (i.e., all forms are varieties). 'Dialect' often conveys the meaning of localized varieties in contrast with wider communication varieties. Often 'dialect' and 'variety' are used interchangeably.

References

ALBERT, M.L. and OBLER, L.K. (1978) *The Bilingual Brain*, New York, NY, Academic Press.
ARMAS, J. (1990) 'Preserving culture: If we want the job done right, do it ourselves', *Alburquerque Journal*, July 1, p. B3.
BAILEY, C.J. (1973) 'The patterns of language variation', in BAILEY, R.W. and ROBINSON, J.L. (Eds) *Varieties of Present Day English*, New York, NY, MacMillan.
BREATNACH, R.B. (1964) 'Characteristics of Irish dialects in process of extinction', *Communications et Rapports du Premier Congres de Dialectologie Generale*, Louvain, France, Centre International de Dialectologie Generale.
CALIFORNIANS UNITED (1987) 'Californians United Against Proposition 63: English-Only Opposition Campaign Kit', San Francisco, CA, Californians United.
CHOMSKY, C. (1968) 'The acquisition of syntax in children from 5 to 10', *Research Monograph*, **57**, Cambridge, MA, The MIT Press.
CHOMSKY, N. (1965) *Aspects of the Theory of Syntax*, Cambridge, MA, The MIT Press.
CLARK, H.H. and CLARK, E.V. (1977) *Psychology and Language*, New York, NY, Harcourt Brace Jovanovich.
COHEN, A. (1974) 'The Culver City Spanish immersion program: How does summer recess affect Spanish speaking ability?', *Language Learning*, **24**, pp. 55–68.
CUBBERLY, E.P. (1909) *Changing Conceptions of Education*, Boston, MA, Houghton Mifflin Co.
DAVIS, P. (1990) *An internationalist focus for the revitalization of Spanish in northern New Mexico*, unpublished manuscript, Albuquerque, NM, University of New Mexico, Department of Linguistics.
DORIAN, N. (1978) 'The fate of morphological complexity in language death', *Language*, **54**, pp. 590–609.

DORIAN, N. (1981) *Language Death*, Philadelphia, PA, University of Pennsylvania Press.

FALTIS, C. (1976) *A Study of Spanish and English Usage Among Bilingual Mexican Americans Living in the Las Calles Barrio of San Jose, California*, MA Thesis, San Jose, CA, San Jose State University.

FERGUSON, C.A. (1973) *Studies of Childhood Development*, New York, NY, Holt, Rinehart and Winston.

FISCHER, J.L. (1958) 'Social influences on the choice of a linguistic variant', *Word*, 14, pp. 47–56.

FISHMAN, J.A. (1972) 'Societal bilingualism: Stable and transitional', in FISHMAN, J.A. *The Sociology of Language*, Rowley, MA, Newbury House.

FISHMAN, J.A. and HOFMAN, J.E. (1966) 'Mother tongue and nativity in the American population', in FISHMAN, J. *et al.* (Eds) *Language Loyalty in the United States*, The Hague, Netherlands, Mouton.

FLOYD, M.B. (1982) 'Spanish language maintenance in Colorado', in BARKIN, F., BRANDT, E.A. and ORNSTEIN-GALICIA, J. (Eds) *Bilingualism and Language Contact: Spanish, English, and Native American Languages*, New York, NY, Teachers' College Press.

FLOYD, M.B. (1985) 'Spanish in the Southwest: Language maintanence or shift?' in ELIAS-OLIVARES, L., LEONE, E.A., CISNEROS, R. and GUTIERREZ, J. (Eds) 'Spanish Language use and public life in the USA', in FISHMAN, J.A. (Ed) *Contributions to the Sociology of Language*, 35, The Hague, Netherlands, Mouton.

FRASER, C., BELLUGI, U. and BROWN, R. (1963) 'Control of grammar in imitation, comprehension, and production', *Journal of Verbal Learning and Verbal Behavior*, 2, pp. 121–35.

GAARDER, A.B. (n.d.) *Language Maintenance or Language Shift: The Prospect for Spanish in the United States*, Mimeo.

GALLOWAY, L. (1978) 'Impairment and recovery in polyglot aphasia', in PARADIS, M. (Ed) *Aspects of Bilingualism*, Columbia, SC, Hornbeam Press.

GILLIAM, H. (1993) 'Bursting at the seams', *This World*, San Francisco Chronicle, February 21, p. 12.

GROSJEAN, F. (1982) *Life With Two Languages: An Introduction to Bilingualism*, Cambridge, MA, Harvard University Press.

GUMPERZ, J. and HERNÁNDEZ-CHÁVEZ, E. (1970) 'Cognitive aspects of bilingual communication', in WHITELY, H. (Ed) *Language Use and Social Change*, London, England, Oxford University Press.

GUTIÉRREZ, J.R. (1980) 'Language use in Martineztown', in BARKIN, F. and BRANDT, E. (Eds) *Speaking, Singing, and Teaching: A Multidisciplinary Approach to Language Variation*, Proceedings of the Eighth Annual Southwestern Area Language and Linguistics Workshop, *Anthropological Research Papers*, 20, pp. 454–459. Tempe, AZ: Arizona State University.

GUTIÉRREZ, M. (1990) 'Sobre el mantenimiento de las cláusulas subordinadas en el español de Los Angeles', in BERGEN, J. (Ed) *Spanish in the United States: Sociolinguistic issues*, Washington, DC, Georgetown University Press.

HAAS, M.R. (1968) 'The last words of Biloxi', *International Journal of Applied Linguistics*, 34, pp. 77–84.

HAYDEN, R.G. (1966) 'Some community dynamics of language maintenance', in FISHMAN, J. *et al.* (Eds) *Language Loyalty in the United States*, The Hague, Netherlands, Mouton.

HELLER, C. (1966) *Mexican-American Youth: Forgotten Youth at the Crossroads*, New York, NY, Random House.

HENZL, V. (1977) 'On similarity between language acquisition and language loss', paper presented at the Second Annual Boston University Conference on Language Development, Boston, MA.

71

Eduardo Hernández-Chávez

HERNÁNDEZ-CHÁVEZ, E. (1978) 'Language maintenance, bilingual education, and philosophies of bilingualism in the United States', in ALATIS, J. (Ed) *International Dimensions of Bilingual Education*, Georgetown University Round Table Monograph, Washington, DC, Georgetown University Press.

HERNÁNDEZ-CHÁVEZ, E. (1979) 'Meaningful bilingual bicultural education: A fairytale', in ORTIZ, R. (Ed) *Language Development in a Bilingual Setting*, Pomona, CA, National Multilingual Multicultural Materials Development Center.

HERNÁNDEZ-CHÁVEZ, E. (1985) 'The inadequancy of English immersion education as an educational approach for language minority students', in *Studies on Immersion Education: A Collection for United States Educators*, Sacramento, CA, California State Department of Education.

HERNÁNDEZ-CHÁVEZ, E. (1989) 'Language policy and language rights in the United States: Issues in bilingualism', in SKUTNABB-KANGAS, T. and CUMMINS, J. (Eds) *Minority Education: From Shame to Struggle*, Clevedon, Multilingual Matters Ltd.

HERNÁNDEZ-CHÁVEZ, E. (1990a) '*Gracias por viniendo*' — *Language Loss in the Spanish of New Mexico*, Paper presented at the Linguistic Association of the Southwest Annual Conference, El Paso, Texas, October 19–21.

HERNÁNDEZ-CHÁVEZ, E. (1990b) 'The role of suppressive language policies in language shift and language loss', Estudios Fronterizos, *Revista del Instituto de Investigaciones Sociales*, 7, 8, pp. 18–19, 123–35.

HERNÁNDEZ-CHÁVEZ, E. (1990c) 'Sociocultural sources of Spanish-English codeswitching in language loss', paper presented at the Rocky Mountain Modern Language Association, 44th Annual Meeting, Salt Lake City, Utah, October 11–13.

HILL, J. and HILL, K.C. (1977) 'Language death and relexification in Tlaxcalan Náhuatl', *International Journal of the Sociology of Language*, 12, pp. 55–70.

HUDSON-EDWARDS, A. and BILLS, G. (1982) 'Intergenerational language shift in an Albuquerque barrio', in AMASTAE, J. and ELIAS-OLIVARES, L. (Eds) *Spanish in the United States: Sociolinguistic Aspects*, Cambridge, England, Cambridge University Press.

KESSEL, F.S. (1970) 'The role of syntax in children's comprehension from ages six to twelve', *Monograph of Social Research and Child Development*, 35, 6.

KLOSS, H. (1977) *The American Bilingual Tradition*, Rowley, MA, Newbury House.

KOIKE, D. (1987) 'Code switching in the bilingual Chicano narrative', *Hispania*, 70, pp. 148–54.

KRASHEN, S.D. (1981) 'Bilingual education and second language acquisition theory', in California State Department of Education, *Schooling and Language Minority Students: A Theoretical Framework*, Los Angeles, CA, Evaluation, Dissimentation and Assessment Center, California State University, L.A.

LABOV, W. (1964) 'Stages in the acqustion of standard English', in SHUY, R.W. (Ed) *Social Dialects and Language Learning*, Champaign, IL, National Council of Teachers of English.

LAOSA, L. (1975) 'Bilingualism in three United States Hispanic groups: Contextual use of language by children and adults in their families', *Journal of Educational Psychology*, 67, 5, pp. 617–27.

LIEBOWITZ, A. (1969) 'English literacy: Legal sanction for discrimination', *Notre Dame Lawyer*, 45, 7, pp. 7–67.

LOPEZ, D.E. (1978) 'Chicano language loyalty in an urban setting', *Sociology and Social Research*, 62, pp. 267–78.

MERINO, B.J. (1983) 'Language loss in bilingual Chicano children', *Journal of Applied Developmental Psychology*, 10, pp. 477–94.

MOSKOWITZ, B.A. (1978) 'The acquisition of language', *Scientific American*, 239, pp. 92–108.

OCAMPO, F. (1990) 'El subjuntivo en tres generaciones de hablantes bilingues', in

BERGEN, J. (Ed) *Spanish in the United States: Sociolinguistic Issues*, Washington, DC, Georgetown University Press.

ORTIZ, L.I. (1975) *A Sociolinguistic Study of Language Maintenance in the Northern New Mexico Community of Arroyo Seco*, Ph.D. dissertation, Albuquerque, NM, University of New Mexico.

OSTYN, P. (1972) *American Flemish: A Study in Language Loss and Linguistic Interference*, Ph.D. dissertation, Rochester, NY, University of Rochester.

PARADIS, M. (1977) 'Bilingualism and aphasia', in WHITAKER, H. and H. (Eds), *Studies in Neurolinguistics*, 3, New York, NY, Academic Press.

PATELLA, V. and KUVLESKY, W.P. (1963) 'Situational variation in language patterns of Mexican American boys and girls', *Social Science Quarterly*, 53, 4, pp. 855–64.

PIATT, B. (1990) *Only English? Law and Language Policy in the United States*, Albuquerque NM, University of New Mexico Press.

POUSADA, A. and POPLACK, S. (1979) 'No case for convergence: The Puerto Rican Spanish verb system in a language contact situation', New York, NY, Centro de Estudios Puertorriqueños, Working Papers No. 5.

PRATELLA, W.C. (1970) 'The retention of first and second year Spanish over the period of the summer vacation', *Dissertation Abstracts*, 31.235-A.

SALTRELLI, M. (1975a) 'Emigrant languages in America: Acquisition, development, and death', *Studies in Language Learning*, 1, pp. 186–87.

SALTRELLI, M. (1975b) 'Leveling of paradigms in Chicano Spanish', in MILAN, W., STACZEK, J.J. and ZAMORA, J.C. (Eds) *Colloquium on Spanish and Portuguese Linguistics*, University of Massachusetts, Washington, DC, Georgetown University Press.

SÁNCHEZ, R. (1983) *Chicano Discourse: A Socio-historical Perspective*, Rowley, MA, Newbury House.

SILVA-CORVALÁN, C. (1983a) 'Tense and aspect in oral Spanish narrative: Context and meaning', *Language*, 59, pp. 60–80.

SILVA-CORVALÁN, C. (1983b) 'Code-shifting patterns in Chicano Spanish', in ELIAS-OLIVARES, L. (Ed) *Spanish in the US Setting: Beyond the Southwest*, Rosslyn, VA, NCBE.

SILVA-CORVALÁN, C. (1986) 'Bilingualism and language change: The extension of *estar* in Los Angeles Spanish', *Language*, 62, pp. 587–608.

SILVA-CORVALÁN, C. (1988) 'Oral narrative along the Spanish-English bilingual continuum', in STACZEK, J. (Ed) *Colloquium on Spanish, Portuguese, and Catalan Linguistics*, Washington, DC, Georgetown University Press.

SILVA-CORVALÁN, C. (1990) 'Current issues in studies of language contact', *Hispania*, 73, pp. 162–76.

SKRABANEK, R.L. (1970) 'Language maintenance among Mexican-Americans', *International Journal of Comparative Sociology*, 11, pp. 272–82.

THOMPSON, R. (1970) 'Mexican American language loyalty and the validity of the 1970 census', in BILLS, G. (Ed) *Southwest Areal Linguistics*, San Diego, CA, Institute for Cultural Pluralism.

TRUDGILL, P. (1976–77) 'Creolization in reverse: Reduction and simplification in the Albanian dialects of Greece', *Transactions of the Philosophical Society*, pp. 32–50.

TRUEBA, H., RODRIGUEZ, C., ZOU, Y. and CINTRÓN, J. (1993) *Healing Multicultural America*, London, England, Falmer Press.

US BUREAU OF THE CENSUS (1990) 'Statistical Abstract of the US, 1990, Washington, DC, US Government Printing Office.

US ENGLISH (1987) 'In defense of our common language', in *Californians United. English-Only Campaign Kit*, San Francisco CA.

WEINREICH, U. (1953) 'Languages in contact: Findings and problems', Publications of the *Linguistic Circle of New York*, 1.

73

WILL, G.F. (1985) 'In defense of the mother tongue', *Newsweek*, July 8, Vol. **VI**, p. 78.

WILLIAMSON, S. (1982) 'Summary chart of findings from previous research on language loss', in LAMBERT, R. and FREED, B. (Eds) *The Loss of Language Skills*, Rowley, MA, Newbury House.

WOLFRAM, W. (1969) *A Sociolinguistic Description of Detroit Negro speech*, Washington, DC, Center for Applied Linguistics.

ENGLISH-ONLY RULES AND THE RIGHT TO SPEAK ONE'S PRIMARY LANGUAGE IN THE WORKPLACE†

Juan F. Perea*

They come from every country in Central and South America, the Caribbean and Spain. They differ in many ways. When they come to the United States, language is perhaps their only true bond.[1]

On May 25, 1920, Robert Meyer, an instructor at the Zion Evangelical Lutheran Congregation's parochial school, taught the reading of biblical stories in the German language to a ten-year-old student at the school. Meyer was subsequently indicted and convicted of violating a Nebraska statute that prohibited the teaching of any language other than English to students who had not passed the eighth grade. Meyer's conviction was upheld by the Supreme Court of Nebraska.[2]

In *Meyer v. Nebraska*,[3] the United States Supreme Court reversed, finding that the statute interfered with the profession of modern language teachers, with the acquisition of knowledge by students, and with the prerogative of parents to control the education of their children.[4] The Court concluded that the statute violated the due process clause of the fourteenth amendment, noting that "the individual has certain fundamental rights which must be respected. The protection of the Constitution extends

† ᶜ 1990 Juan F. Perea, all rights reserved.

* Attorney, National Labor Relations Board, Region One; Adjunct Faculty, Boston College Law School. A.B.,University of Maryland, 1977; J.D., Boston College Law School, 1986. Beginning in the Fall semester, 1990, Mr. Perea will be an Assistant Professor at the University of Florida College of Law.

The author wishes to thank Professor Mark Brodin of Boston College Law School, Ms. Deborah Malamud, Esq., and Ms. Beth Tomasello, Esq., for their helpful and perceptive comments on earlier drafts of this Article. The views expressed in this Article are solely the personal views of the author, expressed in his private capacity, and do not reflect any view of the National Labor Relations Board or any other government agency.

1. Ribadeneira, *From Different Worlds, They Share a Label*, Boston Globe, June 5, 1988, at 40, col. 2.

2. Meyer v. State, 107 Neb. 657, 658-59, 187 N.W. 100, 101 (1922).

3. 262 U.S. 390 (1923).

4. *Id.* at 401.

to all, to those who speak other languages as well as to those born with English on the tongue."[5]

Despite the Court's recognition of a "fundamental right" to language, secured from governmental interference, an employee's right to speak his primary language in the workplace is not yet recognized under Title VII of the Civil Rights Act of 1964.[6] The law on the right to speak one's primary language[7] has developed in cases considering English-only rules, which require the use of English, at least at certain times, while an employee is on the employer's premises. Until very recently, the courts did not recognize the right of Hispanic employees to speak Spanish to each other while on the job.[8] In the leading case on this issue, *Garcia v. Gloor*,[9] the United States Court of Appeals for the Fifth Circuit decided that a rule restricting an employee's use of Spanish while on the job did not violate, or even implicate, Title VII. More recently, the United States Court of Appeals for the Ninth Circuit decided a very similar case, *Gutierrez v. Municipal Court*,[10] concluding that a similar rule did constitute national origin discrimination in violation of Title VII. The Supreme Court, however, vacated the *Gutierrez* decision as moot.[11]

Although the Supreme Court did not reach the merits in *Gutierrez* or consider the legality of English-only rules in the workplace under Title VII, eventually the Court will have to resolve this issue. It is certain to recur. The numbers alone guarantee it.

---

5. *Id. Meyer* has continuing vitality in modern constitutional law. The case stands for the proposition that governmental invasions of personal identity and freedom are likely to be invalid when directed at members of discrete and insular minorities for whom the functioning of normal political processes have been curtailed. L. TRIBE, AMERICAN CONSTITUTIONAL LAW 1319-20 (2d ed. 1988). Language minorities are a discrete and insular minority. *See* S. REP. No. 295, 94th Cong., 1st Sess. 25-32 (1975), *reprinted in* 1975 U.S. CODE CONG. & ADMIN. NEWS 774, 791-98 (discussing the history of discrimination against language minorities that has impeded their participation in the political process; this history of discrimination motivated the extension of the Voting Rights Act of 1965 to include language minorities). *See infra* notes 114-15, 122-26 and accompanying text.

6. *See* 42 U.S.C. §§ 2000e to 2000e-17 (1982) (prohibiting employers from discriminating in employment relationships on the basis of race, color, religion, sex or national origin).

7. Primary language, as used in this Article, refers to a person's native language, usually the language spoken by one's parents in the home and one's first language.

8. Apparently all of the cases on this issue decided by the courts and the Equal Employment Opportunity Commission have involved restrictions upon Spanish-speaking employees. *See infra* notes 212, 215-17. Because of this situation and the large number of Hispanic persons in the United States, this Article will focus principally on the right of Hispanics to speak Spanish in the workplace. The principles stated here apply with equal force to restrictions upon the exercise of any primary language other than English.

9. 618 F.2d 264 (5th Cir. 1980), *cert. denied*, 449 U.S. 1113 (1981).

10. 838 F.2d 1031 (9th Cir. 1988), *vacated as moot*, 109 S. Ct. 1736 (1989).

11. Gutierrez v. Municipal Ct., 109 S. Ct. 1736 (1989).

The United States currently contains the fourth or fifth largest Spanish-speaking population in the world.[12] Estimates of the Hispanic population in the United States range between 18 million and 30 million.[13] By the year 2000, Hispanics will be the largest ethnic minority group in the country.[14] Moreover, this growth is reflected in the workplace. According to one recent study, between 1980 and 1987, the number of Hispanic workers rose dramatically, accounting for almost a fifth of employment growth in the United States.[15] This dramatic increase is expected to continue; projections indicate that, by the year 2000, ten percent of the nation's labor force will be Hispanic.[16]

Many Hispanics currently in the work force, as well as many of the new Hispanic entrants, speak Spanish as their primary language and English as a second language.[17] Generally, one can expect them to speak Spanish to their fellow employees who are Hispanic. Employers and supervisors, not understanding Spanish, may want to restrict its use in the workplace. The question of the legality of English-only rules, therefore, is very likely to recur until the Supreme Court decides the issue.

Employers use English-only rules to restrict the use of languages other than English in the workplace and during working hours. The United States Equal Employment Opportunity Commission (EEOC) recognizes two types of English-only rules: (1) a rule requiring employees to speak only English in the workplace at all times, and (2) a limited English-only rule, requiring that employees speak only in English at certain times.[18] This Article will focus on limited English-only rules, and particularly on those rules that seek to restrict private conversations between employees in languages other than English.[19]

---

12. T. WEYR, HISPANIC U.S.A. 3 (1988).

13. *Id.* at 1.

14. Ribadeneira, *Boom Bypassing Mass. Hispanics,* Boston Globe, June 5, 1988, at 40, col. 4.

15. Cattan, *The Growing Presence of Hispanics in the U.S. Work Force,* MONTHLY LAB. REV., August 1988, at 9.

16. *Id.* at 10.

17. The estimated number of persons claiming Spanish as their mother tongue was 11,400,525 in 1979, an increase of 46% over the figure reported in 1970—7,823,583. *See* J. FISHMAN, THE RISE AND FALL OF THE ETHNIC REVIVAL: PERSPECTIVES ON LANGUAGE AND ETHNICITY 147 (Table 14). The number of persons speaking Spanish is likely to be higher today.

18. 29 C.F.R. § 1606.7(a),(b) (1989). The EEOC presumes that an English-only rule in effect at all times violates Title VII, while a limited English-only rule, properly promulgated, must be justified by business necessity. 29 C.F.R. § 1606.7(a)-(c) (1989).

19. The principal cases on English-only rules have involved rules seeking to restrict private conversations between employees. *See* Garcia v. Gloor, 618 F.2d 264, 266 (5th Cir. 1980), *cert. denied,* 449 U.S. 1113 (1981); Gutierrez v. Municipal Ct., 838 F.2d 1031,

This Article analyzes the issues raised by English-only rules and the decisions discussing these rules. Part I reviews the leading cases on English-only rules. The Article then explores several issues that must be considered in deciding any English-only rule case under Title VII. Part II addresses whether speaking one's primary language should constitute a protected right as an aspect of national origin under Title VII. This Article argues that primary language should be protected under Title VII for several reasons: the courts and the EEOC construe the term "national origin" broadly; primary language constitutes a fundamental aspect of ethnicity and national origin; and the difficulty of second-language acquisition renders primary language practically immutable for many persons whose primary language is not English. Part III argues that English-only rules have an exclusive adverse impact on language minority groups distinct from the nonexclusive effect of facially neutral rules typically considered under disparate impact cases. Part IV analyzes the current burden of proof standards for establishing discrimination under Title VII in light of *Wards Cove Packing Co. v. Atonio.*[20] This Part proposes that courts should hold employers to a stricter standard than the *Wards Cove* standard for proving business justification in recognition of the exclusive impact of English-only rules. Finally, Part V discusses the extent of the business justification that can properly justify an employer's use of a language restriction under the standard established in *Wards Cove.*

I. THE LEADING CASES ON ENGLISH-ONLY RULES

The leading cases on the legality of English-only rules are *Garcia v. Gloor*[21] and *Gutierrez v. Municipal Court.*[22] These

---

1036, *vacated as moot,* 109 S. Ct. 1736 (1989). More restrictive rules can be analyzed using disparate treatment theory, disparate impact theory and the business justification standard recently established in Wards Cove Packing Co. v. Atonio, 109 S. Ct. 2115, 2125-26 (1989). *See infra* Parts III and IV.

20. 109 S. Ct. 2115 (1989).

21. 618 F.2d 264 (5th Cir. 1980), *cert. denied,* 449 U.S. 1113 (1981).

22. 838 F.2d 1031, *vacated as moot,* 109 S. Ct. 1736 (1989). In another case, Saucedo v. Brothers Well Serv., Inc., 464 F. Supp. 919 (S.D. Tex. 1979), the court found that an employee's discharge for speaking Spanish violated Title VII. The case has little precedential value in this context, however, because the court did not analyze the prohibition on speaking Spanish, but instead focused on the unfair treatment of the plaintiff. *Id.* at 921-23. Unlike the rules in *Garcia* and *Gutierrez,* the employer's rule in *Saucedo* was informal. *Id.* at 921-22. Furthermore, the court did not state clearly whether the employer's conduct constituted national origin discrimination or race discrimination. Instead, the court found that Saucedo was discharged "because of racial animus." *Id.* at

cases disagree on whether an English-only rule constitutes national origin discrimination under Title VII.[23] *Garcia*, the only remaining precedent on the issue, establishes the legality of English-only rules. In *Garcia*, the Court of Appeals for the Fifth Circuit decided that an employee fired for speaking Spanish on the job had not stated a claim of national origin discrimination under Title VII.[24] The plaintiff, Hector Garcia, was a Mexican American working as a salesman for Gloor Lumber and Supply, Inc. Seven of the eight salesmen, and thirty-one of the thirty-nine persons employed by Gloor Lumber were Hispanic. The court observed that the high percentage of Hispanic salesmen may have been "a matter perhaps of business necessity, because 75% of the population in its business area is of Hispanic background and many of Gloor's customers wish to be waited on by a salesman who speaks Spanish."[25]

Gloor Lumber had an English-only rule prohibiting its salesmen, including Garcia, from speaking Spanish unless they were speaking with Spanish-speaking customers. Although they could speak as they wanted during breaks, the Hispanic salesmen could not speak to each other in Spanish while working in the store.[26]

On June 10, 1975, a fellow Mexican-American employee asked Garcia about an item requested by a customer. Garcia responded in Spanish that the item was not available. Alton Gloor, an officer of Gloor Lumber, heard Garcia speaking in Spanish and subsequently discharged him. Garcia sued, claiming that his discharge constituted national origin discrimination in violation of Title VII.[27]

---

920. The court held that the employer had breached its "obligation to avoid treating its employees discriminatorily." *Id.* at 922. In dicta, however, the court stated that "a duly and officially promulgated . . . rule absolutely prohibiting the speaking of a foreign language during the drilling of a well or the reworking of a well, and providing for immediate discharge for violation of the rule, would be a reasonable rule for which a business necessity could be demonstrated." *Id.* at 921.

23. *Compare Garcia*, 618 F.2d at 266, 268 with *Gutierrez*, 838 F.2d at 1039-40 (disagreeing on application of Title VII to English-only rules).

24. *Garcia*, 618 F.2d at 270-71. For law review commentaries discussing *Garcia* see the following articles: Note, *Language Discrimination under Title VII: The Silent Right of National Origin Discrimination*, 15 J. MARSHALL L. REV. 667 (1982) (authored by John W. Aniol) (approving result in *Garcia*); Note, Garcia v. Gloor: *Mutable Characteristics Rationale Extended to National Origin Discrimination*, 32 MERCER L. REV. 1275 (1981) (authored by Dwight J. Davis) (also approving the result).

25. *Garcia*, 618 F.2d at 266-67.

26. *Id.* at 266.

27. *Id.*

Affirming the district court, the court of appeals held that there was no national origin discrimination.[28] The basis for the court's decision was its view that, for a bilingual person, the choice of which language to speak at a particular time is purely a matter of individual preference that has no compelling nexus to national origin.[29] The court wrote that "[n]either the statute nor common understanding equates national origin with the language that one chooses to speak."[30] Interpreting national origin as one's birthplace or the birthplace of one's ancestors, the court stated that Title VII "does not support an interpretation that equates the language an employee prefers to use with his national origin."[31]

The court also reasoned that a bilingual employee's desire to speak his native language is not an immutable characteristic like place of birth, race, or sex.[32] Rejecting the argument that Gloor Lumber's rule had a disparate impact on Hispanics, the court stated that "there is no disparate impact if the rule is one that the affected employee can readily observe and nonobservance is a matter of individual preference."[33]

Finding no disparate impact and no violation of Title VII, the court declined to examine the employer's justifications for the English-only rule.[34] The court apparently accepted the district court's finding that Gloor's business reasons for the rule were valid.[35] Gloor Lumber offered several reasons for the rule: its English-speaking customers objected to conversations between employees in Spanish, conversations the customers could not understand; requiring bilingual employees to speak English at all times, other than when they served Hispanic customers, would improve their literacy and fluency in English; and the rule would enable Gloor Lumber's English-speaking supervisors to supervise Hispanic employees more effectively.[36]

While the *Garcia* court found no national origin discrimination and therefore no violation of Title VII, the *Gutierrez* court evaluated a similar rule, enacted under similar circumstances,

---

28. *Id.*
29. *Id.* at 270.
30. *Id.* at 268 (footnote omitted).
31. *Id.* at 270.
32. *Id.* at 269.
33. *Id.* at 270.
34. *Id.* at 271.
35. *Id.* at 267.
36. *Id.*

and came to the opposite conclusion.[37] The plaintiff, Alva Gutierrez, worked as a deputy court clerk in the Southeast Judicial District of the Los Angeles Municipal Court. She, like a number of other deputy clerks, was Hispanic American and spoke both Spanish and English. In addition to their other responsibilities, these deputy clerks translated for non-English-speaking persons who used the court.[38]

In March 1984, the municipal court issued a rule prohibiting employees from speaking any language other than English except when they were translating for persons not fluent in English.[39] Later that year, the municipal court amended the rule to permit employees to speak in their preferred language during breaks and during lunch. During work time, however, unless they were translating, the Hispanic clerks were prohibited from speaking Spanish.[40]

The Court of Appeals for the Ninth Circuit affirmed the district court's grant of a preliminary injunction barring enforcement of the municipal court's rule.[41] The court based its analysis on the theory that the rule had a disparate impact on Hispanics.[42] Accordingly, the court first evaluated whether the rule had a disparate impact on Spanish-speaking employees and then whether the municipal court's rule was justified by business necessity.[43]

The *Gutierrez* court found that language is an important aspect of national origin.[44] The court wrote that "[t]he cultural identity of certain minority groups is tied to the use of their primary tongue."[45] Despite an individual's assimilation into American society, "his primary language remains an important link to his ethnic culture and identity."[46] Furthermore, according to the court, "[t]he mere fact that an employee is bilingual does not

---

37. Gutierrez v. Municipal Ct., 838 F.2d 1031, *vacated as moot*, 109 S. Ct. 1736 (1989).

38. *Gutierrez*, 838 F.2d at 1036.

39. Initially, the municipal court's rule prohibited more Spanish than the Gloor Lumber rule, which permitted employees to speak in the language they preferred during lunch and break times and outside the store. Compare *Gutierrez*, 838 F.2d at 1036 with *Garcia*, 618 F.2d at 266 (showing initial municipal court rule as more restrictive than Gloor Lumber's rule).

40. *Gutierrez*, 838 F.2d at 1036.

41. *Id.* at 1045-46 & n.20.

42. *Id.* at 1038-41.

43. *Id.* at 1038-44.

44. *Id.* at 1038-39.

45. *Id.* at 1039.

46. *Id.*

eliminate the relationship between his primary language and the culture that is derived from his national origin."[47]

Relying on regulations published by the EEOC, the court concluded that English-only rules have a disparate impact:

> We agree that English-only rules generally have an adverse impact on protected groups and that they should be closely scrutinized. We also agree that such rules can "create an atmosphere of inferiority, isolation, and intimidation." Finally, we agree that such rules can readily mask an intent to discriminate on the basis of national origin.[48]

Adopting the EEOC's approach to these rules,[49] as well as the traditional structure of disparate impact analysis, the court concluded that a limited English-only rule must be justified by a business necessity before it can be enforced.[50] The court concluded that none of the justifications offered by the appellants for their English-only rule met the business necessity standard.[51]

The *Gutierrez* decision, before it was vacated as moot by the Supreme Court, created a split in the circuits.[52] The court in *Garcia* found no link between a person's primary language and national origin, no disparate impact upon Hispanics, and, consequently, no violation of Title VII resulting from the enforcement of an English-only rule. While not acknowledging that it was doing so, the *Gutierrez* court differed on each of these issues. Under *Gutierrez*, a person's primary language is vitally linked to his national origin, an English-only rule has a disparate impact upon protected groups whose primary language is not English, and, under circumstances similar to those in *Garcia*, an English-

---

47. *Id.*

48. *Id.* at 1040 (citation omitted).

49. The EEOC regulations provide that "[a]n employer may have a rule requiring that employees speak only in English at certain times where the employer can show that the rule is justified by business necessity." 29 C.F.R. § 1606.7(b) (1989).

50. *Gutierrez*, 838 F.2d at 1040. *Gutierrez*, of course, was decided before Wards Cove Packing Co. v. Atonio, 109 S. Ct. 2115 (1989), which significantly lightened the burden of justification faced by employers, who need not prove the business necessity for a challenged practice any longer. *See infra* Part IV.B.

51. *Gutierrez*, 838 F.2d at 1044-45. The municipal court offered several justifications for its rule: preventing the workplace from turning into a "Tower of Babel"; promoting racial harmony; and enhancing the effectiveness of supervision. Additionally, the court stressed that the United States and California are both English-speaking and that the rule was required by the California Constitution. *Id.* at 1042-43.

52. *See* Gutierrez v. Municipal Ct., 861 F.2d 1187 (9th Cir. 1988) (denying rehearing en banc) (Kozinski, J., dissenting) (pointing out the split among the circuits created by the *Gutierrez* decision).

only rule probably violates Title VII. In reaching its conclusions, the *Gutierrez* court examined the employer's justifications to determine whether a business justification existed for the rule. Although no split exists among the circuits at the moment because the Supreme Court decided to vacate *Gutierrez*, the question of the enforceability of English-only rules is likely to recur.[53] The Supreme Court and the lower courts will need to decide three issues when hearing one of these cases. The first is whether the exercise of one's primary language should constitute a protected right as an aspect of national origin under Title VII. Second, the courts must consider whether English-only rules have a disparate impact upon protected language minority groups and, if so, the appropriate standard for justification of these rules. Third, the courts must consider the proper contours of the business justifications that will support the use of English-only rules in the workplace.[54] This Article will discuss each of these issues in turn.

II. THE TITLE VII ANALYSIS

Title VII prohibits discrimination based on national origin.[55] The statute makes no reference, however, to discrimination on the basis of language. The fundamental question, therefore, is whether a person's primary language warrants protection under Title VII as an aspect of national origin.

The Supreme Court has characterized the legislative history of the statutory phrase "national origin" as "quite meager."[56] The brief congressional debate on the term "national origin" suggests that the legislators contemplated persons who came from, or whose forefathers came from, a particular country.[57] There was

---

53. *See supra* text accompanying notes 12-17.

54. The business justification issue will be analyzed using the framework and burdens of proof enunciated in the recently decided case of Wards Cove Packing Co. v. Atonio, 109 S. Ct. 2115 (1989), which has changed significantly the employer's burden of justification. *See infra* notes 187-205 and accompanying text.

55. 42 U.S.C. § 2000e-2(a)(1) (1982) states that:

> It shall be an unlawful employment practice for an employer-
>
> (1) to fail or refuse to hire or to discharge any individual, or otherwise to discriminate against any individual with respect to his compensation, terms, conditions, or privileges of employment, *because of such individual's* race, color, religion, sex, or *national origin;*

Id. (emphasis added).

56. Espinoza v. Farah Mfg. Co., 414 U.S. 86, 88-89 (1973).

57. During the debate on the amendment adding the phrase 'national origin' to the House bill, Representative Roosevelt explained that " 'national origin' means national. It

no commentary, however, on the meaning of national origin discrimination.[58] Primary language should be protected as an aspect of "national origin" for several reasons. First, the courts and the EEOC have interpreted the phrase "national origin" broadly and have extended the protection of Title VII to bar discrimination against persons with characteristics closely correlated with national origin.[59] Second, the sociology of linguistics establishes the importance of primary language as a fundamental aspect of ethnicity and national origin.[60] Third, although primary language is not immutable in the same sense as protected characteristics like race or sex, primary language is what this writer will term "practically immutable," and thus entitled to statutory protection.[61]

A. Broad Construction of National Origin

The courts have construed "national origin" broadly to include characteristics that are correlated with national origin. Several courts, for example, have concluded that an employee's foreign accent, provided that it does not interfere with the employee's ability to perform his job duties, is not a legitimate justification for discrimination under Title VII.[62] Courts also have invalidated minimum height requirements that have discriminatory impact on Mexican Americans or Asian Americans and that

---

means the country from which you or your forebears came from. You may come from Poland, Czechoslovakia, England, France, or any other country." 110 CONG. REC. 2549 (1964), reprinted in UNITED STATES EQUAL EMPLOYMENT OPPORTUNITY COMM'N, LEGISLATIVE HISTORY OF TITLES VII AND IX OF CIVIL RIGHTS ACT OF 1964, at 3179-80 (1968). See also B. SCHLEI & P. GROSSMAN, EMPLOYMENT DISCRIMINATION LAW 305 (2d ed. 1983).

    58. See Note, A Trait-Based Approach to National Origin Claims Under Title VII, 94 YALE L.J. 1164, 1169 & n.25 (1985) (authored by Stephen M. Cutler).

    59. See infra Part II.A.

    60. See infra Part II.B.

    61. See infra Part II.C.

    62. See, e.g., Carino v. Univ. of Oklahoma Bd. of Regents, 750 F.2d 815, 819 (10th Cir. 1984) (holding that a foreign accent that does not interfere with a person's ability to perform job duties is not a legitimate justification under Title VII for an adverse employment action); Bell v. Home Life Ins. Co., 596 F. Supp. 1549, 1555 (M.D.N.C. 1984) (stating that discrimination because of foreign accent can constitute national origin discrimination); Berke v. Ohio Dep't of Pub. Welfare, 30 Fair Empl. Prac. Cas. (BNA) 387, 391-92, 394 (S.D. Ohio 1978), aff'd per curiam, 628 F.2d 980 (6th Cir. 1980); see also 29 C.F.R. § 1606.6(b)(1) (1989) (EEOC regulations stating that discrimination because of foreign accent may be national origin discrimination).

are not justified by business necessity.[63] The *Gutierrez* court treated primary language as a characteristic essentially linked with national origin[64] and entitled to protection under Title VII.[65]

The federal agency charged with enforcing Title VII, the EEOC, also construes national origin discrimination broadly to include discrimination because an individual has the physical, cultural, or linguistic characteristics of a national origin group.[66] In its Guidelines on National Origin Discrimination,[67] the EEOC wrote that "[t]he primary language of an individual is often an essential national origin characteristic."[68] Specifically, several EEOC decisions hold that rules prohibiting Hispanics from speaking Spanish on the job constitute a form of national origin discrimination.[69] The views of the administrative agency that enforces Title VII are entitled to special deference by the courts.[70]

Accordingly, under the broad construction of "national origin" applied by the courts, and under the explicit guidelines and decisions of the EEOC, primary language should be protected under Title VII.

---

63. *See, e.g.,* Davis v. County of Los Angeles, 566 F.2d 1334, 1341-42 (9th Cir. 1977) (holding minimum height requirement for firemen had a disparate impact on Mexican Americans and was not proven to be job related); Officers for Justice v. Civil Serv. Comm'n, 395 F. Supp. 378, 380-81 (N.D. Cal. 1975) (holding minimum height restriction for police officers had a disparate impact on Hispanics, Asians, and women).

64. Gutierrez v. Municipal Ct., 838 F.2d 1031, 1039, *vacated as moot,* 109 S. Ct. 1736 (1989); *accord* Olagues v. Russoniello, 797 F.2d 1511, 1520 (9th Cir. 1986) (en banc) ("[A]n individual's primary language skill generally flows from his or her national origin."), *vacated as moot,* 484 U.S. 806 (1987). *But see* Garcia v. Gloor, 618 F.2d 264, 268, 270-71 (5th Cir. 1980), *cert. denied,* 449 U.S. 1113 (1981).

65. *Gutierrez,* 838 F.2d at 1038.

66. 29 C.F.R. § 1606.1 (1989).

67. 29 C.F.R. § 1606.1-.8 (1989).

68. 29 C.F.R. § 1606.7(a) (1989). The regulation also states that "[a] rule requiring employees to speak only English at all times in the workplace is a burdensome term and condition of employment." *Id.*

69. *See* EEOC Dec. No. 81-25, 27 Fair Empl. Prac. Cas. (BNA) 1820, 1823 (1981); EEOC Dec. No. 72-0281, EEOC Dec. (CCH) ¶ 6293 (1971); EEOC Dec. No. 71446, 2 Fair Empl. Prac. Cas. (BNA) 1127, 1128 (1970).

70. *See* Albemarle Paper Co. v. Moody, 422 U.S. 405, 431 (1975); Griggs v. Duke Power Co., 401 U.S. 424, 433-34 (1971).

B. Primary Language is a Fundamental Aspect of Ethnicity

Primary language, like accent, is closely correlated and inextricably linked with national origin.[71] Prevailing social attitudes, however, deny any relationship between language and culture or ethnicity, leading to the belief that the restriction of language rights does not interfere with ethnic identity or cultural freedom.[72] The court in *Garcia* adopted this position, reasoning that "[n]either [Title VII] nor common understanding equates national origin with the language that one chooses to speak."[73]

Such attitudes are rejected by scholars of ethnicity and language. One leading scholar, Joshua Fishman, defines ethnicity as "both the sense and the expression of 'collective, intergenerational cultural continuity,' i.e. the sensing and expressing of links to 'one's own kind (one's own people),'" with whom one shares ancestral origins.[74] It is through the expression of ethnicity, one's cultural continuity and cultural traits, that "national origin" has perceptible meaning.[75] Primary language is recognized in sociology and sociolinguistics as a fundamental aspect of ethnicity.[76] Fishman has written that "language and ethnic

---

71. *See* Gutierrez v. Municipal Ct., 838 F.2d 1031, *vacated as moot*, 109 S. Ct. 1736 (1989).

72. N. CONKLIN & M. LOURIE, A HOST OF TONGUES: LANGUAGE COMMUNITIES IN THE UNITED STATES (1983). Conklin and Lourie state:

[P]revailing mainstream attitudes deny any relationship between language and culture, arguing that revocation of language rights in no way compromises the integrity of cultural freedoms upon which our nation was constituted. Paradoxically, while language is generally viewed as nothing but a means of communication, standard English is held up as the only appropriate embodiment of the national character.

Id. at 279.

73. Garcia v. Gloor, 618 F.2d 264, 268 (5th Cir. 1980) (footnote omitted), *cert. denied*, 449 U.S. 1113 (1981).

74. J. FISHMAN, *supra* note 17, at 4.

75. *See* Note, *supra* note 58, at 1166-67 & nn.11, 13 (commenting on cultural traits related to national origin).

76. J. FISHMAN, *supra* note 17. Fishman explains:

Ethnicity is . . . belonging or pertaining to a phenomenologically complete, separate, historically deep cultural collectivity, a collectivity polarized on perceived authenticity. This "belonging" is experienced and interpreted physically (biologically), behaviorally (culturally) and phenomenologically (intuitively). . . . [C]haracterized as it is on all three [of these dimensions] it is a very mystic, moving and powerful link with the past and an energizer with respect to the present and future. It is fraught with moral imperatives, with obligations to "one's own kind," and with wisdoms, rewards and proprieties that are both tangible and intangible. . . . As such, it is language-related to a very high and natural degree, both overtly (imbedded as it is in verbal culture and implying as it does structurally dependent intuitions) and covertly (the supreme symbol system [primary language] quintessentially symbolizes its users and distinguishes

authenticity may come to be viewed as highly interdependent."[77] Some scholars view Hispanic culture as imbedded in the language of Spanish speakers, in the sense that both their culture and their language are derived from the reality in which they live; in turn, the culture and the language create and shape that reality.[78] Language and culture together, therefore, form the basic orientation toward reality of any given person or social group.[79] Expert testimony in *Garcia* also stated that "the Spanish language is the most important aspect of ethnic identification for Mexican Americans."[80]

A number of legal commentators also recognize that language is inextricably linked to national origin.[81] One commentator

---

between them and others). Indeed this is so to such a degree that language and ethnic authenticity may come to be viewed as highly interdependent. *Id.* at 70-71; *see also* N. CONKLIN & M. LOURIE, *supra* note 72, at 279 ("[F]or many Americans, speech is an indicator of cultural identity, second in importance only to physical appearance. Further, accent, language choice, verbal style, choice of words, phrases, and gestures act as a primary vehicle for creative expression by individuals and by groups."); Fishman, *The Sociology of Language: An Interdisciplinary Social Science Approach to Language and Society*, in 1 ADVANCES IN THE SOCIOLOGY OF LANGUAGE 217 (J. Fishman ed. 1971)

> [Language] is not merely a *carrier* of content, whether latent, or manifest. Language itself *is* content, a referent for loyalties and animosities, an indicator of social statuses and personal relationships, a marker of situations and topics as well as of the societal goals and the large-scale value-laden arenas of interaction that typify every speech community.

Id. at 219.

77. J. FISHMAN, *supra* note 17, at 70.

78. Christian & Christian, *Spanish Language and Culture in the Southwest*, in LANGUAGE LOYALTY IN THE UNITED STATES 280, 300 (J. Fishman ed. 1966) [hereinafter LANGUAGE LOYALTY].

79. *Id.*

80. Garcia v. Gloor, 618 F.2d 264, 267 (5th Cir. 1980), *cert. denied*, 449 U.S. 1113 (1981).

81. *See, e.g.*, Karst, *Paths to Belonging: The Constitution and Cultural Identity*, 64 N.C.L. REV. 303, 351-57 (1986); McDougal, Lasswell & Chen, *Freedom from Discrimination in Choice of Language and International Human Rights*, 1 S. ILL. U.L.J. 151, 152 (1976) ("[L]anguage is commonly taken as a prime indicator of an individual's group identifications.") (footnote omitted); Piatt, *Toward Domestic Recognition of a Human Right to Language*, 23 HOUS. L. REV. 885, 898-901 (1986); Note, *"Official English": Federal Limits on Efforts to Curtail Bilingual Services in the States*, 100 HARV. L. REV. 1345, 1355 (1987) ("As a separate basis for finding that language-based classifications implicate suspect criteria, courts might determine that such classifications in fact discriminate on the basis of national origin. Litigants have argued that no factor is more intimately tied to a person's ethnic or national identity than is language.") (footnote omitted) [hereinafter Note, *Official English*]; Note, *supra* note 58, at 1165 & n.5 (1985) ("Differences in dress, language, accent, and custom associated with a non-American origin are more likely to elicit prejudicial attitudes than the fact of the origin itself."); Comment, *Native-Born Acadians and the Equality Ideal*, 46 LA. L. REV. 1151, 1167 (1986) (authored by James Harvey Domengeaux) ("Language is the lifeblood of every ethnic group. To economically and psychologically penalize a person for practicing his native tongue is to strike at the core of ethnicity.").

wrote that language is one of the key characteristics "that define social groups . . . . A distinctive language sets a cultural group off from others, with one consistent unhappy consequence throughout American history: discrimination against members of the cultural minority. Language differences provide both a way to rationalize subordination and a ready means for accomplishing it."[82]

The existence in the United States of a thriving ethnic mother-tongue press, non-English commercial broadcasting, and schools designed to preserve foreign languages, demonstrates that primary language is fundamental to ethnicity. The non-English press, particularly the Hispanic press, increased substantially in the United States between 1960 and 1980.[83] The number of Spanish-language publications grew from 49 to 165.[84] The ethnic mother-tongue press provides a vital forum for ethnic concerns and a vehicle for ethnic pride.[85] Non-English radio and television broadcasting also increased between 1960 and 1980, though not at the same rate as commercial broadcasting as a whole.[86] Mother-tongue schools also illustrate the connection between language and ethnicity. The roughly 6600 mother-tongue schools currently operating in the United States[87] are "unequivocally committed to the view that their particular language and ethnicity linkage is vital and, hopefully, eternal."[88]

None of the important sociological and psychological factors that make primary language an important, indeed crucial, aspect

---

82. Karst, *supra* note 81, at 351-52 (footnotes omitted).

83. J. FISHMAN, *supra* note 17, at 344-45. This increase follows a substantial decrease in the non-English press from the 1930s, when ethnic mother-tongue publications reached a peak, to the 1960s. *See* Fishman, Hayden, and Warshauer, *The Non-English and the Ethnic Group Press,* in LANGUAGE LOYALTY, *supra* note 78, at 51-52.

84. J. FISHMAN, *supra* note 17, at 344-45.

85. *Id.* at 330. *See also* Glazer, *The Process and Problems of Language-Maintenance: An Integrative Review,* in A PLURALISTIC NATION: THE LANGUAGE ISSUE IN THE UNITED STATES 32 (1978). Glazer states:

In America, the immigrant wants to preserve, as far as possible, his heritage from the old country. These (sic) are represented preeminently by his language and his religion. At the same time, he wants to participate in the common life and find a place in the American community. In these two motives, we have at once the problem of the foreign-language press and its solution.

Id. at 33. (quoting R. PARK, THE IMMIGRANT PRESS AND ITS CONTROL (1922)).

86. J. FISHMAN, *supra* note 17, at 224-26. In 1982, there were approximately 275 television stations broadcasting during at least a protion of the day in non-English languages. Approximately 60% of these stations broadcast in Spanish. *Id.*

87. *Id.* at 244 (Table 15), 364.

88. *Id.* at 365. The majority of ethnic mother-tongue schools teach in the languages of Hebrew, Yiddish, Spanish, Pennsylvania German, and Greek. *Id.* at 242.

of ethnicity are different in the case of a bilingual person.[89] Even for a bilingual, links to one's "own people" and ethnicity depend heavily on primary language. A study of Spanish-speaking bilinguals demonstrated that they associate Spanish with family and friendship and values of intimacy.[90] Accordingly, given all of these factors, the *Garcia* court erred in concluding that Gloor Lumber's English-only rule "did not forbid cultural expression to persons for whom compliance with it might impose hardship."[91]

C. *Primary Language is Practically Immutable*

Primary language, therefore, merits protection under Title VII as a fundamental aspect and a crucial expression of national origin and ethnicity. The exercise of a person's primary language also warrants protection under Title VII for another reason. One of the rationales for protecting a personal characteristic under Title VII is its immutability.[92] With the exceptions of religion and pregnancy, all of the characteristics protected under the statute—race, color, national origin, and sex—are immutable. The *Garcia* court viewed a bilingual's choice of language, however, as purely a matter of individual preference and not immutable.[93]

---

89. In contrast, the *Garcia* court reasoned that, for a multilingual person, the matter of which language to speak at a particular time is purely a matter of individual choice and without invidious effects. Garcia v. Gloor, 618 F.2d 264, 270 (5th Cir. 1980), *cert. denied*, 449 U.S. 1113 (1981).

90. Greenfield, *Situational Measures of Normative Language Views in Relation to Person, Place and Topic Among Puerto Rican Bilinguals*, in 2 ADVANCES IN THE SOCIOLOGY OF LANGUAGE 17, 33 (J. Fishman ed. 1972) ("Use of Spanish was claimed primarily in the domain of family, secondarily for the domains of friendship and religion, and least of all in those of education and employment, while the reverse held true for English."). *See also* Fishman, *The Sociology of Language: An Interdisciplinary Social Science Approach to Language in Society*, in 1 ADVANCES IN THE SOCIOLOGY OF LANGUAGE 217, 251 (J. Fishman ed. 1971) (stating that among bilinguals, Spanish is primarily associated with family and friendship, which constitute the intimacy value cluster).

91. *Garcia*, 618 F.2d at 270.

92. *See id.* at 269; Willingham v. Macon Tel. Publishing Co., 507 F.2d 1084, 1091 (5th Cir. 1975).

93. *Garcia*, 618 F.2d at 269-70. Bilingualism can be considered as a spectrum of abilities in a second language, ranging from a minimal ability to communicate in the second language to equal facility in the second language. It is not necessarily the case, therefore, that someone able to speak enough English to meet the minimum requirements of a job is fully bilingual and able to express the full range of what needs to be conveyed to conduct personal relationships with co-workers. *See infra* notes 95-101 and accompanying text.

Although not immutable in the same sense as race or sex, primary language is, for many persons, practically immutable.[94] Even the *Garcia* court conceded that "[t]o a person who speaks only one tongue or to a person who has difficulty using another language than the one spoken in his home, language might well be an immutable characteristic like skin color, sex or place of birth."[95] Moreover, acquiring a new language is especially difficult for adults with limited economic resources.[96]

Studies of second-language acquisition demonstrate the difficulty of acquiring English as a second language. One study, conducted by Portes and Bach, examined the language acquisition of a group of recent Mexican and Cuban male immigrants to the United States.[97] Despite spending six years in the United States and despite instruction in English, over two-thirds (74.3%) of the men studied gained essentially no knowledge of English or only minimal English skills.[98] Another study focused on Hispanic-origin males and females, aged fourteen and over, who reported that Spanish was their mother tongue, the language spoken in their homes when they were children.[99] Of this sample, half of the studied group were still using Spanish as their primary language.[100] Other case studies show that, particularly for older adolescents and adults, acquisition of English is quite difficult; often the result is a bare, minimal level of competence in communication.[101] It is a well-established proposition in the psychology and sociology of language acquisition that the acqui-

---

94. *See* Note, *Official English, supra* note 81, at 1354-55. *See also* W. LONGSTREET, ASPECTS OF ETHNICITY: UNDERSTANDING DIFFERENCES IN PLURALISTIC CLASSROOMS 19-20 (1978) ("Individuals will eventually attain some intellectual control over their ethnically learned behaviors, but that control is likely to remain incomplete. Much of what is learned ethnically is done at a very low level of awareness and in a way that seems to sidestep rationality."). The EEOC also recognizes that it is "common for individuals whose primary language is not English to inadvertently change from speaking English to speaking their primary language." 29 C.F.R. § 1606.7(c) (1989).
95. *Garcia,* 618 F.2d at 270.
96. Note, *Official English, supra* note 81, at 1354.
97. A. PORTES & R. BACH, LATIN JOURNEY: CUBAN AND MEXICAN IMMIGRANTS IN THE UNITED STATES (1985).
98. *Id.* at 174, 180, 198.
99. Grenier, *Shifts to English as Usual Language by Americans of Spanish Mother Tongue,* in THE MEXICAN AMERICAN EXPERIENCE: AN INTERDISCIPLINARY ANTHOLOGY 346, 350 (1985).
100. *Id.* at 356. This study also found that Hispanics "are shifting to English at a relatively fast pace." *Id.*
101. *See* Schumann, *Second Language Acquisition: The Pidginization Hypothesis,* in SECOND LANGUAGE ACQUISITION: A BOOK OF READINGS 256-71 (E. Hatch ed. 1978); Shapira, *The Non-learning of English: Case Study of an Adult,* in SECOND LANGUAGE ACQUISITION: A BOOK OF READINGS 246-55 (E. Hatch ed. 1978). Both articles present case studies of Spanish-speaking adults encountering great difficulty in acquiring English.

sition and mastery of a new language is far more difficult for adults than for children.[102] Several theories attempt to explain this phenomenon. One theory postulates a "critical period" after which physiological changes in the brain make learning a second language much more difficult.[103] Another theory explains difficulties in second-language acquisition by adults as the result of the social and psychological distances between an individual member of a social group and members of another social group that speaks a different language.[104] Social distance, which creates a poor language learning situation, exists when an individual's group is either dominant or subordinate to the group speaking the desired language, when both groups desire preservation of their values and cultural pattern and resist intermingling, or when the two groups hold negative attitudes about each other, among other factors.[105] One can infer a large degree of social distance, and therefore poor language learning conditions, between many persons whose primary language is not English and the English-speaking majority culture based on differences

---

102. See Seliger, *Implications of a Multiple Critical Periods Hypothesis for Second Language Learning*, in SECOND LANGUAGE ACQUISITION RESEARCH: ISSUES AND IMPLICATIONS 11 (W. Ritchie ed. 1978) ("[T]he biological fact of adulthood is enough to establish an insurmountable obstacle in most cases for *complete* language acquisition. The incompleteness of the adult learner's [second-language] system has a physiological basis and concomitant cognitive correlates."); Whitaker, *Bilingualism: A Neurolinguistics Perspective*, in SECOND LANGUAGE ACQUISITION RESEARCH: ISSUES AND IMPLICATIONS 21, 29-30 (W. Ritchie ed. 1978); Shapira, *supra* note 101, at 252-53. *See also* Schumann, *supra* note 101, at 259-67.

103. Professor Lenneberg first proposed this theory. He hypothesized that cerebral dominance, and lateralization of the language functions of the brain to the left hemisphere of the brain, was complete by puberty. *See* E. LENNEBERG, BIOLOGICAL FOUNDATIONS OF LANGUAGE (1967); *see also* S. KRASHEN, SECOND LANGUAGE ACQUISITION AND SECOND LANGUAGE LEARNING 72 (1981) (describing Lenneberg's theory); Seliger, *supra* note 102, at 11-12; Whitaker, *supra* note 102, at 29-30. This critical period appears to end at puberty. *See* Whitaker, *supra* note 102, at 29-30 ("Although there is evidence that under unusual circumstances language acquisition may occur after puberty . . ., possibly by the right hemisphere [of the brain], it is neither as rapid nor as successful as normal language acquisition.") (citations omitted); S. KRASHEN, *supra*, at 72-73 ("[T]here seems to be no question that puberty is an important turning point in language acquisition. . . .").

    Several scholars question the critical period hypothesis. Krashen, while acknowledging that differences in second language acquisition potential do exist between children and adults, questions whether this difference is based on physiological or biological differences between children and adults. S. KRASHEN, *supra*, at 73, 81. *See also* Schumann, *supra* note 101, at 259; Shapira, *supra* note 101, at 252; Snow & Hoefnagel-Hohle, *The Critical Period for Language Acquisition: Evidence from Second Language Learning*, 49 CHILD DEV. 1114-28 (1978) (study failed to support the critical period hypothesis; fastest second-language acquisition occurred in subjects aged 12-15 years, while the slowest occurred in subjects aged 3-5 years).

104. Schumann, *supra* note 101, at 261-67.

105. *Id.* at 261-63.

in socioeconomic status and educational level,[106] as well as on the relative isolation of language minority persons in ethnic minority communities.[107]

Success in acquiring a second language can also depend on the psychological distance between the learner and the group speaking the second language.[108] Psychological distance develops as a language learner is haunted by doubts about his ability to express himself in a different language and when he finds that his problem-solving abilities do not work in a new culture with a different language.[109] An individual's motivation, dependent upon his attitude toward English-speakers and his willingness to adopt both linguistic and nonlinguistic aspects of their behavior, is another important factor in his acquisition of a second language.[110] Second-language acquisition, a complex and difficult task under ideal conditions, is more difficult for members of language minority groups, in part because of a long history of discrimination against members of language minorities.[111] Many

---

106. See infra notes 114-15.

107. This isolation originates from a history of discrimination. See infra note 111.

108. Schumann, supra note 101, at 263-67.

109. Id.

110. R. GARDNER & W. LAMBERT, ATTITUDES AND MOTIVATION IN SECOND-LANGUAGE LEARNING (1972). Gardner and Lambert state:

[E]thnocentric and prejudiced views held students back in various ways, where widely shared negative stereotypes of certain peoples appeared to make the work of a language teacher almost impossible, and where particular profiles of values and motives seemed to make the difference between success and failure at school work in general and language study in particular.

Id. at 144; see also Schumann, supra note 101, at 266-67. Schumann writes:

[F]actors causing psychological distance . . . put the learner in a situation where he is largely cut off from [secondary] language input and/or does not attend to it when it is available. The language which is acquired under these conditions will be used simply for denotative referential communication in situations where contact with speakers of the [secondary] language is either absolutely necessary or unavoidable . . . [and] his use of the [secondary] language will be functionally restricted . . . .

Id.

Prejudice against the language of Hispanics is recognized as a cause of low esteem for the language. N. CONKLIN & M. LOURIE, supra note 72, at 193. "Spanish-influenced English is more often scorned than any other language variety in the Chicano verbal repertoire . . . . Neither Chicanos nor Anglos have much respect or affection for it." Id. at 192 (citation omitted). Attitudes such as these can only make the second language acquisition process more difficult and less successful.

111. There is a long history of discrimination against Mexican-Americans in employment. "[T]he pattern of employment of the Mexican American, dictated through the discrimination encountered, has been the major factor contributing to the isolation of the Mexican American from the majority population." Greenfield & Kates, Mexican Americans, Racial Discrimination, and the Civil Rights Act of 1866, 63 CALIF. L. REV. 662, 718 (1975) (footnote omitted). Mexican Americans have been paid lower starting wages than Anglos, have suffered from curtailed opportunities for promotion, and have

cases have recognized the systematic discrimination in public education against Hispanic[112] and Asian[113] children. For many

---

been subject to discrimination from labor unions as well as employers. *Id.* at 719-20. "In nearly all of the broad occupational classifications . . . Mexicans held poorer jobs paying less money than did native American whites." J. MOORE, MEXICAN AMERICANS 61 (1st ed. 1970). Mexicans tend to hold the poorer and and lower paying jobs even within occupational categories. *Id.* at 62. Even if the representation of Mexican Americans and White Americans were equal in the broad occupational categories, Mexicans would still get lower pay than their Anglo counterparts doing similar work. *Id.* at 62.

In 1959, the median income of all Mexican Americans males in the Southwest United States was only 57% of the median earned by Anglo males in the same area. *Id.* at 60. As described by Professor Joan Moore:

> It is perfectly obvious from the most superficial examination of the data that in general Mexican Americans hold the less desirable jobs in the Southwest because of lack of education, lack of business capital, cultural dissimilarity to the majority, and their obvious role as a low-prestige group. Further, Mexicans are disproportionately forced to work in low-wage or marginal firms—in the less profitable, non-unionized fringes of the high-wage industries. Low job earnings are also associated with the concentration of Mexicans in certain low-wage geographical areas, the lower Rio Grande valley of Texas being an example. (Of course, such areas are "low-wage" partly *because* they are heavily Mexican.)

Id. at 63. A more recent study demonstrates that White Americans still fare better economically than Mexican Americans or Black Americans. Verdugo & Verdugo, *Earnings Differentials Between Mexican American, Black, and White Male Workers,* in THE MEXICAN AMERICAN EXPERIENCE: AN INTERDISCIPLINARY ANTHOLOGY 133 (1985).

> [W]hites fared better than either blacks or Mexican Americans socioeconomically. Whites earned more, had completed more years of schooling, and worked at far better jobs than either blacks or Mexican Americans. Whites also appeared to be more fully employed as they worked more hours than either blacks or Mexican Americans.

Id. at 136.

The under-representation of Hispanics in prestigious and highly paid jobs continues into the present. *See, e.g.,* Davila, *The Underrepresentation of Hispanic Attorneys in Corporate Law Firms,* 39 STAN. L. REV. 1403 (1987):

> Despite many advances, minority representation in the legal profession, as in most prestigious fields, is still not proportionate to the minority presence in the general population. But even within the legal world, corporate law firms have been slower than other professional groups in moving toward a more proportionate racial balance. . . . One survey reported that Hispanics represent less than 1 percent of the attorneys in the 151 biggest law firms in the United States.

Id. at 1404 (footnotes omitted). Hispanics in corporate law firms often experience a strong sense of isolation within the firms. *Id.* at 1415. "[T]his sense of isolation may be rooted in the fact that the Hispanic attorneys' backgrounds and value systems differ so radically from those of their white counterparts." *Id. Cf.* Olagues v. Russoniello, 797 F.2d 1511, 1521 (9th Cir. 1986), *vacated as moot,* 484 U.S. 806 (1987) ("[C]ourts have long recognized the history of discriminatory treatment inflicted on Chinese and Hispanic people.") (citations omitted). Many courts have observed such discrimination against Chinese and Hispanic people. *See, e.g.,* Hernandez v. Texas, 347 U.S. 475, 479-82 (1954) (holding that persons of Mexican descent were discriminated against in jury selection); Yick Wo v. Hopkins, 118 U.S. 356, 373-74 (1886) (holding that Chinese persons were discriminated against by municipal ordinance regulating public laundries).

112. *See* Keyes v. School Dist. No. 1, 413 U.S. 189, 197-98 (1973); Cisneros v. Corpus Christi Indep. School Dist., 467 F.2d 142, 144 (5th Cir. 1972) (en banc); United States v. Texas Educ. Agency, 467 F.2d 848, 853 (5th Cir. 1972) (en banc); Soria v. Oxnard School Dist., 328 F. Supp. 157 (C.D. Cal. 1971); *see generally,* Greenfield & Kates, *supra* note 111, at 711-15 (1975); Rangel & Alcalo, *Project Report: De Jure Segregation of Chicanos in Texas Schools,* 7 HARV. C.R.-C.L. L. REV. 379 (1972).

113. *See* Lau v. Nichols, 414 U.S. 563 (1974); Guey Heung Lee v. Johnson, 404 U.S.

years, state and local officials refused to offer equal educational opportunities to members of language minority groups.[114] According to the Senate Report accompanying the 1975 amendments to the Voting Rights Act of 1965, "[p]ersons of Spanish heritage are the group most severely affected by discriminatory practices, while the documentation of discriminatory practices concerning Asian Americans . . . was substantial."[115]

1215, 1215-16 (1971) (stating that a California statute authorized separate schools for children of Asian descent until its repeal in 1947).

    114. *See* S. REP. No. 295, 94th Cong., 1st Sess. 2 (1975), *reprinted in* 1975 U.S. CODE CONG. & ADMIN. NEWS 774, 794 [hereinafter SENATE REPORT].

    The history of discrimination against members of language minority groups begins early: in the schools. It begins with the banning of languages other than English from the classroom. As one scholar has observed, "[i]n 1919 fifteen states decreed that English must be the sole language of instruction in all primary schools, public and private." J. HIGHAM, STRANGERS IN THE LAND: PATTERNS OF AMERICAN NATIVISM, 1860-1925, at 260 (2d ed. 1988). The Nebraska statute, which stated that "[n]o person . . . shall . . . teach any subject to any person in any language other than the English language," was applied to prohibit teaching in the German language. Meyer v. Nebraska, 262 U.S. 390, 397 (1923). In Louisiana, educators banned the use of French in the classroom. *See* Comment, *supra* note 81, at 1154-55. French-speaking students were severely punished when they spoke their primary language in school. *Id.* Spanish, too, was banned from the classroom. In Texas, as in other parts of the Southwestern United States, "Mexican-American children were prohibited from speaking their native language anywhere on school grounds. Those who violated the 'No Spanish' rule were severely punished." United States v. Texas, 506 F. Supp 405, 412 (E.D. Tex. 1981), *rev'd on other grounds*, 680 F.2d 356 (5th Cir. 1982); J. MOORE, *supra* note 111, at 84. The punishment included corporal punishment. *Id.* "[A]s late as the 1950s children who spoke Spanish in school were made to kneel on upturned bottle caps, forced to hold bricks in outstretched hands in the schoolyard, or told to put their nose in a chalk circle drawn on a blackboard. And this would happen in Texas towns that were 98 percent Spanish-speaking." T. WEYR, *supra* note 12, at 52.

    The forcible suppression of other languages in schools was accompanied by the segregation of children from language minority groups in separate and unequal schools. *See* J. MOORE, *supra* note 111, at 81; *see, e.g.,* United States v. Texas, 506 F. Supp. at 411 ("[S]egregation of Mexican Americans is a historical fact in Texas public schools."); Keyes v. School Dist. No. 1, 413 U.S. at 197-98 (1973); Hernandez v. Texas, 347 U.S. at 479 (1954); Greenfield & Kates, *supra* note 111, at 714 & n.299 (1975); *see generally* Rangel & Alcalo, *supra* note 112.

    During the enactment in 1975 of amendments to the Voting Rights Act, Congress found widespread discrimination against language minority citizens and recognized this as a denial of equal educational opportunity. *See* 42 U.S.C. § 1973b(f)(1) (1982); *cf.* Lau v. Nichols, 414 U.S. at 568 (1974) (holding that Chinese children taught in English-only classes were denied equal educational opportunity).

    115. SENATE REPORT, *supra* note 114, at 797. The isolation of language minority students in segregated, inferior schools, and the suppression of their primary languages, has resulted in low educational attainment and a very high dropout rate for such students. These effects are well documented in the case of Mexican American and other Hispanic children. In 1960, the median number of years of education completed was 12.1 for Anglos, but only 7.1 for Spanish-surname students. J. MOORE, *supra* note 111, at 68 (Table 4-2). In 1970, the problem of low educational attainment was still severe. According to

The courts and the Congress have recognized and responded to the difficulties faced by persons of limited English-speaking ability. Indeed, one can imply the practical immutability of one's primary language from the numerous judicial and statutory accommodations to persons whose primary language is not English. For example, in *Lau v. Nichols*,[116] the Supreme Court interpreted Title VI of the Civil Rights Act of 1964[117] to require a school district to provide language assistance to overcome barriers faced by children whose primary language was Chinese and who spoke no English.[118] In other settings, the courts have held that non-English speakers are entitled to affirmative voting assistance,[119] to translators in criminal proceedings,[120] and to relief from a default judgment entered because the defendant, unable to speak or read English, failed to answer a complaint.[121]

Congress also enacted laws designed to accommodate persons whose primary language is not English. In perhaps the most important accommodation, Congress in 1975 extended the coverage of the Voting Rights Act of 1965[122] to include language minori-

---

the 1970 Census, only 5.5% of the general population over 25 had failed to complete five years of school, compared with more than 18.9% of Hispanic citizens over 25. SENATE REPORT, *supra* note 114, at 794. In Texas, over 33% of Mexican American citizens had failed to complete the fifth grade. *Id.* Over half of the Mexican American children in Texas who enter the first grade never finish high school. *Id.* "In 1981, 30 percent of the Hispanic 18 and 19-year-olds were not high school graduates, a significantly higher dropout rate than [for] white or black students." H. R. REP. No. 748, 98th Cong., 2d Sess. 4 (1984), *reprinted in* 1984 U.S. CODE CONG. & ADMIN. NEWS 4036, 4040 (legislative history of the Education Amendments of 1984, including the Bilingual Education Act). Lest one consider this a problem wholly of the past, the very high dropout rate for Hispanic youngsters, currently measured at 50 percent in the Boston schools, for example, remains a serious source of concern and a major problem in 1988. *See* Ribadeneira, *Hispanics Demand a Better Effort by City Schools: Parents Blame High Dropout Rate on Indifference,* Boston Globe, Nov. 21, 1988, at 15, col. 1; Ribadeneira, *Boom Bypassing Mass. Hispanics,* Boston Globe, June 5, 1988, at 41, col. 1 (Massachusetts state dropout rate for Hispanics about 56%; in Boston, about 51%).

To the extent that English is learned in the schools, these high dropout rates support the argument that, for those students whose primary language is not English, primary language is practically immutable.

116. 414 U.S. 563 (1974).

117. 42 U.S.C. § 2000d (1982) (prohibiting discrimination based on national origin in programs receiving federal financial assistance).

118. *See also* Serna v. Portales Mun. Schools, 499 F.2d 1147, 1154 (10th Cir. 1974).

119. Puerto Rican Org. for Political Action v. Kusper, 350 F. Supp. 606, 611-12 (N.D. Ill. 1972), *aff'd,* 490 F.2d 575 (7th Cir. 1973). *See* Note, *Official English, supra* note 81, at 1349 & n.31.

120. United States *ex. rel.* Negron v. New York, 434 F.2d 386, 390-91 (2d Cir. 1970). *See* Note, *Official English, supra* note 81, at 1350 & n.33.

121. Cota v. Southern Arizona Bank & Trust Co., 17 Ariz. App. 326, 497 P.2d 833 (1972).

122. 42 U.S.C. §§ 1971-74 (1982).

ties.[123] Congress found that "voting discrimination against citizens of language minorities is pervasive and national in scope. Such minority citizens are from environments in which the dominant language is other than English."[124] Congress concluded that "where state and local officials conduct elections only in English, language minority citizens are excluded from participating in the electoral process."[125] To remedy this exclusion, Congress required state and political subdivisions to provide voting materials, instructions, and ballots "in the language of the applicable language minority group as well as in the English language."[126] Congress recognized, therefore, the substantial barriers blocking effective participation in the electoral process for persons whose primary language differs from English.

Congress has taken other affirmative steps to assist language minorities. In the Bilingual Education Act,[127] Congress provided financial assistance for local bilingual projects designed to assist children and adults whose primary language is not English and whose abilities in English are limited. As part of the Bilingual Education Act, Congress recognized "that there are large and growing numbers of children of limited English proficiency . . . many of [whom] . . . have a cultural heritage which differs from that of English proficient persons."[128] Congress also was aware that "because of limited English proficiency, many adults are not able to participate fully in national life, and that limited English proficient parents are often not able to participate effectively in their children's education."[129]

In its regulations implementing the Bilingual Education Act, the Department of Education recognizes explicitly the difficulties faced by individuals whose primary language is different from English. The department defined "limited English proficiency" individuals as including those "not born in the United States or whose native language is other than English" or who come "from a home in which a language other than English is used most for communication . . . ."[130] When such a person

---

123. Voting Rights Act Extension of 1975, Pub. L. No. 94-73, 89 Stat. 400 (1975).
124. 42 U.S.C. § 1973b(f)(1) (1982).
125. *Id.*
126. 42 U.S.C. § 1973b(f)(4) (1982).
127. 20 U.S.C. §§ 3281-3341 (1988).
128. *Id.* § 3282(a)(1)-(2) (1988).
129. *Id.* § 3282(a)(19) (1988); *see also* H. REP. No. 748, 98th Cong., 2d Sess. 7 (1984), *reprinted in* 1984 U.S. CODE CONG. & ADMIN. NEWS 4036, 4042.
130. 34 C.F.R. § 500.4(b)(1)(i)-(ii) (1988). In 1989, the department formally adopted the definitions in the Bilingual Education Act. 34 C.F.R. § 500.4(b) (1989). These definitions contain the same language. *See* 20 U.S.C. § 3283(a) (1988).

"has sufficient difficulty in speaking, reading, writing or understanding the English language" [that they cannot] [p]articipate
fully in our society," the person has "limited English
proficiency."[131]

A number of other federal statutes require the use of different
languages in a variety of contexts, covering situations such as
the use of interpreters in the courtroom,[132] the use of foreign
languages at federally funded migrant and community health
centers,[133] and in federal alcohol abuse and treatment
programs.[134]

Judges and lawmakers recognize, therefore, that full participation in important aspects of American life is difficult for persons
with a different primary language. Access to voting, education,
and simple justice is limited severely for many Americans unless
these rights and services are provided in languages understood
by them. These many accommodations to persons of different
primary language imply that a different primary language, if not
completely immutable, is at least practically immutable for
many Americans to a degree that inhibits full functioning in society. The practically immutable nature of a primary language is
the unstated premise of many of these laws, for if one's primary
language could be so easily changed—if English could be so easily acquired—then there would be little need for national laws
guaranteeing that basic rights will be communicated in different
languages and so made available to many Americans.

D.   Garcia v. Gloor—The Wrong Path

The *Garcia* court's conclusion that Title VII does not support
an interpretation that equates an employee's primary language
with his national origin[135] is therefore misguided for several reasons. The courts and the EEOC have extended the protection of
Title VII to bar discrimination against persons who have characteristics that are closely correlated with national origin.[136] Pri-

---

131.   34 C.F.R. § 500.4(b)(2) (1988).
132.   28 U.S.C. § 1827(d) (1982); *see* Note, *Official English, supra* note 81, at 1350 &
n.37.
133.   42 U.S.C. §§ 254b(f)(3)(J), 254c(e)(3)(J) (1982); *see* Note, *Official English,*
supra note 81, at 1350 & n.37.
134.   42 U.S.C. § 4577(b)(3)(1982); *see* Note, *Official English, supra* note 81, at 1350
& n.37.
135.   *Garcia v. Gloor* 618 F.2d 264, 270 (5th Cir. 1980), *cert. denied,* 449 U.S. 1113
(1981).
136.   *See supra* notes 62-69 and accompanying text.

mary language or mother tongue—English for most Americans, and Spanish, German, Italian, French, Polish, Yiddish and other languages for many Americans[137]—is one of the most important aspects of ethnic identity and national origin.[138] As such, it is properly protected under Title VII as a characteristic closely correlated and inextricably related to national origin.[139] In particular, the courts and the EEOC already protect linguistic characteristics such as foreign accent under the statute.[140] It is difficult to discern a reason for protecting one's foreign accent under the statute while denying protection to one's primary language, the fundamental ethnic trait that gave rise to the accent.

The *Garcia* court also reasoned that a bilingual employee's desire to speak his primary language is not an immutable characteristic like place of birth, race or sex.[141] The foregoing analysis demonstrates, however, that for many persons primary language is practically immutable. Indeed, even the *Garcia* court recognized that language might be immutable for persons who speak only one language or who have difficulty with languages other than their mother tongue.[142]

The established difficulty of second-language acquisition for language minorities in this country and the recognition by the courts and Congress of the need to accommodate persons whose primary language is not English provide compelling evidence that primary language is practically immutable. The practical immutability of primary language justifies its protection under Title VII.

---

137. These are the six languages other than English most frequently claimed as mother tongues in the United States as reported in 1970 and 1979 Bureau of the Census data. J. FISHMAN, *supra* note 17, at 111, 145-48.

138. *See supra* notes 74-80 and accompanying text.

139. *See* Note, *supra* note 58, at 1166 ("Courts should therefore employ a definition of national origin discrimination which includes the concept of discrimination on the basis of national origin-linked (i.e., cultural) traits.") (footnote omitted).

140. *See supra* notes 62 and 69 and accompanying text.

141. Garcia v. Gloor, 618 F.2d 264, 269-70 (5th Cir. 1980), *cert. denied*, 449 U.S. 1113 (1981).

142. *Id.* The plaintiff in *Garcia*, Hector Garcia, testified during the trial that he had difficulty following Gloor Lumber's rule because Spanish was his primary language. Because of his primary language, Garcia tended to speak Spanish inadvertently and had to think carefully before speaking English because he might give the wrong impression at times and could not always express himself fluently. Brief for the EEOC at 3-4, Garcia v. Gloor, 625 F.2d 1016 (5th Cir. 1980) (No. 77-2358) (petition for rehearing). Despite Garcia's difficulty in expressing himself in English, the *Garcia* court did not find that his primary language was immutable. Garcia v. Gloor, 618 F.2d 264, 272 (5th Cir. 1980), *cert. denied*, 449 U.S. 1113 (1981).

III. THE "EXCLUSIVE ADVERSE IMPACT" OF ENGLISH-ONLY RULES

Having established that one's primary language closely correlates with national origin and that its use is entitled to protection under Title VII, we must then determine the proper analysis to apply to restrictions imposed upon the exercise of one's primary language. Although few courts have addressed the legality of English-only rules, the EEOC has advocated[143] the use of the disparate impact theory developed in *Griggs v. Duke Power Co.*[144] The *Gutierrez* court, adopting the EEOC's analysis, analyzed the municipal court's English-only rule under a disparate impact theory.[145]

The disparate impact theory applies when a plaintiff demonstrates that a specific, facially neutral employment policy has a discriminatory impact on protected groups.[146] An English-only rule is a specific and identifiable employment practice, as required by *Wards Cove Packing Co. v. Atonio.*[147] Application of the disparate impact theory to the analysis of English-only rules also rests on the assumption that an English-only rule is a facially neutral employment policy. This assumption, not questioned by the litigants or the courts in *Garcia* and *Gutierrez*, or by the EEOC, has superficial appeal. It can be argued that an English-only rule applies equally to all employees in that every employee must speak English.

An English-only rule, however, differs in kind from the facially neutral rules usually analyzed under the disparate impact model. Facially neutral rules are facially neutral because they operate to disqualify members of both the majority class and the protected minority class. Thus, in *Griggs,* the neutral selection devices of a high school diploma or general intelligence tests would disqualify at least some Whites as well as Blacks.[148]

---

143. *See, e.g.,* EEOC Dec. No. 81-25, 27 Fair. Empl. Prac. Cas. (BNA) 1820 (1981); EEOC Dec. No. 72-0281, EEOC Dec. (CCH) ¶ 6293 (1971).

144. 401 U.S. 424 (1971). The application of the disparate impact theory, particularly the allocation of burdens of proof under the theory, has been changed significantly by the recent decision in *Wards Cove Packing Co. v. Atonio,* 109 S. Ct. 2115 (1989). *See infra* notes 182-95 and accompanying text.

145. Gutierrez v. Municipal Ct., 838 F.2d 1031, 1040, *vacated as moot,* 109 S. Ct. 1736 (1989).

146. *Wards Cove,* 109 S. Ct. at 2119, 2124; *Griggs,* 401 U.S. at 431 (stating that Title VII "proscribes not only overt discrimination but also practices that are fair in form, but discriminatory in operation").

147. 109 S. Ct. 2115, 2124 (1989).

148. *Griggs,* 401 U.S. at 427-28.

In *Dothard v. Rawlinson*,[149] the facially neutral statutory height and weight requirements would disqualify at least some men as well as women.[150] Accordingly, such facially neutral devices show fairness in form, if not in results. Only when the neutral rule disqualifies a disproportionate number of members of a protected class does a disparate impact exist.

Now consider the impact of an English-only rule. No member of the majority class will ever be disqualified because of the operation of the rule. An English-only rule will never have any adverse impact on persons whose primary language is English.[151] The only persons disqualified are members of protected groups whose primary language is not English.[152] The rule's full impact falls exclusively upon members of protected groups. Accordingly, English-only rules have no claim to the fairness in form of other rules analyzed under disparate impact theory.[153] Rather than characterizing them inaccurately as "facially neutral," English-only rules should be described as having an exclusive adverse impact that constitutes the "functional equivalent" of national origin discrimination.[154]

Outside the Title VII context, courts already recognize such an adverse impact upon citizens whose primary language is not English. In *Yu Cong Eng v. Trinidad*,[155] decided in 1926, the Supreme Court declared unconstitutional a Philippine law prohibiting Chinese merchants from keeping their business account books in Chinese, the only language the merchants knew. Finding that the enforcement of the law's criminal penalties against the Chinese merchants "would seriously embarrass all of them and would drive out of business a great number,"[156] the

---

149. 433 U.S. 321 (1977).

150. *See id.* at 329-30.

151. Although it is possible to conceive of a few situations in which persons whose primary language is English could be affected by an English-only rule, for example, if someone studying Spanish wanted to practice Spanish with Spanish-speaking co-workers in the workplace, such situations seem few and trivial. Furthermore, in such a situation there would probably be no correlation between Spanish and such a person's national origin, so there would be no national origin discrimination implicated in limiting such a student's use of Spanish in the workplace.

152. *See Note, Official English, supra* note 81, at 1353.

153. *See* 3 A. LARSON & L. LARSON, EMPLOYMENT DISCRIMINATION LAW § 73.41 (1987) ("As to English language tests, when the issue is one of national origin discrimination they probably are not entitled to be called neutral at all.").

154. *See* Fiss, *A Theory of Fair Employment Laws*, 38 U. CHI. L. REV. 235, 298-99 (1971); Comment, *The Business Necessity Defense to Disparate Impact Liability Under Title VII*, 46 U. CHI. L. REV. 911, 923 (1979) (authored by Marcus B. Chandler) (citing "functional equivalence" theory of Professor Owen Fiss).

155. 271 U.S. 500 (1926).

156. *Id.* at 514-15.

Court held that the law denied to Chinese persons due process and equal protection of the laws.[157] More recently, in *Serna v. Portales Municipal Schools*,[158] the court recognized the negative effect of language and cultural restrictions on school children, heeding expert testimony[159] that "a child who goes to a school where he finds no evidence of his language and culture and ethnic group represented becomes withdrawn and nonparticipating."[160] There is little reason to assume that these negative effects are much different when English-only rules are imposed upon adults whose primary language is not English.[161] One court has recognized recently that the chilling effect upon the Spanish-language speech of Hispanics caused by a state Official-English law is a constitutionally redressable injury, violating the first amendment of the U.S. Constitution.[162]

The United States Senate, in its report on the extension of the Voting Rights Act to include language minority citizens, reviewed the adverse effects of English-only elections upon language minority groups.[163] While the issues involved in English-only elections may be somewhat different from those involved in considering an English-only rule in the workplace,[164] the resulting discouragement, frustration and inhibition of people subject to the rule are the same. Recognizing these adverse effects upon adults, the EEOC published regulations describing the effect of English-only rules:

> Prohibiting employees at all times, in the workplace, from speaking their primary language or the language they speak most comfortably, disadvantages an individual's employment opportunities on the basis of national origin. It may also create an atmosphere of inferiority, isolation and intimidation based on national origin which could result in a discriminatory working environment.[165]

---

157. *Id.* at 524-25.

158. 351 F. Supp. 1279 (D.N.M. 1972), *aff'd*, 499 F.2d 1147 (10th Cir. 1974).

159. *Serna*, 351 F. Supp. at 1282.

160. *Serna*, 499 F.2d at 1150 (summarizing district court expert testimony).

161. *See infra* note 165 and accompanying text.

162. *See* Yniguez v. Mofford, 730 F. Supp. 309 (D. Ariz. 1990) (invalidating Arizona's English-only law as violating the first amendment of the U.S. Constitution).

163. SENATE REPORT, *supra* note 114, at 790-97.

164. *Cf. id.* at 792, 796. In *Gutierrez*, the court noted that the English-only rule greatly disturbed Hispanic employees. Gutierrez v. Municipal Ct., 838 F.2d 1031, 1036, *vacated as moot*, 109 S. Ct. 1736 (1989).

165. 29 C.F.R. § 1606.7(a) (1989) (footnote omitted).

Although a limited English-only rule is less burdensome than a complete prohibition on the use of one's primary language, the negative effects of a more limited rule will differ only in degree, not in kind, from those of a complete prohibition.

One should not assume that these effects are different for bilingual persons. Primary language can be a crucial aspect of the ethnicity of a bilingual person.[166] The term "bilingualism" is defined as the ability "to speak two languages with nearly equal facility."[167] Because of the practical immutability of primary language, and the factors contributing to practical immutability,[168] many persons whose primary language is not English are not bilingual, although they may be thought to be so if they have any ability to communicate in English. It is more realistic to consider bilingualism as a spectrum of abilities in a second language ranging from minimal ability to communicate in a second language to equal facility in two languages. For persons with limited English proficiency, who are "bilingual" only to a limited extent, a restriction on their ability to speak their primary languages may be a serious handicap tantamount to the effect of a restriction forcing a right-handed person to write left-handed.

Those who are more fully bilingual still suffer the adverse effects of a restriction on their ability to speak their primary languages. The sociological and psychological factors that make primary language a crucial aspect of ethnicity[169] are also relevant for more fully bilingual persons. Their links to their "own people," their sense of ethnic identity, and their ability to enjoy a full range of verbal expression in relationships with bilingual co-workers depend heavily on their ability to use their primary language. For bilinguals, then, as well as for those who speak only their mother tongue, the exclusive adverse impact of English-only rules warrants a high burden on employers to justify their discriminatory rules.

IV. THE BURDEN OF PROOF FOR EXCLUSIVE ADVERSE IMPACT
UNDER TITLE VII

In light of the exclusive impact of English-only rules upon protected groups, the business justification standard recently an-

---

166. *See supra* notes 74-80 & 89-90 and accompanying text.
167. RANDOM HOUSE COLLEGE DICTIONARY 133 (1972).
168. *See supra* notes 92-101 and accompanying text.
169. *See supra* notes 74-80 and accompanying text.

nounced in *Wards Cove Packing Co. v. Atonio*[170] is inappropriate. Under *Wards Cove*, employers only have the burden of producing evidence of a business justification that significantly
serves some legitimate employment goal.[171] The exclusive adverse impact of English-only rules upon language minorities
raises the issue of whether the traditional disparate impact theory, as modified by *Wards Cove Packing Co.*, is the most appropriate model for analyzing such rules.

A. *English-Only Rules As Disparate Treatment on the Basis*
of National Origin

A restriction on the use of one's primary language such as an
English-only rule should be analyzed as disparate treatment on
the basis of national origin. Discrimination on the basis of primary language is equivalent to discrimination on the basis of national origin, both because of the very close correlation between
primary language and national origin and the exclusive adverse
impact of restrictions upon the use of primary languages other
than English. The intent necessary to show disparate treatment
can be inferred from the existence of such exclusive adverse
effects.[172]

The statutory treatment under Title VII of pregnancy, a characteristic exclusively associated with women, supports the view
that restrictions on the use of primary languages other than En-

---

170. 109 S. Ct. 2115 (1989).

171. *Id.* at 2125-26.

172. *Cf.* Teamsters v. United States, 431 U.S. 324, 335 n.15 (1977) (" 'Disparate treatment' . . . is the most easily understood type of discrimination. The employer simply
treats some people less favorably than others because of their race, color, religion, sex, or
national origin. *Proof of discriminatory motive is critical, although it can in some situations be inferred from the mere fact of differences in treatment.*") (emphasis added);
Washington v. Davis, 426 U.S. 229 (1976) Regarding a constitutional attack on equal
protection grounds against a test used to select police recruits, the Court wrote
   Necessarily, an invidious discriminatory purpose may often be inferred from the
   totality of the relevant facts, including the fact, if it is true, that the law bears
   more heavily on one race than another. It is also not infrequently true that the
   discriminatory impact . . . may for all practical purposes demonstrate unconstitutionality because in various circumstances the discrimination is very difficult
   to explain on nonracial grounds. . . .
Id. at 242. Justice Stevens's concurrence is also supportive. *Id.* at 253 ("Frequently the
most probative evidence of intent will be objective evidence of what actually happened
rather than evidence describing the subjective state of mind of the actor. For normally
the actor is presumed to have intended the natural consequences of his deeds."). For
further discussion of disparate treatment see M. ZIMMER, C. SULLIVAN, & R. RICHARDS,
CASES AND MATERIALS ON EMPLOYMENT DISCRIMINATION 86-94 (2d ed. 1988).

glish should be treated the same as discrimination because of national origin. In 1978, Congress amended Title VII by adding section 701(k), which provides, in part, that "[t]he terms 'because of sex' or 'on the basis of sex' include, but are not limited to, because of or on the basis of pregnancy, childbirth, or related medical condition; and women affected by pregnancy, childbirth, or related medical conditions shall be treated the same for all employment-related purposes."[173]

Congress enacted this amendment to overrule *General Electric Co. v. Gilbert*,[174] in which the Supreme Court concluded that a benefit plan that discriminated on the basis of pregnancy did not discriminate because of sex in violation of Title VII. The amendment adopted the views of the dissenting Justices, who recognized the exclusive adverse effect of discrimination because of pregnancy upon women and who found that such discrimination violated Title VII.[175] The House Report accompanying the amendment concluded that "the dissenting Justices correctly interpreted the Act."[176]

Accordingly, a correct interpretation of Title VII requires treating characteristics that are closely correlated with a protected characteristic the same as the explicitly protected characteristic when such characteristics are used as the basis for discrimination that results in an exclusive adverse effect upon a protected group. Just as the dissenting Justices in *Gilbert* and members of Congress recognized that discrimination because of pregnancy is the same as discrimination because of sex, so should the courts recognize that discrimination because of primary language is the same as discrimination because of national origin. A proper interpretation of Title VII requires that restrictions on the exercise of primary languages other than English be analyzed as disparate treatment because of national origin.

If restrictions upon primary languages other than English are analyzed as discrimination because of national origin, then em-

---

173. Pregnancy Discrimination Act of 1978, Pub. L. No. 95-555, 92 Stat. 2076 (1978) (currently codified at 42 U.S.C. § 2000e(k) (1982)).

174. 429 U.S. 125 (1976).

175. *Id.* at 147 (Brennan, J., dissenting) (adopting the EEOC's view that the plan violates Title VII "because the omission of pregnancy from the program has the intent and effect of providing that 'only women [are subjected] to a substantial risk of total loss of income because of temporary medical disability' ") (quoting Brief for EEOC at 12); *id.* at 161 (Stevens, J., dissenting) ("[T]he rule at issue places the risk of absence caused by pregnancy in a class by itself. By definition, such a rule discriminates on account of sex; for it is the capacity to become pregnant which primarily differentiates the female from the male.") (footnote omitted).

176. H. REP. No. 948, 95th Cong., 2d Sess. 2 (1978), *reprinted in* 1978 U.S. CODE CONG. & ADMIN. NEWS 4749, 4750.

ployers can only justify such restrictions under the bona fide occupational qualification (BFOQ) defense.[177] The Supreme Court
has described the BFOQ defense as "an extremely narrow exception to the general prohibition of discrimination."[178] It is the
employer's burden to establish the BFOQ defense by a preponderance of the evidence, proving the "reasonable necessity" of
policies that discriminate on the basis of national origin.[179] Furthermore, the discrimination must be reasonably necessary to
the essence of the employer's business.[180]

The courts should require employers utilizing English-only
rules to prove that their rules are necessary under the strict
standards of the BFOQ defense, rather than under the permissive standard of *Wards Cove*. The functional equivalence of primary language and national origin warrants imposing upon employers the burden of proving that restrictions on languages
meet the standards of the BFOQ defense. English-only rules
merit close examination from courts because of the ease with
which employers can use such rules as a pretext to keep Hispanics, and other language minority groups, out of the work force.[181]

B. Disparate Impact Theory and Exclusive Adverse Impact

Under the disparate impact theory, as interpreted most recently in *Wards Cove*, the plaintiff bears the initial burden of
demonstrating the adverse effect of a particular rule or employ-

---

177. Section 703(c) of Title VII describes the defense, stating that "it shall not be an
unlawful employment practice for an employer to hire and employ employees . . . on the
basis of . . . national origin in those certain instances where . . . national origin is a
*bona fide occupational qualification reasonably necessary to the normal operation of
that particular business or enterprise*." 42 U.S.C. § 2000e-2(e) (1982) (emphasis added).

178. Dothard v. Rawlinson, 433 U.S. 321, 334 (1977).

179. Western Air Lines v. Criswell, 472 U.S. 400, 422 (1985).

180. *Id.* at 419; Diaz v. Pan Am. World Airways, Inc., 442 F.2d 385, 388 (5th Cir.
1971) ("[D]iscrimination based on sex is valid only when the *essence* of the business
operation would be undermined by not hiring members of one sex exclusively.").

181. The discharge of Hector Garcia from Gloor Lumber illustrates how enforcement
of such rules can keep members of language minorities out of the work force. *See* Garcia
v. Gloor, 618 F.2d 264, 266 (5th Cir. 1980), *cert. denied*, 449 U.S. 1113 (1981). *See also*
Fragante v. City of Honolulu, 888 F.2d 591 (9th Cir. 1989). The *Fragante* court stated:
    Accent and national origin are obviously inextricably intertwined in many cases.
    It would therefore be an easy refuge in this context for an employer unlawfully
    discriminating against someone based on national origin to state falsely that it
    was not the person's national origin that caused the employment or promotion
    problem, but the candidate's inability to measure up to the communication skills
    demanded by the job. We encourage a very searching look by the district courts
    at such a claim.
Id. at 596 (footnote omitted).

ment practice on a protected group.[182] The plaintiff must identify a specific employment practice or rule that results in a disparate impact.[183] If the plaintiff successfully demonstrates the adverse impact of a specific employment practice, then the inquiry shifts to a consideration of the business justification offered by the employer for its practice.[184] The inquiry consists of a reasoned review of the employer's asserted justification.[185] The challenged practice must serve, in a significant way, the legitimate employment goals of the employer.[186] The employer carries only the burden of producing evidence of a business justification for his employment practice.[187] The plaintiff bears the burden of persuading the court that the employer's proffered justification is invalid.[188] If the trier of fact concludes that the employer's business justification is valid, then the plaintiff may still prevail if he can demonstrate the availability of alternative employment practices that would accomplish the employer's goals with less adverse impact.[189] If the plaintiff can show that such alternatives exist, or that the employer's asserted business justification is a pretext, then the plaintiff prevails.[190]

The Court in *Wards Cove* thus revised the burden imposed upon an employer seeking to establish a business justification. Under the old standard the employer bore the burden of proving

---

182. Wards Cove Packing Co. v. Atonio, 109 S. Ct. 2115, 2124-25 (1989); Watson v. Fort Worth Bank and Trust, 108 S.Ct. 2777, 2784 (1988); Dothard v. Rawlinson, 433 U.S. 321, 329 (1977). *See also* B. SCHLEI & P. GROSSMAN, *supra* note 57, at 1287, 1324-25.
183. *Wards Cove*, 109 S. Ct. at 2124.
184. *Id.* at 2125.
185. *Id.* at 2126.
186. *Id.* at 2125-26.
187. *Id.* at 2126. The recent decision in *Wards Cove* represents a radical departure from the previously settled distribution of burdens of proof in a disparate impact case. Prior to *Wards Cove* if a plaintiff successfully proved the disparate impact of an employer's practice, then the burden of proof shifted to the defendant to prove that its practice was justified by business necessity. *See, e.g.*, Watson v. Fort Worth Bank and Trust, 108 S.Ct. 2777, 2791-97 (1988) (Blackmun, J., concurring) (stating that burden of proof passes to defendant to establish that employment practice is a business necessity); Dothard v. Rawlinson, 433 U.S. 321, 329 (1977) (holding employer required to "prov[e] that the challenged requirements are job related"); Albemarle Paper Co. v. Moody, 422 U.S. 405, 425 (1975) (same); Griggs v. Duke Power Co., 401 U.S. 424, 432 (1971) (stating that Congress placed on the employer the burden of showing that the challenged requirement bears a "manifest relationship to the employment in question").
188. *Wards Cove*, 109 S. Ct. at 2126.
189. *Id.* at 2126-27; *Dothard*, 433 U.S. at 329; *Albemarle Paper*, 422 U.S. at 425. *See also* B. SCHLEI & P. GROSSMAN, *supra* note 57, at 1287.
190. *Wards Cove*, 109 S. Ct. at 2126-27; *Dothard*, 433 U.S. at 332; McDonnell Douglas Corp. v. Green, 411 U.S. 792 (1973); Burwell v. Eastern Air Lines, Inc., 633 F.2d 361, 368 (4th Cir. 1980) (citing Albemarle Paper Co. v. Moody, 422 U.S. 405 (1975)); Robinson v. Lorillard Corp., 444 F.2d 791, 798-800 (4th Cir. 1971), *cert. dismissed sub nom.* Tobacco Workers Int'l Union v. Robinson, 404 U.S. 1007 (1972).

the job-relatedness of an employment practice.[191] This so-called "business necessity" standard received criticism for being varied and inconsistent.[192] The new standard created in *Wards Cove* imposes only a burden of production on the employer to present some evidence of business justification. This is apparently the slightest burden ever imposed upon employers under the disparate impact theory.[193] Although evidence of an insubstantial business justification is not sufficient to meet the employer's burden,[194] an employer no longer needs to prove that a challenged rule or practice is essential to good job performance.[195] Now it is up to the employee to disprove the alleged business justification.

The Supreme Court, in developing its standards in disparate impact cases, has evaluated standardized employment tests and criteria[196] and subjective employment criteria,[197] all of which can

---

191. *See* Griggs v. Duke Power Co., 401 U.S. 424 (1971); *see also* B. SCHLEI & P. GROSSMAN, *supra* note 57, at 1328-29.

192. Commentators and courts have remarked on the varied and inconsistent standards applied to employers attempting to establish a business necessity defense. *See* Rutherglen, *Disparate Impact Under Title VII: An Objective Theory of Discrimination,* 73 VA. L. REV. 1297, 1312 (1987) ("[D]isarray . . . has resulted in the federal courts from uncertainty over what the defense requires the defendant to prove."); Comment, *supra* note 154, at 912 ("[L]ower courts have been afforded a considerable degree of freedom in shaping the contours of the defense."); B. SCHLEI & P. GROSSMAN, *supra* note 57, at 1328-29 & n.139; *see also* Contreras v. City of Los Angeles, 656 F.2d 1267, 1275-76 (9th Cir. 1981) ("[C]ourts differ on just what an employer must prove to discharge its burden."). There is little reason to assume that the application of the new business justification standards established by *Wards Cove,* will be any more uniform than the application of the old business necessity standard.

193. *Wards Cove* creates essentially the same burden of proof for an employer under a disparate impact case that exists for a disparate treatment case. Under the *McDonnell Douglas Corp. v. Green* disparate treatment model, the employer must only "articulate some legitimate, nondiscriminatory reason for the employee's rejection," and the burden then shifts to the plaintiff, who must then demonstrate that the articulated reason is a pretext. McDonnell Douglas Corp. v. Green, 411 U.S. 792, 802-05 (1973). The burden of production imposed upon employers by *Wards Cove,* and the "reasoned review" of the employer's asserted justification, is only slightly more onerous a burden than the mere articulation of a legitimate reason for a business practice.

194. *Wards Cove,* 109 S. Ct. at 2126.

195. This is another example of how *Wards Cove* has lessened significantly the burden of proof on employers. Prior to the decision, employers were required to prove that a challenged practice or rule was essential to good job performance. *See, e.g.,* Dothard v. Rawlinson, 433 U.S. 321, 331 (1977); Albemarle Paper Co. v. Moody, 422 U.S. 405, 431 (1975) (holding that discriminatory tests must be proven to be " 'predictive of or significantly correlated with important elements of work behavior which comprise or are relevant to the job' ") (quoting 29 C.F.R. § 1607.4(c) (1974)); Craig v. County of Los Angeles, 626 F.2d 659, 662 (9th Cir. 1980), *cert. denied,* 450 U.S. 919 (1981).

196. *See* Watson v. Fort Worth Bank and Trust, 108 S. Ct. 2777, 2785 (1988) ("[E]ach of our subsequent decisions, however, like *Griggs* itself, involved standardized employment tests or criteria."); *see, e.g.,* Connecticut v. Teal, 457 U.S. 440 (1982) (written examination); New York City Transit Auth. v. Beazer, 440 U.S. 568 (1979) (policy against employing persons using narcotic drugs, including methadone); Dothard v. Rawlinson, 433 U. S. 321 (1977) (height and weight requirements); Washington v. Davis, 426 U.S. 229 (1976) (written test of verbal skills); Albemarle Paper Co. v. Moody, 422 U.S. 405 (1975) (written aptitude tests).

197. *Wards Cove,* 109 S. Ct. 2115 (1989).

73

be characterized as facially neutral in the sense described earlier.[198] The disparate impact theory, however, should not apply to English-only rules because such rules are not facially neutral and because they have an exclusive adverse impact.[199] The courts, nevertheless, will probably continue to apply this familiar theory to such rules. Even under the disparate impact theory, though, courts should recognize the exclusive impact and hold employers to a higher standard of business necessity.[200] Rules that are not facially neutral warrant a different analysis under the disparate impact theory, with a correspondingly higher burden of justification required from employers seeking to use them. The exclusive adverse impact of English-only rules on language minority groups justifies at least a return to the former burdens of proof under the business necessity defense, which required an employer to prove the business necessity for a challenged practice.[201] This exclusive adverse impact also justifies a more substantial burden upon employers, such as requiring employers using English-only rules to prove that such rules are the least discriminatory alternative that will accomplish their legitimate goals.[202]

English-only rules warrant very close examination by the courts because of the ease with which employers can discriminate against language minority groups through the use of such rules.[203] Such a close examination is appropriate especially in light of past discrimination against language minorities.[204] Employers also can use these rules to subject such groups to discipline and consequently reduced job opportunities. Furthermore,

---

198. *See supra* notes 146-50 and accompanying text.

199. *See supra* notes 151-54 and accompanying text.

200. In contrast to a practice with an exclusive impact, the disparate impact theory that originated in *Griggs* was meant to analyze employer practices that were "fair in form, but discriminatory in operation." Griggs v. Duke Power Co., 401 U.S. 424, 431 (1971).

201. *Wards Cove*, 109 S. Ct. at 2130 (Stevens, J., dissenting).

202. *See* Rutherglen, *supra* note 192, at 1326 (employment practices with larger adverse impact should be harder to justify than practices with little impact). *See also* Robinson v. Lorillard, 444 F.2d 791, 798 (4th Cir. 1971), *cert. dismissed sub nom.* Tobacco Workers Int'l Union v. Robinson, 404 U.S. 1007 (1972) ("[T]here must be available no acceptable alternative policies or practices which would better accomplish the business purpose advanced, or accomplish it equally well with a lesser differential racial impact.") (footnote omitted).

203. *See supra* note 181 and accompanying text.

204. *See supra* note 111 and accompanying text.

such rules may discourage otherwise qualified applicants from applying for positions with employers utilizing such rules. The danger of applying a permissive standard of review, such as that articulated in *Wards Cove*, to English-only rules is that "such a low standard of review would permit discrimination to be practiced through the use of spurious, seemingly neutral employment practices."[205]

V. English-Only Rules Under the Disparate Impact Theory: The Current Standard Applied

Courts may continue to analyze English-only rules under the disparate impact theory, as modified by *Wards Cove*. Even under the current disparate impact theory, however, analysis of justifications offered by employers for English-only rules demonstrates that the rules often will not pass muster. The following section analyzes common justifications offered by employers for English-only rules.

Even if primary language is recognized as a characteristic of national origin protected under Title VII, the right to speak one's primary language is not absolute. Rather, it is a right bounded by the actual requirements of the job and the business at issue. In certain situations, it is clearly inappropriate for someone to speak a language other than English in the workplace.[206] If a bilingual, Spanish-speaking salesperson insisted on speaking in Spanish to a prospective customer who spoke only English, leading to a lost transaction, the employer could properly discipline this salesperson for failing to do his job. Similarly, a bilingual stage actor cast in the role of Hamlet would not have a right to deliver the soliloquy in Spanish, unless the production called for such a delivery. The actor's and the salesman's use of primary language would constitute poor performance, and the employer could properly discipline or discharge a poorly performing employee. In such a situation, it is not the language that needs regulation, but rather the job performance.[207]

---

205. *Wards Cove*, 109 S. Ct. at 2126. It is ironic that these words were written by the Court in *Wards Cove*, which has made it easier for employers to justify seemingly neutral employment practices.

206. *See, e.g.*, Jurado v. Eleven-Fifty Corp., 813 F.2d 1406, 1411-12 (9th Cir. 1987) (finding no violation of Title VII in the discharge of a bilingual radio announcer who refused to comply with the station program director's instructions to broadcast only in English).

207. Accordingly, if one Hispanic, bilingual salesperson insisted on speaking Spanish to English-speaking customers, the appropriate regulation would be exactly the same

Business justification, however, means more than mere business convenience or preference.[208] The challenged practice must serve "in a significant way" the legitimate employment goals of the employer.[209] Accordingly, the challenged practice or rule must carry out the business purpose asserted by the employer effectively and objectively.[210] If a plaintiff can show that less discriminatory alternatives exist that would accomplish the employer's purpose equally well or more effectively with less adverse impact, this proof undermines the justification for the employer's practice.[211] These principles limit, therefore, the potentially acceptable purposes for which employers can enact English-only rules as well as the scope of these rules.

The cases decided by the courts and the EEOC reveal a variety of justifications offered by employers to defend their use of English-only rules. Employers have claimed that such rules reduce the racial tension and fear experienced by customers or fellow employees who do not understand conversations in languages other than English.[212] One employer argued that these

---

kind of discipline that would be meted out to any other employee who performed poorly in a similar manner, say by ignoring customer requests or by being rude. Such poor performance by a bilingual employee would not be grounds for an English-only rule, prohibiting conversations between employees who would understand each other, but would be grounds for whatever discipline is ordinarily imposed for poor performance.

208. *See, e.g., Wards Cove,* 109 S. Ct. at 2126 (stating that a "mere insubstantial justification . . . will not suffice"); Blake v. City of Los Angeles, 595 F.2d 1367, 1376 (9th Cir. 1979) ("Administrative convenience is not a sufficient justification for the employer's practices."); United States v. Jacksonville Terminal Co., 451 F.2d 418, 451 (5th Cir. 1971) (stating that "management convenience and business necessity are not synonomous"); *see also* B. SCHLEI & P. GROSSMAN, *supra* note 57, at 359.

209. *Wards Cove,* 109 S. Ct. at 2125-26.

210. *See, e.g.,* Griggs v. Duke Power Co., 401 U.S. 424, 432 (1971); Robinson v. Lorillard Corp., 444 F.2d 791, 798 (4th Cir. 1971), *cert. dismissed sub nom.* Tobacco Workers Int'l Union v. Robinson, 404 U.S. 1007 (1972); Rutherglen, *supra* note 192, at 1321 (defense of business justification deals with objective reasons for an employment practice); *cf.* Comment, *supra* note 154, at 934 ("[S]tandard of job-relatedness is an objective one. . . . [O]nly if the practice *in fact* serves business purposes can it be deemed 'necessary.' ").

211. *Wards Cove,* 109 S. Ct. at 2126-27. *See* Rutherglen, *supra* note 192, at 1327-28 ("[I]f the defendant has not considered an alternative . . . procedure with obviously greater validity, then it has undermined the procedure that it did choose."); *cf.* Williams v. Colorado Springs, Colo., School Dist. #11, 641 F.2d 835, 841 (10th Cir. 1981); EEOC Dec. No. 71-1418, 3 Fair Empl. Prac. Cas. (BNA) 580, 582 (1971).

212. Gutierrez v. Municipal Ct., 838 F.2d 1031, 1042-43, *vacated as moot,* 109 S. Ct. 1736 (1989); Garcia v. Gloor, 618 F.2d 264, 267 (5th Cir. 1980), *cert. denied,* 449 U.S. 1113 (1981); Hernandez v. Erlenbusch, 368 F. Supp. 752, 754 (D. Or. 1973) (language restriction in tavern allegedly necessary to stem fear on the part of White clientele that Chicanos were talking about Whites); EEOC Dec. No. 81-25, 27 Fair Empl. Prac. Cas. (BNA) 1820, 1821 (1981) (fellow workers and customers annoyed at Spanish conversations between co-workers); EEOC Dec. No. 72-0281, EEOC Dec. (CCH) ¶ 6293 (1971) (Anglo barbers irritated at Spanish conversations of Hispanic barber).

rules reduce disruptions in the workplace.[213] Employers also have claimed that the rules support the use of English in this predominantly English-speaking society.[214] The argument that English-only rules facilitate supervision by those who do not understand languages other than English has been raised as well.[215] Finally, in one reported case, an employer justified such a rule as necessary for safety and efficiency in potentially dangerous areas of the employer's premises and during emergencies.[216] Each of these asserted justifications will be analyzed under the business justification standard to determine whether it can support an English-only rule in the workplace.

For this analysis, a distinction should be made between jobs in which a different language is required and jobs in which there is no such requirement.[217] It will be more difficult for an employer to advance a cogent business justification for a language restriction in a job that requires the use of a different language than in a job with no such requirement. When speaking Spanish is a requirement of the job, such as the sales position in *Garcia* or the municipal court clerk job in *Gutierrez*, the Spanish language is already an established part of the work environment. If fluency in Spanish is required in a job, this must be in order to provide a required or desired service in Spanish. A rational employer, by hiring someone to perform part or all of his job in a different language, has acted to reduce disruptions and confusion and to maximize efficiency. At Gloor Lumber, for example, the employer hired bilingual sales clerks to enhance its appeal to Hispanic customers and maximize revenues.[218] In the municipal

---

213. *Gutierrez*, 838 F.2d at 1042 (stating that the employer contended "the rule [was] necessary to prevent the workplace from turning into a 'Tower of Babel' ").

214. *Id.* at 1042; *Garcia*, 618 F.2d at 267.

215. *Gutierrez*, 838 F.2d at 1043; *Garcia*, 618 F.2d at 267; EEOC Dec. No. 71-446, 2 Fair Empl. Prac. Cas. (BNA) 1127, 1128 (1970) (employer apparently attempted to justify rule based on inability of supervisors to understand Spanish).

216. EEOC Dec. No. 83-7, 2 Empl. Prac. Guide (CCH) ¶ 6836 (1983) (the employer claimed that the English-only rule was necessary to assure effective communication among its employees during emergencies, and that the rule helped to prevent or control fires, explosions and other casualties in a refinery while employees were working with potentially dangerous equipment and materials); *see also* Saucedo v. Brothers Well Serv., Inc., 464 F. Supp. 919, 921 (S.D. Tex. 1979) (employer sought to justify English-only rule during drilling of an oil well).

217. Under appropriate circumstances, it can be lawful to require bilingual ability. *See* Smith v. Dist. of Columbia, 29 Fair Empl. Prac. Cas. (BNA) 1129, 1133 (D.D.C. 1982) (upholding the employer's requirement of bilingual ability in Spanish and English in an action brought under the fifth amendment, Title VII and 42 U.S.C. § 1983).

218. Garcia v. Gloor, 618 F.2d 264 (5th Cir. 1980), *cert. denied*, 449 U.S. 1113 (1981). The court wrote: "Of the eight salesmen employed by Gloor in 1975, seven were Hispanic, a matter perhaps of business necessity, because 75% of the population in its busi-

court, the situation must have been far more chaotic when clerks who did not speak Spanish attempted to conduct court business with persons who did not speak English. In cases such as these, business necessity requires the use of different languages in the workplace. Accordingly, it is illogical for these employers to argue that there is also a business justification for restricting the use of the different language.[219]

For jobs in which a different language is required, some of the potential justifications for a language restriction are illogical and could not, therefore, constitute a business justification. Because a different language is already an established part of the workplace, a language restriction probably cannot effectively reduce disruptions in the workplace. In such a case, whatever additional Spanish or other language results from conversations between employees is unlikely to be significantly more disruptive than the standard work environment.[220] Furthermore, the asserted justification of "supporting the use of English" makes no sense in a job that requires a different language for its proper performance.[221] Nor can supervision of job performance partially or wholly conducted in a different language be enhanced by requiring personal conversations between employees to be in English.[222] Although the requirement of a different language in a job may undermine certain asserted business justifications, the question of the validity of language restrictions in other jobs, and for other reasons, remains.[223]

A. Reducing Racial Tension and Fear

Employers claim that English-only rules promote racial harmony and reduce racial tension and fear.[224] In *Garcia*, for example, the employer stated that customers who understood no

---

ness area is of Hispanic background and many of Gloor's customers wish to be waited on by a salesman who speaks Spanish." *Id.* at 267.

219. *See Gutierrez*, 838 F.2d at 1043. This analysis only works, of course, where the language necessary for the job is the same as the restricted language.

220. *Id.* at 1042.

221. *Id.*

222. *Id.* at 1043.

223. Interestingly, the two principal cases discussing the legality of English-only rules involved jobs in which the ability to speak Spanish was a requirement of the job.

224. *See supra* note 212 and cases cited therein. Although the *Gutierrez* court described it as racial tension and fear, the tension and fear resulting from the use of a language other than English is more properly described as cultural, linguistic, or ethnic tension.

Spanish became irritated when employees spoke Spanish to each other.[225] In *Gutierrez*, the municipal court asserted that its rule reduced racial tension and fear among employees.[226] The municipal court listed a number of very common fears in attempting to justify its rule. The employer was concerned that Spanish might be used to make discriminatory, insubordinate, or belittling comments about fellow employees.[227] The employer also was concerned that Spanish could be used to conceal the substance of conversations.[228] A restriction on the ability of Spanish speakers to speak their primary language was necessary, therefore, to assuage these fears of employees who spoke no Spanish.[229]

Such fears, however, are exactly the kind of stereotyped judgments that Title VII was designed to eliminate from the workplace,[230] and are no different from the many racial or sexual stereotypes that cannot be used as the basis for discriminatory treatment of members of a protected group under Title VII. It is well-established law under Title VII that customer preference does not provide the business justification that will support a discriminatory rule.[231] If customer preference provides no justification, then neither do the discriminatory preferences of fellow employees. As the Supreme Court stated, "[p]rivate biases may be outside the reach of the law, but the law cannot, directly or indirectly, give them effect."[232] Accordingly, the reduction of employees' or customers' racial tensions and fears cannot justify an English-only rule under the business justification standard.[233]

---

225. Garcia v. Gloor, 618 F.2d 264, 267 (5th Cir. 1980), *cert. denied*, 449 U.S. 1113 (1981).

226. *Gutierrez*, 838 F.2d at 1042-43.

227. *Id.* at 1042.

228. *Id.*

229. *Id.*

230. *See infra* note 243 and accompanying text. Courts recognize the problem of lingering stereotypes. *See, e.g.*, Watson v. Fort Worth Bank and Trust, 108 S.Ct. 2777, 2786, (1988) (O'Connor, J.) (plurality opinion) (mentioning "the problem of subconscious stereotypes"); Guardians Ass'n of New York City Police Dept., Inc. v. Civil Serv. Comm'n of New York, 431 F. Supp. 526, 551 (S.D.N.Y. 1977) ("As has been seen in the areas of race and sex discrimination, long-accepted stereotypes too often help perpetuate discriminatory practices even though they have no basis in fact.").

231. *See* Diaz v. Pan Am. World Airways, Inc., 442 F.2d 385, 389 (5th Cir. 1971); *see also* Fernandez v. Wynn Oil Co., 653 F.2d 1273, 1276-77 (9th Cir. 1981) (holding stereotyped customer preferences did not justify sexually discriminatory conduct); Witt v. Secretary of Labor, 397 F. Supp. 673, 678 (D. Me. 1975) (holding customer preference for a male hairdresser was not a bona fide occupational qualification).

232. Palmore v. Sidoti, 466 U.S. 429, 433 (1984); *see also* City of Cleburne v. Cleburne Living Center, 473 U.S. 432, 448 (1985).

233. Indeed, this must be the right result because, otherwise, the "reduction of racial tension" rationale could be used to justify egregious racial or sexual discrimination. There are still many places in the United States where racial or sexual tension would be

Moreover, someone who does not understand Spanish has little basis for reaching negative judgments about the content of conversations in Spanish. The employer, fellow employees, or customers who speak no Spanish simply assume, in the absence of understanding, that Spanish-language conversations are ill-intentioned, discriminatory, insubordinate, belittling, or secretive. There was little or no evidence in the *Gutierrez* case to prove that these fears and concerns were justified.[234] Indeed, the evidence in the case showed that racial tension increased as a result of the English-only rule.[235] The EEOC itself has reached this conclusion. In its regulations discussing national origin discrimination, the EEOC states that restrictions on languages other than English may increase racial tension.[236] Evidence of such racial tension would greatly assist plaintiffs who, under *Wards Cove*, must now disprove an employer's assertion that English-only rules decrease racial tension.[237] Plaintiffs may even be able to prove that racial tension increases as the result of English-only rules. Such racial tension, induced by restricting the ability to speak one's primary language, is apparent in several of the cases that have discussed the issue.[238] If a plaintiff can prove that an English-only rule increases racial tension, it will obviously be difficult for an employer to claim that the reduction of racial tension justifies the rule.[239]

---

reduced for White persons or for males if Blacks, Hispanics or women were denied employment opportunities or the ability to use public accomodations. Yet the fact that such tension may exist cannot provide a justification for discrimination against these protected groups without violating Title VII. *See* Hernandez v. Erlenbusch, 368 F. Supp. 752, 755 (D. Or. 1973) ("Catering to prejudice out of fear of provoking greater prejudice only perpetuates racism.").

234. Gutierrez v. Municipal Ct., 838 F.2d 1031, 1042-43, *vacated as moot*, 109 S. Ct. 1736 (1989).

235. *Id.* at 1042.

236. 29 C.F.R. § 1606.7(a) (1989) (prohibiting employees from speaking their primary language at all times may create an "atmosphere of inferiority, isolation and intimidation based on national origin").

237. Wards Cove Packing Co. v. Atonio, 109 S. Ct. 2115, 2126 (1989). *See supra* notes 186-88 and accompanying text.

238. *See Gutierrez*, 838 F.2d at 1042; Saucedo v. Brothers Well Serv., Inc., 464 F. Supp. 919, 921-22 (S.D. Tex. 1979) (racial tension and fight resulting from employer's discharge of employee for speaking Spanish on the job); Hernandez v. Erlenbusch, 368 F. Supp. 752, 754 (D. Or. 1973) (rule prohibiting foreign languages in a tavern led to racial tension and assault upon Hispanic customers by regular customers of the tavern).

239. The net effect of such an English-only rule, rather than to reduce racial or cultural tension, may be merely to transfer such tension from persons objecting to different language conversations to those persons engaging in such conversations.

B. *Reducing Disruptions in the Workplace*

Employers claim that a limited English-only rule reduces disruptions in the workplace and prevents the workplace from becoming a "Tower of Babel."[240] Suppose that an employer finds that conversations in languages other than English are "disruptive," and seeks to eliminate such conversations with a limited English-only rule. This employer permits employees to enjoy private conversations in English in the workplace and seeks to limit only conversations in Spanish. There is no permissible reason why two employees' private conversation in Spanish would be any more disruptive than the same conversation would be in English. If the employer or fellow employees feel annoyed or threatened by conversations in a different language, or if they feel suspicious about what is being said, these feelings are probably based on negative feelings about persons speaking in languages other than English or on negative assumptions about the content of such conversations. As discussed above, such private fears or biases cannot constitute the business justification for a rule that discriminates against a protected group.[241] An employer who allows private conversations between employees in English should have great difficulty justifying a rule attempting to restrict the same conversations in Spanish to minimize disruptions. The only way to minimize such disruptions, consistent with Title VII, entails prohibiting all private conversations between employees, whether in Spanish, English, or any other language.[242] Although somewhat draconian, at least such a solution is even-handed, creating no greater burden on the protected class than on the majority class. Even-handed treatment is, of course, the very goal of Title VII.[243]

---

240. *Gutierrez*, 838 F.2d at 1042.

241. *See supra* notes 231-33 and accompanying text.

242. Such a prohibition, applied to persons whose primary language is English, is only slightly more burdensome than an English-only rule is for someone with very limited abilities in English.

243. *See* H.R. REP. No. 914, 88th Cong., 1st Sess. 26 (1963), *reprinted in* EEOC, LEGISLATIVE HISTORY OF TITLES VII AND IX OF CIVIL RIGHTS ACT OF 1964 at 2001, 2026, 2150.

C. Supporting the Use of English in the Nation

Employers seek to justify English-only rules on the basis that these rules support the use of English in the nation.[244] The argument may take several forms. An employer, like the municipal court in *Gutierrez*, may argue that an English-only rule is required by state statutes making English the "official" language of a state.[245] A related justification, offered by the employer in *Garcia*, is that an English-only rule improves the English fluency of persons whose primary language is not English.[246]

One can wonder whether an employer's voluntary desire to support perceived national or state policies can constitute a business justification at all, as such a desire may have nothing to do with an employer's business.[247] The fact that a state constitutional provision or statute makes English the "official" language of the state does not automatically provide a business justification for an employer's English-only rule; any such statute, in order to be a valid justification for an employer's English-only rule, must itself be supported by a business justification.[248]

An employer's desire to improve the English fluency of employees by restricting the use of languages other than English may provide a more relevant employer purpose. The Supreme Court, however, has rejected this justification when offered for an English literacy requirement as a qualification for the right to vote.[249] This should make the justification less plausible in the workplace. Furthermore, an English-only rule enacted for this purpose probably cannot survive examination under the business justification standard for at least two reasons. First, a plaintiff can demonstrate that there are less discriminatory alternatives that would more effectively improve an employee's fluency

---

244. *See supra* note 214 and accompanying text. Such English-only statutes may themselves be unconstitutional. *See* Yniguez v. Mofford, 730 F. Supp. 309 (D. Ariz. 1990) (invalidating Arizona's English-only provision as violating the first amendment of the U.S. Constitution).

245. Gutierrez v. Municipal Ct., 838 F.2d 1031, 1042, 1043-44, *vacated as moot*, 109 S. Ct. 1736 (1989).

246. Garcia v. Gloor, 618 F.2d 264, 267 (5th Cir. 1980), *cert. denied*, 449 U.S. 1113 (1981).

247. *Cf.* Burwell v. Eastern Air Lines, Inc., 633 F.2d 361, 371 (4th Cir. 1980) (plurality opinion), *cert. denied*, 450 U.S. 965 (1981) ("If this personal compassion [for pregnant stewardesses] can be attributed to corporate policy it is commendable, but in the area of civil rights, personal . . . decisions not affecting business operations are best left to individuals who are the targets of discrimination.").

248. *Cf.* Dothard v. Rawlinson, 433 U.S. 321, 331-32 & n.14 (1977) (holding that statute itself did not establish a business justification in a sexual discrimination context).

249. Katzenbach v. Morgan, 384 U.S. 641, 654 (1966).

in English. An employer could offer English classes to employees, or offer to reimburse employees for courses they take to improve their English. Both of these alternatives would more effectively accomplish the employer's stated purpose with less adverse impact.[250] Second, a restriction on languages other than English does little to improve an employee's abilities in English. It forces employees to rely exclusively on their English, such as it is, but, absent some instruction or assistance, does little to improve that English. It is questionable, therefore, whether an English-only rule facilitates fluency in English.

D. More Effective Supervision

Another justification offered for English-only rules is that they enable more effective supervision. Like the business justification itself, effective supervision is more important in the essential aspects of a job than in the tangential aspects. In order for more effective supervision to constitute a business justification, the English-only rule must enhance significantly a supervisor's ability to monitor the performance of a job.[251]

---

250. Under *Wards Cove*, the cost of such alternatives to the employer would be relevant in determining whether they are as effective as the challenged rule or practice, but additional cost to the employer would not necessarily defeat them as viable, less-discriminatory alternatives. Wards Cove Packing Co. v. Atonio, 109 S. Ct. 2115, 2127 (1989). Courts will have to determine what costs for less discriminatory alternatives can be imposed upon employers under the business justification standard. Under the former business necessity defense, cost considerations gained greater judicial acceptance as a legitimate defense to liability under the disparate impact theory, posing a danger to the effectiveness of Title VII and the accomplishment of its goals. *See* Brodin, *Costs, Profits, and Equal Employment Opportunity*, 62 NOTRE DAME L. REV. 318, 344-58 (1987):

> The allowance of such cost justification in fair employment law is ill-advised. If Title VII is to operate effectively in the American workplace to extend opportunities to groups traditionally excluded, justification for discriminatory practices must be narrowly confined to situations where job performance, productivity, or the very financial existence of the enterprise is at stake.

Id. at 358 (footnote omitted). The explicit mention in *Wards Cove* of cost considerations as relevant in evaluating the "equal effectiveness" of less discriminatory alternatives offered by plaintiffs sanctions and furthers the cost defense to liability under the disparate impact theory. *See Wards Cove*, 109 S. Ct. at 2127; Watson v. Fort Worth Bank and Trust, 108 S.Ct. 2777, 2790 (1988) (O'Connor, J.) (plurality opinion) ("Factors such as the cost or other burdens of proposed alternative selection devices are relevant in determining whether they would be equally as effective as the challenged practice in serving the employer's legitimate business goals.").

251. *Wards Cove*, 109 S. Ct. at 2125-26 (stating that a challenged practice must serve significantly and substantially the legitimate employment goals of the employer)l; *see also* Robinson v. Lorillard Corp., 444 F.2d 791, 798 (4th Cir. 1971) ("[T]he challenged practice must effectively carry out the business purpose it is alleged to serve.") (footnote omitted); *cf.* United States v. Bethlehem Steel Co., 446 F.2d 652, 662 (2d Cir. 1971)

An English-only rule can enhance supervision in only one way: it allows supervisors without skill in a different language to know the content of employees' conversations. Access to the content of such conversations alone, however, cannot constitute a business justification without a showing that supervision is significantly enhanced by such access. The employer must also show that access to the content of such conversations is somehow job-related. Accordingly, if an English-only rule limits the use of other languages at certain times or in certain areas of the workplace, a business justification exists only if access to the content of conversations at those times and in those areas relates to the job and significantly enhances supervision.

The extent to which knowledge of conversations relates to the job varies depending on the type of job. For example, in a production job such as manufacturing widgets, the essential part of the job is producing widgets. The important ingredients of job performance will be the quantity and quality of widgets produced, efficiency and safety in producing them, reliability, diligence, and other typical factors. Assume that this widget manufacturer institutes a rule prohibiting conversations between employees in languages other than English while they work. The employer asserts that the rule enhances the supervision of employees. This justification should fail because there is no business reason for a supervisor to have access to the content of employee conversations that do not relate to important tasks of the job.[252] As long as job performance is good, measured by the quantity, quality, efficiency, and safety of widget production, the content of employee conversations should make little or no difference to the employer.

If employee conversations interfere with job performance, the interference results from the fact that such conversations occur, not from the fact that they occur in a language other than English. Accordingly, if the employer permits conversations between employees in English, then he can assert no business jus-

---

(stating that to constitute a business necessity, the criteria needs to be "an irresistible demand" of the job); B. SCHLEI & P. GROSSMAN, supra note 57, at 359 (noting that criteria must be reasonably necessary for job performance).

252. Wards Cove, 109 S. Ct. at 2125-26. See Griggs v. Duke Power Co., 401 U.S. 424, 431-32 (1971) ("If an employment practice [that has a disparate impact] cannot be shown to be related to job performance, the practice is prohibited. . . .[A]ny given requirement must have a manifest relationship to the employment in question."). The requirement that an employment practice with disparate impact must be job related still appears to be part of the disparate impact standard. Wards Cove, 109 S. Ct. at 2126 (holding evidence of an insubstantial business justification will not be sufficient to meet an employer's burden).

tification based on more effective supervision for restricting similar conversations in languages other than English. The same outcome holds true in sales jobs. The salesperson sells merchandise and provides good service to customers. The content of an employee's conversations with fellow employees is typically not an important part of the job. If an employee's conversations with his fellow employees interfere with service to customers and job performance, it is because such conversations occur, not because of the language in which they occur or their content. Accordingly, if an employer allows employee conversations in English, more effective supervision will often not furnish a business justification for an English-only rule. If customers are annoyed at conversations in languages other than English, that annoyance is based on private biases and furnishes no justification for an English-only rule.[253]

A recently decided case in the Ninth Circuit, *Jurado v. Eleven-Fifty Corp.*,[254] illustrates how these principles might apply to a job in which the content of the non-English speech is at the core of a job. The plaintiff, Valentine Jurado, was a bilingual disc jockey. For several years he had conducted his radio show in English. Attempting to increase the radio station's Hispanic audience, the program director asked Jurado to use some Spanish words and phrases during his broadcasts. Jurado complied, but his use of Spanish did not increase his Hispanic audience. A consultant hired by the station concluded that the bilingual broadcasts actually hurt the station's ratings by confusing listeners about the station's programming. Accordingly, the program director told Jurado to stop using Spanish during his show. Jurado refused and was fired.[255]

Both the district court[256] and the court of appeals[257] found that Jurado's discharge did not violate Title VII. Although both courts relied on the rationale of *Garcia v. Gloor*,[258] the *Gutierrez* decision discusses *Jurado* and offers a rationale more consistent with the business justification standard.[259] As the *Gutierrez*

---

253. *See supra* notes at 231-33 and accompanying text.

254. 630 F. Supp. 569 (C.D. Cal. 1985), *aff'd*, 813 F.2d 1406 (9th Cir. 1987).

255. *Jurado*, 630 F. Supp. at 570-71.

256. *Id.* at 578-80.

257. Jurado v. Eleven-Fifty Corp., 813 F.2d 1406, 1411-12 (9th Cir. 1987).

258. *Jurado*, 630 F. Supp. at 580; 813 F.2d at 1411-12 (citing Garcia v. Gloor, 618 F.2d 264 (5th Cir. 1980), *cert. denied*, 449 U.S. 1113 (1981). Both courts reasoned that because Jurado was bilingual, he could readily comply with the employer's English-only rules and therefore there was no disparate impact and no violation of Title VII.

259. Gutierrez v. Municipal Ct., 838 F.2d 1031, 1041, *vacated as moot*, 109 S. Ct. 1736 (1989).

court recognized, the content of radio broadcasts is the product produced by a radio station.[260] Because Jurado's use of Spanish had negative effects, the station's business - its ability to broadcast as it chose and to sustain the audience for its broadcasts - was undermined by Jurado's refusal to comply with the program director's instructions.[261]

Although the employer in *Jurado* did not attempt to justify the language restriction as necessary for more effective supervision, the case illustrates how a language restriction may be permissible. Where content is at the core of the job, an employer may be able to sustain the business justification for restrictions on the use of languages other than English.[262]

Courts must evaluate the job-relatedness of language restrictions based on the need for more effective supervision. When evaluating the "more effective supervision" business justification, it may be useful for a court to consider a spectrum ranging from jobs in which the content of employee conversations has no job relation, such as widget production, to jobs in which the content of conversations is at the core of the job and highly job-related, like the disc jockey in *Jurado*. In the former kind of job, it will be difficult for an employer to show the business justification for an English-only rule based on more effective supervision. In the latter kind of job, where content is at the core, an employer may be able to justify a language restriction.

Even when an employer can offer evidence of a business justification based on the need for more effective supervision, a plaintiff may be able to prove the existence of a more effective and less discriminatory alternative. "[T]he best way to ensure that supervisors are apprised of how well . . . bilingual employees are performing . . . their assigned tasks would be to employ Spanish-speaking supervisors."[263] A plaintiff able to offer such proof still may be able to establish that an English-only rule violates Title VII.[264]

---

260. *Id.*

261. *Id.*

262. *See* Fragante v. City of Honolulu, 49 Fair Empl. Prac. Cas. (BNA) 437, 439 (9th Cir. 1989) ("Employers may lawfully base an employment decision upon an individual's accent when—but only when—it interferes materially with job performance. There is nothing improper about an employer making such an honest assessment of a candidate for a job when oral communication skills" are necessary) (citations omitted) (text omitted from amended decision reported at 888 F.2d 591). *See also infra* note 276 and accompanying text.

263. *Gutierrez*, 838 F.2d at 1041.

264. Wards Cove Packing Co. v. Atonio, 109 S. Ct. 2115, 2126-27 (1989).

E. Safety and Efficiency

Although no courts have decided the issue, an employer in a proceeding before the EEOC used safety and efficiency as the basis for justifying a limited English-only rule.[265] Safety and efficiency are well-recognized grounds for establishing a business justification under Title VII,[266] and employers are likely to assert them in support of English-only rules in the future. The requirements of the "safety and efficiency" justification arose in cases prior to *Wards Cove* in the context of the business necessity defense, which required employers to prove the business necessity for a challenged practice. Plaintiffs, now carrying the burden of persuasion on the business justification for an employer's challenged practice, will have to disprove the validity of the employer's offered justification.[267]

The safety and efficiency justification was asserted to support mandatory leave and minimum height requirements in the airline industry,[268] and to justify minimum height or strength requirements for police officers.[269] The analysis in such cases is particularly useful because it illustrates the kind of evidence required by courts analyzing the safety and efficiency justification when a job's duties include managing emergencies. By analogy, the same kind of evidence will be required from plaintiffs seek-

---

265. EEOC Dec. No. 83-7, 2 Empl. Prac. Guide (CCH) ¶ 6836 (1983). The employer claimed that effective communication among its employees was necessary during emergencies and while employees were working with potentially dangerous equipment and materials in order to prevent or control fires, explosions and other casualties; the employer alleged that its English-only rule was narrowly drawn to fit these circumstances. *Id.* The EEOC, however, apparently accepted the employer's claimed necessity for the rule with no showing of proof of the justification for the rule. *Id.*

266. Dothard v. Rawlinson, 433 U. S. 321, 331-32 & n.14 (1977); *see also* Note, *Business Necessity under Title VII of the Civil Rights Act of 1964: A No-Alternative Approach,* 84 YALE L.J. 98, 108 (1974).

267. *Wards Cove,* 109 S. Ct. at 2126-27.

268. *See, e.g.,* Levin v. Delta Air Lines, Inc., 730 F.2d 994, 997 (5th Cir. 1984); Harriss v. Pan Am. World Airways, Inc., 649 F.2d 670, 676-77 (9th Cir. 1980); Burwell v. Eastern Air Lines, Inc., 633 F.2d 361, 365, 371 (4th Cir. 1980) (plurality opinion), *cert. denied,* 450 U.S. 965 (1981); Boyd v. Ozark Airlines, Inc., 419 F. Supp. 1061, 1062 (E.D. Mo. 1976).

269. *See, e.g.,* Dothard v. Rawlinson, 433 U.S. 321, 331-32 (1977); Craig v. County of Los Angeles, 626 F.2d 659, 666-68 (9th Cir. 1980), *cert. denied,* 450 U.S. 919 (1981); Blake v. City of Los Angeles, 595 F.2d 1367, 1374, 1379-81 (9th Cir. 1979); Davis v. County of Los Angeles, 566 F.2d 1334, 1341-42 (9th Cir. 1977); United States v. New York, 21 Fair Empl. Prac. Cas. (BNA) 1286, 1293, 1296 (N.D.N.Y. 1979) (findings of fact not included in decision as reported at 475 F. Supp. 1103); League of United Latin American Citizens v. City of Santa Ana, 410 F. Supp. 873, 882 (C.D. Cal. 1976); Officers for Justice v. Civil Serv. Comm'n of San Francisco, 395 F. Supp. 378, 380 (N.D. Cal. 1975).

ing to disprove the justification for an English-only rule involving hazards or emergencies.

As with the other supposed justifications, the employer carries the burden of production.[270] Merely asserting the rationale should not suffice. As one court stated, "the incantation of a safety rationale is not an abracadabra to which [a] [c]ourt must defer judgment."[271] An employer's subjective belief that a practice is necessary, without any supporting evidence, is insufficient to justify a discriminatory practice.[272]

Assuming an employer can meet its burden, the plaintiff will have to prove that conversations in a primary language different from English do not interfere with the specific job-related tasks he must perform routinely in particularly hazardous areas of the workplace and during emergencies.[273] Courts may also require expert testimony establishing that the use of different languages does not interfere with safety or efficiency.[274]

In evaluating the effectiveness of an English-only rule, the court should consider the purpose of the rule and what the rule actually accomplishes. In a job involving hazards or possible emergencies, the purpose of a limited English-only rule must be to improve communication between employees and to reduce confusion. The English-only rule ensures that all communications will be in English, thus improving the ability of those whose primary language is English to understand all conversations between employees when the rule is in force. By improving communication, so the argument goes, the rule increases safety on the job and improves the employees' ability to respond to an emergency.

---

270. *Wards Cove*, 109 S. Ct. at 2125-26.

271. Maclennan v. American Airlines, Inc., 440 F. Supp. 466, 472 (E.D. Va. 1977).

272. *See* Craig v. County of Los Angeles, 626 F.2d 659, 667 n.8 (9th Cir. 1980), *cert. denied*, 450 U.S. 919 (1981); United States v. Lee Way Motor Freight, Inc., 625 F.2d 918, 941-43 (10th Cir. 1979).

273. In cases challenging mandatory leave requirements for pregnant flight attendants, courts, applying the business necessity standard, have required employers to provide proof of the specific duties of flight attendants, both normally and during emergencies, and of the specific experiences of pregnant attendants in their jobs. *See* Burwell v. Eastern Air Lines, Inc., 633 F.2d 361, 365-66 (4th Cir. 1980) (plurality opinion). Employers also have been required, under the former standard of business necessity, to present considerable expert testimony on the effect of pregnancy on job performance. *Id. See also* Harriss v. Pan Am. World Airways, Inc., 649 F.2d 670, 675 (4th Cir. 1980); Levin v. Delta Air Lines, Inc., 730 F.2d 994, 997 (5th Cir. 1984). Now that the burden of proof on the employer's justification has been shifted to plaintiffs under *Wards Cove*, 109 S. Ct. at 2125-26, plaintiffs presumably will have to offer similar kinds of proof of the invalidity of an employer's asserted justification.

274. *Cf. supra* note 273 and cases cited therein (noting that expert testimony was required in cases based on sexual discrimination).

Upon careful analysis, however, one can question whether an English-only rule effectively carries out its purpose. Although an English-only rule clearly would improve the ability of persons whose primary language is English to understand all conversations in the workplace, such a rule may decrease the effectiveness of communications, and therefore interfere with safety and efficiency for persons whose primary language is Spanish or some other language. The reviewing court, therefore, should consider the composition of an employer's work force to determine whether English-only communication enhances or interferes with safety and efficiency. Furthermore, an English-only rule based on safety and efficiency often may be unnecessary. A rational employer hires and retains employees who are capable of understanding the safety requirements of a job and of performing their jobs satisfactorily. Where ability to speak and understand English is necessary, an employer may properly require such an ability as a prerequisite for employment.[275] In a potentially hazardous job in which lives and equipment may be at risk, it would make no sense for an employer to place his trust in an employee who could not perform the job. Even if his primary language is not English, an employee working in such a job must have been found by the employer to both understand and communicate well enough in English to meet the requirements of the job in the first place. Additionally, a rational employer will train his employees, probably in English, to handle situations that could arise on the job. In a crisis situation, it would be completely irrational for a trained and capable Spanish-speaking employee to defy his experience, training, and common sense by attempting to communicate in Spanish to people who will not

---

275. *See e.g.,* Garcia v. Rush-Presbyterian-St. Luke's Medical Center, 660 F.2d 1217, 1222 (7th Cir. 1981) (holding that ability to speak and read some English is a requirement for virtually every job in a highly sophisticated hospital); Duong Nhat Tran v. City of Houston, 35 Fair Empl. Prac. Cas. (BNA) 471, 472 (S.D. Tex. 1983) (holding that mastery of English could be required in job involving explanation of requirements of city law to building owners); Mejia v. New York Sheraton Hotel, 459 F. Supp. 375, 377-78 (S.D.N.Y. 1978), *modified,* 476 F. Supp. 1068 (S.D.N.Y. 1979) (holding that adequate mastery of English could be required for hotel front office position, which involved contact with guests); Chung v. Morehouse College, 11 Fair Empl. Prac. Cas. (BNA) 1084, 1088-89 (N.D. Ga. 1975) (holding that mastery of English could be required for college faculty position); *cf.* Vasquez v. McAllen Bay & Supply Co., 660 F.2d 686, 688 (5th Cir. 1981) (finding no violation of 42 U.S.C. § 1981 in employer's requirement that truck drivers speak English because the employer lacked discriminatory intent); Frontera v. Sindell, 522 F.2d 1215, 1220 (6th Cir. 1975) (holding that requirement of successful performance on English-language civil service exam for a carpenter position is not a violation of 42 U.S.C. §§ 1981, 1983, 1985 or fourteenth amendment).

understand him.[276] Rationality, therefore, and the need to perform a job or to handle a crisis, may accomplish the same objectives as a limited English-only rule.

To the extent that an English-only rule in a dangerous employment situation is based on an employer's fear that an irrational response to a crisis by a bilingual person will increase the risk of catastrophe, it appears that, under *Wards Cove*, a plaintiff would have to prove that such a fear is unjustified. This could be very difficult.[277] Once an employer has a bilingual work force, the risk that bilingual employees might speak their primary language is always there. The inquiry, therefore, should be whether routine observance of an English-only rule diminishes that risk.

A plaintiff, however, can probably show the existence of less discriminatory measures that accomplish the employer's safety and efficiency purposes. In a hazardous business, an employer concerned about possible confusion due to language differences among his employees should post emergency instructions and offer training in the languages best understood by his employees. Such measures are both less restrictive and probably more effective than an English-only rule for persons whose primary language is not English.[278]

Like the existence of less discriminatory alternatives, the presence of counterexamples provides persuasive evidence of pretext or lack of job relation. A counterexample is a case in which an employer, without any decrease in safety or efficiency, fails to adhere to an allegedly necessary discriminatory practice.[279] In one case an employer attempted to justify a minimum height

---

276. Persons successfully holding jobs requiring ability in English are likely to be at the more fully bilingual end of the bilingual spectrum. *See supra* notes 93-94. Such persons, who are more fully able to express themselves in a second language, are probably less apt to slip inadvertently into speaking their primary languages than persons whose limited abilities in English place them at the less bilingual end of the spectrum.

277. Formerly, under the business necessity standard, employers were required to prove that such fears were justified. For example, employers were required to prove that pregnant flight attendants and short police officers could not perform their jobs safely, which employers were, at least in some cases, unable to do. For cases challenging pregnancy rules for flight attendants, see *supra* note 268. For cases challenging minimum height requirements for police officers, see *supra* note 269.

278. *Cf.* Katzenbach v. Morgan, 384 U.S. 641, 655 (1966) (stating that ability to read or understand Spanish-language newspapers, radio, and television is as effective a means of obtaining political information as ability to read English).

279. *Cf.* Levin v. Delta Air Lines, Inc., 730 F.2d 994, 998 (5th Cir. 1984) ("If it is established that an employer takes a lax approach to safety in comparable matters, the employer may be hard-pressed to convince the court that it deems the contribution to safety effected by the challenged policy to be necessary . . . .") (footnote omitted).

requirement of 5'7" for a truck driver position.[280] Indiscreetly, the employer had hired many nonminority drivers unable to meet the minimum height requirement; one of these drivers, a 5' 4 ½" white man, had performed years of accident-free driving and had received safe driving awards.[281] The court concluded that "if Anglos less than 5' 7" tall could perform safely and efficiently . . ., there is no reason to suppose that Spanish surnamed Americans could not do likewise."[282] Accordingly, in addition to considering the existence of less discriminatory and equally effective alternatives, plaintiffs' lawyers challenging English-only rules should consider the consistency with which the employers have applied their rules.

In some circumstances, employers may be able to justify English-only rules that are not unduly discriminatory, based on safety and efficiency. An English-only rule, however, must actually and significantly contribute to greater safety or efficiency.[283] The employer's mere assumptions or beliefs, like the beliefs that pregnant flight attendants or short police officers cannot do their jobs, are not sufficient to support a discriminatory English-only rule.[284] The presence of more than one language in the workplace does not necessarily make a dangerous workplace less safe. One can be as safe and efficient in Spanish, or any other language, as in English.[285]

---

280. United States v. Lee Way Motor Freight, Inc., 625 F.2d 918, 941-42 (10th Cir. 1979).

281. *Id.* at 941.

282. *Id.* at 942.

283. Wards Cove Packing Co. v. Atonio, 109 S. Ct. 2115, 2125-26 (1989).

284. *Id.* at 2126 (holding that an employer bears the burden of producing evidence of a business justification; a "mere insubstantial justification [offered by an employer] will not suffice, because such a low standard of review would permit discrimination to be practiced through the use of spurious, seemingly neutral employment practices"). Accordingly, although it remains to be seen how the courts will apply the new standard established in *Wards Cove*, mere assumptions about or beliefs in the validity of a challenged practice do not appear to be sufficient to pass muster. *See, e.g.,* Craig v. County of Los Angeles, 626 F.2d 659, 667 n.8 (9th Cir. 1980), *cert. denied,* 450 U.S. 919 (1981) ("Mere opinion testimony by sheriff's department personnel that height is effective in control functions is inadequate to establish the significant correlation that is required under Title VII."); United States v. Virginia, 454 F. Supp. 1077, 1088 (E.D. Va. 1978) (stating that opinions of five members of state police that "height and weight are useful in police work" fail to establish job relatedness, but establish only "a good faith belief of job relatedness").

285. *Cf.* Katzenbach v. Morgan, 384 U.S. 641, 655 (1966) (stating that in exercising the right to vote "an ability to read or understand Spanish is as effective as ability to read English").

F. Summary of Analysis of English-Only Rules Under the Business Justification Standard

This Part of the Article has examined the various justifications offered by employers in support of English-only rules: reducing racial tension and fear; reducing disruptions; supporting the English language and improving employees' English skills; enhancing the effectiveness of supervision; and enhancing safety and efficiency in the workplace. Applying the business justification standard, it appears that three of the potential justifications—reducing racial tension and fear,[286] reducing disruptions,[287] and improving employees' English skills[288]—probably cannot pass muster under the standard. English-only rules simply are not effective for such purposes. English-only rules increase, rather than reduce, racial tensions and fears. Different-language conversations are no more disruptive than conversations in English, except for legally impermissible reasons. And English-only rules do little to improve the English of persons whose primary language is not English.

Some of the other asserted justifications do not fare much better under the business justification standard. It is questionable whether supporting the use of English in this country is a business purpose at all. A desire to enhance the effectiveness of supervision cannot constitute a business justification unless a supervisor's access to the content of different-language conversations relates to the job and enhances supervision. Furthermore, a plaintiff often will be able to show a less discriminatory, and more effective, alternative to an English-only rule: an employer needs only to hire a supervisor conversant in the different language to achieve more effective supervision.[289]

Under appropriate circumstances, an employer may be able to justify an English-only rule on the grounds of safety and efficiency. The new business justification standard requires the plaintiff to disprove the employer's asserted justification. This standard will be as difficult for plaintiffs to meet with regard to the safety and efficiency justification as it was for employers to meet under the business necessity standard. Plaintiffs, however,

---

286. See supra Part V.A.
287. See supra Part V.B.
288. See supra Part V.C.
289. Gutierrez v. Municipal Ct., 838 F.2d 1031, 1043, vacated as moot, 109 S. Ct. 1736 (1989).

may be able to prevail by demonstrating less restrictive and more effective alternatives.

VI. Conclusion

The long history of discrimination against members of language minority groups in the United States suggests that they, like persons whose race or religion differs from those of the majority, warrant protection under Title VII.[290] The strong link between the primary language, ethnicity, and national origin of persons whose primary language is different from English justifies protection for such persons under Title VII. This link between primary language and national origin exists regardless of bilingualism.[291] Furthermore, the difficulty of second-language acquisition makes primary language practically immutable, another basis for protection under the statute. For these reasons, discrimination against persons whose primary language is different from English is a form of national origin discrimination.

English-only rules have a disparate impact on persons whose primary language is not English. Indeed, the impact of these rules is beyond "disparate." The rules result in an exclusive adverse impact because English-only rules can disqualify or affect only members of protected national origin groups. English-only rules, therefore, cannot be facially neutral in the same sense as other neutral rules analyzed under the disparate impact theory. The demographics of the United States indicate that, by the year 2000, Hispanics will be the largest ethnic minority group in the United States.[292] The primary language of many of these persons will be Spanish. They will bear the impact of English-only rules in the workplace along with other persons whose primary language is different from English.

The issues posed in *Garcia* and *Gutierrez,* consequently, are very likely to return to the courts. Courts should recognize the link between primary language, ethnicity, and national origin. Courts also should recognize that English-only rules have an exclusive adverse impact upon protected language minority groups.

---

290. *Cf.* Olagues v. Russoniello, 797 F.2d 1511, 1521 (9th Cir. 1986), *vacated as moot,* 484 U.S. 806 (1987) ("[C]ourts have long recognized the history or discriminatory treatment inflicted on Chinese and Hispanic people.") (citations omitted). *See* Senate Report, *supra* note 114, at 791-97. *See supra* notes 111-15 and accompanying text.

291. *Gutierrez,* 838 F.2d at 1039. *See* Karst, *supra* note 81, at 351-57; J. Fishman, *supra* note 17, at 70.

292. *See supra* note 14 and accompanying text.

Accordingly, courts should evaluate such rules as disparate treatment because of national origin and require employers to establish a bona fide occupational qualification defense for such rules. In the alternative, if a court adheres to the disparate impact theory for analyzing English-only rules, employers should be required to meet a strict standard of business necessity. Even if a court adheres to the permissive standards of *Wards Cove* in analyzing an English-only rule, such a rule should be upheld only when the rule relates to the job and effectuates its asserted purpose, when the rule is not a pretext for discrimination, and when a plaintiff fails to demonstrate the availability of less discriminatory, but equally effective, alternatives.

Conversations in one language need not be more disruptive, nor less safe, than conversations in another language.

94

1 | Generational Status, Family Background, and Educational Attainment Among Hispanic Youth and Non-Hispanic White Youth

VILMA ORTIZ

The rapid growth of the Hispanic population in the United States during the past decade and the economically disadvantaged position of this population have led both policymakers and researchers to realize that there is much to be learned about our country's second largest minority group. One segment of the Hispanic population that merits special attention is its youth. Compared to majority white youth, Hispanic youth are disadvantaged in many respects but especially with regard to educational attainment (Brown, Rosen, Hill, & Olivas, 1980; Borus, Crowley, Rumberger, Santos, & Shapiro, 1980; U.S. Bureau of the Census, 1980). Hispanic youth not only are more likely to have acquired fewer years of schooling but are also disadvantaged along other indicators characterizing the educational process. Two important disparities in the education of Hispanic youth as compared to majority youth are that Hispanics are more likely to be delayed in school and to drop out of high school (Brown et al., 1980). Furthermore, while similar percentages of Hispanic high school graduates and non-Hispanic white high school graduates go on to college, Hispanics are further disadvantaged in that they are considerably more likely to attend two-year colleges and to not complete

This research was supported by a contract from the Department of Labor's Employment and Training Administration (No. 99-1-1588-33-3), to the National Council of La Raza. Institutional support was also provided by the Hispanic Research Center at Fordham University and the Institute for Social Research at the University of Michigan. I gratefully acknowledge comments made by Rosemary Santana Cooney, Douglas Gurak, and Carlos Arce.

29

their college education. Thus research on the educational attainment of Hispanics should focus not only on years of schooling acquired but on educational outcomes, such as the likelihood of dropping out of high school.

A considerable amount of sociological research has focused on factors that influence educational attainment. In the original model developed by Blau and Duncan (1967), the impact of father's education and occupation on son's education was examined. The model was later elaborated on to include number of siblings, the presence of two parents in the household, and characteristics of the mother (Duncan & Duncan, 1968; Duncan, Featherman, & Duncan, 1972; Featherman & Hauser, 1978; Sewell, Hauser, & Wolf, 1980). This research has shown that family background has a sizable impact on years of schooling acquired since it represents the mechanism by which achievement values, economic resources, and information about the world of work are transmitted intergenerationally.

The facts that Hispanics are more likely to come from disadvantaged families and to be recent immigrants have implications for their educational attainment. Recent immigrants are likely to be disadvantaged socioeconomically in comparison to later generations, and socioeconomic background has a strong impact on attainment. Featherman and Hauser (1978) provide evidence on the role of family background in explaining educational differences among generational groups. Foreign-born persons of different nationalities were found to have considerably fewer years of schooling in comparison to second and later generations, with the second and later generations not differing to a large extent. After controlling for family background, the first generation continued to be disadvantaged educationally, although less so, and the second generation was shown to have acquired more years of schooling than later generations. Thus the second generation achieved an educational level similar to or higher than that of later generations from similar backgrounds. Featherman and Hauser make these generational comparisons across national-origin groups as well as for Mexicans (the only national-origin group for which there was a sufficient number of respondents to analyze separately). The results for Mexicans were similar; the first generation had a significantly lower educational level than later generations, and the second generation a significantly higher level than later generations, after controlling for family background.

Featherman and Hauser (1978) also examined the impact of family background on educational attainment separately for generational groups across different national-origin groups. They found that family background was less influential in explaining variability in educational attainment among the second generation than among the first generation or later generations. This effect was due primarily to the weaker impact of father's education on attainment among the second generation. Thus the process by which family background affects achievement was found to vary by generational status.

These results are further supported by findings obtained by Cooney, Rogler, Correale, and Ortiz (1980) where the impact of family background on educational attainment among Puerto Rican immigrants was compared to that of their adult children, who were primarily second-generation or had arrived on the U.S. mainland during their preschool years. Father's characteristics had a significant impact on the educational attainment of the parents but not on the attainment of the children. In addition, Peñalosa and McDonagh's (1966) study of second-generation Mexicans in California found no relationship between parents' occupations and respondents' education, while Hirschman's (1978) study of first-generation Mexicans in Texas found significant relationships between fathers' education and occupational status and the respondents' education. In sum, these studies demonstrate that parental characteristics have a stronger impact on the achievements of the first generation and third generation than on the achievements of the second generation.

The results of these prior studies point to the unique experience of the second generation in the educational process and the intergenerational transmission of socioeconomic status. What implications does this have for the attainment of Hispanic youth? Because of the relatively recent immigration history of Hispanics to the United States, Hispanic youth are mostly first- and second-generation.[1] In addition, because of the socioeconomic position of Hispanics in this society, Hispanic youth are especially likely to come from disadvantaged backgrounds. Thus generational status and family background are certain to be important factors explaining the achievement of Hispanic youth. In this paper, the educational attainment of first-, second-, and third-generation Hispanic youth is compared to that of non-Hispanic white youth before and after controlling for family background. This analysis addresses the question of whether the achievement of second-generation Hispanic youth is greater than that of other Hispanic generational groups and greater than that of non-Hispanic white youth once family background is held constant. In addition, the impact of family-background characteristics on educational attainment is examined separately for Hispanic youth and non-Hispanic white youth and for generational groups within Hispanics, thus addressing the question of whether the *process* of achievement for Hispanic youth, and in particular the second-generation, differs from that of non-Hispanic white youth. Specifically, do parental characteristics, especially parents' educational attainment, have less impact among second-generation Hispanic youth than among first- or third-generation Hispanic youth or non-Hispanic white youth?

DATA AND METHODS

The analysis presented in this paper is based on the Youth Cohort of the National Longitudinal Surveys of Labor Market Experiences conducted by Ohio State University. The data used in this analysis are from the first-year interviews collected in 1979 of a five-year longitudinal survey. This cohort of approximately 12,700 youths was sampled to be nationally representative of youths between the ages of fourteen and twenty-one. In addition, Hispanics and blacks were oversampled; disadvantaged non-Hispanic, nonblack youth were oversampled; and youth enlisted in the military were oversampled.

The focus of this paper is on Hispanic youth and native-born non-Hispanic white youth; therefore, blacks and other nonwhite groups were excluded from the analysis. Race and ethnicity were obtained using a self-identification measure in which respondents could identify with more than one racial or ethnic group. Respondents who identified with a group of Hispanic origin were classified as Hispanics even if they also identified with another group. Respondents were classified as native-born non-Hispanic white if they met the following criteria: identified with a group of European descent or as American; did not identify with a group of Hispanic origin; did not identify as black or with another nonwhite group; were not racially coded as "black" or "other" by the interviewer; and were born in the United States.

The dependent variables to be examined in this paper are highest grade completed, delay in school, and dropping out of high school. The operationalization of highest grade completed is straightforward. Delay in school is the comparison of respondents who have fallen behind their age cohort during their primary or secondary education to those who are at the same level as their age cohort. Since the respondents in this sample were not specifically asked about delays in school, this measure was obtained by calculating the ideal grade the respondents should have completed given their age cohort and comparing the ideal grade to the actual grade enrolled in. Respondents who were two or more years behind their age cohort were considered delayed.[2] High school completion is the comparison of respondents who have dropped out of high school to those who have graduated from high school or are currently enrolled in high school.

The analysis was restricted to respondents who were sixteen years of age or older. The fourteen- and fifteen-year-olds were omitted from the analysis because most are enrolled in high school. Among the remaining subsample, the sixteen- to twenty-one-year-olds, many have not completed their education. Thus the focus of this analysis is on educational outcomes that are especially relevant for this age group—delay in school and dropping out of high school. These measures may be considered indicative of early success in the educational process and serve as proxies for the respondents' eventual educational attainment.

Highest grade completed and age are highly correlated, that is, older respondents are farther along in school than younger respondents. For this reason, age is held constant in all the analysis to be presented.

DESCRIPTIVE ANALYSIS

Descriptive statistics of sex, age, and family-background characteristics for Hispanics and non-Hispanic whites are presented in table 1.1. Females slightly outnumber males among the Hispanic youth, while males slightly outnumber females among the non-Hispanic white youth. There is little difference between the two groups in terms of age. Both groups are, on the average, almost nineteen years old. As expected, Hispanics are disadvantaged relative to non-Hispanic whites in terms of family-background characteristics. For instance, the parents of Hispanic respondents have approximately eight to nine years of schooling on the average, while the parents of the non-Hispanic white respondents have approximately twelve years of schooling. Furthermore, the Hispanics

Table 1.1: Weighted Descriptive Statistics for Hispanics and Non-Hispanic Whites

| | Hispanics | | Whites | |
	Mean	S.D.	Mean	S.D.
Female	.519	.500	.480	.500
Age	18.664	1.792	18.680	1.802
Father's education	8.847	5.100	12.485	3.258
Mother's education	8.383	4.377	12.174	2.310
Father's occ. status	44.706	26.483	62.086	22.138
Mother employed	.464	.499	.493	.500
Intact family	.764	.425	.893	.309
Number of siblings	4.542	2.952	3.032	1.924

are more likely to have fathers with lower-status occupations, mothers who did not work when the respondents were fourteen years old, only one parent in the household at the age of fourteen, and a greater number of siblings.[3]

Table 1.2 presents weighted means and proportions of the educational outcomes disaggregated by ethnicity, national origin, and generational status.[4] As can be seen from table 1.2, the Hispanic youth are considerably disadvantaged educationally in comparison to non-Hispanic white youth. The difference between the two groups in highest grade completed is an entire year; Hispanic youth are more than twice as likely to be delayed in school (20 percent vs. 9 percent) and to have dropped out of high school (30 percent vs. 12 percent). As can also be seen from table 1.2, the first generation is considerably more educationally disadvantaged than later generations, and there is little difference between the second and third generations. The first generation has completed one year less schooling than the second or third generation and is two times more likely than the second or third generation to be delayed and to have dropped out. Generational differences among the Mexicans,

Table 1.2: Weighted Means and Proportions of Educational Outcomes

	Highest Grade Completed	Delay in School	High School Dropout	(N)
Both groups	11.365	.100	.136	(6277)
Non-Hispanic whites	11.455	.086	.118	(4731)
Hispanics	10.515	.197	.305	(1546)
Generation 1	9.799	.312	.411	(536)
Generation 2	10.801	.170	.260	(461)
Generation 3	10.935	.115	.246	(549)
Mexicans	10.283	.212	.316	(955)
Generation 1	8.851	.401	.549	(266)
Generation 2	10.745	.178	.247	(244)
Generation 3	10.805	.131	.229	(445)
Puerto Ricans	10.410	.221	.386	(268)
Generation 1	9.815	.317	.504	(102)
Generation 2	10.761	.165	.247	(166)
Other Hispanics	11.134	.143	.226	(323)
Generation 1	10.965	.200	.194	(168)
Generation 2	11.311	.134	.141	(57)
Generation 3	11.298	.067	.306	(98)

Puerto Ricans, and other Hispanics are similar in that the first generation has the lowest attainment, followed by the second and third generation. Among the Mexicans, the difference between the first and second generation is greater (e.g., a two-year difference in highest grade completed) than among the Puerto Ricans (a one-year difference) or the other Hispanics (less than half a year's difference). Among the other Hispanics, the generational difference in terms of dropping out of school is reversed—the third generation has a higher rate (31 percent) than the first or second generation (19 percent and 15 percent respectively).[5]

When comparing the national-origin groups, we find that Mexican and Puerto Rican youth are similar to each other in highest grade completed (appropriately ten years of school) and being delayed (appropriately 20 percent are delayed). However, the dropout rate among Puerto Ricans is slightly higher than among Mexicans. Furthermore, Mexicans and Puerto Ricans are considerably more disadvantaged than other Hispanics in highest grade completed, delay in school, and dropping out of high school. Among the first generation, Mexicans are the most disadvantaged educationally, followed by Puerto Ricans, with the least disadvantage found among other Hispanics. The difference between Mexicans and Puerto Ricans and between Puerto Ricans and other Hispanics is approximately one year in highest grade completed and ten percentage points in delay in school. However, the difference between Mexicans and Puerto Ricans in dropping out of school is small, while other Hispanics have a considerably lower rate of dropping out. Among the second generation, Mexican and Puerto Rican youth are very similar in their levels of attainment, while the other Hispanic youth have a slightly higher level of attainment. Among the third generation, Mexicans are more disadvantaged than other Hispanics in highest grade completed and delay in school, but the other Hispanics have a higher rate of dropping out of school. Furthermore, the national-origin differences among the first generation are greater than the differences among the second or third generation. In sum, these figures demonstrate the disadvantaged educational profile of Hispanic youth, particularly among Mexican and Puerto Rican youth and among first-generation youth.

MULTIVARIATE ANALYSIS

As was clearly seen from the descriptive statistics presented in table 1.1, the Hispanic youth come from more disadvantaged family backgrounds than the non-Hispanic whites. What role do family background differences play in explaining educational differences between Hispanic youth and non-Hispanic white youth? Table 1.3 presents regression analysis for highest grade completed, delay in school, and dropping out of high school where Hispanic youth are compared to non-Hispanic white youth, controlling for (1) sex and age *without* controlling for family-background characteristics and (2) controlling for sex, age, and family-background characteristics. Comparisons are also made between first-, second-, and third-generation Hispanics and non-Hispanic whites *prior to* and *after* controlling for family-background characteristics.

The results presented in table 1.3 show that prior to controlling for family-background characteristics, the differences between Hispanic youth and non-Hispanic white youth are significant and that ethnicity accounts for a considerable amount of variance in educational attainment (ranging from 2 percent of the variance in dropping out of high school to 4 percent of the variance in highest grade completed). After controlling for family background, the difference between Hispanic youth and non-Hispanic white youth is reduced considerably. The difference in highest grade completed, although it continues to be significant, has decreased from almost a year's difference to approximately a tenth of a year's difference. The Hispanic-white difference in being delayed has decreased from an 11 percent difference to a 2 percent difference and is no longer significant. The ethnic difference in dropping out of high school has decreased from a 15 percent difference to no difference and is, also, no longer significant.

Next, first-, second-, and third-generation Hispanics are compared to non-Hispanic whites *prior to* and *after* controlling for family-background characteristics. As can be seen from table 1.3, all three generation groups differ significantly from non-Hispanic whites. The largest difference is between the first generation and non-Hispanic whites—the first generation has completed 1.7 fewer years of schooling and is approximately 20 percent higher in being delayed and in dropping out of school. The second and third generations are almost half a year behind non-Hispanic whites in highest grade completed, are respectively 9 percent and 5.5 percent more likely to be delayed, and are both 10 percent more likely to drop out of high school. After controlling for family background, we find that although the disadvantaged position of the first generation decreases, that generation continues to have significantly *lower* attainment—.8 fewer years of schooling, 6 percent more likelihood of being delayed, and 4.5 percent more likelihood of dropping out. In contrast, the second-generation Hispanic youth goes from significantly lower attainment before controlling for family background

Table 1.3: Regression Analysis of Educational Attainment on Ethnicity and Generational Status Without and With Family-Background Characteristics

	Highest Grade Completed[a]		Delay in School[b]		High School Dropout[b]	
	Without Background	With Background	Without Background	With Background	Without Background	With Background
Hispanic	-.890***	-.121**	.114***	.016	.150***	.001
Proportion of variance	.043***	.001**	.039***	.000	.024***	.000
Generation 1	-1.729***	-.763***	.174***	.060***	.228***	.045*
Generation 2	-.420***	.360***	.088***	-.010	.092***	-.070***
Generation 3	-.406***	.007	.055***	-.007	.108***	.012
Proportion of variance	.070***	.016***	.054***	.006	.031***	.003

*p<.05
**p<.01
***p<.001

[a] Ordinary least squares regression is used for the analysis of highest grade completed, and unstandardized regression coefficients are presented.
[b] Logit regression is used for the analysis of delay in school and dropping out of high school. This procedure uses an iterative maximum-likelihood solution to predict the logarithm of the probability of delay in school or dropping out of school. First-order partial derivatives are presented. These are computed as b,P' $(1-P')$ where b is the coefficient of the relevant independent variable and P' is the proportion that is delayed or has dropped out. The sample proportion is chosen as a realistic representation of the probability of delay or dropping out (the derivatives would be different if computed at other points in the logistic curve). These derivatives are interpreted as the increment to the average probability of delay or dropping out associated with a one-unit increase in the independent variable.

103

to significantly *higher* attainment in highest grade completed and dropping out of high school after controlling for family background. And the difference between the second generation and non-Hispanic whites in being delayed in school is no longer significant after holding family background constant. The significant differences between the third generation and non-Hispanic whites prior to adjusting for family background decrease to nonsignificant, small differences after adjusting for family background.[6]

Table 1.4 presents the analysis for highest grade completed, delay in school, and dropping out of high school regressed on sex, age, and family-background characteristics separately for Hispanics and non-Hispanic whites. Among the non-Hispanic whites, females have significantly higher attainment than males on highest grade completed, delay in school, and dropping out of high school. This is consistent with U.S. population figures regarding the attainment of males and females (U.S. Bureau of the Census, 1980). Males have lower rates of high school completion and are more likely to drop out at younger ages. However, males are more likely to complete college and to attend graduate school. Therefore, females are advantaged at early points in the educational process while males are advantaged at later points; thus, across all age groups, the median educational attainment for males and females is similar. Among Hispanics, females have a lower rate of being delayed in school but do not differ from males in years of schooling acquired or likelihood of dropping out of high school. In sum, non-Hispanic white females are doing considerably better educationally than non-Hispanic white males, while there is a much smaller difference between Hispanic males and females.

The results presented in table 1.4 also show that age has a strong and significant impact on highest grade completed for both Hispanic youth and non-Hispanic white youth (this is the major reason for the large proportion of variance accounted for in highest grade completed, especially among the non-Hispanic white youth). This is understandable since older respondents are more likely to have acquired more years of schooling. Age does not have a significant impact on delay in school for either Hispanic youth or non-Hispanic white youth. Age does have a significant impact on dropping out of high school, but this effect is not as strong as it is for highest grade completed. In addition, the effect of age on dropping out of school is stronger among Hispanic youth than non-Hispanic white youth. Older Hispanic youth are more likely to drop out of high school than are younger Hispanic youth or non-Hispanic white youth.

What is the direct impact of family-background characteristics on educational attainment? Father's and mother's education have a signifi-

Table 1.4: Regression Analysis of Educational Attainment on Sex, Age, and Family Background for Hispanics and Non-Hispanic Whites

	Highest Grade Completed[a]		Delay in School[b]		High School Dropout[b]	
	Hispanics	Whites	Hispanics	Whites	Hispanics	Whites
Female	.018	.308***	−.052**	−.061***	−.025	−.053***
Age	.339***	.568***	.003	−.003	.048***	.009***
Father's education	.058***	.056***	−.009**	−.006***	−.009*	−.015***
Mother's education	.061***	.108***	−.007*	−.013***	−.006*	−.024***
Father's occ. status	.004	.005***	−.002***	−.001***	−.002*	−.002***
Mother employed	.239*	−.056	−.076***	.006	−.039	.002
Intact family	−.080	.242***	.025	−.016	−.039	−.094***
Number of siblings	−.132***	−.073***	.012***	.007***	.024***	.011
Constant	2.490	−1.590	−.112	.138	−.963	.207
Proportion of variance	.262***	.499***	.073***	.118***	.067***	.107***
Unweighted mean or proportion	10.390	11.415	.206	.073	.312	.151

*$p < .05$
**$p < .01$
***$p < .001$

[a] Ordinary least squares regression is used for the analysis of highest grade completed, and unstandardized regression coefficients are presented.
[b] Logit regression is used for the analysis of delay in school and dropping out of high school, and first-order partial derivatives are presented. These are interpreted as the increment to the average probability of delay or dropping out of school associated with a one-unit increase in the independent variable. See note b to table 1.3 for more detail.

cant impact on all three indicators of educational attainment among both Hispanic youth and non-Hispanic white youth. Father's occupational status affects highest grade completed, being delayed, and dropping out among Hispanic youth and non-Hispanic white youth, with the exception of highest grade completed among Hispanics. Mother's employment leads to higher grade completion and less delay among Hispanics but does not affect dropping out among Hispanics or any of the three achievement measures among non-Hispanic whites. Being in an intact family leads to higher grade completion and less dropping out among Hispanics but does not affect delay in school among Hispanics or any achievement measure among non-Hispanic whites. Number of siblings affects highest grade completed, being delayed, and dropping out among both Hispanics and non-Hispanic whites, with the exception of dropping out of school among non-Hispanic whites. In sum, family-background characteristics account for a significant proportion of variance in educational attainment.

To what extent do the relationships between family-background characteristics and educational attainment differ meaningfully between the groups? By meaningful differences, we mean that the relationship in one group is significantly stronger or weaker than in the other group. While these significance tests are not presented in the tables, the results of these comparisons are discussed in the following sections. Mother's education has a weaker impact on educational attainment among Hispanic youth than among non-Hispanic white youth. The differences between the groups are significant for all three indicators of attainment. One can see an example of this by examining the coefficients for highest grade completed regressed on mother's education. This coefficient among the non-Hispanic whites is almost twice the magnitude of the coefficient among the Hispanics. The impact of father's education differed between Hispanic and white youth only in dropping out of high school. And being in an intact family has a weaker impact on dropping out of school among Hispanic youth. The only instances of stronger relationships among Hispanics are those of mother's employment status to highest grade completed and delay in school and number of siblings to highest grade completed. The most consistent difference in these comparisons is the weaker impact of mother's education on the attainment of Hispanic youth.

If we make finer distinctions among Hispanics with respect to generational status, does the impact of family background vary by generational group? Specifically, is the weaker impact of mother's educational attainment, and to some extent father's, found among Hispanics in general particular to one generational group? Table 1.5 presents

Table 1.5: Regression Analysis of Educational Attainment on Sex, Age, and Family Background for Generational Groups Among Hispanics

	Highest Grade Completed[a]			Delay in School[b]			High School Dropout[b]		
	Gen. 1	Gen. 2	Gen. 3	Gen. 1	Gen. 2	Gen. 3	Gen. 1	Gen. 2	Gen. 3
Female	-.057	-.040	.085	-.025	-.055	-.079**	-.004	-.005	-.052
Age	.197***	.558***	.516***	.014	.003	-.001	.075***	.030**	.036**
Father's education	.098***	-.001	.051**	-.014*	-.000	-.010*	-.016**	-.002	-.011
Mother's education	.088**	.026	.039*	-.006	-.001	-.005	-.019**	.003	.005
Father's occ. status	-.001	.010**	.000	-.002	-.003**	-.001	.000	-.002	-.003*
Mother employed	.469*	-.089	.079	-.108*	-.034	-.046	-.097	.060	-.049
Intact family	-.209	-.162	.320	.123*	.005	-.038	-.056	-.061	-.001
Number of siblings	-.168***	-.060*	-.096***	.001	.015*	.017***	.026**	.019*	.024**
Constant	5.669	.453	.419	-.155	-.115	-.015	-1.322	-.822	-.782
Proportion of variance	.243***	.383***	.430***	.048***	.061***	.116***	.109***	.028*	.062***
Unweighted mean or proportion	9.646	10.761	10.807	.326	.167	.120	.435	.236	.255

*p<.05
**p<.01
****p<.001

[a] Ordinary least squares regression is used for the analysis of highest grade completed, and unstandardized regression coefficients are presented.
[b] Logit regression is used for the analysis of delay in school and dropping out of high school, and first-order partial derivatives are presented. These are interpreted as the increment to the average probability of delay or dropping out of school associated with a one-unit increase in the independent variable. See note b to table 1.3 for more detail.

regression analysis for highest grade completed, delay in school, and dropping out of high school by generational status. As can be seen from this table, the coefficients for both mother's and father's education are smaller among second-generation Hispanics than among first- or third-generation Hispanics. In addition, comparing the coefficients of the generational groups to those of non-Hispanic whites (presented in table 1.4), one can see that the weak relationships for parents' education among second-generation Hispanics are dramatically different from the relationships among non-Hispanic whites. The differences between the second generation and non-Hispanic whites are statistically significant in every instance, that is, for both mother's and father's education and for the three indicators of educational attainment. The comparisons between the first and second generation are also significant in almost every instance. The coefficients among the second generation are smaller than those among the third generation, although these differences are, for the most part, not statistically significant.

While the largest differences are between the second generation and non-Hispanic whites, to some extent the first and third generation also differ from non-Hispanic whites. The relationships between mother's education and the three indicators of achievement among the third generation are significantly weaker than among non-Hispanic whites. However, the impact of father's education on educational attainment does not differ between the third generation and non-Hispanic whites. Both mother's and father's education affect dropping out of school significantly less among the first generation than among non-Hispanic whites, while the effect of parents' education on highest grade completed and delay does not differ between the two groups. In sum, the impact of parents' education on education attainment is least strong among the second generation than any other generation or the non-Hispanic whites. Furthermore, the differences in the impact of parents' education are statistically significant when comparing the second generation to non-Hispanic whites and the first generation.

SUMMARY AND CONCLUSIONS

These findings show that Hispanic youth are considerably more educationally disadvantaged than non-Hispanic white youth. However, the differences between Hispanics and non-Hispanic whites can be partly explained by the disadvantaged family backgrounds of Hispanic youth. In addition, generational status was also found to be important for understanding the achievements of Hispanic youth. Even after controlling for family background, first-generation Hispanic youth are educationally disadvantaged. However, second-generation Hispanic youth have significantly *higher* achievements after controlling for family background, while third-generation youth do not differ significantly from non-Hispanic white youth.

These findings also demonstrate that the process of achievement differs for Hispanics and non-Hispanic whites. When non-Hispanic whites are compared to Hispanics as a group, mother's educational attainment has a weaker impact on educational attainment among Hispanic youth. When finer distinctions are made among Hispanics with respect to generational status, *both* mother's and father's educational attainment have a weaker impact among the second generation. Furthermore, the differences between the second generation and non-Hispanic whites and between the first and second generations are statistically significant in every comparison made, this is, for the three indicators of educational attainment regressed on both mother's and father's education. The relationships among the second generation are weaker than among the third generation, although these differences are largely not significant. Thus these findings are consistent in demonstrating that the impact of parents' education on educational attainment is less strong among the second generation than among other generational groups or non-Hispanic whites and that the largest differences are between the second generation, on the one hand, and non-Hispanic whites and the first generation, on the other hand.

What does it mean that second-generation Hispanics achieve as well as or better than the first or later generations, who are of similar socioeconomic background, although their achievements are less affected by family background than those of the first generation or later generations? To understand the unique educational process among the second generation, it seems one must consider both personal characteristics of the immigrant parents and structural characteristics of the immigration experience.

First, personal characteristics are important since immigrants are a select group in comparison to nonimmigrants. Immigrants choose to immigrate and are successful in immigrating. In addition, many immigrants move for economic goals, and even when these goals may not materialize for themselves, there is still the hope that the goals will be obtained by their children. In light of this, the relatively high achievements of the second generation are not surprising. It is probably true that immigrant parents provide more encouragement and hold higher expectations for their children than do nonimmigrant parents.

Second, structural characteristics are important for understanding why relatively higher status on the part of immigrant parents does not necessarily translate into greater achievement for their children. One characteristic of the immigrant parents' educational experience is that their education has been acquired in a different country. Since educational systems vary greatly from country to country, it may be that an educational advantage on the part of the parents in another country does not translate into an advantage for the child. An additional aspect of the immigrant parents' educational experience is that it is considerably lower than that of the non-Hispanic white parents. Variation in the educational attainment of the parents may be relevant only if this variation is around the educational norms present in that society. Thus differences at the lower end of the educational spectrum in a society where the norms and requirements are for a greater amount of schooling may have fewer implications for the attainment of the child. Therefore the combination of schooling acquired in a different country and schooling that is considerably lower than the U.S. norms may mean that differences in attainment on the part of immigrant parents do not translate into either an advantage or a disadvantage for their U.S.-born children, that is, the second generation. Third-generation youth, on the other hand, have parents who are U.S.-born and U.S.-educated; thus variation in their achievements may have greater relevance for the child. And among the first generation, to the extent that their education is acquired in the country of origin (which depends on their age of arrival), differences in their parents' achievements may be relevant to their achievement.Thus we see that the second generation holds a unique place in the transmission of class position from generation to generation. For the second generation, relatively higher achievement on the part of their parents does not necessarily translate into an advantage for them, yet they still acquire greater achievements than later generations who are of similar background.

NOTES

1. The two major national-origin groups included in the "Hispanic" category (both in this study and in the United States) are Mexicans and Puerto Ricans. Because of the commonwealth status of Puerto Rico, movement from Puerto Rico to the mainland is technically considered not immigration but migration. However, Puerto Rico is most similar to other Hispanic countries in terms of language and culture. Thus, in this discussion, island-born Puerto Ricans are considered immigrants.

2. In constructing this variable, the assumption is made that the oldest age a child will be when enrolling in school is seven years old, which is a fairly

conservative definition since other studies have assumed that children enter school at the age of six. A more conservative criterion is used because there are many instances of children not entering school until the age of seven. For example, in New York State, children may enroll in school in the year they turn six years old, but they are not legally required to enroll in school until the calendar year in which they turn seven.

3. Father's occupation, which was recoded to an occupational status measure of socioeconomic standing (Nam & Powers, 1968), was missing for approximately 20 percent of the sample. Therefore Cohen and Cohen's (1975) procedure for handling the instance where a substantial proportion of the sample has a missing value on an independent variable was employed. The missing value was recoded to the mean and a dummy variable signaling the presence of missing data for father's occupation was created and included in the analysis.

4. Among the Puerto Rican youth, only six respondents were third generation; therefore, the third-generation Puerto Ricans are combined with the second generation.

5. Generational differences among the other Hispanics are difficult to interpret because the generational groups are composed of different national-origin groups. The first generation consists primarily of recent immigrants such as Dominicans, Cubans, and Central and South Americans, while the third generation includes groups such as Hispanos in the Southwest.

6. The results presented in table 1.3 and the following tables are not disaggregated by national origin. Although there are national-origin-group differences in achievement (as demonstrated by table 1.2), there is no reason to believe that the hypothesized relationships regarding generational differences and the role of family background differ by national origin. To ensure that this was true, the results presented in tables 1.3 to 1.5 were redone for the Mexican youth and the Puerto Rican youth (the only national-origin groups where there were sufficient respondents to allow for separate analysis). Since the results for separate groups were similar to the results for combined groups of Hispanics, only the results for all Hispanics are presented.

REFERENCES

Blau, P., & Duncan, O. D. (1967). *The American occupational structure*. New York: Wiley.

Borus, M., Crowley, J., Rumberger, R., Santos, R., & Shapiro, D. (1980). *Pathways to the future: A longitudinal study of young Americans, Preliminary report: Youth and the labor market—1979*. Columbus, OH: Ohio State University Center for Human Resource Research.

Brown, G., Rosen, N., Hill, S., & Olivas, M. (1980). *The condition of education for Hispanic Americans*. Washington, DC: National Center for Educational Statistics, U.S. Government Printing Office.

Cohen, J., & Cohen, P. (1975). *Applied multiple regression/correlation analysis for the behavioral sciences*. Hillsdale, NJ: Erlbaum.

Cooney, R., Rogler, L., Correale, L., & Ortiz, V. (1980). *Intergenerational change in educational attainment among Puerto Ricans: A closer look at the migration experience.* Paper presented at the annual conference of the Population Association of America. Denver, CO.

Duncan, B., & Duncan, O. D. (1968). Minorities and the process of stratification. *American Sociological Review, 33,* 356–364.

Duncan, O. D., Featherman, D., & Duncan, B. (1972). *Socioeconomic background and achievement.* New York: Harcourt Brace Jovanovich.

Featherman, D., & Hauser, R. (1978). *Opportunity and change.* New York: Academic Press.

Hirschman, C. (1978). Prior U.S. residence among Mexican immigrants. *Social Forces, 56,* 1179–1181.

Nam, C., & Powers, M. (1968). Changes in the relative status level of workers in the United States, 1950–1960. *Social Forces, 47,* 635–657.

Peñalosa, F., & McDonagh, E. (1966). Social mobility in a Mexican-American community. *Social Forces, 44,* 498–505.

Sewell, W., Hauser, R., & W. Wolf. (1980). Sex, schooling, and occupational status. *American Journal of Sociology, 86,* 551–583.

U.S. Bureau of the Census. (1980). *Educational attainment in the United States, 1979.* Current population reports, Series P-20, No. 356. Washington, DC: U.S. Government Printing Office.

Bilingual Education as a Status Conflict

Rachel F. Moran†

America has evolved for the better. She will pretty much meet you on your terms. In fact, I think that she has finally come to the conclusion that the Blacks, Mexicans, Indians, etc. are here to stay. And the only way to perceive them is to accept them and their existence as valid. Acceptance, that's really the key word. America is accepting all the people, as one people, the way it was meant to be. Today, at least, you can afford to be yourself.

—Maria, a Hispanic social worker[1]

We have room for but one language here and that is the English language, for we intend to see that the crucible turns our people out as American, of American nationality, and not as dwellers in a polyglot boarding house.

—Theodore Roosevelt, as reprinted in a recent U.S. English brochure[2]

These voices bear witness to the conflict engendered by ethnic, linguistic, and cultural diversity. Especially since the 1960's, this conflict has frequently been addressed through the legal process, rather than through more informal means. Hispanics, for example, have repeatedly expressed concerns about their language and culture in promoting programs for non-English-proficient (NEP) and limited-English-proficient (LEP) children. They have often pressed for bilingual-bicultural education programs, which not only promote proficiency in English but also foster literacy in the native language and respect for the child's cultural heritage.[3] Hispanics have also endorsed transitional bilingual education (TBE) programs that utilize subject-matter instruction in a student's

† Acting Professor of Law, Boalt Hall School of Law, University of California, Berkeley. A.B. 1978, Stanford University; J.D. 1981, Yale Law School. I would like to acknowledge the helpful comments of Richard Buxbaum, Sheldon Messinger, Robert Post, Martin Shapiro, Jan Vetter, and Franklin Zimring. I owe a special debt to Steve Sugarman for support and guidance that went well beyond the call of duty. I would also like to express my gratitude to my research assistant, Martha Jiminez, who cheerfully, methodically, and indefatigably pursued the history of federal bilingual education law with me.

1. Monreal, *Maria, Social Worker, Comments*, in SIGHS AND SONGS OF AZTLAN 100, 101-02 (F. Albi & J. Nieto eds. 1975).

2. U.S. English, *In Defense of Our Common Language* . . . (informational brochure, n.d.).

3. OFFICE FOR CIVIL RIGHTS, TASK-FORCE FINDINGS SPECIFYING REMEDIES AVAILABLE FOR ELIMINATING PAST EDUCATIONAL PRACTICES RULED UNLAWFUL UNDER *Lau v. Nichols*, at

native language until the child is sufficiently proficient in English to participate in a regular classroom. To facilitate acquisition of English, the child typically learns to read in both the native language and English.[4]

Critics of bilingual-bicultural education and TBE programs have argued that schools can best promote proficiency in English by minimizing reliance on the student's native language in the instructional process. They have pushed for English as a Second Language (ESL) and structured immersion programs. In ESL programs, linguistic minority children spend most of the day in regular classes but receive additional instruction in English for part of the day.[5] Structured immersion programs use English to teach subject matter, although the teacher speaks both the native language and English. Children may ask questions about a subject in the native language, but the teacher generally responds only in English. The curriculum is structured so that extensive knowledge of English is not assumed as subjects are taught, and the program may provide thirty to sixty minutes of native-language instruction per day.[6] In addition to advocating these alternative instructional approaches, some opponents of bilingual-bicultural education and TBE programs have supported English-only requirements in the schools to ensure the continuing preeminence of English.[7]

Typically, these disputes have been analyzed as yet another example of special interest groups' bargaining over the allocation of scarce resources. The crudest version of this analysis asserts that Hispanics support bilingual-bicultural education and TBE programs because they provide them with jobs as teachers and teachers' aides.[8] For example, in an extremely influential article published in Harper's magazine in 1979, Tom Bethel stated that "[t]he bilingual education program is more or less the Hispanic equivalent of affirmative action."[9] This view fails to explain why Hispanics have concluded that elementary and secondary schools provide a particularly fertile source of employment, especially in light of overall shrinking student enrollments.[10] Perhaps Hispanics are

---

§ IX, pt. 1 (1975), *reprinted in* BILINGUAL EDUCATION 213, 221 (K. Baker & A. de Kanter eds. 1983).

    4. *Id.* at § IX, pt. 5, *reprinted in* BILINGUAL EDUCATION, *supra* note 3, at 221; Baker & de Kanter, *Federal Policy and the Effectiveness of Bilingual Education*, in BILINGUAL EDUCATION, *supra* note 3, at 33, 35.

    5. Baker & de Kanter, *supra* note 4, at 34.

    6. *Id.*

    7. *See infra* notes 55-64 and accompanying text.

    8. N. EPSTEIN, LANGUAGE, ETHNICITY AND THE SCHOOLS 38 (1978) (remarks of A. Bruce Gaarder, former chief of the United States Office of Education's Modern Foreign Language Section); Bethell, *Against Bilingual Education: Why Johnny Can't Speak English*, HARPER'S, Feb. 1979, at 30.

    9. Bethell, *supra* note 8, at 30; *see also* San Miguel, *Conflict and Controversy in the Evolution of Bilingual Education in the United States—An Interpretation*, 65 SOC. SCI. Q. 505, 512-13 (1984).

    10. Levin, *An Analysis of the Federal Attempt to Regulate Bilingual Education: Protecting Civil Rights or Controlling Curriculum?*, 12 J.L. & EDUC. 29, 52 (1983). In California, there was a steady

unconcerned about this general decline because the population of NEP and LEP pupils is growing.[11] Still, it seems unlikely that these activists wholly failed to anticipate that English-speaking teachers would lodge objections based on their seniority if they were displaced by a bilingual education "jobs program" for Hispanics.[12]

Moreover, bilingual education statutes have typically included waiver provisions that enable English-speaking teachers to instruct NEP and LEP students while acquiring bilingual teaching skills.[13] These provisions have been necessary because of the lack of qualified bilingual teachers.[14] The prevalence of waiver provisions raises two troubling problems for those who treat bilingual education as merely a "jobs program" for Hispanics. First, it seems surprising that Hispanics would concentrate on generating employment opportunities in a field in which a pool of qualified Hispanics is not readily available.[15] Second, once waiver

---

decline in enrollments during the 1970's but a gradual increase in the early 1980's. This increase is expected to continue as children of the "baby boomlet" enter the public schools. ASSEMBLY OFFICE OF RESEARCH, CALIFORNIA 2000, at 15 (June 1986).

11. *The Hispanic Population: Hearings Before the Subcomm. on Census and Population of the House Comm. on Post Office and Civil Service*, 98th Cong., 1st Sess. 91 (1983) (statement of Dr. Gloria Zamora, President, National Association for Bilingual Education); *Bilingual Education: Hearing on H.R. 11 and H.R. 5231 Before the Subcomm. on Elementary, Secondary, and Vocational Educ. of the House Comm. on Educ. & Labor*, 98th Cong., 2d Sess. 124-25 (1984) [hereinafter *1984 House Hearings*] (prepared statement of Dr. M. Joan Parent, President, National School Boards Association). In California, a recent report indicated that by the 1990's, at least 15% of the students would arrive at school without any knowledge of English. ASSEMBLY OFFICE OF RESEARCH, *supra* note 10, at 15 (basing estimate on paper presented to California Board of Education by Norman G. Gold in 1985).

12. In fact, such objections did quite predictably materialize. *See, e.g.*, Morris v. Brentwood Union Free School Dist., 52 A.D.2d 584, 383 N.Y.S.2d 542, *leave to appeal denied*, 40 N.Y.2d 802 (1976) (granting tenured English-speaking teachers' petitions for reinstatement when they were dismissed while more junior bilingual teachers were retained); 60 Op. Cal. Att'y Gen. 80 (1977) (upholding district's right to retain junior nontenured teachers with bilingual competency while terminating senior tenured teachers without such competency where the district had adopted a bilingual education program pursuant to the California Education Code); 59 Op. Cal. Att'y Gen. 73 (1976) (same).

13. *See* R. IRIZARRY, BILINGUAL EDUCATION 24-25 (1978) ("Where teachers are not available with the established qualifications, provisions in the legislation frequently allow for exemptions."); ASSEMBLY OFFICE OF RESEARCH, BILINGUAL EDUCATION 18 (1986) (approximately 40% of the teachers in bilingual education programs in California have waivers; 60% of them are "non-Hispanic white.")

14. *1984 House Hearings, supra* note 11, at 56-57 (prepared statement of Gumecindo Salas, Chairperson, Michigan State Board of Education); *id.* at 72 (prepared statement of Dr. Gloria Zamora, President, National Association for Bilingual Education); *id.* at 84 (prepared statement of Nguyen Ngoc Bich, President-Elect, National Association for Vietnamese American Education); *id.* at 113 (prepared statement of Guillermo Lopez, State Director of Bilingual Education Office, California Department of Education).

15. Schoolteachers must be college graduates. Hispanics complete 10.5 years of schooling compared with 12.5 years for the non-Hispanic white population. The high school dropout rate for Hispanics is 18%, and in large urban areas, the rate is often found to be as high as 50%-70%. Of Hispanic high school graduates, fewer than 30% go on to college, a drop from 35.5% during 1975 to 1982. Of these, fewer than 50% actually graduate from college. Sotomayor, *Demographic*

provisions became a fairly uniform feature of bilingual education statutes, their potential as a source of jobs for Hispanics was considerably diminished. Yet advocates did not reduce their vigorous commitment to bilingual education by redirecting their attention to other programs for increasing Hispanic employment.[16] Thus, although bilingual education programs have undoubtedly generated some jobs for Hispanics, this simple form of interest-group bargaining analysis hardly provides a comprehensive explanation of Hispanics' efforts to promote bilingual education reforms.

A more sophisticated interest-group bargaining analysis attributes the government's endorsement of bilingual education programs to Hispanics' growing political clout. According to this view, as Hispanics have grown in numbers,[17] they have been able to exercise more influence over the political process in promoting their self-interest. Not only have legislators in general become more responsive to Hispanic views, but more Hispanics have also been elected or appointed to political office. In addition, Hispanic lobbying groups have become increasingly experienced and effective as they have gained greater access to the governmental decisionmaking process.[18]

While this view provides some helpful insights into the bilingual education controversy, it too is not a completely satisfying analysis. To

---

Characteristics of U.S. Hispanic Populations, in HISPANICS IN AN AGING SOCIETY 15, 17-18 (Torres-Gil ed. 1986).

16.   Although Hispanics have always pursued other avenues of reform, such as employment discrimination claims, they continue to participate heavily in legislative hearings and litigation related to bilingual education. *See, e.g.*, Avila, *Equal Educational Opportunities for Language Minority Children*, 55 U. COLO. L. REV. 559, 559, 569 (1984) (describing Mexican American Legal Defense and Educational Fund's investment of over one million dollars to identify and promote educational programs providing the greatest opportunities for Hispanic students).

17.   Sotomayor, *supra* note 15 (projecting that by the year 2000, the Hispanic population will be the fastest growing major ethnic group in the United States based on Bureau of the Census figures).

18.   For various analyses of bilingual education policy that reflect interest-group bargaining considerations, see A. LEIBOWITZ, THE BILINGUAL EDUCATION ACT 9-10 (1980); E. MOSHER, A. HASTINGS & J. WAGONER, JR., PURSUING EQUAL EDUCATIONAL OPPORTUNITY 13 (1979); M. REBELL & A. BLOCK, EDUCATIONAL POLICY MAKING AND THE COURTS 193-94 (1982); San Miguel, *supra* note 9, at 506. The analysis here is representative of these approaches without exhaustively describing their subtle variations.

Although the number of Hispanics elected to local, state, and national offices increased from 3,128 to 3,202 between 1980 and 1985, Hispanics still hold fewer than 1% of the nation's elected offices. Sotomayor, *supra* note 15, at 18. Moreover, although the number of Hispanic women who were eligible to vote and went to the polls increased between 1978 and 1982, overall registration and voting participation for presidential elections during this period was lower than in 1972. In the last presidential election, 36% of Hispanics 18 years old and over indicated that they had registered to vote, but only 30% voted. *Id.* The consistently low voter turn-out among Hispanics presents some serious difficulties for an interest-group bargaining model that relies on Hispanics' growing political clout. It is possible, however, that legislators based their actions on a belief that Hispanics would mobilize more effectively in the future.

begin with, this approach does not explain why Hispanics consider bilingual-bicultural education and TBE programs to be of such central importance in advancing their interests. Hispanics have remained strong adherents of these programs, although empirical studies have produced mixed evidence on their effectiveness in promoting academic achievement.[19] Even taking into account the methodological weaknesses of some of these studies,[20] an interest-group bargaining analysis does little to clarify Hispanics' unswerving support for these programs and their reluctance to substitute ESL and structured immersion programs.

Similarly, this analysis does not explain why English speakers with no direct stake in the dispute have dedicated themselves to imposing English-only requirements that would potentially eliminate bilingual-bicultural education and TBE programs. Obviously, English-speaking teachers whose jobs are threatened by such programs could be expected to intervene to protect their economic interests. More baffling, however, is the heavy involvement of English-speaking individuals who have little or no direct contact with the schools or with bilingual-bicultural education and TBE programs.[21] Again, because interest-group bargaining analysis fails to address the underlying process of preference formulation, it can shed little light on this question.

To address these deficiencies in interest-group bargaining approaches, this Essay will utilize status conflict analysis to describe how participants in the bilingual education controversy have used language as a proxy for the status of their culture, customs, and values. It will argue that the participants' preoccupation with the respect and deference accorded to their way of life has strongly influenced the debate over bilingual education. Part I will first briefly recount the history of bilingual education policymaking at the federal level, examine two case studies of bilingual education litigation, and describe the bilingual education and English-only movements. After a review in Part II of earlier work on status conflicts, Part III will apply this theoretical framework to the poli-

---

19. *E.g.*, AMERICAN INSTITUTES FOR RESEARCH (AIR), EVALUATION OF THE IMPACT OF ESEA TITLE VII SPANISH/ENGLISH BILINGUAL EDUCATION PROGRAM (1977-78); Baker & de Kanter, *supra* note 4, at 50-51; Baker & de Kanter, *Assessing the Legal Profession's Contribution to the Education of Bilingual Students*, 1 LA RAZA L.J. 295, 309-15 (1986).

20. *See, e.g.*, INTERCULTURAL DEVELOPMENT RESEARCH ASSOCIATION, THE AIR EVALUATION OF THE IMPACT OF ESEA TITLE VII SPANISH/ENGLISH BILINGUAL EDUCATION PROGRAMS (Eric Ed No. 151-435, 1977); Cardenas, *Response I*, in N. EPSTEIN, *supra* note 8, at 74-75. Recently, a General Accounting Office draft report concluded that the Department of Education had misinterpreted bilingual education research, thereby downplaying the benefits of native-language instruction for NEP and LEP children. May, *U.S. Faulted on Bilingual Education*, L.A. Times, Nov. 8, 1986, § I, at 20, col. 1.

21. For example, one of the leaders in the push for English-only reforms is an opthalmologist from Petoskey, Michigan. Only about 200 of Petoskey's 6,100 residents are nonwhite, and almost all of them speak English. Trombley, *Prop. 63 Roots Traced to Small Michigan City*, L.A. Times, Oct. 20, 1986, § I, at 3, col. 1. *See infra* notes 58, 177-78 and accompanying text.

cymaking and litigation processes in the bilingual education field. It will also evaluate how status concerns have influenced the evolution of the bilingual education and English-only movements. Part IV will close with some tentative suggestions about the future of bilingual education policymaking and litigation, as well as the prospective development of the bilingual education and English-only movements.

I

AN OVERVIEW OF THE BILINGUAL EDUCATION
CONTROVERSY

The debate over bilingual education has raged since the 1960's before a variety of governmental decisionmakers.[22] This controversy will first be examined by reviewing the process through which relevant federal statutes were enacted and applied. Because Hispanics have frequently brought suit to enforce bilingual education provisions, this Part will next describe two empirical studies of such cases. It will then contrast the reform strategies employed by the bilingual education and English-only movements.

A. The Policymaking Process

In 1968, amid considerable fanfare, Congress enacted the Bilingual Education Act, the first piece of federal legislation devoted exclusively to the special educational needs of NEP and LEP children.[23] Witnesses expressed high hopes for the bill. They argued that bilingual education programs would promote academic achievement, thereby enabling Hispanics to participate more fully in the social, economic, and political life of the nation.[24] Several witnesses indicated that bilingual education programs were significant for Hispanics because they represented the schools' acceptance of the Spanish language and the best hope for mutual

---

22. There have been earlier disputes over language issues in the United States. The Founders decided not to establish an official language in the Constitution, in part because they feared that such a provision would infringe on the religious freedom of churches conducting services in languages other than English. Heath, *English in Our Language Heritage*, in LANGUAGE IN THE U.S.A. 6, 6-7, 12 (C. Ferguson & S. Heath eds. 1981). During the late 1800's and early 1900's, controversy arose over German instruction in public and private schools. *Id.* at 14-17; *see generally* H. KLOSS, THE AMERICAN BILINGUAL TRADITION 45, 46-47, 52-53, 60-61, 67-74 (1977) (describing early efforts to suppress use of German in the United States).

23. Bilingual Education Act of 1968, Pub. L. No. 90-247, 81 Stat. 816 (codified as amended at 20 U.S.C. §§ 3221-3262 (1982)).

24. *See, e.g., Bilingual Education Programs: Hearings on H.R. 9840 and H.R. 10224 Before the General Subcomm. on Educ. of the House Comm. on Educ. & Labor*, 90th Cong., 1st Sess. 144-47 (1967) (statement of Rep. Edward Roybal); *id.* at 245-47 (statement of Herman Badillo, President, Borough of the Bronx, New York City); *see also* C. HARRINGTON, BILINGUAL EDUCATION IN THE UNITED STATES 2-3 (1980); A. LEIBOWITZ, *supra* note 18, at 20-23; E. MOSHER, A. HASTINGS & J. WAGONER, JR., *supra* note 18, at 13.

understanding and respect.[25]

For all this stirring rhetoric, the Bilingual Education Act was actually a quite modest grant-in-aid program designed to meet the needs of NEP and LEP children by promoting research and experimentation.[26] The Act never clearly defined bilingual education, in part because of an unresolved ambiguity about the programs' proper objectives. Some supporters saw the legislation simply as a way to maximize proficiency in English, while others viewed it as a means of furthering proficiency in both the native language and English and of instilling respect for the child's cultural heritage.[27] From 1968 to 1974, appropriations under the Act were significantly lower than authorized expenditures, but no popular outcry ensued.[28]

Between 1968 and 1974, bilingual education proponents struggled to create and enforce an entitlement to special educational services for NEP and LEP children. Title VI, an omnibus civil rights bill enacted in 1964, provided that "[n]o person in the United States shall, on the basis of race, color, or national origin, be excluded from participation in, be denied the benefits of, or be subjected to discrimination under any program or activity receiving federal financial assistance."[29] Congress left to the Office of Civil Rights (OCR) the task of elaborating on this broad, but rather ill-defined, mandate by promulgating and enforcing regulations.[30] Although Congress had not explicitly considered the problems of NEP and LEP children in enacting title VI, OCR issued a 1970 memorandum concluding that the provision barred discrimination against national origin-minority group children on the basis of language.[31] How-

---

25. *Bilingual Education: Hearings on S. 428 Before the Special Subcomm. on Bilingual Education of the Senate Comm. on Labor and Public Welfare*, 90th Cong., 1st Sess. 327 (1967) [hereinafter *1967 Senate Hearings*] (remarks of Joe Bernal, Texas State Senate); *id.* at 382 (remarks of Tony Calderon, Representative of the Federation for the Advancement of Mexican Americans).

26. The Act "provide[d] financial assistance to local educational agencies to develop and carry out new and imaginative elementary and secondary school programs designed to meet the special educational needs [of NEP and LEP children]." 20 U.S.C. § 880b (as amended by Pub. L. No. 93-380, § 105(a)(1), 88 Stat. 503 (1975); omitted in codification by Pub. L. No. 95-561, § 701, 92 Stat. 2268 (1978)). According to the Senate Committee Report, the Act did not prescribe a specific type of program because of the need for extensive research. S. REP. NO. 726, 90th Cong., 1st Sess. 50 (1967), *reprinted in* 1967 U.S. CODE CONG. & ADMIN. NEWS 2730, 2781.

The Act authorized $15 million in appropriations for the fiscal year ending June 30, 1968; $30 million, for the fiscal year ending June 30, 1969; $40 million for the fiscal year ending June 30, 1970; $80 million for the fiscal year ending June 30, 1971; $100 million for the fiscal year ending June 30, 1972; and $135 million for the fiscal year ending June 30, 1973. 20 U.S.C. § 880b-1(a).

27. D. RAVITCH, THE TROUBLED CRUSADE 273 (1983).

28. EXECUTIVE OFFICE OF THE PRESIDENT, OFFICE OF MANAGEMENT AND BUDGET, THE BUDGETS OF THE UNITED STATES GOVERNMENT FISCAL YEARS 1969-1975 (1968-1973).

29. 42 U.S.C. § 2000d.

30. Rabkin, *Office for Civil Rights*, in THE POLITICS OF REGULATION 307-13 (J. Wilson ed. 1980).

31. Identification of Discrimination and Denial of Services on the Basis of National Origin, 35

ever, this memorandum went largely unenforced.[32]

In 1974, the Supreme Court adopted OCR's interpretation of title VI in its widely publicized decision in *Lau v. Nichols*.[33] In *Lau,* a class action brought by Chinese NEP and LEP children in the San Francisco schools, the plaintiffs established that approximately 1,800 Chinese-speaking children were receiving no special assistance whatsoever. The Court concluded that under title VI as interpreted by OCR, the district was obligated to take some steps to rectify the language barrier when English-only instruction had the effect of excluding NEP and LEP children from meaningful participation in the educational program.[34] However, it left the task of designing a remedy to local school officials.[35]

Lau triggered a number of responses. It had significant effects on the allocation of resources to bilingual education. Following discussions on whether school districts could marshall the resources necessary to comply with *Lau,* Congress began to authorize and appropriate more funds under the Bilingual Education Act.[36] State legislatures also

---

Fed. Reg. 11595 (1970) (requiring school districts to take affirmative steps to rectify a language barrier where it excluded national origin-minority group children from effective participation in the educational program); *see also* Margulies, *Bilingual Education, Remedial Language Instruction, Title VI, and Proof of Discriminatory Purpose: A Suggested Approach,* 17 COLUM. J.L. & SOC. PROBS. 99, 115 (1981) (history of administrative interpretations of title VI's protection of NEP and LEP children).

32. San Miguel, *supra* note 9, at 507. For a general description of some of the enforcement problems that have plagued OCR, see Rabkin, *supra* note 30, at 304-53.

33. 414 U.S. 563 (1974).

34. *Id.* at 566-69. The Court asserted:

Imposition of a requirement that, before a child can effectively participate in the educational program, he must already have acquired those basic skills is to make a mockery of public education. We know that those who do not understand English are certain to find their classroom experiences wholly incomprehensible and in no way meaningful.

Id. at 566. The Court went on to conclude that "the Chinese-speaking minority receives fewer benefits than the English-speaking majority from [the] school system which denies them a meaningful opportunity to participate in the educational program." *Id.* at 568.

35. *Id.* at 564-65. The Court stated that although no specific remedy was requested, "[t]eaching English to the students of Chinese ancestry who do not speak the language is one choice. Giving instructions to this group in Chinese is another. There may be others." *Id.* at 565.

36. For some representative statements on the problems of complying with *Lau,* see *Bilingual Education Act: Hearings on H.R. 1085, H.R. 2490, and H.R. 11464 Before the General Subcomm. on Educ. of the House Comm. on Educ. & Labor,* 93d Cong., 2d Sess. 7 (1974) (remarks of Rep. Lloyd Meeds); *id.* at 7-9 (remarks of Stanley Pottinger, Assistant Attorney General, Civil Rights Division, U.S. Department of Justice); *id.* at 20-32 (remarks of Martin Gerry, Acting Director, Office for Civil Rights, Department of Health, Education, and Welfare).

Amendments to the Bilingual Education Act in 1974 authorized $135 million for the fiscal year ending June 30, 1974; $135 million for the fiscal year ending June 30, 1975; $140 million for the fiscal year ending June 30, 1976; $150 million for the fiscal year ending June 30, 1977; and $160 million for the year ending June 30, 1978. Bilingual Education Act of 1974, § 702(b)(1), Pub. L. No. 93-380, § 105(a)(1), 88 Stat. 484, 504 (1974). In addition, the amendments authorized $7.75 million for technical assistance in the fiscal year ending June 30, 1976; $8.75 million in the fiscal year ending June 30, 1977; and $9.75 million in the fiscal year ending June 30, 1978. *Id.* § 702(b)(2). More importantly, actual appropriations in 1974 and later years more closely approximated authorized

enacted their own bilingual education acts and appropriated monies under these provisions.[37]

OCR stepped up its enforcement efforts by promulgating guidelines for districts to use in complying with *Lau* and applying these guidelines in negotiating consent agreements.[38] These guidelines went well beyond the minimal entitlement recognized in *Lau* by endorsing bilingual-bicultural education and TBE programs and deeming ESL programs inappropriate for elementary school students.[39]

Congress also expressed its approval of *Lau* by passing the Equal Educational Opportunity Act (EEOA), which included a provision that explicitly adopted the decision's approach. The provision stated, "No State shall deny equal educational opportunity to an individual on account of his or her race, color, sex, or national origin, by . . . (f) the failure by an educational agency to take appropriate action to overcome language barriers that impede equal participation by its students in its instructional programs."[40] Because the measure was enacted as an amendment from the floor, there was little legislative history to guide its interpretation.[41]

After 1974, Hispanics turned to the federal district courts to enforce NEP and LEP students' entitlement to special educational services.[42] While these lawsuits were being brought with varying degrees of success

---

levels of expenditure. EXECUTIVE OFFICE OF THE PRESIDENT, OFFICE OF MANAGEMENT AND BUDGET, THE BUDGETS OF THE UNITED STATES GOVERNMENT FISCAL YEARS 1976-1980 (1974-1978).

37.   E. MOSHER, A. HASTINGS & J. WAGONER, JR., *supra* note 18, at 16. *See generally* R. IRIZARRY, *supra* note 13, at 45-128 (collecting data on state bilingual education legislation). In general, state bilingual education acts declare the state's commitment to meeting the needs of NEP and LEP students, provide for the identification and assessment of these students, describe the kinds of programs that will meet these needs, set forth requirements for staffing and parental involvement, and authorize state funding. *See* Kobrick, *A Model Act Providing for Transitional Bilingual Education Programs in Public Schools,* 9 HARV. J. ON LEGIS. 260, 274-300 (1972).

38.   OFFICE FOR CIVIL RIGHTS, *supra* note 3, *reprinted in* BILINGUAL EDUCATION, *supra* note 3, at 213-21; *see also* E. MOSHER, A. HASTINGS & J. WAGONER, JR., *supra* note 18, at 16 (federal enforcement efforts increased after *Lau*).

39.   OFFICE FOR CIVIL RIGHTS, *supra* note 3, at III, *reprinted in* BILINGUAL EDUCATION, *supra* note 3, at 215-18. *See generally* Margulies, *supra* note 31, at 116 (describing how HEW drafted and disseminated the *Lau* guidelines).

40.   20 U.S.C. § 1703(f) (1982).

41.   United States v. Texas, 506 F. Supp. 405, 431-32 (E.D. Tex. 1981), *rev'd,* 680 F.2d 356 (5th Cir. 1982); Haft, *Assuring Equal Educational Opportunity for Language-Minority Students: Bilingual Education and the Equal Educational Opportunity Act of 1974,* 18 COLUM. J.L. & SOC. PROBS. 209, 233 (1983).

42.   *See, e.g.,* Guadalupe Org. v. Tempe Elementary School Dist., 587 F.2d 1022 (9th Cir. 1978); Cintron v. Brentwood Union Free School Dist., 455 F. Supp. 57 (E.D.N.Y. 1978); Rios v. Read, 73 F.R.D. 589 (E.D.N.Y. 1977); Otero v. Mesa County Valley School Dist., 408 F. Supp. 162 (D. Colo. 1975), *vacated,* 568 F.2d 1312 (10th Cir. 1977); Aspira of New York v. Board of Educ., 394 F. Supp. 1161 (S.D.N.Y. 1975); Keyes v. School Dist. No. 1, 380 F. Supp. 673 (D. Colo. 1974), *modified,* 521 F.2d 465 (10th Cir. 1975), *cert. denied,* 423 U.S. 1066 (1976), *on remand,* 576 F. Supp. 1503 (1983).

around the country, the federal government commissioned a systematic inquiry into the effectiveness of programs funded under the Bilingual Education Act. The results of this study, known as the AIR evaluation, were released in 1977-78. They indicated that the programs were not effective in promoting English proficiency and resulted in classroom segregation of Hispanic children.[43] Despite protests that the study was methodologically unsound, these results had a sobering effect on Congress as it reconsidered its commitment to the Bilingual Education Act.[44] After 1978, Congress became increasingly receptive to efforts to broaden the range of programs that would be funded under the Act. In particular, it expressly acknowledged that structured immersion and ESL programs might be viable alternatives to bilingual-bicultural education and TBE programs.[45] Concomitantly, funding under the Act steadily declined.[46]

In 1978, the Supreme Court also began to retreat from the *Lau* decision by suggesting that it would no longer find a title VI violation when a program merely had the effect of excluding a disproportionate number of racial or ethnic minorities. In *Regents of the University of California v. Bakke,*[47] a majority of the Court appeared ready to treat title VI and the equal protection clause as coextensive, thereby requiring plaintiffs to prove discriminatory intent as well as an adverse effect under both provisions. Although the Court did not expressly overrule *Lau,* the *Bakke* decision cast serious doubt on its holding.[48]

Shortly thereafter, the demise of the *Lau* guidelines further eroded

43.   III AMERICAN INSTITUTES FOR RESEARCH (AIR), *supra* note 19, at IV-2 to IV-4.

44.   For critiques of the study, see INTERCULTURAL DEVELOPMENT RESEARCH ASSOCIATION, *supra* note 20; Cardenas, *supra* note 20, at 74-75. For evidence of the effect that the study had on legislators, see *Bilingual Education: Hearings on H.R. 15 Before the Subcomm. on Elementary, Secondary, and Vocational Educ. of the House Comm. on Educ. & Labor,* 95th Cong., 1st Sess. 352 (1977) [hereinafter *1977 House Hearings*] (remarks of Christopher Cross, Minority Senior Education Consultant) ("[Critics] have indicated . . . that we should not use the AIR report to base our judgments on changes. If not, what should we use?").

45.   *See, e.g., 1984 House Hearings, supra* note 11, at 99-100 (remarks of Reps. Steve Bartlett and Ron Packard); *id.* at 131-32 (prepared statement of Rep. Norman Shumway); *id.* at 132-33 (prepared statement of Rep. William Whitehurst); *The Bilingual Education Improvement Act of 1983: Hearings on H.R. 2682 Before the Subcomm. on Elementary, Secondary, and Vocational Educ. of the House Comm. on Educ. & Labor,* 98th Cong., 1st Sess. 22-23 (1983) [hereinafter *1983 House Hearings*] (prepared statement of Terrel H. Bell, Secretary of Education); *id.* at 31 (remarks of Rep. Ron Packard). In 1984, the Act was amended to reserve a specified percentage of funds for ESL, structured immersion, and similar programs. The total amounts that could be allocated to these programs were carefully limited. 20 U.S.C. § 3222(b)(3)-(4) (Supp. III 1985).

46.   Orum & Yzaguirre, *Secretary Bennett's Bilingual Education Initiative: Historical Perspectives and Implications,* 1 LA RAZA L.J. 225, 235 (1986). The Undersecretary of Education has suggested that if the cap on funds that can be allocated to ESL and structured immersion programs were lifted, the Department of Education would increase funding for programs for NEP and LEP children. *Id.* at 239.

47.   438 U.S. 265 (1978).

48.   *Id.* at 304-05; Margulies, *supra* note 31, at 130; *see also* Guardians Ass'n v. Civil Service

NEP and LEP children's entitlement to special educational services under title VI. In 1978, an Alaska school district challenged the validity of the *Lau* guidelines in federal district court, alleging that they were tantamount to rules and had not been published for notice and comment as required by the Administrative Procedure Act. Pursuant to a consent agreement, the federal government agreed to publish the guidelines.[49]

Rather than publish the *Lau* guidelines, the newly formed Department of Education published a Notice of Proposed Rulemaking (NPRM) in 1980. The regional hearings on the NPRM were a political free-for-all, rife with stinging accusations. Opponents, including influential teachers' unions, bitterly attacked the regulations, and newspaper articles likening the Department of Education's approach to that in Quebec heightened the tension.[50] The controversy became so unmanageable that the NPRM was never finalized.[51] Later, the *Lau* guidelines were quietly withdrawn, and the controlling administrative regulation under title VI is now OCR's 1970 memorandum.[52]

Because of these developments, most bilingual education litigation today is decided under the EEOA, which looks only at whether a program has the effect of excluding NEP and LEP students from the educational program and does not require proof of discriminatory intent.[53] Although the EEOA allows plaintiffs to establish a violation more easily, its remedial consequences are different from those under the *Lau* guidelines. In contrast to the guidelines, which strongly endorsed bilingual-bicultural education and TBE programs, the EEOA's "appropriate action" requirement is arguably broad enough to encompass ESL and structured immersion programs as well.[54]

In 1981, Senator S.I. Hayakawa began introducing proposals to amend the Constitution to declare English the official language of the United States.[55] Hayakawa argued that among other things, an English language amendment would counter the divisive effects of bilingual-bicultural education and TBE programs.[56] He feared that failure to pro-

---

Comm'n, 463 U.S. 582, 589-93 (1983) (opinion of White, J.) (analyzing whether *Bakke* overruled *Lau* by making title VI coextensive with the equal protection clause).

49. Northwest Arctic School Dist. v. Califano, No. A-77-216 (D. Alaska Sept. 29, 1978).

50. Levin, *supra* note 10, at 51-52.

51. *Id.* at 39-40, 50, 56-57.

52. Baker & de Kanter, *supra* note 19, at 307.

53. Haft, *supra* note 41, at 211-15 (1983); Margulies, *supra* note 31, at 108-09.

54. *See* Castaneda v. Pickard, 648 F.2d 989, 1008-09 (5th Cir. 1981) ("Congress' use of the less specific term 'appropriate action,' rather than 'bilingual education,' indicates that Congress intended to leave state and local educational authorities a substantial amount of latitude in choosing the programs and techniques they would use to meet their obligations under the EEOA."). *But cf.* Haft, *supra* note 41, at 263 (arguing that Congress in enacting the EEOA intended to advance already existing legislative and administrative policies favoring the use of bilingual-bicultural methods).

55. S.J. Res. 72, 97th Cong., 1st Sess., 127 CONG. REC. 7444-45 (1981).

56. *The English Language Amendment: Hearing on S.J. Res. 167 Before the Subcomm. on the*

mote a common language would produce instability and unrest as it had in other countries with balkanized language groups.[57] Hayakawa also founded U.S. English, a national organization devoted to preserving English as the official language of the United States. Its membership is composed primarily of individuals who have also worked to curb immigration, first-generation immigrants who learned English as a second language, and English-speaking schoolteachers.[58] When Hayakawa's repeated efforts to amend the Constitution failed, U.S. English attempted to have English declared an official language at the state and local level through popular referenda and legislative action.[59]

These efforts have stirred deep emotional responses. For example, when the California chapter of U.S. English used the referendum process to make English the state's official language, opponents contended that the measure conveyed a symbolic message that culturally and linguistically different groups were unwanted.[60] They alleged that the campaign was a thinly veiled form of racism and derived from anti-immigrant sentiment.[61] The proposal's supporters argued that it was a common sense way to ensure that California's population remained politically cohesive.[62] After spirited debate, the proposal passed by an overwhelming majority in November 1986.[63] Hayakawa's followers succeeded in mak-

---

Constitution of the Senate Comm. on the Judiciary, 98th Cong., 2d Sess. 54-56 (1984) (statement of Sen. Hayakawa). Hayakawa also expressed concern about the widespread use of bilingual ballots and election materials. *Id.* at 53.

57. *See generally* Note, *The Proposed English Language Amendment: Shield or Sword?*, 3 YALE L. & POL'Y REV. 519 (1985) (describing recent efforts to make English the official language, analogizing these attempts to the Americanization movement of the early twentieth century, and urging that such an amendment would be inappropriate despite the possible validity of some of its supporters' concerns).

58. A. GALVAN, R. MACIAS, R. MAGALLAN & L. ORUM, ARE ENGLISH LANGUAGE AMENDMENTS IN THE NATIONAL INTEREST? 2-3 (1986); Cahan, *English Spoken Here,* 13 STUDENT LAW. 6 (Apr. 1985); Trombley, *supra* note 21.

59. Cahan, *supra* note 58, at 6; Nakao, *Battle of Words Heats Up over 'English Only,'* San Francisco Examiner, Sept. 21, 1986, at A1, col. 1.

60. L.A. Times, Oct. 3, 1986, § II, at 4, col. 1; L.A. Times, Aug. 21, 1986, § I, at 23, col. 3.

61. Trombley, *English Ballot: Opinions Transcend Language*, L.A. Times, Oct. 12, 1986, § I, at 1, col. 2; del Olmo, *Se Habla Ingles: Prop. 63, a Cruel Joke, Could Cost Us Dearly*, L.A. Times, Aug. 28, 1986, § II, at 5, col. 1; Shaw, *Minority Groups Protest 'English Only' Movement*, San Francisco Examiner, Aug. 21, 1986, at A2, col. 1. In fact, according to a 1986 November general election survey conducted by Mervin Field, 46% of those who opposed the English language amendment considered it racist and discriminatory against new immigrants. Among Hispanics, 72% of those who rejected the measure expressed this view. The California Poll: 1986 November General Election Survey 196, 200 (directed by Mervin Field) (on file with author) [hereinafter California Poll].

62. Trombley, *supra* note 61; Nakao, *supra* note 59.

63. According to Field's 1986 November general election survey, 68% of those who voted on the proposal favored it, while 32% opposed it. While 72% of the white voters and 67% of the black voters endorsed the measure, 41% of the Hispanic voters and 56% of the Asian voters did so. California Poll, *supra* note 61, at 186, 188. Of those who cast ballots, 14% did not vote on the English language amendment. Ten percent of the white voters and 20% of the black voters did not

ing English the official language in California just as they have in at least
seven other states and numerous cities and counties.[64]

B. The Litigation Process

The foregoing analysis illuminates the general tenor and complexity
of the bilingual education controversy, but this account would be incomplete without a closer examination of the lawsuits that Hispanics have
brought to enforce federally created entitlements. Rather than enumer-
ate the outcomes in various cases, this Section will explore the underlying
dynamics of the litigation process by examining empirical studies of two
bilingual education cases. Because of the paucity of empirical research in
this area, it is not possible to say whether these studies are representative
of most bilingual education litigation.[65] Still, their detailed inquiries provide some useful insights into the bilingual education debate.

The first case, *Otero v. Mesa County Valley School District No. 51*,[66]
was brought in 1974 in a Colorado federal district court by a coalition of
attorneys from the Mexican American Legal Defense and Education
Fund (MALDEF), the Chicano Education Project (CEP), and Colorado
Rural Legal Assistance (CRLA).[67] Brought on behalf of a class of Mexican-American parents and their children residing in Grand Junction,
Colorado, the suit alleged that the district's educational program and hiring practices discriminated against Chicanos. To remedy the problem,
the plaintiffs requested that the district implement a far-ranging bilingual-bicultural education program and institute affirmative action hiring
programs for Chicano personnel.[68]

Several years before the lawsuit was filed, there had been a marked
increase in local Chicano political activism. The group primarily responsible for the increased political activity, La Voz de la Raza, spearheaded
the lawsuit, and the traditionally nonpoliticized Chicano community
associated the case with militancy. The school board thought that La
Voz was run by outside "agitators" who wanted to use the litigation as a

---

register an opinion on the measure. Twelve percent of the Hispanic voters and 9% of the Asian
voters did not do so. *Id.* at 188. For further discussion of these results, see *supra* note 61 and *infra*
note 148.

64. *See* Note, *supra* note 57, at 519; *Harper's Index,* HARPER'S, Apr. 1987, at 15; Trombley,
Assemblyman Vows to Carry the Ball for English-Only Action, L.A. Times, Nov. 6, 1986, § I, at 3,
col. 5.

65. In an effort to increase the available data on bilingual education litigation, I am currently
undertaking a case study of Keyes v. School Dist. No. 1, 576 F. Supp. 1503 (D. Colo. 1983).

66. 408 F. Supp. 162 (D. Colo. 1975), *remanded on other grounds,* 568 F.2d 1312 (10th Cir.
1977), *on remand,* 470 F. Supp. 326 (1979), *aff'd,* 628 F.2d 1271 (1980). The case study was done by
Michael A. Rebell, a visiting lecturer in law at the Yale Law School, and Arthur A. Block, a lecturer
in law at Columbia Law School. M. REBELL & A. BLOCK, EQUALITY AND EDUCATION (1985).

67. M. REBELL & A. BLOCK, *supra* note 18, at 147.

68. *Id.*

national test case, rather than advance the interests of local Chicanos. Consequently, the board was reluctant to negotiate as a means of avoiding a lawsuit, believing that La Voz would only be satisfied if the board completely abdicated its responsibility to design a curriculum responsive to the entire community's needs.[69]

Because *Lau* had only recently been decided, the litigants had no well-developed precedents to guide in its interpretation. Understandably, the plaintiffs and the school district in *Otero* presented markedly different views about *Lau*'s holding. The plaintiffs contended that *Lau* supported their position that Chicano schoolchildren were discriminated against by a curriculum that did not account for their linguistic and cultural needs. To remedy such discrimination and ensure that Chicanos reaped equal benefits from the educational process, they claimed that the district had to adopt a bilingual-bicultural education program.[70]

In contrast, the district interpreted *Lau* as prohibiting the exclusion of NEP and LEP students from the curriculum based on language. To remedy such exclusion, the district argued that it was simply obligated to furnish special instruction in English until children were sufficiently proficient to participate in the regular curriculum. According to the district, it had no obligation to ensure that NEP and LEP students actually performed as well as other children after their return to English-only classrooms.[71]

The case was bitterly contested. The discovery process was highly acrimonious, confused, and excessively litigious. Even the usual professional courtesies among lawyers failed to temper the parties' distrust and hostility. These problems were exacerbated by the uncertainty surrounding a relatively novel case and the trial judge's desultory efforts to address complex discovery issues and facilitate compromise.[72]

The case also engendered deep emotional responses in the community. Although no violence actually occurred in connection with the trial, two Chicanos who planned to testify on the school district's behalf claimed that they had received anonymous death threats. The courtroom was also cleared several times because of bomb threats following accusations that the judge was biased against the plaintiffs.[73]

On a more positive note, the case served an important educational function. The local newspaper covered the proceedings in considerable detail, even publishing school-by-school dropout statistics. Based on this publicity, one Chicano businessman decided to testify for the plaintiffs

---

69. *Id.* at 148-50.
70. *Id.* at 152-53.
71. *Id.* at 151-52.
72. *Id.* at 153-55.
73. *Id.* at 282 n.15.

because their ideas were gaining wider acceptance in the Chicano community.[74] At the end of the trial, the local newspaper observed that regardless of its outcome, the case had demonstrated the importance of responding to individual student needs, rather than "cramming [all children] into a common Anglo mold."[75]

The trial court eventually rejected the plaintiffs' claim that Chicano students were entitled to a comprehensive bilingual-bicultural education program. A civil rights conservative, the judge had been unsympathetic to this argument from the outset.[76] Moreover, the plaintiffs were unable to produce convincing evidence that their suggested remedy was a workable response to the special needs of Chicano children in Grand Junction. The court was never persuaded that the plaintiffs' program was essential enough to override the school district's discretion in structuring the curriculum.[77]

In *Zambrano v. Oakland Unified School District,*[78] the plaintiffs, a class of Cambodian, Filipino, Hispanic, and Asian linguistic minority children, alleged that the Oakland school system in California had failed to implement an adequate bilingual education program as required by federal and state law. The suit asked for injunctive relief to ensure compliance and the appointment of an independent auditor to monitor the district's progress.[79] The case was filed by Public Advocates, a San Francisco public interest firm, and the plaintiffs received additional assistance from attorneys at MALDEF and the Legal Aid Society of Alameda County.[80]

Filed in 1984, *Zambrano* differs significantly from *Otero* because in the intervening ten years, an administrative and judicial framework had developed to address NEP and LEP students' demands for special educational services. California had also enacted a comprehensive bilingual education act, while the Colorado legislature had not addressed such concerns at the time of the *Otero* decision.[81] Moreover, the

---

74. *Id.* at 150.

75. *Id.* (footnote omitted).

76. *Id.* at 155, 167, 290 n.85.

77. *Id.* at 172-74. The case generated a plethora of social science evidence regarding the linguistic abilities of Chicano schoolchildren in the district, their educational achievement, and the potential benefits of bilingual-bicultural education. The district enjoyed several advantages in presenting evidence on these questions. It had easier access to the relevant data, its principal expert was thoroughly familiar with the conditions in the district, and it was strongly committed to using social science evidence to refute the plaintiffs' expert testimony. *Id.* at 155-68, 171.

78. No. 584503-9 (Alameda Sup. Ct. May 1, 1985). The case study was done by Brenda Reyes and Marsha Siegel in conjunction with a seminar on children's rights and test-case litigation at Boalt Hall School of Law.

79. B. Reyes & M. Siegel, Zambrano v. Oakland Unified School District 1, 60 (1985) (unpublished manuscript) (on file with author).

80. *Id.* at 47-55.

81. *Id.* at 10-12. The Colorado legislature did enact a bilingual education act shortly after the

demographics of the classroom had changed, and Hispanics were more likely to be joined by Asian language groups in seeking special assistance for NEP and LEP children.[82] What remained unchanged, however, was the animosity that such lawsuits provoked.

During the eight years before *Zambrano* was brought, four administrative complaints were filed with OCR, and at least two were filed with the California State Department of Education. These complaints consistently resulted in findings of noncompliance, and the district was repeatedly ordered to prepare plans and submit progress reports. The district did so, but it failed to implement adequately plans that on paper appeared fully operational.[83]

Critical in catalyzing the lawsuit was the creation of a bilingual district advisory committee (BDAC) in Oakland pursuant to California's bilingual education act. Although the district had ignored the BDAC for several years, two activist parents were elected chair and vice-chair and ambitiously sought to develop and implement a bilingual master plan.[84] With help from two curriculum specialists in the district's Office of Bilingual Education, the BDAC prepared a plan for submission at a public hearing before the school board. Noting the BDAC's "advisory" character, the district rejected the plan and presented one of its own. The district's plan, which read the relevant statutes and regulations as narrowly as possible, expressed a strong preference for ESL instruction and utilized bilingual instructional aides and volunteers, rather than certified bilingual teachers.[85]

Public hearings on the plans attracted as many as 200 to 300 parents and generated media coverage sympathetic to the BDAC's position. In light of this strong interest, the school board was unwilling to approve the district's plan, which many viewed as an illegitimate substitute for the BDAC's proposal. The district superintendent therefore appointed a committee of parents and school personnel to draft yet another plan. The committee's proposal favored native-language instruction as a bridge to learning English and required the district actively to recruit certified

---

Otero decision. M. REBELL & A. BLOCK, *supra* note 18, at 175. While the Colorado act originally endorsed bilingual-bicultural education for kindergarten through third grade, it was amended in 1977 to provide for TBE programs. *Id.* at 184. More recently, Colorado repealed its bilingual education law, substituting an ESL requirement. Levin, *supra* note 10, at 57 n.72.

82. According to the Assembly Office of Research, most NEP and LEP children in California schools speak Spanish, but many speak Asian languages, and the latter constitute the fastest growing segment of the linguistic minority population. ASSEMBLY OFFICE OF RESEARCH, *supra* note 13, at 1.

83. B. Reyes & M. Siegel, *supra* note 79, at 28-37, 46.

84. *Id.* at 36-40. Most BDAC members were linguistic minority parents, but some were education professionals. *Id.* at 36-38.

85. *Id.* at 40-41.

bilingual education teachers.[86]

At a meeting attended by 300 supporters of the new plan and a number of reporters, the school board approved the committee's plan after heated debate.[87] The district responded by dismantling its Office of Bilingual Education and reassigning its personnel to positions in which they would be less able to do "politicking" for bilingual education. Thus, the district had a bilingual master plan but no central staff to implement it. Although the superintendent eventually established a new Office of Bilingual Education in response to public pressure, *Zambrano* was filed less than a year after the district instituted its purge.[88]

In keeping with events leading up to the case, *Zambrano* generated considerable hostility and distrust among the parties. Although some district officials treated the suit as a predictable response to the district's history of noncompliance, others were outraged and thought the litigation had undermined their efforts to reorganize the Office of Bilingual Education and implement the new master plan. The district's formal response reflected the view that the plaintiffs' request for an injunction was unnecessary and highly intrusive, although its counsel faced the unenviable task of explaining away eight years of administrative violations.[89]

The relationship between the attorneys in the case grew increasingly acrimonious. Shortly after the first court hearing, the district's counsel questioned whether a document drafted by plaintiffs' counsel accurately set forth an oral order in the case. Disputes arose about whether the district had provided the plaintiffs with adequate notice of motions and hearings and had served them with copies of orders it obtained.[90] These problems were aggravated when the court vacated an injunction requiring the district to conduct prompt language assessments. The district insisted that the plaintiffs post open-ended personal surety bonds as well as a corporate bond to provide for potential damages should the injunctive relief prove unwarranted. Not surprisingly, the plaintiffs were unable to meet this demand because of their limited incomes.[91]

Eventually, the district filed a countersuit against the plaintiffs and their attorney for $250,000 in general damages and $4 million in punitive damages, alleging that *Zambrano* was the product of a conspiracy to

---

86. *Id.* at 41-44.

87. *Id.* at 42.

88. *Id.* at 44-46.

89. *Id.* at 65-66, 73.

90. *Id.* at 83.

91. *Id.* at 79-80, 83. The plaintiffs lost their appeals to reinstate the injunction. When they subsequently petitioned the trial court for a new injunction, the district did not demand personal surety bonds. The court granted the injunctive relief. *Id.* at 81-82.

"harass, impede, embarrass and obstruct" district operations.[92] The countersuit claimed that the plaintiffs and their attorney had instigated the suit to "generat[e] negative publicity based on facts known to [them] to be false; pursu[e] destructive, senseless and unnecessary preliminary injunctive relief while totally refusing to take recourse to their plain and fully adequate administrative remedy; and unreasonably withhold[] cooperation necessary to complete the process of staff appointments and organizational restructuring."[93] Ultimately, a superior court judge dismissed the countersuit and imposed sanctions on the district for bringing a frivolous claim in bad faith.[94]

The district's counsel later deemed the countersuit "a gross political error."[95] When a popular outcry followed the district's action, it found itself in a peculiarly untenable position because it had filed the countersuit without first consulting the school board.[96] The brouhaha that attended the countersuit's filing may well have pushed the district to the settlement table. Ironically, by this point, the plaintiffs were reluctant to negotiate because they wanted the complete victory that a trial could provide. Eventually, however, they were persuaded that negotiations might prove fruitful.[97]

Although a mediator had to be appointed to oversee the settlement negotiations because of continuing mistrust among the parties, an agreement was ultimately hammered out. This successful resolution was in part attributable to ongoing political pressure placed on the school board by community supporters of bilingual education.[98] The plan required that all NEP and LEP elementary schoolchildren have daily access to some form of bilingual instruction. It also expressed a "preference" for a bilingual classroom where thirty or more NEP and LEP secondary students attended a school. In addition, the plan ordered the district to take steps to hire all needed bilingual education teachers and instructional aides.[99] While the plan has been implemented under the supervision of a court-appointed monitor, an expert auditor, and the judge, some named plaintiffs have remained active in bilingual education affairs, primarily through the BDAC.[100]

While these two cases are in many ways quite different, they share some important characteristics. In *Otero,* the parties confronted a rela-

---

92. *Id.* at 84.
93. *Id.* at 85.
94. *Id.* at 89.
95. *Id.* at 85.
96. *Id.* at 85-88.
97. *Id.* at 104-06.
98. *Id.* at 101-03.
99. *Id.* at 116-17.
100. *Id.* at 119, 124-36.

tively novel entitlement to special assistance for NEP and LEP students; the uncertainty surrounding the interpretation of this claim might have provoked the confusion and ill-will that permeated the proceedings. By the time *Zambrano* was filed, however, there had been longstanding efforts to define this entitlement more precisely. Nevertheless, the parties voiced fundamental disagreements about the scope of the district's obligation to NEP and LEP children. Moreover, the proceedings were characterized by the same type of deep-seated animosity observed in *Otero.* Although lawsuits are by definition adversarial, this cannot completely explain the parties' highly contentious behavior, for even the traditional courtesies among lawyers broke down during each case.

C.   The Bilingual Education and English-Only Movements

The bilingual education movement first pursued reforms at the federal level and then used its successes to press more effectively for changes at the state and local level. It has sought to achieve its objectives through a mix of legislative, administrative, and judicial action. While Congress initially provided a useful forum for publicizing the educational problems of NEP and LEP children, it was ultimately necessary to turn to a nonelective and less visible decisionmaker, OCR, to establish an entitlement to special educational services for NEP and LEP students. These less publicized efforts culminated in a highly visible Supreme Court decision in *Lau.* This decision in turn provided bilingual education advocates with additional leverage in seeking further legislative and administrative reforms.

To attain their objectives, bilingual education supporters relied on omnibus civil rights bills, such as title VI and the EEOA, as well as more narrowly focused legislation, such as the Bilingual Education Act. These omnibus bills did not concentrate on the problems of NEP and LEP children. Title VI was enacted primarily in response to continuing racial discrimination against blacks; it was passed shortly after a brutal assault on civil rights marchers in Birmingham, Alabama and the 1963 March on Washington.[101] The EEOA was enacted mainly out of concern about the widespread use of busing as a remedy for past segregation in the schools. Special educational services for NEP and LEP children were simply an example of the kind of "quality" educational programs that might be substituted for unpopular busing remedies.[102]

To benefit from these omnibus civil rights bills, Hispanics had to ally themselves with other civil rights groups and engage in multiple-issue politics.[103] That is, they diversified their political portfolio by

---

101.   Rabkin, *supra* note 30, at 309.
102.   Haft, *supra* note 41, at 233-34.
103.   C. HARRINGTON, *supra* note 24, at 2; A. LEIBOWITZ, *supra* note 18, at 9. One can also

expressing support for a broader array of civil rights reforms. Moreover, to bring themselves within the coverage of these omnibus bills, bilingual education advocates had to argue that language barriers were a proxy for racial and ethnic discrimination. Because this approach sensitized activists to different forms of discrimination and various potential remedies, it naturally limited their ability to engage in single-issue politics.

Despite pressures to rely on coalitions, compromises, and multiple-issue politics, advocates continued to press for special attention to the needs of NEP and LEP children. They supported the Bilingual Education Act, pursued administrative and judicial recognition of an entitlement to special services for linguistic minority students, and urged enactment of state bilingual education acts. Perhaps in part to distinguish themselves from black civil rights groups, Hispanics pressed decisionmakers to accord particular importance to language issues.[104]

In contrast, the English-only movement has been unsuccessful in seeking reforms at the federal level. It has therefore attempted to change state and local government practices. Rather than pursue a mix of legislative, administrative, and judicial action, English-only adherents have relied exclusively on popular political processes, including referenda and legislative enactments. By achieving success at the state and local level, English-only supporters hope to create momentum for their national reform agenda.[105]

The English-only movement has remained committed to single-issue politics, focusing exclusively on language issues without embracing a more generalized reform agenda.[106] Its proposals continue to treat lan-

---

analyze bilingual education advocates as "free riders" who benefited disproportionately from the black civil rights movement's investment of resources. *Cf.* M. OLSON, THE LOGIC OF COLLECTIVE ACTION 9-16 (1965) (analysis of "free rider" effects where individuals will benefit from activity of groups acting in the collective interest, whether or not the individual gives any support to the group). Certainly, in light of the black civil rights movement's successes at the federal level and potential roadblocks at the state and local level, Hispanics advocating bilingual education could have reasonably concluded that their resources would be optimally deployed at the federal level. *See* U.S. COMM'N ON CIVIL RIGHTS, A BETTER CHANCE TO LEARN 15-19 (1975) (describing educational neglect of linguistic minority children prior to federal intervention in the 1960's); U.S. COMM'N ON CIVIL RIGHTS, THE EXCLUDED STUDENT 14-20 (1972) (describing local schools' use of no-Spanish rules and punitive enforcement techniques). *See generally* A. OBERSCHALL, SOCIAL CONFLICT AND SOCIAL MOVEMENTS (1973) (theoretical analysis of how social movement groups maximize the use of their scarce resources).

104. See *infra* note 142.

105. Trombley, *supra* note 21. The English-only movement is certainly aware that its reforms can command broad support in some regions, in light of the long history of state and local legislation restricting the use of languages other than English. *See generally,* Leibowitz, *English Literacy: Legal Sanction for Discrimination,* 45 NOTRE DAME L. REV. 7, 41-42, 51-67 (1969) (noting numerous state laws establishing English as the exclusive language of instruction in the school system). By first pursuing state and local victories through popular political processes, the English-only movement is arguably optimizing the use of its scarce organizational resources.

106. *See, e.g.,* J. Barzun, *Language & Life* (undated essay published by U.S. English) (stressing

guage as uniquely significant and make no effort to link it to other characteristics, such as race, ethnicity, or socioeconomic status.

II

A THEORETICAL FRAMEWORK FOR ANALYZING THE BILINGUAL EDUCATION CONTROVERSY

Participants in the debate over bilingual education have often responded in deeply emotional ways that seem to transcend immediate concerns with the allocation of scarce resources. Some have openly acknowledged that more than pedagogy is at stake because government support of bilingual education signals acceptance of and respect for the Hispanic community.[107] A study of bilingual education that overlooks this symbolic component is arguably incomplete. Yet, legal scholars have not scrutinized this impact closely, presumably because such inquiries seem less systematic and scientific than interest-group bargaining analyses.[108] To address this omission, the Essay will draw on Joseph Gusfield's well-known efforts to develop a framework for understanding status conflicts in the context of the Temperance movement.

Gusfield asserts that status conflicts occur when groups clash in the political arena over the approval, respect, admiration, or deference that they are able to command by virtue of their way of life, including their culture, customs, and values.[109] When status groups compete with each other to change or defend their prestige allocation, they do so through symbolic actions. The significant meanings derive not so much from the intrinsic properties of the action but from what it has come to represent for the participants. The action is ritualistic and ceremonial because the goal is reached in the behavior itself, rather than in any desired state that

---

need to speak standard English); Tanton, *Bilingual Education: Is It Threatening to Divide the United States Along Language Lines?*, 33 VITAL ISSUES (1984) (arguing that linguistic diversity engenders conflict, while a common language promotes socially beneficial cooperation). Although some of the English-only movement's leaders are personally interested in curbing immigration, this has not yet become an organizational objective. Trombley, *supra* note 21.

107.   *See supra* notes 24-25 and 60-61 and accompanying text.

108.   For an important exception, see Karst, *Paths to Belonging: The Constitution and Cultural Identity*, 64 N.C.L. REV. 303, 314-15 (1986), which touches upon the symbolic components of cultural politics by relying in part on Gusfield's status conflict analysis. *See also* K. LUKER, ABORTION AND THE POLITICS OF MOTHERHOOD 7-8, 193, 242-43 (1984) (applying status conflict analysis to the abortion controversy).

109.   J. GUSFIELD, SYMBOLIC CRUSADE 17-19 (1963); *see also* Gusfield, *Moral Passage: The Symbolic Process in Public Designations of Deviance*, 15 SOC. PROBS. 175, 176-78 (1967). Gusfield's work draws upon Max Weber's earlier distinctions among three factors influencing the distribution of power: class, status group, and party. "Classes" are economic groups composed of persons with roughly the same life chances as determined by market forces. "Status groups" are somewhat amorphous communities composed of individuals whose life chances are similarly influenced by social estimations of honor or prestige. "Parties" are oriented to exercising power by influencing communal actions, whatever their content. H. GERTH & C. MILLS, FROM MAX WEBER: ESSAYS IN SOCIOLOGY 180-95 (1946).

it brings about.[110] Conflict resolution in symbolic terms is not necessarily irrational; in fact, it can be a highly useful institutionalized response in the face of social conflicts and tensions manifested in a disarray of the status order as well as other areas of action.[111]

When concerns about status are translated into political disputes, issues are frequently framed in moral terms that seem antithetical to bargaining in a pluralistic process.[112] The association of an issue with its supporters' way of life can increase the tendency of political issues to turn into matters of "face," freezing the adherents to a given program and diminishing the possibility of compromise or graceful defeat. Because the dispute involves opposition over ways of life, each side feels compelled to degrade the other's cultural content.[113] Where status elements are implicated, they often impart an erratic, highly emotional, and disturbing character to the dispute.[114] Moreover, because status conflicts are highly symbolic, support and opposition frequently come from diverse coalitions that attach broad-ranging connotations to the issues. Status conflicts consequently emerge in diffuse, unfocused forms.[115]

Gusfield carefully distinguishes his treatment of status conflicts from Murray Edelman's analysis of symbolic politics.[116] Edelman focuses on how legislative, administrative, and judicial decisionmakers resort to symbolic-expressive cues to appease those who in fact have lost out in the contest for tangible benefits.[117] Because of symbolic reassurances that their interests are being protected, groups that do not obtain desired objectives nevertheless acquiesce in a decision.[118] Edelman has treated reliance on symbolic cues as a commonplace, while Gusfield considers status conflicts a rarity in institutionalized politics under the American two-party system.[119] As Gusfield also makes clear, a symbolic victory in a status conflict does more than assuage fear and resentment: It also affects important status interests. Any governmental action can be an act of deference because it confers power on one group and limits some other group.[120] Moreover, the relative status of groups is affected by actions

---

110. J. GUSFIELD, *supra* note 109, at 21.
111. *Id.* at 175-76.
112. *Id.* at 177-78, 183-84.
113. *Id.* at 184-85.
114. *Id.* at 186.
115. *Id.* at 186-87.
116. *Id.* at 182.
117. *Id. See generally* M. EDELMAN, THE SYMBOLIC USES OF POLITICS (1964); M. EDELMAN, POLITICS AS SYMBOLIC ACTION (1971); M. EDELMAN, POLITICAL LANGUAGE (1977) (describing how the formal appearance of an equal opportunity to participate in a seemingly rational governmental decisionmaking process induces acquiescence among losing groups who do not obtain desired tangible resources).
118. J. GUSFIELD, *supra* note 109, at 182.
119. *Id.* at 185-86.
120. *Id.* at 182.

that bear on their ways of life.[121] Legislation that affirms a group's way of life is of particular importance to those attempting to defend or enhance their status.[122]

Gusfield developed this framework as a way of understanding the American Temperance movement's drive to establish Prohibition. According to Gusfield, the Temperance movement originated in the 1820's as a reaction by the Federalist aristocracy to its loss of political, social, and religious standing.[123] Although the Federalists' efforts to vindicate a norm of abstinence reflected underlying changes in the status order, advocates of temperance did not attempt to legislate their morality during this period, instead relying solely on moral suasion.[124] Although these leaders did not seek a political resolution of the underlying status conflict, they openly asserted that intemperance had dangerous political consequences, including increased risks of "disobedience, renunciation, and rebellion."[125]

Later, the Temperance movement was assimilated to a wave of religious revivalism during the 1830's and 1840's. As part of this revivalism, temperance was held up as a moral virtue, a means of self-improvement that would enable the worker or farmer to establish middle-class respectability.[126] In contrast to the earlier movement in the 1820's, the push for abstinence was no longer an effort to reform others but was instead an avenue of personal advancement for adherents.[127] The promotion of temperance was not politicized; rather, it reflected a stable status order with a clear hierarchy of values, which made strategies for achieving upward mobility plain.

During the 1840's and 1850's, however, support for the Temperance movement again shifted. Increasing urbanization and immigration threatened the social, moral, and cultural preeminence of rural Protestant Americans.[128] Once again, the drive for Temperance reflected an effort to maintain waning group status. Not surprisingly, the Temperance movement was closely allied with the nativist movement, which reflected similar concerns about urbanization and immigration. During this period, the Temperance movement first sought to resolve these uncertainties about status through legislative intervention. Temperance leaders successfully pursued Prohibition legislation in a number of states,

---

121. *Id.* at 182-83.

122. *Id.* at 180.

123. *Id.* at 37-44.

124. *Id.* at 51.

125. *Id.* at 42-43.

126. *Id.* at 44-47.

127. *Id.* at 46-47 (personal development was also affected through participation in fraternal temperance lodges that provided certain economic benefits to members).

128. *Id.* at 55-57.

although by the early 1890's, the laws had been largely eliminated.[129]

The declining emphasis on Prohibition legislation after the 1850's and 1860's paralleled yet another shift in the Temperance movement. In 1872, the movement adopted a humanitarian orientation that emphasized assimilative reform.[130] In contrast to the earlier religious revivalists, Temperance leaders of the 1870's considered abstinence not as a means of personal improvement, but as a vehicle for improving the lives of the poor and working classes.[131] During this period, the movement embraced wide-ranging platforms of social reform. To pursue these broader goals, the Women's Christian Temperance Union (WCTU) and the national Prohibition party were founded.[132] According to Gusfield, these efforts reflected a basic satisfaction with the status order. Relatively secure in their social position, Temperance leaders responded to the problems of urban industrialization and immigration with pleas for ameliorative reforms within the system.[133]

By the early 1900's, however, the increasing salience of urban centers and immigrant populations presented a growing challenge to the dominance of rural Protestant Americans. Earlier humanitarian reform efforts had failed to deflect this threat.[134] Once again, the fight to establish Prohibition became the proxy for an underlying concern about status. As in the 1850's and 1860's, support for Prohibition was strongest in areas that were Protestant, rural, and nativist; in fact, as the Temperance movement became more single-mindedly committed to Prohibition reforms, it grew increasingly isolated from progressive reform movements that had shared its earlier humanitarian objectives.[135] A new wave of Prohibition campaigns began, again culminating in restrictive legislation in a large number of states.[136] After these state and local victories, the drive for Prohibition took on national dimensions, resulting in the enactment of

---

129. The Massachusetts Legislature passed the first major Temperance bill in 1838. Called the Fifteen-Gallon law, it prohibited the purchase of liquor in quantities of less than 15 gallons. The bill's primary effect was to restrict drinking among the poor, and it was repealed two years later. *Id.* at 52-53. The drive to restrict liquor and beer consumption intensified during the 1850's, and by 1856, eight states had passed some form of Prohibition legislation. *Id.* at 51. Between 1843 and 1893, 15 states passed legislation prohibiting statewide sale of intoxicants, but by 1906 these laws remained in force in only three states. *Id.* at 100.

130. Gusfield, *Social Structure and Moral Reform: A Study of the Woman's Christian Temperance Union*, 61 AM. J. Soc. 221 (1955), *reprinted in* SOCIAL MOVEMENTS AND SOCIAL CHANGE 61-64 (R. Lauer ed. 1976).

131. *Id.* at 63-68.

132. The WCTU in particular adopted far-reaching plans for social reform. *Id.* at 62-64; J. GUSFIELD, *supra* note 109, at 94.

133. Gusfield, *supra* note 130, at 64, 67.

134. *Id.* at 64-65, 67-68.

135. J. GUSFIELD, *supra* note 109, at 100-10.

136. Seven states passed Prohibition laws between 1906 and 1912. By 1919, when Prohibition was elevated to a constitutional mandate, 19 more states had passed restrictive legislation. *Id.* at 100.

the eighteenth amendment, which stood as a testament to rural, Protestant American values for over a decade.[137]

The eighteenth amendment's proscriptions against trafficking in intoxicating liquors were not stringently enforced; one observer has gone so far as to characterize this lackluster effort as "nullification by non-enforcement."[138] Underenforcement did not provoke a major outcry among Temperance leaders, who appeared satisfied with constitutional vindication of the norm of abstinence, regardless of whether it was fully observed.[139] Gusfield argues that this complacency confirms the highly symbolic character of status conflicts.[140]

III
ANALYZING THE BILINGUAL EDUCATION CONTROVERSY AS A STATUS CONFLICT

Gusfield's analysis of status conflicts can illuminate the bilingual education controversy if Hispanics have used language as a proxy for their culture, customs, and values. Under these circumstances, government support of bilingual-bicultural education and TBE programs represents the deference accorded Hispanics' way of life.[141] Termination of this support would undermine Hispanics' recently acquired and hard-won status.

To evaluate the merits of this approach, this Part will use status conflict analysis as a framework for explaining bilingual education policymaking, litigation, and the development of the bilingual education and

---

137. *Id.* at 106-07, 118-19.

138. Gusfield, *Prohibition: The Impact of Political Utopianism*, in CHANGE AND CONTINUITY IN TWENTIETH-CENTURY AMERICA: THE 1920'S 257, 269-70 (J. Braeman, R. Bremmer & D. Brody eds. 1968) (quoting C. MERTZ, THE DRY DECADE 120 (1937)). The eighteenth amendment gave Congress and the states concurrent power to enforce its requirements by appropriate legislation. The major federal enforcement effort was the National Prohibition Act, or Volstead Act. The Act imposed responsibility for detection and suppression of violations on the Commissioner of Internal Revenue in the Treasury Department, rather than on the Department of Justice. The Prohibition Bureau was not brought under the Civil Service, and the salaries of Prohibition agents were considerably lower than those of other personnel. Federal and state appropriations were seldom large enough to establish an effective legal and police organization. Ineffective organization and weak morale were further aggravated by a succession of appointed Prohibition commissioners. Only after Herbert Hoover was elected President in 1928 did the Bureau become regularized by requiring recruits to pass the Civil Service examination and by bringing its activities under the supervision of the Justice Department. *Id.* at 270-71.

139. J. GUSFIELD, *supra* note 109, at 120-21.

140. *Id.* at 122-24; Gusfield, *supra* note 138, at 286-90.

141. Bilingual-bicultural education programs most clearly vindicate Hispanics' way of life because they place the Spanish language and related cultural values on a par with English and its attendant cultural norms. TBE programs provide a more ambiguous affirmation since children are ultimately returned to English-speaking classrooms. However, some deference is still accorded to distinctive linguistic and cultural heritages. Certainly, TBE programs display a greater sensitivity to these concerns than ESL and structured immersion programs.

English-only movements.[142] Applying Gusfield's work in each of these areas will also enrich his original observations.

A. *The Policymaking Process Revisited*

In 1968, the wide publicity and emotionally charged rhetoric surrounding passage of the Bilingual Education Act reflected the participants' belief that more was at stake than a modest grant-in-aid program to fund research on bilingual education. As the testimony indicated, proponents viewed the Act not only as a vehicle for upward mobility but also as an endorsement of their language, culture, customs, and values.[143] The Act's symbolic impact far exceeded its initially small effect on the allocation of resources to programs for NEP and LEP children. Yet, just as Temperance leaders did not protest the nullification of the eighteenth

---

142. Neither Gusfield's analysis nor this Essay examines why certain disputes over status become politicized and others do not. The dispute over bilingual education is clearly politicized, perhaps in part because it centers around a state-provided service, public education. Of course, in choosing to focus on a public service, the participants also may have implicitly decided to politicize the dispute. By contrast, the Temperance movement focused on the consumption of alcohol, a largely private activity that was not inherently politicized. In fact, the dispute over temperance that arose in the 1820's did not become a political issue until the 1840's. See *supra* notes 123-29 and accompanying text.

The readiness with which a status conflict becomes politicized may depend on the general tendency to address disputes in the public forum. For example, some commentators have noted the growing trend to address a variety of issues, including those relating to special education, by elaborating substantive rights and developing trial-type procedural protections. Neal & Kirp, *The Allure of Legalization Reconsidered: The Case of Special Education*, in SCHOOL DAYS, RULE DAYS 343-45 (D. Kirp & D. Jensen eds. 1986). *But cf.* Gusfield, *The Modernity of Social Movements: Public Roles and Private Parts*, in SOCIETAL GROWTH 302-07 (A. Hawley ed. 1979) (arguing that the state will become a less vital arena for social movements and that the civil rights movement may be the last major movement to rely on centralized state power to effect its demands). The push to convert educational problems into legalistic terms may have increased the likelihood that the status conflict underlying the bilingual education controversy would become politicized.

A related issue is why Hispanics selected bilingual education to serve as the proxy for their status. This choice may in part have been dictated by resource mobilization considerations. Hispanics needed an issue that would unite, rather than divide, them along ethnic lines. Their shared language heritage was a logical choice. See Padilla, *On the Nature of Latino Ethnicity*, 65 SOC. SCI. Q. 651, 653, 655, 658-60 (1984); *see also* Rodriguez, *'Latino'—A Label Too Wide and Too Narrow for Reality*, L.A. Times, Jan. 8, 1987, § II, at 5, col. 1. They also needed to ensure that the issue was of sufficient concern to their constituents that they would mobilize to support it. Recent studies suggest that education is of critical importance to Hispanics, among both long-time residents and more recent immigrants. Garcia & de la Garza, *Mobilizing the Mexican Immigrant: The Role of Mexican-American Organizations*, 38 W. POL. Q. 551, 559 (1985) (citing generally low rates of political and community involvement for Mexican immigrants but noting surprisingly high participation in PTA chapters); Romo, *The Mexican Origin Population's Differing Perceptions of Their Children's Schooling*, 65 SOC. SCI. Q. 635, 637, 648-49 (1984) (noting that all Mexican-origin groups value education, although their expectations of and degree of alienation from the school system vary with length of residence). In addition to satisfying resource mobilization requirements, bilingual education enabled Hispanics to distinguish their demands from those of black civil rights groups, who had dominated many of the efforts to combat racial discrimination. Rodriguez, *supra*.

143. *See supra* notes 23-27 and accompanying text.

amendment by nonenforcement, bilingual education advocates refrained from loudly decrying the Act's consistent underfunding.

However, bilingual education advocates could not simply acquiesce in the Act's underenforcement. Unlike Temperance supporters who were defending their status against the threat of growing urban immigrant populations, bilingual education supporters sought to enhance their status despite a longstanding history of exclusion and prejudice. A symbolic victory for the Temperance movement was probably more resilient in the face of underenforcement because the message conformed to the traditional status order. The affirmation of rural, Protestant American values merely confirmed people's preexisting beliefs about status. By contrast, the vindication of Hispanics' language, culture, and way of life in the Bilingual Education Act was designed to revise the status order. Because the Act's message challenged most people's assumptions about status, its symbolic impact was extremely fragile in the absence of any significant changes in school district practices.[144] A wholly discretionary grant program therefore could not fully vindicate Hispanics' status: A mandatory entitlement to bilingual education was necessary.

The Act's supporters turned to administrators and the courts to establish an entitlement that would ensure that schools devoted a greater share of their resources to programs for NEP and LEP children. These efforts succeeded when OCR issued its 1970 memorandum extending title VI's protections to NEP and LEP students, and the Supreme Court endorsed OCR's position in *Lau*. By proceeding before administrative decisionmakers whose deliberations on title VI's coverage of NEP and LEP children received relatively little attention, proponents avoided the serious consequences of a widely publicized defeat in the political arena. Had these advocates loudly criticized the underfunding of the Bilingual Education Act, their protests might have been ignored, and the symbolic impact of the Act would have been undermined.

The *Lau* decision had some symbolic consequences when announced and significant effects on the allocation of resources as applied. Its declaration of rights affirmed the value of according NEP and LEP children a meaningful opportunity to participate in an educational program. Because the opinion did not specify a remedy for the exclusion of NEP and LEP children from the curriculum, however, it did

---

144. In his analysis of the Temperance movement, Gusfield did not distinguish between the strategies of groups seeking to enhance their status and those seeking to defend it. Apparently, rural Protestant Americans organized around the issue of abstinence, but burgeoning urban immigrant populations did not. The liquor industry mounted the primary opposition to Prohibition laws, but its arguments were predicated on economic self-interest, rather than on concern for a particular way of life. *See* Gusfield, *supra* note 138, at 303-04. Consequently, Gusfield's examination of the Temperance movement did not afford him an opportunity to compare status groups based on whether they were improving or preserving their position.

not clearly vindicate the language, culture, and way of life of linguistic minorities. In fact, the decision expressly acknowledged that teaching English to NEP and LEP children might be an acceptable alternative, regardless of whether they received native-language instruction or information about their cultural heritage. The *Lau* decision became associated with a commitment to programs that relied heavily on native-language instruction only because of the later interpretive gloss in the *Lau* guidelines, which established a strong preference for such programs over structured immersion and ESL programs.[145] OCR's interpretation not only affected how resources were allocated to programs for NEP and LEP children but also altered the symbolic impact of the *Lau* decision.

Originally, congressional enactment of the EEOA was nothing more than a sympathetic gesture since it merely reiterated the standard under title VI set forth in *Lau* and OCR's 1970 memorandum. The EEOA's original symbolic impact on the linguistic minority community was probably quite small compared to the effect of the Bilingual Education Act in 1968. After all, the provision relating to NEP and LEP children was added as an amendment from the floor with little discussion and was embedded in an omnibus civil rights bill. Moreover, most linguistic minorities preferred to obtain relief under title VI because of the availability of the *Lau* guidelines, which endorsed bilingual-bicultural education and TBE programs. Only later, when title VI's coverage became more ambiguous and the *Lau* guidelines were withdrawn, did the EEOA begin to have important symbolic and instrumental consequences. Although the EEOA has permitted litigants to continue to sue successfully for special educational assistance, it less clearly vindicates the language, culture, and values of linguistic minorities since it seems to permit ESL and structured immersion programs.[146]

As enforcement efforts produced an increasingly important reallocation of resources to bilingual education programs, adversely affected groups organized around both economic interest and status. In 1977-78, when empirical research failed to demonstrate the effectiveness of bilingual education programs, opponents were able to challenge federal support for the programs successfully. The free-for-all surrounding the NPRM in 1980 reflected both interest-group and status politics. English-speaking teachers, who were probably concerned about their employment security in a shrinking job market, mounted a strong attack on the requirements. At the same time, concerns about official bilingualism and separatism reflected a preoccupation with the status of English as the preeminent language of the United States.[147]

---

145. *See supra* notes 33-35 and 38-39 and accompanying text.
146. *See supra* notes 40-41 and 53-54 and accompanying text.
147. *See supra* notes 43-46 and 50-51 and accompanying text.

The movement to make English the official language of the United States even more clearly derives from a desire to preserve English and the "American" way of life from encroachment by a growing number of linguistic minority groups. The membership is composed of long-time citizens who want to curb immigration that may strain America's resources and undermine its standard of living. Other members are immigrants who learned English as a second language and want to ensure that their newfound and perhaps tenuous hold on respectability through assimilation is not undermined. They may believe that learning English and adopting American values is the only legitimate route to upward social mobility.[148] Although some supporters are English-speaking teachers with an economic interest in eliminating bilingual education programs, these interests have been subordinated to status concerns in the drive to make English the official language.[149]

Only when bilingual education advocates had achieved a significant reallocation of resources did this "status backlash" develop. The symbolic victory associated with the Bilingual Education Act's passage in 1968 did not trigger a strong adverse reaction. The English-only movement mobilized only after funding for bilingual-bicultural education and TBE programs had greatly increased, and empirical evidence had failed to document the programs' benefits. The mixed research findings made it difficult to justify the programs as purely pedagogical devices designed to promote proficiency in English and achievement in other subjects. The continuing commitment to these programs plainly reflected other objectives, including the vindication of the language, culture, and values of

---

148. Among voters who favored making English the official language of California, 62% believed that "everyone living here should speak English," and 56% said that it was "important for immigrants to learn English." Interestingly, among Hispanics who favored the proposal, 68% endorsed these propositions, a rate nearly 10% higher than that among white voters who supported the measure. While 50% of the general voters who supported the English language amendment contended that it is "important to society to speak the same language," 58% of Hispanics who voted for the measure agreed with this statement. Apparently, for a substantial segment of the Hispanic electorate, learning English was seen as a key element to participation in American society. Significantly, however, the poll does not indicate whether these voters favored the elimination of bilingual services as a means to achieve an English-speaking society, nor does it report on the degree to which they wanted to encourage proficiency in Spanish and an awareness of their cultural heritage in addition to acquiring English language skills. California Poll, *supra* note 61, at 191, 193.

Interestingly, the results among Asian voters who endorsed the measure were somewhat different. Of these voters, 75% believed that "everyone living here should speak English," but only about 35% stated that it is "important for immigrants to learn English" or "important to society to speak the same language." Apparently, these voters did not attach peculiar significance to the need for immigrants to learn English nor did they believe that fundamental societal needs were at stake. Only further study can illuminate precisely why Asian voters endorsing the measure thought everyone should speak English. *Id.* at 193.

149. Note, *supra* note 57, at 520-21 (primary emphasis of English-only movement is need for common bond of English to ensure political stability); see *supra* note 58 and accompanying text.

linguistic minorities, especially Hispanics.[150] As these political implications became clearer, English-only adherents found the programs increasingly threatening to their chosen way of life. They therefore mobilized to promote English-only reforms.

Although the English-only movement has succeeded in enacting reforms in a number of cities, counties, and states, it is unclear whether these measures will be effectively enforced. Like Temperance adherents, the English-only movement seeks to preserve its place in the established status order against a perceived threat. It has relied on symbolic victories through popular political processes. Because these victories conform to expectations about status, their immediate impact will not be undermined by a lack of enforcement. Consequently, there is a real possibility that, like the eighteenth amendment, English-only reforms will also be at least partially nullified by nonenforcement.

B. The Litigation Process Reexamined

Both *Otero* and *Zambrano* share characteristics consistent with the view that the bilingual education controversy embodies a status conflict. In each case, the plaintiffs demanded bilingual-bicultural education or TBE programs, while the districts typically favored heavier reliance on ESL instruction. These differences arose despite ongoing legislative, judicial, and administrative efforts to define a school district's obligations to NEP and LEP students. Because ESL is a less expensive instructional program,[151] the school districts' claims can be partly explained in terms of budgetary constraints. However, the plaintiffs' strong preference for native-language instruction is consistent with a desire to vindicate their culture, customs, and values, and the districts' choice of ESL programs may also reflect a tendency to uphold the traditional status order.[152]

Both cases certainly had a strong symbolic impact on the surrounding community, at least in part because they attracted considerable media attention. In *Otero*, the plaintiffs may have favorably influenced

---

150. For example, John Molina, the director of the Office of Bilingual Education, responded to the AIR evaluation by explaining:

> You actually can't evaluate a bilingual education program. It is philosophy and management. You can evaluate courses. For example, evaluation should be limited to reading, mathematics, science and social science. I think we need a tremendous amount of research in order to determine what are the best methods and if children learn in languages other than English.

D. RAVITCH, *supra* note 27, at 278. Professor Ravitch termed Molina's answer "a blunt admission that bilingual education proceeded from ideological grounds, and not as a result of research validating the best methods of teaching children of limited English-speaking ability." *Id.*

151. Birman & Ginsburg, *Introduction: Addressing the Needs of Language-Minority Children,* in BILINGUAL EDUCATION, *supra* note 3, at xvi-xvii; B. Reyes & M. Siegel, *supra* note 79, at 41.

152. *See* D. TYACK, THE ONE BEST SYSTEM 104-09 (1974) (when immigrant groups sought to influence school policies by imposing their values or affirming their subcultures, school personnel typically endorsed traditional values, which they took for granted as self-evident).

the status accorded their way of life, even though they failed to persuade the court that bilingual-bicultural education should be required. That a politically moderate Chicano businessman testified for the plaintiffs indicated that their views were gaining wider acceptance in the Chicano community. The local newspaper acknowledged that whatever the decision, the case had demonstrated the importance of recognizing the special needs of linguistically and culturally different children.[153]

In *Zambrano,* not only did the media generate interest in the dispute, but the BDAC also used the bilingual master plan as a rallying cry to spark widespread community involvement. Supporters appeared by the hundreds at public hearings, and popular outrage at the district's countersuit may ultimately have forced it to the bargaining table. Moreover, continuing public pressure on the school board probably improved the plaintiffs' chances to obtain a favorable agreement.[154]

Although these machinations may appear to be nothing more than another example of interest-group bargaining over educational resources, evidence suggests that more than pedagogy was at stake for the *Zambrano* plaintiffs. The plaintiffs were initially reluctant to enter into settlement negotiations with the district because they wanted a full trial and complete victory "to teach the [d]istrict a lesson."[155] After the agreement was reached, the plaintiffs hailed it as a great triumph. Now that the consent decree is being implemented, linguistic minority parents, including some of the named plaintiffs, remain heavily involved in BDAC meetings. The parents value this involvement because "[i]t marks their right to participate in decisions affecting their children's schooling and confers dignity on their linguistic heritage."[156] These parents demonstrate a high degree of ethnic and linguistic consciousness at the meetings.[157]

Otero and *Zambrano* also demonstrate the polarization and heated emotional responses that often accompany a status conflict. In each case, the litigation was highly acrimonious, and even traditional professional courtesies broke down. In *Zambrano,* the animosity among the parties culminated in the district's filing of a countersuit alleging harassment by the plaintiffs and their attorney.[158] The cases also sparked deeply felt reactions in the community at large. In *Otero,* these feelings manifested themselves most virulently in threats of violence. In *Zambrano,* they were evidenced by the heavy attendance and heated debate at public

---

153. *See supra* notes 74-75 and accompanying text.
154. *See supra* notes 86-87 and 95-98 and accompanying text.
155. B. Reyes & M. Siegel, *supra* note 79, at 104.
156. *Id.* at 137.
157. *Id.* at 140.
158. *See supra* notes 72, 90-94 and accompanying text.

hearings and by the outcry that followed the countersuit.[159]

The plaintiffs' substantial involvement in *Otero* and *Zambrano* may have significantly influenced the symbolic impact of the litigation. Although in both cases the school district portrayed the attorneys as outside "agitators," the lawyers reportedly had responded to the plaintiffs' vigorous request for representation, rather than stirring up the lawsuits.[160] Moreover, the attorneys worked closely with the named plaintiffs throughout each case.[161] In *Zambrano*, the plaintiffs even served as liaisons to their broader ethnic, linguistic, and cultural communities.[162] Because the plaintiffs played a substantial part in the litigation process, they may have been more likely to conclude that the cases enhanced their community's status. After all, sophisticated attorneys had deferred to their values.

By contrast, if clients are co-opted or become passive when confronted with counsel's superior expertise, litigation may do little to bolster the community's status. A favorable outcome is apt to be interpreted as a triumph of legal acumen, rather than as an act of deference to Hispanics' way of life.[163] NEP and LEP clients may be especially vulnerable to co-optation, making it more likely that a lawsuit will not vindicate their community's status. Typically, these clients are poor ethnic minorities who speak little or no English, have little formal education, and may have distinctive cultural values.[164] Confronted with an alien legal process, they are apt to defer to attorneys who are well-educated, financially secure, often white, and sometimes non-Spanish-speaking.[165] At least in *Otero* and *Zambrano*, counsel apparently overcame

---

159. *See supra* notes 73, 86-87, 95-97 and accompanying text.

160. The plaintiff's lead attorney in *Otero* thought that Grand Junction was a poor site for a test case because other districts had more NEP and LEP children and had engaged in more overt acts of discrimination. Yet he concluded that "his primary obligation was to La Voz, a local client attempting to overcome what it saw as concrete aggrievements, rather than to a more abstract national litigation strategy." M. REBELL & A. BLOCK, *supra* note 18, at 282 n.11. In *Zambrano*, the BDAC parents consulted with several attorneys before finding a public-interest lawyer both willing and able to take their case. B. Reyes & M. Siegel, *supra* note 79, at 46-51.

161. M. REBELL & A. BLOCK, *supra* note 18, at 171 (describing how plaintiff's attorneys adjusted their strategies and theories to fit the needs and perceptions of their clients); B. Reyes & M. Siegel, *supra* note 79, at 93-95.

162. B. Reyes & M. Siegel, *supra* note 79, at 101-03.

163. *See* S. OLSON, CLIENTS AND LAWYERS 28 (1984). Lawyer domination occurs when: (1) lawyers control the content and management of the case without sufficient input from their clients; and (2) clients become so dependent on lawyers that their capacity to function as an organization is impaired in the long run. *Id. See generally* Denvir, *Towards a Political Theory of Public Interest Litigation,* 54 N.C.L. REV. 1133, 1144-46 (1976) (analyzing how litigation affects community organization).

164. L. ORUM, THE EDUCATION OF HISPANICS 6-25 (Eric Ed. No. 262-121, 1985).

165. Parents may also be overshadowed by English-speaking representatives of the Hispanic community, such as Chicano educators, who become involved in the case. *Cf.* Post-Trial Brief of Defendant at 43-47, Keyes v. School Dist. No. 1, 576 F. Supp. 1503 (D. Colo. 1983) (discussing

the barriers to meaningful client involvement that such differences in language, culture, ethnicity, education, and social status frequently present.

C. The Development of the Bilingual Education and English-Only Movements

In addition to illuminating the policymaking and litigation processes, status conflict analysis is helpful in evaluating the evolution of the bilingual education and English-only movements. Because the bilingual education movement sought to enhance its status, it was less able to rely on popular political processes that are apt to affirm the longstanding, generally accepted status order. Moreover, the movement had limited resources available with which to overcome this popular inertia. Still, it had to ensure that any fragile symbolic victories it achieved were bolstered by some subsequent reallocation of resources to bilingual education. Otherwise, a purely symbolic impact could be eroded by school district practices that continued to conform to the traditional status order.

To stand any chance of success in the legislature, bilingual education proponents had to ally themselves with other civil rights groups. Yet, these alliances typically resulted in omnibus bills that relegated bilingual education to the background. During legislative deliberations, bilingual education was consistently overshadowed by other civil rights issues, such as segregation and busing. Only during deliberations on the Bilingual Education Act did Congress focus exclusively on the problems of NEP and LEP children. The modest grant-in-aid program that emerged from these discussions arguably demonstrates the limited potential of this narrow legislative reform effort.[166]

Bilingual education advocates therefore confronted a dilemma: They could demand specific legislative consideration of their needs and reap extremely limited reforms, or they could join civil rights coalitions to gain more sweeping reforms that accorded little special attention to their concerns. Neither outcome was satisfactory for Hispanics who accorded a unique importance to language as a proxy for their way of life. To achieve a more meaningful endorsement of their language, culture, and values, these advocates had to turn to decisionmakers that were

---

standing, typicality, and commonality requirements of class action brought by an organization of Hispanic educators as well as students and their parents) (on file with author).

166.   Bilingual education proponents may have traded their support on other issues for favorable consideration of the Bilingual Education Act, thereby using coalitions to promote a more single-minded focus on the issue. Because the Act benefited a much narrower class, however, bilingual education supporters probably expended much of their political capital on catapulting the issue to prominence. They were therefore unable to extract more stringent legislation. Again, interest-group bargaining plays a role in explaining the legislative process, but status conflict analysis illuminates why proponents were willing to trade off a great deal to make bilingual education a salient issue.

not directly accountable through the electoral process: the courts and administrative agencies. Relieved of some of the need to forge broader coalitions, proponents could insist more narrowly on explicit approval of bilingual-bicultural education and TBE programs as a means of affirming their way of life.[167] As they achieved judicial and administrative victories, they were able to use them to persuade the legislature that its choices in enacting a bilingual education act or in funding programs were quite limited.[168] This strategy enabled bilingual education supporters to highlight bilingual education as a singularly important symbol of their status.

In contrast to bilingual education proponents who have relied heavily on judicial and administrative as well as legislative intervention, English-only reformers have typically relied on legislative action and popular referenda. Because the English-only movement seeks to preserve the existing status order, it is better able to capitalize on popular political processes than are bilingual education advocates, who challenge that order.[169] The high visibility of these processes, especially the popular referendum, makes them particularly useful in symbolically affirming the value of the English-only reformers' way of life.

However, the message sent by these measures is often clouded by the need to generate widespread sympathy for the proposals and the opportunity for broad-ranging participation in the referendum process. In California, for example, one survey found that few voters had any clear idea of what the official language proposal meant. Some even simultaneously supported the English-only amendment and bilingual education or bilingual ballots.[170] The English-only movement may therefore achieve highly salient symbolic victories with extremely ambiguous connotations.[171] In the short run, this ambiguity may not greatly trouble the

---

167. Although the plaintiffs in *Lau* did not request a specific remedy, most litigants, like those in *Otero* and *Zambrano*, have demanded bilingual-bicultural education or TBE programs. Baker & de Kanter, *supra* note 19, at 299-305; Levin, *supra* note 10, at 37-39. Of course, these demands were significantly shaped by the *Lau* guidelines, *id.* at 37, but even after the guidelines' demise, plaintiffs have pressed for such programs under the EEOA. Baker & DeKanter, *supra* note 19, at 302-05; Roos, *Implementation of the Federal Bilingual Education Mandate: The Keyes Case as a Paradigm*, 1 LA RAZA L.J. 257, 265-66 (1986).

168. *See, e.g.*, M. REBELL & A. BLOCK, *supra* note 18, at 193.

169. *See supra* notes 101-06 and accompanying text.

170. Trombley, *Latino Backing of 'English-Only' a Puzzle*, L.A. Times, Oct. 25, 1986, § II, at 6, col. 1.

171. In fact, even some of the popular referenda themselves have been loosely worded. For example, in California, the state constitutional amendment provides simply that "English is the official language of the State of California." CAL. CONST. art. III, § 6(b) (amended 1986). It goes on to require the legislature to "enforce this section by appropriate legislation" and mandates that the legislature and state officials "take all steps necessary to insure that the role of English as the common language of the State of California is preserved and enhanced." *Id.* § 6(c) (amended 1986). It further prohibits the legislature from passing any law "which diminishes or ignores the role of English as the common language of the State of California." *Id.* The amendment also provides for a

supporters of English-only reforms. Disagreements about the provision's meaning are likely to become manifest only while implementing it; yet, as previously noted, English-only reformers who seek to affirm the established status order are less pressed to enforce their symbolic triumphs. In fact, they may shy away from enforcement efforts that are apt to disrupt their support by making clear the diverse interpretations of the measures.[172]

IV

SOME PREDICTIONS AND SUGGESTIONS ABOUT BILINGUAL EDUCATION AND ENGLISH-ONLY REFORMS BASED ON STATUS CONFLICT ANALYSIS

This Essay would not be complete without using status conflict analysis to indulge in some speculation about the future of bilingual education policymaking and litigation as well as the prospective development of the bilingual education and English-only movements. These predictions are offered only tentatively, however, in light of the myriad factors that can influence these complicated events.

A.   *The Policymaking Process Projected*

So far, the English-only movement has pursued highly symbolic affirmations of its values without evincing much concern about subsequent enforcement. The English-only movement is unlikely to address the allocation of educational resources except when bilingual education supporters press for bilingual-bicultural education and TBE programs.[173] These battles are most likely to occur when legislatures are deliberating on bilingual education acts or appropriating funds under them.[174] The English-only movement's "reactive" posture is wholly consistent with its effort to defend, rather than alter, its status.

---

private right of action to enforce its provisions. *Id.* § 6(d) (amended 1986). The amendment's all-encompassing wording is apt to spark a number of competing interpretations. Trombley, *supra* note 61; L.A. Times, Oct. 3, 1986, § II, at 4, col. 1.

172. For example, efforts to eliminate foreign language advertising have created considerable dissension within the English-only movement. May, *Opposition Intensifies to Ads Using Spanish*, L.A. Times, Sept. 8, 1986, § I, at 21, col. 1.

173. After the passage of the English-only amendment in California, leading officials were reluctant to enact legislation to implement its requirements. Ingram, *Prop. 63 Backers Aim at Bilingual Education*, L.A. Times, Nov. 24, 1986, § I, at 3, col. 1. Even an assemblyman who introduced bills to eliminate a wide range of bilingual services after the amendment's passage expressed doubts as to whether the legislature would endorse his proposals. Trombley, *supra* note 64; San Francisco Examiner, Nov. 6, 1986, at A3, col. 1.

174. In California, there is general agreement that English-only advocates will strenuously oppose efforts to extend the state's bilingual education provisions, which expire on June 30, 1987. Ingram, *supra* note 173; Trombley, *supra* note 64; San Francisco Examiner, *supra* note 173.

The English-only movement will probably have far less impact on omnibus civil rights statutes, such as title VI and the EEOA, because they treat language barriers as a proxy for discrimination on the basis of race or ethnicity. This framework makes it more difficult for bilingual education advocates or English-only proponents to elevate language to a position of singular importance. Moreover, these statutes are supported by a coalition of civil rights groups. Because of its single-issue orientation, the English-only movement may be less able to forge the alliances necessary to challenge this coalition.

The English-only movement is unlikely to file many administrative complaints and lawsuits to change bilingual education programs, although it would undoubtedly respond to any challenges to the validity of English-only measures. Instead, organizational resources are currently being devoted to political campaigns for English-only reforms across the country.[175] These campaigns have produced widely publicized, discrete changes with a strong symbolic impact. By contrast, administrative actions and litigation tend to be drawn out and may produce only mixed results for English-only supporters, given the strictures of title VI and the EEOA.[176] Because administrative proceedings are typically less publicized than higher court decisions, they are particularly unattractive avenues of change for English-only adherents because of their limited symbolic impact.

Moreover, few members of U.S. English have any direct stake in how English-only measures are enforced in the schools. Having had little direct contact with bilingual education programs, they are not likely to devote the time and energy necessary to investigate and challenge program implementation; in any event, mere passage of English-only measures vindicates their way of life.[177] The one exception is English-speaking teachers whose jobs may be threatened by bilingual education programs. Again, English-speaking teachers are apt to assume a "reac-

---

175. For instance, U.S. English loaned its California chapter $385,000 to finance the English-only initiative. Trombley, *Prop. 63 Finance Infraction Alleged*, L.A. Times, Sept. 19, 1986, § I, at 25, col. 1; Nakao, *Prop. 63 Opponents Complain About Loan to Plan's Backers*, San Francisco Examiner, Sept. 19, 1986, at A6, col. 5.

176. Obviously, districts will remain bound by consent decrees negotiated pursuant to title VI. Baker & de Kanter, *supra* note 19, at 307-08. Moreover, the EEOA, which is now the principal source of federal protection for linguistic minority schoolchildren, only requires that districts take "appropriate action" to meet their needs. In the short term, this would clearly seem to allow properly implemented ESL and structured immersion programs. *See supra* note 54 and accompanying text. However, the prevailing interpretation of the requirement also requires districts to evaluate their programs and modify them if they do not improve NEP and LEP students' academic achievement. Castaneda v. Pickard, 648 F.2d 989, 1009-10 (5th Cir. 1981). In the longer term, ESL and structured immersion programs might run afoul of the EEOA if ongoing evaluation revealed that they did not adequately enhance NEP and LEP students' opportunity to participate in the educational curriculum.

177. *See supra* notes 21, 58, 149 and accompanying text.

tive" posture, filing complaints only in response to bilingual education advocates' efforts to reallocate resources. Moreover, while displaced teachers may rely on the English-only measure, they are also apt to invoke their vested interests based on seniority.[178]

To the extent that the English-only movement interjects itself into bilingual education debates, it will probably rigidify policy discussions by insisting on the unique role of English. Each side will increasingly view language as an absolute value that can not be traded off against other goods. As both sides grow more inflexible in their demands for vindication of their language's value, they will insist more vehemently on specific remedies that validate their ways of life. Each will be even less willing to consider empirical evidence on the effectiveness of different approaches to teaching NEP and LEP children. Instead, English-only advocates will invariably demand structured immersion and ESL programs because they promote the status of English. By the same token, Hispanics and perhaps other linguistic minority groups will demand bilingual-bicultural education and TBE programs that endorse their language, culture, and customs.[179] It will become increasingly difficult to mask this deep-seated conflict through compromises that advance neither side's status objectives.

B.   The Litigation Process Predicted

Bilingual education advocates have relied heavily on the litigation process to ensure that programs for NEP and LEP children are adequately funded. However, this process has been increasingly complicated by tensions between bilingual education and desegregation and by the proliferation of linguistic minority groups. Bilingual education conflicts with desegregation in two ways. First, implementation of a desegregation decree often threatens bilingual education programs that require a minimum number of NEP and LEP students in a particular school to trigger program requirements. Even where programs continue after implementation of the decree, they are more likely to rely on ESL because bilingual-bicultural education and TBE programs are not utilized with a small number of students.[180] Second, to the extent that linguistic minority students must be separated from their English-speaking classmates for special instruction, bilingual education programs can result in racially or ethnically identifiable classrooms and undesirable

---

178. *See supra* note 12 and accompanying text. Of course, to the extent that claims based solely on seniority have proven unsuccessful, English-speaking teachers are apt to rely more heavily on English-only reforms.

179. The polarization of the bilingual education conflict along these lines is already beginning to emerge in California. Ingram, *supra* note 173; Trombley, *supra* note 64.

180. Roos, *Bilingual Education: The Hispanic Response to Unequal Educational Opportunity*, LAW & CONTEMP. PROBS., Autumn 1978, at 135.

isolation.[181]

Courts have responded to these tensions in a variety of ways. Some have simply accorded a higher priority to desegregation than bilingual education. Others have allocated NEP and LEP children among the schools covered by a desegregation decree in a way that preserves bilingual education programs.[182] To avoid classroom segregation, Congress has provided that up to forty percent of the students in a federally funded bilingual education program can be English-proficient.[183] The courts and Congress have also required integrated classes in music, art, physical education, and other elective subjects.[184]

The conflict between bilingual education and desegregation diminishes the symbolic impact of lawsuits in vindicating Hispanics' way of life. The litigation process makes clear the trade-offs required among different approaches to combatting racial and ethnic discrimination in the schools. In fact, these trade-offs reflect the omnibus character of the statutes that have spawned the litigation. By treating language as a proxy for race and ethnicity, these provisions acknowledge that children are vulnerable to various forms of discrimination, which may require distinctive remedies.

What remains uncertain is whether compromises forged in the legislature will endure the litigation process. When omnibus civil rights bills are passed in Congress, the trade-offs are abstract and remote, but in a lawsuit, they become concrete and immediate. Moreover, litigants are often more deeply committed to specific remedies than are lobbyists who regularly employ a wide range of tools to achieve an organizational objective.

Public-interest attorneys who litigate a number of bilingual education or desegregation cases can help to prevent the factionalization of plaintiffs along these lines by placing the plaintiffs' efforts in a broader perspective. Without divesting clients of ultimate decisionmaking authority, these attorneys can inform them about the wide range of approaches that have been used to fight racial and ethnic discrimination and the continuing commitment to each. If attorneys can persuade plaintiffs seeking desegregation and those seeking bilingual education

---

181. *1977 House Hearings, supra* note 44, at 355-37 (remarks of Professor Gary Orfield, Political Science Department, University of Illinois at Urbana).

182. Roos, *supra* note 180, at 135-37 (describing approaches adopted in cases involving desegregation and bilingual education).

183. Bilingual Education Act, 20 U.S.C.A. § 3223(a)(4)(B) (Supp. 1986).

184. *E.g.*, Cintron v. Brentwood Union Free School Dist., 455 F. Supp 57, 63 & n.9, 64 (E.D.N.Y 1978); *see also* OFFICE FOR CIVIL RIGHTS, *supra* note 3, §§ IV, VI, *reprinted in* BILINGUAL EDUCATION, *supra* note 3, at 218-20 (no longer enforced); Bilingual Education Act, 20 U.S.C.A. § 3223(a)(4)(C) (requiring participation of NEP and LEP children in regular classes in elective courses, such as art, music, and physical education).

that cooperation is mutually beneficial, then the in-fighting that can potentially stymie meaningful judicial intervention may be prevented.[185] To some extent, the attorneys' success in preserving these alliances will depend on the degree to which the English-only movement rigidifies the focus on language as a basis for vindicating Hispanics' way of life. The more vigorously bilingual education advocates insist on the symbolic affirmation of their language, culture, and customs, the more likely that legislative trade-offs will not survive the litigation process.

The increasing number of linguistic minority groups also complicates the litigation process in bilingual education cases. Hispanic plaintiffs have played a leading role in many bilingual education cases, even where a number of other linguistic minority groups were potentially affected by the decree.[186] These other groups have seldom participated actively in formulating litigation strategies. Courts have frequently ignored their lack of involvement by assuming an identity of interest among language groups during the liability phase of a bilingual education case. Judges have, however, suggested that broader participation by these groups is required once liability is established and a remedy is being formulated.[187] Such protection at the remedial phase is probably more illusory than real. Once a school district has been found liable, it typically negotiates with the plaintiffs to draft a consent agreement subject to judicial approval. It is unclear whether previously uninvolved language groups meaningfully participate in this negotiation process.[188]

If judges mandate more active participation by a wide range of affected linguistic minorities, Hispanic plaintiffs will have to forge new alliances with these groups to ensure successful litigation of their claims. If these coalitions fail to materialize, the lawsuit's potential to vindicate Hispanics' way of life will be seriously diminished. Not only will the suit's symbolic impact be diluted if groups bicker over the desired relief, but the case also will probably fail to produce any significant reallocation

---

185. This problem can be analyzed as a permutation of the Prisoners' Dilemma game, where both parties are better off in the long term by cooperating but believe that they can advance their short-term interests by competing. Because both respond competitively, each suffers both short-term and long-term disadvantages. Perhaps this feature of bilingual education litigation could appropriately be labeled Plaintiffs' Dilemma. *See* Elliott, Ackerman & Millian, *Toward a Theory of Statutory Evolution: The Federalization of Environmental Law*, 1 J.L. ECON. & ORG. 313, 324-26 (1985).

186. *See, e.g.,* Moran, *Foreword—The Lessons of* Keyes: *How Do You Translate "The American Dream"?,* 1 LA RAZA L.J. 195, 201-02 (1986) (Spanish-speaking intervenors and their counsel directed bilingual education case with little or no input from other potentially affected language groups).

187. *See, e.g.,* Keyes v. School Dist. No. 1, 576 F. Supp. 1503, 1506-08 (D. Colo. 1983) (although Hispanic plaintiff-intervenors were found to represent adequately the interests of Indochinese children during the liability phase of the trial, the court reserved authority to order separate representation during the remedy phase).

188. *See* Moran, *supra* note 186, at 202.

of resources. Eventually, litigation will cease to be an effective tool except in jurisdictions characterized by a relatively homogeneous linguistic minority population.

Even if alliances are forged, the very process of coalition building will alter the dynamics of the litigation process. In contrast to the tensions between desegregation and bilingual education, the tensions among linguistic minorities have not been extensively addressed during legislative deliberations. Congress paid scant attention to bilingual education issues during discussions of title VI and the EEOA, and Hispanics have overshadowed other groups at hearings on the Bilingual Education Act.[189] Moreover, the tensions between bilingual education and desegregation have promoted multiple-issue politics by highlighting the fact that the plaintiffs have suffered discrimination not only on the basis of language but also on the basis of race or ethnicity. In building coalitions among linguistic minorities, however, it will be necessary to emphasize the common denominator of language. By promoting single-issue politics, the formation of these alliances may intensify the commitment to language as a proxy for linguistic minorities' ways of life and rigidify demands for governmental intervention to vindicate these values. Under these circumstances, language will develop broader, more diffuse connotations for the participants and will provoke deeper emotional responses.

C. The Development of the Bilingual Education and English-Only Movements Divined

As previously noted, because bilingual education proponents sought to alter the status order by enhancing the deference accorded to their way of life, they had to engage in multiple-issue politics, joining with other civil rights groups to promote the reallocation of resources to bilingual education programs. Because English-only advocates are defending their place in the traditional status order, they have been able to pursue single-issue politics without an immediate concern about underenforcement of their reform measures.[190]

---

189. *See supra* notes 101-06 and accompanying text. Several commentators have noted that the Bilingual Education Act primarily responded to Hispanic demands. *See, e.g.,* C. HARRINGTON, *supra* note 24, at 2; A. LEIBOWITZ, *supra*, at 9; S. SCHNEIDER, REVOLUTION, REACTION, OR REFORM: THE 1974 BILINGUAL EDUCATION ACT 6-7 (1976). In fact, the bilingual education bill as originally introduced in the Senate covered only Spanish-speaking students but was later broadened to cover other linguistic minority groups, presumably to avoid legal challenges and an appearance of inequity. A. LEIBOWITZ, *supra*, at 15-17; S. SCHNEIDER, *supra*, at 22, 24. At the 1967 Senate hearings, over 60 people with a Spanish surname testified, while no Asian-surnamed persons appeared. *1967 Senate Hearings, supra* note 25, at iii-vi. In recent years, however, other linguistic minority groups have played a greater role in the development of bilingual education legislation. L. ORUM, THE BILINGUAL EDUCATION ACT OF 1984: COMMUNITY INVOLVEMENT IN POLICY DEVELOPMENT 6 (1984).

190. For a description of another group that has engaged in single-issue politics, see Kristin

The prevalence of coalition-building and multiple-issue politics may have significant implications for each group's long-term resiliency. The bilingual education movement, by participating in coalitions and concerning itself with a number of civil rights issues, has diversified its political portfolio in a way that may improve its chances for survival. That is, if advocates encounter defeat in pursuing a particular reform, they can redirect their energies to other issues that promise greater opportunities for success. Conversely, if they succeed in one reform effort, supporters will not disband as readily as would a single-issue group because other reforms will remain on the agenda.[191] Of course, if the English-only movement's emphasis on language forces bilingual education advocates to adopt a more single-minded commitment to this issue, their organizational resiliency may be impaired.

The English-only movement's exclusive focus on promoting the English language could jeopardize its chances for long-term survival. If a single-issue political group consistently fails to achieve desired reforms, it is more likely to lose members who become pessimistic about the possibilities for change and cannot devote themselves to alternative organizational objectives. For example, the WCTU's membership declined markedly after the repeal of Prohibition. Faced with a changed social and political environment that was more hostile to a norm of total abstinence, the WCTU nevertheless retained its single-minded commitment to temperance. As a consequence, its support, especially among the middle and upper middle classes, steadily diminished. The WCTU's former adherents could no longer identify with the largely discredited and unattainable goal of mandatory abstinence.[192] On the other hand, if a single-issue group succeeds in promoting desired reforms, its membership is more likely to become apathetic and quiescent. For example, the

---

Luker's analysis of the anti-abortion movement. K. LUKER, *supra* note 108, at 223-24. Interestingly, until recently, adherents of the "right to choose" have been less likely to be single-issue voters. *Id.* at 286 n.11.

191. For a general description of the life cycle of social movements, including a discussion of their organizational decline, see C. STEWART, C. SMITH & R. DENTON, PERSUASION AND SOCIAL MOVEMENTS 37-50 (1984). Of course, economies of scale may also lead groups to diversify when start-up costs are prohibitive. Elliott, Ackerman & Millian, *supra* note 185, at 323. Multi-purpose organizations may confer other advantages as well. For example, groups that deal with multiple issues may better understand how various problems relate to one another and may more accurately predict the diverse ramifications of reform.

192. Gusfield, *supra* note 130, at 62-63, 72-75. Current WCTU members express moral indignation at the defection of middle and upper middle class members. *Id.* at 70-73. This new emphasis on moral outrage may signal a shift in the WCTU's relevant audience. Political appeals to establish Prohibition were undoubtedly directed at both members and nonmembers, while angry moralizing about the defection of former adherents is probably aimed at the remaining membership. Rather than shaming middle and upper middle class defectors into rejoining, these denunciations are designed to retain the current membership by promoting in-group solidarity. This change in focus may represent an implicit acknowledgment that the WCTU's temperance objective no longer can command broad political appeal.

WCTU's broad-ranging commitment to humanitarian reforms in the 1870's may have been designed to stave off apathy among members after the successful pursuit of Prohibition legislation in the 1840's through the 1860's.[193] So far, the English-only movement has successfully pursued reforms at the state and local level. Whether it will become apathetic after these initial successes or will broaden its reform agenda to maintain an active membership remains an open question.[194]

CONCLUSION

Analyzing the bilingual education and English-only movements as part of a status conflict provides a useful supplement to interest-group bargaining analysis. Status conflict analysis is especially helpful in understanding why ongoing government intervention and empirical research have done relatively little to temper the highly emotional quality of the debate. Much more is at stake for the participants than optimizing the allocation of educational resources based on current pedagogical theories. For each side, language has become a proxy for their culture, customs, and values. If, for the foreseeable future, the United States will remain what Theodore Roosevelt termed a polyglot boarding house, the clash over bilingual education and English-only reforms will continue to reflect the status we accord its dwellers.

---

193. *See supra* notes 130-33 and accompanying text. Of course, this does not explain why the WCTU was able to diversify its goals in the 1870's after the successful pursuit of Prohibition legislation, but was not able to do so in the 1930's after the repeal of Prohibition. Perhaps, the WCTU was able to consider supplemental objectives so long as temperance remained a central organizing principle. Once abstinence became a discredited norm, however, the WCTU could not turn to other goals as substitutes for its self-proclaimed primary goal.

194. Regulating immigration would be a likely topic for a broadened reform agenda as several leaders of the English-only movement have expressed concern about this issue. Trombley, *supra* note 21 (both the chairman and executive director of U.S. English were active in an organization that lobbied for more stringent immigration laws and lower immigration quotas).

MEXICAN-AMERICANS AND THE DESEGREGATION OF SCHOOLS IN THE SOUTHWEST

I. INTRODUCTION

On June 4, 1970, Federal District Judge Woodrow Seals, in *Cisneros v. Corpus Christi Independent School District*,[1] held that Mexican-Americans are an "identifiable ethnic minority group" for the purpose of public school desegregation.[2] Because Mexican-Americans are an identifiable group and have been subjected to discrimination in the Corpus Christi, Texas area, Judge Seals stated that Mexican-Americans are entitled to the same protection afforded Negroes under the landmark decision of *Brown v. Board of Education*.[3] The court found that the school district segregated Mexican-Americans, as well as Negroes, to such an extent that a dual school system resulted.[4] The parties were then asked to submit a desegregation plan which considered the three major ethnic groups: Negro, Mexican-American, and Anglo, that is, other whites besides Mexican-Americans.[5]

Cisneros is unique in that it is the first case in which a court officially recognized Mexican-Americans as an *indentifiable ethnic minority group* for purposes of public school desegregation. Before proceeding with a discussion of the significance of being an *identifiable ethnic minority group*, a definition of the phrase may be conducive to a better understanding of the court's holding. Mexican-Americans are considered by some to be a non-white racial group. However, the predominant view is that Mexican-Americans are white, even though many are *mestizos* (a hybrid of white and Indian). Nevertheless, like other white nationality groups who have been victims of discrimination, for example, the Jewish and Italian-Americans, Mexican-Americans have inherent characteristics which make them easily identifiable and susceptible to discrimination. Among these characteristics are brown skin color, a Spanish surname, and the Spanish language. The fact that this group is of Mexican descent and has certain inherent characteristics makes it an *identifiable ethnic group*.

Judge Seals characterized Mexican-Americans as an ethnic *minority* group. Mexican-Americans definitely are a numerical minority in the United States, representing about 2.5 percent of the population.[6] In Texas, this ethnic group comprises 14.5 percent of the population.[7] In Corpus Christi,

---

1. Civil Action No. 68-C-95 (S.D. Tex., June 4, 1970) [hereinafter cited as *Cisneros*], noted, 49 TEX. L. REV. 337 (1971).
2. *Id.* at 9-10.
3. 347 U.S. 483 (1954). *See also* Swann v. Charlotte-Mecklenburg Bd. of Educ., 91 S.Ct. 1267 (1971).
4. *Cisneros* at 13-14.
5. *Id.* at 20-21.
6. *See* THE NEW YORK TIMES ENCYCLOPEDIC ALMANAC 35, 288 (2d ed. 1970).
7. *Id.* at 245, 288.

where *Cisneros* arose, Mexican-Americans comprise 35.7 percent of the population.[8] However, Judge Seals does not rely on mere numbers to determine whether an ethnic group is a minority group. His principal test is whether the group is discriminated against in the schools through segregation, a discrimination facilitated by the group's economic and political impotence.[9] Thus, Mexican-Americans are an *identifiable ethnic minority group*, even in areas where they are the majority since many are economically and politically disadvantaged.

The court's holding, that Mexican-Americans are entitled to the protection given Negroes by *Brown*, is significant because it introduces a new group into the desegregation process. Federal courts should consider Mexican-American students in determining whether a unitary school system is in operation. More importantly, the court's recognition of Mexican-Americans should serve as a restraint on school districts which utilize the Mexican-American's classification of white by integrating them with Negroes to satisfy court desegregation orders. Further discussion about the mixing of Negroes and Mexican-Americans in minority schools is presented in parts IV and VI-B.

This comment seeks to analyze whether Mexican-Americans should be considered an identifiable ethnic minority group for purposes of public school desegregation. After providing a brief history of the American of Mexican descent, the writer will discuss various civil rights problems encountered by Mexican-Americans and, more importantly the evolution of the desegregation doctrine as it pertains to Mexican-Americans.

II. HISTORICAL BACKGROUND OF THE MEXICAN-AMERICAN

Mexican-Americans are the second largest minority group in the United States.[10] In the Southwest (an area including Arizona, California, Colorado, New Mexico, and Texas), where 87 percent of this minority group resides, Mexican-Americans are the largest minority group.[11]

In the 1500's the Spanish began to settle this area, many years before the English established the first settlement at Jamestown in 1607. This early Spanish influence is evidenced in the number of States, cities, and rivers with Spanish names.[12] These Southwestern States came under Mexican rule after Mexico won her independence from Spain in 1821.

However, the vast Mexican nation encountered internal problems when

---

8. *Cisneros* at 10 n.34.
9. *Id.* at 8 n.28.
10. L. GREBLER, J. MOORE, & R. GUZMAN, THE MEXICAN-AMERICAN PEOPLE 14-15 (1970) [hereinafter cited as GREBLER, MOORE, & GUZMAN]. The authors cite the Mexican-American population in 1960 as 3.8 million and estimate the 1970 count to be 5.6 million.
11. *Id.* at 15.
12. *E.g.*, States: Arizona, California, Colorado, Texas; cities: San Antonio, Del Rio, San Francisco, Santa Fe, Pueblo; rivers: Rio Grande, Brazos, Guadalupe.

Texas seceded in 1836 and again when the United States Congress voted in 1845 to allow Texas to enter the Union. Mexico had warned that admission into the Union would be equivalent to an act of war. In spite of Mexico's relative military weakness compared to the United States, the two countries engaged in armed conflict. The result was the defeat of Mexico and the signing of the Treaty of Guadalupe Hidalgo on February 2, 1848.[13] By the terms of the treaty, Mexico acknowledged the annexation of Texas and ceded the rest of the Southwest to the United States. In addition, the treaty guaranteed civil and property rights to those who became American citizens.[14]

Approximately 75,000 Mexicans decided to remain and receive American citizenship.[15] These Mexican-Americans were later supplemented by vast emigrations from Mexico. The first influx, precipitated by the social revolution in Mexico, began in 1910. A second wave of immigrants resulted in the increase of the Mexican-American population by nearly one million from 1910 to 1930. During and after World War II, attracted by the agricultural labor market, a third group of Mexicans came to the United States.[16] In addition, about 3500 Mexicans immigrate to this country each month, thus continuing the steady growth of the Mexican-American population.[17]

With the increase of the Mexican-American population, there was an increase in the prejudice of the predominant Anglo society. For example, Mexican-Americans, as well as Mexican nationals, were deported during the Great Depression to reduce the welfare rolls.[18] This prejudice resulted in the "largest mass trial for murder ever in the United States."[19] Such prejudice also led to the so-called "zoot suit" riots of 1943 in Los Angeles. The riots began when city police refused to intervene while over a hundred sailors roamed the streets for nearly a week beating and stripping Mexican-American youths in retaliation for the beating some sailors had received earlier from a gang of "zoot suiters."[20]

As a result of these and similar discriminatory practices, Mexican-American interest groups began to organize in order to defend *La Raza* (the race), as Mexican-Americans call themselves. In 1927 the League of United Latin American Citizens (LULAC) was formed in Texas. Shortly

---

13.   9 Stat. 922 (1848).
14.   *Id.* at 929-30, art. VIII.
15.   C. McWilliams, North From Mexico 52 (1948) [hereinafter cited as McWilliams].
16.   L. F. Hernandez, A Forgotten American 8 (1969).
17.   U.S. Bureau of the Census, We the Mexican Americans 2 (1970).
18.   McWilliams 193.
19.   R. Daniels & H.H.L. Kitano, American Racism 74 (1970). The authors refer to People v. Zammora, 66 Cal. App. 2d 166, 152 P.2d 180 (1944), in which 17 Mexican-American youths were indicted and convicted for murder, without any tangible evidence, in the death of another youth who was killed in a gang fight. The California appellate court reversed and remanded all the convictions.
20.   *Id.* at 77. The name "zoot suiters" was derived from the gaudy clothing worn by some of the *Chicano* youths.

thereafter LULAC helped fund the first challenge against the segregation of Mexican-American school children.[21] In 1948, a Mexican-American war veteran, Dr. Hector P. Garcia, founded the American GI Forum for the purpose of protecting Mexican-American veterans from discriminatory practices which they "were being subjected to in the areas of education, employment, medical attention and housing . . . ."[22] The American GI Forum, which now has many chapters throughout the United States, has also helped support civil rights litigation.

In spite of the successes which LULAC and the GI Forum have accomplished, many Mexican-American youths have not been satisfied. Unlike their elders, Mexican-American youth activists, or *Chicanos* (the term is a derivation of *mejicano,* which is the Spanish term for Mexican), as they like to be called, refuse to be satisfied with justice on the installment plan, that is, gradual social progress. Instead, this new breed demands justice and equality for *La Raza* now. If there has been any validity to the sociologists' *mañana* stereotype, which infers that Mexican-Americans will always wait until tomorrow to do what could be done today, today's *Chicano* readily dispels that idea.

In order to promote the advancement of Mexican-Americans, *Chicanos* throughout the Southwest have organized in recent years, mainly on college campuses.[23] For example, the Mexican-American Youth Organization (MAYO), which was founded in 1967 by San Antonio college students,[24] is currently organized at the two largest universities in Texas, The University of Texas and the University of Houston. In addition, MAYO chapters are active in the *barrios* (neighborhoods where the Mexican-American population is predominant).

The Mexican-American Legal Defense and Educational Fund (MALDEF), a *Chicano* (the term is not limited in its application to the youth activists) civil rights organization which was created in 1968,[25] is even more effective than these political groups. The previous lack of a legal defense organization perhaps best explains why Mexican-Americans have not been too active in civil rights litigation. In fact, the Supreme Court of the United States has decided a *Chicano* civil rights issue on only one

21. *See* Independent School Dist. v. Salvatierra, 33 S.W.2d 790 (Tex. Civ. App. —San Antonio 1930), *cert. denied,* 284 U.S. 580 (1931).
22. AMERICAN GI FORUM, 21st ANNUAL CONVENTION, July 4, 1969. The incident leading to the creation of the GI Forum was the refusal in 1948 of Anglo citizens in Three Rivers, Texas to have a deceased Mexican-American veteran buried in the city's cemetery. The soldier, Felix Longoria, was buried with honors in Arlington National Cemetery. San Angelo Standard-Times, July 6, 1969, § 1, at 1, col. 1.
23. Judge Seals listed MAYO, LULAC, and the GI Forum as products of discriminatory practices. *Cisneros* 12.
24. Steiner, Chicano Power, THE NEW REPUBLIC, June 20, 1970, at 17.
25. The Texas Observer, April 11, 1969, at 6, col. 1. MALDEF is operating under an 8-year, $2.2 million Ford Foundation grant.

occasion.[26] However, legal activities of MALDEF prompted a newspaper to note that "[m]ore legal attention has been focused on the problems of Texas' nearly two million Mexican-Americans during the past 11 months than during the entire history of *La Raza* in Texas."[27] This statement is applicable as well to the rest of the Southwest.[28]

III.   THE MEXICAN-AMERICAN—AN IDENTIFIABLE ETHNIC MINORITY GROUP

A.   *The Mexican-American*

Mexican-Americans, as a group, have been widely discriminated against. As a result, many Mexican-Americans have easily been able to identify with *La Raza*. On the other hand, there are many Mexican-Americans who have never personally experienced an act of discrimination and thus, find it difficult to empathize with the civil rights movement. Many of these adamantly assert that they are Americans and fail to identify with Mexican-Americans. In many cases, a light-skinned complexion has helped make life more "American" for them.[29] In addition, there are some who feel a stigma or a handicap if the term "Mexican" is used to describe them and who prefer a euphemistic label like Latin American or Spanish-speaking American. Finally, there is a group who, because of their ancestry of early Spanish colonists, call themselves Spanish-Americans and Hispanos. Nevertheless, in spite of what Spanish-surnamed Americans of the Southwest prefer to be called, the name Mexican-American is perhaps the best designation which can be applied objectively. Regardless of what they call themselves, one fact is clear—either they or their ancestors, including the Spanish colonists, came "north from Mexico."[30]

B.   *Discrimination in Areas Besides Education*

1.   *Employment*

Mexican-Americans, like Negroes, have encountered discriminatory practices by employers in hiring and promotion. What is worse, is that much of this discrimination is subtle. Employers often use the "high school

---

26. *See* Hernandez v. Texas, 347 U.S. 475 (1954). The Supreme Court found that Mexican-Americans had been discriminated against in the selection of jurors in Jackson County, Texas. *See also* Tijerina v. Henry, 48 F.R.D. 274 (D.N.M.), *appeal dismissed*, 90 S. Ct. 1718 (1969) (Douglas, J., dissenting).
27.   The Texas Observer, April 11, 1969, at 6, col. 1.
28.   As of December 1969, MALDEF had filed civil rights suits against discrimination in hiring and promotion, the enforcement of the laws, voting rights, public accommodations, and education. See MALDEF Docket Report (Dec. 1969) [hereinafter cited as Docket Report).
29.   One author contends that the "brown skin color" of most Mexican-Americans makes them susceptible to Anglo prejudice against darker-skinned persons. *See* Forbes, *Race and Color in Mexican-American Problems*, 16 J. HUMAN REL. 55 (1968).
30.   McWILLIAMS.

diploma" or "we'll call you" tactics since they can no longer discriminate openly with impunity. As a result, it is often difficult to maintain a civil rights action. Since the Civil Rights Act of 1964[31] was passed, at least one Mexican-American has been successful, and many more cases have been filed. The one successful claim is the agreement reached in the case of *Urquidez v. General Telephone Co.*[32] The suit, a class action, resulted from the fact that Urquidez applied for employment, passed the tests, and had more job-related experience and education than several Anglo applicants who were subsequently hired. The settlement agreement acknowledged that Urquidez had a prima facie case of discrimination, awarded him $2,000, and provided that General Telephone would take definite steps to remedy past discriminatory practices.

In spite of the unusually small number of cases in the field of employment discrimination, the statistics and evidence indicate that discriminatory practices are very prevalent. For example, considering the Southwest alone, the unemployment rate among Mexican-Americans is double the Anglo rate —a statistic which understates the severity of the situation since farm workers are not included in unemployment statistics.[33] In addition, in 1960, 79 percent of all Mexican-American workers held unskilled and semi-skilled jobs.[34]

While some of the employment problems facing Mexican-Americans are attributable to their relatively low educational attainment,[35] there are indications of discrimination to offset much of that argument. For instance, in comparing the income of Mexican-Americans and Anglos who have completed the same number of school years, the income of Mexican-Americans is only 60 to 80 percent of the Anglo income.[36] Since passage of the Civil Rights Act of 1964, employers have resorted to more subtle practices, such as promoting Anglos before Mexican-Americans, even if the former are less educated and less skilled. Many employers, when questioned about such practices, rationalize that Anglo workers will not take orders from Mexican-Americans.[37] Consequently, the Mexican-American is denied the equal

---

31. 42 U.S.C. § 2000e-2 (1964).
32. Civil Action No. 7680 (D.N.M., Sept. 24, 1969), discussed in 1 MALDEF Newsletter 1, Nov., 1969.
33. H. ROWAN, THE MEXICAN AMERICAN 38, (Paper prepared for U.S. Comm'n on Civil Rights 1968).
34. *Id.* at 39.
35. The median school years completed by Mexican-Americans is 8.1, much lower than the 12.0 years achieved by Anglo students. GREBLER, MOORE, & GUZMAN 143.
36. W. FOGEL, MEXICAN AMERICANS IN SOUTHWEST LABOR MARKETS 191 (U.C.L.A. Mexican-American Study Project: Advance Report No. 10, 1967).
37. H. ROWAN, THE MEXICAN AMERICAN 45, U.S. Comm'n on Civil Rights (1968).

protection of the laws as guaranteed him by the Constitution of the United States[38] and by the Civil Rights Act of 1964.

As previously stated, many employment discrimination cases have been instituted, mostly by MALDEF-assisted plaintiffs. Two of these cases were delayed by motions to dismiss which have been denied,[39] and the cases are set for a hearing on the merits. MALDEF lists 15 additional pending cases.[40] Among the grounds urged for relief are: (1) refusal to hire because of national origin; (2) failure to promote over less-educated and less-experienced Anglos; (3) hiring Mexican-Americans only for low-paying positions; (4) paying different wages to Mexican-Americans and Anglos; and (5) underemployment while Anglos with less seniority are allowed more work time.[41]

One pending case, *Quiroz v. James H. Matthews & Co.*,[42] challenges some of the subtle, covert practices employers commonly use to deny Mexican-Americans equal opportunity. Quiroz alleges violation of his equal employment rights under Title VII of the Civil Rights Act of 1964.[43] The plaintiff, who had 16 years' experience, was replaced by an Anglo who had less job-related experience. Furthermore, Quiroz contends that the defendant pays Mexican-American employees less than fellow Anglo employees receive for doing the same kind of work.[44]

2. Spanish and Mexican Land Grants

Mexican-Americans have also suffered unjustly in the area of Spanish and Mexican land grants, an issue encountered generally in New Mexico and Colorado. The issue is whether Mexican-American land grantees or the heirs of these grantees, who by some means were defrauded of their land by various state officials, are entitled to compensation.

This issue was raised in *Vigil v. United States*,[45] a class action filed for those descendants of Spanish-surname Americans who lived in areas ceded

---

38. U.S. Const. amend. XIV provides: "No State shall . . . deny to any person within its jurisdiction the equal protection of the laws." The Justice Department has sued an Arizona copper company for job opportunity discrimination against Mexican-Americans and Indians. Arizona Daily Star, Mar. 4, 1971, § B, at 1, col. 6.

39. *See* Vigil v. American Tel. & Tel. Co., 305 F. Supp. 44 (D. Colo. 1969); Pena v. Hunt Tool Co., 296 F. Supp. 1003 (S.D. Tex. 1968). In another employment case, Moreno v. Henckel, 431 F.2d 1299 (5th Cir. 1970), the plaintiff was fired for circulating a petition of grievances concerning dissatisfaction with the rate of promotion for Mexican-American workers. The case was remanded since the district court incorrectly dismissed the case.

40. *See generally* Docket Report, Tit. 2, Job Discrimination. The Justice Department has sued an Arizona firm and some unions for job opportunity discrimination against Mexican-Americans and Indians. Arizona Daily Star, Mar. 4, 1971, § B, at 1, col. 6.

41. *Id.*

42. Civil Action No. 69H-1082 (S.D. Tex., filed Nov. 4, 1969).

43. 42 U.S.C. § 2000e-2 (1964) makes it unlawful for an employer to discriminate because of race, color, religion, sex, or national origin.

44. Docket Report, Tit. 2, at 7.

45. 293 F. Supp. 1176 (D. Colo. 1968).

to the United States by Mexico in 1848. The plaintiffs sought $1 million actual damages and $1 million punitive damages for each individual who was part of the class. However, the court held that the vague allegations in the complaint failed to satisfy the Federal Tort Claims Act and that there was no claim against the United States under the Civil Rights Acts for deprivation of property.

Although that complaint was vague, one *Chicano* writer has been more specific.[46] He claims Mexican-Americans have lost nearly four million acres of land.[47] This loss has occurred even though Article VIII of the Treaty of Guadalupe Hidalgo provides:

> The present owners, the heirs of these, and all Mexicans who may hereafter acquire said property by contract, shall enjoy with respect to it guaranties equally ample as if the same belonged to citizens of the United States.[48]

The writer argues that the shift from the Mexican legal system, where grant lands were immune from taxation and titles were unregistered, to the Anglo legal system of land taxation and title recordation was the major factor in the land losses which Mexican-Americans suffered.[49] Many landowners were divested of title by wealthy Anglo ranchers purchasing deeds at tax sales or by recording a claim to the property before the true owner.[50] Perhaps federal courts will grant relief to these aggrieved heirs of the land grantees when and if the complaints are clarified.

3. Public Accommodations

Mexican-Americans have been excluded from public accommodations. Fortunately the practice has subsided since the 1940's when Mexican-Americans were segregated from restaurants, theaters, and swimming pools.[51] Nevertheless, prejudice and overt acts of discrimination have contributed to making Mexican-Americans an identifiable ethnic minority group.

In 1944 Texas upheld the right of a proprietor to exclude any person for any reason whatsoever, including the fact that the person was of Mexican descent.[52] However, that same year, a federal court in California held that Mexican-Americans *are* entitled to public accommodations such as other citizens enjoy.[53] In spite of this ruling and the Civil Rights Act of 1964, a

---

46. Valdez, *Insurrection in New Mexico*, 1 EL GRITO 14 (Fall, 1967).
47. *Id.* at 19-20.
48. 9 Stat. 922, 929-30 (1848).
49. Valdez, *Insurrection in New Mexico*, 1 EL GRITO 14, 20-21 (Fall, 1967).
50. *See* McWILLIAMS 76-78, *supra* note 15.
51. For actual cases of ethnic discrimination in Texas see A. PERALES, ARE WE GOOD NEIGHBORS? 139-227 (1948) [hereinafter cited as PERALES].
52. Terrell Wells Swimming Pool v. Rodriguez, 182 S.W.2d 824 (Tex. Civ. App.—San Antonio 1944, no writ); *cf.* Lueras v. Town of Lafayette, 100 Colo. 124, 65 P.2d 1431 (1937).
53. Lopez v. Seccombe, 71 F. Supp. 769 (S.D. Cal. 1944).

federal court in 1968 found it necessary to enjoin the exclusion of Mexican-Americans from public swimming pool facilities.[54]

4. Administration of Justice

Mexican-Americans also face serious discrimination in the administration of justice. This discrimination, as well as the personal prejudice of police officers, often leads to physical and psychological injury to Mexican-Americans.[55] However, Mexican-Americans, like other minority groups, have encountered difficulty in getting grand juries to return indictments against police officers who use excessive force and insulting, derogatory language.[56] In one case a Mexican-American woman won a civil damages suit against a police officer.[57] The plaintiff claimed she had suffered physical and mental damages because of being forcefully undressed by two policewomen and two policemen to see if she had any concealed narcotics. Earlier, when the officers had entered the plaintiff's residence without a search warrant, the plaintiff demanded respect for her constitutional rights, but one officer told her to "go back to Mexico."[58]

Besides the treatment received from law enforcement officials,[59] Mexican-Americans are often inadequately represented on juries. Consequently, the juries hearing cases involving Mexican-American defendants are not "impartial"[60] juries since they fail to represent the community. These inequities still occur frequently, even though the United States Supreme Court held in *Hernandez v. Texas*[61] that "[t]he exclusion of otherwise eligible [Mexican-Americans] from jury service solely because of their ancestry or national origin is discrimination prohibited by the Fourteenth Amendment."[62] The Court stated that the absence of a Mexican-American juror for 25 years in a county where this ethnic group comprised 14 percent of the population "bespeaks discrimination, whether or not it was a conscious decision on the part of any individual jury commissioner."[63]

Prior to *Hernandez*, Texas courts refused to recognize the Mexican-American as a separate class—distinct from other whites—for purposes of

---

54. Beltran v. Patterson, Civil Action No. 68-59-W (W.D. Tex. 1968), cited in Brief for MALDEF as Amicus Curiae at 3, Ross v. Eckels, 434 F.2d 1140 (5th Cir. 1970).

55. U.S. COMM'N ON CIVIL RIGHTS, MEXICAN AMERICANS AND THE ADMINISTRATION OF JUSTICE IN THE SOUTHWEST 2-6 (1970) [hereinafter cited as ADMINISTRATION OF JUSTICE].

56. *Id.* at 4 n.15.

57. Lucero v. Donovan, 258 F. Supp. 979 (C.D. Cal. 1966).

58. Lucero v. Donovan, 354 F.2d 16, 18 (9th Cir. 1965). Mrs. Lucero was a native-born citizen of the United States.

59. For an insight into the distrust of the Texas Rangers by South Texas *Chicanos*, see ADMINISTRATION OF JUSTICE 16-17.

60. *See* U.S. CONST. amend. VI.

61. 347 U.S. 475 (1954).

62. *Id.* at 479.

63. *Id.* at 482.

determining whether there was an unconstitutional exclusion from juries.[64] The Texas courts limited the application of the equal protection clause to two classes, whites and Negroes. Since Mexican-Americans were legally considered white, the equal protection clause did not apply.

Nevertheless, this weak argument was overruled by the Supreme Court in *Hernandez* when it held that Mexican-Americans are a separate class, distinct from whites. The Court noted that historically "differences in race and color have defined *easily identifiable* groups which have at times required the aid of the courts in securing equal treatment under the laws."[65] Since *Hernandez*, courts have recognized Mexican-Americans as an identifiable ethnic group, although they have not always found discrimination.[66]

Recently, the Fifth Circuit overturned the 1942 rape conviction of a Mexican-American in El Paso County, Texas, because the juries that indicted and convicted him had excluded persons of his ethnic group.[67] Only 18 of the 600 grand jurors who served from 1936 to 1947 were Mexican-Americans, even though the county population was 15 to 20 percent Mexican-American.[68] The court stated that these figures "cry out 'discrimination' with unmistakable clarity."[69]

Although the discussion of discrimination towards Mexican-Americans dealt only with the issues of employment, land grants, public accommodations, and the administration of justice, this in no way limits the areas in which Mexican-Americans encounter injustices.[70] The issues discussed were selected to justify the holding in *Cisneros,* that Mexican-Americans are an identifiable ethnic minority group entitled to the protection of the 14th amendment in the area of school desegregation in the Southwest.

C. *Non-Judicial Recognition*

The Mexican-American has been recognized as a separate, identifiable group not only by the courts but also by other governmental institutions. For

---

64.   Hernandez v. State, 160 Tex. Crim. 72, 251 S.W.2d 531 (1952); Sanchez v. State, 156 Tex. Crim. 468, 243 S.W.2d 700 (1951); Salazar v. State, 149 Tex. Crim. 260, 193 S.W.2d 211 (1946); Sanchez v. State, 147 Tex. Crim. 436, 181 S.W.2d 87 (1944).
65.   347 U.S. 475, 478 (1954) (emphasis added).
66.   See United States v. Hunt, 265 F. Supp. 178 (W.D. Tex. 1967); Gonzales v. State, 414 S.W.2d 181 (Tex. Crim. App. 1967); Montoya v. People, 345 P.2d 1062 (Colo. 1959).
67.   Muniz v. Beto, 434 F.2d 697 (5th Cir. 1970).
68.   *Id.* at 703.
69.   *Id.* at 702.
70.   *E.g.,* Voting rights: Mexican-American Federation v. Naff, 299 F. Supp. 587 (E.D. Wash. 1969), *rev'd,* 39 U.S.L.W. 3296 (U.S. Jan. 12, 1971) (English literacy requirement upheld by the lower court); Castro v. State, 2 Cal. 3d 223, 466 P.2d 244, 85 Cal. Rptr. 20 (1970) (English literacy requirement held unconstitutional). Housing: Valtierra v. Housing Authority, 313 F. Supp. 1 (N.D. Cal. 1970), rev'd *sub nom.* James v. Valtierra, 91 S.Ct. 1331 (1971). Judicial prejudice: *Judge Gerald S. Chargin Speaks,* 2 EL GRITO 4 (1969). In this juvenile court proceeding, Judge Chargin denounced a *Chicano* youth, who was charged with incest, and the "Mexican people"

instance, the Civil Rights Act of 1964, by use of the term "national origin,"[71] impliedly includes Mexican-Americans and other "national origin" minority groups such as Puerto Ricans. Furthermore, recognizing the problems facing many Mexican-American school children, Congress passed the Bilingual Education Act[72] which seeks to facilitate the learning of English and at the same time allow the Spanish-speaking child to perfect his mother language and regain self-esteem through the encouraged learning of Spanish.[73] In addition, Congress created a cabinet committee whose purpose is to assure that federal programs are reaching Mexican-Americans and all other Spanish-speaking groups.[74] Also, through the creation of the United States Civil Rights Commission in 1957, Congress and the public have become better informed as to the injustices Mexican-Americans endure.[75] Other governmental agencies have researched the living conditions of the Mexican-American.[76] Finally, the Department of Health, Education, and Welfare (HEW) has issued regulations which prohibit the denial of equal educational opportunity on the basis of English language deficiency. The regulations apply to school districts accepting federally assisted programs and having at least 5 percent Mexican-American enrollment.[77]

IV.   THE CHICANO SCHOOL CASES

Since all three branches of government recognize Mexican-Americans as a minority group, the question which must be answered is whether

---

for acting "like an animal" and for being "miserable, lousy, rotten people." Chargin also stated that "[m]aybe Hitler was right" about having to destroy the animals in our society.

71.   42 U.S.C. § 2000(a) (1964).

72.   20 U.S.C. § 880b (Supp. V, 1970).

73.   The Mexican-American student has suffered serious emotional scars because of the "No Spanish" rule, whose violation by speaking Spanish on school grounds often has led to scolding and/or detention after school as punishment. The rule was probably derived from Tex. Laws 1933, ch. 125, § 1, at 325 (repealed 1969), which required all school business, except foreign language classes, to be conducted in English.

74.   42 U.S.C. § 4301 (Supp. V, 1970).

75.   For example, the following reports have been published: U.S. COMM'N ON CIVIL RIGHTS, MEXICAN AMERICAN EDUCATION STUDY, REPORT I: ETHNIC ISOLATION OF MEXICAN AMERICANS IN THE PUBLIC SCHOOLS OF THE SOUTHWEST (1970); U.S. COMM'N ON CIVIL RIGHTS, MEXICAN AMERICANS AND THE ADMINISTRATION OF JUSTICE IN THE SOUTHWEST (1970); H. ROWAN, THE MEXICAN AMERICAN, U.S. Comm'n on Civil Rights (1968); U.S. COMM'N ON CIVIL RIGHTS, HEARING HELD IN SAN ANTONIO, TEXAS, DECEMBER 9-14, 1968 (1968).

76.   U.S. BUREAU OF THE CENSUS, WE THE MEXICAN AMERICANS (1970); F. H. SCHMIDT, SPANISH SURNAMED AMERICAN EMPLOYMENT IN THE SOUTHWEST (1970) (A Study Prepared for the Colorado Civil Rights Comm'n under the auspices of the Equal Employment Opportunity Comm'n).

77.   Pottinger, Memorandum to School Districts with More Than Five Percent National Origin-Minority Group Children, May 25, 1970. Memorandum on file in Univ. of Houston Law Library. See also 35 Fed. Reg. 13442 (1970). The Department of Health, Education, and Welfare suggested to the Houston school district that Mexican-Americans be appointed to the district's biracial committee. Houston Chronicle, Dec. 18, 1970, § 1, at 1, col. 8.

Chicano students have been discriminated against by school districts to such an extent as to warrant their inclusion as a separate ethnic group in the desegregation plans for public schools in the Southwest. In other words, does the history of Mexican-American school children in the predominantly Anglo school systems of the Southwest demand recognition of this educationally disadvantaged group as being separate and distinct from whites?

The practice of maintaining separate schools throughout the Southwest was never sanctioned by any State statute, although in California, a statute allowing separate schools for "Mongolians" and "Indians" was interpreted to include Mexican-Americans in the latter group.[78] Generally, the segregation of Mexican-Americans was enforced by the customs and regulations of school districts throughout the Southwest. Nevertheless, the segregation was de jure since sufficient State action was involved.

The struggle by Mexican-Americans against separate and unequal schools has been lengthy. In 1930 a Texas appellate court held in *Independent School District v. Salvatierra*[79] that school authorities in Del Rio, or anywhere else, have no power to segregate *Chicano* children "merely or solely because they are [Mexican-Americans]."[80] However, the school district successfully argued that the children's language deficiencies warranted their separate schooling, even though the superintendent conceded that "generally the best way to learn a language is to be associated with the people who speak that language."[81] The Attorney General of Texas later supported this holding by justifying education of the linguistically deficient in separate classrooms and even in separate buildings if necessary.[82]

The first federal district court decision in this area was *Mendez v. Westminister School District*[83] in 1946. The court held that the equal protection of the laws pertaining to the public school system in California is not met by providing "separate schools [with] the same technical facilities"[84] for Mexican-American children—words which are strikingly similar to the Supreme Court's holding in *Brown* 8 years later that "[s]eparate educational facilities are inherently unequal."[85] The court observed that "[a] paramount requisite in the American system of public education is social equality. It must be open to all children by unified school association regardless of lineage."[86]

---

78. T. I. EMERSON, 2 POLITICAL AND CIVIL RIGHTS IN THE UNITED STATES 1734 (3d ed. 1967), *citing* NATIONAL ASS'N OF INTERGROUP RELATIONS, *Public School Segregation and Integration in the North*, J. INTERGROUP REL. 1 (1963).
79. 33 S.W.2d 790 (Tex. Civ. App.—San Antonio 1930), *cert. denied*, 284 U.S. 580 (1931).
80. *Id.* at 795.
81. *Id.* at 793.
82. TEX. ATT'Y GEN. OP. No. V-128 (1947), reported in J. C. HINSLEY, TEXAS SCHOOL LAW 1109 (4th ed. 1968).
83. 64 F. Supp. 544 (S.D. Cal. 1946), *aff'd*, 161 F.2d 774 (9th Cir. 1947).
84. *Id.* at 549.
85. Brown v. Board of Educ., 347 U.S. 483, 495 (1954).
86. 64 F. Supp. at 549.

On appeal, the Ninth Circuit affirmed *Mendez,* finding that the school officials had acted "under color of State law" in segregating the Mexican-American students.[87] The appellate court reasoned that since the California segregation statute did not expressly include Mexican-Americans, their segregation denied due process and the equal protection of the laws.[88]

Following the landmark ruling in *Mendez,* a federal district court in Texas, in *Delgado v. Bastrop Independent School District,*[89] held that the segregation practices of the district were "arbitrary and discriminatory and in violation of [the 14th amendment]."[90] In addition, the court's instructions to Texas school districts stipulated that separate classes for those with language deficiencies must be on the same campus with all other students,[91] thereby denying school officials the power to justify completely separate Mexican-American schools by use of the language deficiency argument.

Nevertheless, the *Delgado* requirement did not prevent the creation of evasive schemes in order to maintain segregated school facilities. For example, in Driscoll, Texas, school authorities customarily required a majority of the Mexican-American children to spend 3 years in the first grade before promotion to the second.[92] After the *Delgado* case, Driscoll abandoned the maintenance of separate schools for Anglos and Mexican-Americans. However, the school district exploited the *Salvatierra* doctrine by drawing the line designating who must attend the language deficiency classes on a racial rather than a merit basis.[93] In *Hernandez v. Driscoll Consolidated Independent School District*[94] a Mexican-American child who could not speak Spanish was denied admission to the Anglo section until a lawyer was contacted. The court held that abusing the language deficiency of the Mexican-American children is "unreasonable race discrimination."[95] In a situation similar to *Driscoll,* Judge Seals, who later wrote the *Cisneros* opinion, enjoined the Odem Independent School District from operating and maintaining a separate school solely for Mexican-American children.[96]

After *Brown v. Board of Education*[97] the *Chicano* school cases began to assume a new dimension. Since Mexican-Americans were generally classified as whites, school districts began to integrate Negroes and Mexican-Americans while Anglos were assigned to all-Anglo schools. As a result, two

---

87.   School Dist. v. Mendez, 161 F.2d 774, 779 (9th Cir. 1947), *aff'g* 64 F. Supp. 544 (S.D. Cal. 1946).
88.   *Id.* at 781.
89.   Civil Action No. 388 (W.D. Tex., June 15, 1948) (unreported); *accord,* Gonzales v. Sheely, 96 F. Supp. 1004 (D. Ariz. 1951).
90.   *Id.* at 1.
91.   *Id.* at 2.
92.   *See* Hernandez v. Driscoll Consol. Ind. School Dist., 2 RACE REL. L. REP. 329 (S.D. Tex. 1957).
93.   *Id.* at 331.
94.   2 RACE REL. L. REP. 329 (S.D. Tex. 1957).
95.   *Id.* at 331-32.
96.   Chapa v. Odem Ind. School Dist., Civil Action No. 66-C-92 (S.D. Tex., July 28, 1967) (unreported).
97.   347 U.S. 483 (1954).

educationally disadvantaged minority groups have been prevented from having maximum interaction with students of the predominant Anglo group. For example, in 1955 Negro and Mexican-Americans sued the El Centro School District in California for alleged "ethnic and racial discrimination and segregation by regulation, custom and usage."[98] In a rather narrow reading of *Brown*, the district court stated that *Brown*, which involved constitutional and statutory provisions, did not apply in situations where only customs and regulations were alleged. The court dismissed the complaint, claiming that where no specific regulation was set forth, plaintiffs must seek construction of the regulation in a State court.[99] On appeal, the Ninth Circuit reversed and remanded the case,[100] holding that when the complaint alleged segregation of public school facilities on the basis of race or color, a federal constitutional issue had been raised, requiring the district court to exercise its jurisdiction. Instead of going to trial, the case apparently was settled out of court, but the segregation of Negroes and Mexican-Americans has continued in most of the Southwest.

Whether integrating Negroes and Mexican-Americans produces a unitary school system was the issue raised in *Keyes v. School District Number One*.[101] In *Keyes*, the court questioned the permissibility of adding the number of Negroes and Hispanos (as Mexican-Americans are referred to in Colorado) to reach a single minority category in order to classify the school as a segregated school.[102] Nevertheless, the court stated that "to the extent that Hispanos . . . are isolated in concentrated numbers, a school in which this has occurred is to be regarded as a segregated school, either *de facto* or *de jure*."[103] Failing to find de jure segregation, the court held that where de facto segregated schools exist, they must provide equal educational opportunity, or a constitutional violation may exist.[104] As a result, the *Keyes* court revived the separate-but-equal doctrine[105] as to de facto segregated schools.

While *Keyes* did not answer whether mixing Blacks and *Chicanos* satisfies constitutional requirements, *Cisneros* did, holding that placing Negroes and Mexican-Americans in the same school did not achieve a unitary system.[106] However, *Keyes* involved de facto segregation, whereas *Cisneros* involved de jure segregation in the form of (1) locating schools in

---

98. Romero v. Weakley, 131 F. Supp. 818, 820 (S.D. Cal.), *rev'd*, 226 F.2d 399 (9th Cir. 1955).
99. *Id.* at 831.
100. 226 F.2d 399 (9th Cir. 1955).
101. 313 F. Supp. 61 (D. Colo. 1970). (This opinion deals only with the issue of segregation in the school.)
102. *Id.* at 69.
103. *Id.* On the issue of the desegregation plan, the court expressed that apportionment of the three ethnic groups was desirable but not required. *Id.* at 98.
104. *Id.* at 82-83. For another de facto case involving *Chicanos* and Blacks, see United States v. Lubbock Ind. School Dist., 316 F. Supp. 1310 (N.D. Tex. 1970).
105. *See* Plessy v. Ferguson, 163 U.S. 537 (1896). The separate-but-equal doctrine was repudiated as to de jure school segregation by Brown v. Board of Educ., 347 U.S. 483 (1954).
106. *Cisneros* at 13.

the Negro and Mexican-American neighborhoods; (2) bussing Anglo students to avoid the minority group schools; and (3) assigning Negro and Mexican-American teachers in disproportionate ratios to the segregated schools.[107]

In *Ross v. Eckels*[108] the Fifth Circuit appears to have disregarded the arguments advanced by Mexican-Americans and Negroes that mixing these minorities does not provide the equal educational opportunity of a unitary school system. In *Ross* the court implemented a pairing plan for the elementary schools of Houston, Texas, resulting in merging predominantly Negro schools with predominantly Mexican-American schools. Judge Clark, dissenting, relied on *Cisneros* in stating:

> I say it is a mock justice when we "force" the numbers by pairing disadvantaged Negro students into schools with members of this equally disadvantaged ethnic group [Mexican-Americans].[109]

Ross is an important case. First, *Ross* involves the sixth largest school district in the United States, having approximately 235,000 students.[110] Second, *Ross* involves a Southwestern city which, like Corpus Christi, has a tri-racial rather than a bi-racial student population. This tri-racial situation was recognized by the Houston school board when they voted unanimously to appeal the *Ross* case to the United States Supreme Court.[111]

Another case involving segregation of Mexican-Americans, *Perez v. Sonora Independent School District*,[112] held that the Sonora, Texas schools were operating in a "unitary, nondiscriminatory, fully desegregated school system."[113] MALDEF had offered evidence to show that in 1938 the Sonora school board passed a resolution enrolling Mexican-American children in the "Mexican School."[114] *Perez* is an important case for Mexican-Americans and the desegregation of schools in the Southwest in that it is the first desegregation case in which the Justice Department has intervened on behalf of Mexican-Americans.[115]

---

107. *Id.* at 14-15.
108. 434 F.2d 1140 (5th Cir. 1970).
109. *Id.* at 1150 (dissenting opinion).
110. *Id.* at 1141.
111. Houston Chronicle, Sept. 15, 1970, § 1, at 1, col. 1.
112. Civil Action No. 6-224 (N.D. Tex., Nov. 5, 1970). Sonora, Texas had a "Mexican" elementary school which was 2 percent black and an all-Anglo elementary school.
113. *Id.* at 2.
114. Plaintiff's Motion for a Preliminary Injunction at 4, Perez v. Sonora Ind. School Dist., Civil Action No. 6-224 (N.D. Tex., Nov. 5, 1970).
115. Houston Chronicle, Nov. 6, 1970, § 1, at 9, col. 7. The United States has also objected to the adoption of a desegregation plan in Austin, Texas whereby Blacks and *Chicanos* were integrated to the exclusion of Anglos, thus maintaining ethnically and racially identifiable schools. United States v. Texas Educ. Agency, Civil Action No. A-70-CA-80, (W.D. Tex., filed Aug. 7, 1970), cited in Brief for MALDEF as Amicus Curiae at 14, Ross v. Eckels, 434 F.2d 1140 (5th Cir. 1970).

Since *Salvatierra* in 1930 the Mexican-American desegregation struggle has progressed slowly, considering the injustices which resulted first, from almost total segregation by the regulations of the various school districts, and second, from exploitation of the classification of Mexican-Americans as white. As *Brown* held, it is unconstitutional to segregate Blacks in the public school systems. Similarly, cases from *Mendez* in 1947 to *Perez* in 1970 have held that it is a violation of the equal protection clause of the 14th amendment to maintain by "custom or regulation" segregated schools for Mexican-Americans. Consequently, assigning Negroes and Mexican-Americans to the same schools and excluding Anglos accomplishes an end that is exactly opposite to the goal desired by the educationally disadvantaged, that goal being the social encounters and interactions between the identifiable minority groups and Anglo-Americans. As a result, the desegregation or assignment plans, which school districts in the Southwest formulate in tri-racial situations, should include the three ethnic groups on a more or less proportionate basis. The necessity for this can perhaps be demonstrated by an analogy from criminal law:

1. If it is a crime to commit *A*, and
2. If it is a crime to commit *B*, then
3. One cannot commit *A* and *B* simultaneously and be absolved of the crimes.

The same applies to school districts which continue to segregate Negroes and Mexican-Americans from predominantly Anglo schools on the theory that a unitary school system is achieved by integrating the two minority groups, merely because one is technically classified as white. Actually the public school system remains a dual one with identifiable white schools and identifiable minority schools, thus justifying intervention of courts in situations where either identifiable minority group seeks relief.

Forty-one years have passed since Mexican-Americans first sought an equal educational opportunity by attendance at racially integrated schools. In many cases this goal has not been realized, even though Mexican-Americans have been successful in almost every case since *Mendez*.[116] Consequently, an affirmative answer is required for the question whether the history of the Mexican-American school children in the predominantly Anglo school systems of the Southwest demands recognition of them as an identifiable ethnic minority group.

---

116. One case where Mexican-Americans and Negroes were denied relief is United States v. Lubbock Ind. School Dist., 316 F. Supp. 1310 (N.D. Tex. 1970), where the court found the segregation to be de facto.

V. Factors Leading to the Segregation of
Mexican-American Children

A. *Residential Segregation*

Residential segregation, whether resulting from economic necessity or discriminatory racial covenants, is a substantial factor in the de facto school segregation of Mexican-Americans. The residential segregation of Mexican-Americans ranges from a low of 30 percent in Sacramento, California to a high of 76 percent in Odessa, Texas.[117] The *Chicano* school cases can be compared to the amount of residential segregation in the areas where the cases arose, perhaps establishing a correlation between the residential segregation and allegations of unequal protection in the public school system:

Cases	Areas	Percentage of Mexican-American Residential Segregation[118]
Mendez (1946)	San Bernardino, California	67.9
Delgado (1948)	Austin, Texas	63.3
Gonzalez (1951)	Phoenix, Arizona	57.8
Keyes (1970)	Denver, Colorado	60.0
Cisneros (1970)	Corpus Christi, Texas	72.2
Ross (1970)	Houston, Texas	65.2
Perez (1970)	San Angelo, Texas	65.7

This table reflects a positive correlation between de jure segregated schools and substantial residential segregation. This should be sufficient to shift the burden of proof to the defendant school districts in cases where de facto segregation is alleged.

Furthermore, *Dowell v. School Board*,[119] which holds that a neighborhood school policy is invalid when superimposed on residential segregation which was initiated by State enforcement of racial covenants, should be an aid to the Mexican-American's quest for an equal educational opportunity. There is support for the view that Mexican-Americans have been denied access to homes and apartments in predominantly Anglo areas.[120] These denials are aggravated by the economic reality that when one settles for a home in a residentially segregated neighborhood, the home is usually retained for some time.[121]

---

117. Grebler, Moore, & Guzman 274, *supra* note 10. Zero percent segregation connotes a random scattering throughout the population; 100 percent represents total segregation.
118. *Id.* at 275.
119. 244 F. Supp. 971 (W.D. Okla.), *aff'd sub nom.* Board of Educ. v. Dowell, 375 F.2d 158 (10th Cir. 1965), *cert. denied*, 387 U.S. 931 (1967).
120. Perales 139-46, *supra* note 51.
121. Kaplan, *Segregation Litigation and the Schools—Part II: The General Northern Problem*, 58 Nw. U.L. Rev. 157, 212 (1964).

In 1948 *Shelley v. Kraemer*[122] held that State enforcement of private racial covenants is unconstitutional. As a result, State courts in California[123] and Texas[124] refused to enforce racial convenants which provided that "[n]o person or persons of the Mexican race or other than the Caucasian race shall use or occupy any buildings or any lot."[125] The patterns that developed prior to *Shelley* have not receded. School districts in the Southwest should not be allowed to allege that school segregation is merely de facto if there has been State action in pre-*Shelley* days. A plaintiff should not be required to prove any specific act of residential discrimination where a pattern of segregation appears. Requirements of actual proof allow unjustifiable delay in the immediate transformation to unitary school systems, an issue the Supreme Court considers to be of "paramount importance."[126]

B. *Ability Grouping*

Like residential segregation, ability grouping (grouping students according to their talents and aptitudes) often leads to segregated education. However, unlike residential segregation, a factor external to the public school system, ability grouping is practiced within the school system. In schools that are to some extent desegregated, the tests and guides which are used indirectly lead to classes in which many Negroes, Mexican-Americans, or both are grouped into segregated classrooms. The results are by no means attributable to any inherent inadequacy on the part of minority group children. Instead, ability grouping which leads to ethnic and racial segregation can be traced to the nature of the social and environmental conditions which minority group children experience. When their aptitude is measured by a standardized national test, which is geared to represent the average white middle class student, the results are inherently biased against children who are culturally different from whites.[127]

In *Hobson v. Hansen,*[128] Judge Skelly Wright held that the school district's track system, a method of ability grouping, must be abolished because "[i]n practice, if not in concept, it discriminates against the disadvantaged child, particularly the Negro."[129] Judge Wright did not condemn all forms of ability grouping. However, he did question ability grouping

---

122.   334 U.S. 1 (1948).
123.   Matthews v. Andrade, 87 Cal. App. 2d 906, 198 P.2d 66 (1948).
124.   Clifton v. Puente, 218 S.W.2d 272 (Tex. Civ. App.—San Antonio 1948, writ ref'd n.r.e.).
125.   87 Cal. App. 2d 906, 198 P.2d 66 (1948). The language in *Clifton* was similar to that cited here.
126.   396 U.S. 19, 20 (1969). *See generally* Wright, *Public School Desegregation: Legal Remedies for De Facto Segregation,* 16 W. RES. L. REV. 478 (1965).
127.   Hobson v. Hansen, 269 F. Supp. 401, 484-85 (D.D.C. 1967), *appeal dismissed,* 393 U.S. 801 (1968), *aff'd sub nom., Smuck v. Hobson,* 408 F.2d 175 (D.C. Cir. 1969).
128.   *Id.*
129.   *Id.* at 515; *accord,* Dove v. Parham, 282 F.2d 256, 261 (8th Cir. 1960).

when it unreasonably leads to or maintains continuous racial or socio-economic segregation. In cases of such segregation, the effect is unreasonable and discriminatory because it fails to accomplish its aim—the grouping of pupils according to their capacities to learn. Because minority group children have had an educationally disadvantaged experience does not mean they must be permanently restricted to low achievement.

Hobson may contribute much to the fall of the track systems employed in the Southwest. After all, when tests are given which result in highly disproportionate numbers of Mexican-Americans in the retarded or below average category, the classification is constitutionally suspect. The Supreme Court's language in *Hernandez* applies by analogy to the discriminatory effects of ability grouping in the Southwest:

"The result [of an overrepresentation of Mexican-Americans in the below average category] bespeaks discrimination, whether or not it was a conscious decision on the part of any individual [school official]."[130]

Besides the language deficiency argument, other devices result in the segregation of Mexican-Americans, even in racially mixed schools. For example, standardized tests fail to judge accurately the Mexican-American's innate capacity to learn. The national tests may ask the *Chicano* child to match a picture with a word that is foreign to him but may be quite common to the middle class white child, who may have encountered its use within his environment. One must realize that these tests are geared to measure the average middle class white American. Consequently, *Chicano* children continue to score very low and to be placed in the lower intelligence sections, from which escape is practically impossible.[131]

An even more damaging practice is common in California. Mexican-American children, many of whom come from homes where Spanish is spoken daily, are given tests in English to determine their grouping level. Consequently, the language obstacle hinders the Spanish-speaking child and contributes to his lower score. As a result, many children score low enough to be classified as "Educable Mentally Retarded" (EMR). Once a child is placed in a special education class, his chance of escaping is minimal. In the San Diego, California school district, Mexican-Americans have challenged the unfair testing schemes which are employed and which result in disproportionate numbers of *Chicanos* in the EMR classes.[132]

In order to realize how examinations such as these deny equal protection to the Mexican-American student, one must perceive the discrepancy which

---

130. Hernandez v. Texas, 347 U.S. 475, 482 (1954).
131. A suit has been filed in Texas against a district alleging segregation resulting both from design and from a rigid system of ability grouping. Zamora v. New Braunfels Ind. School Dist., Civil Action No. 68-205-SA (W.D. Tex., filed Aug. 28, 1968), *cited in* Docket Report, Tit. 3, Education, at 1.
132. Covarrubias v. San Diego Unified School Dist., Civil Action No. 70-394-T (S.D. Cal., filed Dec. 1, 1970).

results when the *Chicano* child is tested under varying conditions. Using the Wechsler Intelligence Scale for Children, 44 scored below 80 when tested in English. But when the test was administered to the same group in Spanish, only 20 scored below 80.[133] Consequently, when applied to children with a limited background in English, these tests are inadequate since they are unable to measure a child's capacity to learn and thus result in harmful discrimination to the Mexican-American child in the public schools of the Southwest.

VI.   MEXICAN-AMERICAN DESEGREGATION—THE FUTURE

A.   *The Southwest Generally*

Overall, there are many areas of the Southwest where segregated schools should be challenged as denying the equal protection of the laws. For example, Del Rio, Texas, the scene of the *Salvatierra* case in 1930, although it is a rather small town, has two school districts within the city limits: The Del Rio Independent School District, which is predominantly Anglo, and the San Felipe Independent School District, which is almost entirely Mexican-American.[134] Since the Del Rio schools are much better, the Anglo children from a nearby Air Force base are bussed at State expense to the Del Rio district schools, even though the base is located in the San Felipe district.[135] Although there are two technically separate school districts in Del Rio, they should be treated as one for purposes of school desegregation. The obvious reluctance of the Del Rio district to accept Mexican-Americans is evidenced by the fact that this school district's accreditation was questioned in 1949 for failure to integrate Mexican-American students.[136] This may support a claim of unconstitutional State action. However, assuming the Del Rio public school system is segregated on a de facto basis, the *Keyes*[137] separate-but-equal formula may play a decisive role in the desegregation of these schools. *Keyes* demands that segregated schools offer equal educational opportunity if they are to be constitutionally allowable. However, both physically and academically, the Del Rio district schools are superior. Besides being newer, Del Rio High School (mostly Anglo) offers 75 to 100 courses. On the other hand, San Felipe High School (Mexican-American) offers only 36 courses and cannot afford a vocational program.[138]

San Antonio, Texas, which is nearly 50 percent Mexican-American,

---

133.   M. WEINBERG, DESEGREGATION RESEARCH: AN APPRAISAL 265-66 (2d. ed. 1970).
134.   U.S. COMM'N ON CIVIL RIGHTS, HEARING HELD IN SAN ANTONIO, TEXAS, December 9-14, 1968, at 295-304 (1968).
135.   *Id.* at 304.
136.   *Id.* at 305.
137.   313 F. Supp. 61 (D. Colo. 1970).
138.   2 Civil Rights Digest 16, 20 (1969).

employs a similar public school system. There are 13 school districts in and around the San Antonio area, of which five are predominantly Mexican-American and eight are predominantly Anglo-American.[139] Ninety percent or 82,000 of the Mexican-American students attend school in five predominantly Mexican-American districts. Because of the financial and educational inequities which result from having various independent school districts, residents of a nearly 100 percent Mexican-American school district have sued all the school districts in the San Antonio area.[140] The plaintiffs allege the Texas system of school financing, which allows each school district to collect taxes for use exclusively within that particular school system, violates the constitutional rights of children in the poorer districts to an equal educational opportunity. In a case of this type, *Hobson,* which also held that school boards cannot discriminate on the basis of poverty,[141] may be controlling, since the financing scheme does result, whether intentionally or not, in an unreasonable discrimination against the poor.

Ethnic isolation or concentration, as it exists in the Del Rio and San Antonio, Texas systems, is similar to that found throughout the Southwest, although it is least serious in California and most serious in Texas.[142] It is interesting to note that there is an inverse relationship between the educational level of Mexican-Americans in these two States.[143] In other words, where the ethnic segregation increases, the educational level decreases, and vice versa. This reaffirms the accepted view in desegregation cases that segregated educational facilities fail to offer an equal educational opportunity.[144]

B. Ross v. Eckels—The Houston Situation

As previously mentioned *Ross v. Eckels*[145] is a Fifth Circuit case in which a pairing order was issued for some Houston, Texas elementary schools. The result was the pairing of 27 predominantly Black and *Chicano* schools, whose segregated facilities resulted mostly from the de jure segregation of pre-1954 years and from the de facto segregation which developed as a result of the high rate of residential segregation in Houston. In many areas of the city, Negro neighborhoods are adjacent to Mexican-American *barrios.* Consequently, much of the neighborhood school "integration"

---

139. U.S. COMM'N ON CIVIL RIGHTS, MEXICAN AMERICAN EDUCATION STUDY, REPORT I: ETHNIC ISOLATION OF MEXICAN AMERICANS IN THE PUBLIC SCHOOLS OF THE SOUTHWEST 26 (1970) [hereinafter cited as ETHNIC ISOLATION].

140. Rodriguez v. San Antonio Ind. School Dist., 299 F. Supp. 476 (W.D. Tex. 1969) (issue here limited to whether a three-judge panel should hear the case).

141. 269 F. Supp. at 513.

142. ETHNIC ISOLATION 30.

143. *See* GREBLER, MOORE, & GUZMAN 144, *supra* note 10.

144. A Connecticut Department of Education study shows that children bussed to suburban classrooms from inner-city schools accelerate their reading ability as much as 18 months ahead of their urban counterparts who remain behind. Houston Chronicle, Nov. 8, 1970, § 1, at 2, col. 7.

145. 434 F.2d 1140 (5th Cir. 1970).

which Houston does have is black-brown integration, lacking the white student population necessary in order to make the school system responsive both politically and educationally to the needs of the minority group population of Houston.

In the Southwest more than 50 percent of the Mexican-American students at the elementary school level attend predominantly Mexican-American schools.[146] For this reason, and since the *Ross* pairing order involved only elementary school children, this discussion will be limited to the elementary schools in Houston.

Judge Clark, in his dissenting opinion in *Ross*, denounced the pairing order as "mock justice" because it paired Negroes with another educationally disadvantaged group. An anlysis of the school populations may prove Judge Clark's dissent to be more consistent with the prior development in the desegregation cases involving Blacks and *Chicanos*.[147]

The elementary grade level students in the Houston public schools number approximately 143,400.[148] Of these, 66,612 are Anglo; 53,875 are Negro; and 23,000 are Mexican-American. The respective percentages of each group in relation to the total student population in the elementary schools are 46.5 percent Anglo, 37.5 percent Negro, and 16 percent Mexican-American. Comparing the Anglo with the combined minority groups, Black and *Chicano* students comprise 53.5 percent of the student population. In addition, in 23 of the 170 elementary schools, the Mexican-American student population exceeds 50 percent, thus leading to ethnic imbalance. This does not include the many other schools where the combined minority group population greatly exceeds the 53.5 percent this combined group represents. In these 23 elementary schools, Mexican-Americans account for 74.9 percent of the total enrollment (13,300 out of a total of 17,750). In comparison to the entire Mexican-American school population, the 13,300 students in these ethnically concentrated schools account for 57.8 percent of the total *Chicano* population in elementary schools. As a result, Houston is typical of the elementary school segregation norm in the Southwest: Over 50 percent ethnic isolation.

Of the 27 schools involved in the *Ross* pairing order, only one was predominantly (50 percent or more) Anglo. It appears that the desegregation order excluded any meaningful integration of the Anglo student with the other identifiable groups in Houston. Overall, there were 2,368 Anglo, 6,233 Mexican-American, and 14,942 Negro students involved in the pairing

---

146. ETHNIC ISOLATION 35.
147. *E.g.*, Cisneros v. Corpus Christi Ind. School Dist., Civil Action No. 68-C-95 (S.D. Tex. June 4, 1970); Keyes v. School Dist. Number One, 313 F. Supp. 61 (D. Colo. 1970); Romero v. Weakley, 131 F. Supp. 818 (S.D. Cal.), *rev'd*, 226 F.2d 399 (9th Cir. 1955). These three cases involved segregation of Negroes and Mexican-Americans into minority schools.
148. Houston Chronicle, Oct. 1, 1970, § 1, at 13, col. 1-2. All figures and percentages used in the analysis of the Houston elementary schools were derived from this article.

plan. Consequently, 21,175 of the total 23,543 students, or 89.9 percent, were children of educationally disadvantaged backgrounds. The purpose of the desegregation cases, which is to establish unitary school systems and thereby provide meaningful social and educational encounters between students of all racial backgrounds, is not achieved by the *Ross* pairing order.[149]

VII. CONCLUSION

Throughout the Southwest, the approximately 1.4 million Mexican-American students represent 17 percent of the total enrollment. Thus, *Chicanos* constitute the largest minority student group in this part of the United States.[150] These students have been neglected, both educationally[151] and legally. The low educational levels of Mexican-Americans imply that the school systems have failed to deal with this bilingual, bicultural group. Legally, the past failure of courts to require total disestablishment of dual school systems, such as in Del Rio, Texas after *Salvatierra*, has provided much support to the publicly-elected school boards in their attempt to maintain the segregation of Mexican-Americans.

As a result, Judge Seals' landmark ruling in *Cisneros* is cause for much optimism on the part of the Mexican-American population in the Southwest regarding the educational future of their children. In all respects, the holdings in *Brown* and its progeny apply to Mexican-Americans as well as to any other identifiable minority group.

Cisneros is consistent with prior judicial development. Historically, Congress and the courts have granted Mexican-Americans protection from unreasonable discrimination in housing, employment, public accommodations, voting, the administration of justice, and in the field of equal educational opportunity. This protection has resulted from a recognition that Mexican-Americans are an identifiable ethnic minority group, whether because of physical characteristics, language, predominant religion, distinct culture, or Spanish surname[152] and are entitled to equal protection of the laws in the area of public school desegregation.

Guadalupe Salinas°

---

149.   Ross v. Eckels, 434 F.2d 1140 (5th Cir. 1970) was appealed to the Supreme Court of the United States by the Houston Independent School District because the court pairing order integrated two minority groups. Houston Chronicle, Sept. 15, 1970, § 1, at 1, col. 1. A motion to stay the pairing order was denied by the Supreme Court. Houston Chronicle, March 1, 1971, § 1, at 1, col. 1.
150.   ETHNIC ISOLATION 89.
151.   *See* T. P. CARTER, MEXICAN AMERICANS IN SCHOOL: A HISTORY OF EDUCATIONAL NEGLECT (1970).
152.   Cisneros v. Corpus Christi Ind. School Dist., Civil Action No. 68-C-95, at 10-11 (S.D. Tex. June 4, 1970).

° *Richard S. Garfinkel, Editor*

MEXICAN AMERICAN ORGANIZATIONS AND THE CHANGING POLITICS OF SCHOOL DESEGREGATION IN TEXAS, 1945 TO 1980

Guadalupe SAN MIGUEL, Jr., *University of California, Santa Barbara*

The following documents the efforts Mexican American organizations have made to influence educational policy over time. More specifically, this study provides a history of the campaign to eliminate the segregation of Mexican American children in the Texas public schools and emphasizes the strategies and tactics utilized by several community organizations in their attempts to desegregate the public schools.

Little, if any, emphasis has been placed on the efforts Mexican American organizations have made to influence educational policy over time.[1] This study provides a history of the campaign to eliminate the segregation of Mexican American children in the Texas public schools and a focus on the strategies and tactics utilized by several community organizations in their attempts to desegregate the public schools.

Mexican American organizations have played a significant and increasing role in challenging discriminatory school policies and practices since 1929. Led and inspired by the League of United Latin American Citizens (LULAC)[2] and the American G.I. Forum[3] during the first half century and by special interest groups, principally the Mexican American Legal Defense and Education Fund (MALDEF),[4] begin-

[1] For a useful and insightful account of the legal campaign to desegregate the public schools in Texas see Alcala and Rangel (1972). For a history of the American G.I. Forum's participation in the desegregation campaign see Allsup (1977).

[2] For a general history of these organizations see Tirado (1974). Garza (1951) and Sandoval (1979) provide a comprehensive view of LULAC's organizational history and its activities.

[3] See the American G.I. Forum (1950a) for a brief historical overview of the organization, (hereinafter cited as AGIF).

[4] Orfield (1978:211) argued that by 1978 ". . . MALDEF had the oldest tradition of litigation for Hispanics and represented the largest group."

Social Science Quarterly, Vol. 63, No. 4, December 1982
©1982 by the University of Texas Press   0038-4941/82/040701-15$01.50

ning in the mid-1960s, the challenge to discrimination in education has focused on eliminating segregated schools and on abolishing student assignment and classification policies and practices which have served to maintain or increase segregation. The assignment of Mexican students to separate and inferior education facilities based on national origin and the classification of Mexican students as "linguistically" or "educationally" handicapped for instructional purposes historically have been used to deny Mexican Americans an equal educational opportunity and to "keep them in their place." In their campaign to eradicate school segregation and discriminatory assignment and classification policies and practices, Mexican American organizations, acting as traditional American pressure groups, have pursued a politics of accommodation. The politics of accommodation was a broad strategy aimed at bringing pressure to bear on local and state officials to eliminate educational discrimination and segregation. At no point has there been any attempt to question the basic structure of educational institutions in particular or of social and economic institutions in general. There has also been no effort to replace Anglo public school officials with Mexican Americans, as was the case during the period of educational ferment in the late 1960s among the Chicano activists.

The Campaign to Desegregate the Schools, 1945–68

Although LULAC sought to end the practice of establishing separate and unequal elementary schools for Mexican American children during the 1930s (Sandoval, 1979), it was not until the mid-1940s that these efforts increased significantly. These new efforts were influenced by a California desegregation court case declaring unconstitutional the practice of segregation based on national origin, by the administrative responses of different state agencies to the California court case, and by the emergence in 1948 of the American G.I. Forum, a militant and vocal Mexican American organization comprised of World War II veterans conscious of inequitable treatment at home.

On 2 March 1945, several Mexican Americans challenged the practice of school segregation in the Federal District Court in Los Angeles (*Mendez* v. *Westminster School District*, 1946). They claimed that their children and 5,000 other children of "Mexican and Latin descent" were being denied their constitutional rights by being forced to attend separate "Mexican" schools in the Westminster, Garden Grove, Santa Ana, and El Modeno School Districts of Orange County. Judge Paul J. McCormick ruled in favor of the Mexican American parents on 18 February 1946. Fourteen months later, on 14 April 1947, McCormick's ruling was upheld by the Ninth Circuit Court of Appeals in San Francisco. This case, which brought an end to *de jure* school segregation in California, attracted national attention. During the original court proceedings the American Civil Liberties Union and the National Lawyers Guild had filed *amicus curiae* briefs on the side of the Mexican American parents. By the time the appeal was brought before the Ninth Circuit Court of Appeals in San Francisco a variety of organizations and prominent state officials had sided with the plaintiffs.[5] A *New York Times* correspondent, Lawrence Davis, also wrote that the court case was being "closely watched as a guinea pig case," since the ACLU and NAACP briefs asked the court to strike down the "separate but equal" doctrine itself (Wollenberg, 1974:327).

On 8 April 1957, in response to the California federal court case which found segregation of Mexican origin students to be unconstitutional, the Attorney General of Texas, Price Daniel, issued a legal opinion forbidding the separate placement of Mexican American children in the state's public schools. Segregation based on national origin or racial ancestry was prohibited, Daniel reported, but if "based solely on language deficiencies or other individual needs or aptitudes, separate classes or schools may be maintained for pupils who, after examinations equally applied, come within such classifications (Alcala and Rangel, 1972:335). Gus Garcia, a member of LULAC, sought clarification of the Attorney General's opinion on segregation in the schools. Garcia inquired whether the opinion prohibited all segregation except that based on scientific tests that were equally applied to all students regardless of national origin, and whether it also prohibited provision of inferior facilities to Mexicans. The Attorney General replied in the affirmative, saying, "We meant that the law prohibits discrimination against or segregation of Latin Americans on account of race or descent, and that the law permits no subterfuge to accomplish such discrimination" (Alcala and Rangel, 1972:336). But the legal opinion on segregation was ineffective, for no mechanisms to secure compliance were established and no guidelines for implementing these steps were provided to local school officials. Allsup (1977:32) notes that in October 1947 three University of Texas student groups—the Laredo Club, the Alba Club, and the American Veterans Committee—charged local school districts in Beeville, Sinton, Elgin, Bastrop, and Cotulla with segregation. The local and state school officials dismissed their charges after conducting an investigation, and no further action was taken either by the student groups or the officials. Allsup does not discuss the ethnic composition of the student groups but implies that they were Mexican American in origin.

Consequently, additional legal efforts aimed at the establishment of the unconstitutionality of segregation practices were pursued by LULAC. In January 1948, LULAC filed a desegregation suit aimed at clarifying the constitutional issues involved in the segregation of Mexicans in the public schools. Two months later, the newly formed American G.I. Forum joined LULAC to provide moral support and to elicit finan-

[5] Some of the organizations filing *amicus curiae* briefs on the side of the plaintiffs were the National Association for the Advancement of Colored People (NAACP), the American Jewish Congress, and the Japanese American Citizens League. Robert W. Kennedy, Attorney General of California, also filed an *amicus curiae* brief. See *Westminster School District of Orange et al.* v. *Mendez et al.* (1947) for the list of names.

cial aid from numerous Mexican American communities in south and south central Texas (Allsup, 1977:33). In *Delgado* v. *Bastrop Independent School District* (1948), the parents of school aged Mexican American children charged that school officials in four communities in central Texas were segregating Mexican Americans contrary to the law. As in the case of California, the United States District Court for the Western District of Texas ruled that the placing of students of Mexican ancestry in different buildings was arbitrary, discriminatory, and illegal. Judge Ben H. Rice declared on 15 June 1948 that:

> The regulations, customs, usages and practices of the defendants, Bastrop Independent School District of Bastrop County, et al., and each of them insofar as they or any of them have segregated pupils of Mexican or other Latin American descent in separate classes and schools within the respective school districts heretofore set forth are, and each of them is, arbitrary and discriminatory and in violation of plaintiff's constitutional rights as guaranteed by the fourteenth Amendment to the Constitution of the United States, and are illegal. (*Delgado* v. *Bastrop Independent School District*, 1948:1)

Of additional significance, especially for the continued antisegregation efforts of LULAC and the American G.I. Forum, was the stipulation by the district court that permanently restrained and enjoined the local school boards and the superintendents

> from segregating pupils of Mexican or Latin American descent in separate schools or classes within the respective school districts of said defendants and each of them, and from denying said pupils use of the same facilities and services enjoyed by other children of the same age or grades. . . . (*Delgado* v. *Bastrop Independent School District*, 1948:1)

Exception, however, was granted in cases where children did not know English and were placed in separate classes on the same campus for the first grade only. The placement of non-English-speaking students in separate classes, would be determined on the basis of "scientific and standardized tests, equally given and applied to all pupils" (*Delgado* v. *Bastrop Independent School District*, 1948:1). The sanctioning of segregation of Mexican American children in the first grade "solely for instructional purposes" weakened the potential impact of this federal decision. As Allsup noted in his study of the American G.I. Forum, "even though this decision undermined the rigid segregation of the pre-1948 Texas school system," the Delgado proviso provided a legal loophole "that gave school districts opportunities to circumvent the goals of Gus Garcia, LULAC, and the American G.I. Forum" (Allsup, 1977:34).

In response to the Delgado case, the State Superintendent of Public Instruction and the Texas State Board of Education (1948) issued regulations regarding the illegality of discriminatory school practices such as segregation. The new instructions to the school districts stipulated that segregation as mandated by the state constitution and by judicial and legislative decree only applied to blacks and not to members of any other race. These instructions and regulations also stated the following three major points: (1) segregation practices based on national origin were unconstitutional, arbitrary, and discriminatory; (2) separate classes would be formed in the first grade only for instructional purposes, "for any students who have language difficulties whether the students be of Anglo American, Latin American or any other origin"; and (3) all educational agencies, including the State Department of Education "will take all necessary steps to eliminate any and all segregations that may exist" in these districts.[6]

One year after this desegregation policy was issued, the Mexican American community embarked on a plan to enforce the ruling by seeking the disaccreditation of the Del Rio School District for failure to comply with the new policy. On 7 January 1948, a Mexican American student group at the University of Texas filed a complaint with the State Department of Education against the segregated school district in Del Rio (Alderete, 1979). Within a month, T. M. Trimble, the Assistant State Superintendent of Public Instruction, personally inspected the Del Rio public schools. In his report to the State Superintendent, Trimble recommended that accreditation be withheld. According to the report, "the elementary children of the two races were, by board regulation, not permitted to mix" (Del Rio Decision, 1949). On 12 February 1949, Superintendent L. A. Woods canceled Del Rio's accreditation. The Del Rio school officials requested a reconsideration, but after reviewing their practices, the Superintendent reaffirmed the earlier decision to withdraw accreditation. During the summer, as part of a general reorganization of the public school system in Texas, the state legislature transferred the powers of the State Superintendent of Public Instruction, an elected position, to the newly created office of Commissioner of Education, an appointive position (*Texas, General and Special Laws*, 1949). Woods, an elected official sympathetic to desegregation concerns, was replaced with J. W. Edgar, a professional educator less willing to use the state's power to dismantle segregated schools at the local level (Alcala and Rangel, 1972:340–42). Del Rio school officials then appealed the decision to withdraw accreditation to the State Board of Education. This time they were successful. The Woods decision to withdraw accreditation was reversed. Mexican American efforts to enforce court-ordered desegregation policy in Del Rio were blunted. Undaunted by these state actions, Mexican American leaders in Del Rio resorted to mobilizing the community in that particular city and circumventing specific discriminatory practices aimed at maintaining segregation in education (Alderete, 1979).

Besides increasing public awareness of existing patterns of racial discrimination and segregation in schools and filing legal challenges, the Mexican American organizations, especially the American G.I. Forum, also documented the extent of segregation in Texas during the

---

[6] Subject to legislative mandates and prohibitions the Texas State Board of Education is the principal agency charged with policy formation and planning for the public school system. The State Department of Education is an administrative agency responsible for implementing the policies formulated by the State Board of Education.

late 1940s and early 1950s. For instance, a year after the Delgado case, the Corpus Christi chapter of the American G.I. Forum conducted a survey of 14 school districts adjoining Corpus Christi. The survey (American G.I. Forum, 1950b) indicated that although segregation was still the rule in all of the school districts, it had now assumed new forms. According to the report the response of local school officials to the decree issued by the State Superintendent forbidding discrimination ranged from indifference to helplessness. Of the 14 school districts visited, six did not make an effort or did not even promise to eliminate segregation. One school district promised to do away with separate educational facilities for Mexican Americans and Anglos but at a later date. Another one stated that segregation was too far advanced to do anything about it. The rest of the school districts used various evasive schemes to maintain segregated facilities. These included the following: (1) three districts resorted to segregating Mexican American children by allowing Anglo but not Mexican American children the option of choosing the school they wished to attend, (2) one district provided token transfer of Mexican origin children to the Anglo schools whenever there were any vacancies available, (3) one district had established separate classes for Mexican Americans within the Anglo school, and (4) one district had segregation based on the "language handicap" of the non-English-speaking children. The American G.I. Forum charged that through the development of evasive schemes local school districts in South Texas were circumventing the decisions of the court and the antisegregation decree of the State Superintendent of the Public Instruction. As the Mexican American educational survey stated:

> It is the consensus of opinion of the Latin leaders and myself to conclude that the school board officials are purposely and stubbornly trying to get around the law by many rules, actions, etc., which are not only unconstitutional but also done on purpose to deprive the Latin American children of their God given right of the advantages to which they are entitled to under our great liberal constitution. (American G.I. Forum, 1950b:1)

The leader of the Corpus Christi chapter of the American G.I. Forum, Dr. Hector P. Garcia, continued his attacks on segregation in the months to follow. In a sworn affidavit dated 13 April 1950, Dr. Garcia (1950) alleged that segregation existed in 10 South Texas cities which he had personally surveyed. The affidavit plus a letter listing 12 other school districts in South Texas found to be segregated was sent to the Commissioner of Education.

These investigations, however, only exposed the inherent weakness of the existing regulations and instructions regarding segregation. Hence, both LULAC and the American G.I. Forum moved to strengthen the policy of desegregation. On 8 May 1950, Gus Garcia of the American G.I. Forum and George I. Sanchez of LULAC appeared before the State Board of Education and discussed the continued existence of segregation despite the *Delgado* case. They recommended that a state policy of desegregation be declared and that the appropriate mechanisms be established to ensure the implementation of that policy (Texas State Board of Education, 1950a:3). In response to Garcia's and Sanchez's presentations, the State Board of Education issued a "Statement of Policy Pertaining to Segregation of Latin American Children." This policy recognized the illegality of segregation, but it asserted the right of local districts to handle the complaints and grievances of local citizens alleging discriminatory treatment. "Consistent with this board's belief in local self government to the fullest extent possible," the policy statement read,

> this board deems it proper, in cases where it has alleged there exists a practice of segregating Latin American children from Anglo American children that the local boards of school trustees be given the opportunity to eliminate such segregation prior to the bringing of such cases to the Commissioner of Education where such matters would be handled only on the basis of appeal. (Texas State Board of Education, 1950b)

The State Board of Education's desegregation policy led to the creation of an elaborate bureaucratic redress mechanism whereby Mexican Americans could voice their complaints to their local schools. If these local school officials failed to eliminate segregation, the Mexican American community could appeal to the State Department of Education, which would then investigate the charges and issue an opinion. The entire process, which was challenged by Mexican Americans in 1952, was tedious, time-consuming, extremely bureaucratic, and apparently intended to impede efforts to eliminate school segregation of Mexican American children.[7] Between 1950 and 1957 nine local school districts were brought up before the Commissioner of Education for special hearings (Alcala and Rangel, 1972; Allsup, 1977), although hundreds of school districts throughout the state were segregating Mexican American students (American G.I. Forum, 1957). Of the handful of cases heard by the Commissioner of Education little was done to eliminate the assignment of Mexican American children to separate schools or classes. In fact, evidence indicates that the state's actions in two particular cases actually had the effect of contributing to rather than eliminating segregation based on national origin (Alcala and Rangel, 1972).

While willing to abide by the State Board's administrative remedies, the Mexican American organizations did not hesitate on taking recalcitrant school districts to court, although they preferred not to. "Reluctantly," said two Mexican American lawyers,

---

[7] American G.I. Forum (1952:3) states that LULAC and the AGIF asked the Commissioner of Education, J. W. Edgar, to revise the procedure in appealing school segregation cases to his office. They sought to eliminate appeals to the local school officials "on the grounds that it is like asking a jury to reconsider the case of a man it has already found guilty." Allsup (1977:38) also argues that the intent of the state official's actions "was to impede the attempts of the American G.I. Forum and other organizations to eliminate segregation."

we have been compelled to resort to litigation in our federal courts. .... We have waited a long time to file these lawsuits, we do so with a heavy heart. But we have no recourse except to appeal to the public conscience of our Anglo American friends and to the justice of our federal judiciary. (Garcia and Lopez, 1955:1)

During the late 1950s, approximately 15 cases of discrimination in public schools were filed. In all cases favorable decisions were received (American G.I. Forum, 1957). But the court's finding of discrimination based on national origin grounds were circumvented by the formulation and implementation of creative discriminatory practices by the local school districts. The mid and late 1950s can probably be called the era of subterfuges since it was during this period that a multitude of evasive practices, e.g., "freedom-of-choice" plans, selected student transfer and transportation plans, classification systems based on language or scholastic ability, and others, were utilized by local school districts to maintain segregated schools (Alcala and Rangel, 1972). Although there is evidence indicating that some small school districts did eliminate separate schools for Mexican Americans, the LULAC and the American G.I. Forum leaders perceived further litigation after 1957 to be futile since "there were so many subterfuges available to bar effective relief (Alcala and Rangel, 1972:345). No further desegregation litigation was initiated by LULAC or the American G.I. Forum until political and economic circumstances changed in the late 1960s.

Results were disheartening after the first set of desegregation cases were won during the 1940s and 1950s. As late as 1968, a nationwide survey on the education of Mexican Americans in the southwest reported that while ethnic isolation of Mexican Americans in general was high, it was most pronounced in Texas. Approximately 40 percent of the Mexican American school age population was attending schools which were 80 percent or more Mexican American (U.S. Commission on Civil Rights, 1970). Segregation thus continued to be a way of life for many Mexican American students in Texas. Promises were made to end segregation, but little was actually done. In fact, local school officials managed to expand segregation to the secondary level after the late 1940s. The creation of junior and senior high schools attended primarily by Mexican American students in different parts of the state during the 1950s and 1960s testifies to the expansion of the segregated public school system (San Miguel, 1978:82–6).

The New Politics of Desegregation in the Contemporary Era, 1969–80

During the 1960s and 1970s several important developments occurred which changed the character of the campaign to desegregate the schools in Texas. Of utmost importance during this period were the participation of a variety of interest groups in the desegregation campaign, the ascendancy of the Mexican American Legal Defense and Education Fund (MALDEF) as the most important of these new actors, and the declining influence of LULAC and the American G.I. Forum in the desegregation issue. As a result of the participation of new groups in the desegregation process a successful shift in legal strategy was made, and the trend toward greater dependence on litigation for affecting educational policy increased. By the end of the 1970s a diminishing interest in desegregation and growing interest in other issues, especially bilingual education, was apparent.

Within this brief period of approximately three years between 1967 and 1970, LULAC and the American G.I. Forum appeared to have lost control over the campaign to desegregate the schools. As late as 1967 LULAC and the American G.I. Forum, in consultation with community groups, were the two major groups determining the nature and character of the desegregation campaign. By 1970, these two organizations were conspicuously absent from desegregation cases. Of the approximately 15 desegregation cases filed during the 1950–60 period all of them were filed by LULAC or the American G.I. Forum (American G.I. Forum, 1957; San Miguel, 1979). In the period from 1969 to 1971, LULAC and the American G.I. Forum were not the principal initiators of the approximately 13 new desegregation cases filed in Texas.[8] Although both groups continued to be involved in the education of the Mexican American, they were replaced by other specialized interest groups which had emerged as a result of the heightened civil rights activities of the racial and cultural groups, the active participation of the federal government in civil rights activities, and the funding for community organizations by both private and governmental agencies (Orfield, 1978). New groups such as the American Steel Workers Union, the Justice Department, the Department of Health, Education, and Welfare, the Mexican American Legal Defense and Education Fund, and others took the initiative in filing desegregation cases, in determining the nature of the legal arguments to be used, in deciding the conditions under which a settlement would or would not be reached, and in deciding whether or not to appeal an unfavorable decision to a higher court. In essence, these new interest groups, of which MALDEF was the largest, were now determining the direction of the campaign to desegregate the schools (Orfield, 1978:211). MALDEF as well as all the other interest groups continued the desegregation efforts begun by LULAC and the American G.I. Forum, but their approach to the desegregation campaign differed from the "older" Mexican American organizations. Whereas LULAC and the American G.I. Forum attempted to influence educational policy directly by either persuading or pressuring school officials into eliminating discriminatory policies and practices,

[8] The cities in which desegregation suits were filed included New Braunfels (1968), San Antonio (1969), Corpus Christi (1970), Lubbock (1970), Austin (1970), Midland (1970), Sonora (1970), San Diego (1970), Uvalde (1970), Dallas (1971), El Paso (1971), Del Rio (1971), and Bryan (1971). This list might be incomplete, but efforts are under way to verify its completeness. Taken from San Miguel (1979).

MALDEF and others sought to influence educational policy indirectly. For MALDEF and the other interest groups, litigation was the primary instrument to affect educational policy. For LULAC and the American G.I. Forum, litigation was to be utilized once all other remedies—administrative, political, and personal—had failed.

The new interest groups, wanting to take advantage of the legal principals developed in the *Brown* findings for desegregating the southern schools (*Brown* v. *Board of Education*, 1954), changed the legal strategy that had been used by LULAC and the American G.I. Forum. Until 1968 Mexican American desegregation efforts had developed independent of the *Brown* findings. Black desegregation cases argued that segregation on a constitutional or statutory basis was inherently unequal, and contrary to the equal protection clause of the Fourteenth Amendment. But Mexican American desegregation cases, taking advantage of the Texas Constitution, which provided for segregation only of "colored children," and of the *Plessy* v. *Ferguson* (1896) decision which sanctioned the social separation of blacks from whites, sought to have Mexican Americans declared to be part of the "white" race. Neither the Texas Constitution, legislative law, nor any other public document formally stipulated that members of the same race could or should be segregated. Mexican Americans thus sought acceptance of their own group as Caucasian or "other white" in order to prove that "absent a statute allowing segregation of Chicanos, any attempt by local officials to do so exceeded their powers (Alcala and Rangel, 1972:334). During the late 1960s this "other white" legal strategy was replaced by the equal protection argument used in black desegregation cases. Several school districts had begun to use the legal arguments in the "other white" strategy to circumvent the desegregation of the schools. In some districts, e.g., Houston, the court treated Mexican Americans as part of the white race in its desegregation plan.[9] This allowed the Houston school officials to desegregate blacks with Mexican Americans while leaving the all-Anglo schools intact (*Ross* v. *Eckels*, 1970). Alcala and Rangel, in their report on segregation in Texas, also state that some school districts, including Austin, attempted to disprove the de jure segregation requisite to *Brown* relief, as stipulated in the *Swann* case (1971), by arguing that "Texas has never required by law that Mexican American children be segregated (Alcala and Rangel, 1972:348). In order to undermine these efforts at circumvention and also to take advantage of the *Brown* findings, the new interest groups shifted the legal strategy from the "other white" to the equal protection argument.

In order for Mexican Americans to apply the *Brown* findings of Fourteenth Amendment violations to them it was necessary to win judicial recognition as a separate class or as an identifiable minority group, i.e., a group classified as having unalterable congenital traits, political impotence, and the attachment of a stigma of inferiority (Harvard Law

[9] Orfield (1978:203) notes that the courts also allowed local school officials in Miami, Florida, to count Cubans as white for desegregation purposes.

Review, 1969). This was accomplished in the *Cisneros* v. *Corpus Christi Independent School District* case in 1970 where Mexican Americans were declared to be an "identifiable ethnic minority with a past pattern of discrimination (1970:606). By winning judicial recognition as an identifiable minority group, the reach of the 1954 *Brown* decision was extended to Mexican Americans. More importantly, it introduced a new social group into the desegregation process. In the next several years, the *Cisneros* findings were upheld in all Mexican American desegregation cases, with the exception of the Houston case. In 1973, the Supreme Court also acknowledged the separate legal status of Mexican Americans as an identifiable minority group in the Denver case (*Keyes* v. *School District No. 1*, 1973). The invigorating dose of success, though, was dampened in the mid-1970s as the pace of desegregation litigation decreased and the interest in it diminished. Between 1973 and 1978 most desegregation cases, e.g., El Paso, Corpus Christi, etc., were held up as local school districts appealed to the higher courts for reprieve. Once a court's determination was final, disagreement over the constitutionality and legality of appropriate remedies further delayed the dismantling of segregated schools. In some school districts, such as Austin, desegregation efforts did not begin until the fall of 1980.

In addition to the pace of desegregation coming to a near halt, new issues focusing on different aspects of educational policy emerged in the Mexican American community. While the dismantling of dual school systems was perceived by Mexican American leaders in earlier periods to be the primary obstacle to achieving educational opportunity, this was not the case by the mid-1970s. Bilingual education was gaining ascendance and becoming the primary issue in the Mexican American community (Pifer, 1979:5). "It is interesting to note that almost without exception," stated Jose Cardenas, a leading Mexican American educator, "Hispanic interest in desegregation cases since *U.S.* v. *Texas* (the Del Rio case) has gone beyond pupil assignment plans and into instructional practices" (Cardenas, 1977:61).

Bilingual education, unlike desegregation, had been promoted by the federal government since 1968. Congress had passed the Bilingual Education Act of 1968 and the Department of Health, Education, and Welfare had issued regulations in 1970 requiring all school districts with significant numbers of non-English-speaking children to develop special programs designed to meet their language needs. Bilingual education was also actively supported by the Mexican American community in Texas. Carlos Truan, a state representative from Corpus Christi, authored the passage of the first bilingual education law in Texas in 1968.[10] In 1971, Mexican Americans successfully argued for the establishment of bilingual programs in the San Felipe–Del Rio school sys-

[10] Hardgrave and Hinojosa (1975:5) state that the bilingual education bill passed by the state legislature did not augment federal funding, but "it did give the Texas Education Agency permission to encourage the development of bilingual education in Texas schools."

tem (*United States* v. *Texas*, 1971). Two years later, the *Lau* decision upheld the right of linguistic groups to receive special language train- ing in the public schools (*Lau* v. *Nichols*, 1974).

These developments in bilingual education appeared to clash with the constitutional requirement to desegregate the public schools. The deseg- regation cases had successfully argued that Mexican Americans were a "victimized minority whose deprivation could be remedied by inclusion through integration" (Orfield, 1978:211). The *Lau* case, on the other hand, argued that the linguistic groups in the United States were denied their rights by an Anglo-oriented and English-speaking public school (*Lau* v. *Nichols*, 1974). The remedy to this was not integration but rather, to use Orfield's term, group solidarity. Bilingual advocates wanted public schools to assist in the maintenance and preservation of the native languages and cultures of the linguistic groups discriminated against in the public schools as well as increase the English proficiency among them. The remedy to language discrimination in the schools "could best be accomplished by separating children by language background and concentrating the necessarily limited number of bilingual teachers in the schools where the children were concentrated" (Orfield, 1978:211).

MALDEF, as the principal Mexican American organization in charge of desegregation and bilingual education litigation, did not perceive the statutory requirement to provide special language programs to cultural and linguistic groups as clashing with the constitutional requirement to desegregate the public schools. It believed that the two issues were complimentary. MALDEF was committed to desegregation but with bilin- gual instruction. "If you have a bilingual education program," stated a MALDEF lawyer, "this will help desegregate the school district" (Orfield, 1978:214).

The efforts to incorporate bilingual education into the desegregation process indicated, among other things, that there was a diminishing interest in desegregation. This coupled with the complexities of finding and implementing appropriate legal remedies for dismantling segre- gated schools suggested that the pace of desegregation had slowed down tremendously as the campaign to eliminate separate and inferior schools entered its sixth decade of activity in the 1980s.

Conclusion

The campaign to desegregate the schools had gone through signifi- cant transformations since it began in 1929. The old Mexican Ameri- can organizations had been replaced by new, more aggressive interest groups; the legal strategy had shifted from the "other white" to the equal protection argument, and the dependence on litigation as a more effective instrument for shaping educational policy had in- creased. But while the actors and the strategies and tactics in the poli- tics of education had changed over the years, the ideological basis of the campaign remained constant. Guided by the ideals of political lib- eralism, especially the belief in using particular institutions as effective instruments of educational and social reform, Mexican Americans devised solutions to the problems confronting them without raising basic questions concerning the nature of the society they lived in. The reform strategy of Mexican American organizations actually reinforced the liberal belief that institutions could become effective instruments of social reform without significantly modifying the existing socioeconomic and political structure of American society. The emphasis on using the judiciary or on pressuring the state educational agencies to eliminate local patterns of school segregation though did bring about some significant changes in American society. First, the campaign to desegregate the schools established the unconstitutionality of segregation based on national origin. This campaign also outlawed the formulation of discriminatory policies by legislative, educational, and other state agencies. Finally, the desegregation campaign inspired individuals and organizations to challenge and eliminate the most blatant patterns of educational inequity.

But solutions framed within the liberal tradition of using institutions as instruments of social and educational reform were limited in several important respects. By focusing on legal and administrative challenges to segregation, Mexican American organizations narrowed the political and social struggle of educational inequality to technical legal issues of Constitutional principles. One major unintended consequence of this shift in emphasis from modifying school policies to protecting the civil rights of individuals in the public schools was the further exclusion of community persons from participation in the campaign to provide equal and integrated schools for Mexican Americans. The further exclusion of community participation was accomplished by allowing professionals, e.g., lawyers, to dominate the direction the desegregation campaign would take and by depending on them for arguing the case against unfair treatment of Mexican American school children before the courts and before the state educational agencies. Also, emphasis on legal and administrative challenges to segregation served to deflect serious analysis of the complexity and of the sources of inequality in the society. Failure to understand the complexities and sources of inequality led to the development of certain types of strategies, e.g., litigation, aimed at modifying segregation practices in the public schools rather than to the development of long- and short-term strategies aimed at comprehensively attacking the root causes of structural inequalities, of which school segregation was one particular manifestation.[11]

In sum, one can argue that the desegregation campaign eliminated old patterns of discriminatory treatment of Mexican American school children but failed to eliminate the structural causes of educational inequality. Close to half a century after the campaigns to desegregate

[11] For a discussion of how education can contribute to comprehensive social change see Carnoy (1976) and Bowles and Gintis (1976), especially chapter 11, "Education, Socialism, and Revolution."

the schools were initiated, the obstacles which LULAC and the American G.I. Forum perceived to be limiting access to and participation in American life—discriminatory school policies and inferior and separate schools—were still present. As the community entered the decade of the 1980s the prospects for substantial changes in the educational status of the Mexican American were not great. More of the same appeared to be in store for the community as MALDEF, the American G.I. Forum, LULAC, and other Mexican American organizations turned their focus to other issues such as bilingual education. SSQ

REFERENCES

Alcala, Carlos M., and Jorge C. Rangel. 1972. "Project Report: De Jure Segregation of Chicanos in the Texas Public Schools," *Harvard Civil Rights–Civil Liberties Law Review*, 7 (March):307–91.

Alderete, Cristobal. 1979. Personal interview. Washington, D.C. 26 July 1979.

Allsup, Carl. 1977. "Education Is Our Freedom: The American G.I. Forum and the Mexican American School Segregation in Texas, 1948–1957," *Aztlan*, 8 (Spring, Summer, Fall):27–50.

American G.I. Forum. 1950a. *The American G.I. Forum and What It Stands For.* American G.I. Forum Central Office Files, Corpus Christi, Tex.: pp. 1–8.

_____. 1950b. "School Inspection: Report on Fourteen Schools," American G.I. Forum Central Office Files, Corpus Christi, Tex.

_____. 1952. *News Bulletin,* 1 (15 December 1952).

_____. 1957. *News Bulletin,* 5 (15 December 1957).

Bilingual Education Act, P.L. 90-247, (2 Jan. 1968), 81 Stat. 816, 20 U.S.C.A. 880(b).

Bowles, Samuel, and Herbert Gintis. 1976. *Schooling in Capitalist America* (New York: Basic Books).

Brown v. Board of Education, 347 U.S. 483 (1954).

Cardenas, Jose. 1977. "Desegregation and the Mexican American," in National Institute of Eduction, ed., *Desegregation and Education Concerns of the Hispanic Community* (Washington, D.C.: U.S. Government Printing Office).

Carnoy, Martin. 1976. "The Role of Education in a Strategy for Social Change," in Martin Carnoy and Henry M. Levin, eds., *The Limits of Educational Reform* (New York: David McKay): pp. 269–90.

Cisneros v. Corpus Christi Independent School District, 324 F. Supp. 599 (S.D. Tex., 1970)

Delgado v. Bastrop Independent School District (1948), Civil Action No. 333, District Court of the United States, Western District of Texas (Abstract of Principal Features).

Del Rio Decision of L. A. Woods, State Superintendent of Public Instruction, 23 April 1949. Texas Education Agency Library, Austin, Tex.

Garcia, Gus. C., and Homero M. Lopez, "Statement," Attorneys for the Plaintiffs in the Salinas School Segregation Case, 28 April 1955. American G.I. Forum Central Office Files, Corpus Christi, Tex.

Garcia, Hector P. 1950. "Report of Personal Inspection Trip," 13 April 1950. American

G.I. Forum Central Office Files. Corpus Christi, Tex.

Garza, Edward D. 1951. "LULAC: League of United Latin American Citizens," M.A. thesis, Southwest Texas State Teachers College, San Marcos, Tex.

Hardgrave, Robert L., Jr., and Santiago Hinojosa. 1975. *The Politics of Bilingual Education* (Manchaca, Tex.: Sterling Swift).

Harvard Law Review. 1969. "Developments in the Law—Equal Protection," *Harvard Law Review*, 82 (March):1065–1127.

Keyes v. *School District No. 1*, 413 U.S. 189 (1973).

Lau v. *Nichols*, 414 U.S. 563 (1974).

Mendez et al. v. *Westminster School District of Orange County et al.*, 64 F. Supp. 544 (S.D. Calif. 1946).

Orfield, Gary. 1978. *Must We Bus?* (Washington, D.C.: Brookings Institution).

Pifer, Alan. 1979. *Bilingual Education and the Hispanic Challenge, Annual Report* (New York: Carnegie Corporation).

Plessy v. *Ferguson*, 163 U.S. 537 (1896).

Ross v. *Eckels*, 434 F. 2d. 1140 (1970).

Sandoval, Moises. 1979. *Our Legacy: The First Fifty Years* (Washington, D.C.: LULAC).

San Miguel, Guadalupe, Jr. 1978. "Endless Pursuits: The Chicano Educational Experience in Corpus Christi, Texas, 1880–1960." Ph.D. dissertation, Stanford University.

———. 1979. "List of Desegregation Cases in the Southwest, 1930–1971." Personal research file. University of California, Santa Barbara, School of Education.

Swann v. *Charlotte-Mecklenburg Board of Education*, 402 U.S. 1 (1971).

Texas, General and Special Laws, Public Free Schools, Art. V, Ch. 299, 51st Legis., Reg. Sess. (11 January–6 July 1949): pp. 543–44.

Texas State Board of Education. 1948. "Instructions and Regulations of the Texas State Superintendent of Public Instruction," Texas State Board of Education Correspondence, American G.I. Forum Central Office Files, Corpus Christi, Tex.

———. 1950a. "Agenda and Minutes," 14 April 1950. Texas Education Agency Library, Austin.

———. 1950b. "Statement of Policy Pertaining to Segregation of Latin American Children," 8 May 1950. State Board of Education Correspondence, American G.I. Forum Central Office Files, Corpus Christi, Tex.

Tirado, Miguel David. 1974. "Mexican American Community Political Organization: The Key to Chicano Political Power," in F. Chris Garcia, ed., *La Causa Politica: A Chicano Politics Reader* (Notre Dame: University of Notre Dame Press): pp. 105–27.

United States v. *Texas*, 321 F. Supp. 1043 (S.D. Tex.. 1971), *aff'd and modified*, 447 F. 2d 441 (5th Cir., 1971).

U.S. Commission on Civil Rights. 1970 *Mexican American Education Study, Vol. I: Ethnic Isolation of Mexican Americans in the Public Schools of the Southwest* (Washington, D.C.: U.S. Government Printing Office).

Westminster School District of Orange et al. v. *Mendez et al.*, 161 F. 2d 775 (9th, Calif., 1947).

Wollenberg, Charles. 1974. "Mendez v. Westminster: Race, Nationality and Segregation in California Schools," *California Historical Quarterly*, 53 (Winter):326–48.

COMMENTARY

CHICANOS IN THE SCHOOLS: AN OVERVIEW OF THE PROBLEMS AND THE LEGAL REMEDIES

Joe C. Ortega* and Peter D. Roos**

I. Introduction

Unequal educational opportunity and segregation in American schools are commonly associated with black Americans. These problems, however, extend beyond blacks to other minorities, as the Chicanos who live in a school district like the one in Oxnard, California, know only too well:

> To implement the "principle of segregation," the minutes for November 1936 to June 1939 show how Oxnard's School Board not only established and maintained segregated schools, but also established and maintained segregated classrooms within a school. Where segregated classrooms existed within a school, the Board had the additional problem of keeping children of different ethnic groups from playing together. In addressing this problem, the Board debated the feasibility of staggered playground periods and release times. Feasibility also dictated some exceptions to the Board's general principle of segregation. In some cases the "brightest" and "cleanest" of the "Mexican children" were placed in "white classes when the white class (was) small and the Mexican class (was) too large." . . . In 1940, after considering the matter for a number of years, the Board built the Ramona Schoolhouse "for the convenience of the Mexican population." But the conveniences of the Ramona School were few. Its floor consisted of blacktop rolled over bare earth, its illumination came from a single bare bulb, its roof leaked, its toilet facilities were deplorable. Eleven years later, in 1951, to relieve Ramona's overcrowded conditions, the Board constructed the Juanita School within one block of Ramona. Before this court's remedial order went into effect, few so-called "Anglo" youngsters ever attended these two segregated barrio schools . . . . During the 1960's, a number of desegregation plans, which were administratively and educationally sound and feasible, were presented to the Board and rejected by it . . . . Ironically, during that period, the School Board did take positive action to aggravate segregation. . . . For example, in the mid 1960's, under the guise of pursuing a neighborhood school policy, the Board situated three new schools — Sierra Linda, Marina West, and Rose Avenue — within the district so that these schools were segregated on the very day they opened their doors.[1]

The 1974 case which detailed this instance of deliberate segregation, *Soria v. Oxnard School District*,[2] illustrates the deep-seated resistance in many areas of

* Member, California Agricultural Labor Relations Board; previously executive director, Model Cities Center for Law & Justice; J.D., U.C.L.A., 1968; B.A., University of Chicago, 1957.
** Senior Staff Attorney, Center for Law and Education, Harvard University; Research Associate, Graduate School of Education, Harvard University; J.D., Hastings College of Law, 1967; A.B., Occidental College, 1964.
1 Soria v. Oxnard School Dist., 386 F. Supp. 539 (C.D. Cal. 1974).
2 *Id.* \

the country to inclusion of Mexican Americans in the educational process on an equal basis with Anglos. While segregation of Chicanos has long existed in many Southwestern school districts,[3] it has not been attacked in the courts as vigorously as has that of blacks. Recently, however, the significance[4] and, in some respects, uniqueness of the Chicano situation have been increasingly recognized by the federal government, the courts, and the Chicanos themselves. Consequently, there are prospects now for greater activity in this arena of the civil rights effort.

Deliberate physical segregation is only one way Chicano pupils are denied equal educational opportunity. Since Spanish is the native tongue of these children, they often do not speak and read English as fluently as their white peers. This leads to segregation by ability grouping and special slow-learning classes, a more subtle but nonetheless serious form of segregation. Chicanos also are excluded or suspended as disciplinary problems in disproportionate numbers, and many Mexican born students are excluded from schools by the threat of deportation.

Even if these problems are overcome, the Chicano student faces an alien culture with unfamiliar values and expectations. Many teachers, ignorant of cultural differences, believe they are helping a Chicano child by asking him to ignore his native language and culture. Textbooks depict the virtues of middle-class Americanism without reference to the contributions of blacks, Chicanos, and other minorities, reinforcing the Chicano's cultural disorientation. In all these ways, the Mexican American child is denied the educational experience available to children of middle-class Anglo background. While not as susceptible to successful legal challenge as deliberate segregation, these other obstacles to equal education are being increasingly attacked, and new remedies are being considered.

II. Segregation

A. *The Current Status*

Although segregation of Mexican American children was recognized as a violation of the fourteenth amendment even before the *Brown* decision,[5] segre-

---

3 Ironically, the same court which condemned discrimination against Mexican Americans in Oxnard in 1974 had ruled against it 30 years earlier and, indeed, eight years before Brown v. Board of Educ. 347 U.S. 483 (1954). *See* Mendez v. Westminster School Dist., 64 F. Supp. 544 (S.D. Cal. 1946), *aff'd*, 161 F.2d 774 (9th Cir. 1947).

4 In purely numerical terms, the Chicano's problems are significant. Spanish-surnamed Americans are the second largest minority group in the nation, numbering 10.8 million in 1974. Over half of these, 6.15 million, are of Mexican origin ("Chicano"). Over five million Chicanos live in the Southwest (Arizona, California, Colorado, New Mexico, and Texas). *See* U.S. DEP'T OF COMMERCE, CURRENT POPULATION REPORTS: PERSONS OF SPANISH ORIGIN IN THE UNITED STATES (1974); U.S. BUREAU OF THE CENSUS, SUBJECT REPORT: PERSONS OF SPANISH SURNAME (1973).

Since the Spanish-surnamed population is younger than the general population, the percentage of Chicano children in school is even higher than these numbers indicate. Thirteen percent of Spanish-surnamed Americans are less than five years old, as compared to eight percent of the general population.

Furthermore, the second largest school district in the country, the Los Angeles Unified School District, had 148,000 Chicano students in 1972, or 24 percent of its total enrollment. The district projects that by 1977, 215,000 pupils, or 35 percent of its enrollment, will be Chicano.

5 *See* Gonzales v. Sheely, 96 F. Supp. 1004 (D. Ariz. 1951); Mendez v. Westminster School Dist., 64 F. Supp. 544 (S.D. Cal. 1946), *aff'd*, 161 F.2d 774 (9th Cir. 1947).

gation is very much alive in the Southwest today. In many districts, it survives as a remnant of officially recognized "Mexican Schools." In Texas, for example, prior to 1954 the "Mexican School" was part of most school districts.[6] Today those identical schools, though no longer called Mexican Schools, invariably are all Chicano.[7]

In addition to these remnants of an officially created and undisguised dual system, the usual indicia of de jure policies are found in many towns and cities in the Southwest. Boundaries are drawn to segregate Chicanos; schools are intentionally located to separate the races; portable classrooms are utilized to keep students apart; student transfer programs and optional attendance zones allow Anglos to escape from predominantly Chicano schools. In addition, teachers are assigned by race, and feeder patterns are created to ensure that students in Anglo elementary schools advance to Anglo junior and senior high schools and, likewise, that Chicanos in Chicano elementary schools advance to racially similar junior and senior high schools.[8]

B. Recent Cases

Although desegregation has generally proceeded slowly in the Southwest, several recent cases portend increased activity. Most important among them is *Keyes v. School District*.[9] *Keyes* dismissed any lingering doubts about whether *Brown* applies to racial or ethnic groups other than blacks.

> [O]ne of the things which the Hispano has in common with the Negro is economic and cultural deprivation and discrimination. . . . [T]hough of different origins, Negroes and Hispanos in Denver suffer identical discrimination. . . .[10]

Another encouraging decision is the supplemental order filed in *Adams v. Weinberger*.[11] In *Adams*, the court ordered the Department of Health, Education, and Welfare to make certain that unlawful segregation was not being practiced in various Southern States. HEW was directed to obtain information from specified school districts, including 41 districts in Texas. If the information shows improper segregation, HEW must initiate legal action. Most of the Texas districts are Chicano-segregated districts. While the history of HEW efforts in

---

6 *See, e.g., Project Report, De Jure Segregation of Chicanos in Texas Schools,* 7 HARV. CIV. RIGHTS-CIV. LIB. L. REV. 307, 313-14 (1972).
7 An example is the Aoy School in El Paso, a former "Mexican School," which today has approximately 900 elementary school students, all Chicano.
8 *See, e.g.,* Keyes v. School Dist., 413 U.S. 189 (1973); Soria v. Oxnard School Dist., 328 F. Supp. 155 (C.D. Cal. 1971), *vacated and remanded,* 488 F.2d 579 (9th Cir. 1973), *aff'd on remand,* 386 F. Supp. 539 (C.D. Cal. 1974); United States v. Texas, 342 F. Supp. 24 (E.D. Tex. 1971), *aff'd,* 466 F.2d 518 (5th Cir. 1972); Cisneros v. Corpus Christi Ind. School Dist., 324 F. Supp. 599, 617-20 (S.D. Tex. 1970), *aff'd in part, modified in part,* 467 F.2d 142 (5th Cir.), *cert. denied,* 413 U.S. 920 (1972). *Cf.* Alvarado v. El Paso Ind. School Dist., 445 F.2d 1011 (5th Cir. 1971).
9 413 U.S. 189 (1973).
10 *Id.* at 197-98.
11 391 F. Supp. 269 (D.D.C. 1975).

this area does not inspire much hope, it is possible that the pressure of these lawsuits could finally result in enforcement of the law.[12]

Actually, most desegregation lawsuits have been brought not by HEW or other governmental agencies but by private attorneys and organizations. Currently, litigation is under way which will affect school districts in El Paso, Texas;[13] Uvalde, Texas;[14] Austin, Texas;[15] Tucson, Arizona;[16] and Los Angeles, California.[17]

III. Testing and Ability Grouping

To many teachers, the important difference about Chicanos is their language: they don't speak "American." This difference has been the basis of much discrimination against the Chicano student, and has sometimes been cited openly as the rationale for placing Chicanos in different schools.[18] Language difference was also used in the past to justify segregation by classes within a school or by groups within classes.

Language is the basis for a more subtle method of discrimination as well. Many school districts still use tests written in English to determine the aptitude of all pupils, both Anglos and Chicanos. Chicano students, who naturally do poorly on tests not in their native tongue, are then assigned to retarded or slow-learning classes (or "tracks") because of this poor performance.

In addition to language differences, cultural differences have played a part in denying equal educational opportunities to Chicano children. I.Q. tests such as the Stanford-Binet and the Wechsler, often used in assessing children's abilities, contain a strong cultural bias toward the middle-class Anglo child.[19] As stated by Judge J. Skelly Wright:

> Because these tests are standardized primarily on and are relevant to a white middle-class group of students, they produce inaccurate and misleading test scores when given to lower-class and Negro students. As a result, rather than being classified according to ability to learn, these students are in reality being classified according to their socio-economic or racial status, or — more precisely — according to environmental and psychological factors which have nothing to do with innate ability.[20]

---

12 These suits against the Department of Health, Education, and Welfare, and particularly against the Office of Civil Rights, are predicated upon the Civil Rights Act of 1964, 42 U.S.C. § 2000(d) et seq. (1970), amending 42 U.S.C. § 2000(d) et seq. (1964). These provisions prohibit discrimination by any recipient of federal funds and require HEW to ensure that such discrimination does not occur.

13 Alvarado v. El Paso Ind. School Dist., 445 F.2d 1011 (5th Cir. 1971).

14 Morales v. Shannon, 366 F. Supp. 813 (W.D. Tex. 1973), appeal docketed, No. 73-3096, 5th Cir., ——, 1973.

15 United States v. Texas Educ. Agency, 467 F.2d 848 (5th Cir. 1972).

16 Mexican Americans for Equal Educ. Opportunity v. Tucson School Dist., Civil No. 74-204 (D. Ariz., filed ——, 1974).

17 Crawford v. Board of Educ., Civil No. 37750 (Los Angeles County, Cal. Super. Ct., filed ——, 1973).

18 See, e.g., Mendez v. Westminster School Dist., 64 F. Supp. 544 (C.D. Cal. 1946).

19 See Cardenas, Bilingual Intelligence Testing (paper presented to the Education Task Force of the Mexican American Legal Defense Fund, June 6, 1975).

20 Hobson v. Hansen, 269 F. Supp. 401 (D.D.C. 1967), appeal dismissed, 393 U.S. 801 (1968), aff'd sub nom. Smuck v. Hobson, 408 F.2d 175 (D.C. Cir. 1969).

Cultural bias due to intelligence testing occurs in several ways. A person's intelligence is not quantifiable like height and weight. It must be measured indirectly, by noting how intelligence influences behavior in certain situations. Cultural bias occurs when the tester assumes that all children faced with a certain situation will respond in the same way, depending only on their intelligence. For example, a child may be asked what he should do if a younger child hits him. While Anglo children may choose the "correct" answer ("walk away from him"), the upbringing of children from other cultures may lead them to respond differently and receive a "wrong" score.

Tests also show cultural bias by assuming that all the individuals being tested have been exposed to certain common experiences, and that intelligence can be measured by determining how much they have retained from these experiences. Obviously, if a child is ignorant of the experience being tested, he has retained nothing and will score poorly. Actually, a Chicano child has many experiences which are different from those of an Anglo, but the tests ask no questions about such experiences; consequently, Chicanos are denied a chance to demonstrate their ability to use retained knowledge.

Finally, I.Q. tests assume that the child being tested has certain mechanical test-taking skills. The Chicano child, besides being linguistically limited in an English-language test, may also not have been in school as long as his Anglo counterpart, and may lack the skills assumed for a child of his age or grade.

Grouping based on testing only reinforces the differences between Chicanos and Anglos. Whites are assigned to the academic and commercial courses, Chicanos to shop and homemaking ones. Similarly, schools built in the Anglo sections of town contain chemistry and physics labs; in the Chicano section, there are wood and auto shops.[21]

Despite the language barrier, should a Chicano youngster score high on intelligence and achievement tests, he is still often channeled into shop courses on the benevolent theory that since his parents cannot afford to send him to college, it is cruel to give him expectations that cannot be met. Yet Chicanos assigned to shop classes are still better off than those with lower test scores who

---

21   One way to show this is to consider the following courses offered at Bowie High School, El Paso (97.6 percent Mexican American), and compare those offered at Coronado High School (12 percent Mexican American) during the 1971-72 school year. Courses offered at Bowie but not at Coronado included: Art IV — Fine Arts, Bookkeeping II, Business Communications, English Lab IV, English IV (M), Int. Language Dev., Portuguese I, Portuguese II, Portuguese III, Beginning Band, Beginning Orchestra, Music History, Literature, Biology I (M), Physical Science (M), Economics, Mexican American Studies, CVAE Cooperative I, CVAE Cooperative II, CVAE—Boys (General Mechanical Trades), CVAE—Girls (Home & Community Services), Distributive Ed. II, Homemaking II, Industrial Cooperative Training I, Industrial Cooperative Training II, Vocational Office Ed. (The CVAE designation represents a special vocational program.)
The following courses were offered at Coronado and not at Bowie: Business Org. and Mgt., English I (E), English II (E), English III (E), English IV (E), Language Advancement, Speech IV, Drama I, Drama II, Drama III, German I, German II, German III, Latin I, Latin II, Latin III, Spanish I, Spanish II, Spanish III, Spanish IV, Spanish V, Horticulture, Machine Drafting I, Machine Drafting II, Pre-Engineering Drafting, Analysis, Alg. I (E), Alg. II (E), Geometry (E), Trig., Prob. and Stat., Music Theory I, Advanced Science, Aerospace, Biology I (E), Biology II, Geology, Physical Science (E), American History (M), American Indian Studies, Anthropology, World History (M), Sociology, Philosophy, World Geography, and Child Development Lab.

are assigned to classes for the mentally retarded—children whose language and cultures are so different from those of the test and the tester that they are relegated to an education of playing with clay and simple toys.

A legal challenge to such testing and class assignment was brought by Chicano parents in *Arreola v. Santa Ana Unified School District*.[22] The plaintiffs alleged that the defendant school district violated the equal protection and due process clauses of the fourteenth amendment of the Constitution in that Mexican American pupils were denied an equal educational opportunity on the basis of faulty, biased, and discriminatory testing. They contended that the tests and testers were geared to a different language and culture than Chicano test subjects. The plaintiff children were retested by bilingual psychologists using a variety of tests; it was found that children assigned to mentally retarded classes were of normal and in some cases above normal intelligence. The suit ended in a stipulated settlement.

While the *Arreola* suit was pending, the California Legislature revised its statutes dealing with mentally retarded classes. The new law[23] requires that the psychological evaluation be conducted in the primary home language of the pupil and administered by a certified psychologist fluent in the pupil's language. The statutes also require written consent of the parent in the parent's own language before the child can be placed in retarded classes.

Other suits[24] have been brought in California and other Southwestern States. In San Diego, a challenge similar to that in *Arreola* was brought on behalf of both Chicano and black children alleging that the tests were culturally biased against both groups of children.

Ability grouping (or "tracking") is still prevalent in many school districts, and perpetuates a caste system the effects of which last far beyond the school years. Most challenges[25] have attacked the basis of "tracking": the testing devices which determine what level of education a student is capable of. Psychological tests are vulnerable to legal challenge only when there is sufficient evidence to show that they are unfair and discriminatory toward the non-English-speaking. There have been no challenges to the more subtle, undemocratic aspects of ability grouping per se. Nevertheless, various courts have placed school districts under a heavy burden of educational justification when there is a showing of racial segregation.[26] This is a hopeful sign that courts are beginning to look at the realities behind educational labels.

---

22 Civil No. 160-577 (Orange County, Cal. Super. Ct., filed June 7, 1968).
23 CAL. EDUC. CODE § 6902-085 (West 1975).
24 *See* Covarrubias v. San Diego Unified School Dist., Civil No. 70-394-S (S.D. Cal., filed Aug. 21, 1972); Guadalupe Organization, Inc. v. Tempe Elementary School Dist., Civil No. 71-435 PHX (D. Ariz., filed Jan. 25, 1972); Diana v. State Bd. of Educ., Civil No. C-70 37 REP (N.D. Cal., filed June 18, 1971).
25 *See, e.g.,* Hobson v. Hansen, 269 F. Supp. 1101 (D.D.C. 1967), *appeal dismissed,* 393 U.S. 801 (1968), *aff'd sub nom.* Smuck v. Hobson, 408 F.2d 175 (D.C. Cir. 1969).
26 McNeal v. Tate County School Dist., 508 F.2d 1017, 1020 (5th Cir. 1975). *See also* P. v. Riles, 343 F. Supp. 1306 (N.D. Cal. 1972); Moses v. Washington Parish School Bd., 330 F. Supp. 1340 (E.D. La. 1971), *aff'd,* 456 F.2d 1285 (5th Cir.), *cert. denied,* 409 U.S. 1013 (1972); Hobson v. Hansen, 269 F. Supp. 401 (D.D.C. 1967), *appeal dismissed,* 393 U.S. 81 (1968), *aff'd sub nom.* Smuck v. Hobson, 408 F.2d 175 (D.C. Cir. 1969).

IV. Teachers and Their Understanding of Chicano Culture

When a Chicano child first enters an American classroom, he meets a foreign environment that minimizes his chances of success. The most foreign element is often the teacher. Until very recently, even in predominantly Mexican neighborhoods, almost all teachers were Anglo. While some inroads have been made, the small number of Chicano teachers remains vastly disproportionate to the number of Chicano students. For instance, in *Aguilar v. Los Angeles City Unified School District*,[27] now pending in a federal district court, plaintiffs allege that only six percent of the district's teachers are Spanish-surnamed, as compared to 30 percent of its pupils. This district has been "educating" more Chicanos than any other district in the country, and has the benefit of several state universities and colleges in the area which train local people to serve the community. Other districts fare much worse in their ratio of Spanish-surnamed teachers to Spanish-surnamed students.

Moreover, the various civil rights acts and regulations prohibiting discrimination and requiring affirmative action plans have not substantially increased the number of Chicano teachers.[28] One major reason Chicanos are not being hired is the use of testing and certification devices which tend to keep minorities out; however, there have recently been some successful challenges to the use of these devices.[29]

While Anglo teachers can be effective with Chicano pupils, the majority, because they bring to their teaching stereotypes of the Chicano, are not. White middle-class values are different from those of the Chicano, and Anglo teachers generally are ignorant of a Chicano child's cultural background. They try to "Americanize" the child, and consequently Chicano children are often criticized for exhibiting "foreign" traits.

> Children are provided with examples of the social roles they are expected to play. They are frequently shown that Anglos are best in everything and Mexicans are worst. Mexican American children are rewarded in school . . . when they look and act like Anglos and punished (or ignored) if they look and act like Mexicans.[30]

---

27 Civil No. CV7434-WMP (C.D. Cal., filed Sept. 2, 1974).
28 In Texas, 20.1 percent of the students are Mexican American, compared to 4.9 percent of the teachers. The comparable figures for the other Southwestern states are: California, 14.4 percent Mexican American students, 2.2 percent Mexican American teachers; New Mexico, 38 percent Mexican American students, 16.2 percent Mexican American teachers; Arizona, 19.6 percent Mexican American students, 3.5 percent Mexican American teachers; Colorado, 13.7 percent Mexican American students, 2.3 percent Mexican American teachers. U.S. COMM'N ON CIVIL RIGHTS, ETHNIC ISOLATION OF MEXICAN-AMERICANS IN THE PUBLIC SCHOOLS OF THE SOUTHWEST 43 (1971) (Report I of the Mexican-American Education Study). The percentages grow even starker as one goes higher up the ladder to principal and superintendent.
  See also U.S. COMM'N ON CIVIL RIGHTS, TEACHERS AND STUDENTS 17 (1973). This report, fifth in the series, outlines the subtle within-class discrimination which takes place. It was found, for example, that teachers are 35 percent more likely to praise or encourage an Anglo student than a Mexican student, and 40 percent more likely to accept or use his ideas. Conversely, it was found that a teacher was 5.5 percent more likely to criticize Mexican American students, or to justify the use of authority in disciplining them.
29 *See* Morgan v. Hennigan, 379 F. Supp. 410 (D. Mass. 1974); Baker v. Columbus Municipal Separate School Dist., 329 F. Supp. 706 (N.D. Miss. 1971). *Cf.* Chance v. Board of Examiners, 330 F. Supp. 203 (S.D.N.Y. 1971), *aff'd*, 458 F.2d 1167 (2d Cir. 1972).
30 T. CARTER, MEXICAN AMERICANS IN SCHOOL: A HISTORY OF NEGLECT 82 (1970).

Even the speaking of Spanish was for many years cause for disciplinary action in many Southwestern schools. Often, then, the child learns that to be Mexican is to be a failure while to be American means success.

Well-meaning Anglo teachers may also create a negative image of the Chicano child's culture by some of their attempts to help. Some teachers tell their pupils that a good breakfast consists of orange juice, cereal, eggs, and bacon (the ideal American breakfast), and that a breakfast of coffee, beans, and tortillas is bad. Although the teacher means well by such advice, it in fact causes deterioration of the child's view of himself, his parents, and his culture. Likewise, when a teacher criticizes large families, or slick, greasy-appearing hair, the Chicano child's chances of attaining a healthy, positive self-image is unwittingly subverted.

V. Textbooks

In addition to coping with teachers who do not understand his culture, the Chicano child must read textbooks that ignore his cultural identity. According to many history books, for instance, the white man alone discovered this country and by his hard labor made it great. In other textbooks, the Chicano student reads about and sees pictures of the normal white, middle-class family: father goes to work in a suit while mother bakes cookies. Seldom, if ever, is the Chicano culture portrayed. In fact it is only recently, due in part to legislative mandates[31] and public pressure, that textbook writers have started to portray the contributions of Native Americans, Asians, Mexicans, blacks, and other minorities.

While textbook challenges are difficult to sustain due to first amendment problems, at least one case has had an impact in this area. In 1972, Chicanos filed suit in California under a state law which prohibited textbooks from incorrectly portraying ethnic groups.[32] A preliminary injunction was obtained which prohibited the California Department of Education from signing contracts with the books' publishers. Although the injunction was ultimately dissolved, it put publishers on notice that they could no longer ignore the concerns of minority groups.

VI. Disciplinary Methods

Recent studies have shown minority students are more frequently the objects of school discipline than their Anglo counterparts.[33] While most documentation

---

31   Section 9240 of the California Education Code requires that instructional materials "accurately portray the culture and racial diversity of our society, including . . . . [t]he role and contributions of American Indians, American Negroes, Mexican Americans, Asian Americans, European Americans, and members of other ethnic and cultural groups. . . ." Section 9243 prohibits instructional materials which contain "[a]ny matter reflecting adversely upon persons because of their race, color, creed, national origin, ancestry, sex or occupation." CALIF. EDUC. CODE §§ 9240, 9243 (West Supp. 1974).

32   Gutierrez v. State Bd. of Educ., Civil No. 221086 (Sacramento County, Cal. Super. Ct., filed Dec. 15, 1972).

33   See, e.g., CHILDREN'S DEFENSE FUND, CHILDREN OUT OF SCHOOL IN AMERICA (1974); SOUTHERN REGIONAL COUNCIL & THE ROBERT F. KENNEDY FOUNDATION, THE STUDENT PUSHOUT, VICTIM OF CONTINUED RESISTANCE TO DESEGREGATION (1974).

on this question has concerned black students, attorneys working with Chicanos have noted a lack of due process when Chicanos are expelled or suspended from school.

At other times, cultural differences make ostensibly equal treatment unequal. Typically, a white middle-class boy and a Chicano boy caught fighting are both told that they are suspended until they come in with their parents. The white parents come in the next day. The Chicano parents, who speak little or no English, and who are afraid of the authorities, may never show up. These feelings may be based on the very real history of discrimination inside and outside the school. Fortunately, requests made by attorneys for hearings, other due process procedures, and disciplinary standards have had some limited results.[34] In some instances, legislatures and school boards have amended procedures for exclusion and suspension of students to conform with due process standards.

VII. Bilingual-Bicultural Education

The Supreme Court in *Lau v. Nichols* stated:

> Basic English skills are at the very core of what the public schools teach. Imposition of a requirement that before a child can effectively participate in the educational program he must already have acquired those basic skills is to make a mockery of public education. We know that those who do not understand English are certain to find their classroom experiences wholly incomprehensible and in no way meaningful.[35]

The *Lau* decision, based upon Title VI of the Civil Rights Act of 1964,[36] was merely one step, albeit an important one, in the quest for bilingual-bicultural education for Chicanos.[37] Without specifying a remedy, the Court held that the failure to give special attention to English language deficiencies constituted national origin discrimination.

Many advocates of bilingual education see it as more than a device to overcome language "deficiencies." Indeed, they argue that while a child should be taught English, it is imperative that he receive instruction in his native language while he is learning English so that he can compete with English-dominant children on a substantive level, and receive instruction in the history and culture of his people so that he can know and appreciate his origins. Some would argue further that children should be given the option to study in their native language throughout their school years and that a bilingual-bicultural education should be provided to all children of Mexican heritage, irrespective of English language "deficiencies."

Although some of these positions might appear extreme to those who have not studied the educational programs for Chicanos, they are gaining more and more credence among those who have. One need only look at the small per-

---

34   Goss v. Lopez, 95 S. Ct. 729 (1975).
35   414 U.S. 563 (1974).
36   42 U.S.C. § 2000(d) (1970).
37   For a historical picture of the efforts to secure bilingual education, see Gonzales, *Coming of Age in Bilingual/Bicultural Education: A Historical Perspective*, 19 INEQUALITY IN EDUC. 5 (1975).

centage of Chicanos graduating from high school to realize that there is something terribly wrong with the education they are receiving. One leading Chicano educator has identified what he considers to be "incompatibilities" between middle-class Anglo and Chicano children.[38]

> Black and Mexican-American children have not enjoyed the same success in school as that of the typical middle-class American. The Cardenas-Cardenas Theory of Incompatibilities is a tested belief that the failure of such children can be attributed to a lack of compatibility between the characteristics of typical instructional programs.[39]

He believes that these incompatibilities can only be alleviated by a true bilingual-bicultural program.

While *Lau* mandates, at a minimum, some form of instruction in English as a second language, several courts have ordered true bilingual-bicultural programs. In *Serna v. Portales Municipal Schools,*[40] the district court ruled that it was a denial of equal protection to educate Spanish-speaking children in English. As a remedy, the court rejected the school district's program of English as a second language and ruled, after hearing expert testimony, that a bilingual program would more effectively overcome past discrimination. This ruling was upheld by the Tenth Circuit,[41] with the court basing its decision on Title VI rather than on equal protection. It ruled that the trial court's broad equitable discretion to correct legal wrongs was not abused by requiring adoption of a bilingual program.

The "Cardenas Plan" for full-scale bilingual-bicultural education was also ordered on a pilot basis in *Keyes v. School District.*[42] The court, in adopting this plan, called it "a very sensible method" for meeting the educational needs of the Chicano population.[43] Whether the district court exercised discretionary power or fulfilled a mandatory duty to adopt a bilingual approach as a response to prior de jure segregation is a question that will likely be decided in the near future; the adoption of the "Cardenas Plan" has been appealed to the Tenth Circuit.[44]

While the bilingual movement is gaining momentum[45] through court orders and legislation, it can be argued that the cart has been placed before the horse. The majority of Chicanos in the Southwest speak English sufficiently well to

---

38 Cardenas & Cardenas, *Chicano—Bright-Eyed, Bilingual, Brown, and Beautiful,* TODAY'S EDUCATION, February 1973, at 49. Dr. Cardenas also prepared a plan to provide a remedy in Keyes v. School Dist. 380 F. Supp. 673 (D. Colo. 1974).

39 *Id.*

40 351 F. Supp. 1279 (D.N.M. 1972).

41 Serna v. Portables Municipal Schools, 499 F.2d 1147 (10th Cir. 1974).

42 380 F. Supp. 673 (D. Colo. 1974), *modified,* Civil Nos. 74-1349-51 (10th Cir., filed Aug. 11, 1975). The Tenth Circuit ruled that the record below concerning discrimination on the basis of language was insufficient to justify the massive bilingual remedy which the district court had prescribed.

43 380 F. Supp. at 692.

44 *See* note 42 *supra. See also* United States v. Texas, 342 F. Supp. 24 (E.D. Tex. 1971), *aff'd,* 466 F.2d 518 (5th Cir. 1972) (bilingual education ordered in a desegregated context in San Felipe Del Rio District).

45 In addition to the litigation mentioned, various states have adopted some form of bilingual legislation. *See, e.g.,* CAL. EDUC. CODE §§ 5761-5764.6 (West Supp. 1974); TEXAS CODE ANN. §§ 21.451-.460 (Supp. 1974). *See also* MASS. GEN. LAWS ch. 71A, § 5 (Supp. 1975) (the first and most expansive bilingual legislation).

understand the curriculum offered, but because of the incompatibilities observed by Cardenas—the curriculum, the ethnic composition of faculties, and other factors—the distinctive cultural needs of these children are still not being met. Litigation concerning this lack of cultural education might be possible on a theory that imposing a middle-class Anglo curriculum on a Chicano population constitutes national origin discrimination under Title VI.

VIII. The Illegal Alien

No discussion of Chicano educational issues is complete without mention of the illegal alien. Driven by the poverty of Mexico and drawn by the affluence of the United States, hundreds of thousands of Mexicans cross the imaginary line between Mexico and this country without legal permission. Although these Mexicans are here illegally and subject to deportation if apprehended, few are actually deported. The Immigration and Naturalization Service estimates that over four million illegal aliens live in the Southwest.[46] They live and work here, and have their families—including school-aged children—with them. Because their parents accept any job available, many children come from migrant farm families. Even those aliens who live in the cities are also migrant, moving constantly, following one temporary job to another. A teacher in Los Angeles lamented that the class picture taken in September is seldom bought by the children when it comes in December because most of those in it have left the school.

Coming from the poorest of the poor, speaking no English or even the *patois* of the Chicano, these children have all the disadvantages of the Chicano multiplied many times. They are resented by school authorities and politicians, who feel that tax-supported schools should not be used by "aliens." Some school districts actually refuse to admit such children, and it is estimated that thousands of these children never attend school.

The most common device for excluding children of illegal aliens from school is the district residency requirement. A school district can argue, with sound legal but questionable moral merit, that a child in the United States illegally cannot establish legal residence in the district. California has recently passed legislation that requires school districts to admit illegal aliens, but also requires that they be reported to the Immigration and Naturalization Service.[47] In this ironic situation, children are admitted to the schools only to be deported from the country.

While legal challenges to these practices are difficult, if not impossible,[48] to sustain, it does seem a ripe area for federal legislation. Excluding these children from school is a terrible waste, for the country as well as the children themselves.

---

46   Statement of Attorney General William B. Saxbe, estimating that four to seven million and possibly 12 million illegal aliens reside in the U.S. *See* L. A. Times, Oct. 31, 1974, at 6, col. 3.

47   Cal. Education Code §§ 6950, 6957 (West Supp. 1974).

48   The implementation of the California statute is being challenged in one district. The challenge, a highly technical one, and applicable only to an aberration in that district, is primarily based upon the recently adopted Family Educational Rights and Privacy Act, 20 U.S.C.A. § 1232 g (Supp. 1975).

IX. Conclusion

Although the Chicano constitutes a significant part of the American scene, he is still educationally deprived. If he is to participate equally in the opportunities of American life, he must have access to the quality of education available to the Anglo majority. The courts and the legislative bodies can and should be the catalyst for progress toward this goal.

Harvard Civil Rights-Civil Liberties Law Review

Volume 7, Number 2   March, 1972

PROJECT REPORT:
DE JURE SEGREGATION OF
CHICANOS IN TEXAS SCHOOLS*

"They are an inferior race, that is all"[1] was the justification asserted by Nueces County, Texas, school officials for segregating Chicanos[2] in 1929.[3] Such remarks and practices are not merely reflections of society's past indiscretions. Public officials continue to inveigh against Mexican Americans.[4]

---

* This Comment is dedicated to Dr. Hector P. Garcia, founder of the American G.I. Forum and former member of the United States Commission on Civil Rights, in recognition of his relentless efforts, spanning twenty-five years, to eradicate Chicano school segregation in Texas. Acknowledgement is also extended to the Institute of Politics of the John F. Kennedy School of Government at Harvard University and the New World Foundation in New York for the research grants which made this study possible.

[1] P. Taylor, AN AMERICAN MEXICAN FRONTIER 219 (1934) [hereinafter cited as *Taylor*].

[2] The term Chicano derives from *Mejicano*, the Spanish term for Mexican. Chicano is herein used interchangeably with Mexican American, Spanish American, Latin American, and Spanish-surnamed individual. It refers to persons born in Mexico and now United States citizens or whose parents or ancestors immigrated to the United States from Mexico. It also refers to persons who legitimately trace their lineage to Hispanic or Indo-Hispanic forebears who resided in Spanish or Mexican territory now part of the Southwestern United States. *See* U.S. Comm'n on Civil Rights, MEXICAN-AMERICAN EDUCATION STUDY, REPORT 1: ETHNIC ISOLATION OF MEXICAN AMERICANS IN THE PUBLIC SCHOOLS IN THE SOUTHWEST 7 n.1 (1971) [hereinafter cited as ETHNIC ISOLATION]. The term Anglo refers to white persons not Mexican American or members of other Spanish-surnamed groups. *Id.*

[3] Segregated schools in a Nueces County district occasioned a recent landmark decision holding that Chicanos are an identifiable minority victimized by *de jure* segregation. Cisneros v. Corpus Christi Ind. School Dist., 324 F. Supp. 599 (S.D. Tex. 1970), *appeal docketed*, No. 71–2397 (5th Cir., filed July 16, 1971), *noted in* 49 TEX. L. REV. 337 (1971).

[4] Judge Chargin of the California Superior Court, at the sentencing of a 17-year-old juvenile charged with incest, recently stated: "Mexican people after thirteen years of age, think it is perfectly all right to go out and act like an animal . . . . We ought to send you out of the country—send you back to Mexico . . . . You ought to commit suicide. That's what I think of people of this kind. You are lower than animals . . . just miserable, lousy, rotten people . . . . Maybe Hitler was right. The animals in our society probably ought to be destroyed because they have no right to live among human beings." 115 CONG. REC. 32358 (1969). For a discussion of the prejudice shown by Los Angeles

Chicanos have suffered from invidious discrimination at all levels of interaction with the dominant society.[5] The west Texas city of Ozona is illustrative. Drugstores were closed to Mexican Americans until the late 1940's. Chicanos were not served in restaurants or allowed into movie theaters until the early 1950's. Hotels were exclusive until about 1958. Residents complain that barber and beauty shops were segregated until late 1969, and have advised the Office for Civil Rights of the Department of Health, Education, and Welfare that the bowling alley, cemeteries and swimming pools remain segregated even today.[6]

Chicanos have also received prejudicial treatment in the administration of justice.[7] Although early efforts to litigate the issue were unsuccessful,[8] the Supreme Court ruled such discrimination unconstitutional in 1954.[9]

Housing reflects similar discrimination. Overcrowding among Chicanos in the Southwest[10] in 1960 was more than four times that among Anglos.[11] Nearly 875,000 Chicanos lived in overcrowded housing.[12] An estimated thirty percent of all housing units occupied by Chicanos in 1960 were dilapidated, but only seven and a half percent of Anglo units were so classified.[13]

Superior Court Judges, particularly in Grand Jury selections, see Note, El Chicano Y The Constitution: The Legacy of Hernandez v. Texas: Grand Jury Discrimination, 6 U. SAN FRAN. L. REV. 129, 142−45 (1971) [hereinafter cited as El Chicano].

[5] See generally U.S. Comm'n on Civil Rights, MEXICAN-AMERICANS AND THE ADMINISTRATION OF JUSTICE IN THE SOUTHWEST (1970).

[6] U.S. Dep't of Health, Educ. & Welfare, On-Site Review of Ozona ISD 7 (Mar. 1970).

[7] The discrimination is of course not limited to Texas. See El Chicano, supra note 4.

[8] Sanchez v. State, 156 Tex. Crim. 468, 243 S.W.2d 700 (1951); Bustillos v. State, 152 Tex. Crim. 275, 213 S.W.2d 837 (1948); Salazar v. State, 149 Tex. Crim. 260, 193 S.W.2d 211 (1946); Sanchez v. State, 147 Tex. Crim. 436, 181 S.W.2d 87 (1944). But see Carter v. Texas, 177 U.S. 442 (1900) (where exclusion of Blacks from Texas juries was held unconstitutional).

[9] Hernandez v. Texas, 347 U.S. 475 (1954) (finding exclusion of Chicanos from juries in Jackson County, Texas, unlawful).

[10] Arizona, California, Colorado, New Mexico and Texas.

[11] L. Grebler, J. Moore, & R. Guzman, THE MEXICAN AMERICAN PEOPLE 250 (1970) [hereinafter cited as Grebler, Moore, & Guzman]. Of Chicano families, 34.6% lived in overcrowded housing, compared to 21.8% of nonwhite families and only 7.7% of Anglo families. In Texas, conditions were even worse. A study shows that 46.5% of Chicano families, 25.9% of nonwhite families, and only 9.4% of Anglo families occupied overcrowded housing. F. Mittelbach & G. Marshall, THE BURDEN OF POVERTY, MEXICAN AMERICAN STUDY PROJECT, UCLA Advance Report 5, at 44 (July, 1966) [hereinafter cited as Mittlebach & Marshall].

[12] Grebler, Moore, & Guzman 250.

[13] Id at 251−52. See also Mittelbach & Marshall, supra note 11, at 45 (9% of Chicano housing, 7.9% of nonwhite housing, and only 1.3% of Anglo housing in Southwestern metropolitan areas was found to be in a dilapidated condition).

Again a particular city illustrates the problem. A 1967 study of El Paso, Texas revealed

The employment picture is just as dismal.[14] Unemployment among Chicanos is over fifty percent higher than among Anglos.[15] Forty-seven percent are unemployed, underemployed or earning less than $3,200 per year.[16] Among United States cities whose populations exceed 100,000, the three poorest are San Antonio, El Paso, and Corpus Christi, Texas, each approximately forty percent Chicano.[17]

While there are many causes of Mexican-American unemployment and resulting poverty, discrimination is the root. It is embodied in many forms, both explicit and subtle, ranging from irrelevant test requirements to unnecessary height and weight specifications.[18] Such discriminatory practices pervade all institutions with which Mexican Americans must contend. It is against this background that Chicano school segregation in Texas must be assessed.

Historically, Texas educators have viewed public education as a vehicle for "Americanizing" the "foreign element".[19] Their efforts to eliminate Chicano culture,[20] however, have met tenacious resistance

---

that 10,500 of the 21,000 residents in a Chicano *barrio* (neighborhood) lived in 238 tenements, only eight of which were of quality comparable to public housing. Only twenty-four of the tenements had hot and cold running water; 101 had no indoor water. Still more disheartening, only 18 of the 238 tenements had inside toilets. The combined total of showers and bathtubs was 120. El Paso Dep't of Planning, SOUTH EL PASO 3—5 (1969).

[14] *See* Comment, *Mexican-Americans and the Desegregation of Schools in the Southwest,* 8 HOUS. L. REV. 929, 933—35 (1971) [hereinafter cited as *Houston*]. A good description of employment discrimination in the metropolitan area of Houston is found in Equal Empl. Oppor. Comm'n, AN EQUAL EMPLOYMENT OPPORTUNITY REPORT—HOUSTON HEARINGS (1970).

[15] Mexican American Leg. Def. and Educ. Fund, THE FORGOTTEN MINORITY (1971).

[16] *Id.* More than half the rural Chicano families in the Southwest (54%) and about one third of urban Chicano families (31%) have annual incomes less than $3,000, a figure below the poverty line. U.S. Comm'n on Civil Rights, MEXICAN-AMERICANS AND THE ADMINISTRATION OF JUSTICE-SUMMARY 2 (1970).

[17] OEO, U.S. CITIES WITH THE HIGHEST POVERTY INCIDENCE 1965 (1966).

[18] *See, e.g.,* Griggs v. Duke Power Co., 401 U.S. 424 (1971), where the Court held unlawful the requirement of either a high school diploma or passage of a battery of tests for employment when each had an adverse effect on employment opportunities of minority workers and neither was relevant to job performance. *See also Houston, supra* note 14, at 933—35.

[19] The general philosophy was expressed by a former Texas State Superintendent of Public Instruction in a chapter entitled "Foreign Problems in Texas". A. Blanton, A HANDBOOK OF INFORMATION: EDUCATION IN TEXAS—SCHOLASTIC YEARS 1918—1922, at 22 (1923). As late as 1946 the Abilene Independent School District (ISD) reported the existence of an "Americanization School". State Dep't of Educ., PUBLIC SCHOOL DIRECTORY, NO. 472, at 13 (1947).

[20] Illustrative of this prevalent attitude is the sworn statement of a young Chicano student: "A Mexican-American boy who used to raise the American flag each morning was told by Mr. Neil, the English teacher and assistant principal, that he couldn't raise

from the Mexican-American community.[21] In the resulting conflict, public school officials and Chicano students have rejected each other, with education the major casualty. The Chicano dropout rate is eighty-nine percent.[22] Median education for Chicanos twenty-five and over is 4.8 years.[23] Institutional rejection has resulted in a pattern of historically segregated schools.

This Comment reports the findings of a ten-month study of Mexican-American educational discrimination in Texas. It will show that the contemporary pattern of Chicano school segregation is a vestige of *de jure* segregation necessitating *de jure* relief. Examination of school officials' activities will demonstrate that separate schools resulted from state action.[24] A survey of judicial decisions will reveal an inadequate response to such segregation. Review of federal executive responses, primarily those of the Department of Health, Education and Welfare, will show similar inadequacy. The Comment concludes with a discussion of remedies needed to attain the dual objectives of integration and education meeting the unique needs of Chicano students.

---

the flag anymore because he wasn't an American." Affidavit of Juventino Dominquez, Jr., March 26, 1970. Filed in Perez v. Sonora Ind. School Dist., Civil No. 6 – 224 (N.D. Tex., Nov. 5, 1970).

This attitude helps to explain the strict application of rules against speaking Spanish on school grounds. The rules apparently derived from Tex. Laws 1933, ch. 125, § 1, at 325 (repealed 1969), which required all school business, except courses in foreign languages, to be conducted in English. Even today, some schools in Texas have what is referred to as Spanish detention, whereby a child caught speaking Spanish is usually held after school. Persistence by the child in using his native language may result in a spanking from the principal or even expulsion. T. Carter, MEXICAN AMERICANS IN SCHOOL: A HISTORY OF EDUCATIONAL NEGLECT 98 (1970).

[21] *See* C. Heller, MEXICAN-AMERICAN YOUTH: A FORGOTTEN YOUTH AT THE CROSSROADS 84 (1966).

[22] S. Steiner, LA RAZA: THE MEXICAN AMERICANS 215 (1970). *See also El Chicano, supra* note 4, at 132 – 33. The Director of Migrant Education for the Southwest Educational Development Laboratory has estimated the dropout rate for migrant children, who are predominantly Chicano, to be about 90%. More shocking is the fact that 20% of those eligible never enroll in school at all. R. Salazar, STRANGER IN ONE'S LAND 28 (U.S. Comm'n on Civil Rights, Pub. No. 19, May, 1970) [hereinafter cited as *Salazar*].

[23] *Grebler, Moore & Guzman, supra* note 11, at 152. In Texas, median education in 1960 for persons 25 years or older was 11.5 years for Anglos, 8.1 years for nonwhites, and 4.8 years for Chicanos. Similar figures for the entire Southwest were 12.1, 9.0, and 7.1, respectively. *Id* at 150. Testimony before the U.S. Commission on Civil Rights, meeting in Texas in 1968, indicated that persons of Spanish surnames, 17 years and older, averaged 4.7 years in school, while Blacks averaged 8.1 and the figure for the entire population was over 10. *Salazar* at 23.

[24] Thus, the statement from a recent law review note that "Mexican-Americans never had the benefit of *de jure* separate but equal education, only of substandard education" is, at least in Texas, incorrect in its first assumption. But it is a dubious "benefit" in any case. *El Chicano, supra* note 4, at 132, citing *Houston, supra* note 14, at 929. In fact, the

I. SEGREGATION OF CHICANO STUDENTS BY OFFICIAL DESIGN

In assessing the constitutionality of school officials' actions, the terms *de jure* and *de facto* have progressively blurred, sometimes signifying little more than legal conclusions.[25] School officials cannot avoid making decisions regarding school boundaries, school construction, and transfer policies, which increase or decrease racial and ethnic separation. The modern trend in what may be termed the Northern cases is that courts find the necessary state action if these decisions increase segregation.[26] Even in the context of Southern Black school segregation, courts have not distinguished racial separation mandated by state law from that resulting from a series of actions by school officials.[27] Nonetheless, although school authorities are accountable for the natural, foreseeable, and probable segregative impact of their recurring operational decisions,[28] courts are more receptive to school desegregation suits based on official intentions and explicit policy statements favoring segregation. This is particularly true in the application of broad-ranging remedies, including busing and redistricting of school attendance zones, sanctioned by the Supreme Court in *Swann v. Charlotte-Mecklenburg Board of Education.*[29] The situation of Chicanos in Texas is a hybrid: while statutory segregation as in the traditional Southern case cannot be shown, it is possible, unlike the usual Northern situation, to show official intent to segregate.

Evidence from widely separated parts of the state indicates that some districts did not originally provide public education for Chicanos.[30] When they did admit Chicanos to public schools, local authorities

---

latter specifically says that "the segregation was de jure since sufficient State action was involved." *Id* at 940.

[25] *See* Comment, *The Evolution of Equal Protection-Education, Municipal Services, and Wealth,* 7 HARV. CIV. RTS.-CIV. LIB. L. REV. 103, 139 (1972) ("*de facto* and *de jure* are less than helpful") [hereinafter cited as *Evolution-Equal Protection*]. *See generally,* Dimond, *School Segregation in the North: There Is But One Constitution,* 7 HARV. CIV. RIGHTS-CIV. LIB. L. REV. 1 (1972); Fiss, *Racial Imbalance in the Public Schools: The Constitutional Concepts,* 78 HARV. L. REV. 564 (1965).

[26] *See* cases cited in note 441, *infra. But see* Keyes v. School Dist. No. 1, 445 F.2d 990 (10th Cir. 1971), *cert. granted,* 40 U.S.L.W. 3329 (U.S. Jan. 17, 1972).

[27] *See* note 25 *supra*

[28] *See* Fiss, *The Charlotte-Mecklenburg Case—Its Significance for Northern School Desegregation,* 38 U. CHI. L. REV. 697, 706 (1971).

[29] *See, e.g.,* Swann v. Charlotte-Mecklenburg Bd. of Educ., 402 U.S. 1 (1971).

[30] One author has implicitly stated that this was the case in El Paso. E. Morrel, THE RISE AND GROWTH OF PUBLIC EDUCATION IN EL PASO 39, 40 (1936). In his study of Nueces County, Paul Taylor states that Mexican Americans first entered the schools in 1891, even though public schools were founded in the early seventies. P. Taylor, AN AMERICAN MEXICAN FRONTIER 192 (1934).

charged with policy-making responsibilities established separate "Mexican" schools,[31] encouraged by the explicit sanction of racial school segregation in the 1876 State Constitution: "Separate schools shall be provided for the white and colored children and impartial provision shall be made for both."[32] Not until 1930 was this provision held not to authorize segregation of Mexican Americans,[33] and not before a 1948 federal district court order[34] did state authorities repudiate segregation of Chicano students as an expression of official policy.[35] No affirmative effort to minimize or eliminate segregation of Chicanos has yet been made.[36]

Public school policy is entrusted to officials at both state and local levels in Texas. State administrative officials are granted general supervisory duties and powers,[37] and are charged with policy formation and planning for the public school system, subject to legislative mandates and prohibitions. The State Board of Education, the principal executive body, often carries out its planning function without explicit legislative directive. In such cases, the legislature's role is merely negative: to check

---

[31] *See generally* W. Little, SPANISH SPEAKING CHILDREN IN TEXAS (1944) [hereinafter cited as *Little*]. *See also* E. Clinchy, Jr., Equality of Opportunity for Latin-Americans in Texas (1954) (unpublished Ph.D. thesis in Columbia University Library); G. Sanchez, CONCERNING SEGREGATION OF SPANISH-SPEAKING CHILDREN IN THE PUBLIC SCHOOLS (Inter-American Educ. Occasional Papers No. IX, 1951) [hereinafter cited as *Sanchez*]. Describing segregated schools in Texas, one Chicano authority stated that "the public school system in Texas was not established to meet the needs of our people; it has only served to rape us of our culture and to permanently maim the minds of our children." Interview with Dr. Hector P. Garcia, founder of the American G.I. Forum and former member of the U.S. Commission on Civil Rights, in Corpus Christi, Texas, Aug. 10, 1971.

[32] Tex. Const. art. 7, § 7 (1876). *Cf.* Free Schools, ch. 124, §§ 93–96 (1905) Tex. Laws (repealed by Acts 1969, 61st Leg., ch. 129, § 1). The 1876 provision was a compromise between the constitutions of 1866 and 1869. The 1866 constitution limited the use of public funds to white schools only, with a separate provision for the taxation of "Africans" to maintain African schools. The Reconstruction constitution of 1869 provided for equal distribution of funds among all school districts, without providing for separate schools.

[33] Independent School Dist. v. Salvatierra, 33 S.W.2d 790 (Tex. Civ. App., 4th Dt. 1930), *cert. denied*, 284 U.S. 580 (1931). The court struck down only the practice of segregating Chicanos regardless of their English language proficiencies, while sanctioning separate schools where language barriers precluded a uniform curriculum.

[34] Delgado v. Bastrop Ind. School Dist., Civil No. 388 (W.D. Tex., June 15, 1948); *accord*, Gonzales v. Sheely, 96 F. Supp. 1004 (D. Ariz. 1951); Mendez v. Westminister School Dist., 64 F. Supp. 544 (C.D. Cal. 1946), *aff'd*, 161 F.2d 774 (9th Cir. 1947).

[35] Sup't of Pub. Instr., Instructions to Regulations (1948): "[T]here has never been any requirement or authority for segregation of Latin American children . . . ." The Instructions do not enunciate a policy of integrating Chicano and Anglo students; they merely deny the existence of any legislative sanction for a segregative policy.

[36] *See* pp. 339–41 *infra*.

[37] Tex. Educ. Code Ann. §§ 11.23–11.35 (1971).

abuses or practices that contravene the duty to provide a meaningful education. General management and control of schools is delegated to local officials, either elected county school boards[38] or boards of trustees for "common"[39] and "independent"[40] school districts. At both state and local levels, the assignment of pupils, creation of school attendance zones, construction of school facilities, and employment and retention of teaching staff have been conducted so as to deny educational opportunities to Mexican-American children, stamping them with a badge of inferiority by unreasonable segregation.

Local school trustees instigated the phenomenon of the "Mexican" school as early as 1902 in the Seguin Independent School District (ISD).[41] As the practice spread, the "tri-ethnic" school system with separate institutions for Anglo, Black and Chicano school children became dominant across the state.[42] By the twenties, operating Mexican

---

[38] *Id.* at §§ 17.01 – 17.02, 17.21 – 17.31.

[39] *Id.* at §§ 22.01 – 22.12.

[40] *Id.* at §§ 23.25 – 23.31.

[41] Seguin ISD, BOARD MINUTES, vol. 1, at 111 (June 9, 1902). *See also* McAllen ISD, BOARD MINUTES, vol. 2, at 11 (Feb. 18, 1919) (discussing the building of a new Mexican School). School board trustees generally provided funds for the construction of such separate facilities. Pharr-San Juan-Alamo ISD, BOARD MINUTES, vol. 1, at 54 (July 14, 1919)(where a committee was appointed to approve architect's plan for a Mexican School in Pharr and San Juan). Anglo hostility to any such expenditure of funds for Chicanos was never lacking, and often had a telling impact on trustees' decisions. For example, in 1919, after several citizens in the Pharr district objected to the presence of Mexican-American students in the district's brick school building, the Pharr Board accepted a proposal to transfer these students to a nearby Mexican church. The citizens had arranged to secure its use as a Mexican School. Pharr-San Juan-Alamo ISD, BOARD MINUTES, vol. 1, at 59 (Sept. 8, 1919). Such practices distinguish Chicano school segregation from both "Southern" Black segregation, which was mandated by state statute, and "Northern" Black segregation, which resulted from administrative decisions. Uniquely, Chicanos were usually relegated to Mexican schools by rules and regulations which *required* them to attend separate schools. For example, an HEW review of the Kingsville ISD includes school board minutes for December 29, 1929 where a "[m]otion was made and carried not to allow any Mexican to attend Flato School, but to attend Stephen F. Austin School where special arrangements had been made for teaching." U.S. Dep't of Health, Educ. & Welfare, On-Site Review of Kingsville ISD, June 23 – 24, 1971.

[42] In 1923, the following cities reported one or more Mexican elementary schools: Amarillo, Bishop, Kennedy, Kerrville, Kingsville, Lockhart, New Braunfels, Pharr-San Juan, Rio Hondo, Robstown, Runge, San Marcos, Sonora, Taft, Taylor, Temple, and Weslaco. State Dep't of Educ., PUBLIC SCHOOL DIRECTORY, NO. 158 (1923). Chicanos and Blacks were often relegated to inferior facilities but not always treated identically. For example, in Pharr, Texas, when there were not enough Blacks to merit a separate school, they were bussed to another city. But Mexican-Americans, when few in number above fourth grade (due to dropout rate), were grudgingly placed in classes on the same campus with Anglos: "The Mexican students of the Alamo Mexican School in the fifth and sixth grades are to be permitted and may attend the Alamo American School, as there are not sufficient number of such students in the fifth and sixth grades in the Alamo

Ward Schools existed in North, Central, West, and South Texas.[43] The state school directory for 1931–32 evidences a wide-spread pattern of locally established Mexican schools wherever Mexican Americans were a part of the school age population.[44] The number of Mexican Ward Schools in independent school districts alone doubled between 1922–23 and 1931–32, to a total of forty.[45] By 1942–43, separate schools for Mexican Americans were maintained by at least 122 districts in fifty-nine widely distributed and representative counties across the state.[46] Under the tri-ethnic system, during the formative period of the Mexican school (the decades from 1920 to 1940), Chicano pupils were often required to register at the Mexican school regardless of residential proximity.[47]

Explicit segregation of Chicano students by local authorities during this initial period was limited to the elementary grades. This was not due to laudable or benign motives. Local policy often limited Chicano

---

Mexican School at the present time to warrant the addition of an extra teacher, and with the proviso that this resolution shall and will be effective for the remainder of the scholastic year only." Pharr-San Juan-Alamo ISD, Board Minutes, vol. 1 at 226, 230 (Feb. 2, 19, 1925). *See also* notes 48 and 50 *infra*.

[43] State Dep't of Educ., Public School Directory Bulletin 158 (1923). In 1929, Nueces County in South Texas alone had twelve school districts providing separate schools for Mexican children. *Taylor, supra* note 1, at 215.

[44] State Dep't of Educ., PUBLIC SCHOOL DIRECTORY, NO. 296, at 7 (1931).

[45] *Id.* at 12–57. The listings in the Directory represented only those in Independent school districts, not those in Common school districts, which were administered by county-wide boards and were generally in rural areas. In addition some independent districts failed to report the existence of Mexican schools. *See* Harlingen ISD, BOARD MINUTES, vol. 3, at 46 (Aug. 14, 1928) (referring to a "Mexican Ward School building" not listed in the 1931–32 Directory). Finally, some districts like the Kingsville ISD, listed in the 1922–23 Directory as having a Mexican school, renamed the facility so that it did not appear as Mexican in the 1932–33 figures. An HEW review of the Kingsville ISD refers to the district's Board Minutes of April 5, 1927, recording that the "Mexican Ward School" was thereafter to be referred to as the Stephen F. Austin School.

[46] *Little, supra* note 31, at 59–60. A clear example of the dual system is reflected in the following entry of total salaries for each of the schools in the Pharr San Juan Alamo district:

Pharr Grammar Sch.	$9165.00
San Juan Gr. Sch.	5310.00
Alamo Gr. Sch.	3105.00
Pharr Mexican Sch.	8635.00
San Juan Mexican Sch.	4185.00
Alamo Mexican Sch.	1035.00

Pharr San Juan Alamo ISD, BOARD MINUTES, vol. 1, at 80 (Sept. 14, 1927).

[47] *E.g.*, U.S. Dep't of Health, Educ. & Welfare, On-Site Review of Uvalde ISD (June, 1970). Harlingen ISD, BOARD MINUTES, vol. B, at 115 (Sept. 14, 1920) (All Chicanos below fifth grade had to attend the Mexican School). Alice ISD, BOARD MINUTES, vol. 5, at 197 (Aug. 24, 1939) (In 1939 the Board of Trustees required that "all Latin Americans attend Nayer School through the elementary grades and Anglo Saxons attend the Hobbes Strickland school through the elementary grades.") References to the Mexican

children to elementary education.[48] Pressures were put on Mexican-American students not to go beyond the elementary level. And where local officials opened secondary schools to Chicanos, so few progressed beyond the elementary level[49] that it was impractical to establish separate high schools. However, when significant numbers did enroll in secondary schools during the mid-1940's, local officials expanded the concept of the Mexican school to include high schools.[50]

State authorities have compounded local segregation of Mexican-American children in two ways. First, they have failed to restrain local authorities, to whom substantial policy-making powers have been delegated, from ignoring their constitutional responsibilities. Second, they have undertaken several actions that in themselves contributed to increased segregation of Chicano students.

A state court recognized the arbitrary nature of Chicano segregation as early as 1930.[51] Holding that only "rational" segregation based on educational (primarily linguistic) needs of Mexican-American students was permissible, it ruled that the constitutional mandate of 1876 for separate schools did not authorize local authorities to segregate for any

school in the Alice District can be found as far back as 1915. *Id.*, vol. 1, at 8 (May 8, 1915).

[48] In the Pecos ISD: "Prior to 1938, no Mexican-American had attended junior or senior high school. . . . According to reliable community contacts, before this time there was a policy of not permitting Mexican-Americans to go beyond the sixth grade." U.S. Dep't of Health, Educ. & Welfare, On-Site Review of Pecos ISD, at 5 (June, 1969). Prior to 1941, no Chicano had graduated from high school in the Pecos district. Only four did so between 1941 and 1944 when fifty-six percent of school age children in Reeves County, where the Pecos district is located, were Mexican-American. *Id.*

Exclusion of Chicanos from the high school in the Sonora ISD prior to 1948 was a finding of fact in Perez v. Sonora Ind. School Dist., Civil No. 6–224 (N.D. Tex., Nov. 5, 1970). In the Bishop district, Chicanos were forced to attend high schools in neighboring districts or not at all. U.S. Dep't of Health, Educ. & Welfare, On-Site Review of Bishop ISD, at 2–3 (Jan. 1970).

[49] During 1942–43, over ninety percent of the Mexican-American school population was enrolled at the elementary level. *Little, supra* note 31, at 37 (Table 15), 41 (Table 16). Little reached this figure by counting the number of Spanish-surnamed school age children on the State Department of Education census rolls for that year. The census itself made no such ethnic breakdown, since Mexican-American children were included in the "White" category. *Id.* at 5. In 1955–56, this proportion had only dropped to seventy-seven percent. H. Manuel, SPANISH SPEAKING CHILDREN OF THE SOUTHWEST 57 (1965). Throughout this period, the first three grade levels contained more than half of all Chicano school children. *Little* 64–65.

[50] In 1942–43, four districts provided separate, segregated high school facilities. *Little, supra* note 31, at 8. In the Ozona ISD, eleven students attended the Mexican high school. That school graduated its first Chicano in 1944, with three more in 1945, one in 1946, and three in 1948, when the Chicano High School closed. The local paper then headlined: "Latin American High School to be Discontinued." Ozona Stockman, July 15, 1948. U.S. Dep't of Health, Educ. & Welfare, On-Site Review of Ozona ISD, 3 (Mar. 1970).

[51] Independent School Dist. v. Salvatierra, 33 S.W.2d 790 (Tex. Civ. App., 4th Dt.

other purpose. Yet the state took no steps to implement the decision beyond the facts of the case.

Arbitrary segregation was later held to violate the fourteenth amendment in the 1948 case of *Delgado v. Bastrop Independent School District*,[52] which should have put an end to the tri-ethnic system. But the response of the State Department of Education muffled its impact. Instructions and regulations promulgated by the Superintendent of Public Instruction[53] were inadequate to cope with the problem of dismantling the deeply entrenched tri-ethnic school system. While declaring a policy of desegregation, they neither established machinery to secure compliance nor provided guidelines for "necessary steps" by local officials to desegregate. Consequently, these regulations were not implemented by local officials.[54] A 1950 Texas Education Agency policy statement[55] appears to have been similarly ignored.[56] Furthermore it appears that the state's decrees were not even communicated to all affected districts.[57]

1930), *cert. denied,* 284 U.S. 580 (1931).

[52] Civil No. 388 (W.D. Tex., June 15, 1948). The court enjoined several defendant school districts from segregating Chicanos from facilities available to Anglo students. First graders who demonstrated a lack of functional familiarity with English were excepted from this order. The state superintendent was enjoined from "directly or indirectly" participating in these segregative practices. The judgment is remarkable for its lack of specificity, failure to retain jurisdiction to assure compliance, and ambiguity.

[53] Sup't of Pub. Instr., Instructions to Regulations (1948).

[54] The Corpus Christi Chapter of the American G.I. Forum, under the leadership of Dr. Hector P. Garcia, asserted in 1949 that segregation was still the rule in fourteen school districts around Corpus Christi. These findings were included in a report of investigations at the following schools: Rio Hondo, Del Rio, Encinal, Beeville, Robstown, George West, Mathis, Orange Grove, Bishop, Driscoll, Sinton, Taft, Three Rivers and Edcouch Elsa. Am. G.I. Forum, SCHOOL INSPECTION REPORT (1949). Similarly, in a sworn affidavit dated April 13, 1950, which Dr. Garcia sent to the Commissioner of Education, he alleged that segregation existed in ten cities which he had personally surveyed: Robstown, Driscoll, Bishop, Banquete, Mathis, George West, Gonzalez, Sinton, Rivera and Taft. The letter included a list of twelve other cities reported to be segregated by other chapters of the G.I. Forum: Alpine, McAllen, Edinburg, Nixon, Seguin, Beeville, Edcouch, Lubbock, Sonora, Marathon, Pecos, and Rockspring. These investigations may have prompted the statement of policy issued by the Texas Education Agency on May 8, 1950. *See* note 55 *infra.*

[55] Texas Bd. of Educ., Statement of Policy Pertaining to Segregation of Latin-American Children (May 8, 1950) (on file with the authors).

[56] *See* pp. 344 – 46 *infra.*

[57] *E.g.,* Kingsville ISD, BOARD MINUTES, vol. 5, pt. 2, at 478 (Sept. 2, 1954) (wherein the school trustees professed ignorance of the *Delgado* decision, in response to protests over a proposed attendance zoning plan). The incipient state of the law regarding the powers and duties of lower federal courts to assure implementation of desegregation orders may have added to the ineffectiveness of *Delgado.* One apparent consequence of the decision and the state response is that local school officials ceased designating schools as Mexican for purposes of the PUBLIC SCHOOL DIRECTORY. The 1948 – 49

These omissions by state officials gain added meaning in light of their thorough awareness and approval of separate local schools. State officials long considered the Mexican school and resulting tri-ethnic system of education symbols of progress. Development of public education was premised upon their continued existence and improvement.[58] Efforts to improve their physical facilities reflected the desire of state school officials to nurture the growth of separate systems.

Awareness by state officials of local segregation is further evidenced by work of the Texas Educational Survey Commission between 1921 and 1925.[59] Its final report to the Governor and Legislature devoted an entire chapter to non-English-speaking children and public schools.[60] The Commission detailed some of the local officials' discriminatory abuses, such as misallocating their appropriated state funds to provide disproportionate amounts of money to "American schools."[61] Thus, while the existence of the Mexican school was the pretext for additional funds, these funds were not spent to educate Mexican pupils. Not only does the state's toleration of this abuse reflect intent to encourage denial of equal educational opportunities, but its acceptance of the tri-ethnic premise was itself the construction of an "inherently unequal"[62] system. The sin of omission is present at two levels: failure to eliminate such an unconstitutional system, and failure to correct abuses of that very system.[63]

Involvement of state officials transcended acquiescence to and support of local segregative policies. State responsibility—"that somewhere, somehow, to some extent, there be an infusion of conduct by officials panoplied with state power . . ."[64]—existed in the past and

DIRECTORY included only one district, Midland, with a Mexican School. State Dept. of Educ., PUBLIC SCHOOL DIRECTORY, Bulletin 499, at 48 (1949).

[58] See, e.g., A. Blanton, A HANDBOOK OF INFORMATION: EDUCATION IN TEXAS, 1918–1922, at 69 (1923)(where the State Superintendent of Public Instruction declared that "schools for Mexicans and Negroes have greatly improved").

[59] The Commission was created to survey the public educational system, including all schools supported in whole or part by public tax moneys. Tex. Rev. Civ. Stat. Ann. arts. 2675a-2675f (1965).

[60] Tex. Educ. Survey Comm., TEXAS EDUCATIONAL SURVEY REPORT VIII: GENERAL REPORT 207 (1925).

[61] Id. at 125.

[62] Brown v. Board of Educ., 347 U.S. 483, 495 (1954). See also Black, The Supreme Court, 1966 Term, Foreword: "State Action," Equal Protection and California's Proposition 14, 81 HARV. L. REV. 69, 95 (1967); Peters, Civil Rights and State Non-Action, 34 NOTRE DAME LAW. 303, 328 (1958).

[63] Cf. Davis v. School Dist., 309 F. Supp. 734, 741 (E.D. Mich. 1970), aff'd, 443 F.2d 573 (6th Cir.), cert. denied, 92 S. Ct. 233 (1971) ("When the power to act is available, failure to take the necessary steps so as to negate or alleviate a situation which is harmful is as wrong as is the taking of affirmative steps to achieve that situation.").

[64] Terry v. Adams, 345 U.S. 461, 473 (1953) (Frankfurter, J., concurring).

continues today. Officials of the State Board periodically review the facilities of all public schools, in order to accredit their status as meeting the Board's educational standards.[65] These reviews have encouraged the development of separate (and supposedly equal) facilities for Mexican-American children. State authorities have directed their efforts to alleviate such problems as overcrowding and half-day sessions, praising local authorities whose operation of Mexican schools approached that of Anglo schools.[66] There is also evidence that state reviewers defined quality education for Chicanos by reference only to other Mexican schools.[67] Little effort was made to assure facilities equal to those of comparable Anglo schools. Accreditation policies therefore sanctioned the existence of tri-ethnic discrimination,[68] while failing to assure that the three separate groups of schools equally fulfilled the goal of quality education.

A second set of discriminatory state practices derives from the process for approving bond proposals. The state attorney general is required by law to "carefully inspect and examine" any proposal for school financing, to assess its "validity."[69] The concept of "validity" has long permitted approval of construction funds for separate school facilities for Anglos, Blacks and Chicanos. The attorney general has approved local issues of construction bonds both explicitly to finance Mexican schools[70] and in cases where school board minutes reveal that

---

[65] Tex. Educ. Code, § 11.26 (1971).

[66] For instance, state officials praised the Harlingen district's high school, and its efforts to structure the Mexican (elementary) schools so that "no crowded condition" existed and that there were no "half-day sessions." Harlingen ISD, BOARD MINUTES, vol. 6 (Oct. 8, 1935). Letters from the State Department of Education to other districts revealed a similar attitude. For example, in 1921, the Chief Supervisor of the public high schools wrote the Alice school board, that he "was very glad that immediate steps will be taken to bring the laboratory up to standard and to increase the teaching force in the Mexican School." Alice ISD, BOARD MINUTES, vol. 1, at 186 (May 14, 1921).

[67] A 1946 Report by the State Department of Education on the Beeville schools concluded that "[p]rovisions for the Latin-American school building and equipment measure up favorably with the best the supervisor has found in twenty-four counties." Corpus Christi Caller Times, Oct. 5, 1947, at 12, col. 1.

[68] See Texas State Dep't of Educ., BULLETIN NO. 428: SUPPLEMENT TO STANDARDS AND ACTIVITIES NO. 416 OF THE DIVISION OF SUPERVISION 1942—43, at 5 (instructing the Director of Supervision to consider the standards and efficiency of the elementary, junior and senior high schools of all *"Anglo-American, Latin-American,* and *Negro* institutions") (emphasis added).

[69] Tex. Rev. Civ. Stat. Ann. art. 2670, § 1 (1965) (renumbered as Art. 709d by Acts, 1969, 61st Leg. Ch. 889, § 2).

[70] Thus, in 1925 the Harlingen district issued an election order calling for the issuance of construction bonds which included "building and equipping an addition to the Mexican School Building." Harlingen ISD, BOARD MINUTES, vol. B, at 277—78 (March 3, 1925). The bond election was successful and the Attorney General approved it on May

bonds were for the purpose of constructing or repairing Mexican schools.[71]

Even after the 1948 disavowal of "required or authorized" separate schools for Chicanos, public monies were used to construct separate schools, since neither state law nor State Board policy contained any prohibition of segregation. Thus, school location and construction reflected a policy of ethnic separation and was "a potent weapon for creating and maintaining a state segregated system."[72] The intentions of state and local officials, throughout the history of public education in Texas, explicitly embraced the concept of segregation with its concomitant deleterious effects upon school children of all ages.

II. THE SURVIVAL OF A SEGREGATED SYSTEM

A. Vestiges of De Jure Segregation

Segregation of Chicano pupils in Texas has harmed not only the students, but the educational system itself. Despite growing judicial, educational, and social awareness of the indelibility of these harms, the tradition of separate schools for Chicanos has continued in full force since *Brown*.

1. Mexican School Revisited. The most obvious reminder of the past is the now institutionalized Mexican school. Although school officials have resorted to more benign appellations, such as J. Luz Saenz, Juan Seguin, and Lorenzo de Zavala, they have not eliminated the most distinctive characteristic of Mexican schools—a predominantly Chicano enrollment.[73] As of 1968, over sixty-six percent of all Texas Chicanos

---

27, 1925. Texas Att'y Gen'l, BIENNIAL REPORT: SEPT. 1, 1924-AUG. 31, 1926, at 89 (1927).

[71] The Seguin ISD is a noteworthy example. In 1916, the Board conducted a bond election to provide funds for various projects, among which was the construction and equipping of a public school with the "building to be used as a school house for Mexican children." Seguin ISD, BOARD MINUTES vol. 2, at 12 – 14 (March 22, 1916). The bond election was later defeated. *Id.*, (May 15, 1916). However, the next year the Board ordered another election. This time the language did not refer to the Mexican school. It stated merely that the funds were for the purpose of constructing a ward school and for additions to the Negro school. *Id.* at 31, 32 (April 11, 1917). The intention of the school board became apparent at a meeting later called to receive "bids for building the Mexican and Negro schools." *Id.* at 39 (July 27, 1917). *See also* McAllen ISD, BOARD MINUTES, vol. 3, at 27 (Sept. 18, 1926) and 55 (July 15, 1927).

[72] Swann v. Charlotte-Mecklenburg Bd. of Educ., 402 U.S. 1, 21 (1971).

[73] Kingsville, McAllen, Harlingen, Sequin, Pecos, Alice, and Midland are only a few of the cities whose original Mexican or Latin-American schools are still predominantly Chicano.

attended predominantly Chicano schools.[74] Of these, forty percent are in schools 80—100 percent Chicano and nearly twenty-one percent attend schools 95—100 percent Chicano.[75] Such general ethnic imbalance is greatest in the elementary grades. This is primarily because the Mexican school concept was initially developed for elementary children,[76] although there are other contributing factors.[77]

A second indicator, "school district" imbalance, connotes an even more invidious official policy. This figure compares the ethnic constituency of each school with that of the entire district. As one would expect, nearly seventy-nine percent of Chicano students attending predominantly Mexican-American schools reside in predominantly Chicano districts.[78] Over thirty-four percent of all Chicano students in Texas, or nearly 173,051 pupils, however, attend schools in ethnic imbalance with the constituency of the district.[79] The pervasiveness of this imbalance removes the segregation from the realm of chance.

Moreover, statistics indicate that identifiable Mexican schools are no longer restricted to elementary grades. Some districts have succeeded in developing Chicano intermediate and secondary schools. In 1969 over eighty-six percent of Anglo high school students in the El Paso district attended predominantly Anglo schools and over eighty-one percent of Chicano high school students were enrolled at predominantly Chicano schools. These figures closely approximated those for comparable elementary grades.[80] At least three choices of educational policy have

---

[74] ETHNIC ISOLATION, *supra* note 2, at 26. For the five Southwestern states of Arizona, California, Colorado, New Mexico, and Texas, this figure is forty-five percent. *Id.* at 26. In 1968, of the eight million public school pupils in the Southwest, seventy-one percent were Anglo, seventeen percent were Chicano, ten percent were Black, and two percent were Asian or Native American. Thirty-six percent of all Southwestern Spanish-surnamed students are in Texas. *Id.* at 16—17. Student enrollment in Texas by ethnic group in 1968 was 64.4 percent Anglo, 20.1 percent Chicano, 15.1 percent Black and 0.3 percent Native American or Asian. *Id.* at 17 (rounded figures).

[75] *Id.*

[76] *See* pp. 314—15 *supra*

[77] Notable are the disincentive effects upon pupils created by a failure of the educational process at these early age levels. Vestiges of this high level of elementary segregation are reflected in statistics for Texas which reveal that in 1968, while 69.9 percent of Chicano elementary students were in predominantly Chicano schools, 59.6 percent of Chicano intermediate students and 61.5 percent of Chicano secondary pupils were similarly segregated. ETHNIC ISOLATION, *supra* note 2, at 28.

[78] *Id.* at 29. Again we refer to 1968 statistics, assuming no significant change since then.

[79] *Id.* at 30. A school is ethnically imbalanced under this definition when the ethnic composition of the group deviates by 15 percent or more from the composition of the district.

[80] U.S. Dep't of Health, Educ. & Welfare, On-Site Review of El Paso ISD, at 24 (April 1970). The figures for elementary grade levels were 81.8 percent (Anglo) and 85.8 percent (Chicano).

assisted this spread of segregation. Implementation of the "feeder" school plan has channeled isolation from the elementary to the secondary level. New schools have been located to conform to increasing patterns of residential separation. Finally, freedom-of-choice plans have encouraged whites to transfer out of schools with large proportions of Chicanos.[81]

2. Chicano Achievement. The history of Chicanos in the segregated educational facilities of Texas has been one of "educational neglect."[82] Segregated schools have provided Chicano students with sub-standard facilities[83] and stamped them with a badge of inferiority.[84] Achievement statistics demonstrate that segregation has not provided an educational setting conducive to success.

In Texas, Chicanos have been one of the groups most estranged from the public schools.[85] A recent study has shown that Chicanos drop out

[81] For example, because of the construction of neighborhood schools and the adoption of a freedom-of-choice plan, four of the seven elementary schools in the Alice district were at least ninety-seven percent Chicano in 1970. This enrollment accounted for ninety-five percent of the entire population of Chicano students. U.S. Dep't of Health, Educ. & Welfare, Elementary and Secondary School Civil Rights Survey, Form OSCCR-102 (1970). *Cf.* U.S. Dep't of Health, Educ. & Welfare, On-Site Review of Bishop ISD, at 49 (Jan. 1970).

[82] *See generally* T. Carter, MEXICAN AMERICANS IN SCHOOL: A HISTORY OF EDUCATIONAL NEGLECT (1970).

[83] In a 1947 survey of ten school systems, it was found that "[t]he physical facilities, equipment, and instructional materials in the schools for Spanish-name children were found to be generally inferior and inadequate as compared with those existing in the Anglo schools." Strickland & Sanchez, *Spanish Name Spells Discrimination,* THE NATION'S SCHOOLS, at 22 — 24 (Jan. 1948). Substandard facilities for Chicanos are not altogether a thing of the past. In 1971 Dr. Garcia complained to the State Department of Health about conditions at three predominantly Chicano schools. In a post-inspection letter, the Commissioner of Health stated that "major overall repair and improvement including outside and inside painting, replacement of all broken windows, roof repair, etc., is needed at all three schools." Letter from V.E. Peavy to Dr. Hector P. Garcia, June 29, 1971. Compare this with a 1951 letter to the State Department of Health in which Dr. Garcia complained of the health and safety hazards at the Sonora Mexican school. Letter from Dr. Hector P. Garcia to Dr. George W. Cox, May 2, 1951, on file with the authors.

[84] In Mendez v. Westminister School Dist., 64 F. Supp. 544, 559 (N.D. Cal. 1946), the court found that "the methods of segregation prevalent in the defendant school district foster antagonisms in the children and suggests inferiority among them where none exists." *See, e.g.,* Brown v. Board of Educ., 347 U.S. 483 (1954).

[85] One authority has described the estrangement in these terms: "The high dropout rate among Spanish-American students, the high degree of overageness in grade placement, the low academic achievement, the un-motivated and disinterested students, and the low educational attainment among the Spanish-surnamed population suggests that some degree of educational alienation exists among members of this subculture." Cordova, *The Relationship of Acculturation, Achievement, and Alienation Among Spanish-American*

before completing high school at a rate 3.2 times greater than that of Anglo students.[86] The proportion of Chicano high school graduates enrolling in institutions of higher education (30.7 percent) is also dismally low in comparison to that for Anglos (62.2 percent).[87]

A clearer indication that ethnically segregated schools have been ineffective is found in reading ability statistics. By the end of the twelfth grade, 64.7 percent of Chicanos are deficient in their reading ability as compared with twenty-one percent of Anglo students.[88] Verbal ability statistics for Chicanos are equally inferior.[89] Segregated schools which isolate Chicanos from their English-speaking peers have a harmful effect on the Spanish-speaking child's verbal ability in English. Any diminution of the opportunity to improve oral language skills has a parallel effect on reading ability. In spite of this educational system's appalling performance, segregation persists.

3. Instructional and Administrative Staff. Another vestige of the segregated school in Texas is the distribution of Chicano professional staff.[90] The Table titled "Teacher Distribution" includes figures for twenty school districts of varying size and geographical location, and is illustrative of present disparities. The table reveals that the percentage of Chicano teachers in a school district is never equal to the percentage of Chicano students.[91] More significantly, some districts with substantial numbers of Chicano students have not hired a single Chicano teacher.[92] A third troubling statistic reveals that Anglos have a substantially lower

---

Sixth Grade Students, in EDUCATING THE MEXICAN AMERICAN 163 (H. Johnson & W. Hernandez eds. 1971).

[86] U.S. Comm'n on Civil Rights, MEXICAN-AMERICAN EDUCATIONAL SERIES, REP. II: THE UNFINISHED EDUCATION 20 (1971) [hereinafter cited as UNFINISHED EDUCATION].

[87] *Id.* at 22.

[88] *Id.* at 25.

[89] *Id.* at 89. The two statistics are interrelated. *See generally* J. Moffett, A STUDENT-CENTERED LANGUAGE ARTS CURRICULUM, GRADES K-13: A HANDBOOK FOR TEACHERS (1968).

[90] ETHNIC ISOLATION, *supra* note 2, at 42.

[91] Additional support for this conclusion is found in a letter which Dr. Garcia sent to J. Stanley Pottinger, Director of the Office for Civil Rights of the U.S. Dep't of Health, Educ. & Welfare. Dr. Garcia included a list of 224 school districts in Texas which had a Chicano enrollment. In none of the districts was the percentage of Chicano teachers equal to or greater than the corresponding percentage of Chicano students. Letter from Dr. Hector P. Garcia to J. Stanley Pottinger, October 2, 1970, on file with Dr. Garcia in Corpus Christi.

[92] The list which accompanied Dr. Garcia's letter to Mr. Pottinger included the following districts which have a majority of Chicano enrollments, but no Chicano teachers: Hondo, Fort Hancock, O'Donnell, Ozona, and Karnes Independent School Districts.

student-teacher ratio than Chicanos in each of the districts,[93] regardless of the district's ethnic character.

The underrepresentation of Chicanos in the teaching profession is due to many factors, but the history of ineffective education of Chicanos must bear primary responsibility. There are simply too few Chicanos who meet the educational prerequisites for state authorization to teach, because segregated schools in Texas have provided Chicanos with an inadequate education.[94]

Chicano teachers in Texas are segregated even more than are Chicano pupils. Eighty percent of the teachers, compared to two-thirds of the students, are in predominantly Chicano schools.[95] Non-teaching, professional staff are similarly segregated.[96] For example, prior to 1969, Chicanos had never been hired as counselors or librarians in the Pecos district.[97] Similarly, as of 1970 one Crockett County Common School District had not hired a single Mexican-American principal or teacher's aide in its history.[98]

These policies exacerbate segregation in public schools by making possible, and encouraging, ethnic identification of schools on the basis of staff composition. Moreover, they do not comply with the dictates

---

[93] The figures for pupil-teacher ratios in the state as a whole are 1 to 98 (Chicano), 1 to 31 (Black), and 1 to 19 (Anglo). ETHNIC ISOLATION, *supra* note 2, at 42.

[94] Other factors contributing to the scarcity of Chicano teachers reflect deeper alienation of the Chicano from the entire educational system. These include a lack of junior colleges and Chicano colleges that may provide a bridge to professional education and careers, and a near 100 percent dropout rate from high school until the late 1940's. Interview with Carlos Vela, former staff member, Office of Civil Rights, U.S. Dep't of Health, Educ. & Welfare, in Brownsville, Tex., Aug. 9, 1971. *See also* UNFINISHED EDUCATION *supra* note 86, at 22.

[95] ETHNIC ISOLATION, *supra* note 2, at 44–45. The situation in the Alice district is illustrative. In 1970, 94.7 percent of the Chicano elementary teachers were assigned to schools with at least ninety-seven percent Chicano enrollments. Similarly, the four Chicano principals are at schools which are at least ninety-seven percent Mexican-American. U.S. Dept. of Health, Educ. & Welfare, Fall 1970 Elementary and Secondary School Civil Rights Survey.

[96] A study of Texas districts with ten percent or more Chicanos showed that all Chicano professional librarians and about eighty percent of the counselors and assistant principals are assigned to predominantly Mexican-American schools. ETHNIC ISOLATION, *supra* note 2, at 50. A 1970 review of the Uvalde district has shown that the district employed no Chicano principals and no Chicano counselors. In addition, none of the Chicano elementary teachers were assigned to the predominantly Anglo school; all (except for the Head Start and special education teachers) were given positions at the Chicano elementary schools. U.S. Dep't of Health, Educ. & Welfare, On-Site Review of Uvalde ISD, SS d, f, and g of findings (June 1970).

[97] U.S. Dep't of Health, Educ. & Welfare, On-Site Review of Pecos ISD, § II of findings (June 1969).

[98] U.S. Dep't of Health, Educ. & Welfare, On-Site Review of Crockett County Cons. School Dist. (Ozona), at 27 (Jan. 1970).

SEGREGATED TEXAS SCHOOL
DISTRICTS

TEACHER DISTRIBUTION*

School District	Teachers				Students				Teacher-Student Ratio		
	M/A†	A/A††	Other	Total	M/A	A/A	Other	Total	M/A	A/A	Other
Alice	99 30.8%	221 68.8%	1 .40%	321	4458 66.2%	2226 33.0%	50 .80%	6734	1:45	1:10	1:50
Brownsville	365 53.9%	299 44.2%	12 1.9%	676	15611 87.3%	2255 12.5%	17 .20%	17933	1:43	1:7	1:1
El Paso	562 21.3%	1967 74.8$	99 3.9%	2628	35215 57.4%	23840 38.8%	2273 3.8%	61328	1:63	1:12	1:23
Harlingen	127 27.8%	323 70.8%	6 1.4%	456	7527 70.9%	2957 27.8%	123 1.3%	10607	1:59	1:9	1:20
Karnes City	0	72 100%	0	72	595 43.2%	699 50.8%	83 6.0%	1377	0	1:9	0
Kingsville	119 33.6%	225 63.5%	10 2.9%	354	3670 56.2%	2601 39.8%	257 4.0%	6528	1:31	1:11	1:26
La Feria	8 12.1%	58 87.9%	0	66	1245 76.6%	371 22.8%	10 60%	1626	1:55	1:6	0
McAllen	155 33.2%	311 66.8%	0	466	8482 74.7%	2838 25.0%	22 .30%	11342	1:74	1:9	0
Midland	22 2.9%	676 89.7%	55 7.3%	753	2343 13.5%	12785 74.1%	2128 12.3%	17247	1:106	1:19	1:39
New Braunfels	7 4.0%	164 95.3%	1 .7%	172	1707 42.8%	2168 54.4%	105 2.8%	3980	1:244	1:13	1:105
Odessa	28 2.4%	1018 90.8%	75 6.6%	1121	4059 17.0%	18128 76.1%	1627 6.8%	23814	1:145	1:18	1:22
Ozona	0	60 100%	0	60	553 53.0%	472 45.3%	15 1.7%	1042	0	1:7	0
Pecos	14 6.8%	187 91.2%	4 2.0%	205	2755 61.1%	1590 35.2%	162 3.7%	4507	1:197	1:8	1:40
Pharr-San Juan-Alamo	218 51.2%	206 48.4%	1 .40%	425	7208 85.8%	1183 14.0%	5 .20%	8396	1:33	1:6	1:5
San Benito	76 31.1%	165 67.6%	3 1.3%	244	5053 86.6%	738 12.8%	40 .60%	5831	1:66	1:4	1:13
Seguin	13 5.2%	212 85.8%	22 9.0%	247	2083 40.6%	2316 45.2%	723 14.2%	5122	1:160	1:11	1:33
Snyder	1 .40%	214 96.8%	6 2.7%	221	780 20.5%	2817 74.1%	204 5.3%	3801	1:780	1:13	1:34
Uvalde	18 9.2%	175 90.2%	1 .50%	194	2468 63.3%	1415 36.3%	12 .30%	3895	1:137	1:8	1:12
Victoria	26 4.7%	496 89.6%	31 5.6%	553	4292 34.9%	6933 56.4%	1060 8.6%	12285	1:165	1:14	1:34
Ysleta	206 15.2%	1120 82.7%	28 2.1%	1354	22005 62.2%	12097 34.2%	1250 3.6%	35352	1:107	1:11	1:45

* With the following exceptions, all figures have been compiled from the U.S. Dep't of Health, Educ. & Welfare, Fall 1971 Elementary and Secondary School Civil Rights Survey, Form OS/CR 101 – 1:

Figrues for Alice—Fall 1970 Survey, Form OS/CR101 – 1;

Figures for La Feria and Karmes City—Fall 1969 Survey, Form OS/CR 101 – 1;

Figures for Ozona—U.S. Dep't. of Health, Educ. & Welfare, On-Site Review of Crockett County Consol. Common School Dist., at 1 (March 9, 1970);

Figures for Pecos—U.S. Dep't. of Health, Educ., & Welfare, On-Site Review of Pecos ISD, at 4 – 5 (June 3 – 5, 1969).

† M/A = Mexican American

†† A/A = Anglo American

of *Swann* that administrative choices result in schools of similar quality and staff.[99] By superimposing segregation of professional personnel on the existing pattern of separate schools for Anglo and Chicano students, school officials reveal their calculated efforts to maintain a wall between communities.

B. Perpetuation of a Dual School System

Segregation of Chicano students is as prevalent today, twenty-four years after *Delgado*, as it was during the 1940's. Freedom-of-choice plans,[100] gerrymandered zones,[101] option zones,[102] transfer policies,[103] construction of neighborhood schools[104] and public transportation plans[105] are utilized by school officials to perpetuate separation. These arrangements have been condemned as "calculted to . . . maintain and promote a dual school system,"[106] both in Northern school systems[107] and in situtations involving Chicanos.[108]

1. School Construction. Segregation was initially achieved by constructing identifiable Mexican school buildings. It was maintained simply by repairing and expanding these schools to accommodate increasing Chicano enrollment.[109] Improvements of dilapidated facilities were made to satisfy the pressing need for space. When these failed, more extensive repairs or alterations of physical plant were undertaken. Only when schools became grossly overcrowded was new construction undertaken.[110]

---

[99] Swann v. Charlotte-Mecklenberg Bd. of Educ., 402 U.S. 1, 19 (1971). *See also* Dimond, *supra* note 25, at 3.

[100] *E.g.,* Alice district. Interview with Lewis Davis, Director Pupil Personnel and Services, in Alice, June 8, 1971).

[101] *E.g.,* Pecos district. U.S. Dept. of Health, Educ. & Welfare, On-Site Review of Pecos ISD, at S Ib (June 1969).

[102] *E.g.,* Seguin district. Seguin ISD, BOARD MINUTES (Sept. 8, 1959).

[103] *E.g.,* El Paso district. U.S. Dep't of Health, Educ. & Welfare, On-Site Review of El Paso ISD, at 23 (Apr. 1970).

[104] *E.g.,* Harlingen district. Harlingen ISD, BOARD MINUTES, vol. I (Feb. 22, 1962).

[105] *E.g.,* El Paso district. *See* U.S. Dep't of Health, Educ. & Welfare, On-Site Review of El Paso ISD, at 23 (Apr. 1970).

[106] Cisneros v. Corpus Christi Ind. School Dist., 324 F. Supp. 599, 620 (S.D. Tex. 1970).

[107] *See* Dimond, *supra* note 25, at 3.

[108] Cisneros v. Corpus Christi Ind. School Dist., 324 F. Supp. 559 (S.D. Tex. 1970). *Cf.* Keyes v. School Dist. 1, 445 F.2d 990 (10th Cir. 1971), *cert. granted,* 40 U.S.L.W. 3329 (U.S. Jan. 17, 1972).

[109] *E.g.,* McAllen ISD, BOARD MINUTES, vol. 2, at 21 (Oct. 4, 1919). The entry reveals that the Board was concerned with conducting a bond election for the purpose of erecting school buildings, especially one in the Mexican part of town.

[110] *Eg.,* Harlingen ISD, BOARD MINUTES, vol. 14, at 2. (Oct. 2, 1945). Attendance

By creating Mexican schools, local Boards established the foundation for a pattern of segregation that continues to the present. These initial decisions also had an impact in determining the composition of neighborhoods, because people gravitate toward the schools to which their children are assigned.[111] The original segregation has been maintained by repairing and constructing schools in Mexican *barrios*, contravening the local board's duty to eliminate a dual school system.[112] The El Paso district is a good example. Beginning with the erection of two high schools in 1930, the effect of new construction has consistently been to further isolate Mexican-American students.[113] Similarly, the Alice district purposefully perpetuated a dual school system when it built two elementary schools in 1963: one on the "Mexican" side of town with an exclusively Chicano opening enrollment and a completely Chicano staff, the other predominantly Anglo.[114] Such construction activity is unconstitutional because it impedes the creation of a unitary system.[115]

2. Freedom-of-Choice Plans. Freedom-of-choice plans have merited close scrutiny in situations involving Black segregation.[116] Such plans are even less workable where Chicanos are involved. Fear of the Anglo-dominated environment outside the barrio, additional transportation burdens placed upon already meager budgets, and administrative failure to make any choice available are compounded by an additional obstacle: the language barrier. These pressures, combined with a policy of encouraging Anglos to exercise their choice, augment ethnic segregation. Only three times have such plans worked to integrate Anglo and Chicano

---

at the Mexican elementary school had swollen to an average of 1186. Figures for Anglo elementary schools were 500, 210, 150, and 195 pupils respectively. The Harlingen Board decided to remodel the Mexican school and to build a new "Latin-American" school. *See* Alice ISD, BOARD MINUTES, vol. 6, at 11 (Sept. 17, 1946) (plans to build another Latin-American school in the Mexican part of town).

[111] *See, e.g.,* Swann v. Charlotte-Mecklenburg Bd. of Educ., 402 U.S. 1, 20 (1971) ("the location of schools may . . . influence the patterns of residential development").

[112] *E.g.,* Carter v. West Feliciana Parish School Bd., 396 U.S. 290, 292 (1970) (per curiam) (mem.) ("extirpate any lingering vestiges of a constitutionally prohibited dual school system") (Harlan, J., concurring); Alexander v. Holmes County Bd. of Educ., 396 U.S. 19, 20 (1969) (per curiam) ("the obligation . . . is to terminate dual systems at once and to operate now and hereafter only unitary schools"); Green v. County School Bd., 391 U.S. 430, 437–38 (1968) ("affirmative duty to take whatever steps might be necessary to convert to a unitary system").

[113] U.S. Dep't of Health, Educ. & Welfare, Compliance Review of El Paso ISD, at 18 (Mar. 1971).

[114] Alice ISD, BOARD MINUTES, vol. 11, at 7, 67 (July 9, 1963).

[115] *Cf.* Bradley v. School Bd., 324 F. Supp. 456, 462 (E.D. Va. 1971) (patterns of new school construction must affirmatively promote the creation of a unitary school system).

[116] Green v. County School Bd., 391 U.S. 430 (1968); *cf.* Raney v. Board of Educ., 391 U.S. 443 (1968).

school children, and then only after a strong community-wide effort by Chicano parents.[117]

The freedom-of-choice policy was not established to benefit the entire community. Recent litigation involving the Sonora district has exposed instances where school officials have thwarted efforts by Chicano parents to exercise options.[118] The policy has evidently been designed to allow Anglo children residing near a predominantly Mexican-American school to choose to attend an Anglo school. Examples of this segregative result are legion. In the Bishop district, students at the predominantly Anglo elementary school were sent "choice forms" in the spring preceding the applicable school year, while students at the Mexican elementary school were never given the opportunity to exercise a choice.[119] Another discriminatory application of the policy was found in Ozona. When freedom-of-choice was implemented, there was no publication of the plan in either the board minutes or newspapers. There was only the Anglo superintendent's insistence that he had told "everybody in town" about it.[120] Finally, there exist situations like Abilene, where a geographic zoning policy was grafted onto the freedom-of-choice plan. There the ninety-nine percent Black school and the ninety-five percent Mexican-American school were located in the same zone, just six blocks apart, and their pupils' choice was limited to one or the other of the two schools.[121]

"Choice" plans rarely encourage Anglo children to attend predomi-

---

[117] In 1970, parents of Chicano pupils in the Alpine district joined together to exercise their choice to transfer their elementary-age children to the school which contained over eighty-five percent Anglo children. They were leaving a school that was 98.9 percent Chicano. School officials responded by converting one school into a junior high school, housing all elementary pupils in the other. Interview with Mr. Pete Gallegos, Board Member, Alpine ISD, in Alpine, Tex., July 6, 1971. See Sanchez, supra note 31, at 20−21 (mass exercise of choice by Chicano parents in Del Rio district in 1949 resulted in termination of plan and consolidation of schools). Chicano parents in Cotulla, Texas, integrated the Mexican school (Welhausen) where Lyndon B. Johnson held his first teaching job when they exercised their freedom of choice. When all Chicanos chose the Anglo school in September, 1970, the district was forced to pair. Integration resulted in better equipment and facilities for the former Mexican school. Telephone interview with Alfredo Zamora, former mayor of Cotulla, Texas, Apr. 3, 1972.

[118] See Affidavit of V.C. Chavez, Perez v. Sonora Ind. School Dist., Civil No. 6−224 (N.D. Tex., Nov. 5, 1970). When Ms. Chavez attempted to enroll her child at the Anglo Central Elementary School, she was told by the Superintendent that the only people who have freedom-of-choice are those who live in ranches and must ride a school bus. Few Mexican Americans are able to meet this criterion.

[119] U.S. Dep't of Health, Educ. & Welfare, On-Site Review of Bishop ISD, at 25 (Jan. 1970).

[120] U.S. Dep't of Health, Educ. & Welfare, On-Site Review of Crockett County Cons. Common School Dist., at 5 (May 1970).

[121] U.S. Dep't of Health, Educ. & Welfare, On-Site Review of Abilene ISD, at 2 (Feb. 1969).

nantly Mexican-American schools. On the contrary, they encourage Anglo children to flee predominantly Chicano "neighborhood schools."[122] This "white flight" and the homogeneity of identifiable Chicano schools will persist so long as local officials utilize freedom-of-choice schemes to maintain segregation.

3. Transfer Policies. Permissive transfer plans have results similar to those achieved by freedom-of-choice plans, but with little pretense that anyone is offered a choice. An excellent example of a "free transfer" plan that served to segregate is that which existed in Seguin, Texas. The 1960 school board minutes reveal the thoughts of local officials:

> The crux of the problem is this, the Latin-Americans look upon Juan Seguin as a segregated school because we have in the past permitted Anglos to transfer out of that area while at the same time we have been trying to insist on Latins going to Juan Seguin School. Sooner or later the Latins will force our hand on it a·.d I know what the State Commissioner of Education will do. He will order the School Board to zone school areas.[123]

A variation of this technique is the "inter-district transfer." Under this plan, students are allowed to transfer to schools in neighboring districts if overcrowding is thereby alleviated. The Texas Commissioner of Education has complied with a court order enjoining his approval of such inter-district transfers when they perpetuate or increase ethnic segregation by resulting in transfer only of Anglos out of predominantly Black or Chicano schools.[124] The primary abusers of "inter-district" transfer plans have been school officials of districts with enclaves of United States military personnel (predominantly Anglo),[125] and there is evidence that they and other local authorities are managing to evade the

---

[122] *E.g.,* Alice District has a freedom-of-choice policy for seven elementary schools. A school official stated that he knew of no case where an Anglo child had decided to attend one of the four predominantly (97 – 100 percent) Mexican-American schools. Interview with Lewis Davis, Director Pupil Personnel and Services, in Alice, June 8, 1971.

[123] Seguin ISD, BOARD MINUTES, at 2 (June 14, 1960).

[124] Order of Aug. 13, 1971, in Del Rio ISD intervention in United States v. Texas, 321 F. Supp. 1043 (E.D. Tex. 1970), *modified,* Civil No. 5281 (E.D. Tex., July 16, 1971).

[125] *Id.* The case involved a plan creating racially segregated schools. Two contiguous districts (San Felipe and Del Rio) collaborated to transfer over 800 children who were dependents of personnel at Laughlin Air Force Base. Most of the children were Anglo. In 1956 the Texas Education Agency approved the transfer, and thereafter assisted in paying for necessary transportation. Because of the transfer to the Del Rio district, additional federal funds were received by that district, which were used to construct a new high school. The federal district court ordered the districts consolidated as of August 7, 1971.

Commissioner's order.[126]

4. Attendance Zones. School trustees rely on varied schemes for the necessary task of drawing boundary lines to distribute the student population. However, this discretionary tool has historically been utilized to isolate Mexican-American students in many Texas communities. The zoning policies of the Uvalde district illustrate the abuse. A recent re-drawing of attendance zones when a new elementary school opened in the "Chicano area" raised the proportion of Chicanos attending Mexican schools from sixty-three to seventy-four percent of total Chicano enrollment.[127]

Because demarcation of school zones is a complicated procedure dependent upon balancing many interests, one should not too readily infer discriminatory intention from such statistics. However, since trustees must select one plan which reflects their evaluation of the relative importance of interests, their plan reveals the weight attributed to integrated education. When school authorities choose the one zoning plan from among four admitted to be pedagogically sound which maximizes resulting ethnic and racial segregation, one infers they value integration least of all.[128] That such a value choice is intolerable is now abundantly clear.[129] In particular, the purity of motive professed by many local school authorities, who stress devotion to the neighborhood school concept,[130] cannot be accepted in light of their current transportation

---

[126] On July 21, 1971, the San Antonio district was cautioned against accepting 316 transfers from the Kelly Air Force Base, located within the neighboring Edgewood district. The Commissioner of Education warned that continued acceptance would result in a loss of state funds and a loss of accreditation. San Antonio Express, July 22, 1971, at 8, col. 1. However, the practice of accepting transfers persists. Telephone interview with Mauro Reyna, Deputy Superintendent of Edgewood ISD, November 5, 1971.

Districts surrounding the Crystal City district are impeding integration by accepting such inter-district transfers. After Board elections in which La Raza Unida (the Chicano party) swept into office, Anglo parents sought to transfer their children elsewhere. Three school districts agreed to accept the transferees: Uvalde, La Pryor, and Carrizo Springs. These three districts have also been warned by the state Commissioner. San Antonio Express, July 22, 1971, at 18, col. 1. But the warnings have been unsuccessful in arresting the practice. Telephone interview with Amanzio Cantu, Assistant Superintendent of Crystal City ISD, November 5, 1971.

[127] U.S. Dep't of Health, Educ. & Welfare, On-Site Review of Uvalde ISD, at 5 − 6 (June 1970).

[128] This is exactly what happened in Kingsville in 1954. Kingsville ISD, BOARD MINUTES, vol. 5, pt. 2, at 478 (Sept. 2, 1954). *See also* Harlingen ISD, BOARD MINUTES, vol. 1, (Feb. 22, 1962) (where a similar controversy ensued when the Board decided to zone the two junior high schools).

[129] *See, e.g.,* Bradley v. School Bd., 40 U.S.L.W. 1105 (E.D. Va., Jan. 5, 1972); *cf.* Dimond, *supra* note 25, at 27.

[130] In the Kingsville situation, note 128 *supra,* school officials insisted they were drawing boundary lines to make it more convenient for students to attend their neighborhood

policies.

5. *Busing.* School officials' transportation programs have perpetuated the identifiability of Mexican-American schools. One of the most frequent situations involves busing Anglo children across town to predominantly Anglo schools. A special irony results when the bus carrying Anglo students makes several stops at schools which are identifiably Mexican-American.[131] Here again, school officials use their discretionary powers to transport Anglo students out of neighborhoods in which they are an ethnic minority.

The desire to bus is so strong in some districts that local authorities insist upon it even when state assistance is not provided.[132] For instance, in El Paso, elementary schools have been zoned to establish a "feeder" pattern for intermediate and high schools. Predominantly Chicano Jones elementary school is zoned to feed predominantly Chicano El Paso High School. Students in the Jones attendance zone are actually closer to an elementary, intermediate, and high school now predominantly Anglo. Because of this and the availability of public transportation, state assistance to bus Mexican Americans to the Chicano High School is unavailable. Nevertheless, local authorities do so with district funds. They adamantly insist on the fairness of their policies, arguing that Mexican-American students are not the only ones bused at local expense. In fact, they point out, Anglo students who reside near Chicano schools are similarly bused to predominantly Anglo elementary and intermediate schools.[133] Thus, local officials combine liberal transfer policies and a busing scheme to further isolate Chicano students.

6. *Remedial Classes (Tracking).* In many instances, tracking continues to separate Chicanos from Anglos on the same campus. Separate classrooms, operated without regard for linguistic abilities of students, were often introduced in response to abolition of the Mexican school.[134]

---

schools. Reliance on the composition of neighborhoods to justify zoning plans was untenable, however, because the officials, by establishing Mexican schools, had been intimately involved in the forging of the ethnic composition of those neighborhoods. *See* U.S. Dep't of Health, Educ. & Welfare, On-Site Review of Kingsville ISD (June 23—24, 1971).

[131] *See* U.S. Dep't of Health, Educ. & Welfare, On-Site Review of Alice ISD, at 6 (Sept. 1968), reporting the busing of a substantial number of Anglo students past Mary Garcia School (99% Mexican-American) to Noonan Elementary School which had a significantly larger number of Anglo students.

[132] Tex. Educ. Code §§ 16.51—16.61 (1971) (provision of state aid for busing).

[133] U.S. Dep't of Health, Educ. & Welfare, Compliance Review of El Paso ISD, at 10 (Mar. 1971) (affidavit of Carlos F. Vela).

[134] *E.g.,* Wharton ISD historically operated a separate school for Chicanos. The

This segregation has been perpetuated by so-called ability-grouping, which produces over-representation of Chicanos in lower-achieving sections.[135] For example, during the 1970 school year, the fourth grade remedial class at Bishop District's Eastside elementary was composed solely of Blacks and Chicanos, while the fifth grade remedial class was entirely Chicano. This was the case even though there were Anglos in both grades with lower test scores.[136]

Intentional segregation is also evident where "lower ability" Chicanos are housed in separate facilities. The process involves the administration of a general achievement test, and utilizing the resulting scores as the basis for selecting students for the "special" facilities. In some instances, tests are given only to Chicanos.[137] Ability grouping, or tracking, perpetuates any ethnic imbalance that may exist in the lower grades. It "locks-in" those classed as "low achievers" by systematically destroying their self-image and expectation of academic success.[138]

The purposeful segregation becomes more apparent where Chicanos are classified as "educationally mentally retarded" (EMR) partially on the basis of intelligence tests given in English.[139] Recent studies have cast doubt on the validity of these intelligence tests, especially with respect to Chicanos.[140] However, blind adherence to IQ tests by school officials reveals that their interest is not in effectively measuring intelligence, but

---

evidence indicates that when the Mexican School was abandoned in 1948 the district contemporaneously initiated an ability grouping program. U.S. Dep't of Health, Educ. & Welfare, On-Site Review of Wharton ISD, at 12 (June 1970). In the 1969 – 70 school year, fifty-two percent of Anglo and four percent of Chicano first grade students were in "accelerated" classes.

[135] The extent of segregation in the Wharton district is demonstrated by the fact that ninety-three percent of Chicano first graders were in predominantly Chicano classes and sixty-three percent of Anglos were in predominantly Anglo classes. Segregation was even greater in the second and third grades. A sampling of upper grades indicated that grouping continued to promote segregation. *Id.* at 3 – 11. *See* Zamora v. New Braunfels Ind. School Dist., Civil Action No. 68 – 205-SA (W.D. Tex., filed Aug. 28, 1968) (alleging discrimination against Chicanos in the use of a system of ability grouping).

[136] U.S. Dep't of Health, Educ. & Welfare, On-Site Review of Bishop ISD, at 52 – 53 (Jan. 21 – 23, 1970).

[137] *See* Statement of Liberal Club of the United Citizens of Donna Educ. Comm., at 3, 1962 (condemning practice of giving the general achievement test only to Chicanos), on file with the authors.

[138] *See* Hobson v. Hansen, 269 F. Supp. 401 (D.D.C. 1967), *aff'd sub nom.* Smuck v. Hobson, 408 F.2d 175 (D.C. Cir. 1969). *See also* Chapa v. Odem Ind. School Dist., Civil No. 66-C-72 (S.D. Tex., July 28, 1967), (high school classes were divided into two divisions, college and terminal, with the preponderance of the latter group being Chicano).

[139] *See* pp. 360 – 61 *infra.*

[140] A study by the California State Department of Education concluded that Chicanos have been placed in educationally mentally retarded classes solely on the basis of their performance on an invalid IQ test. The test was deemed invalid because Chicanos did not

rather in purposefully segregating Chicanos.[141] By relying on this allegedly "objective" instrument, educators attempt to exonerate themselves from any intentional culpability. The invalidity of tracking schemes resulting in discriminatory segregation of minority children has been established,[142] but school officials in Texas have chosen segregation as their guide.

These types of official actions have played a primary role in continued Chicano school segregation. The historical inadequacy of legal and administrative responses also bear a significant part of the responsibility.

III. JUDICIAL AND QUASI-JUDICIAL RESPONSE

A. Early Decisions: 1930—1954

Early civil rights strategem sought treatment of Chicanos as part of the "white race." Theory conformed to the jurisprudence of the times[143] and took advantage of the Texas Constitution[144] which provided for

---

have the facility and understanding of English required by the test. *Hearings on Mexican-American Education before the Senate Select Committee on Equal Educational Opportunity,* 91st Cong., 2nd Sess., pt. 4, at 2504 (1970) [hereinafter cited as *Hearings*].

[141] Illustrative of the success of this technique is the El Paso district, where EMR classes are eighty-one percent Chicano although Chicanos comprise only fifty-six percent of the student population. U.S. Dep't of Health, Educ. & Welfare, On-Site Review of the El Paso ISD: Special Education, at 3—4 (1969). *See also* Covarrubias v. San Diego Unified School Dist., Civil Action No. 70—394-T (S.D. Cal., filed Dec. 1, 1970) (challenging the testing methods which result in disproportionate representation of Chicanos in EMR classes). One possible explanation for this practice, aside from the desire to segregate, is that there are financial incentives for having a large number of EMR students. *Hearings, supra* note 140, at 2394. School districts then utilize the funds to provide EMR curriculum to students who find the program stultifying.

[142] *See* Hobson v. Hansen, 269 F. Supp. 401, 484—85 (D.D.C. 1967), *appeal dismissed,* 393 U.S. 801 (1968), *aff'd sub nom.,* Smuck v. Hobson, 408 F.2d 175 (D.C. Cir. 1969).

[143] *See* Gong Lum v. Rice, 275 U.S. 78, 80 (1927). The Court upheld the state court interpretation of § 207 of the 1890 Mississippi Constitution ("[s]eparate schools shall be maintained for children of the white and colored races") which found § 207 "divided the educable children into those of the pure white or Caucasian race, on the one hand, and the brown, yellow, and black races, on the other hand, and therefore Martha Lum of the Mongolian or yellow race could not insist on being classed with the whites under this constitutional division." *Cf.* Wong Him v. Callahan, 119 F. 381 (C.C.N.D. Cal. 1902)(upholding separate schools in San Francisco for children of Mongolian descent); C. Vose, CAUCASIANS ONLY 83—84, 129—131 (1967). Vose describes the Black strategy in restrictive covenant cases of the late 1940's, arguing that covenants against colored people could not validly be enforced as there was no constant characteristic by which to identify Negro people. *See also* note 265 *infra. But see* Westminister School Dist. v. Mendez, 161 F.2d 774 (9th Cir. 1947) (statute providing for segregation of Asiatics and Indians could not be applied to Chicanos).

[144] Article VII, § 7 of the Texas Constitution reads as follows: "Separate schools shall

segregation only of "colored children."

In 1930, the first Chicano desegregation case set the pattern for the next forty years. In *Independent School District v. Salvatierra,*[145] plaintiffs sought to prove that actions of Del Rio, Texas school authorities were designed to effect, and did accomplish, "the complete segregation of the school children of Mexican and Spanish descent (in certain elementary grades) from the school children of *all other white races* in the same grade."[146] The trial court granted an injunction which prohibited "segregating the children of plaintiffs . . . from children of Anglo-Saxon parentage of like ages and educational attainments within the school district."[147] The Texas Court of Civil Appeals agreed in theory: "school authorities have no power to arbitrarily segregate Mexican children, assign them to separate schools, and exclude them from schools maintained for children of *other white races,* merely or solely because they are Mexicans."[148] But the judgment was reversed and the injunction dissolved.

The appellate court referred to plaintiffs' "constitutional or statutory rights, privileges, or immunities"[149] and agreed with Chicano attorneys that absent a statute allowing segregation of Chicanos, any attempt by local officials to do so exceeded their powers.[150] But where there was no proof of intent to discriminate, the court held, segregation of the first three grades on wholly separate campuses was a reasonable exercise of the board's discretionary powers,[151] justified by the Del Rio Superintendent's judgment that an overwhelming majority of Chicano children needed special training because of language difficulties.[152] In dictum the court recognized that such separation would have to be applied with equal force to both white and "Mexican race" students.[153] But if so applied, separation to meet individual needs was permissible[154] and the

---

be provided for white and colored children and impartial provision shall be made for both."

[145] 33 S.W.2d 790 (Tex. Civ. App., 4th Dt. 1930), *cert. denied,* 284 U.S. 580 (1931).

[146] 33 S.W.2d at 794 (emphasis added).

[147] *Id.* at 793 – 94.

[148] *Id.* at 795 (emphasis added).

[149] *Id.* at 794, 796.

[150] *Id.* at 795. Ironically, it was this argument on which the state later relied in an attempt to show the absence of *de jure* segregation of Chicanos. *See* p. 349 *infra.* Thus, "[t]he hardest thing in a [Chicano education] suit is establishing *de jure* segregation." Interview with John Serna, staff attorney for the Mexican-American Legal Defense and Education Fund (MALDEF), in San Antonio, Texas, July 19, 1971.

[151] 33 S.W.2d at 795.

[152] *Id.* at 792. The school district also argued that Chicanos were segregated to avoid disrupting classes several months into the school year when large numbers of migratory workers returned to the district. This rationale was rejected because English-speaking children who entered late were not segregated. *Id.* at 795.

[153] *Id.* at 795.

[154] *Id.* at 794. Later courts have noted that meeting individual need based on language

pedagogical wisdom of local administrators, rather than tests, was held to be adequate to identify children with language problems.[155]

It appears that no Chicano school integration suits were filed between 1930 and 1948. The situation in Pearland, Texas in 1942 illustrates the reason for this. Bishop Patrick Flores of the San Antonio diocese recalls that in his childhood he was compelled to attend the segregated Mexican school outside the Pearland limits. He was not allowed to ride the school bus carrying Anglos to the white school even though it passed in front of his house. Instead, he was restricted to the one-room, one-teacher, seven-grade building outside the city limits. When the school district considered building a new Mexican school the bishop and all his classmates began an eighteen month school boycott. After two years the superintendent compromised by moving the Mexican school next to the Anglo school.[156] Primarily because the Mexican building was an eyesore, the children were eventually integrated to avoid embarrassment to the district. Attorneys in Pearland never went to court because the environment was not conducive to integration, and because no funds were available for such litigation.[157]

The *Salvatierra* doctrine was emphasized in 1947 by an Attorney General's Opinion forbidding segregation Of Latin Americans.[158] In response, the late Gus Garcia inquired of Attorney-General Price Daniel whether the opinion forbade segregation except that based on scientific tests "equally applied to all students regardless of racial ancestry," and whether it forbade inferior facilities.[159] Daniel responded unequivocally: "I am certainly pleased to know that your interpretation of this opinion agrees with ours. We meant that the law prohibits discrimination against or segregation of Latin Americans on account of race or descent, and

---

handicap may be a euphemism for segregation. Hernandez v. Texas, 347 U.S. 475, 479 (1954).

[155] 33 S.W.2d at 794—96.

[156] Telephone interview with Bishop Patrick Flores, Mar. 3, 1972.

[157] Telephone interview with John Herrera, counsel for Pearland, Texas citizens, Mar. 3, 1972.

[158] The text of the opinion, dated April 8, 1947, reads as follows: "The Cuero Independent School District [DeWitt County] may not segregate Latin-American pupils, as such. Based solely on language deficiencies or other individual needs or aptitudes, separate classes or schools may be maintained for pupils who, after examinations equally applied, come within such classifications. No part of such classification or segregation may be based solely upon Latin-American or Mexican descent. Independent School District v. Salvatierra, 33 S.W.2d 790, *cert. denied,* 284 U.S. 580 (*See* opinion for additional authorities)." DIGEST OF OPINIONS OF THE ATTORNEY GENERAL OF TEXAS, V-128, at 39 (1947) [hereinafter cited as OP. ATT'Y GEN. TEXAS].

[159] Letter from Gus C. Garcia to Price Daniel, Aug. 18, 1947, *quoted in* G. Sanchez & V. Strickland, STUDY OF THE EDUCATIONAL OPPORTUNITIES PROVIDED SPANISH-NAME CHILDREN IN THE TEXAS SCHOOL SYSTEMS 7 (1947).

that the law permits no subterfuge to accomplish such discrimination."[160] Yet scholars continued to document extensive *de jure* segregation and lack of enforcement.[161]

In a 1947 California case, *Westminister School District v. Mendez*,[162] the Ninth Circuit added a theoretical dimension to the problem of Chicano segregation. It found that defendant school districts were segregating under color of law even though segregation of Chicanos was not provided for by state law.[163] Segregation, it said, was allowed in California only as to children of "one or another of the great races of mankind;"[164] it was not permitted within one of the great races. Chicanos were part of the white race.[165] Yet the court did not hold that segregation of Mexican-American children violated the fourteenth amendment *per se*. On the contrary, California could pass a law to segregate Mexican-American children. But absent such a law, Chicano segregation was unconstitutional.[166]

The combination of the *Mendez* decision and the Attorney General's Opinion generated a major suit in Texas. Like California, Texas had no *state* law requiring segregation of Mexican children, although the practice remained prevalent.[167] Gus Garcia combined these elements in 1948 in *Delgado v. Bastrop Independent School District*.[168] The complaint alleged that four Texas school districts[169] segregated Mexican children from "other white children,"[170] without sanction of state law[171] and contrary to the Attorney-General's Opinion.[172] The argument suc-

---

[160] Letter from Price Daniel to Gus. C. Garcia, Aug. 21, 1947, *in* Sanchez & Strickland, *supra*.

[161] *Id.* at 7. "It seems clear, then, that the segregation of Spanish-name children, as practiced in eight of the ten school systems surveyed in this study, is contrary to the laws of Texas." Sanchez & Strickland, *supra*.

[162] 64 F. Supp. 544 (S.D. Cal. 1946), *aff'd*, 161 F.2d 774 (9th Cir. 1947).

[163] 161 F.2d at 778. *Cf.* Screws v. United States, 325 U.S. 91 (1945); United States v. Classic, 313 U.S. 299 (1941).

[164] 161 F.2d at 780. The "three great races" generally recognized are mongoloid, caucasoid, and negroid.

[165] *Id.* at 780.

[166] *Id.* at 781. The court distinguished the segregation cases, Cumming v. Board of Educ., 175 U.S. 528 (1899); Plessy v. Ferguson, 163 U.S. 537 (1896); Ward v. Flood, 48 Cal. 36, 17 Am. R. 405 (1874); Roberts v. City of Boston, 59 Mass. 198, 5 Cush. 198 (1849), on the ground that they applied only to segregation of "the great races of man." 161 F.2d at 780.

[167] *Little, supra* note 31.

[168] Civil No. 388 (W.D. Tex., June 15, 1948) (*semble*); *accord*, Gonzales v. Sheely, 96 F. Supp. 1004 (D. Ariz. 1951).

[169] Bastrop ISD of Bastrop County, Elgin ISD of Bastrop County, Martindale ISD of Caldwell County, and Travis County Schools of Travis County.

[170] Civil No. 388 (W.D. Tex. June 15, 1948). Findings of fact and conclusions of law were waived by stipulation of the parties. The court recognized the suit as a proper class

ceeded. The district court permanently enjoined each district from segregating pupils of Mexican descent, ordering districts to comply, if necessary, through new construction or relocation of buildings "in no event beyond *September 1949.*[173] However, a proviso permitted segregation in the first grade "solely for educational purposes" if on the same campus and only "as a result of scientific and standardized tests."[174]

To comply with the order,[175] Superintendent of Public Instruction L.A. Woods issued regulations forbidding segregation of Chicanos in separate classes, schools, or extra-curricular activities with the *Delgado* first grade proviso.[176] Woods' original order stated: "The above reference to colored children has been interpreted by the Texas courts and the Texas Legislature as including only members of the Negro race or persons of Negro ancestry. The courts have held that it does not apply to members of any other race."[177] Subsequent publications omitted these sentences but stated categorically that there was no support in Texas law

---

action. *See also* Alvarado v. El Paso Ind. School Dist., 445 F.2d 1011 (5th Cir. 1971) (class action for Mexican-American students found permissible); Romero v. Weakly, 226 F.2d 399 (9th Cir. 1955); Gonzales v. Sheely, 96 F. Supp. 1004 (D. Arix. 1951); Westminister School Dist. v. Mendez, 64 F. Supp. 544 (S.D. Cal. 1946), *aff'd* 161 F.2d 774 (9th Cir. 1947) (sustained class action on behalf of Mexican children). *Cf.* Independent School Dist. v. Salvatierra, 33 S.W.2d 790, 796 (Tex. Civ. App., 4th Dt. 1930). *Contra,* Tijerina v. Henry, 398 U.S. 922 (1970) (dismissing an appeal from the District Court of New Mexico which had found that the class "designated as Indo-Hispano, also called Mexican, Mexican-American, and Spanish-American, [which is] generally characterized by Spanish surnames, mixed Indian and Spanish ancestry and . . . Spanish as a primary or maternal language" was "too vague to be meaningful.").

[171] Complaint § 1, Delgado v. Bastrop Ind. School Dist., Civil No. 388 (W.D. Tex., June 15, 1948).

[172] *Id.* S 2.

[173] Civil No. 388 (W.D.Tex., June 15, 1948) (emphasis added); *cf.* Singleton v. Jackson Municipal Separate School Dist., 426 F.2d 1364 (5th Cir. 1970) (ordering immediate integration to take effect by Fall, 1970); Alexander v. Holmes County Bd. of Educ., 396 U.S. 19 (1969) (immediate relief).

[174] Civil No. 388 (W.D. Tex., June 15, 1948).

[175] *Delgado* permanently enjoined the Superintendent from participating in segregation of pupils of Mexican descent. *Cf.* United States v. Texas, 321 F. Supp. 1043 (E.D. Tex. 1970), *modified,* 330 F. Supp. 235 (E.D. Tex. 1971), *aff'd in part,* 447 F.2d 441 (5th Cir. 1971), *stay denied,* 92 S. Ct. 8 (Black, Circuit Justice, 1971), *cert. denied,* 40 U.S.L.W. 3313 (Jan. 11, 1972), where the Texas Education Agency (TEA) was enjoined from participating in segregation and ordered to aid integration efforts. *See also* pp. 375 – 83 *infra.*

[176] Texas State Dep't of Educ., STANDARDS AND ACTIVITIES OF THE DIVISION OF SUPERVISION AND ACCREDITATION OF SCHOOL SYSTEMS, Bulletin No. 507, at 45 – 6 (1948 – 49) [hereinafter cited as TEXAS EDUCATION STANDARDS].

[177] The original text of the order as mailed can be found in G. Sanchez, CONCERNING SEGREGATION OF SPANISH SPEAKING CHILDREN IN THE PUBLIC SCHOOLS 74 – 75 (1951).

for segregation of children of Mexican or other Latin-American descent.[178] Several contemporaneous Texas decisions assaulted other strongholds of Chicano segregation—restrictive covenants,[179] restricted public swimming pools,[180] and exclusive juries.[181] Similar thrusts were made in other states.[182]

Following *Delgado*, civil rights attorneys moved to enforce court-ordered desegregation by seeking disaccreditation of segregated school districts. The approach was novel and effective. In January of 1949, a complaint[183] was filed against the particularly obdurate district in Del Rio, Texas.[184] Less than a month later, a report by the Assistant State Superintendent recommended that accreditation be withheld because students were segregated and Latin-American teachers were "unacceptable" in the Anglo school. The report indicated that "elementary children of the two races were, by board regulation, not permitted to mix."[185] Superintendent Woods cancelled Del Rio's accreditation on February 12, 1949.[186]

After granting Del Rio's request for reconsideration, the Super-

---

[178] TEXAS EDUCATION STANDARDS, *supra* note 176, at 45.

[179] Clifton v. Puente, 218 S.W.2d 272 (Tex. Civ. App. 1948) (invalidated restrictive covenants in the sale or lease of property to "persons of Mexican descent"); *accord,* Matthews v. Andrade, 87 Cal. App. 2d 906, 198 P.2d 66 (Dist. Ct. App. 1948); *cf.* Shelley v. Kraemer, 334 U.S. 1 (1948)(restrictive covenants against Blacks held unenforceable).

[180] "A lease by the Board of Directors of Pecos County Water Improvement District No. 1 and Pecos County for bathing, swimming, and other purposes of like kind by the public may not lawfully carry a provision that no person or persons of Latin-American race shall be permitted to use said property for swimming, bathing, drinking, or for any other purpose." OP. ATT'Y GEN. TEXAS, V-150, *supra* note 158 at 45 (1947); *accord,* Valle v. Stengel, 176 F.2d 697 (3rd Cir. 1949); Lopez v. Seccombe, 71 F. Supp. 769 (S.D. Cal. 1944) (holding exclusion of Chicanos from public swimming pools unconstitutional).

[181] Hernandez v. Texas, 347 U.S. 475 (1954); *cf.* Patton v. Mississippi, 332 U.S. 463 (1947) (racial discrimination in jury selection a denial to both Negro defendants and potential Negro jurors of the equal protection of the laws).

[182] *E.g.,* Gonzalez v. Sheely, 96 F. Supp. 1004 (D. Ariz. 1951). Finding separate schools for Anglos and Chicanos, with unequal physical plants, a denial of equal protection, the court took a path independent from the "white" versus "colored" distinction. Suggesting a principle later to become law in *Brown,* the district judge reasoned that "segregation suggests inferiority where none exists." *Id.* at 1007.

[183] Cristobal P. Aldrete, a Del Rio citizen, made the complaint on January 7, 1949. Del Rio Decision of L.A. Woods, State Supt. of Pub. Instr., at 1 (April 23, 1949), on file with Dr. H. Garcia in Corpus Christi, Texas.

[184] Del Rio had been the defendant in Independent School Dist. v. Salvatierra, 33 S.W.2d 790 (Tex. Civ. App., 4th Dt. 1930).

[185] Del Rio Decision, *supra* note 183, at 3—4. (Assistant Superintendent Trimble personally inspected Del Rio on January 21, 1949).

[186] *Id.* Woods had, first, unsuccessfully attempted to sidestep the controversy by reopening *Delgado. Id.* The cancelling of accreditation also meant that teachers would have

intendent reaffirmed his decision to withdraw accreditation and made specific findings:[187]

1. The children were segregated to separate the two groups.
2. Latin-American teachers were confined to the Chicano school.
3. Freedom-of-choice did not solve the segregation problem because only Chicano children were given a choice and schools that had been all Chicano remained so.[188]

Success was short-lived. On June 1, 1949, the Texas legislature transferred the powers of the State Superintendent of Public Instruction to the newly created position of Commissioner of Education.[189] Woods, an elected official,[190] was continued as adviser to the new Commissioner for the remainder of his term, when both the Superintendent's position and the advisory position were abolished.[191] Declaring the act an emergency measure, the legislature rendered it effective as of July 7, 1949[192] (two months before Del Rio would start its school year). Del Rio then appealed to the State Board of Education which reversed the Woods decision.[193] The man selected to replace Woods is the current Commissioner of Education, J. W. Edgar.

Chicano leaders continued to complain of segregation.[194] In less than nine months complaints against at least twenty-two cities were sent to the new commissioner.[195] But state educational authorities became decidedly less cooperative after the Legislature's 1949 "emergency

---

their certificates cancelled if they taught in Del Rio in 1949—1950.

[187] Del Rio Decision, *supra* note 183, at 4—5.

[188] *See also* Green v. County School Bd., 391 U.S. 430 (1968) (finding freedom-of-choice plans unlawful if they perpetuate segregation).

[189] Public Free Schools Administration Act, ch. 299, art. V, Texas Laws (1949) *as amended* Tex. Educ. Code §§ 11.25, 11.51, 11.52 (Vernon Supp. 1971).

[190] Free Schools, ch. 124, § 24, Texas Laws (1905)[*repealed* Public Free Schools Administration Act, ch. 199, art. VII (1949)] *as amended* Tex. Educ. Code § 11.25 (Vernon Supp. 1971).

[191] Public Free Schools Administration Act, ch. 299, art. VII, Tex. Laws (1949) *as amended* Tex. Educ. Code §§ 11.13, 11.14, 11.25(f) (Vernon Supp. 1971).

[192] State Board of Education-Members Act, General and Special Laws, Texas ch. 546, § 12 (1949).

[193] Letter to the authors from Cristobal Alderete, Del Rio attorney, February 3, 1972. Mr. Alderete helped the Chicanos of Del Rio short-circuit the freedom-of-choice scheme. When school opened in September, over a thousand Chicano children were at Central Elementary (Anglo) to greet the principal. The resulting crisis ended in a pairing of schools. *Id. See also* The Daily Texan (Austin, Texas), March 1, 1949.

[194] Letter from Dr. Hector Garcia, M.D., to the Commissioner of Education, J.W. Edgar, and the State Board of Education, April 13, 1950, on file with Dr. H. Garcia in Corpus Christi, Texas.

[195] *Id.* A partial list of these cities appears in note 54 *supra*.

measure"—a fact that was to assume special significance because civil rights attorneys now felt it necessary to exhaust administrative remedies prior to filing federal suit.[196]

This uncooperative attitude was exemplified by the state's response to segregation in the Hondo school district. The district had supposedly ended segregation in grades two through eight in 1952–53, but Chicano parents complained that the schools reverted to segregation in these grades in separate classes and continued to segregate first graders on a separate campus. The Commissioner admitted the school had changed from sectioning alphabetically to sectioning by achievement test, but held the change not arbitrary because there was neither sufficient evidence of intent to segregate nor of segregation itself.[197] He held that the district was illegally segregating Chicano first graders because they were on separate campuses, rather than in separate classrooms on the same campus. As of September 8, 1953, Hondo agreed to segregate as specified by the Commissioner. In a cease and desist order Edgar additionally required Hondo to test all first graders.[198]

The Commissioner reacted similarly to a protest by Chicano parents

---

[196] The change of strategy was not entirely voluntary. According to Albert Armendariz, co-counsel in *Barraza v. Pecos,* note 199 *infra,* they were required to exhaust administrative remedies before going to federal court. Telephone interview with Albert Armendariz in El Paso, Texas, October 19, 1971; *accord,* telephone interview with Cristobal Alderete, counsel in Perez v. Terrell County Common School Dist., Jan. 31, 1972. *Cf.* Texas Law provided a free right of appeal to the Commissioner of Education in disputes arising with school boards, Public Free Schools Administration Act, ch. 299, art. VII S 1, Tex. Laws (1949) *as amended* Tex. Educ. Code § 11.13 (Vernon Supp. 1971); Salinas v. Kingsville Ind. School Dist., Civil No. 1309 (S.D. Tex., filed Feb. 25, 1956) (memorandum opinion of September 19, 1955 staying federal court action until State Commissioner ruled on the case). *But see* Romero v. Weakley, 226 F.2d 399 (9th Cir.), *rev'ing* 131 F. Supp. 818 (S.D. Cal. 1955).

[197] Orta v. Hondo Ind. School Dist., decided by Commissioner of Education, J.W. Edgar, September, 1953, at 2, on file with Dr. H. Garcia in Corpus Christi, Texas. A similar situation was found in Sanderson, Texas. Plaintiffs charged that first graders were segregated and grades two through six were divided into homogenous achievement groups which had the same segregative effect. Petition in Perez v. Terrell County Common School Dist. to J.W. Edgar, Texas Commissioner of Education, reprinted in The Sanderson Times (Sanderson, Texas), June 26, 1953, at 1. Although the school superintendent testified that Chicanos were usually average, The Austin Statesman (Austin, Texas), July 8, 1953, at 1, col. 2, Commissioner Edgar nonetheless approved a grouping plan based on chronological age although he stated it would probably result in segregation. Perez v. Terrell County Common School Dist. No. 1, decided by J.W. Edgar, Texas Commissioner of Education, July 10, 1953 on file with Cristobal Alderete in Washington, D.C.

[198] Orta v. Hondo Ind. School Dist., *supra* note 197 at 3. At least as late as 1968, Hondo maintained an identifiable Mexican school. Although 58% of the student body was Chicano there was not a single Chicano faculty member. U.S. Dep't of Health, Educ. & Welfare, DIRECTORY OF PUBLIC AND SECONDARY SCHOOLS IN SELECTED DISTRICTS—ENROLLMENT AND STAFF BY RACIAL/ETHNIC GROUP-FALL 1474 (1968).

of a 1953 zoning plan in Pecos. The parents contended that the school board's construction of East Pecos Junior High in the Latin-American section of the city was intended to, and did effect, segregation of Chicano children from "other white" children.[199] The zoning plan placed the Mexican section in the East Pecos Junior High district, but created no other zone, simply declaring that all other students, in and out of the city limits, would attend Pecos Junior High.[200] East Pecos Junior High was to be 96% Latin American and Pecos Junior High 77% Anglo.[201] The school board's reaction to the complaint was to propose a zoning plan in which three of the four elementary schools were to become even more segregated than before the complaint.[202] Giving the school board's actions a presumption of legality despite *Delgado*, Edgar failed to find sufficient evidence of intent to segregate.[203]

Time proved Chicano parents in Pecos correct.[204] In 1968 – 69, East Pecos Junior High was 100% Chicano.[205] Eight of the nine Chicano teachers were in schools 99.6 – 100% minority.[206] Though arguably the state had no standard by which to judge the Pecos plan, the plan upheld

---

[199] Barraza v. Pecos Ind. School Dist., decided by J.W. Edgar, Commissioner of Education, Nov. 25, 1953, on file with the Texas Education Agency.

[200] *Id.* at 2.

[201] The Latin American Junior High school was much more overcrowded, *id.* at 2, and the Anglo Junior High had an attendance area three times larger than the Mexican-American school. U.S. Dep't of Health, Educ. & Welfare, On-Site Review of Pecos ISD, at 1, June 12, 1969. The junior high school zones have never been changed. *Id.* at 12. Geographic zoning appears to have been particularly unfair because Mexican-American housing in Pecos was segregated. *Id.* at 8; *cf.* Henry v. Clarksdale Municipal Separate School Dist., 409 F.2d 682 (5th Cir.), *cert. denied,* 396 U.S. 940 (1969) (a district may not use geographic zoning to freeze past discrimination patterns).

[202] Barraza v. Pecos Ind. School Dist., *supra* note 199, at 46. For example, Earl Bell Elementary, which was to be 94% Latin American under the old plan, became 96% Latin American under the new plan.

[203] *Id.* at 45. *But see* United States v. Board of Instr., 395 F.2d 66 (5th Cir. 1968).

[204] A 1969 HEW review revealed that: "Prior to 1953 the district operated at the elementary level, 3 elementary schools on a completely segregated basis—Pecos Elementary, Earl Bell (Mexican-American) Elementary, and Carver (Negro) Elementary," and that "[t]he geographic attendance zone method of assignment has been ineffective in removing the identifiability of the Mexican-American schools." U.S. Dep't of Health, Educ. & Welfare, On-Site Review of Pecos ISD, at 6, June 12, 1969. Although the school board argued in *Barraza* that Chicanos had segregated themselves, the HEW review team found that Mexican Americans were historically segregated in a community around the Santa Rosa Catholic Church within the Earl Bell-East Pecos Junior High zones. According to the Superintendent, all other areas within the city were restricted for Anglos. In 1953 – 54, Mexican-Americans began to spread to the area zoned for the North Pecos Elementary School. This school is now 87% Mexican-American and 13% Anglo. The other areas of town did not open to Mexican-Americans until 1965. *Id.* at 8.

[205] *Id.* at 6 – 7.

[206] *Id.* at 4 – 5.

was blatantly discriminatory and even more segregationist than the prior school board proposal.

With separate-but-equal still the law, early Chicano attorneys sought acceptance of the mestizo race as white. Chicano cases, therefore, stressed fourteenth amendment due process and statutory violations, emphasizing segregation in the *absence* of state law, while Black cases were stressing the fourteenth amendment equal protection, arguing that segregation in the *presence* of state law was inherently unequal.

B. Strategies After Brown

Brown v. Board of Education[207] should have changed the strategy of Chicano attorneys. With the segregation cases overruled, their efforts could have been directed solely at showing *de jure* segregation and seeking fourteenth amendment relief. However, as late as 1970[208] attorneys argued the old and proven "other white" theory.

Strategy did not change after *Brown* because of the peculiarities of *Hernandez v. Texas* in 1954.[209] In that case a Chicano was sentenced to life imprisonment upon conviction of murder by an all-white jury. No Chicano had served on a jury for at least the previous twenty-five years.[210] Texas courts had repeatedly held that nationality and race were not identical under the fourteenth amendment and would not so decide in the absence of a Supreme Court ruling.[211] They reasoned that since Chicanos were white and the Constitution forbids only racial discrimination, Chicanos were not within the aegis of the fourteenth amendment.[212]

In *Hernandez,* the only Mexican-American discrimination case ever

---

[207] 347 U.S. 483 (1954).

[208] *See* Complaint, Cisneros v. Corpus Christi Ind. School Dist., 324 F. Supp. 599 (S.D. Tex. 1970), *appeal docketed,* No. 71 – 1297 (5th Cir., filed June 16, 1971).

[209] 347 U.S. 475 (1954). The opinion of the Texas appellate court, 251 S.W.2d 531 (Tex. Crim. App. 1952), was critically analyzed in 31 TEX. L. REV. 581 (1953).

[210] 347 U.S. at 481. This was true even though 14% of the population, 11% of the males over 21, and 6% or 7% of free holders on county tax rolls were Chicano. *Id.* at 480 – 81.

[211] Sanchez v. State, 147 Tex. Crim. 436, 181 S.W.2d 87, 90 (1944). A blind, nineteen-year-old, retarded youth with the mind of a five-year-old was convicted by an all-white jury of the murder of an Anglo farmer he heard attack his aging father. Although 50% of Hudspeth county was Chicano, there had been no Chicano on a jury for at least six years. The Texas court refused to reverse the conviction on the basis of Chicano exclusion from juries. *Accord,* Bustillos v. State, 152 Tex. Crim. 275, 213, 213 S.W.2d 837 (1948); Salazar v. State, 149 Tex. Crim. 260, 193 S.W.2d 211 (1946).

[212] Sanchez v. State, 156 Tex. Crim. 468, 243 S.W.2d 700 (1951). *But cf.* Clifton v. Puente, 218 S.W.2d 272 (Tex. Civ. App. 1948), where the Texas court refused to enforce restrictive covenants on the sale of land to persons of Mexican descent.

decided by the Supreme Court,[213] Chicanos were held to be among those protected by the fourteenth amendment:

> Throughout our history differences in race and color have defined easily identifiable groups which have at times required the aid of the courts in securing equal treatment under the laws. But community prejudices are not static, and from time to time other differences from the community norm may define other groups which need the same protection. *Whether such a group exists within a community is a question of fact.* When the existence of a distinct class is demonstrated, and it is further shown that the laws as written or as applied single out that class for different treatment not based on some reasonable classification, the guarantees of the Constitution have been violated. The Fourteenth Amendment is not directed solely against discrimination due to a "two-class theory"—that is, based upon differences between "white and Negro."[214]

Although the defendant established that Chicanos comprised "a separate class in Jackson County",[215] the Court refused to reach the broader question of whether Chicanos are generally to be recognized as an identifiable ethnic minority group.[216] However, only once since *Hernandez* has a court refused to recognize Mexican Americans as a distinct class on the particular facts before it,[217] although discrimination has not always been found.

---

[213] 347 U.S. 475 (1954). But the Court has granted *certiorari* in Keyes v. School Dist. 1, 445 F.2d 990 (10th Cir. 1971), *cert. granted,* 40 U.S.L.W. 3335 (U.S. Jan. 18, 1972), involving segregation of both Blacks and Chicanos. *See also* Tijerina v. Henry, 48 F.R.D. 274 (D.N.M.), *appeal dismissed,* 398 U.S. 922 (1970) (Douglas, J., dissenting).

[214] 347 U.S. at 478 (emphasis added); *accord,* Montoya v. People, 141 Colo. Rep. 9, 345 P.2d 1062 (1959).

[215] 347 U.S. at 479–80. The finding was based on such community practices as segregated schools; segregated courthouse toilets for white, colored, and Mexican; and at least one restaurant which did not serve Mexicans.

[216] As emphasized *supra,* the Court stated that "[w]hether such a group exists within a community is a question of fact," *id.* at 478, and that "[t]he petitioner's initial burden . . . was to prove that persons of Mexican descent constitute a separate class in Jackson County, distinct from 'whites'." *Id.* at 479. Footnote 19 specifically says that "[w]e do not have before us the question whether or not the Court might take judicial notice that persons of Mexican descent are there [Jackson County?] considered as a separate class." *Id. Contra Houston, supra* note 14, at 938.

[217] *See, e.g.,* Muniz v. Beto, 434 F.2d 697 (5th Cir. 1970) (reversal of a 1942 conviction by an all-white jury because Chicanos had been excluded from juries in El Paso County, Texas); United States v. Hunt, 265 F. Supp. 178, 188 (W.D. Tex. 1967): "It appears and the court so finds that there is in Bexar County an identifiable ethnic group referred to as Mexican Americans, which group must be taken into consideration in connection with jury selection." One exception is the recent Houston case of Ross v. Eckels, Civil No. 10444

Defendant Hernandez relied upon statistical inferences rather than direct evidence of discrimination. Texas courts had previously required direct proof of discrimination to show a denial of equal protection to Chicanos.[218] But the United States Supreme Court had long accepted systematic exclusion of qualified Blacks from Texas juries as sufficient evidence of discrimination.[219] Thus the Texas courts were drawing a fictitious line between the type of proof required to show discrimination against Blacks, and what was needed to show the same thing in Chicano cases.[220]   Chief Justice Warren disposed of the evidentiary problem, stating that "it taxes our credulity to say that mere chance resulted in there being no members of this class among the over six thousand jurors called in the past 25 years."[221]

While winning the evidentiary point, Chicanos recognized that the main reason for the fifty-four-year delay between the opening of Texas juries to Blacks[222] and the inclusion of Chicanos was reluctance to recognize Chicanos as a separate class. The Supreme Court's equivocation on this point, refusing to take judicial notice and instead making a limited factual determination,[223] led civil rights attorneys in the late fifties to return to the *Salvatierra* "other white" strategy and the *Delgado* case.[224] These were readily available precedents requiring no proof of a separate class and seemed to afford relief as adequate as *Brown*.

Thus in the cases argued immediately after *Brown*, Chicano civil rights attorneys did not change the "other white"—"no state law" strategy.[225] With the exception of *Hernandez v. Driscoll Consolidated*

(S.D. Tex., May 24, 1971). *But see* Tijerina v. Henry, 48 F.R.D. 274 (D.N.M.), *appeal dismissed,* 398 U.S. 922 (1970).

[218] *See* Bustillos v. State, 152 Tex. Crim. 275, 213 S.W.2d 837 (1948); Sanchez v. State, 147 Tex. Crim. 436, 181 S.W.2d 87 (1944); Carasco v. State, 130 Tex. Crim. 659, 95 S.W.2d 433 (1936); Ramirez v. State, 119 Tex. Crim. 362; 40 S.W.2d 138 (1931).

[219] Ross v. Texas, 341 U.S. 918 (1951); Cassell v. Texas, 339 U.S. 282 (1950); Hill v. Texas, 316 U.S. 400 (1942); Smith v. Texas, 311 U.S. 128 (1940); *accord,* Patton v. Mississippi, 332 U.S. 463 (1947); Norris v. Alabama, 294 U.S. 587 (1935).

[220] *See* Note, 31 Tex. L. Rev. 581, 583 (1953). *Compare* the Texas double standard *with* the Justice Department's position in its Brief to the Fifth Circuit in *Cisneros v. Corpus Christi Ind. School Dist., appeal docketed* No. 71–2397 (5th Cir., filed July 16, 1971), where the government requested immediate relief for segregated Black children but remand for more evidence concerning segregated Chicano children.

[221] Hernandez v. Texas, 347 U.S. 475, 482 (1954).

[222] Carter v. Texas, 177 U.S. 442 (1900).

[223] *See* note 216 *supra.*

[224] Added support for the proposition that courts would be reluctant to apply *Brown* to Chicano segregation not sanctioned by state law can be found in recent cases discussed at pp. 348–49 *infra.*

[225] *See* Complaint in Salinas v. Kingsville Ind. School Dist., Civil No. 1309 (S.D. Tex., February 25, 1956)(dismissed without prejudice), on file with Dr. Hector Garcia, Corpus Christi, Texas. Gus Garcia stressed Mexican descent, but nevertheless used the "other

Independent School District[226] in 1957, which made unlawful the segregation of Chicanos in the first grade in the absence of standardized tests,[227] no significant Chicano school cases were filed in the decade following *Brown.*[228]

The sparsity of Chicano desegregation cases following *Brown* might be explained on the basis that the law became so settled that school boards capitulated.[229] More plausible is that Chicano attorneys saw litigation as futile because there were so many subterfuges available to bar effective relief. Through 1957 Chicanos were able only to desegregate

---

white" strategy, arguing that no state law allowed segregation of Chicanos. This may be the first case in which school board minutes were used as the complaint cited segregation policies dating back to 1914. *See also* Cortez v. Carrizo Springs Ind. School Dist., Civil No. 832 (W.D.Tex., filed April 20, 1955). Despite *Brown,* the complaint continues the "other white"—"no state law" strategy. *Cortez* was dismissed on June 13, 1955, on plaintiff's motion after the board agreed to cooperate in every respect. Letter from Cristobal P. Alderete, attorney in *Cortez,* to Anastacio Soliz, August 1, 1955, on file in Mr. Alderete's office in Washington, D.C.

[226] 2 Race Rel. L. Rep. 329 (S.D. Tex., Jan. 11, 1957).

[227] *Id.* at 333. Defendant school district's claim that Latin children were segregated for four years in the first two grades because of language handicap was rejected after plaintiffs produced a little girl, Linda Perez, who had been segregated in a non-English speaking classroom even though she could speak only English. *Id.* at 331.

[228] *See* Villareal v. Mathis Ind. School Dist., Civil No. 1385 (S.D. Tex., May 2, 1957). This case was filed on the same day as Hernandez v. Driscoll Consol. Ind. School Dist., 2 Race Rel. L. Rep. 329 (S.D. Tex. 1957), by the same attorney—James DeAnda. *Villareal* was dismissed and an agreed order entered because the expert witness was afraid to testify. Mr. DeAnda did not pursue the suit because at the time there was no requirement for balancing and no law on tracking. Telephone interview with James DeAnda, Oct. 20, 1971. Shortly thereafter, the Mexican school was closed, but the Chicano children were put in segregated classes. The cause of the change was apparently a Texas Education Agency threat to take away the Mathis district's accreditation, rather than the *Villareal* filing. Commissioner Edgar ordered the district to cease its arbitrary retention and segregation of Chicano pupils for two years in the first grade. They were also ordered to comply with *Delgado* in the upper grades. Guerrero v. Mathis Ind. School Dist., decided by J.W. Edgar, Texas Commissioner of Education, May 11, 1955. The district was slow to comply with the first two parts of the Commissioner's order and ignored the third. Only after suit was threatened against TEA did it revoke the Mathis district's accreditation. In order to regain accreditation, the West Side school (Mexican) was closed and some classes were matched: half Anglo and half Chicano. But, because the school was 80% Chicano, 60% of the Chicano children remained completely segregated. Chicano migrants were restricted to Mexican classes. Telephone interview with Mr. James DeAnda, Oct. 20, 1971.

[229] For example, Chicano parents in Crystal City, Texas, packed a school board meeting in 1960 demanding an end to two segregated elementary schools. Zavala County Sentinel (Crystal City, Texas), July 15, 1960, at 1, col. 6. As a result the grade schools were paired. *Id.* July 22, 1960, at 1, col. 5. However, the school board refused to adopt rules dealing with the discriminatory treatment of migrants. Letter from R.C. Tate, Crystal City ISD Superintendent, to Cristobal Alderete, August 9, 1960, on file in Mr. Alderete's offices in Washington, D.C.

Anglo schools, not to integrate Chicano schools.[230] Such evasions of integration as "freedom-of-choice" were not struck down until 1968 in *Green v. Board of Education.*[231] Many school districts with large numbers of Chicanos operated with gerrymandered zoning and freedom-of-choice plans well past 1968.[232] Some such plans are currently in effect.[233] While faculty segregation has long been unlawful,[234] not until *Singleton*[235] was it clear that the teaching staff in each school should reflect the composition of the teaching staff in the district as a whole.

A parallel hiatus in change was evident for Blacks. Though they brought a significantly greater number of desegregation cases following *Brown,*[236] results were disheartening—only 2.3 percent of Southern Black children were in desegregated schools ten years after *Brown.*[237] It was the Civil Rights Act of 1964[238] that served as catalyst for major

---

[230] One partial exception is the shortlived pairing of schools in Del Rio in 1949 by Supt. L.A. Woods. *See* note 183 *supra. Cf.* Pate v. County School Bd., 434 F.2d 1151 (5th Cir. 1970); Allen v. Board of Pub. Instr., 432 F.2d 362 (5th Cir. 1970); Bradley v. Board of Pub. Instr., 431 F.2d 1377 (5th Cir. 1970); Manning v. Board of Pub. Instr., 427 F.2d 874 (5th Cir. 1970) (all holding that pairing is a permissive tool of affirmative action to dismantle a dual system).

[231] 391 U.S. 430 (1968) (freedom-of-choice plan found unacceptable where it does not convert a dual system to a unitary system—immediately.). *See* Raney v. Board of Educ., 391 U.S. 443 (1968). Earlier decisions had not disturbed such plans. United States v. Jefferson County Bd. of Educ., 372 F.2d 836 (5th Cir. 1966), *noted in* 2 HARV. CIV. RIGHTS-CIV. LIB. L. REV. 328 (1967). *Cf.* Youngblood v. Board of Pub. Instr., 430 F.2d 625 (5th Cir. 1970), *cert. denied,* 402 U.S. 943 (1971), holding that zone lines must affirmatively promote desegregation.

[232] *E.g.,* El Paso, Texas, eliminated its freedom-of-choice plan between Chicano and Anglo High Schools on Dec. 4, 1970. The announcement came four days after a suit was filed. Defendant's Answer in Alvarado v. El Paso Ind. School Dist., 326 F. Supp. 674 (W.D. Tex.), *rev'd and remanded* 445 F.2d 1011 (5th Cir. 1971).

[233] La Feria, Texas, currently operates with freedom-of-choice zones between its elementary schools. Interview with Mr. Vail, Superintendent La Feria ISD, in La Feria, Texas, Aug. 7, 1971. One of these two schools, Sam Houston Elementary, was 99% Chicano in the 1969—70 school year. The other elementary school contained 97—100% of all Anglo students in the same grades. U.S. Dep't of Health, Educ. & Welfare, Office for Civil Rights, Individual School Campus Report, Fall, 1969, Form OSCR-102, La Feria ISD, Sam Houston Elementary.

[234] *See* United States v. Montgomery County Bd. of Educ., 395 U.S. 225 (1969); Bradley v. School Bd., 382 U.S. 103 (1965); Wheeler v. Board of Educ., 363 F.2d 738, 740 (4th Cir. 1966); Betts v. County School Bd., 269 F. Supp. 593, 602 (W.D. Va. 1967).

[235] Singleton v. Jackson Municipal Separate School Dist., 419 F.2d 1211, 1217—18 (5th Cir. 1970), *cert. denied,* 402 U.S. 943 (1971). An earlier Fifth Circuit opinion in the same case was *noted in* 1 HARV. CIV. RIGHTS-CIV. LIB. L. REV. 171 (1966).

[236] *See generally* Comment, *The Courts, HEW and Southern School Desegregation,* 77 YALE L.J. 321 (1967).

[237] N.Y. Times, May 23, 1966, at 16, col. 4.

[238] 28 U.S.C. § 1447; 42 U.S.C. §§ 1971, 1975a-1975d, 2000a-2000h-6 (1970).

change by injecting administrative action into desegregation efforts.[239] HEW enforcement pushed the figure to six percent in 1965 – 66.[240] However, HEW did not aid in Chicano cases until 1969.

In 1967 the evolution of school integration law coupled with renewed fervor in the Mexican-American community brought inequities in Chicano education back to court. James deAnda,[241] the attorney in the *Driscoll* case, filed *Chapa v. Odem Independent School District*,[242] the first Chicano suit to test subterfuges adopted by school districts in the milieu of sophisticated civil rights law. The complaint used both "other white" and equal protection language without clearly invoking either.[243] The school board defense was the familiar combination of language handicap and achievement tests.[244] But for the first time, a court refused to accept unquestioningly a classification system based on properly administered achievement tests. Instead, while accepting an agreed

---

[239] Comment, *The Courts, HEW, and Southern School Desegregation,* 77 YALE L.J. 321, 322 (1967). *See* United States v. Jefferson County Bd. of Educ., 372 F.2d 836, 847 (5th Cir. 1966), where Judge Wisdom states: "A national effort, bringing together Congress, the executive, and the judiciary may be able to make meaningful the right of Negro children to equal educational opportunities. *The Courts acting alone have failed."* (emphasis by court). HEW had accepted freedom-of-choice plans prior to *Green,* necessitating the holding in *Green* because of the weight courts in the Fifth Circuit gave to the HEW position. "[W]e hold again in determining whether school desegregation plans meet the standard of *Brown* and other decisions of the Supreme Court, the courts of this circuit should give great weight to HEW Guidelines." *Id.*

[240] N.Y. Times, May 23, 1966, at 16, col. 4.

[241] Mr. James deAnda of Corpus Christi, Texas, has a long history of litigation on behalf of Chicano civil rights. He was an attorney in 1954 in *Hernandez v. Texas,* and is presently an attorney in Cisneros v. Corpus Christi Ind. School Dist., 324 F. Supp. 599 (S.D. Tex. 1970), *appeal docketed,* No. 71 – 2397 (5th Cir., filed July 16, 1971).

[242] Civil No. 66-C-72 (S.D. Tex., July 28, 1967).

[243] *Id.* The language of the order is what might be expected from a due process decision, placing it in the line of "other white" cases. *Brown* was not cited in the briefs, although Hobson v. Hansen, 269 F. Supp. 401 (D.D.C. 1967), *aff'd sub nom.,* Smuck v. Hobson, 408 F.2d 175 (D.C. Cir. 1969), was cited in plaintiffs' memorandum of law regarding remedies.

[244] Complainants' Memorandum Brief in Motion for Summary Judgement of June 30, 1967, at 2, in Chapa v. Odem Ind. School Dist., Civil No. 66-C-72 (S.D. Tex., July 28, 1967). First, plaintiffs presented evidence to show that language handicap separation was a mere sham: no teacher or principal had special training to deal with the problem; two of the three first grade teachers at the Mexican school had neither college degrees nor teaching certificates; and the same books and materials were used at both schools. *Id.* at 4. Second, the Superintendent admitted that most children were sectioned without achievement tests and when tests were given in 1965 and 1966 only Mexican-American children were tested, and even then only after sectioning. *Id.* at 3. When Anglos were finally tested, the superintendent did not send those scoring in the lower range to the Mexican school because of a custom and policy of keeping Anglo children together. *Id.* at 3 – 4.

order, the court expressed a desire for additional evidence on the question of testing.[245]

Despite such apparent progress, the "other white" strategy continued in *Odem* has recently come to haunt Chicano civil rights attorneys. Now local school boards, rather than plaintiff Chicanos, avail themselves of the argument that no state law has ever sanctioned segregation,[246] in their attempt to disprove the *de jure* segregation prerequisite to *Brown* relief.[247] But while the bare absence of such a state law once sufficed for Chicano attorneys to prove that segregation of Chicanos exceeded school officials' statutory powers, it is no defense to an equal protection suit. All such a suit need show is that past segregation by school officials was under "color of law." "Color of law" extends to action by officials under guise of state authority regardless of statutory powers, even action which is malevolent abuse of power.[248] Yet other, more serious questions arise from Chicano equal protection strategy. These questions are considered in the next section.

IV. THE DEVELOPING EQUAL PROTECTION ARGUMENTS

A. Suspect Classification Treatment for Chicanos

To avail themselves of the equal protection clause and *Brown v. Board of Education*, Chicanos must win judicial recognition as an *identifiable minority group*.[249] There has been no Supreme Court ruling that they constitute such a class throughout the Southwest, despite overwhelming evidence that they do.[250] *Hernandez v. Texas*,[251] often cited

---

[245] Civil No. 66-C-72 (S.D. Tex., July 28, 1967).

[246] United States v. Texas (Austin ISD), Civil No. A-70-CA-80 (W.D. Tex., June 28, 1971), where the court, in ruling against Mexican American relief, took notice of the fact that "Texas has never required by law that Mexican-American children be segregated."

[247] *See, e.g.*, Swann v. Charlotte-Mecklenburg Bd. of Educ., 402 U.S. 1 (1970).

[248] Monroe v. Pape, 365 U.S. 167 (1961); Screws v. United States, 325 U.S. 91 (1945).

[249] A group may be classified as an identifiable minority because of unalterable congenital traits, political impotence, and the attachment of a stigma of inferiority. *See Developments in the Law-Equal Protection*, 82 HARV. L. REV. 1065, 1126 – 1127 (1969) [hereinafter cited as *Developments-Equal Protection*]. The Supreme Court has accepted evidence of community prejudice in school segregation of Chicanos as proof that they are an identifiable minority group in regard to juries in Jackson County, Texas. Hernandez v. Texas, 347 U.S. 475, 479 (1954).

[250] *See* Alvarado v. El Paso Ind. School Dist., 445 F.2d 1011 (5th Cir. 1971), where the court found Chicanos a proper class. Though initially the fourteenth amendment was judicially limited to Blacks in the *Slaughter-House Cases*, 83 U.S. (16 Wall.) 36, 81 (1873), by 1886 the Court in Yick Wo v. Hopkins, 118 U.S. 356, 369 (1886), extended fourteenth amendment protection to Chinese, and even to a corporation. County v. Southern Pac. R.R., 118 U.S. 394, 396 (1886).

[251] 347 U.S. 475 (1954).

as declaring Mexican Americans a separate class,[252] reserved the question.[253] Although some hastily adjudicated post-*Brown* decisions ruled that *la raza* did not constitute a separate class,[254] Chicanos have recently been declared an identifiable minority group in *Cisneros v. Corpus Christi Independent School District.*[255] While not the first post-*Brown* finding of *de jure* segregation of Chicanos,[256] it was the first case to apply *Brown* to Chicanos. With the notable exception of court-ordered "integration" of Chicanos and Blacks in Houston,[257] most decisions have rejected arguments that Chicanos are simply other whites,[258] and agreed with the *Cisneros* finding of an identifiable minority group.[259]

The *Cisneros* court premised its finding on their distinctive physical, cultural, linguistic, religious and Spanish-surname characteristics.[260] The

---

[252] *See, e.g., Houston, supra* note 14, at 938; Brief for the United States at 8, Cisneros v. Corpus Christi Ind. School Dist., No. 71–2397 (5th Cir., filed July 16, 1971).

[253] *See* pp. 343–44 *supra.*

[254] *See* Memorandum on motion to intervene in Ross v. Eckels, Civil No. 10444 (S.D. Tex., May 24, 1971): "The Houston Independent School District (as I believe has been true generally for school purposes throughout this state) has always treated Latin-Americans as of the Anglo or White race." Although that premise appears to be clearly wrong, Judge Connally went on to conclude that even if Chicanos were an identifiable minority group they were not entitled "to escape the effects of integration [with blacks]" because they had not been subjected to "*state-imposed segregation.*" *Id.*

In a previous appeal to the Fifth Circuit, Judge Clark stated in dissent that: "Approximately 36,000 students in the Houston, Texas system are Spanish surnamed Americans. They have been adjudicated to be statistically white. As the majority states, we know they live in the very areas required to be paired with all or predominantly Negro schools. I say it is mock justice when we 'force' the numbers by pairing disadvantaged Negro students into schools with numbers of this equally disadvantaged ethnic group." 434 F.2d 1140, 1150 (5th Cir. 1970).

[255] 324 F. Supp. 599, 606 (S.D. Tex. 1970); *cf.* Alvarado v. El Paso Ind. School Dist., 445 F.2d 1011 (5th Cir. 1971); United States v. Austin Ind. School Dist., Civil No. A-70-CA-80 (W.D. Tex., June 28, 1971); Tasby v. Estes, Civil No. CA-3–4211 (N.D. Tex., July 16, 1971).

[256] *See* Chapa v. Odem Ind. School Dist., Civil No. 66-C-92 (S.D. Tex., July 29, 1967).

[257] Ross v. Eckels, 317 F. Supp. 512 (S.D.Tex.), *aff'd,* 434 F.2d 1140 (5th Cir. 1970) (which included Chicanos as white for purposes of integration).

[258] *Contra,* Ross v. Eckels, 434 F.2d 1140 (5th Cir. 1970).

[259] *See* United States v. Austin Ind. School Dist., Civil No. A-70-CA-80 (W.D. Tex., June 28, 1971); Tasby v. Estes, Civil No. CA-3–4211 (N.D. Tex., July 16, 1971); *cf.* Romero v. Weakley, 131 F. Supp. 818 (S.D. Cal. 1955). (Plaintiffs had alleged segregation of Chicano and Black children in El Centro, California. The case was settled out of court.); Keyes v. School Dist. 1, 313 F. Supp. 61 (D. Colo. 1970), *rev'd,* 445 F.2d 990 (10th Cir. 1971), *cert. granted,* 40 U.S.L.W. 3335 (U.S. Jan. 18, 1972)(The district court found that overwhelmingly Hispano schools might be considered segregated, but was puzzled by Hispano-Black schools. This bewilderment was needless, for a standard which can apply to them severally must also apply to them jointly. The Tenth Circuit did not consider this issue).

[260] 324 F. Supp. at 608.

same characteristics that render Chicanos an identifiable minority group render classifications discriminating against them "suspect," subject to "strict scrutiny," and justifiable only by a showing that they are necessary to promote a compelling state interest.

One argument that Chicanos constitute an identifiable minority group is simply that they are a separate race. Because the Chicano gene pool is eighty percent Native American with the remaining twenty percent about equally divided between European and Black,[261] it has been argued that Chicanos should be considered as Indian.[262] So considered, Chicanos would correspond to a Black of one-eighth or one-sixteenth Anglo ancestry.[263] The high percentage of Native American blood in most Chicanos has produced a people characteristically having an easily identifiable brown skin color, black hair, and brown eyes.[264] However, the difficulty[265] and nonessentiality of the argument outweigh its value. Although racial classifications are accorded the strictest scrutiny,[266] classifications based on national ancestry[267] or alienage[268] are also suspect. A court could apply a suspect classification test without reaching the race issue.

Chicanos are also readily identifiable because they retain many

---

[261] H. Driver, INDIANS OF NORTH AMERICA 602 (1961). The possibility that any given Chicano is a descendent of "pure Spanish ancestors" is extremely tenuous since "[a]bout 90 percent of the Spanish immigrants were men who came over single or cohabited with Indian women." Moreover the bulk of European and Black immigration took place prior to 1810.

[262] Forbes, *Race and Color in Mexican-American Problems*, 16 J. HUM. REL. 57 (1968) [hereinafter cited as *Forbes*]. *But cf.* Westminster School Dist. v. Mendez, 161 F.2d 774 (9th Cir. 1937) (school districts erred in separating Chicanos on the basis of a statute allowing segregation of Indians and Asiatics).

[263] *Forbes* at 57.

[264] At least one author has attributed much of the discrimination against Chicanos to their color characteristics. *See generally Forbes, supra* note 262.

Indeed "Mexicans" were a racial category in the 1930 census. U.S. Bureau of the Census, U.S. Census of Population: 1960, Subject Reports, Persons of Spanish Surname at viii (Final Report PC [2]-1B, 1963).

[265] *See* C. Vose, CAUCASIANS ONLY 83 – 84, 87, 129 – 31 (1967), where the author relates the strategy of Black civil rights attorneys. They sought to prove that there was no constant characteristic by which Black people could be positively identified as a separate race for purposes of restrictive covenants. Neither hair texture, nor skin color, nor head size, nor blood type was constant for all Black people. Much the same is true of Chicanos. Like Black people their physical characteristics defy an inviolable stereotypic description.

[266] *See, e.g.,* Hunter v. Erickson, 393 U.S. 385 (1969); Loving v. Virginia, 388 U.S. 1 (1967); McLaughlin v. Florida, 379 U.S. 184 (1964); Strauder v. West Virginia, 100 U.S. 303 (1880).

[267] *See, e.g.,* Korematsu v. United States, 323 U.S. 214 (1944).

[268] *See, e.g.,* Takahishi v. Fish and Game Comm'n, 334 U.S. 410 (1938); Sei Fujii v. State, 38 Cal. 2d 718, 242 P.2d 617 (1952).

customs inherited from their Indian and Spanish ancestors.[269] Most importantly, Chicanos characteristically speak Spanish as a mother tongue. Although language classifications are not themselves suspect, at least one state court has applied strict scrutiny to strike down language classifications burdening the right to vote.[270] Where Californians, literate in Spanish but not English, were denied the right to vote on the basis of English literacy tests, the California Supreme Court applied the strict test. It is unclear whether its basis was a suspect racial classification, the fundamental interest in the franchise, or both.[271]

Chicanos are particularly susceptible to exclusion based on English literacy testing. Although Congress has suspended literacy test requirements for voting in any federal, state or local election until August 6, 1975,[272] temporarily unenforceable English tests remain on the books in fifteen states.[273] Specifically mentioning discrimination against "Spanish-Americans," the Supreme Court has unanimously upheld the

---

[269] *See generally* A. Paredes, WITH HIS PISTOL IN HIS HAND (1958).

[270] Castro v. State, 2 Cal. 3d 223, 466 P.2d 244, 85 Cal. Rptr. 20 (1970) (*semble*).

[271] *Id.*, 2 Cal.3d at 229, 232 – 33, 466 P.2d at 247, 250, 85 Cal. Rptr. at 23, 26.

[272] Voting Rights Act, 42 U.S.C. § 1973aa (1970).

[273] Ala. Const. amend. 223, § 1 (suspended by § 4c of the Voting Rights Act of 1965, United States v. Alabama, 252 F. Supp. 95 (M.D. Ala. 1966)); Ariz. Rev. Stat. Ann. § 16 – 101 (1956); Conn. Gen. Stat. Ann. § 9 – 12 (1958); Del. Const. art. 5, § 2; Ga. Const. art. 2, § 704; Miss. Const. art. 12, § 244 (suspended by § 4c of the Voting Rights Act of 1965, United States v. Mississippi, 256 F. Supp. 344 (S.D. Miss. 1966)); Miss. Code Ann. §§ 3212, 3235 (1942)(also suspended); N.H. Rev. Stat. Ann. §§ 55:10, :12 (1955); N.Y. Const. art. 2, § 1(provision seriously limited in its discriminatory effect on Puerto Ricans by § 4(e) of the 1965 Voting Rights Act, Katzenbach v. Morgan, 384 U.S. 641 (1966)); N.Y. Election Law § 168 (McKinney Supp. 1968) (also limited); N.C. Const. art. VI § 4 (suspended as to a county where court applied § 4(c) of Voting Rights Act of 1965, Gaston County v. United States, 395 U.S. 285 (1969); N.C. Gen. Stat. § 163 – 58 (1964) (also limited); Ore. Const. art. II, § 2 (Oregon voters will vote in 1972 on whether to delete this section, 5 Ore. Rev. Stat. 1146); Ore. Const. art. VIII, § 6 (school board elections) (also to be decided upon in 1972); S.C. Code Ann. § 23 – 62(4) (1962); Wash. Const. amend. 5; Wyo. Const. art. 6, §9. Curiously, Louisiana allows a literacy test to be taken in one's mother tongue in lieu of English. La. Const. art. § 1(c); La. Rev. Stat. § 18:31(3) (1969). *But see* Minn. Stat. Ann. §§ 204.13, 206.20 (1962), which requires aid for non-English speaking voters. The California law (Cal. Const. art. II, § 1) was ruled unconstitutional by the state Supreme Court in Castro v. State, 2 Cal. 3d 223, 466 P.2d 244, 85 Cal. Rptr. 20 (1970). The constitutionality of the Washington law (Wash. Const. amend. 5) was upheld in Mexican-American Federation v. Naff, 299 F. Supp. 587 (E.D. Wash. 1969). However, the decision was vacated and remanded by the U.S. Supreme Court, 400 U.S. 986 (1971), citing the 1970 Voting Rights Act and Oregon v. Mitchell, 400 U.S. 112 (1970). Five states, Alaska, Hawaii, Maine, Massachusetts, and Oregon have repealed English literacy tests for voting since 1968. *See generally* Liebowitz, *English Literacy: Legal Sanction for Discrimination*, 45 NOTRE DAME LAW. 7 (1969). *See also* Garza v. Smith, Civil No. SA = 70-CA-169 (May 17, 1971), *rev'd in part*, ___ F.2d ___ (5th Cir. 1971) (requiring aid for illiterate Chicano voters).

Congressional prohibition of literacy tests for voting.[274] Four states require English speaking ability to hold some state or local offices.[275] Three states restrict foreign language instruction,[276] and twenty-nine states and territories including Arizona, California, Colorado, New Mexico, New York and Illinois specify English as the main language of instruction in public and private schools, although some have added provisions permitting bilingual education.[277] Other states and territories require that legislative proceedings,[278] court proceedings,[279] official

---

[274] Oregon v. Mitchell, 400 U.S. 112, 118, 131 – 34 (1970); cf. Katzenbach v. Morgan, 384 U.S. 641 (1966) (§ 4[e] of the Voting Rights Act of 1965 which enfranchised non-English-speaking citizens who had attended American flag schools upheld). See also NOTE, The Impact of Katzenbach v. Morgan on Mexican-Americans 7 HARV. J. LEGIS. 154 (1969). But see Camacho v. Rogers, 199 F. Supp. 155 (S.D.N.Y. 1961) (dicta to the effect that English literacy tests are valid).

[275] Ariz. Const. art. XX, § 8; Ariz. Rev. Stat. Ann. § 11 – 402 (1956); Cal. Elections Code § 1611 (West 1961); Ind. Ann. Stat. § 19 – 3201 (1969); Minn. Stat. Ann. § 203.22(4) (1962). See also Cal. Elections Code 14217 (West 1961)(requiring elections officials to speak only English); Iowa Code Ann. § 365.17 (1946) (restricting people illiterate in English from Civil Service positions).

[276] Conn. Gen. Stat. Ann. § 10 – 17 (1958); Minn. Stat. Ann. §§ 120.10(2), 126.07 (1960); Wis. Stat. Ann. § 118.01(1) (West 1970).

[277] Ariz. Const. art. XX, § 7; Ariz. Rev. Stat. Ann. § 15 – 202 (Supp. May, 1969); Ark. Stat. Ann. § 80 – 1605 (1947); Cal. Educ. Code § 71 (West 1969)(providing also for bilingual education); Colo. Rev. Stat. Ann. § 123 – 21 – 3 (1963); Conn. Gen. Stat. Ann. § 10 – 17 (1958); Del. Code Ann. tit. 14, § 122(b)(5)(1958); Guam Gov't Code § 11200 (1970); Idaho Code Ann. § 33 – 1601 (1949); Ill. Ann. Stat. ch. 122, § 27 – 2 (Smith-Hurd 1969); Iowa Code Ann. § 280.5 (1946); Kan. Stat. Ann. § 72 – 1101 (1963); La. Const. art. 12, § 12; Me. Rev. Stat. Ann. tit. 20, § 102 (1964) as amended (Supp. 1972); Mich. Stat. Ann. § 15.3360 (1968); Minn. Stat. Ann. §§ 120.10(2), 126.07 (1960); Mont. Rev. Codes Ann. § 75 – 7503 (1947); Neb. Const. art. I § 27; Nev. Rev. Stat. § 394.140 (1967); N.H. Rev. Stat. Ann. §§ 189:19 – 21 (1955) as amended (Supp. 1971)(proviso for bilingual education); N.M. Const. art. XXI, § 4; N.Y. Educ. Law § 3204 (1953); N.C. Gen. Stat. § 115 – 198 (1965) as amended (Supp. 1971); N.D. Cent. Code § 15 – 47 – 03 (1971); Okla. Stat. Ann. tit. 70, § 11 – 2 (1966); Ore. Rev. Stat. § 336.074 (1971)(proviso for bilingual education); Pa. Stat. Ann. tit. 24, § 15 – 1511 (1962) as amended (Supp. 1971); S.D. Comp. Laws § 13 – 33 – 11 (1968); Wash. Rev. Code Ann. § 28A.05.010 (1970)(providing also for bilingual education); W.Va. Code Ann. § 18 – 2 – 7 (1971); Wis. Stat. Ann. § 118.01(1) (West 1970).

[278] Neb. Const. art. 1, § 27.

[279] Ark. Stat. Ann. § 22 – 108 (1962); Cal. Civ. Pro. Code § 185 (West 1954); Colo. Rev. Stat. Ann. § 37 – 1 – 22 (1963); Idaho Code Ann. § 1 – 1620 (1947); Mo. Ann. Stat. § 476.050 (1949); Mont. Rev. Codes Ann. § 93 – 1104 (1947); Neb. Const. art. I, § 27; Nev. Rev. Stat. § 1.040 (1969); Utah Code Ann. 78 – 7 – 22 (1953); Vt. Stat. Ann. tit. 4, § 731 (1972); Wis. Stat. Ann. § 256.18 (1971). But see Tex. Rev. Civ. Stat. Ann. art. 3737d-1 (Supp. 1972).

records,[280] or legal notices[281] be in English. Finally, although the Supreme Court has held that one cannot be denied employment because of alienage,[282] three states require English entrance examinations to enter regulated occupations.[283] English literacy tests, having their origins in anti-immigrant feelings, are today used to discriminate against minorities that are readily identifiable by color: Chicanos, Blacks, Indians, and Boricuas (Puerto Ricans).[284]

A further identifying trait of Chicanos is that most are Catholic, albeit in past times attending segregated churches.[285] Religious classifications have of course been held suspect, requiring strict judicial review.[286]

Another common means of identifying Chicanos in Texas is by Spanish-surname. The United States Bureau of the Census has used this means to compile census statistics since 1950.[287] Spanish surname has at times been the principal means for segregation.[288]

These identifying characteristics fall into two categories: alterable—

---

[280] Ark. Stat. Ann. § 22 – 108 (1962); Cal. Civ. Pro. Code § 185 (West 1954); C.Z. Code tit. 3, § 278 (1963); Guam Code Civ. Proc. § 185 (1953); Idaho Code Ann. § 1 – 1620 (1947); Ky. Rev. Stat. Ann. § 446.060(2) (1969); Mo. Ann. Stat. § 476.050 (1949); Mont. Rev. Codes Ann. § 93 – 1104 (1947); Neb. Const. art. I, § 27; N.J. Rev. Stat. Ann. § 52:36 – 4 (1955); Utah Code Ann. § 78 – 7 – 22 (1953); Vt. Stat. Ann. tit. 4, § 732 (1972); Wis. Stat. Ann. § 256.18 (1971).

[281] Ariz. Rev. Stat. Ann. § 39 – 204 (1956); Cal. Corp. Code § 8 (West 1955); Ind. Stat. Ann. Stat. §§ 2 – 4706 (1968); Iowa Code Ann. § 618.1 (1946); Ky. Rev. Stat. Ann. § 446.060 (1971); La. Rev. Stat. §§ 1:52, 43:201 to :202 (1950) *as amended* (Supp. 1972); Me. Rev. Stat. Ann. tit. 1, §§ 353, 601 (1964) *as amended* (Supp. 1972); Mass. Gen. Laws Ann. ch. 200A, § 8(b) (1955) *as amended* (Supp. 1972); N.J. Rev. Stat. § 35:1 – 2.1 (1968); N.D. Cent. Code § 46 – 06 – 02 (1960); Ohio Rev. Code Ann. § 3905.11 (1971); Wash. Rev. Code Ann. § 65.16.020 (1966); Wis. Stat. Ann. § 324.20 (1958) *as amended* (Supp. 1971). *But see* N.M. Stat. Ann. § 10 – 2 – 11 (1953); N.M. Stat. Ann. § 10 – 2 – 13 (1953) *as amended* (Supp. 1972).

[282] Truax v. Raich, 239 U.S. 33 (1915).

[283] Conn. Gen. Stat. Ann. §§ 20 – 108 (1958); Okla. Stat. Ann. tit. 59, § 806 (1971); Utah Code Ann. §§ 58 – 12 – 11, 58 – 5 – 3 (1953). *See also* N.Y. Gen. Bus. Law § 434.3 (McKinney 1968) *as amended* (Supp. 1971)(barbering test may now be translated on request and need into other languages); Tex. Educ. Code § 13.034 (Vernon Supp. 1971)(requiring teaching certificate applicants to demonstrate an ability to use English easily and readily) *formerly* Tex. Rev. Civ. Stat. Ann. art. 2880 (1965).

[284] Leibowitz, *English Literacy: Legal Sanction for Discrimination*, 45 NOTRE DAME LAW. 7, 37, 50 (1969).

[285] For example, Catholic Churches in Alice, Texas were segregated until the 1950's. Interview with Fortino Trevino, Alice civil rights activist, in Alice, Texas, July 19, 1971.

[286] *See, e.g.,* Juarez v. State, 102 Tex. Cr. R. 297, 277 S.W. 1091 (1925) (exclusion of Roman Catholics from juries barred by the fourteenth amendment).

[287] U.S. Bureau of the Census, *supra* note 264. *See also* Little, *supra* note 31.

[288] *See* Hernandez v. Driscoll Consol. Ind. School Dist., 2 RACE REL. L. REP. 329 (S.D. Tex. 1957).

culture, language, religion, Spanish-surname; and unalterable, or "congenital,"—physical characteristics and national origin. Because one of the three primary rationales for applying the suspect criteria test is classification based on congenital traits,[289] discrimination against Chicanos deserves judicial treatment as "suspect."

The other two rationales of this doctrine of strict judicial review are the protection of politically disadvantaged minority groups[290] and the attachment of a stigma of inferiority to a classification.[291] Politically disadvantaged minority groups deserve special protection because state legislatures fail to represent them, often giving less than full consideration to their interests. Chief Justice Stone suggested this rationale in *United States v. Carolene Products Co.:*[292] "[P]rejudice against discrete and insular minorities may be a special condition which tends seriously to curtail the operation of those political processes ordinarily to be relied upon to protect minorities, and which may call for a correspondingly more searching judicial inquiry." Since it is uncontrovertible that Chicanos in Texas are politically disadvantaged,[293] they deserve strict review under this second rationale also.

Finally, the stigma of opprobrium that attaches to Chicanos in Texas is much like that which attaches to Blacks in other parts of the South.[294] Based on the premise of white superiority, exclusion of Chicanos from jobs, housing, schools, restaurants, theaters, and swimming pools[295]

---

[289] *See, e.g.,* McLaughlin v. Florida, 379 U.S. 184 (1964).

[290] *See* Hobson v. Hansen, 269 F. Supp. 401, 507–08 n. 198 (D.D.C. 1967), *aff'd sub nom.* Smuck v. Hobson, 408 F.2d 175 (D.C. Cir. 1969); *Evolution-Equal Protection, supra* note 25, at 132; *Developments-Equal Protection, supra* note 249, at 1125.

[291] *See, e.g.,* Black, *The Lawfulness of the Segregation Decisions,* 69 YALE L. J. 421, 424 (1960); *Evolution-Equal Protection* at 132–135; *Developments-Equal Protection, supra* note 249, at 1127.

[292] 304 U.S. 144, 153 n. 4 (1938). *See* Hobson v. Hansen, 269 F. Supp. 401, 503 (D.D.C. 1967) (the power structure "may incline to pay little heed to even the deserving interests of a politically voiceless and invisible minority.").

[293] *E.g.,* There are only 11 Chicanos in the 150-member Texas House of Representatives and of the 31 Texas Senators only one is Chicano. Their influence is so attenuated that a Bilingual Education Bill never reached the floor because of opposition from people who felt it to be un-American. Telephone interview with Paul Moreno, Texas State representative, December 17, 1971. *See also,* U.S. Comm'n on Civil Rights, MEXICAN-AMERICANS AND THE ADMINISTRATION OF JUSTICE IN THE SOUTHWEST (1970).

[294] *Cf.* Local 53 of Int. Ass'n of Heat and Frost I. A. Wkrs. v. Vogler, 407 F.2d 1047 (5th Cir. 1969) (The 5th Cir. affirmed a lower court finding that Blacks and Mexican Americans had been excluded from the Louisiana local).

[295] *E.g.,* Texas courts upheld a proprietor's right to refuse service to a Chicano in Terrel Wells Swimming Pool v. Rodriguez, 182 S.W.2d 824 (Tex. Civ. App. 1944) *cf.* Lueras v. Town of Lafayette, 100 Colo. 124, 65 P.2d 1431 (1937). *But see,* Lopez v. Seecombe, 71 F. Supp. 769 (S.D. Cal. 1944); Beltran v. Patterson, Civil No. 68–59-W (W.D. Tex. 1968),

aggravated the stigma of inferiority,[296] a result concommitant with the general effect of segregation in America.[297] The Supreme Court seems to have accorded this rationale overriding importance. Even when a legislature meets the second test—majoritarian consideration of minority interests—by providing separate but equal facilities, the Court refuses to legitimize segregated schools because separation of some children "from others of similar age and qualifications solely because of their race generates a feeling of *inferiority as to their status* in the community that may affect their hearts and minds in a way unlikely ever to be undone."[298]

Chicanos in the Southwest have historically been viewed as inferior. As a result they have suffered much abuse, often at the hands of law enforcement personnel.[299] In the 1930's an Arizona newspaper referring to segregation of Mexicans reported them to be "both strangers belonging to an alien race of conquered Indians, and persons whose enforced status in the lowest economic levels make [sic] them less admirable than other people."[300] The stigma of inferiority can be traced to the pervasive stereotype of Chicanos as "lazy, dirty, and ignorant." One glaring manifestation of this stigma occurred as recently as 1971. In Seguin, Texas, Chicano children were being expelled[301] allegedly for having lice despite recurrent doctors' examinations showing the allegations to be greatly exaggerated. Local OEO workers were instructed by their superiors to use Gulf spray on the heads of those children

---

cited in brief for MALDEF as *amicus curiae*, at 3, Ross v. Eckels, 434 F.2d 1140 (5th Cir. 1970), where the court enjoined the exclusion of Chicanos from a public swimming pool.

[296] A. Perales, ARE WE GOOD NEIGHBORS 139−227 (1948).

[297] *See* Black, *supra* note 291, at 425; *Developments-Equal Protection, supra* note 249, at 1127.

[298] Brown v. Educ., 347 U.S. 483, 494 (1954) (emphasis added); *cf.* McLaughlin v. Florida, 379 U.S. 184 (1964); Loving v. Virginia, 388 U.S. 1 (1967). A pre-*Brown* court reached this same conclusion regarding Chicanos who were segregated in schools solely and exclusively for them. Gonzalez v. Sheely, 96 F. Supp. 1004 (D. Ariz. 1951). *See Evolution-Equal Protection* at 31−42.

[299] *See, e.g.,* Cavazos v. State, 143 Tex. Crim. 564, 160 S.W.2d 260 (1942) (conviction reversed where Texas Rangers beat and tortured a Chicano prisoner to secure a confession). *See generally* A. Parades, *supra* note 269, at 7−32.

[300] Quoted in McWilliams, NORTH FROM MEXICO 41 (1948).

[301] *E.g.,* The mother of one eight-year-old expelled from school for "lice" found none on her daughter. She reported: "The next day I took her to school. The nurse examined [the daughter] and claimed that she found one [lice] which she placed in an envelope but she refused to allow me to see it. I left.

That night [daughter] started complaining of stomach pains and has been sick for the last three weeks. [Daughter] says that she is reluctant to go back to school because she was afraid of being embarrassed or humiliated again by the teachers." Statement of [mother of expelled girl], February 25, 1971, taken by Alberto Huerta, MALDEF administrative assistant, in San Antonio, Texas.

suspected of having lice. Field workers questioned this order, calling the school nurse before proceeding. She explained that this spray was to be used in the homes.[302] Children reported ridicule by teachers, examination in front of class for examples of lice, examination only of Chicanos or in separate lines, public declarations of infestation, and, in at least one case, expulsion for three weeks for dandruff.[303]

Courts should be no less able than the Anglo citizens of Texas to recognize Chicanos as an identifiable ethnic minority. And because their identity is unalterable, stigmatized, and abused by the majority in Texas' political processes, classifications discriminating against Chicanos are suspect and courts must review them with strict scrutiny.

B. Proving Segregation Once "Suspect" Treatment Is Accorded

Once a suspect classification argument is accepted, a plaintiff could proceed to establish a *prima facie* case of discrimination based upon direct evidence of segregative state action and statistical evidence of an unconstitutional degree of segregation.[304] Plaintiffs in *Cisneros* made out a *prima facie* case of unconstitutional segregation by establishing that: (1) Mexican Americans are an identifiable minority group, (2) they are segregated, and (3) state action caused their present segregation.

Cisneros demonstrated the kind of direct evidence of segregative state action which may be presented. The school district had argued that there had never been a dual system since there was no history of a state law requiring segregation of Chicanos. Judge Seal found unconstitutional state action in school board decisions, which,

> in drawing boundaries, locating new schools, . . . renovating old schools in the predominantly Negro and Mexican parts of town, in providing an elastic and flexible subjective, transfer system that resulted in some Anglo children being allowed to avoid the ghetto, or 'Corridor' school, by bussing some students [to avoid Mexican and Negro schools], by providing one or more optional transfer zones which resulted in Anglos being able to avoid Negro and Mexican-American schools, not allowing Mexican-Americans or Negroes the option of going to Anglo schools, by spending extraordinarily large sums of money which resulted in

---

[302] Interview with Alberto Huerta, MALDEF administrative assistant, in San Antonio, Texas, July 19, 1971.

[303] *See generally* Statements of parents and children from Seguin, Texas, taken in February, 1971 by MALDEF on file in MALDEF offices in San Antonio, Texas.

[304] *Cf.* Hawkins v. Town of Shaw, 437 F.2d 1286 (5th Cir. 1971). *See also* Fessler & Haar, *Beyond the Wrong Side of the Tracks: Municipal Services in the Interstices of Procedure,* 6 HARV. CIV. RIGHTS-CIV. LIB. L. REV. 441, 442 – 456 (1971).

intensifying and perpetuating a segregated, dual school system, by assigning Negro and Mexican-American teachers in disparate ratios to these segregated schools, and further failing to employ a sufficient number of Negro and Mexican-American teachers and failing to provide a majority-to-minority transfer rule, were, regardless of all expressions of good intentions, calculated to, and did, maintain and promote a dual school system.[305]

Although these grounds have been held sufficient to support a finding of *de jure* segregation,[306] the school board's assertion of no constitutional requirement to affirmatively correct racial imbalance remained an arguable defense,[307] because the plaintiffs did not explore school board minutes for additional evidence of pre-1954 violations.[308] While the Justice Department, as plaintiff-intervenor, has not taken a position as strong as the school board's, it has nonetheless asked the Fifth Circuit to remand for more data on Chicano segregation.[309]

In previous cases relying on evidence from school board minutes courts have found historical *de jure* segregation of Mexican Americans.[310] This is especially persuasive when coupled with witnesses of that time, newspaper accounts, and other historical data. However, school board minutes have not universally sufficed. One difficulty is that board minutes are subject to the attrition[311] of time and may be lost or

---

[305] 324 F. Supp. at 617–20.

[306] *See* cases cited in notes 441–443 *infra.*

[307] Brief for Corpus Christi ISD at 18, in Cisneros v. Corpus Christi Ind. School Dist., No. 71–2397 (5th Cir., filed July 16, 1971).

[308] Telephone interview with James deAnda, counsel in *Cisneros,* Oct. 20, 1971.

[309] Brief for United States at 13, in Cisneros v. Corpus Christi Ind. School Dist., No. 71–2397 (5th Cir., filed July 16, 1971).

[310] Perez v. Sonora Ind. School Dist., Civil No. 6–224 (N.D. Tex., Nov. 5, 1970). The court found that by rules and regulations of the Sonora ISD formulated on August 4, 1938, "all Mexican children were to be enrolled in Mexican schools." *Id.* Pre-Trial Order of May 13, 1970, at 4. All Mexican children were required to attend the Mexican school until 1948 when *Delgado* forced the repeal of the resolution and zone lines were instituted. However, these were gerrymandered sufficiently to make one of the two elementary schools 100% Anglo and the other 100% Mexican. *Id.* at 6–7. Chicano high school students were not permitted onto the present Sonora High campus until 1948. *Id.* No Chicano or Black child attended the white school until 1964—although the two schools were only 1.2 miles apart. *Id.* at 7 and 10. *See also* United States v. Lubbock Independent School District, 316 F. Supp. 1310 (N.D. Tex. 1970). The court found that five of the thirty-eight elementary schools were vestiges of a *de jure* system of segregation toward Chicanos and Blacks. Two of these were predominantly Chicano. One was built in the pre-*Brown* era, the other in 1961. *Id.* at 1318. An additional thirteen of the remaining thirty-three elementary schools were racially identifiable. *Id.* at 1317. Although the court found *de jure* segregation in at least five elementary schools, the court did not disturb the composition of any elementary school. *Id.* at 1319.

[311] A school official in Kingsville, Texas, told the authors that the school board minutes

burned. Courts may fail to give probative value to ambiguous statements referring to "Mexican schools," interpreting them as schools located in Mexican neighborhoods.[312] But many egregious decisions holding that Chicanos have never been segregated appear contrary to evidence and unsupported by findings of fact.[313] To date *Cisneros* is the only contemporary Texas case finding *de jure* segregation of Chicanos absent

---

prior to 1940 had been destroyed by a fire a few years ago. Interview with Mr. Gillett, Superintendent Kingsville ISD, August 9, 1971. Subsequent to this interview the authors had access to a HEW document which referred to Kingsville Board Minutes dating back to May 16, 1908. The review was conducted on June 23−24, 1971. U.S. Dep't of Health, Educ. & Welfare, *On-Site Review of Kingsville ISD, Texas on June 23−24, 1971*, at 8, submitted to John Bell, Chief, Education Branch OCR, Aug. 5, 1971. The Superintendent of La Feria ISD informed the authors that he had no quarrel with the concept of school board minutes as public, but reasoned that this applied only to citizens of La Feria. Thus, the authors were denied access to these minutes. Interview with Clyde E. Vail, Superintendent of La Feria ISD, August 7, 1971. El Paso, Texas, is divided into two districts: El Paso ISD and Ysleta ISD. References to Mexican schools in the El Paso ISD were found prior to 1930. *See, e.g.*, El Paso ISD Board Minutes, March 25, 1924 (copied and read by Carlos Vela on file in Brownsville, Texas). *See generally* P. Horn, SURVEY OF THE CITY SCHOOLS OF EL PASO TEXAS (1922)(In this study for the El Paso Public Schools, Horn made much of the unequal education in the American and Mexican Districts). *See also El Paso City Schools*, THE SCHOOLS OF EL PASO 24 (1928)(Aoy elementary school described as "historic school for Mexican pupils."). When the authors asked to see the Ysleta ISD minutes prior to 1930, they were told that these were with the county recorder downtown. Interview with Dr. J.W. Hanks, Superintendent, Ysleta ISD, July 12, 1971. No one could locate them. Interview with Al Morales, El Paso County Clerk, July 13, 1971.

[312] United States v. Austin Ind. School Dist., Civil No. A-70-CA-80 (W.D. Tex., June 18, 11971) *appeal docketed*, No. 71−2508 (5th Cir., filed Aug. 3, 1971). There were board references to a Mexican school as early as 1916. A second Mexican school was built in 1924, a third in 1935. While separation was not rigidly enforced when children were distant from these schools, Chicano children in zones overlappling Anglo zones were required to attend the Mexican school. Mexican schools were built to accommodate Mexican children attending Anglo schools. The district did not attempt to segregate Chicano high school students because the extremely high dropout rate made this unnecessary. "Mexican" housing projects were located near the Mexican school. Zone lines, construction and transfer policies were designed to and did accomplish segregation of Chicano children. Chicano schools in Austin are so overcrowded that space per pupil is only about 40 percent of that in Anglo schools. Brief for United States as Appellant at 10−32, United States v. Austin Ind. School Dist., No. 71−2508 (5th Cir., filed Aug. 3, 1971).

[313] *E.g.*, United States v. Midland Ind. School Dist., Civil No. MO-70-CA-67 (W.D. Tex., Aug. 25, 1970), *vacated*, 443 F.2d 1180 (5th Cir. 1971), *rehearing*, 334 F. Supp. 147 (N.D. Tex. 1971), *appeal docketed*, No. 71−3271 (5th Cir., *filed* Nov. 5, 1971). Evidence showed that the school board provided a "separate school for Mexicans" as early as 1914. Until 1948, Chicanos in Midland were not permitted past eighth grade, and all schooling was in the Latin-American school. The first Chicano to attend an integrated junior high school did so in 1946. Six years later in 1952, the city had its first Chicano high school graduate. Brief for United States as Appellant at 6−9, United States v. Midland Ind. School Dist., *appeal docketed*, No. 71−3271 (5th Cir. *filed* Nov. 5, 1971). In spite of overwhelming evidence to the contrary, Judge Guinn found: "As Texas has never required

proof of historical educational segregation.[314]

Interestingly, the *Cisneros* complaint also used the "other white" argument.[315] This was an improvident inclusion, for it works against a showing of an identifiable minority group. Fortunately, the court chose to ignore the implications of the argument. A court unaware of the civil rights origins of the "other white" argument might have stretched it to include Chicanos as "other whites" for purposes of statistical integration. Instead, the *Cisneros* court, relying on *Brown*, held integration of Chicanos and Blacks not a constitutional means of eliminating dual school systems.[316] It ordered pairing and busing.[317]

Once a *prima facie* case of unconstitutional segregation is established, the burden of going forward shifts to the defendant. The defendant may then make one or all of three answers: (1) challenge the validity of the evidence, (2) concede the evidence and offer proof of a rationale for its existence which would override an inference of illegal discrimination, or (3) challenge the scope of the plaintiffs' mandate for equality.[318]

To preempt the first defense plaintiffs need only be cautious enough to use valid and sufficient evidence. To forestall the second, plaintiffs may offer proof of a previous dual system not sufficiently dismantled or a presumption to that effect. As to the third, the state would have to show a compelling state interest for continued segregation; and only war-time necessity has ever been found sufficiently "compelling" to justify invidious racial or national origin classification.[319]

C. State Interest in Chicano Segregation

Many arguments have been proferred for separating Mexican-

---

by law that Mexican-American children be segregated and the Midland Independent School District has never enacted regulations to this effect and from the evidence, the Court finds that there has been no history of discriminary practices against Mexican-Americans by the school district." 334 F. Supp. 147, 150−51 (W.D. Tex. 1971).

[314] *See* Tasby v. Estes, Civil No. CA-3−4211 (N.D. Tex., July 16, 1971) (Dallas) (*de jure* segregation of Chicanos not found). Plaintiffs failed to explore school board minutes for the origins of Mexican schools. Interview with R. Surrat, counsel in *Tasby*, in Dallas, July 15, 1971; *cf.* Ross v. Eckels, Civil No. 10444 (S.D. Tex., May 24, 1971) (motion to intervene on behalf of Chicano plaintiffs denied in the absence of historical data such as school board minutes).

[315] Complaint at 4, Cisneros v. Corpus Christi Ind. School Dist., 324 F. Supp. 599 (S.D. Tex., 1970).

[316] 324 F. Supp. at 611.

[317] *Id.* at 618−24; *accord* Uresti v. School Bd., Civil No. 70-B-100 (S.D. Tex., Sept. 14, 1971) (busing may be used by a school board to integrate Mexican-American schools).

[318] *See* Fessler & Haar, *supra* note 304, at 447−48.

[319] *See* Korematsu v. United States, 323 U.S. 214, 216−18 (1944).

American school children from their Anglo peers.[320] For equal protection purposes, the validity of these reasons can be analyzed in terms of both strict[321] and permissive[322] standards of review.

1. Strict Standard

The justifications given for segregating Chicano students generally fall within one of four classifications.

Prejudice. Many of the articulated bases of segregation have been overtly racist. One study of Nueces County quoted school executives who stated that they "segregate for the same reason that the southerners segregate the Negro. They are an inferior race that is all."[323] Because racial or ethnic prejudice is not a legitimate governmental objective, a classification designed for its promotion is unconstitutional.[324]

Mexican-American Preference for Segregation. This assertion is based on an inference that silence and acceptance of a *fait accompli* by Chicano parents amounts to exercising a preference. The inference ignores the fact that very few people in the Chicano community have been in a position to mount effective opposition to the "Mexican School."[325] Furthermore, those outspoken Mexican Americans who did raise their voices expressed protest, not approval, of segregation, though few were able to change school board policy.[326] In proffering this rationale, the state fails to meet its burden of justification for a suspect classification.

Mexican Americans are Underachievers. The argument is that since Chicano students generally fall behind in class, integration would slow the progress of Anglos.[327] The notion that Chicanos are "slower" derives

---

[320] *See* Little, *supra* note 31, at 60−61.

[321] Suspect classifications are subject to strict scrutiny and the state carries a heavy burden of justification. *See* Korematsu v. United States, 323 U.S. 214, 216 (1944); Hirabayashi v. United States, 320 U.S. 81 (1943). *See* pp. 348−56, *supra.*

[322] Under permissive or traditional review, a classification is not held invalid unless it is without any reasonable basis. Morey v. Doud, 354 U.S. 457 (1957).

[323] Taylor, *supra* note 1, at 219.

[324] *See, e.g.,* Korematsu v. United States, 323 U.S. 214, 223 (1944). *Cf.* Tussman & tenBroek, *The Equal Protection of the Laws,* 37 CALIF. L. REV. 341, 374 (1949).

[325] Taylor, *supra* note 1, at 230−240.

[326] There were some efforts by organizations like the American G.I. Forum and the League of United Latin American Citizens (founded in 1929). There were also instances when members of the local Chicano community came before school officials and requested changes. *See, e.g.,* Alice ISD, BOARD MINUTES, vol. 7, at 74 (1948) (where Fortino Trevino led a delegation to discuss segregation).

[327] Significantly, the comprehensive Coleman Report has documented the achievement of white children to be less affected by characteristics of fellow students than are Blacks, Chicanos or Orientals. U.S. Dep't of Health, Educ. & Welfare, EQUALITY OF EDUCATIONAL OPPORTUNITY 303, 306 (1966).

from their lower scores on standardized intelligence tests.[328] However, most of these tests are culturally and linguistically biased, reflecting ethnicity rather than true ability.[329] It is doubtful whether "intelligence" can ever be meaningfully tested. It is too deeply enmeshed in the web of history and human relations to be isolated numerically with the accuracy needed to shape social policy. Moreover, to the extent Chicano underachievement is due to previous educational deprivation caused by psychological discrimination and inferior schools, segregation simply perpetuates the effect of past discrimination.[330] Finally, the justification fails because the classification of Mexican Americans as underachievers is both underinclusive and overinclusive. It excludes low achieving Anglos, but includes high achieving Chicanos. The underachievement argument therefore fails to meet its "heavy burden of justification."[331]

Language Problem. The justification meriting most serious attention is that Mexican-American children are segregated to learn English better. By not mixing them with English-speaking pupils until they are proficient in English, it is argued, Chicano students can avoid falling behind in other subjects.[332] But courts generally reject segregative classifications even when they promote legitimate governmental purposes, if substitute avenues are available.[333] Here, there are alternative means to accomplish the objective—if, indeed, it is better education—which are at least as feasible and, some educators argue, more beneficial to the learning process.[334]

---

[328] *See Hearings Before the Senate Select Committee on Equal Educational Opportunity,* 91st Cong., 2d Sess. 2504 (1970) [hereinafter cited as *1970 Hearings*]. At least one recent study, conducted by Dr. Jane R. Mercer, associate professor of sociology at the University of California in Riverside, concluded that underachievement among white, Black and Chicano children is attributable to non-racial and nonhereditary causes. Boston Globe, Nov. 19, 1971, at 1, col. 2 [hereinafter cited as Mercer study]. It is also misleading to compare the achievement of Mexican-American students with their Anglo peers, because Chicanos have historically been relegated to school buildings where conditions have been less than ideal. *See, e.g.,* Harlingen ISD Board Minutes, vol. 4 (Oct. 25, 1932): "The worst conditions we have are in West Ward. In the beginners there, we have 108 enrolled. We are handling this at present by dividing the room into sections and by keeping one or two sections on the playground at all times."

[329] Mercer Study, *supra* note 328.

[330] United States v. Jefferson County Bd. of Educ., 372 F.2d 836 (5th Cir. 1966), *cert. denied* 389 U.S. 840 (1967).

[331] *See, e.g.* Loving v. Virginia, 388 U.S. 1, 9 (1967); McLaughlin v. Florida, 379 U.S. 184 (1964).

[332] *E.g.,* San Benito ISD, BOARD MINUTES, vol. 2, at 71 (Sept. 20, 1915). "It was ordered on account of the widely different methods that must be used in teaching non-English speaking peoples and English-speaking people, that all pupils that do not speak English natively, be required to attend the First Ward until they have been promoted to the Fifth grade. . . ."

[333] *E.g.,* Carrington v. Rash, 380 U.S. 89 (1965).

[334] Educators argue that Chicano students can learn English better if they are mixed

The historical implementation of segregation discredits its assertedly beneficent purpose. The situation presented in 1957 in *Hernandez v. Driscoll Consolidated Independent School District*[335] is illustrative. In *Driscoll*, the local board's requirement that all Mexican-American students attend segregated classes for *four* years in the first *two* grade levels was a purposeful and "unreasonably discriminatory" act.[336] Its arbitrariness was apparent because the board did not have testing facilities to measure progress of Chicano students in language proficiency. Additionally, in one instance a Chicano student who could not speak Spanish had been summarily assigned to the segregated Chicano classroom.[337]

If this segregation were really intended to meet the need for different instructional methods, the educational resources and facilities of Mexican schools would be equal, if not superior, to those at Anglo schools. There is no evidence that they are. On the contrary, Mexican-American children historically have been provided inferior facilities, often drastically over-crowded,[338] in some instances necessitating half-day classes.[339] In 1948, the Mexican Chamber of Commerce of Harlingen submitted to the local board a report[340] outlining in detail conditions at the Alamo School (originally the Mexican School). These included broken windows, rooms without lights, three-inch cracks in the side of the building and loose ceilings "just about ready to fall."[341]

---

with the English-speaking students. Interview with Dr. George Sanchez, Professor of Education, University of Texas at Austin, in Austin, July 17, 1971. *See generally* pp. 384−91 *infra.* One conference of educators emphatically reported that segregation of Chicano children "is pedagogically unsound, socially dangerous, and unquestionably unamerican." *See Sanchez, supra* note 31, at 44. Thus, Dr. Sanchez concludes that educational reasons offered by school administrators must in the end be regarded "either as professional blunders or worse still, as evidence that educational principle is being prostituted to racialism [sic]." *See Sanchez, supra* note 31, at 58.

[335] 2 Race Rel. L. Rep. 329 (S.D. Tex., Jan. 11, 1957).

[336] *Id.* at 333.

[337] *Id.* at 331. Overinclusive classifications are most difficult to justify because they place added burdens on those who are not similarly situated for purposes of the designated class. *See, e.g.,* Carrington v. Rash, 380 U.S. 89 (1965). *See also Developments-Equal Protection, supra* note 249, at 1086.

[338] *E.g.,* McAllen ISD, BOARD MINUTES, vol. 2, at 21 (Oct. 4, 1919) (The Mexican school had one teacher in one classroom with 190 pupils).

[339] *E.g.,* U.S. Dept. of Health, Educ. & Welfare Compliance Review of El Paso ISD, at 11−12 (Mar. 1971).

[340] Letter from A.C. Lozano, President of the Mexican Chamber of Commerce, to the Harlingen School Board, March 12, 1948.

[341] Letter from Alamo School Investigating Committee to A.C. Lozano, President of Mexican Chamber of Commerce in Harlingen, March 10, 1948, on file with Dr. Garcia in Corpus Christi. *See also* letter from Hector P. Garcia, Chairman of the American G.I.

Comparison of the length of school terms originally provided Chicano, Black, and Anglo students in some districts casts additional doubt upon the allegedly beneficent purpose behind historical segregation.[342] Discrimination in length of school year was evidenced by findings of the Texas Education Survey Commission in 1923.[343] In its review of twenty-five school districts in twelve counties, the Commission found differences between white and Black school terms of almost five months, with an average of 1.6 months more education per year provided in Anglo schools. Similarly, the difference in length of school terms for white and Mexican-American students averaged 2.4 months.[344] Although part of the difference was because many Chicanos and Blacks pursued migratory labor, not all were migrants. Yet in the usual situation they were all required to attend Mexican or Black schools.[345] Thus, Chicano children were denied equal educational opportunities by the shortened school year for reasons inapplicable to them as individuals.

When subjected to "rigid scrutiny,"[346] the ethnic classification fails because it is not necessary to achieve any compelling state interest. But, should a court fail to apply the stricter suspect criteria test, the more permissive standard of review must also be considered.

2. Permissive Standard

Under permissive review, school officials must meet two requirements: there must be a conceivable legitimate purpose for

---

Forum, to Texas Commissioner of Education, April 11, 1948, on file at Dr. Garcia's office, Corpus Christi, Texas. This report of the conditions of the schools in three cities (Mathis, Orange Grove, Sandia) is accompanied by photographic evidence of the buildings. Similar conditions were described by the Texas Educational Survey Commission as occurring in 1925 "[i]n a village of about 1500 [where] there was found a fairly good public school for the English speaking children. 'Across the tracks' was the Mexican School. It was a dilapidated, two or three room building. The toilets were unscreened and the grounds poorly kept." Texas Educ. Survey Comm'n, *supra* note 60, at 214.

[342] The Uvalde ISD minutes reveal that the date for closing public schools in 1911 would be Friday, May 19, except that the Mexican and colored schools would be closed on April 21. U.S. Dept. of Health, Educ. & Welfare, On-Site Review of Uvalde, at 8 (June 1970).

[343] Texas Educ. Survey Comm'n, 7 TEXAS EDUCATIONAL SURVEY REPORT: GENERAL REPORT 207 (1925).

[344] *Id.* at 125.

[345] One school district in reporting its statistics of pupil enrollment at the beginning of the 1906−07 school session noted that: "To the enrollment at the time this pamphlet goes to the printer there will be large additions—especially in the Mexican School and the Negro schools, many of which are picking an extraordinarily large cotton crop." Victoria ISD, ORGANIZATION AND COURSE STUDY OF THE PUBLIC SCHOOLS OF THE VICTORIA INDEPENDENT SCHOOL DISTRICT, 1906−07, at 3 (1907).

[346] Korematsu v. United States, 323 U.S. 214, 216 (1944).

segregating Chicano students, and the resulting classifications must have a rational relation to that purpose.[347] This formula immediately eliminates segregation based on prejudice, because the purpose underlying the classification is itself impermissible.[348]

Similarly, compliance with the wishes of the Mexican community does not legitimize state-imposed ethnic discrimination. Only if the ethnic classification were benign could it arguably be constitutional. Moreover, even if some Mexican parents did favor segregation, establishment of separate Mexican schools was not reasonably related to the purpose of meeting Chicano community preference.[349] There were also parents who did not want a Mexican school, yet their children were assigned to the separate school. Its overinclusiveness renders the classification unconstitutionally discriminatory.[350]

If the purpose of separation is to prevent Chicano students from retarding the progress of Anglo children, an admittedly legitimate purpose, the classification is similarly arbitrary, because of both over- and under-inclusiveness. The classification is underinclusive because some Anglo underachievers also hold back a class's progress. It is overinclusive because it includes Chicano high achievers who do not retard class progress.

Finally, the validity of segregation for purposes of improving English proficiency of Chicanos is also questionable under the permissive standard of review. Although this purpose is legitimate, classifications of Mexican-American students often have no reasonable relation to it. Blanket categorization of Chicanos, without considering the abilities of individuals, is arbitrary. The segregative classification is also irrational when Chicano schools do not have facilities to cope with the "language problem." If school officials assert this purpose without including specific programs to realize their alleged goal, the presumption of legitimate governmental purpose is overcome. As in *Hernandez v. Driscoll Consolidated Independent School District,*[351] a court should find that intentional segregation was not based on pedagogical considerations, but, rather, was "arbitrary and discriminatory."

---

[347] *See* Shapiro v. Thompson, 394 U.S. 618, 658 (1969); Morey v. Doud, 354 U.S. 457, 464–465 (1947); *See also Developments-Equal Protection, supra* note 249, at 1077–1087.

[348] Yick Wo v. Hopkins, 118 U.S. 356 (1886) (racial hostility not permissible purpose).

[349] "[C]ourts must reach and determine the question of whether the classifications drawn in a statute are reasonable in light of its purpose." McLaughlin v. Florida, 379 U.S. 184, 191 (1964).

[350] *Developments-Equal Protection, supra* note 249, at 1086.

[351] 2 Race Rel. L. Rep. 329, 333 (S.D. Tex., Jan. 11, 1957).

V. FEDERAL AGENCIES LOOK ELSEWHERE

A. Department of Health, Education, and Welfare

To contend with persisting segregation, Congress enacted Title VI of the Civil Rights Act of 1964,[352] which provides that "[n]o person in the United States shall, on the ground of race, color, or national origin, be excluded from participation in, be denied the benefits of, or be subjected to discrimination under any program or activity receiving Federal financial assistance."[353] Administrative action[354] was to be the catalyst for change; "[t]he courts acting alone [had] failed."[355] Responsibility for executive enforcement of the 1964 Act rests with the Office for Civil Rights of the Department of Health, Education and Welfare. Its Education division is charged with eliminating discrimination in public schools.[356]

The Office for Civil Rights has been severely criticized for neglect of Chicano integration problems.[357] Prior to the 1967—68 school year, HEW required racial school statistics only for Blacks and whites.[358] Only then was the category "other" added to its statistical forms and defined to include all "significant 'minority groups' in the community" and specifically Mexican Americans.[359] Not until 1968—69 were separate statistics collected for "Spanish Surnamed Americans."[360] It is not

---

[352] Civil Rights Act of 1964, §§ 601—05, 42 U.S.C. §§ 2000d to 2000d-4. (1970) [hereinafter cited as 1964 Act]. *See generally* Dunn, *Title VI, the Guidelines and School Desegregation in the South,* 53 VA. L. REV. 42 (1967).

[353] 1964 Act, § 601, 42 U.S.C. § 2000d (1970).

[354] 1964 Act, § 602, 42 U.S.C. § 2000d-1 (1970): "Each Federal department and agency which is empowered to extend Federal financial assistance to any program or activity by way of grant, loan, or contract other than a contract of insurance or guaranty, is authorized and directed to effectuate the provisions of section 2000d of this title . . . ." *See generally* Comment, *The Courts, HEW and Southern School Desegregation,* 77 YALE L. J. 321 (1967).

[355] United States v. Jefferson County Bd. of Educ., 372 F.2d 836, 847 (5th Cir. 1966), *cert. denied,* 389 U.S. 840 (1967).

[356] 35 FED. REG. 10927 (1970).

[357] *See, e.g.,* Letter from Dr. Hector P. Garcia to Mr. Stanley Pottinger, Nat'l Director, Office for Civil Rights, U.S. Dep't of Health, Educ. & Welfare, in *1970 Hearings, supra* note 328, at 2581.

[358] *1970 Hearings, supra* note 328, at 2552 (statement of C. Vela).

[359] U.S. Dep't of Health, Educ. & Welfare, Fall 1967 Summary of Enrollment and Staff of School System, Form OE 7001: "Other—Should include any racial or national origin group for which separate schools have in the past been maintained or which are recognized as significant 'minority groups' in the community (such as Indian American, Oriental, Eskimo, Mexican-American, Puerto Rican, Latin, Cuban, etc.)"

[360] U.S. Dep't of Health, Educ. & Welfare, Fall 1968 Elementary and Secondary School Survey, Form OS/CR 101. This method is subject to criticism on two grounds: it is inexact,

surprising, then, that HEW found such districts as Pecos, Texas, in compliance with the 1964 Act when they had done no more than transfer Black students to Chicano schools.[361]

HEW's on-site review practices were as negligent and ineffective as its statistical oversight. Even where the Department had initiated its cumbersome administrative process, all too often real enforcement was left to others. There are indications, for example, that HEW reviewed New Braunfels, Texas, for Chicano segregation as early as 1965,[362] an anomaly in its custom of neglect; but the resulting relief was not so anomalous—nothing was done.[363] The Mexican American Legal Defense and Educational Fund (MALDEF)[364] recently filed suit against New Braunfels to compel integration.[365]

In 1968, HEW undertook "Mexican-American studies" of Chicano districts with migrant problems.[366] Pecos was reviewed in August 1968.[367] Significant violations were found in student assignment, facilities, tracking, and faculty assignment. Yet there followed no administrative actions or negotiations toward compliance. Oddly the report made no mention of migrant problems. Alice, Texas, was reviewed on August 21–22, 1968. The review found four of seven elementary schools at least ninety-seven percent Chicano,[368] and a freedom-of-choice scheme in use at the elementary level.[369] School Board minutes sanctioning the

---

and it fails to differentiate among different Spanish surnamed groups. Anglo surnamed Chicanos are counted as Anglos and Spanish surnamed Anglos are counted as Chicanos for purposes of integration. Thus, for example, some districts that do not hire Chicanos may nonetheless indicate that they have Spanish surnamed employees. Secondly, in areas such as Chicago which have concentrations of Chicanos and Boricuas (Puerto Ricans), it is impossible to adequately meet the needs of either. At the higher education level, problems of differentiation are even more acute due to greater mobility of students and faculty.

[361] See U.S. Dep't of Health, Educ. & Welfare, On-Site Review of Pecos ISD, at 8 (Sept. 1968). See also, U.S. Dep't of Health, Educ. & Welfare, On-Site Review of Bishop ISD, at 49 (Jan. 1970).

[362] Letter from Aguinaldo Zamora to the Equal Employment Opportunity Commission, May 3, 1968, on file in Dr. Hector Garcia's office in Corpus Christi, Texas.

[363] Interview with anonymous HEW official.

[364] MALDEF was funded by a $2.2 million Ford Foundation grant in 1968. THE TEXAS OBSERVER, April 11, 1969, at 6, col. 1.

[365] Zamora v. New Braunfels Ind. School Dist., Civ. No. 68–205-SA (W.D. Tex., filed Aug. 28, 1968).

[366] There had been reviews in eight of ten districts originally chosen for "Mexican-American Studies," dealing with migrant problems and not Title VI compliance. Interview with Carlos Vela, former Texas Coordinator for HEW, Office for Civil Rights, in Brownsville, Texas, August 10, 1971.

[367] U.S. Dep't of Health, Educ. & Welfare, On-Site Review of Pecos ISD (Sept. 1968).

[368] U.S. Dep't of Health, Educ. & Welfare, On-Site Review of Alice ISD, at 2 (Sept. 1968).

[369] Id. at 3.

existence of a Mexican school as far back as 1915, and restricting Latin-American children to that school in 1939,[370] were ignored by HEW. Despite the Supreme Court's holding three months earlier that freedom-of-choice plans which do not eliminate segregation are unconstitutional,[371] the reviewers told the Superintendent that the district "appeared to be in compliance with the law."[372] HEW later commended the Board "for the leadership . . . taken in providing a quality education for all students in the Alice Independent School Districts."[373] HEW did request additional efforts to eliminate the identifiability of the four elementary schools. By the 1970—71 school year, all had enrollments at least ninety-seven percent Chicano. Despite additional complaints of segregation in Alice, nothing more has been done.[374]

After the HEW review of Alice, the Commission on Civil Rights held hearings in December, 1968, in San Antonio, and requested "prompt action" to alleviate educational disparities between Anglos and Chicanos in San Antonio and across the Southwest. Low achievement scores, ethnic isolation, and cultural discrimination were among problems highlighted for prompt HEW action.[375]

The Sonora review in February, 1969, demonstrated HEW's ominously slow response.[376] The Sonora district received a letter of non-compliance on May 5, 1969.[377] Following this, as is the general procedure, negotiations began in an attempt to achieve voluntary compliance. However, at a time when the negotiator felt school officials were about to capitulate,[378] HEW suspended negotiations. In spite of

[370] *E.g.*, Alice ISD, BOARD MINUTES (May 8, 1915). *See also id.* for May 14, 1921, May 2, 1941, and Sept. 17, 1946. In the minutes for August 24, 1939 is a resolution: "Motion was duly made, seconded, and carried that all Latin Americans attend Nayer school through elementary grades and Anglo Saxons attend Hobbs-Strickland School . . . ." The Nayer school was ninety-nine percent Chicano in 1970—71. U.S. Dep't of Health, Educ. & Welfare, 1970 Individual School Campus Report, Form OS/CR 102—1.

[371] Green v. Board of Educ., 391 U.S. 430 (1968).

[372] U.S. Dep't of Health, Educ. & Welfare, On-Site Review of Alice ISD, at 6 (Sept. 1968).

[373] Letter from Jerald D. Ward, Chief, Dallas Education Branch, Office of Civil Rights. to Mr. Dewey G. Smith, Superintendent Alice ISD, September 9, 1968.

[374] Letter from Alfredo Arriola, Chairman, Alice G.I. Forum, to Mrs. Dorothy Stuck, Director, Region VII Office for Civil Rights, October 15, 1970.

[375] Letter from Howard A. Glickstein, Acting Staff Director, U.S. Comm'n on Civil Rights, to Robert H. Finch, Secretary of U.S. Dep't of HEW, Feb. 5, 1969, on file with Carlos Vela in Brownsville, Texas.

[376] U.S. Dep't of Health, Educ. & Welfare, On-Site Review of Sonora ISD (Feb. 1969). *See* p. 368 *infra.*

[377] Letter from Roberto Gonzalez, Acting Chief Education Branch, Office for Civil Rights, to Ralph J. Finklin, Superintendent Sonora ISD, May 5, 1969.

[378] *1970 Hearings, supra* note 328, at 2253 (statement of C. Vela).

requests for immediate action from Civil Rights Commissioner Hector P. Garcia, HEW agreed only to conduct further reviews. Within ten days, MALDEF filed what proved to be a successful suit to desegregate the Chicano schools.[379]

A second review of the Pecos district was conducted contemporaneously with Sonora. As in Sonora, HEW issued a letter of non-compliance, but despite continuing complaints,[380] has not followed with administrative enforcement.[381] Three years have since passed, yet nothing has been done to enroll the first Anglo pupil in the Chicano school.[382] Rather, it was MALDEF that entered into agreements designed to produce prompt action in Pecos, threatening litigation should these agreements fail.[383]

Before the end of 1969, HEW teams visited two more school districts in Texas, Wilson and Shallowater, and several in New Mexico: Carlsbad, Clovis, Hobbs, and Las Cruces. They found segregation of Chicanos in the Texas districts and of both Chicanos and Blacks in the New Mexico districts. Nothing has been done concerning any of these districts.[384] When one Texas superintendent called the HEW Dallas office to ask whether he would have to eliminate a segregated class, he was referred to Washington.[385]

In the first six months of 1970, HEW conducted reviews in at least six more cities: Crystal City,[386] Bishop,[387] Ozona,[388] Wharton,[389] El Paso,[390] and Uvalde.[391] Desegregation plans were negotiated for Bishop and Ozona. HEW has taken no further administrative action on the remaining four cities in spite of violations.[392] As a result, MALDEF filed suit against El Paso.[393]

---

[379] Perez v. Sonora Ind. School Dist., Civil No. 6—224 (N.D. Tex., Nov. 5, 1970).

[380] *E.g.*, Letter from Dr. Hector Garcia to J. Stanley Pottinger, August 13, 1970, on file with Dr. Garcia in Corpus Christi, Texas.

[381] Interview with anonymous HEW official.

[382] Letter from Dr. Hector Garcia to J. Stanley Pottinger (undated Fall, 1970) (the letter describes the deplorable conditions in Pecos ISD and requests immediate action). *Cf.* U.S. Dep't of Health, Educ. & Welfare, On-Site Review of Pecos ISD (June 1969).

[383] Telephone interview with Albert Armendariz, MALDEF Director, in El Paso, Texas, Oct. 19, 1971.

[384] *1970 Hearings, supra* note 328, at 2553 (statement of C. Vela).

[385] *Id.*

[386] *Id.*

[387] U.S. Dep't of Health, Educ. & Welfare, On-Site Review of Bishop ISD (Jan. 1970).

[388] U.S. Dep't of Health, Educ. & Welfare, On-Site Review of Ozona ISD (Mar. 1970).

[389] U.S. Dep't of Health, Educ. & Welfare, On-Site Review of Wharton ISD (June 1970).

[390] U.S. Dep't of Health, Educ. & Welfare, On-Site Review of El Paso ISD (Apr. 1970).

[391] U.S. Dep't of Health, Educ. & Welfare, On-Site Review of Uvalde ISD (Aug. 1970).

[392] *1970 Hearings, supra* note 328, at 2553—54 (statement of C. Vela). However, Uvalde did recieve a letter of non-compliance.

[393] Alvarado v. El Paso Ind. School Dist., 445 F.2d 1011 (5th Cir. 1971). This was done

The year 1970 saw a turn in the course of administrative action. Indeed, HEW officials today freely admit that prior to 1970 both HEW and the courts largely ignored Chicano problems.[394] They point to events of 1970 as building a new era of sensitivity to Chicano problems.[395] The impetus for sudden administrative interest appears to have arisen from two sources. Progress in the rest of the South left more resources available for work in Texas. However it is premature to expect newly unburdened staff to concentrate on Chicano desegregation.[396] Second, rising Chicano militancy, characterized by school boycotts, created pressure for action. The Crystal City review followed a four-week student walk-out.[397] Of the eight Texas cities involved in school boycotts prior to August, 1970, seven have since been the scene of HEW action. Two have had their plans for compliance with Title VI accepted by HEW.[398] Two more are presently involved in negotiations.[399] Three others have been reviewed by HEW.[400]

On May 25, 1970, HEW published a memorandum[401] listing four

---

in conjunction with El Paso Legal Assistance and referral attorneys Fred Weldon and Richard Baca.

[394] Gerry, Cultural Freedom in the Schools, at 4 (May 21, 1971)(unpublished article done for HEW Office for Civil Rights where Mr. Gerry is special assistant to the director) [hereinafter cited as *Cultural Freedom*]. "From 1965 to early 1969 the Office for Civil Rights, Education Branch, was primarily pursuing the elimination of the Southern dual (black-white) school systems.

Desegregation plans accepted from Texas school districts in most cases failed to significantly effect the discriminatory treatment of Mexican-American students. 'Desegregation' of blacks and Mexican-Americans (rather than desegregation among blacks, Anglos, and Mexican-Americans) often resulted.

To summarize, between 1954 — 1970 neither the courts nor the Executive Branch seriously attacked either the segregation of the Mexican-American, Puerto Rican, and native American children or the invidious discriminatory practices utilized by school districts in the operation of educational programs within schools." *Id.* at 4 — 5.

[395] Even HEW hiring practices have been subjected to charges of discrimination against not only Chicanos but all Spanish-surnamed minorities. *1970 Hearings, supra* note 328, at 2552 (statement of C. Vela). *See id.* at 2416 (letter from J. Stanley Pottinger to Senator Mondale).

[396] There are indications that the shift will instead be to other parts of the country. Eighty of the 132 Office for Civil Rights staff are already assigned to areas outside the South. 117 CONG. REC. S 5478 (daily ed. April 22, 1971).

[397] *1970 Hearings, supra* note 328, at 2553 (statement of C. Vela). *See also 1970 Hearings, supra* note 328, at 2486 (Exhibit C). Boycotts have brought vastly inconsistent results. The boycott in Crystal City prompted the election of four Chicanos to the school board and the appointment of a Chicano Superintendent. Boycotts in Kingsville resulted in the arrest of 110 students and no concessions were made. El Paso, Edcouch-Elsa, Abilene, Uvalde, Sierra Blanca, and Lockhart also experienced Chicano school boycotts.

[398] Sierra Blanca and Lockhart. Interview with anonymous HEW official.

[399] El Paso and Uvalde. However, negotiations are dormant in both of these cities. *Id.*

[400] Kingsville, Crystal City, and Abilene. *Id.*

[401] U.S. Dep't of Health, Educ. & Welfare, Memorandum from J. Stanley Pottinger

criteria by which performance toward elimination of discrimination against Chicanos would henceforth be judged:

—Where there are sufficient language problems, school districts must make affirmative efforts to rectify the language deficiency.
—Assignment to mentally retarded classes and exclusion from college preparatory courses must not be based on criteria which measure English language skills.
—Tracking to meet the language deficiency should not constitute a permanent track.
—Adequate notice of school activities should be given to national origin minority group parents in their own language if necessary.

To supplement the Memorandum, HEW proposed a timetable for implementation. Four phases of action were contemplated between spring 1970 and spring 1971.[402] HEW also scheduled reviews of ten more districts across the Southwest.[403]

The May 25 Memorandum is subject to two major criticisms. First, it was not mailed to all Texas districts that should have received it, namely those with Chicano student populations greater than five percent.[404] Second, the Memorandum is a watered-down version of a draft proposed before the resignation of Leon E. Panetta as Director of the Office for Civil Rights. The earlier draft had also included the following compliance standards:[405]

—Failure to undertake affirmative recruitment and development through in-service programs of teachers, counselors and administrators who possess a sensitivity for and understanding of the cultural background of the minority pupils . . . .
—Failure to include in the curriculum courses which recognize and illustrate the contributions made to the development of this country by the forbearers of the district's minority pupils . . . .
—Failure to provide bi-lingual personnel in schools with

to School Districts With More than Five Percent National Origin-Minority Group Children (May 25, 1970) (at *1970 Hearings, supra* note 328, at 2579 — 80) [hereinafter cited as May 25 Memorandum].

[402] U.S. Dep't of Health, Educ. & Welfare, Initial Report—Proposed Timetable, from the Task Force on Implementation of National Origin-Minority Group Policy Statement, to J. Stanley Pottinger, Director, Office for Civil Rights, May 28, 1970, on file with Carlos Vela in Brownsville, Texas.

[403] *1970 Hearings, supra* note 328, at 2556 (statement of C. Vela).

[404] *Id.* at 2579. It is reported that this oversight has since been rectified. Interview with anonymous HEW official.

[405] U.S. Dep't of Health, Educ. & Welfare, Memorandum from Leon E. Panetta, Director, Office for Civil Rights, to School District with More Than Five Per cent Spanish Surname or Other Disadvantaged National Origin Minority, (undated draft), on file with Carlos Vela in Brownsville, Texas.

significant Spanish-speaking enrollment and in other district contact positions.

Between May 25, 1970 and April, 1972, the Office for Civil Rights secured compliance plans in line with the May 25 Memorandum from at least fourteen districts.[406] In addition, HEW has reviewed twelve other districts for compliance with the May 25 memorandum but has not yet secured an acceptable plan.[407]

The plan for Beeville is an excellent model of the necessary relief. The HEW study showed that a substantial number of Chicano children in Beeville enter school with English deficiencies.[408] Because tests used to group or track students were based on criteria which measured English language skills, there was great underinclusion of Chicanos in advanced tracks and overinclusion in mentally retarded and lower tracks. As Chicano children progressed in years of attendance their performance on standardized tests actually declined, compared with both their *own prior performance* and that of their Anglo peers.[409] These factors prompted HEW to require bilingual and bicultural education.[410]

These efforts are but a small beginning. On September 25, 1970, HEW was sent a list of twelve cities which had been reviewed and not acted upon. Eighteen months later, HEW had accepted a plan in compliance with its standards from only one of these districts.[411] On October 2, 1970 the Office for Civil Rights was sent a list compiled from an HEW publication[412] of 224 districts with schools ninety to a hundred percent Mexican American which had a minimal number of Chicano

---

[406] These districts are: Ozona-Crockett County, Bishop, Lyford, Rotan, Sierra Blanca, Los Fresnos, Lockhart, San Marcos, Beeville, Weslaco, and Carne. Additionally, the list should include the districts of Sonora and Del Rio-San Felipe which are under court order, the latter composed of two consolidated districts.

[407] *Id.* Reviews have been initiated in: El Paso, Karnes City, Uvalde, Fort Stockton, La Feria, South San Antonio, Santa Maria, Victoria, Harlingen, Pawnee, and Taft, Texas, as well as Hobbs, New Mexico.

[408] U.S. Dep't of Health, Educ. & Welfare, Letter of non-compliance from John Bell, Chief, Education Branch, Region VI, Office for Civil Rights to Archie A. Roberts, Superintendent of the Beeville ISD, Feb. 17, 1971.

[409] *Cultural Freedom, supra* note 394, at 9–14.

[410] For a history of the development of techniques to show a need for bilingual-bicultural education, see *id.*

[411] The districts listed were: Pecos, Wilson, Shallowater, El Paso, Wharton, Uvalde, Crystal City, and Beeville, Texas, and Hobbs, Las Cruces, Carlsbad, and Clovis, New Mexico. Letter from Dr. Hector Garcia to Elliot Richardson, Sec'y, U.S. Dep't of Health, Educ. & Welfare, September 25, 1970, on file with Dr. Garcia in Corpus Christi, Texas. Beeville is the only district for which a compliance plan has been accepted.

[412] U.S. Dep't of Health, Educ. & Welfare, Directory of Public and Secondary Schools in Selected Districts, "Enrollment and Staff by Racial/Ethnic Group, Fall, 1968."

teachers.[413] One hundred nine districts with Chicano students employed no Chicano teachers. In at least six districts hiring no Mexican-American teachers, Chicano pupils were more than fifty percent of enrollment.[414] As indicated above, the Department has since reviewed only a small proportion of these districts. HEW's "new era of sensitivity to Chicano problems" is not yet credible.

B. Department of Justice

The Department of Justice first intervened on behalf of Chicanos in Sonora, Texas in early 1970.[415] Although the district capitulated, the Department's intervention was a mixed blessing for the original plaintiffs. The Department submitted a plan, objectionable to the plaintiffs,[416] which was finally agreed upon by the defendant school district and the court.[417]

A desire to sensitize the Justice Department to Chicano problems prompted J. Stanley Pottinger, Director of HEW's Office for Civil Rights, to suggest that Justice Department negotiations for Black desegregation in forty-eight Texas school districts should also seek to desegregate Chicanos. A list of twenty-five of these districts apparently discriminating against Chicanos was sent to the Department.[418] Yet when Justice filed suit against thirteen of these districts in August of 1970,[419] it included allegations of discrimination against Chicanos in only five districts.[420] In a severed suit involving one of the districts, Midland, evidence of a Mexican school operating from 1914 to the present was

[413] Letter from Dr. Hector Garcia, former member, U.S. Comm'n on Civil Rights, to J. Stanley Pottinger, Director, Office for Civil Rights, October 2, 1970, on file with Dr. Garcia in Corpus Christi, Texas.

[414] *Id.* The predominantly Chicano districts hiring no Chicano teachers are listed at note 92 *supra*.

[415] Press Release from MALDEF, May 27, 1970, at 1, on file in MALDEF offices in San Antonio, Texas.

[416] Telegram from Pete Tijerina and Ed Idar, attorneys for plaintiffs, to John F. Conroy, attorney, Education Section, Justice Dep't, Nov. 10, 1970, on file in MALDEF offices in San Antonio, Texas.

[417] Supplemental Order of November 16, 1970, Perez v. Sonora Ind. School Dist., Civil No. 6 – 224 (N.D. Tex., Nov. 5, 1970).

[418] Letter from J. Stanley Pottinger to Jerris H. Leonard, Assistant Attorney General, (undated), on file with Carlos Vela, in Corpus Christi, Texas (twenty-five of the forty-eight districts were listed as having elements of Chicano discrimination).

[419] United States v. Texas Educ. Agency, Civil No. 3 – 4076-A (N.D. Tex., filed Aug. 7, 1970)(the six districts obtained separate hearing dates); United States v. Texas Educ. Agency, Civil No. A-70-CA-80 (N.D. Tex., filed Aug. 11, 1970)(the seven districts obtained separate hearing dates).

[420] Lubbock, San Angelo, Austin, Ector County and Midland. Discrimination in hiring of Chicano teachers in the other districts sued was not contested.

revealed, yet the court failed to find *de jure* segregation.[421]

Other actions illustrate the Department's insufficient efforts. It failed to appeal in *United States v. Lubbock Independent School District*, where vestiges of a dual system were left untouched, discriminatory optional zones remained in effect, and Chicano imbalances in a high school and junior high were reduced only from ninety-nine and ninety-eight to sixty-three and eighty-eight percent, respectively.[422] It also failed to appeal a San Angelo Case, in which it alleged segregation of Chicanos[423] but the court's order failed to provide any remedy, even though there was no trial on the merits and, as one government attorney said, the decision "did not significantly change segregation."[424] In a 1970 Odessa case,[425] the Department accepted an agreed order with no provisions for rezoning, busing, or pairing. As a result, four schools that were 99 − 100% minority in 1969 remained 97 − 100% minority in 1971 − 72.[426] Finally, in *United States v. Austin Independent School District*,[427] the Department did appeal a court ruling, contrary to overwhelming evidence, that Chicanos had not suffered *de jure* segregation. But on appeal, the Department disavowed[428] an HEW plan for system-wide dismantling of *de jure* Chicano segregation, adopting the position that not all predominantly Chicano schools were vestiges of *de jure* segregation. One administration critic has charged that the disavowal was politically inspired.[429]

The Justice Department's role as intervenor is even more disturbing than its losing record as plaintiff. In *Cisneros*, the Department was asked

---

[421] United States v. Midland Ind. School Dist., 334 F. Supp. 147 (W.D. Tex. 1971), *appeal docketed*, No. 71−3271 (5th Cir., *filed* Nov. 5, 1971). Judge Guinn was reversed by the Fifth Circuit in a similar case. Alvarado v. El Paso Ind. School Dist., 445 F.2d 1011 (5th Cir. 1971). *See also* note 313 *supra.*

[422] 316 F. Supp. 1310 (N.D. Tex. 1970).

[423] Complaint at 4, United States v. Texas Educ. Agency, Civil No. 6−245 (N.D. Tex. Aug. 24, 1970).

[424] Telephone interview with anonymous staff attorney, Civil Rights Division, Justice Department, October 15, 1971.

[425] Order of August 26, 1970, United States v. Ector County Ind. School Dist., Civil No. MO-70-CA-64 (W.D. Tex., Aug. 26, 1970).

[426] Dep't of Health, Educ. & Welfare, Elementary and Secondary School Civil Rights Survey, Odessa ISD: Carver Elem., Hays Elem., Milam Elem., Blackshear Jr. H.S., Forms OS/CR 102−1, Fall 1971. Four other schools with overwhelmingly minority student populations in 1969 remained so. *Id.* (Ector Jr. Sr. H.S., Rusk Elem., Travis Elem., Zavala Elem.).

[427] Civil No. A-70-CA-80 (N.D. Tex., June 28, 1971), *appeal docketed*, No. 71−2508 (5th Cir. Aug. 3, 1971).

[428] Brief for Appellant at 50, United States v. Texas Educ. Agency, No. 71−2508 (5th Cir., filed Aug. 3, 1971).

[429] Brown, *"Busing: Leaving the Driving to U.S. . . .,"* INEQUALITY IN EDUCATION, Dec. 1971, at 4−5.

to intervene after partial final judgement that Corpus Christi had imposed a *de jure* segregated system upon Chicanos as well as Blacks.[430] In its brief before the Fifth Circuit, the Department admitted that it intervened "after the basic evidentiary hearings had been entered; we are not in a position to provide a detailed analysis of the facts." Discussing only legal issues, it termed the case "basically a factual inquiry." After questioning the relief ordered by the district court, the Department concluded: "For these reasons we think that an appropriate disposition would be a remand by this Court for further findings and, if necessary, the taking of further evidence regarding discrimination against Mexican-Americans. However under the Supreme Court decision in *Alexander v. Holmes County Board of Education* 396 U.S. 19 (1969), immediate relief should be accorded to the students in the black schools."[431]

This was a startling recommendation for a plaintiff intervenor against the principal plaintiff, Cisneros.[432] Admitting incapacity to evaluate the findings of facts, Justice based its recommendation on conceded ignorance. It is difficult to understand why the government would remand for the district court to review more data only to reaffirm its *de jure* finding. The district court had heard evidence of segregative school construction and improvements, optional zones, free transfer, gerrymandered zoning, and failure to act, all of which have been held sufficient evidence of *de jure* segregation.[433] Both departments charged with enforcing Title VI have failed to make educational civil rights a reality for the Chicano community.

---

[430] Cisneros v. Corpus Christi Ind. School Dist., 330 F. Supp. 1377 (S.D. Tex. 1971), *appeal docketed,* No. 71−2397, (5th Cir., filed July 16, 1971).

[431] Brief for United States as intervenor at 13, Cisneros v. Corpus Christi Ind. School Dist., No. 71−2397, (5th Cir., filed July 16, 1971).

[432] Justice Department intervention in opposition to comprehensive integration orders has not been limited to Chicanos. *See* The Washington Post, Feb. 2, 1972, § C, at 1, col. 1 (statements of then Attorney General Mitchell regarding possible intervention into the Richmond, Va., situation, to prevent cross-boundary busing).

[433] Cisneros v. Corpus Christi Ind. School Dist., 324 F. Supp. 599, (S.D. Tex. 1970). *See* Brewer v. School Bd., 397 F.2d 37 (4th Cir. 1968); United States v. Board of School Comm'rs, 332 F. Supp. 655 (S.D. Ind. 1971); Spangler v. Pasadena Bd. of Educ., 311 F. Supp. 501 (C.D. Cal. 1970). Since the government's own plan, that of HEW, provided for busing 15,000 students, including large numbers of Chicano students, the *Cisneros* court's plan hardly seems "extreme" and "an abuse of discretion." It was based on the HEW plan with some modifications to further minimize ethnic isolation. The court used HEW's estimation of the number of students to be bused. *See* 330 F. Supp. at 13.

VI. DILEMMA OF RELIEF

Both means and goals of relief in Chicano school integration suits are complex. A statewide suit against the Texas Education Agency would provide much of the necessary relief; it would not eliminate the need for local suits, although it would facilitate them. Integration may be the goal, but what is to be the scope of the decree? The needs of Chicano pupils for integrated experiences may conflict with their unique needs for bilingual-bicultural education. This section addresses first the strategy of a statewide suit, and second the need for bilingual-bicultural education.[434]

A. Statewide Suit

1. *General Objectives.* By compelling state education officials to exercise their powers to desegregate schools for Chicanos, a statewide suit would conserve time and legal resources which would otherwise be expended on district-by-district suits.[435] In addition, such a suit could facilitate local litigation. It is the best vehicle to secure a determination that Chicanos are an identifiable minority group on whose behalf the

---

[434] This Comment deals only with those questions of relief having special importance to Chicano desegregation efforts. Thus, no attempt is made to deal with many important problems such as the currently burning issue of busing. Recent writings regarding busing include: *Perspectives on Busing,* INEQUALITY IN EDUCATION, Mar. 1972; Fiss, *The Charlotte-Mecklenburg Case-Its Significance for Northern School Desegregation,* 38 U. CHI. L. REV. 697 (1971); Note, *Busing-A Permissable Tool of School Desegregation,* 49 J. URBAN L. 399 (1971); Note, *Swann v. Charlotte-Mecklenburg Board of Education: Roadblocks to the Implementation of Brown,* 12 WIL. AND MARY L. REV. 838 (1971); *See also* 5 HARV. CIV. RIGHTS-CIV. LIB. L. REV. 488 (1970) (regarding one-way busing: minority to majority). It should, however, be noted that President Nixon's expressed desire to reduce busing has, in Texas, come at the expense of Mexican-American children. For example, in Corpus Christi, where a large percentage of the school population is Chicano, but a relatively small percentage is Black, the Government has opposed broad busing orders as to Chicanos but made no objection as to Blacks. *See* p. 374.

[435] *See* United States v. Texas, 447 F.2d 441 (5th Cir. 1971); Reeves v. Board of Educ., 430 F.2d 1334 (5th Cir. 1970); United States v. Georgia, 445 F.2d 303 (5th Cir. 1971); Lee v. Macon County Bd. of Educ., 267 F. Supp. 458 (M.D. Ala.) (three-judge court), aff'd mem., 389 U.S. 215 (1967). If Texas state and local officials proved particularly obstreporous, the statewide suit might eventually have to be dismembered into separate local suits. *See* Lee v. Macon County Bd. of Educ., Civ. No. 604-E (W.D. Ala., June 24, 1970)(three judge court); O. Fiss, INJUNCTIONS II-143 (rev. ed. 1971)(unpublished teaching materials, University of Chicago Law School).

suspect criteria test should be applied.[436] And establishing past[437] and present[438] state involvement in segregation would help local attorneys answer assertions that there has never been a state law permitting the segregation of Chicanos.[439] By creating a persuasive inference of previous *de jure* segregation, a statewide suit would overcome difficulties inherent in the evidentiary use of old school board minutes.[440] Aided by such an inference, local attorneys could establish a contemporary *de jure* segregated system by showing segregationist construction policies,[441] discriminatory busing, option zones and free transfer policies,[442] and gerrymandered zone lines.[443] A caveat to the statewide suit approach is that its utility lies in making law and precedent, rather than in integrating individual districts. It is not necessarily a talisman to district-by-district litigation.

2. *Specific Means.* Chicanos may secure the benefits of a statewide suit either by bringing an original action or by intervening in *United States v. Texas,*[444] in which much of the needed relief has already been

---

[436] *See* pp. 348 − 64 *supra.*

[437] *See* pp. 311 − 19 *supra.*

[438] *See* pp. 319 − 33 *supra.*

[439] *See, e.g.,* United States v. Austin Ind. School Dist., Civil No. A-70-CA-80 (W.D. Tex., June 28, 1971).

[440] *See* pp. 356 − 59 and note 311 *supra.*

[441] United States v. School Dist. 151, 404 F.2d 1125 (7th Cir. 1968), *modified,* 432 F.2d 1147 (7th Cir. 1970), *cert denied,* 402 U.S. 943 (1971) (South Holland, Illinois); Spangler v. Pasadena Bd. of Educ., 311 F. Supp. 501 (C.D. Cal.), *intervention denied,* 427 F.2d 1352 (9th Cir. 1970) (Pasadena); Kelley v. Brown, Civil No. LV-1146 (D. Nev., Dec. 2, 1970)(Las Vegas); Davis v. School Dist., 309 F. Supp. 734 (E.D. Mich. 1970), *aff'd,* 443 F.2d 573 (6th Cir.), *cert. denied,* 92 S. Ct. 233 (1971) (Pontiac, Michigan); Johnson v. San Francisco Unified School Dist., Civil No. C-70−1331 SAW (N.D. Cal. 1971) (San Francisco); Soria v. Oxnard School Dist. Bd. of Trustees, 328 F. Supp. 155 (C.D. Cal. 1971) (involving Chicanos and Blacks in Oxnard, California); United States v. Board of School Comm'rs, 332 F. Supp. 655 (S.D. Ind. 1971) (Indianapolis); Bradley v. Milliken, Civil No. 35257 (E.D. Mich. 1971) (Detroit); Crawford v. Board of Educ., Civil No. 822854 (Sup. Ct. L.A. Cty., Feb. 11, 1970) (Los Angeles). *See generally* Dimond, *supra* note 25.

[442] *Id.*

[443] *See, e.g.,* Taylor v. Board of Educ., 294 F.2d 36 (2d Cir. 1961). A district may not use zone lines superimposed on residential segregation to accomplish a dual system. Brewer v. School Bd., 397 F.2d 37, 42 (4th Cir. 1968). Residential segregation may be inferred from restrictive covenants and refusal on the basis of race to sell. Dowell v. School Bd., 244 F. Supp. 971, 980 (N.D. Okla. 1965), *aff'd,* 375 F.2d 158 (10th Cir. 1967).

[444] 321 F. Supp. 1043 (E.D. Tex. 1970), *modified,* 330 F. Supp. 235 (E.D. Tex.), *aff'd in part,* 447 F.2d 441 (5th Cir.), *stay denied* 92 S. Ct. 8 (1971) (Black, Circuit Justice), *cert. denied,* 40 U.S.L.W. 3313 (U.S. Jan. 11, 1972). Integration problems in Houston, Dallas, and Austin illustrate the fact that isolation of Chicanos and Blacks is so intertwined that any plan ordered for one group has substantial ramifications upon the other. This phenomenon necessitates a common suit whose relief will adequately meet the needs of each, and gravitates against separate suits and uncoordinated remedies.

granted. *Texas* was a Black desegregation suit against the Texas Education Agency and eleven school districts.[445] Nine districts were all Black, while the remaining two white districts were contiguous gerrymandered districts.[446] The district court granted broad relief against the TEA because of its failure to safeguard minority rights across the state. It also gave specific relief to the nine Black districts.[447] The Fifth Circuit affirmed with limited modifications.[448] The district court then entered a modified order, at least as broad as the original,[449] and retained jurisdiction over the matter for all purposes.[450]

[445] 321 F. Supp. at 1045–46.

[446] *Id.* at 1049.

[447] *Id.* at 1045–46, 1060–62.

[448] United States v. Texas, 447 F.2d 441 (5th Cir. 1971).

[449] Order of July 13, 1971, United States v. Texas, Civil No. 5281 (E.D. Tex. 1971).

[450] *Id.* The relief approved in *Texas* limited student transfers, changes in school district boundaries, school transportation, extra-curricular activities, faculty and staff, student assignment, curriculum and comprehensive education. 447 F.2d at 441–42. The modified order enjoined TEA from either accrediting or giving state funds to districts discriminating in any of these areas on the basis of "race, color, or national origin." Order of July 13, 1971, in United States v. Texas, Civil No. 5281 (E.D. Tex. 1971). It prohibits TEA from permitting, arranging or supporting transfers whose effect "will be to reduce or impede desegregation," and requires TEA to review all transfers, to notify districts of those found unlawful, and to deprive recalcitrant transferee districts of state funds. This is a significant threat in Texas because a substantial part of a school district's funds come from state sources.

TEA was further barred from permitting either extracurricular activities which result in segregation or discriminatory hiring, assigning, or treatment of faculty and staff "who work directly with children." Penalties for violations include loss of accreditation, state funds for salaries, and operating expenses, at the rate of ten percent for each semester the violations continue.

Most importantly, TEA is enjoined from supporting school and classroom segregation. As in other sections, the court provided extensive review provisions. All districts maintaining schools whose student enrollment is sixty-six percent or greater minority must be reviewed by TEA, which shall evaluate the school's compliance with Title VI of the Civil Rights Act. Additionally, TEA is required to review all districts of fewer than 250 students which are sixty-six percent or more minority and show cause why they should not be consolidated to eliminate their "existence as a racially or ethnically separate educational unit." TEA must file a report with the court each October 1, submitting findings and describing steps taken to eliminate identifiable minority schools. This automatic review requirement should significantly transform the state's role from investigator to initiator of complaints. Once a district is under review, the state must check for other violations. All complaints must be investigated.

Judge Justice ordered balanced curriculums including: "[S]pecific educational programs designed to compensate minority group children for unequal educational opportunities resulting from past or present racial *and ethnic isolation as well as programs and curriculum designed to meet the special educational needs of students whose primary language is other than English.*" Order of July 13, 1971, at 14, in United States v. Texas, Civil No. 5281 (E.D. Tex. 1971)(emphasis added). In ordering some form of bilingual-

Because the broad language of the *Texas* order covers segregation by "race, color or national origin,"[451] it bars the Texas Education Agency from complicity in local segregation of Chicanos. The order has already been applied to uphold TEA's refusal to approve inter-district transfers which segregate Chicanos.[452] However, there remains some question as to the decree's *res judicata* effect with regard to Chicanos, which determines whether it can be collaterally attacked. Close analysis indicates that it cannot be,[453] but, in any event, Chicano plaintiffs should intervene to insure enforcement and extend relief. They might move to clarify the

bicultural education as an element of equal educational opportunity, Judge Justice required TEA to develop sanctions for school districts that fail to participate in compensatory programs.

[451] 321 F. Supp. at 1060.

[452] Order of Aug. 13, 1971, Intervention of Del Rio Ind. Sch. Dist. in United States v. Texas, 321 F. Supp. 1043 (E.D. Tex. 1970).

[453] Apparently the complaint and all evidence in the trial proper referred only to Blacks, although there were a few Chicanos in some affected districts. Telephone interview with David Vanderhoof, attorney for the Civil Rights Division of the Justice Department in United States v. Texas, Washington, D.C., Mar. 24, 1972. Generally a judgment may be attacked in any court on the ground that it is void because entered by a court lacking jurisdiction over the subject matter. F. James, Jr., CIVIL PROCEDURE 534 – 35 (1965) [hereinafter cited as *James*]. The general rule is, however, subject to many qualifications and exceptions. *Id.* at 535. Fed. R. Civ. P. 60(b) provides that a motion to vacate a judgment as void must be "made within a reasonable time." However, where a judgment is void, this "must generally mean no time limit." 7 Moore, FEDERAL PRACTICE ¶ 60.25[4] (2d ed. 1955). *See also* Lichter v. Scher, 4 Ill. App. 2d 37, 123 N.E.2d 161 (1954); Langer v. Wiehl, 207 Misc. 826, 140 N.Y.S.2d 298 (Sup. Ct. 1955). In default cases, jurisdiction has been found lacking when the court has decided an issue which the parties did not put to it by pleadings or in any other way. *James* at 537. *See, e.g.*, Looper v. Looper, 34 Cal. Rptr. 912, 222 Cal. App. 2d 247 (1963). Professor James says at one point that this is because of an absence of jurisdiction over the subject matter, *James* at 537, but at another that, even if there is subject matter jurisdiction, the court lacks jurisdiction to enter judgment in the described situation. *Id.* at 614. While the Restatement of Judgments limits the rule to default cases, § 8, Comment c, Professor James argues that it should not be so limited, *James* at 614. The Restatement's position appears to be the sounder because, in non-default cases, the losing party still has the opportunity to directly appeal the point. Where, as here, the losing party fails to appeal, the need to conserve judicial resources indicates that he should be barred from making a collateral attack.

Even if a court were to apply the rule in question to non-default cases it should not apply to the *Texas* litigation. While in the trial proper no evidence regarding Chicanos was submitted, at the hearing on desegregation plans the basis for upholding the District Court's decree was laid. TEA Commissioner Edgar was asked, on the stand, whether he would apply the court's order equally to Chicanos as well as to Blacks, and he replied that the TEA would accept similar responsibilities toward them. Vanderhoof interview *supra*. This statement will support the applicability of Judge Justice's decree to Chicanos, because it must be interpreted either as a consent to the decree or as an admission that Chicanos are officially segregated just as Blacks, so that there is evidence of Chicano segregation which supports the judgment. *See generally Developments in the Law-Res Judicata*, 65 HARV. L. REV. 818 (1952).

judgment[454] and move for supplemental relief.[455] Chicano intervenors could then present further evidence of past and present segregation,[456] as well as the great need for additional bilingual-bicultural education.[457] When granted party status, Mexican Americans could initiate proceedings to enforce existing requirements of the decree upon TEA, rather than having to rely upon TEA self-enforcement or enforcement by the present plaintiff, the United States.[458]

Mexican Americans may apply for intervention either of right[459] or permissively.[460] In neither case would there be a problem of jurisdiction over the person of intervenors,[461] nor over any new defendant Texas school districts joined as defendants.[462] Neither would there be any prob-

---

[454] *See, e.g.*, Public Utilities Comm'n v. Gallop, 143 Me. 290, 299−300, 62 A.2d 166, 171 (1948).

[455] *See, e.g.*, United States v. Lynd, 349 F.2d 790 (5th Cir. 1965).

[456] *See* pp. 311−33 *supra.*

[457] Just as any district with an identifiable minority school must be investigated, *see* note 450 *supra*, a similar triggering mechanism should be provided for bilingual education. For example, the court might order a review of compensatory programs in any district with twenty or more children in need of bilingual education. *See generally* Massachusetts Bilingual Education Act, Advance Sheets Acts and Resolves of the General Court, ch. 1005, at 943 (1971), (requiring bilingual education in any district where 20 or more children are in need of such services). *See generally* pp. 384−91 *infra.*

[458] Enforcement could be sought by further motions for clarification or supplemental relief, or, in an extreme case, by a petition for contempt. *See, e.g.*, Williams v. Iberville Parish Sch. Bd., 273 F. Supp. 542 (E.D. La. 1967). Although civil contempt proceedings are usually commenced by a party to the suit, *see, e.g.*, Secor v. Singleton, 35 F. 376 (C.C. Mo. 1888), such an action could be brought by Chicanos even if they were not allowed to intervene, because civil contempt proceedings may be brought by a stranger to the action. The test to be applied is, first, whether the moving party has some right under the court order that is being violated. Annot., 61 A.L.R.2d 1086 (1958); *cf.* Middleton v. Tozer, 259 S.W.2d 80 (Ct. of App. Mo. 1953). Clearly Chicanos would have a legal right in the *Texas* order which forbids discrimination by TEA on the basis of "race, color, or national origin." The second prerequisite is that the movant has sustained an injury due to the alleged contemnor's violation of the order. Annot., 61 A.L.R.2d 1088 (1958); *cf.* Terminal R.R. Ass'n v. United States, 266 U.S. 17 (1924). The latter test is an easily surmountable hurdle for Chicano plaintiffs in Texas. And although the court could not itself initiate civil contempt proceedings, MacNeil v. United States, 236 F.2d 149 (1st Cir.), *cert. denied*, 352 U.S. 912 (1956), it could of its own accord initiate criminal contempt proceedings to vindicate its authority. *Id. See generally Developments in the Law-Multiparty Litigation in the Federal Courts*, 7 HARV. L. REV. 874 (1958) [hereinafter cited as *Developments-Multiparty Litigation*].

[459] Fed. R. Civ. P. 24(a). *See also Developments-Multiparty Litigation* at 898−903.

[460] Fed. R. Civ. P. 24(b); Atkins v. Board of Educ., 418 F.2d 874, 876 (4th Cir. 1969) ("Intervention in suits concerning public schools has been freely allowed."). *See also Developments-Multiparty Litigation* at 903−04.

[461] 6 FEDERAL PRACTICE MANUAL § 7369 (M. Volz ed., 2d ed. 1970). *See generally Developments-Multiparty Litigation, supra* note 358, at 905−06.

[462] 4 C. Wright & A. Miller, FEDERAL PRACTICE AND PROCEDURE § 1075

lem of service of process upon defendants within the territorial limits of Texas.[463] The individual school districts would not be indispensable parties, and thus inability to join them would not bar Chicano intervention.[464]

If intervention is of right, interveners need not satisfy independent requirements of venue;[465] and the intervention should be held timely.[466] But if the court were to allow only permissive intervention, Chicano plaintiffs might face problems both of venue[467] and timeliness.[468] Nonetheless, since exceptions to the venue requirement for intervenors are a matter of reasoned policy rather than binding rule,[469] and timeliness is a matter within the discretion of the court, neither hurdle should bar permissive intervention. The special judicial solicitude for school desegregation cases extends protection from ordinary procedural technicalities whenever possible.[470] Moreover, Chicano intervention in *Texas* meets the criteria for timeliness recently set out by the Fifth Circuit in *Diaz v. Southern Drilling Co.*.[471]

(1969). *See* Aftanase v. Economy Baler Co., 343 F.2d 187 (8th Cir. 1965); *cf.* Mississippi Publishing Corp. v. Murphree, 326 U.S. 438, 442—43 (1946). Permissive joinder could be sought under Fed. R. Civ. P. 20. It would entail no problems of jurisdiction over the persons of, or service upon, joined districts. *See* pp. 379-80 *supra.* However, if intervention were only permissive, venue might impede joinder unless there is a school district within the Marshall Division of the Eastern District of Texas, where *United States v. Texas* was litigated, that is segregating Chicanos. 28 U.S.C. §§ 1393(b). Even if no districts were joined, the suit might proceed against TEA because the threat of a cut-off of state funds is a very potent weapon in Texas. *See generally Developments-Multiparty Litigation, supra* note 358, at 879—97.

[463] Fed. R. Civ. P. 4(f).

[464] Lee v. Macon County Bd. of Educ., 267 F. Supp. 458, 479 (M.D. Ala. 1967)(local school districts held not indispensible where a statewide integration plan is sought).

[465] 3 B. Moore, FEDERAL PRACTICE ¶ 24.19 (2d ed. 1969) [hereinafter cited as *Moore*]; *cf.* International Ass'n of Machinists v. Smiley, 76 F. Supp. 800 (D. Pa. 1968).

[466] 3B *Moore* ¶ 24.13(1).

[467] *Id.*; 28 U.S.C. §§ 1391—93 (1970).

[468] *See* Fed. R. Civ. P. 24; 3B *Moore* ¶ 24.13(1). *See generally Developments-Multiparty Litigation, supra* note 358, at 904—05.

[469] 3B *Moore* ¶ 24.19.

[470] *Cf.* United States v. Georgia, 428 F.2d 377, 378 n.1 (5th Cir. 1970).

[471] 427 F.2d 1118, 1125—26 (5th Cir. 1970). Chicano intervention would meet the two tests of timeliness. The length of time the intervener has known about his interest in the suit without intervening should not bar Chicano intervenors because they have only recently elicited the extensive factual evidence and sophisticated legal understanding needed to realize and act upon their interest in *United States v. Texas.* More important, considerations of delay and concomitant harm to parties caused by intervention, *Id.* at 1126, should not bar intervenors who, like Chicanos, seek no delay in existing relief or litigation, but merely attempt to extend the scope of that relief. *See* Pate v. Dade County School Bd., 303 F. Supp. 1068 (S.D. Fla. 1969) (intervenors allowed to re-open school desegregation suit nine years after original court decree); United States v. Jefferson County

Even so, Chicano litigators should argue for intervention of right under which venue, timeliness and joinder problems are more easily overcome. Intervention of right requires an interest in the transaction involved in the suit, which may as a practical matter be impaired or impeded by denial of intervention, and which is not adequately represented by existing parties.[472] Chicano interest in the statewide school desegregation order is pronounced.[473] Without additional evidence regarding Chicanos, the decree may arguably be collaterally attacked. Further, their interest in bilingual-bicultural programs to provide equal educational opportunity[474] is impaired by the present inadequate relief. Although there are numerous school desegregation cases denying intervention of right, nearly all involve white or other parents seeking to intervene as defendants opposing integration, and nearly all deny intervention of right not on the ground of insufficient interest or impairment, but on the ground that existing party school boards adequately represent their interest.[475] Chicano intervenors in the instant case could hardly be considered to have received adequate representation by present plaintiff,

---

Bd. of Educ., 372 F.2d 836, 896 (5th Cir. 1966) (intervention timely after school board submitted plan in compliance with court decree); cf. Robinson v. Shelby County Bd. of Ed., 330 F. Supp. 837 (W.D. Tenn. 1971)(dicta)(intervention would have been timely after two district court, and one appellate court, decisions); Atkins v. Board of Educ., 418 F.2d 874 (4th Cir. 1969) (intervention timely where delay due to lack of funds). *But see* United States v. Carroll County Bd. of Educ., 427 F.2d 141 (5th Cir. 1970)(intervention, five years after suit filed and five months after desegregation plan ordered into effect, held untimely).

[472] Fed. R. Civ. P. 24(a).

[473] This interest is even more pronounced than that of the national teachers organization which sought to intervene in *Bennett v. Madison County Bd. of Educ.*, 437 F.2d 554 (5th Cir. 1970). There, Judge Wisdom, in dissent, observed that the possibility of the *Bennett* suit affecting via *stare decisis* a second, later suit, was a sufficient interest to require intervention of right. *Id.* at 556, *citing*, Atlantis Development Corp. v. United States, 379 F.2d 818 (5th Cir. 1968). He continued: "[A] second separate suit . . . would be unsound for the court and the parties. The court should handle school cases as units. . . . The types of discrimination which a school board must abjure and undo are inherently interrelated. . . . The fundamental policy of Rule 24 to encourage simultaneous adjudication of related claims, is the same policy that underlies the practice of considering together all school desegregation issues." 437 F.2d at 556 (Wisdom, J., dissenting), *citing* Smuck v. Hobson, 408 F.2d 175, 179 (D.C. Cir. 1969). *See* note 444 *supra.*

[474] *See* notes 450 & 457 *supra* and pp. 384−91 *infra.*

[475] *See, e.g.,* Hatton v. County Sch. Bd., 422 F.2d 457 (6th Cir. 1970); Hobson v. Hansen, 44 F.R.D. 18 (D.D.C. 1968). For these same reasons the Houston court's denial of intervention to Chicano plaintiffs, Tasby v. Estes, Civil No. 10444, at 5−10 (S.D. Tex., May 24, 1971), appears to be clearly wrong, especially in its reliance on previous cases of attempts by white parents to intervene and intervention attempts of the National Education Association, *see* note 473 *supra.* The court's reasoning that the intervention would not be timely, Tasby v. Estes, Civil No. 10444, at 10 (S.D. Tex., May 24, 1971), is just as erroneous. *See* p. 380 and note 471 *supra.*

the United States, which presented no evidence of need to protect Chicano interests. Government representation of Chicano interests has historically been less than adequate.[476] In the unlikely event that intervention was held to be only permissive and venue to bar intervention, proper disposition of the application would be to dismiss without prejudice to Chicanos' right to bring independent suit in another district against TEA and school districts, or simply to transfer intervenor's case to the district and division of proper venue.[477]

Either intervention or a separate statewide suit against TEA might force it to fill the administrative review gap left by HEW's insensitivity to Chicano educational problems.[478] Since court orders frequently request aid from HEW and Title IV personnel,[479] the suit might also bring HEW's active assistance. Sanctions provided in *United States v. Texas,* depriving non-complying districts of state funds and accreditation, are considerable. Once applied to Chicanos, future litigation would focus on the applicability of the order to particular districts. If these sanctions were energetically applied by TEA, only the most obdurate districts would have to be brought to court. Such an allocation of enforcement responsibility is just and efficient. Since TEA has considerably more manpower than private litigants, the burden of dismantling the vestiges of dual systems rightly falls on its shoulders. It must take care that state funds and policies do not perpetuate a dual educational system.[480]

The major flaw in the strategy is the doubtfulness that TEA will vigorously investigate charges of discrimination.[481] TEA's present director took office in the midst of a similar suit twenty-two years ago.[482] The propensities of TEA were demonstrated by its 1953 *Hondo*[483] and

---

[476] See pp. 372−74.

[477] 28 U.S.C. § 1406(a) (1970).

[478] See pp. 365−72 *supra*

[479] See, e.g., Order of July 13, 1971, United States v. Texas, Civil No. 5281 (E.D. Tex., July 16, 1971) (ordering cooperation between TEA and Title IV personnel of the Office of Education); cf. Whittenberg v. Greenville County School Dist., 298 F. Supp. 784 (D.S.C. 1969) (3 judge court).

[480] See pp. 329−30 *supra* for a list of districts ordered by TEA to cease accepting transfers that impede integration of Chicanos and Anglos. The Chicano Community had been attempting to stop the transfers in Del Rio for several years. The TEA threat of a loss of accreditation for Del Rio schools precipitated a suit which resulted in substantial integration. See note 125 *supra*

[481] One of the Government attorneys in the *Texas* case, however, reports that although he is no longer personally working on the case, he has been told that TEA is enforcing the judgment as to Chicanos. See Vanderhoof interview, note 453 *supra* The Del Rio School District's intervention into the *Texas* case, see note 452 *supra,* came after TEA ordered the district to comply with the *Texas* order regarding Chicanos.

[482] See pp. 336−39 *supra*

[483] Orta v. Hondo Ind. School Dist. was a decision of the State Commissioner of Education, J.W. Edgar, Sept., 1953, on file in Dr. Hector Garcia's office in Corpus Christi,

Pecos[484] decisions. If HEW has lagged, can one expect TEA to do better? There exists a partial check on the possibility of a recalcitrant TEA supervising recalcitrant districts. TEA has less lawful discretion than HEW[485] to ignore supervision of Chicano integration because it disperses state funds and grants state accreditation, and because its directors might be held in contempt of court for failure to supervise desegregation.[486] But the sobering influence of contempt charges, while deterring procrastination, could dictate neither eagerness nor favorable decisions. Each adverse ruling would then have to be relitigated in the context of judicial review. This difficulty, however, would not arise as to any local districts joined as defendants in the Chicano statewide suit.[487]

Chicano plaintiffs would not be barred by an adverse administrative judgment from bringing a separate action in federal court. A state administrative action would pit state authorities against local school boards so that plaintiffs' class would not be adequately represented. In any event, the administrative process is not the exclusive remedy.[488] Plaintiffs seeking relief from an adverse TEA judgment would still have the benefit of inferences arising from the wider suit.

A successful statewide suit via intervention or separate action would facilitate local suits. It would destroy "other white" and "no state law" defenses because they are premised on official noninvolvement. While providing for TEA enforcement, it would not limit a plaintiff's right to bring separate suit in federal court.[489] On the contrary, plaintiff's position would be enhanced by persuasive inferences established by the statewide suit, as well as the protection of suspect criteria review.[490]

Texas. The decision did little to alleviate discrimination. *See* pp. 339–40 *supra*.

[484] Barraza v. Pecos Ind. School Dist., decided by J.W. Edgar, Commissioner of Education, Nov. 25, 1953, on file in the offices of Albert Armendariz, Sr., in El Paso, Texas. Commissioner Edgar found no intent to segregate. *See* pp. 340–42 *supra*.

[485] Because it is a federal agency, HEW is afforded a great deal more administrative discretion than is TEA. TEA actions constitute state action in furtherance of a previous state policy of segregating Chicanos.

[486] Lee v. Macon County Bd. of Educ., 267 F. Supp. 458 (M.D. Ala. 1967)(3 judge court), *aff'd sub nom.*, Wallace v. United States, 389 U.S. 215 (1967)(responsibility for insuring Title VI compliance placed on a state agency); *cf.* United States v. Georgia, 445 F.2d 303 (5th Cir. 1971).

[487] *See* note 462 *supra*.

[488] *See* Order of July 13, 1971, United States v. Texas, Civil No. 5281 (E.D. Tex. 1971).

[489] The order in *United States v. Texas* clearly stated that the decision would not foreclose relief otherwise available to plaintiffs. Order of July 13, 1971, Civil No. 5281 (E.D. Tex. 1971) (*passim*).

[490] If the statewide suit were to fail, it should have no worse effect than to leave the *status quo* untouched. Attorneys would be forced to continue on a district by district basis, unaided by TEA or inferences to be won from a statewide suit, and demonstrate that current segregation in each district is the vestige of a dual system.

B. Bilingual-Bicultural Education

Chicanos have historically denounced segregated schools in Texas for not providing them educational opportunities afforded Anglos. On finding *de jure* segregation of Mexican Americans, courts have recently ordered dismantling of dual and establishment of unitary systems.[491] Implicit in these orders is the assumption that integration furnishes Chicanos with equal educational opportunity. Integration without accompanying compensatory programs, however, does not provide equal opportunities because Chicanos have special educational needs impairing their ability to succeed in the English-language environment of public schools.[492] Since ability to learn is directly related to knowledge of English, the state is obliged to assure that all students have an equal opportunity to acquire this vital tool.

The Department of Health, Education and Welfare recognized the special needs of non-English speaking children in its landmark memorandum of May 25, 1970, specifically requiring that: "[w]here inability to speak and understand the English language excludes national origin minority group children from effective participation in the educational program offered by a school district, the district must take affirmative steps to rectify the language deficiency in order to open its instructional program to these students."[493]

Courts have also focused on particular needs of students with different backgrounds. For example, in *United States v. Jefferson County Board of Education,*[494] the Fifth Circuit ordered remedial education

---

[491] *E.g.,* Cisneros v. Corpus Christi Ind. School Dist., 324 F. Supp. 599 (S.D. Tex. 1970), *appeal docketed,* No. 71−2397 (5th Cir., filed July 16, 1971).

[492] *See generally* V. John & V. Horner, EARLY CHILDHOOD BILINGUAL EDUCATION xxii, xxv (1971) [hereinafter cited as EARLY CHILDHOOD BILINGUAL EDUCATION]; U.S. Comm'n on Civil Rights, CIVIL RIGHTS DIGEST 13 (Dec. 1971); *Hearings on S. 428 Before the Special Subcomm. on Bilingual Educ. of the Senate Comm. on Labor and Pub. Welfare,* 90th Cong., 1st Sess. (1967). Consequences of neglecting these special needs were dramatically stated in a study by the National Education Association: "The harm done the [non-English-speaking] child linguistically is paralleled—perhaps even exceeded—by the harm done to him as a person. In telling him that he may not speak his native language, we are saying to him by implication that his language and culture which it represents are of no worth. Therefore [it follows] the people who speak [his language] are of no worth. It would come as no surprise to us, then, that he develops a negative self-concept—an inferiority complex. If he is no good, how can he succeed? And, if he can't succeed, why try?" Nat'l Educ. Ass'n, THE INVISIBLE MINORITY (1966), reprinted in *Hearings on H.R. 9840 and H.R. 10224 Before the Gen. Subcomm. on Educ. of the House Comm. on Educ. and Labor,* 90th Cong., 1st Sess., 182 (1967).

[493] 35 Fed. Reg. 11595 (1970).

[494] 380 F.2d 385, 394 (5th Cir. 1967).

programs to help students who had attended segregated schools overcome inadequacies of their earlier educational environment. Similarly, *Hobson v. Hansen*[495] ordered implementation of a plan of "compensatory education sufficient to at least overcome the detriment of segregation, and thus provide, as nearly as possible, equal educational opportunity to all school children."

On the other hand, a federal district court recently decided that a school district had no obligation to provide compensatory language instruction (bilingual education) to non-English speaking Chinese students.[496] The opinion argued that:

> Chinese-speaking students—by receiving the same education made available on the same terms and conditions to the other tens of thousands of students in the San Francisco Unified School District—are legally receiving all their rights to an education and to equal educational opportunities. Their special needs, however acute, do not accord them special rights above those granted other students.[497]

The court recognized the need of Chinese children "to have special instruction in Chinese." But it concluded that this special need was not legally cognizable because it involved special privileges and not equal educational opportunity.

Seemingly neutral state action, however, can contravene the fourteenth amendment.[498] Under strict review courts have held that identical treatment of persons not similarly situated can violate the equal protection clause.[499] In a school utilizing the English language as the medium

---

[495] 269 F. Supp. 401, 515 (D.D.C. 1967), aff'd, 408 F.2d 175 (D.C. Cir. 1969).

[496] Lau v. Nichols, Civil No. C-70 627 LHB (N.D. Cal., May 26, 1970). *But see* United States v. Texas, Civil No. 5281, at 14 (E.D. Tex., July 13, 1971) (requiring specific educational programs and curriculum designed to meet the special educational needs of students whose primary language is other than English). One factor leading to the California suit was fear in the Chinese community, which is achieving for the first time a significant voice in its schools, that it will be included in a black-white desegregation plan being submitted in Johnson v. San Francisco Unified School Dist., Civil No. C-70–1331 SAW (N.D. Cal. 1971), and that such inclusion will reduce existing bilingual-bicultural programs. Exelrod, *Chicano Education: In Swann's Way?*, INEQUALITY IN EDUCATION, Aug. 3, 1971, at 28.

[497] Lau v. Nichols, Civil No. C-70 627 LHB, at 3 (N.D. Cal., May 26, 1970).

[498] *See, e.g.,* Franklin v. Parker, 223 F. Supp. 724 (M.D. Ala. 1963), *opinion adopted and order aff'd as modified,* 331 F.2d 841 (5th Cir. 1964) (graduation from accredited college as prerequisite to admission to state graduate school where state maintained accredited colleges for Whites only); Meredith v. Fair, 298 F.2d 696 (5th Cir. 1962) (alumni sponsorship as prerequisite to admission to university where Blacks had previously been excluded from attending).

[499] *See, e.g.,* Harper v. Virginia Bd. of Elections, 383 U.S. 663 (1966); Douglas v.

of instruction, a child who cannot comprehend English is not in the same situation as one who can. Thus, strong arguments can be made that bilingual programs for Chicanos are not only permitted but required by the equal protection clause. Under an output standard of equality of education, bilingual programs provide Chicanos merely equal, not extra, education.[500] Similarly, if one measures equality of educational input by effective teaching resources rather than by dollars per pupil, bilingual programs provide Chicanos equal, not extra, educational resources.[501] Even an input standard does not necessarily foreclose the provision of greater educational resources to minority groups. Where, as in Texas, there is previous history of a dual school system, compensatory educational programs are constitutionally required to undo effects of past inferior education.[502]

Most educators contend that the special needs of Mexican-American students can be met through bilingual-bicultural programs.[503] Bilingual education, as envisioned in the federal Bilingual Education Act,[504] is "the

California, 372 U.S. 353 (1963); Griffin v. Illinois, 351 U.S. 12 (1956).

[500] See Evolution-Equal Protection, supra note 290, at 174—77.

[501] See J. Silard & S. White, Intrastate Inequalities in Public Education: The Case for Judicial Relief Under the Equal Protection Clause, 1970 WIS. L. REV. 7. See also Evolution-Equal Protection, supra note 290, at 174—80.

[502] See notes 494, 495, supra. At the very least, such programs when instituted by the state should be upheld as benign racial or ethnic classifications. Evolution-Equal Protection, supra note 290, at 180—84. Strict review of such non-stigmatizing, non-injurious racial programs are reasonable classifications constitutional under "rational basis" review. Even under strict review, bilingual programs may be upheld as necessary to attain the "compelling" state interest in education of Chicanos. See also Note, Beyond The Law-To Equal Educational Opportunities For Chicanos and Indians, 1 N. MEX. L. REV. 336, 345 (1971)("culture conscious programs and policies are not only constitutional, they may be constitutionally required").

[503] See, e.g., A. Gaarder, Teaching the Bilingual Child: Research, Development, and Policy in EDUCATING THE MEXICAN AMERICAN 257 (H. Johnson & W. Hernandez, eds. 1971); Former U.S. Commissioner of Education Harold Howe stated that: "Bilingual education projects . . . show great promise in meeting the special needs of non-English-speaking children. These projects which use both English and the children's mother tongue to teach the entire curriculum, have been the subject of considerable research and experimentation in the United States, Puerto Rico, Canada, Mexico, and South America. It is generally agreed that bilingual projects tend to eliminate the handicap suffered by children whose native language is not the language of the school. Some of these experiments show that children in bilingual programs do better even than those taught in their mother tongue." Hawkins, An Analysis of the Need for Bilingual Education, in EDUCATING THE MEXICAN-AMERICAN 279 (H. Johnson & W. Hernandez eds. 1971) [hereinafter cited as HAWKINS].

[504] Bilingual Education Act, 20 U.S.C. § 880 (b)(1968). Under the Act, the Federal Government supplies funds for a limited number of pilot programs. Appropriations have been insufficient to meet the needs of Spanish-speaking children. Although about half of Mexican-American first graders do not speak English, only a small percentage are enrolled

use of two languages, one of which is English, as mediums of instruction,"[505] with a bicultural curriculum including "history and cultural heritage which reflect the value systems of speakers of both languages."[506] In the past, schools have often been more interested in assimilating the non-English speaking child than in educating him.[507] The bilingual approach views the child's native language as an asset to be developed. It nurtures a positive self-image in Spanish-speaking children, increasing their ability to achieve. Such compensatory programs are necessary if schools are to provide Chicanos the same opportunities presently afforded Anglos.[508]

Given the necessity of bilingual-bicultural programs, problems of implementation remain. School districts with significant numbers of migrant children, who are normally in the area for less than the entire school year, will encounter structural problems in devising a bilingual program.[509] Yet, such a program is, in general terms, required in plans financed under the Bilingual Education Act.[510] And the Texas Project for Education of Migrant Children has shown that administrative problems are not insuperable.[511] In that project, special curricula, including extended class hours, have been developed. Districts could include similar provisions in a bilingual program. Circumstances differ from district to district, and plans should reflect this diversity. But "[w]hatever plan is followed should be one that judges each . . . [child] on his individual merits by the same criteria and with the resultant same treatment as applied to the rest of the children of his age, grade, educational status,

---

in any type of bilingual education program. U.S. Comm'n on Civil Rights, CIVIL RIGHTS DIGEST 13 (Dec. 1971). Massachusetts has also enacted a statute requiring bilingual programs in all school districts having twenty or more non-English-speaking children. Massachusetts Bilingual Education Act, Advance Sheets Acts and Resolves of the General Court, ch. 1005, at 943 (1971).

[505] U.S. Dep't of Health, Educ. & Welfare, PROGRAMS UNDER BILINGUAL EDUCATION ACT 1, 3 (1971).

[506] *Id.* at 3.

[507] *See* Bernal, *I Am A Mexican-American* in A DOCUMENTARY HISTORY OF THE MEXICAN AMERICANS 367 (W. Moquin, C. Van Doren, F. Rivera, eds. 1971).

[508] Senator George Murphy, one of the co-sponsors of the federal Bilingual Education Act, stated that bilingual instruction "provides a solution to the educational problems of [non-English] speaking children who in fact do not have an equal opportunity, an equal chance because of their inability to speak English." 115 CONG. REC. 37, 830 (1969).

[509] Realities of the migrant's work require his children to enter school in late fall and leave in early spring. *See* p. 363 *supra*

[510] U.S. Dep't of Health, Educ. & Welfare, PROGRAMS UNDER BILINGUAL EDUCATION ACT 9 (1971).

[511] The Texas Project for Education of Migrant Children administered by the Texas Education Agency is a special program for some 21,000 children of migrant agricultural workers in some 41 school districts in Texas. U.S. Dep't of Health, Educ. & Welfare, REPORT OF REVIEW-TEXAS PROJECT FOR MIGRANT EDUCATION 4 (1968).

or date of enrollment. . . . Therefore, even though these late entrants do present unusual difficulties to school authorities, they cannot be segregated or offered an education that is not substantially that offered other children."[512]

A bilingual program will be, at least initially, more expensive than present programs. But denial of equal educational opportunities resulting from failure to implement such programs must be balanced against any justifications offered. The state interest must be compelling, not only because a "fundamental interest"—education[513]—is involved, but because the discrimination is based on national origin, which makes the suspect criteria test applicable.[514] The argument that a state can deny equal educational opportunities to conserve public monies is unpersuasive. Although a state has a legitimate interest in limiting its expenses, it "may not accomplish such a purpose by invidious discrimination between classes of citizens."[515]

The most difficult question in devising a truly bilingual-bicultural program is the extent to which Anglo children are to participate. It is questionable whether a court can constitutionally require Anglo students to attend bilingual classes, even though courts have determined that Anglo children must attend integrated schools conducted in English. The burden imposed on Anglo students attending classes partially conducted in Spanish is much greater. There may also be Chicano parents who do not want their children to attend bilingual classes. Consequently, a workable bilingual program should include an element of free choice for both Anglos and Chicanos.[516]

Courts could avoid most administrative burdens by foregoing integration and ordering implementation of bilingual-bicultural programs only at predominantly Mexican-American schools. This position is espoused by some members of the Chicano community who wish to maintain control over their *barrio* schools.[517] Furthermore, some edu-

---

[512] Sanchez, *supra* note 31, at 17. *See also* Cal. State Dept. of Educ., *The Educational Needs of Migrant Children,* in EDUCATING THE MEXICAN AMERICAN 333 (H. Johnson & W. Hernandez, eds. 1971).

[513] *See Evolution-Equal Protection, supra* note 290, at 115–130.

[514] *See* pp. 348–59 *supra.*

[515] Shapiro v. Thompson, 394 U.S. 618, 633 (1969); *cf.* Hosier v. Evans, Civil No. 322–1969 (D.V.I. June 20, 1970) (state cannot deny education to aliens simply because it requires spending public funds).

[516] Free choice may raise fears that Anglos will exercise it to separate themselves from classes conducted in Spanish—and thus from Chicanos. In part, such fears are justified; but even under a bilingual program, all schools and some classes are mandatorily integrated. *See* p. 390 *infra.*

[517] Exelrod, *Chicano Education: In Swann's Way?,* INEQUALITY IN EDUCATION, Aug. 3, 1971, at 28.

cators contend this is a pedagogically sound approach,[518] because it affords Chicano children a homogenous setting, avoiding the negative aspects of confrontation with the dominant group. They argue that the decrease in tension is conducive to higher motivation. Higher motivation coupled with the cultural emphasis of a bilingual experience creates a more positive self-image which prepares the child to face future conflicts.

Close scrutiny of these arguments reveals a plethora of weaknesses. Isolation of Chicano children would result in corresponding segregation of Anglo children who would continue to form attitudes toward Chicanos in situations devoid of interaction. Confrontation is not eliminated, only postponed. If the conflict is faced at an early age, before attitudes are fully formed, it will be more likely to produce positive results. The segregated situation has the additional disadvantage of limiting English input at school to that spoken in the classroom. There would be no peer group reinforcement.

> Isolation and segregation of children for the purposes of instruction deny interaction and exchanges among children of diverse backgrounds. They rob the child of the opportunity to see himself and his neighbor in a realistic environment in which social differences coexist and to respect one another in social harmony. This adultaretion of the classroom with its corresponding weakness and myopia penalizes all children: the Spanish-speaking child because it deprives him of making a contribution among his peers; the Anglo child because it deprives him of the benefits derived from exchanges with his Hispanic classmates.[519]

The most negative aspect of a segregated schools scheme is that it continues to inflict psychological damage on children.[520] Given the historically separate societies in Texas, the argument that schools should continue as the vehicle for separation is dubious. Chicanos in Texas are not unfamiliar with the "different instructional methods" rationale for separate educational facilities. The history of this justification should be carefully examined by those calling for separate schools.

Yet, the courts are confronted with a dilemma when the goal of integration is coupled with the necessity for bilingual-bicultural education. How can both objectives be maximized? A plausible solution is

---

[518] Interview with Heidi Dulay, Teaching Fellow in Bilingual Education at Harvard University, in Cambridge, Massachusetts, Nov. 19, 1971. *But see* M. Guerra, *Language Instruction and Intergroup Relations,* in EDUCATING THE MEXICAN AMERICAN 247 (H. Johnson & W. Hernandez, eds., 1971) [hereinafter cited as Guerra].

[519] Guerra, *supra* note 518, at 247.

[520] *See, e.g.,* Brown v. Board of Educ., 347 U.S. 483, 494 (1954).

found in the bilingual program of Dade County, Florida.[521] The program was developed in 1963 in response to the needs of Cuban refugee children. Admission to the program is voluntary. Cuban and Anglo parents are given the choice of enrolling their children in the program or in an English-only classroom. Parents also have the option of withdrawing their children from the program at any time.[522]

A bilingual program would focus on elementary grades. During the initial year, there would be an equal number of bilingual classes in each of the first three grades, in addition to the regular English-speaking classes. Half the classes would consist of English-speaking children and half of Spanish-speaking children. These bilingual classes, with varying degrees of integration after the third grade, would be extended to the fourth, fifth, and sixth grades during each of the next three years.

The curriculum at the elementary level would begin with basic instruction in the child's native tongue for all participating children. Morning sessions in language arts, social studies, math, and science would be taught in the student's primary language. Knowledge in these areas would then be reinforced in the second language during the afternoon. Music, art, and physical education would be required integrated activities from first to sixth grade. After the third grade, classes would be increasingly integrated. Subject matter would be presented in either language, depending on which best suits the lesson plan. Two teachers would be assigned to each classroom, one a native English speaker and one a native Spanish speaker.

The ultimate goal of such a program would be to equip each child, by the sixth grade, with sufficient linguistic knowledge of both English and Spanish to succeed in either language. In addition, use of Spanish as a medium of instruction and presentation of materials which reflect Chicanos' historical contributions and customs would elevate the Spanish-speaking child's culture to the same status as the dominant culture.[523] The ensuing positive impact on the child's self-image would be immeasurable.

Some school districts will encounter initial difficulties in attempting to implement such a program, because they have a dearth of Mexican-American teachers.[524] This will necessitate an effort to affirmatively re-

---

[521] EARLY CHILDHOOD BILINGUAL EDUCATION, *supra* note 492, at 28−9. *See also* A. Gaarder, *Teaching the Bilingual Child: Research, Development, and Policy,* in EDUCATING THE MEXICAN AMERICAN 262 (H. Johnson & W. Hernandez, eds. 1971).

[522] EARLY CHILDHOOD BILINGUAL EDUCATION, *supra* note 492, at 29.

[523] *See* Rodriguez, *Bilingual Education-Profile '70* in 116 CONG. REC. E1364 (daily ed. Feb. 26, 1970).

[524] *See* pp. 322−26 *supra.* A state educational official has recently stated that "[t]here aren't enough Mexican-American teachers . . . there is only one Mexican-American

cruit Chicano teachers. Teacher retraining programs would also be a component of an effective bilingual program. Districts should distribute personnel to maximize the operation of a bilingual program. The problems of teacher recruitment and training may mean that the number of classes in the program will initially be small, but a start has to be made. The burden should be on school officials to show that good faith efforts to employ Chicano teachers have been unsuccessful.

Bilingual-bicultural education is not a theoretical concept beyond the parameters of practical implementation. Difficulties exist but do not justify inaction. The continued absence of such systematic programs is causing Chicanos to view the Texas educational system as an institution having no relevance to them.

VII. CONCLUSION

Among grievances included in the 1836 Texas Declaration of Independence from Mexico was the failure of the Mexican government "to establish an adequate public system of education although possessed of almost boundless resources."[525] Thus, from its inception as a political entity, Texas pledged itself to provide all citizens with an adequate system of education. Yet the state has historically disregarded this pledge with respect to its citizens of Mexican ancestry, continuing to treat them as a vanquished people.

It is incumbent upon courts to vindicate the Chicano's right to equal educational opportunities by ordering eradication of segregated schools and implementation of bilingual-bicultural education. The public school system, which has perpetuated separate societies in Texas, must now aid in dismantling the wall between Anglos and Chicanos. Social justice can no longer tolerate treatment of the Chicano people as strangers in their own land.

—Jorge C. Rangel
—Carlos M. Alcala

---

teacher for each 100 Mexican American children." Corpus Christi Caller-Times, Nov. 20, 1971, § A, at 10, col. 1. *See also* Rodriguez, *Speak Up, Chicano,* in EDUCATING THE MEXICAN AMERICAN 287 (H. Johnson & W. Hernandez, eds. 1971).

[525] J. Sayles, THE CONSTITUTIONS OF THE STATE OF TEXAS (ANN.) 152 (1888).

EQUAL EDUCATIONAL OPPORTUNITIES FOR LANGUAGE MINORITY CHILDREN

Joaquin G. Avila

I. Introduction

Over the past fifteen years, the Mexican American Legal Defense and Educational Fund, Inc. (MALDEF) has invested over a million dollars for the identification and promotion of educational programs providing the greatest opportunities for Hispanic[1] students. In furtherance of its goal to remove barriers to the eduation of Spanish-speaking students, MALDEF has employed researchers, legal experts, litigators and advocates. MALDEF is pleased to report considerable progress in the establishment of bilingual educational programs during the fifteen years the organization has been in existence.

During the last fifteen years, ten states have passed laws making bilingual education mandatory for limited English proficient students residing in those states. An additional sixteen states permit bilingual education under the aegis of state-funded education programs. Moreover, in 1969 Congress funded Title VII ESEA to provide "transitional" bilingual educational programs in school districts in 42 of the 50 states.

This article will present a very brief overview of the changes that have occurred during the last fifteen years and MALDEF's role in bring about these changes. It will conclude with some predictions of possible future confrontations and problems which MALDEF must prepare to meet.

II. Major Court Decisions

The recent history of bilingual education is replete with many instances of confrontation between school administrators and Hispanics, prompting Hispanics to resort to the adversiarial process of litigation. This is unfortunate. Whenever Hispanics resort to the courts, they undermine some of the general support for the educational programs they are seeking. However, as a review of the major

---

1. For the purpose of this paper, Hispanic is used interchangeably with other terms denoting persons of Hispanic descent, such as Latino, Mexican American, Chicano, etc.

court decisions will demonstrate, many of the legal confrontations were justified.

The United States Supreme Court first spoke to the issue of educational opportunities for language-minority children in *Lau v. Nichols*.[2] The *Lau* plaintiffs consisted of a class of non-English speaking Chinese students in San Francisco. The students claimed that the failure of the city's public school system to educate non-English speaking students in a language they could understand constituted discrimination in violation of both Title VI of the Civil Rights Act of 1964 and the Equal Protection Clause of the Fourteenth Amendment to the United States Constitution. The Supreme Court observed that students who do not understand English and are placed in all-English classrooms are "certain to find their classroom experiences wholly incomprehensible and in no way meaningful." According to the Court, the placement of non-English speaking students in all-English classrooms resulted in those students being "effectively foreclosed from any meaningful education."

The *Lau* decision is significant for language-minority students for several reasons. First, the Supreme Court decision showed the Court's concern with language barriers to educational opportunity. Second, the *Lau* decision placed the responsibility of addressing the language barrier problem squarely on the shoulders of school officials. Third, the Court looked closely at federal regulations requiring school authorities to rectify any loss of educational attainment due to language barriers.

The chief criticism of the *Lau* decision is that it lends support to the notion that non-English speaking students need remedial education. Rather than viewing a student's first language as a special talent or gift, the decision in *Lau* and other cases, classifies language-minority students as persons with deficiencies, handicaps and limitations.

The Court of Appeals for the Tenth Circuit, following the Supreme Court's reasoning in *Lau*, mandated meaningful instruction for non-English speaking students in Portales, New Mexico.[3] The evidence concerning the Portales public schools was striking. For example, at trial plaintiffs proved that until 1970 none of the teachers in the Portales schools were Spanish surnamed, including those teaching the Spanish language in junior and senior high school. Further, evidence showed that at Lindsey, a Portales public school

---

2. 414 U.S. 563 (1974).
3. Serna v. Portales Municipal Schools, 499 F.2d 1145 (10th Cir. 1974).

whose student body was 86 percent Hispanic, only four students with Spanish surnames in the first grade spoke English as well as the average non-minority first grader. Yet, the school district had neither applied for funds under the federal Bilingual Education Act, nor accepted funds for instruction of non-English speaking students when offered by the State of New Mexico. Undisputed evidence showed that Hispanic students did not reach similar achievement levels attained by their white counterparts. The same disparity occurred in school attendance and drop-out rates. In response, the trial court ruled in the plaintiffs' favor, and ordered a bilingual program for the students. The Court of Appeals upheld the lower court's decision, and held that the trial court had a duty to fashion a program which would provide adequate relief for Spanish-surnamed children. Bilingual education thus evolved from a permissive program to a mandatory form of instruction.

The year 1975 proved to be an extremely active year for decisions concerning bilingual education. For example, in *United States v. Board of Education of Waterbury*,[4] Hispanics intervened in a school desegregation case in Waterbury, Connecticut. The court allowed Hispanics to participate in designing remedial measures that would address the needs of non-English speaking persons even though a consent agreement had been filed by the parties almost two years before the Hispanics intervention. That same year, Hispanics joined a class action in *Aspira v. Board of Education of the City of New York*.[5] The parties in *Aspira* settled, and entered a consent agreement providing for bilingual education, as well as bilingual vocational education and bilingual special education. A third decision, in Massachusetts,[6] addressed the objections of Hispanic parents to a student assignment plan calling for the desegregation of the Madison Park public schools. The parents, forming *El Comite de Padres Pro Defensa de la Educacion Bilingue*, alleged that the assignment of students caused an excessive dispersal of bilingual students. The district court agreed and ordered the school district to assign the bilingual students in such a way as to meet the goals of the state-mandated bilingual program. Finally, in *Morales v. Shannon*,[7] the Court of Appeals for the Fifth Circuit cautioned the district court supervising the desegregation of the public schools in Uvalde, Texas that:

---

4. Civil Action No. 13, 465 (D. Conn., May 6, 1975).
5. 394 F.Supp. 1161 (S.D.N.Y. 1975).
6. Morgan v. Kerrigan, 401 F. Supp. 216 (D.C. Mass. 1975).
7. 516 F.2d 411 (5th Cir. 1975), *cert. denied* 423 U.S. 1034 (1976).

"[I]t is now an unlawful educational practice to fail to take appropriate action to overcome language barriers."[8] By this time, however, plaintiffs arguing for mandatory bilingual programs no longer needed to rely solely on the Civil Rights Act or the United States Constitution, the Equal Educational Opportunities Act of 1974 provided a strong and additional source of law for advocates of language-minority students' rights.

Congress adopted the Equal Educational Opportunities Act of 1974 as a floor amendment to the omnibus Education Amendment. Section 1703 of the Act prohibits a state from denying equal educational opportunity through "the failure by an educational agency to take appropriate action to overcome language barriers that impede equal participation by its students in its instructional program."

The presidential message proposing the legislation referred to the law as a "bill of rights":

> School authorities must take appropriate action to overcome whatever language barriers might exist, in order to enable all students to participate equally in educational programs. This would establish, in effect, an educational bill of rights for Mexican Americans, Puerto Ricans, Indians, and others who start under language handicaps, and ensure at last that they too would have equal opportunity.[9]

The Equal Educational Opportunity Act, however, did not help plaintiff's counsel in the Mesa County Valley public schools case. Counsel began the action before the Act took effect, and sought relief soley on constitutional grounds. After plaintiff expended a massive effort in bringing the case, including 3003 pages of depositions, 257 pages of pleadings, 654 pages of interrogatories and answers thereto, 1058 pages of briefs, 360 pages of documents, 3000 pages of reporters' transcripts and 492 exhibits totaling more than 10,000 pages, Colorado District Court Judge Winner declined to rule that the failure to provide a bilingual program violated the Constitution. The court's ruling relied on defendant's expert who testified that an extremely small number of Mexican American students had any problem speaking or comprehending English. Judge Winner looked for guidance from Justice Blackmun's concurring opinion in *Lau* where Justice Blackmun stated:

> I merely wish to make plain that when, in another case, we

---

8. *Id.* at 415.
9. 118 CONG. REC. 8931 (1972).

are confronted with a very few youngsters, or with just a single child who speaks only German or Polish or Spanish or any language other than English, I would not regard today's decision . . . as conclusive. . . . For me, numbers are at the heart of this case and my concurrence is to be understood accordingly.[10]

Thus, the court would not afford a remedy to Hispanic children until a certain numerical threshhold was met.

Fortunately, later courts interpreted the applicable statutes with far less conservatism. The passage of the Equal Educational Opportunities Act sparked decisions that furthered congressional intent to find effective solutions to learning barriers. In particular, courts have interpreted the meaning of the term "appropriate action" in Section 1703(f) of the Act to require positive results.

Two cases in 1978, *Rios v. Read*[11] and *Cintron v. Brentwood Union Free School District*,[12], interpreted Section 1703(f) of the Equal Educational Opportunities Act to require substantive results, rather than mere compliance by the school officials with any specific processes. In each case, the trial court found that the school district's programs did not adequately meet the needs of the language-minority students. As a result, the courts ordered defendant's school districts to implement more effective programs.

The leading case analyzing the term "appropriate action" in Section 1703(f) of the Equal Educational Opportunities Act is the Fifth Circuit's opinion in *Castaneda v. Pickard*.[13] In *Castaneda*, the trial court received abundant evidence on the low quality of the school district's language assistance program. Although the school population of this district in South Texas was 85 percent Mexican American, at least one-half of the teachers assigned to the bilingual education program were merely graduates of a 100-hour emergency certification course designed to impart a limited Spanish vocabulary of 700 words to each teacher. Plaintiff's expert testified that the emergency certification course was "a dismal failure in the development of sufficient proficiency in a language other than English to qualify the people for teaching bilingual programs." The Fifth Circuit Court of Appeals agreed The court articulated a three-step analysis for assessing compliance with the Equal Educational Oppor-

10. Otero V. Mesa County Valley School Dist. No. 51, 408 F.Supp. 162 (D.Colo. 1975).
11. 480 F.Supp. 14 (E.D.N.Y. 1978).
12. 455 F.Supp. 57 (E.D.N.Y. 1978).
13. 648 F.2d 989 (5th Cir. 1981).

tunities Act:

First, the court should examine carefully evidence in the record concerning the soundness of the educational theory or principle behind the challenged program to determine whether the school system is pursuing a program recognized as sound by educational experts.[14]

Second, the court should inquire whether the program and practices actually used by the school system are reasonably calculated to effectively implement the educational theory adopted by the school district. This includes practices, resources, and personnel necessary to transform the theory into reality.[15]

Third, having designed an adequate theory and implemented it thoroughly, a system is subject to the scrutiny of the court if it persists in maintaining the same approach over time when it is evident that the approach is failing.[16]

The overall goal is one of "parity of participation in the standard instructional program," or as the court put it in another context, a system in which "all students can acquire a community-defined level of knowledge and skills . . .without being restricted by an identification with any racial or ethnic groups."

The goal of "parity of participation" incorporates two components. First, the school district must overcome the language barrier and give the limited English proficient students a command of the English language that is comparable to that of the average native speaker. Second, the school district must overcome any academic deficits in substantive coursework that may have occurred as a result of the language barrier. Bilingual programs are not inevitably required by section 1703(f) and a court may approve a system that has as its principal goal the rapid development of literacy in English. Thus, some academic deficiencies may result. However, the court in the *Castaneda* decision made it clear that if academic deficiencies did occur, "interim" sacrifices were not to become permanent deficits. Thus, if a school district does not opt for bilingual education, then the district must provide an intensive academic program to assist the student in achieving parity with her/his native English-speaking classmates.

In the December, 1983, *Keyes* case in Denver, Colorado, a federal judge applied the *Castaneda* three-prong analysis and ruled in favor of the plaintiffs. The court held that the school district's bilin-

---

14. *Id.* at 1009.
15. *Id.* at 1010.
16. *Id.*

gual program was inadequate in identifying students with language difficulties, assessing their proficiencies, assigning teachers, and following through after completion of the bilingual program. The court scheduled a remedial hearing to consider further relief. In June 1984, the school district agreed to a powerful consent decree which incorporated all the aspects of the court's decision.

To conclude, the quality of rights of language minority students has advanced greatly over the last 15 years. Clearly, though, progress could not have been made without the efforts of advocates in the judicial process. It has been through a combination of judicial and legislative channels that advocates for the rights of language-minority students have been successful.

III. REGULATION CONCERNING LANGUAGE-MINORITY STUDENTS

The field of instructional services to language-minority students is regulated at both the federal and state level. The intensity of the monitoring and enforcement of the access to education varies greatly from state to state, and even from district to district. The reasons for this variation in regulation are discussed below.

A. Federal Regulation by the Department of Education

In 1982, Secretary of Education Terrel Bell "de-regulated" bilingual education as his first official public action upon taking office. Advocates for language-minority students perceived this action as a casting down of the gauntlet in direct challenge to their hard efforts. Rather than surrender to the superior resources of the United States Department of Education, however, the plucky advocates have made serious inroads in Washington.

One key success for language-minority advocates has been in resisting the inclusion of Title VII bilingual education funding in the federal block grants program. Although the Reagan administration succeeded in substantially reducing the level of funding for Title VII assistance to bilingual education programs, the monies are separate and apart from other block grants. As a result, the states are still accountable for their expenditures for language-minority students.

At present, MALDEF is continuing to apply pressure to the Department of Education to monitor and enforce the civil rights laws in a case known as *Adams v. Bell*.[17] The plaintiffs in *Adams* seek to

---

17. Civil Action No. 75-1068 (D.D.C.).

compel the Office of Civil Rights of the Department of Education to enforce the nation's civil rights laws. On March 6, 1983, the District Court for the District of Columbia issued an order citing the Department of Education for excessive delays in enforcing the civil rights laws and admonishing the United States to adhere to a strict timetable. The Department of Education appealed this order, oral arguments were held on March 27, 1984, and MALDEF anticipates that the appellate decision will force the Department of Education to play a stronger role in defending the rights of language-minority children.

Presently, the regional offices of the Department of Education have been applying local standards and guidelines for language-minority student assistance. The Department of Eduation has withdrawn its own standards. In most instances, the regional guidelines closely follow state law. Thus, in California and Texas, for example, the regional guidelines are stronger than the national guidelines proposed by Secretary Hufstedler during the Carter Administration.

In sum, the federal regulation of educational opportunities for language-minority students has reached its nadir. Despite isolated instances where Department of Education regional offices continue to enforce the law, advocates have little confidence in the ability of that agency to make meaningful gains for language-minority students.

B. State Laws

In 1980, only eight states mandated that all grade levels from kindergarten through 12th grade make bilingual education available for students needing the program. No state offered instruction in both languages in what is known as a maintenance program, i.e. a program that continues to develop both languages even after the students have learned English. Of the eight states mandating bilingual education, six states established maximum participation limits of three years. It is illuminating to discuss the development in some of the major states.

Texas

In 1981, Texas legislators enacted amendments to the state bilingual education law in response to litigation brought by MALDEF in federal court. The legislative changes assisted Texas in winning a reversal of MALDEF's victory in the district court. However, the court of appeals required the district court to satisfy itself that the new legislation met the three-part test announced in *Castaneda*. The new Texax law mandates:

1) Doubling the scope of the program by including all

elementary grades, instead of only grades kindergarten to third grade as before;

2) Doubling the level of expenditures and enforcement of state regulations by the State education agency, including on-site visits of all 1,100 districts at least once every three years;

3) Establishing model programs; and

4) Requiring a plan for identifying and training bilingual and ESL teachers.

The new law was welcomed in Texas by bilingual advocates who estimate that there are as many as 660,000 limited English proficient students in the state in need of bilingual instruction.

California

While the *Lau* guidelines suffered attacks from opponents of bilingual education on the federal level, in California, several legislative proposals attempted to modify or repeal that state's Bilingual Bicultural Act of 1976. In California, where the language-minority student population is estimated at aproximately 900,000, the initiative resulted in a compromise measure. The State still purports to adhere to a policy of delivering educational programs designed to meet the individual needs of the students, but a full bilingual program is not available unless ten or more students of the same language attend the same school in the same grade. In effect, numbers spoke and legislators listened.

The major criticisms of the California bilingual program have been directed at the state's failure to monitor and enforce the programs. This problem has been largely resolved through litigation in *Comite v. Riles* (a MALDEF and California Rural Legal Aid case) and through the legislative process. The single most pressing problem in the California public schools with language-minority programs is the lack of certified bilingual teachers. Some of the bilingual teachers have been on waivers of teaching credentials for three or four years. MALDEF is presently exploring both legal and legislative solutions to this problem.

Colorado

Language-minority students in Colorado have also had their share of intense debate concerning mandatory bilingual education. The culmination has been the repeal of the Colorado Bilingual Education Law. While a great majority of the limited English proficient students reside in Denver, and must be served by School District No.

1 pursuant to the December 30, 1983, federal court order in the *Keyes* case mentioned previously, a number of language-minority students have found their rights curtailed by the legislative action.

By reducing the scope of the bilingual education program, the Colorado legislature is imposing an irremedial injustice on language-minority students. It is unconscionable for the legislature to withhold resources from these students at the time of their educational careers when they can best benefit from these expenditures. There is no doubt that the State of Colorado will pay dearly for this mistake in the near future, when the academic deficiencies of the language-minority students who have been deprived of an adequate education begin to manifest themselves as increases in drop-out rates and poor graduation rates.

In sum, the lack of educational leadership at the federal administrative level has resulted in a broad range in the quality of services available to language-minority students. Regardless of the outcome of the federal initiatives, conscientious advocates at the state level will continue to pursue full educational programs for language-minority students.

IV. FUTURE ISSUES

The field of educational services for language-minority students has evolved during the last fifteen years in many ways. It is no longer solely an issue reserved for educators; it is now an issue commonly discussed by lawyers, legislators and laypersons. One new sub-issue has been added to the field and should be addressed now. That new issue is "immersion."

Before bilingual education began to enjoy acceptance, an overwhelming number of schools adopted a transitional bilingual education approach. This process attempts to move a student from the language assistance program into the all-English curriculum as early as possible. However, while the student is acquiring English proficiency, he or she receives substantive schoolwork instruction in his or her native language.

In the 1970's, educators began to research the effectiveness of a Canadian practice know as "immersion." This technique involves instructing language majority students in a second language by immersing them in that language. The Canadian immersion proved to be a success provided the school district included the following components:

1) Students who speak the majority language;

2) Students who have an upper middle class

background;

3) Teachers who are bilingual; and

4) Instruction given in both languages even after proficiency is acquired in the majority language.

Students participating in the Canadian immersion model demonstrated gains in achievement that exceeded those of students in the control groups.

The single most important issue for the future is whether the Canadian "immersion" method can be revised and applied to language-minority students from economically disadvantaged backgrounds. Understandably, though, there will be much debate in this area.

The investment that MALDEF has made in identifying the best programs that would provice access to language minority students to equal educational opportunities does not inevitably mean that the best program is bilingual-bicultural. However, the techniques advocated by Senator Hayakawa and his allies have not yet been proven to be effective tools for educating language minority students in the United States. Therefore, MALDEF will continue to insist that language minority students receive a bilingual-bicultural education — at least until a more effective solution arises. We owe it to the students to deliver a full program that works *now*, rather than subject them to experimental programs that may work sometime in the distant future.

ACADEMIC ACHIEVEMENT IN MEXICAN AMERICANS: SOCIO-LEGAL AND CULTURAL FACTORS

Anthony J. Cortese[*]

The purpose of this paper is to explore possible explanations for the extremely low rate of participation for Mexican American in higher education. Data on enrollment, persistence, and achievement are presented as an indication of the extent to which Mexican Americans are underrepresented. The Socio-legal background of minority education is sketched. Next, the cultural factors are discussed, highlighting alienation. Finally, suggestions for the future policy are offered.

The last shall be first.
The King James Bible

If not now, when?
Hillel

"Affirmative action consists of actions to end discrimination and to remedy the effects of past discrimination. It includes such activities as notifying women's and minority groups about job openings, advertising job openings rather than relying on word-of-mouth notification, developing recruitment procedures aimed at women and minorities as well as other qualified applicants, and providing equal opportunities for advancement" (Vetter, et. al., 1982:3).

In institutions of higher education, protected class members must be afforded more than simple "equal opportunity." For example, physically handicapped persons must be provided not only with "equal access" to physical facilities but with means of access that they can effectively use. Likewise, persons in other protected classes also have differences that may hinder access to information about the processes of institutions of higher education. They too must be provided with more than "equal treatment" with respect to understanding the standards and expectations by which they will be judged and with respect to preparation to meet those standards and expectations.

Our society is heavily involved with certification. This means that one needs to have a written guarantee, diploma, or other type of formal documentation that guarantees qualification to practice a certain profession. Although

* All correspondence should be sent to: Professor Anthony J. Cortese, Director, Mexican American Studies, Southern Methodist University, Dallas, Texas 75275-0142.

LATINO STUDIES JOURNAL   JANUARY 1992

31

someone may be self-educated and intelligent, it is virtually impossible for that individual to enter many professional schools and white-collar professions without a college degree. Consequently, college academic performance is perceived to be an important initial step toward occupational attainment and the subsequent process of social stratification (Watson, 1979). This makes persistence in college especially salient for minorities. We will examine evidence which indicates that minority students are more likely than non-minority students to withdraw from colleges and universities.

The access, admission, and retention of racial and ethnic minority students to institutions of higher education involve complex and controversial issues and problems that bear substantially on social policy. Hispanics are expected to increase in number within the next decade at a rate that will place them as the nation's largest racial-ethnic minority (Estrada, et. al., 1981). This is due to immigration trends and the high birthrate. Consequently, issues of access, retention and achievement will become critical if members of this group are to begin to approach parity in decision-making processes. While structural discrimination in all facets of society must yet be dismantled, the focus of this paper is the denial of access of Mexican Americans to higher education. Accordingly, data are presented on the extent to which Mexican Americans are underrepresented in institutions of higher education. There are indeed many factors—institutional, economic, political, social, cultural, educational—which work to deny access. In this paper, socio-legal and cultural factors will be analyzed in depth. These two factors have been selected because of their particular saliency for social policy.

Any discussion of this nature must certainly include the U. S. Supreme Court decision in the case of the *Regents of the University of California v. Bakke* (1978), which has affected undergraduate, graduate, and professional schools' admissions programs. Although the court struck specific quota systems as unconstitutional, it did not prohibit affirmative action and the consideration of race or ethnicity as a criterion for admission. Nonetheless, the winds of unwelcome admissions retrenchment for minorities filled the air. In response, the Office for Civil Rights (1978) of the then Department of Health, Education and Welfare (OCR-DHEW) released a policy interpretation which indicated that race and ethnicity could be considered as a positive factor in the admissions process.

Presently, affirmative action procedures, or the lack thereof, vary from campus to campus. In 1980, an ad-hoc group of forty Deans prepared a proposal to be submitted to the Association of American Colleges reemphasizing "more rigorous standards of admissions" (Chronicle of Higher Education, January 19, 1981). Given the current trend away from vigorous enforcement of civil rights, the use of traditional tests, predictive criteria and standards will be raised by more than one professional organization. Mexican Americans are once again on the receiving end of the debate. As noted by the U. S. Commission on Civil Rights:

If many educational systems from kindergarten through college had not historically favored white males, more minorities and women would hold advanced degrees and thereby be included among those involved in deciding what academic tests should test (1981:10).

Institutional racism and discriminatory practices are still deeply imbedded in the characteristics of this society. This invidiousness will end only when the experiences of those previously excluded are represented by "the last" themselves, i.e., when the names, faces, and genders of the decision-makers change.

The Denial of Access

It has been established that Mexican American students generally achieve less academically than their Anglo American peers (Carter and Segura, 1979). Yet, Mexican American students have high educational aspiration levels (Carter, 1968). There seems to be no support for the notion that late-adolescent Mexican American students are predisposed to lower self-regard in terms of academic success than their non-Mexican American counterparts (Frazier and DeBlassie, 1982). It has been widely documented that standardized measures of ability (e.g., ACT) or achievement (e.g., GPA) are heavily influenced by such extraneous factors as socioeconomic status, disparity of educational quality, teacher stereotypes, and language differences (DeBlassie, 1976). When ability level (i.e., ACT) is controlled for, differences between Mexican Americans and non-Mexican Americans dissolve (Frazier and DeBlassie, 1982). This means that given equal ability, they should do equally well in college.

Gandara (1982) found that high-achieving Mexican American women had: a) mothers who provided strong role models; b) the emotional support of their families; and, c) attended highly integrated schools. Vasquez (1982) concluded that sex role restrictions and the oppressive effects of low socioeconomic status, rather than culture or language, partially accounted for the relatively low participation of Mexican American women in college.

The measurement of access of any group to the benefits of educational opportunities requires a review of statistics on enrollment, persistence and degrees. Data displayed in this section are used to compare Hispanics with other minorities and whites. The analysis of persistence and degrees also includes sex as a factor. Recently compiled data on enrollments of American Indian, Asian, black, Hispanic, and white students for Carnegie Research I, land grant institutions with veterinary medicine programs in fall 1982 is shown in Table 1. This consortium of universities was selected for analysis because of its relatively diverse geographical representation (i.e., North Central, Midwest, Atlantic, Southwest, Rocky Mountain, and Pacific) and based on the reputations of its members as major research institutions. Each university has veterinary medicine, physical science, and engineering programs of national stature. Most also have solid medical schools. These are examples of institutions where minority access is crucial if such groups are to approach parity in professional occupational categories.

Table 1. MINORITY ENROLLMENTS AT CARNEGIE RESEARCH I, LAND GRANT INSTITUTIONS WITH VETERINARY MEDICINE PROGRAMS AND MINORITY STATEWIDE REPRESENTATION.

Minority Enrollments State Population, Net Representation	American Indian %	Asian %	Black %	Hispanic %	White %	Total
California, Davis	0.5	11.9	2.8	4.4	76.1	19,321
	0.1	5.5	7.7	19.2	67.5	23,688*
	0.4	6.4	−4.9	−14.8	8.6	
Colorado State, Fort Collins	0.4	1.4	1.2	2.6	91.7	18,909
	0.1	1.2	3.5	11.8	83.4	2,890*
	0.3	0.2	−2.3	−9.2	8.3	
Florida	0.1	1.5	5.1	4.6	84.4	34,252
	0.1	0.6	13.8	8.8	76.7	9,746*
	0.0	0.9	−8.7	−4.2	7.7	
Georgia	0.2	0.7	5.0	0.8	90.2	25,886
	0.1	0.5	26.8	1.1	71.5	5,463*
	0.1	0.2	−21.8	−0.3	18.7	
Illinois, Urbana-Champaign	0.2	3.9	3.3	1.5	86.5	34,914
	0.1	1.5	14.7	5.6	78.1	11,427*
	0.1	2.4	−11.4	−4.1	8.4	
Purdue (Indiana)	0.2	1.2	3.3	1.0	90.5	32,635
	0.1	0.4	7.6	1.6	91.1	5,490*
	0.1	0.8	−4.3	−0.6	−0.6	
Michigan State	0.3	1.0	5.6	1.0	88.1	42,730
	0.1	0.7	12.9	1.8	84.5	9,262*
	0.2	0.3	−7.3	−0.8	3.6	
Minessota, Minneapolis-St. Paul	0.4	2.1	1.5	0.7	91.8	64,515
	0.1	0.8	1.3	0.8	96.6	4,076*
	0.3	1.3	0.2	−0.1	−4.8	

continued page 35

Continued from page 34.

Table 1. MINORITY ENROLLMENTS AT CARNEGIE RESEARCH I, LAND GRANT INSTITUTIONS WITH VETERINARY MEDICINE PROGRAMS AND MINORITY STATEWIDE REPRESENTATION.

Minority Enrollments State Population, Net Representation	American Indian %	Asian %	Black %	Hispanic %	White %	Total
Missouri, Columbia	0.4	1.0	3.6	0.7	89.3	24,763
	0.1	0.5	10.5	1.1	87.8	4,917*
	0.3	0.5	-6.9	-0.4	1.5	
North Carolina State	0.3	1.5	7.5	0.7	86.3	22,669
	0.1	0.4	22.4	1.0	75.8	5,882*
	0.2	1.1	-14.9	-0.3	10.5	
Ohio State, Columbus	0.1	1.3	4.5	0.7	89.2	53,438
	0.1	0.5	10.0	1.1	88.3	10,798*
	0.0	0.8	-5.5	-0.4	0.9	
Oregon State	1.5	4.5	1.1	1.0	89.2	16,754
	0.1	1.6	1.4	2.5	94.4	2,633*
	1.4	2.9	-0.3	-1.5	-5.2	
Texas A&M, College Station	0.1	1.3	1.2	3.8	89.0	36,127
	0.1	0.9	12.0	21.0	66.0	14,229
	0.1	0.4	-10.8	-17.2	23.0	
Wisconsin, Madison	0.3	1.5	2.0	1.1	89.1	42,230
	0.1	0.5	3.8	1.3	94.0	4,707
	0.2	1.0	-1.8	-0.2	-4.9	

* in thousands

Sources: *Fall Enrollment in Colleges and Universities* (1982), National Center for Education Statistics, Washington, D.C.: U. S. Government Printing Office: U. S. Census (1980).

There is an acute underrepresentation of Hispanics and blacks enrolled in the sampled universities. Hispanics are underrepresented at each school, blacks all but one. American Indians and Asians are not underrepresented in any school; whites were overrepresented in all but four.

Student persistence patterns two years after college entry is presented in Table 2. Whites are the only racial category that display an overrepresentation on full-time persistence. American Indians and Asians show no change, Puerto Ricans a slight decrease. Mexican Americans and blacks indicate the largest drop.

Whites and American Indians have proportionately less erratic persisters. There is no change for Puerto Ricans, while Mexican Americans, blacks and Asians show an overrepresentation. In terms of withdrawals, Mexican Americans have the worst record, followed by blacks, Puerto Ricans, and American Indians. Whites have the fewest drop-outs, followed by Asians.

ACADEMIC ACHIEVEMENT

35

Comparing men and women, the latter are underrepresented in enrollment, more erratic persisters, and withdraw at higher rates than men who are better full-time persisters.

Table 2. STUDENT PERSISTENCE PATTERNS TWO YEARS AFTER COLLEGE ENTRY (in percentages)

Characteristics	Total	Full-time Persisters	Erratic Persisters	Withdrawals
Sex				
Men	53.1	54.3	52.4	50.1
Women	46.9	45.7	47.6	49.9
Race				
White	87.9	89.0	86.8	84.9
Black	8.1	7.6	8.9	8.9
American Indian	0.7	0.7	0.5	1.0
Asian	1.1	1.1	1.6	0.8
Mexican American	1.2	0.7	1.3	2.7
Puerto Rican	1.0	0.8	1.0	1.7
Financial Aid				
Have Aid 1975-76	58.3	58.5	52.6	62.9
Have Aid 1976-77	56.5	56.4	48.8	66.8

Soure: Unpublished Study by Helen S. Astin, Higher Education Research Institute, 1979.

Data on Bachelor's, Master's and Doctor's degrees by race/ethnicity and sex are presented in Table 3. U. S. population figures are also given as comparative anchors. Historically, it has been the case that the higher the type of degree, the fewer are the number of Hispanics receiving the degree. The data support this pattern for both men and women. Black males also fit the pattern.

Whites, whether male or female, are increasingly overrepresented with the attainment of each degree. Asians generally follow that same pattern while data on American Indians indicate virtually no change. Overall, whites are substantially overrepresented at all degree levels when compared with national demographic figures. Asians are also overrepresented, but to a much lesser extent than whites. Hispanics and blacks are moderately to strongly underrepresented at all levels, especially black men. There is a slight underrepresentation of American Indians at all levels, regardless of sex.

TABLE 3

1979 BACHELORS, MASTERS, AND DOCTORS DEGREES
BY RACE/ETHNICITY AND SEX AND MINORITY NATIONAL REPRESENTATION

| | AMERICAN INDIAN | | ASIAN | | BLACK | | HISPANIC | | WHITE | | TOTAL | |
	Men	Women	Men	Women	Men	Women	Men	Women	Men	Women	Men	Women
Bachelor's												
Number	1,736	1,674	8,319	7,223	24,675	35,626	14,331	15,388	418.271	384,394	467,332	444,305
Percent	0.4	0.4	1.8	1.6	5.3	8.0	3.1	3.5	89.5	86.5	100.0	100.0
Net Representation	−0.2	−0.2	0.2	0.0	−6.4	−3.7	−3.3	−2.9	9.8	6.8		
Master's												
Number	495	504	3,331	2,188	7,071	12,351	3,152	3,318	124.080	125,321	138,129	143,682
Percent	0.4	0.4	2.4	1.5	5.1	8.6	2.3	2.3	89.8	87.2	100.0	100.0
Net Representation	−0.2	−0.2	0.8	−0.1	−6.6	−3.1	−4.1	−4.1	10.1	7.5		
Doctor's												
Number	69	35	646	165	734	534	302	151	18,433	7,705	20,184	8,590
Percent	0.3	0.4	3.2	1.9	3.6	6.2	1.5	1.8	91.3	89.7	100.0	100.0
Net Representation	−0.3	−0.2	1.6	0.3	−8.1	−5.5	−4.9	−4.6	11.6	10.0		
U.S. Population	0.6		1.6		11.7		6.4		79.7		100.0	

SOURCES: Earned Degree Series, 1878–79, National Center for Education Statistics, Unpublished Data U.S. Census (1980).

Socio-Legal Context

It is impossible to appreciate the question of access without considering the social context through which institutional practices and processes have evolved. This social context has been inimical to the rights of minorities, as illustrated by the legal sanction of "separate but equal" facilities granted by the U. S. Supreme Court (*Plessy v. Ferguson*, 1896 and *Cumming v. Richmond County Board of Education*, 1899, until the historical *Brown v. Board of Education*,

ACADEMIC ACHIEVEMENT

37

1954). In spite of recognition of their rights under the Treaty of Guadalupe Hidalgo in 1848, Mexican Americans living in the annexed Southwest and West suffered under similar conditions as black Americans, i.e., separate educational facilities which were underfunded, understaffed, and subject to shorter school terms. Administrative rulings such as that made by the state of New Mexico, declaring that English would be the sole language of public instruction, were not atypical. As concluded by the U. S. Commission on Civil Rights: "Mexican Americans received a second-rate education which left large numbers of students no alternative to the manual labor that had been the lot of their parents" (1978:3).

With the passage of the Civil Rights Act of 1964, minority enrollment in institutions of higher education became an important issue; and participation, if not parity, was increased. Nor is there evidence that the Bakke decision dissuaded professional organizations from persisting in their belief that race should be considered a relevant factor in the admissions process (Association of American Medical Colleges, Law School Admission Council, Carnegie Commission on Policy Studies, and American Association of University Professors). As well, the then OCR-DHEW issued a policy interpretation of Title VI assuring that race could be taken into consideration as a positive factor in determining applicants' qualifications for admission.

If the social context in the late sixties and early to mid-seventies inspired confidence that the nation was alert to the need to eliminate racist and discriminatory practices, the climate of the late seventies and early to mid-eighties dictates caution and overcoming adversity. In a study of the effects of desegregation released in September of 1981, Dr. Willis D. Hawley of Vanderbilt University asserted that desegregation of schools "has had positive effects for all children, especially for minority students, and has improved educational opportunity" (*Denver Post*, 1981:8a). It is now, in the midst of these messages coupled with cuts in federal funding and challenges of reverse discrimination and preferential treatment, that Mexican Americans who have been slower than blacks to realize their potential, must prepare as a group to claim their rights to equal educational opportunity.

Rather than relying on a social context which is superficially friendly and affirmative, there is much work yet to be done within the Hispanic community to determine what factors in addition to discrimination, or engendered by it, have hindered their participation in education at the higher levels. This is a formidable challenge, when one considers the comparative dearth of research on the Hispanic experience within the United States. Nonetheless, this work must be undertaken if the past is not to be a presage of the future. What factors, for example, set the potential or present Mexican American student apart from his/her black, Native American Indian or Asian American counterpart as s/he faces decisions concerning what schools to apply to and what professions and careers s/he will pursue?

It has been argued repeatedly that America's schools are failing to provide equal educational opportunities for Mexican Americans. A report of the U. S. Commission on Civil Rights (1974) documented this assertion: 1) Mexican Americans attend schools separated from their Anglo counterparts; 2) they are underrepresented as teachers and counselors and in decision making positions, e.g., principal, school board; 3) the language and culture of Mexican American children are ignored or even suppressed by schools; 4) Mexican American parents are largely excluded from participation in school affairs; 5) schools with predominantly Mexican American enrollments are under-financed in comparison to "Anglo" schools; 6) many teachers fail to involve Mexican American children as active participants in the educational process. Possibly the most salient demonstration of the failure of our schools is mirrored in the educational attainment of Mexican American students as discussed above.

Because of common practices, Mexican Americans are disproportionately retained in grades, placed in low ability groups, or shunted off to classes for the educable mentally retarded. These students are typically taught by teachers of a different cultural background whose educational training leaves them ignorant and insensitive to students' educational and personal needs. Rarely are counselors trained to provide guidance on the unique circumstances of Mexican Americans. Even with adequate training, there is the problem of accessibility. Approximately 1.6 million students are affected by these conditions (U. S. Commission on Civil Rights, 1974).

The vast majority of the Mexican American labor force is in low-skilled manual labor categories. Moreover, 70 percent of Spanish surnamed families in the U. S. fall below median income levels (Garcia, et. al., 1984). Thus, it is clear that education is not the only arena where problems are located. But it may be the major root of economic and political problems. Garcia et. al. used the term "educational nonaccomodation" to refer to the failure of our educational institution to maximally accumulate information from and otherwise relevant to the Mexican American. When it has gathered information it has failed to respond to that information. The effect has been a poorer quality and quantity of education for Mexican Americans. The Mexican American has yet to use the courts to secure educational justice, but their use is likely if substantial change does not occur.

Current noted paradigms of the lower performance of Mexican Americans emphasize that they are a non-English-speaking minority and that their culture differs substantially from the dominant Anglo culture. Other variables

ACADEMIC ACHIEVEMENT

39

commonly linked to lower achievement are lack of family and community support for education, the "culture of poverty" and "culture deprivation," and the educational platforms and tactics of the schools attended by Mexican Americans. In the 1960s, cultural deprivation explanations were dominant. Such views affected compensatory educational policies which did little to improve school performance. Today's linguistic and cultural explanations imply the development and implementation of bilingual and bicultural education. Yet education programs are heading in the opposite direction.

Language and cultural differences are important in school performance, but perhaps more important is the caste-like status of the Mexican Americans who were conquered and stripped of power in the southwestern states. "This process of conquest and colonization involved violence and brutality on the part of the conquerors, a system of privilege based on racism, and the exploitation of the labor of Mexicans and other poor people" (Acuña, 1981:1). Since the nineteenth century Mexicans have been socialized to accept their low status and "the American way." Education has been and continues to be a tool to legitimize those in power. Anglo attitudes towards Mexican Americans are affected by the folk ideologies or stereotypes supporting the latter's historically subordinate status and by phenotypical differences. Hence discriminatory practices have become institutionalized. And, as discriminatory practices continue, so does the cycle of structural discrimination:

> Discrimination in education denies the credentials to get good jobs. Discrimination in employment denies the economic resources to buy good housing. Discrimination in housing confines its victims to school districts providing inferior education, closing the cycle in a classic form (U. S. Commission on Civil Rights, 1981:11).

This cycle reinforces and compounds the sense of alienation experienced by Mexican Americans in the Anglo dominated society.

Cultural Factors

Anglo dominated environments alone generally are insignificant in encouraging alienation and negative ethnic self attitudes. In fact, they appear to enhance ethnic salience in self identification (Iadicola, 1981). Nevertheless, high socioeconomic status dominated environments foster negative ethnic self attitudes and promote alienation by diminishing the level of ethnic salience in self identification. Iadicola also notes that Hispanic students' own socioeconomic status level either insulates the individual from the negative effects of a high socioeconomic status school environment or enhances the negative effect of school socioeconomic status upon ethnic attitudes. In sum, it is not the presence of Anglo students alone as much as it is the presence of upper-middle class students which animates alienation in Mexican American students.

Iadicola's (1981) findings suggest more emphasis on socioeconomic status desegregation and less on ethnic desegregation. One of the major consequences of an overall pattern of educational segregation has been the failure of Anglos to accept Mexican Americans as peers, even in those cases where Mexican Americans have attended schools with Anglos. This nonacceptance by Anglos in the public schools in turn has had a devastating psychological impact on Mexican American children (Garcia, et. al., 1984). It has engendered a sense of shame among them toward their history, their heritage, and their culture and personality (San Miguel, 1978; Taylor, 1934). In sum, historically equal educational opportunity for Mexican Americans meant repudiation of their cultural background, perhaps too large an expense to pay for access.

Pragmatically, affirmative action in higher education involves two incongruent goals: assimilation and the improvement of intergroup relations through equal status relations. A college or university which is conducive to assimilation, one with a high level of Anglo students and socioeconomic status, creates status inequalities between Anglo and Mexican American students. Through such assimilation, improvement in intergroup relations results from the absorption of the subordinate group into the dominant culture. But why must Mexican Americans assimilate in order to achieve meritocracy? A conflict perspective would focus on the process of regulating dominated social classes and cultural categories through the basic institutions and organizations of our society. In addition to types of control, one must determine what it is about the social system which makes these particular systems of control necessary. Indeed, the denial of access to Mexican Americans in higher education is part of this larger issue.

Cultural traditions socialize individuals through family activity, peer group, common literature, formal associations, ingroup marriage and segregation. Mexican American children develop stronger group enhancement and cooperative and altruism motives than Anglo children, who develop stronger competitive motives (Madsen, 1971). The cooperative orientation of Mexican American children may not be conducive to success in school. A competitive atmosphere in the classroom pervades our educational institutions. Success in taking standardized and rigidly administered examinations is a requisite for academic advancement. Individual achievement is strongly encouraged and is paramount for capturing the attention of one's mentor. We have offered

ACADEMIC ACHIEVEMENT

41

evidence suggesting that the Mexican American culture socializes individuals in much the opposite manner. Consequently, the Mexican American often faces the choice of remaining true to oneself and one's background or attempting to succeed in the Anglo-dominated educational environment.

It may not be simple demographics (e.g., family size and birth order) that result in the relatively prosocial or cooperative behavior among Mexican American children. Perhaps the strength of familial interdependence and the patterning of relationships between family members is more important (McClintock, et. al., 1979). The effect that family size and ordinal position has on the social behavior of children may be affected by the nature of responsibility that children are given, family conflict resolution style, and familial rules (Knight and Kagan, 1982). In a large family, if, for example, older siblings are handed responsibility characterized by dominance, the family handles conflict with direct aggression, and the family employs authoritarian rules, then the children may exhibit a very competitive or aggressive rather than a prosocial or cooperative nature. In contrast, a cooperative orientation may be the consequence of cultural norms and prescriptions which are selectively reinforced and/or modeled by parents.

Kagan et. al. (1982) experimented with open-ended verbal conflict resolution questions asked of Anglo American, Mexican American, and Mexican children. Previous conclusions regarding Anglo-Mexican American differences in the development of cooperation and competition were supported at early childhood age ranges. However, cultural differences diminished with age. With increasing age, all children responded more to imaginary conflict situations with conflict. Moreover, Mexican American and Anglo children did not vary on verbal conflict resolution questions. Perhaps different cognitive dimensions are tapped by verbal conflict resolution questions and experimental games. For example, Mexican American children may be inhibited about competing for material rewards in gamelike situations. Such inhibitions may not hold for other forms of interpersonal interactions. Accordingly, behavioral choices in experimental games may lack ecological validity. That is, they are not representative of real-life judgments in Mexican American environments. Thus, children are force to choose between what for them may be unusual or even meaningless alternatives.

Kagan et. al.'s (1982) use of open-ended questions to study replies to presumably universal situations is quite in contrast to previous methodologies which may force children to react in culturally unrepresentative ways to culturally unrepresentative situations. Historically, the question has been: Will the children create conflict? But Kagan et. al. presented the children with conflict. The question then becomes: How will they resolve an existing conflict? Perhaps Mexican Americans and Anglos are equally willing to respond to conflict with conflict, but they are not likely to create a conflict. Accordingly, an early adaptation of Mexican American cultural values to acculturation pressures may be to replace the development of a cooperative orientation with the development of a reactive conflict orientation (i.e., a willingness to respond to conflict with conflict).

I have examined evidence suggesting that there are structural factors which differentially affect academic performance in Mexican American students. Also affecting achievement is the fact that schools convey different messages to Mexican American and Anglo students. The communication to the Anglo student is similar to the American belief that perseverance in school results in economic success, self-improvement and prestige. The Mexican American student receives a double message: Persevere and you will succeed and since the economic reality is that Mexican Americans do not succeed, they are left to blame themselves for their lack of success. It simply is another example of our individualistic "blame the victim" cultural bias.

That the Mexican American observes and responds to the obstacles in future employment and social status perhaps induces "mental withdrawal" (Carter, 1970). Economically disadvantaged conditions dictate the culture of poverty, but it is not the Mexican American culture that dictates the mental withdrawal and the low academic performance of Mexican American students. Though the Mexican American may not linger behind his/her Anglo counterpart in school performance in the first several grades, his/her achievement during the intermediate grades plunges acutely (Carter, 1970:178). While a middle class background supplies the type of support and rewards that proliferates high academic performance, a Mexican American or lower-class heritage does not breed such returns. Thus, middle-class Anglo children do well in school because of anticipatory socialization. Mexican American parents, in contrast, may not mislead their children by promising them substantial future social payoffs for high academic achievement.

In conclusion, for Mexican Americans, the relatively few cases of educational attainment has not resulted in the same economic and social premiums that Anglos reap. A lower educational performance by Hispanics might be an adjustment of their social and occupational statuses in society. Such institutional discrimination enhances problems instigated by cultural and languages differences.

Policy Implications

Mexican Americans are underrepresented in institutions of higher education in terms of enrollment and completion of degrees. Affirmative action programs, as sponsored and enforced by the federal government, as well as voluntary and court-ordered affirmative action efforts by institutions cannot, given the current social climate, be relied upon as the sole instrument which Mexican Americans might use to increase their access to institutions of higher education. Because Hispanics as a group are the fastest growing minority within the United States, access to higher education is critical if Hispanics, including Mexican Americans, are to participate in decision-making forums and enjoy higher status and higher paying positions in the employment arena. Structural discrimination, as well as institutional racism, persist within the United States. Accordingly, group entitlement cannot be expected to be bestowed upon Mexican Americans by benevolent forces. Rather, it must be gained by continual pressure from within the Hispanic community as a whole. Higher education has been, and will continue to be, the major route to greater participation in the benefits of living in a post-industrial society.

Given these conclusions, it is critical to focus more attention on possible explanations for the underrepresentation of Mexican Americans in higher education. Objective data on enrollment, persistence, and completion are sufficient to indicate a problem. As well, Mexican Americans within the United States have experienced discrimination, and will no doubt continue to experience discrimination. The task then is to continue to examine the socio-legal factors and cultural elements within the traditional community which may act as barriers to participation in higher education. I do not suggest that all potential culture barriers which may be discovered should be eliminated. In fact, there may be attributes, such as the cooperative orientation, which are more suitable to decision-making in an inter-dependent world of nations than are the individualistic, competitive modes that characterize the Anglo model.

Equal opportunity alone will not remedy the denial of access to higher education for Mexican Americans. The means to access such equal opportunity must also be provided. Each ethnic minority should be afforded the means of access. The data presented in this paper suggest that a strong case can also be made for black males. There has been much evidence that points to offsetting the negative impact of low socioeconomic status, not the Mexican American culture, as the major objective of educational policy involving Mexican Americans. An examination of the socio-legal context reveals what an up-hill struggle equal educational opportunity has been for Mexican Americans. The current administration has formulated and implemented policy which has only increased the educational and economic gaps between whites and minorities. The negative psychological effects of adverse educational situations on Mexican American students are devastating. The cooperative orientation, so

318

well documented in research, may dissolve in real-life conflict situations.

Policy implications point to programs that enhance educational quality for Mexican Americans. Rather than trying to enhance self concept in their Mexican American students, educators should instead compensate for the potentially deleterious effects of low socioeconomic status. Positive steps have included studies of the effects of the unique linguistic patterns of Mexican Americans (LeVine and Franco, 1980), curriculum changes that include the Mexican historical/cultural heritage (Hernandez, 1973), and the amelioration of the stereotypic responses of Anglo educators (Padilla and Ruiz, 1978).

Future policy should involve the cognitive-linguistic patterns of Mexican Americans, curriculum changes recognizing the diversity of the minority experience (this permits and reinforces a positive ethnic identification for minorities and provides Anglos with a greater appreciation for diversity), and curriculum changes in educator training programs so that teachers, as well as students, develop a greater appreciation for diversity. Empowerment is also necessary — giving the Mexican American community more rights and responsibilities in the educating of their children. The empowerment of the Hispanic community and aggressive affirmative action programs, respectively, represent cultural and socio-legal factors that are needed to break the cycle of structural discrimination.

References

Acuña, R. 1981. *Occupied America* (2nd ed.). (New York: Harper & Row).

Brown v. Board of Education of Topeka. 1954. 347 U. S. 483.

Carter, T. 1968. "Negative Self-Concept of Mexican American Students," *School and Society*, 96:217-219.

Carter, T. 1970. *Mexican Americans in School: A History of Educational Neglect.* (New York: College Entrance Examination Board).

Carter, T. P. and R. D. Segura. 1979. *Mexican Americans in the School: A Decade of Change.* (New York: College Entrance Examination Board).

Chronicle of Higher Education, January 19, 1981.

DeBlassie, R. 1976. *Counseling with Mexican-American Youth.* (Austin: Learning Concepts, Inc.).

Denver Post, September 16, 1981:8a.

Estrada, F., F. C. Garcia, R. F. Macias, and L. Maldonado. 1981. "Chicanos in the United States: A History of Exploitation and Resistance," *Daedalus*, 110:103-131.

Frazier, D. and R. DeBlassie. 1982. "A Comparison of Self-Concept in Mexican American and Non-Mexican American Late Adolescents," *Adolescence*, 17:327-334.

ACADEMIC ACHIEVEMENT

45

Gandara, P. 1982. "Passing Through the Eye of the Needle: High Achieving Chicanos," *Hispanic Journal of Behavioral Sciences*, 4:167-180.

Garcia, E., F. Lomeli, and I. Ortiz, eds. 1984. *Chicano Studies: A Multidisciplinary Approach*. (New York: Teachers College Press).

Hernandez, N. 1973. "Variables Affecting Achievement of Middle School Mexican American Students," *Review of Educational Research*, 43:1-39.

Iadicola, P. 1981. "Peer Group Contextual Factors and Hispanic Students' Attitudes Toward Their Own Ethnic Group." Paper presented at the meeting of the Southern Sociological Society, April, at Louisville, Kentucky.

Kagan, S., G. Knight, and S. Martinez-Romero. 1982. "Culture and the Development of Conflict Resolution Style," *Journal of Cross-Cultural Psychology*, 13:43-58.

Knight, G. and S. Kagan. 1982. "Siblings, Birth Order, and Cooperative-competitive Social Behavior," *Journal of Cross-Cultural Psychology*, 13:239-249.

Kutner, P. B. 1979. "Keyes v. School District Number One: A Constitutional Right to Equal Educational Opportunity?" *Journal of Law and Education*, 8 (January):1-43.

Levine, E. and J. Franco. 1980. *New Dimensions in Cross-Cultural Counseling: Some Anglo/Hispanic Comparisons*. New Mexico State University College of Education Dialogue Series.

Madsen, M. C. 1971. "Developmental and Cross-Cultural Differences in the Cooperative and Competitive Behavior of Young Children," *Journal of Cross-Cultural Psychology*, 4:365-371.

McClintock, E., M. Bayard, and C. McClintock. 1979. "Socialization of Prosocial Orientation in the Mexican American Family." Paper presented at the National Symposium on the Mexican American Child, University of California, Santa Barbara, CA.

Office for Civil Rights, Department of Health, Education and Welfare. 1978 Nondiscrimination in Federally Assisted Programs; Title VI of the Civil Rights Act of 1964; Policy Interpretation, 45 CFR Part 80.

Padilla, A. and R. Ruiz. 1978. "Prejudice and Discrimination." In M. Wertheimer and L. Rappoport, eds., *Psychology and the Problems of Today*. (Dallas: Scott, Foresman, & Co.).

San Miguel, G. 1978. "Endless Pursuits: The Chicano Educational Experience in Corpus Christi, Texas, 1880-1960." Ph.D. dissertation, Stanford University.

Taylor, P. 1934. *An American-Mexican Frontier*. (Chapel Hill: University of North Carolina Press).

United States Commission on Civil Rights. 1974. *Toward Quality Education for Mexican Americans*. Reports IV and VI: Mexican American Education Study, February.

United States Commission on Civil Rights. 1978. *Toward Equal Educational Opportunity: Affirmative Admissions Program at Law and Medical Schools*. Clearinghouse Publication 55, June:7, 21.

United States Commission on Civil Rights. 1981. *Affirmative Action in the 1980s: Dismantling the Process of Discrimination*. Clearinghouse Publication 70, November:11.

Vasquez, M. 1982. "Confronting Barriers to the Participation of Mexican American Women in Higher Education," *Hispanic Journal of Behavioral Sciences*, 4:147-166.

Vetter, B., E. Babco, and S. Jensen-Fisher, eds. 1982. *Professional Women and Minorities: A*

Manpower Data Resource Service. Washington, D. C.: Scientific Manpower Commission.

Watson, B. 1979. "Through the Academic Gateway," *Change*, 11:25-28

ACADEMIC ACHIEVEMENT

47

Hispanic Journal of Behavioral Sciences
1982, Vol. 4, No. 2, 147–165

Confronting Barriers to the Participation of Mexican American Women in Higher Education

MELBA J. T. VASQUEZ
Colorado State University

The purpose of this review was to identify and examine barriers purported to prevent the participation of Mexican American women in higher education as well as strategies to confront those barriers. Sex-role restrictions and the oppressive effects of low socioeconomic status, rather than culture or language, partially accounted for the relatively low participation of Chicanas in postsecondary education. The fact that Chicanas must generally seek and obtain financial sources of support because of parental inability to aid further deters chances of obtaining a degree. The alienation and isolation that Chicanas often experience because of the lack of "fit" and support in the college environment can also discourage participation of this underrepresented group. The traditional admissions criteria such as tests scores and high school achievement are often erroneously used to prevent the entrance of many Mexican American women who might indeed have potential to succeed. Motivation and positive self-expectations have been found to mediate the barriers that many Chicanas face. These variables result from support and encouragement, particularly from mother encouragement, teacher expectations, and positive identification with one's language and culture. Programs designed to provide financial and emotional support as well as provide an advocacy role are clearly desirable.

Problems for ethnic minorities and women are still pervasive in general and especially on the nation's campuses despite gains made in the last two decades (Women's Equity Action League Educational and Legal Defense Fund, Note 1). In particular, educational status for Mexican American women, Chicanas (for the purposes of this article, the term "Chicana" will be synonymous with Mexican American and is defined as a female American citizen of Mex-

---

Requests for reprints should be sent to Melba J. T. Vasquez, University Counseling Center, Colorado State University, Ft. Collins, Colorado 80523.

ican ancestry), remains low. The United States Commission on Civil Rights (1978) reported a March 1976 study that revealed that while 32% of all Mexican American men who entered college completed a degree, only 15% of all Mexican American women did so. In comparison, approximately 50% of every nonminority who enters college completes a degree. Moreover, fewer Chicanos than nonminorities enroll in college after high school graduation (*Chronicle of Higher Ecucation*, 1975). Clearly, while both male and female Chicanos are at an educational disadvantage, Chicanas fare less well.

There is a strong ethos in this country that suggests that education is a means to socioeconomic mobility and independence. Yet, the figures that reflect the educational attainment of Chicanas at all levels (undergraduate, graduate, and faculty) in higher education are bleak (Escobedo, 1980). Hence, the effectiveness of higher education for Chicanas may be improved if we learn more about why a large proportion of students do not participate fully in higher education.

The purpose of this article is to identify the barriers that contribute to the low numbers of undergraduate Chicanas in higher education as well as to identify practical measures to minimize Chicana students' chances of dropping out. The research literature in the area of Chicana academic achievement is extremely limited. Thus, many issues, hypotheses, or generalizations will be extrapolated from the general literature on attrition and retention as well as from the meager research on women, Mexican Americans, and other ethnic minority groups in higher education. First, the effects of sex-role restrictions on Chicanas will be discussed. Then the myths about the effects of culture and language on academic achievement will be critiqued. It seems important to address and clarify the negative stereotypic myths that have been perpetuated by studies that have utilized a pathological model of cultural deficit to account for low educational achievement and whose interpretations of data are biased. The deleterious effects of low economic status as well as sources of financial support in college will also be discussed. The notion of environmental fit and the stress from alienation and isolation for Chicanas in all-white institutions will be addressed. The inappropriate use of traditional admissions criteria and the importance of motivation, expectations, and self-esteem to mediate barriers to success for Chicanas are final considerations.

Sex Differences

Does sex-role socialization restrict participation of Chicana women in higher education? Stereotyped attitudes about role definitions for women (e.g., childbearers) and role definitions for men (e.g., the "machismo" image) in traditional Latin cultures are examples of sex-role factors suggested to restrict educational aspirations and levels of achievement for Chicanas. While the traditionally high value placed on *La Familia* has its positive rewards (Keefe, Padilla, & Carlos, 1978), Mexican American women, often first-generation college students, experience role conflict as they attempt to balance the relative rewards and costs of marriage and children with an education and, ultimately, a career.

In their study on Chicanos in higher education on four California campuses, for example, Munoz and Garcia-Bahne (Note 2) found sex differences for academic performance. Forty-two percent of the males compared to 30% of the females in their sample reported that they had been on academic probation at some time. Chicanas received superior grades than Chicanos in high school and in college. Yet, figures reported earlier reflect the relatively low rates of persistence to graduation for Chicanas.

Women and men in general are found to differ in their educational and intellectual development (Maccoby & Jacklin, 1974). One would assume that different needs and role expectations for men and women would result in differences in academic performance. Cope and Hannah (1975) concluded that the variable of sex in predicting withdrawal from college is a complex one. They reported that most studies investigating sex as a variable related to attrition found more men withdrawing than women, but when an adequate follow-up study including reentry and transfer was conducted, only slightly different variations in the attrition rate for men and women were found. While women tended to graduate on schedule more often than men, men were more likely to complete degree requirements eventually.

More information about sex differences in academic performance was reported by Astin (1971, 1977). In a presentation of selectivity data for 2,300 American colleges, Astin reported that women received higher grades than men in both high school and in college. He found that the academic performance of the female freshman surpasses that of the average male freshman, even when they were matched on high school grades and aptitude test scores, a finding similar to that of Munoz and Garcia-Bahne (Note 2) for Chicanas. Despite their superior academic performance, women were more likely to drop out of college after the freshman year.

Astin reported similar conclusions in his later (1977) study. He found that although women earned higher grades than men, they were less likely to persist in college and to enroll in graduate or professional school. Moreover, women's aspirations for higher degress declined, while men's aspirations increased during the undergraduate years.

The socialization process that often perpetuates or reinforces roles for girls and women results in a serious limitation of choices for them. Russo (1976) points out the psychological constraints that sex-role socialization, and particularly the "motherhood mandate," has on women. Dixon (1975) described the very real limitations that marriage and children have on the pursuit of an education. Women who were high school seniors in 1965 were interviewed in 1971. Of those who had started college, 75% of the married women with children had dropped out of school, compared with 52% of married men with children, 22% of single women, and 27% of single men. Sex-role restrictions thus limit the actualization of potential that women have.

Apparently, while women—both Chicana and non-Chicana—perform better academically, persistence to graduation is lower compared to men within respective ethnic groups. The social, economic, and cultural factors common to all women exert great influence on educational attainment. The extent to which cultural elements, in addition, influence the educational attainment of Chicanas is difficult to determine. Because she is often the first generation to enter higher education, the Chicana often experiences stresses resulting from sex-role conflicts. Because of the traditionally high value placed on the Chicano family, the struggle between pursuit of education and the traditional roles of wife and mother may cause many Chicanas to doubt the pursuit of an education. They have often seen their own mothers dedicate their lives to the home and children. Chicanas must thus receive support in dealing with those conflicts and stresses.

Culture and Language

What are the effects of the Mexican American culture and the use of Spanish language on Chicanas' academic performance? While we should not underestimate the possible effects on Chicanas of traditional sex-role restrictions, interpretation of the research regarding the effects of culture on Mexican Americans in general is fraught with difficulties. In a review of vocational education research of minority group needs, Hamilton (1975) concluded that the research was generally based on a social pathology model of cultural deficit and on stereotypes of cultural disadvantage without identifying positive attributes. Martinez (1977) points out that "psychological formulations that adequately explain the behavior of Anglos within the Anglo culture may not necessarily explain the behavior of Chicanos within the Chicano culture" (p. 11). The concept of cultural relativism—that human behavior can be understood only if it is viewed within the cultural context in which it occurs—sensitizes people to the importance of careful interpretation of various studies. Unfortunately, many discussions imply that identification with the values, attitudes, behaviors, and language of the Chicano culture is a liability to educational achievement and that acculturation—the process of "giving up" of one's subculture and adapting to the values, attitudes, and behaviors of the majority culture—should be the guiding philosophy of educational programming and interventions (Heller, 1968; Madsen, 1964; Schwartz, 1971). As Escobedo (1980) points out, the deficit model fails to examine the environmental impact on individuals that limits educational resources.

In a review of several studies negatively relating cultural factors to educational achievement and personality adjustment, for example, Ramirez (1971) concludes that socioeconomic variables are central to the issue. Being "educationally disadvantaged" refers to those environmental deficiencies that are detrimental to an individual's performance in education regardless of ethnic or racial status. Low socioeconomic status, a negative family environment, and limited exposure to cultural and intellectual resources may be properly considered indications of a disadvantaged situation. However, while these conditions may be associated with a portion of the Mexican American population for economic and social reasons, they should not be construed as arising from the group's culture per se (National Board on Graduate Education, 1976; Ryan, 1971).

Language is a culturally related factor that may be a disadvantage if a child does not understand English. The relationship of bilingualism and academic achievement has been recognized as a problem by educators. The National Center for Education Statistics (1978) reported, for example, that "language-minority persons" had lower grade attainment for age and a higher dropout rate. Persons of Hispanic origin were found to be even more disadvantaged than language-minority persons in general. These findings were based on an analysis of data from the nationwide survey of income and education (SIE), conducted in the spring of 1976, by the Bureau of the Census. However, it is suggested by Long and Padilla (Note 3) that bilingualism, itself, is not the problem. Rather, additional factors result in "dual-cultural deprivation." Those factors may include educational deprivation, which is related to low socioeconomic status, which in turn is related to a large proportion of the bilingual population.

Long and Padilla (Note 3), recognizing that little research had concentrated on assessing the role of bilingualism in the academic achievement of college-age students, surveyed successful (Ph.D. recipients) and unsuccessful (dropouts) Chicano graduate students at the University of New Mexico. They found that 94% of the successful students but only 7% of the unsuccessful students reported coming from a bilingual background; most of the unsuccessful students reported that English was the only language in their childhood homes. Long and Padilla concluded that the finding of the high rate of bilingualism in the sample of successful Spanish American students implied that these students may have been better able to interact readily with members of both their own culture and that of the dominant American culture. They further suggested that these individuals may simply be better adjusted members of both cultures, hence, their tendencies to be more successful. The lack of bilingual background of the unsuccessful student may reflect a tendency in the homes to reject their Spanish American background, and the ensuing conflict may lead to a general maladjustment.

The reports of several studies have, in fact, challenged the assumption that acculturation is a cure-all and that identification with one's culture is damaging (Henderson & Merritt, 1968; Ramirez, 1971; Ramirez & Castañeda, 1974; Cordova, Note 4; Long & Padilla, Note 3). A more appropriate philosophy—that of cultural democracy—maintains that identification with one's ethnic group is, in fact, a necessary ingredient of academic success and psychological adjustment. Researchers have begun to indicate that active participation in two or more cultures may, in fact, provide the basis for a more flexible and sophisticated psychological adjustment (Henderson & Merritt, 1968; Ramirez & Castañeda, 1974; Cordova, Note 4; Ramirez, Castañeda, & Cox, Note 5).

Thus, while some studies imply that Chicano culture and use of the Spanish language are barriers to educational attainment (National Center for Educational Statistics, 1978; Schwartz, 1971), others propose a positive relationship between a bilingual, bicultural identity and academic success, psychological adjustment, and social flexibility (Henderson & Merritt, 1968; Ramirez & Castañeda, 1974; Cordova, Note 4; Long & Padilla, Note 3). Other factors, such as low socioeconomic status resulting in limited exposure to cultural and intellectual resources, may partially account for low academic performance and attainment of Mexican American men and women.

Effects of Socioeconomic Status on Academic Performance of Chicanas

Perhaps one of the primary barriers to higher education for Chicanas is the effect of low socioeconomic status. Mexican American women in particular are at the lowest levels of occupational, educational, and financial indices (Vasquez, 1978; Vasquez & Banning, Note 6), and a large portion of the Mexican American population falls in the lower social class (Carter, 1970; U.S. Commission on Civil Rights, 1971). Various indices of social class and their relationship to academic performance have been investigated. Socioeconomic status (SES), as measured by parents' education, occupation, and income, mediates a large number of academic values, attitudes, opinions, and patterns of behavior. The findings frequently reported are that the lower the level of parental education, occupational position, and income, the lower the academic performance. Students from higher SES backgrounds tend to obtain higher grades and persist in college (Astin, 1971, 1975; Astin, Astin, Bisconti, & Frankel, 1972; Cope & Hannah, 1975; Pantages & Creedon, 1978; Vasquez, 1978).

Vasquez (1978), for example, examined factors that influenced and mediated grade point average, persistence, and attrition of Chicana and Anglo University of Texas women. The results of a discriminant analysis showed that socioeconomic status was one of three major variables that contributed to differences between the "successful" and "nonsuccessful" groups. Descriptive data showed that both Anglo and Chicana students who were persisters also had higher parental educational, occupational, and income levels. For the total sample, Chicanas generally reflected lower SES levels than Anglo women.

The process of socialization means that children acquire many of the hopes and expectations of their parents within the social class; they also acquire verbal and auditory skills that have an effect on their ability to adjust to the academic and social demands of college (Cope & Hannah, 1975; Anderson & Johnson, Note 7). Poverty causes stress, particularly in the family structure which has been cited to be the most important facet of life for Chicanos (Cuellar & Moore, 1970). Poor people are also the victims of discrimination in schools and other environments. Thus poverty and discrimination may combine to limit the development of predispositions, habits, knowledge, and experiences that promote academic achievement for Mexican American students (Hernandez, 1973).

Hernandez concluded in a review of two studies that SES is not as significant a predictor for achievement for Mexican American students as for the general population. In an extensive study of Chicanos at four California universities, Munoz and Garcia-Bahne (Note 2) found no significant differences between college grade point average and socioeconomic standing of the family. In a study investigating the sociocultural determinants of Mexican American high school students, Anderson and Johnson (Note 7) found that when achievement motivation was controlled, the previously discovered relationship between SES and grades almost disappeared. These studies suggest that while social and economic indices do relate to academic performance, achievement motivation of Mexican American students mediates the otherwise deleterious effects of SES. However, since need achievement is supposedly one of the attitudinal factors negatively affected by low SES, the question of why some low SES students acquire achievement motivation and others do not remains.

The extent of academic preparation for Chicanos is a related issue that should be explored. Mexican American students in general, and women in particular, are often "tracked" into taking noncollege preparatory courses. The National Academy of Sciences (1977) made visits to 29 engineering campuses with active programs to increase minority student enrollment and found insufficient preparation in mathematics and the physical sciences as one of several reasons for attrition among minority engineering students. Basic study skills are often lacking in minority students who otherwise have the academic potential to succeed in higher education.

While it seems that the academic performance of many students is adversely affected by factors associated with low SES (e.g., stereotypic societal messages, lack of resources, inadequate preparation, different academic values and attitudes, patterns of behavior), other students prevail despite those negative associations. Perhaps the ambition to better oneself mediates the usual disadvantaged situation of the Chicano student from the low SES family. How that ambition is acquired despite negative environmental limitations remains a question, particularly for Chicanas. Yet, many more Chicanos who have potential to succeed are adversely effected. It may well be important to focus energies on alleviating the poverty cycle that so many Mexican American families find themselves. The negative effect of poverty on academic performance is just one of the deleterious consequences of the stresses of poverty.

Financial Situation

Related to low economic status is the resultant problem of financial support in school. Financial situation has a greater impact on Chicano students than on majority students. The U.S. Bureau of the Census (1970) reports that Mexican American families earn about 70% as much income as nonminority families (Table 266, U.S. Bureau of the Census). In a comprehensive study, the National Board on Graduate Education (1976, pp. 77–81) reported that Chicanos anticipate a much lower median parental contribution toward the cost of college ($194 per year) compared to white students ($1,145 per year). These figures are alarming in view of the fact that Astin (1975) concluded that receiving support from parents for college expenses generally enhances the student's ability to complete college (except for women from high-income brackets).

While Munoz and Garcia-Bahne (Note 2) found no differences between college grade point average and socioeconomic status (using parental educational and occupational levels), they did find a negative relationship between family income and dropping out of school. Low family income had a detrimental effect on the Chicano college student's chances of completing college.

Financial concerns do indeed predominate as major problem areas for minority students, as evidenced by reports of a needs assessment conducted at the University of Texas (Baron, Valdez, Vasquez, & Hurst, Note 8) and one conducted at Colorado State University (Vasquez & Banning, Note 6). These two studies found that the area of greatest concern to minority students was that of finances. For the Texas study, those students reporting inadequate income also reported significantly higher mean concerns for 58 of the 63 items on the survey. The extent to which financial aid and other student assistance programs have compensated for disparities in financial circumstances remains unclear. Minorities in general place greater reliance on scholarships, workstudy programs, and loans in financing their undergraduate education, in contrast to nonminority students who receive more parental assistance.

The way in which various types of financial aid affects student performance was investigated by Astin (1975). He concluded that scholarships or grants are associated with small increases in student persistence rates; participation in workstudy programs also appears to enhance student persistence. Reliance on loans, on the other hand, is associated with decreased persistence among men in all income groups while the effects are highly variable among women. Reliance on savings or other assets also appears to decrease the students' chances of finishing college. We can thus hypothesize that one of the barriers to higher educational participation for Mexican American women is primarily the lack of funds and secondarily the common necessity of students to rely on loans. We could conclude that activities designed to make scholarships and grants more available to Chicanas might enhance tendency to enter and remain in school.

Geographic Location, Size of High School, and "Culture Shock" Phenomenon

A Chicana student's hometown location and size are also factors in academic performance. In a review of three studies, Summerskill (1974) concluded that higher attrition rates were found among students from rural homes than among students from cities or towns. Astin (1975) and Cope (1972) found that growing up in a small town was most consistently related to dropping out. "Out of state" students were "underachievers"; students from cities with populations of more than 100,000 were "overachievers." However, in their review of several studies, Cope and Hannah (1975) found conflicting results: some studies indicated that school size makes no difference or that students from smaller high schools do better in college, whereas others showed that students from larger, more urban high schools performed better. The location and size of home communities in themselves probably do not determine a student's academic performance. Yet, variation in quality of secondary schools and in the number and range of the cultural and educational activities among different cities and towns may be influential.

The "culture shock" phenomenon may account in part for the difficulty many Chicana students encounter, especially at large all-white universities. Students report alienation and isolation as a result of being the only minority student in a class of 300 students or in a large residence hall. Astin (1975) and Cope and Hannah (1975) concluded that the "fit" between the size and nature of the student's hometown and the college is important to student academic performance, particularly persistence. Indeed, many students report preferring to return to smaller colleges or community colleges in order to feel more comfortable. Establishment of effective cultural programs, organizations, and other student services can help offset the alienation that Chicana students experience.

Admissions Criteria

The use of traditional admissions criteria as a barrier to the participation of minorities has been recognized by many. Very few studies have attempted to investigate the possible differential relationship of admissions criteria to college grade point average and persistence for Mexican American students, and this author was not able to locate any studies that identified differences for Chicanas. The few studies that have been completed report dissimilar and occasionally contradictory results, possibly due to differences in methodology, selected variables, and populations (Cole & Hanson, 1973; Dalton, 1974; Goldman & Hewitt, 1976; Goldman & Richards, 1974; Sedlacek & Brooks, 1976; Thomas & Stanley, 1969).

Generally, studies reported that the use of admission test scores and high school grades work disproportionately against minority groups. Goldman and Hewitt (1976), for example, found that the accuracy of college grade point average prediction by the combined use of high school grade point average and SAT scores was considerably weaker for black and Chicano students than for white or Asian students in their sample. Goldman and Hewitt (1976) concluded that "if a given *predicted* grade point average were used to select college applicants, then proportionately fewer Black and

Chicano applicants would be admitted than would actually surpass this grade point average criterion" (p. 116).

Some researchers conclude that high school achievement is a better predictor than admissions tests scores for minorities. Yet, high school achievement is a less effective predictor of college grades for minority students than for nonminorities (Dalton, 1974). Others who found test scores to be better predictors of academic success than high school achievement also caution that they are not as predictive for minority students as for majority students (Cole & Hanson, 1973; Thomas & Stanley, 1969). Obviously, the conflicting findings are likely due to problems and differences in methodology. For example, studies that do find the traditional predictors valid for ethnic minorities use subjects who are largely unrepresentative of the larger number of minority students with the potential to do college work, since minority students attracted to higher education tend to be relatively homogeneous on the admissions criteria.

Clearly, university admissions offices that continue to use the traditional criteria prevent many Chicana students and other minorities who have college potential from even entering school. Admissions and other counseling personnel should thus be aware of the lack of predictability of such criteria for Chicanas and other groups.

Motivation, Self-Expectations, and Self-Esteem

As indicated earlier, motivation is one of the identified variables that mediate barriers to the participation of Chicanas in higher education. Personal commitment to either an academic or occupational goal has been identified as one of the single most important determinants of persistence in college. Cope and Hannah (1975) concluded that the commitment to finish college resulting partly from the motivational climate of the family was far more important than having enough money. The literature is conflicted regarding the aspirations, expectations, and motivational climate for Mexican Americans and their families to attend college. Some studies that utilize the pathological model of cultural deficit reported low educational aspirations and expectations (Heller, 1968; Madsen, 1964); others suggested that aspirations and expectations were just as strong for Mexican American students and their parents as for their Anglo counterparts when socioeconomic status and educational circumstances were controlled (Anderson & Johnson, Note

7; Ulibarri, Note 9). A study by Moerk (1974) found that while aspirations were high, expectations to attend college, in reality, were relatively lower.

One of the most recent studies on Chicanos in higher education by Munoz and Garcia-Bahne (Note 2) found that 55% of the Chicano students in their sample from four California universities began thinking of attending college during the 10th grade or later, and more than 26% did not consider the possibility until 12th grade or later. In contrast, the vast majority of Anglo students had planned to attend college during their elementary or junior high school years. This finding implied differences in the *development* of aspirations and expectations to attend college.

In order to have positive expectations for oneself, one must first experience positive feelings and perceive oneself to be skillful in interacting in the Anglo world, such as the generally all-white institutions of higher education. Self-esteem and one's image is developed primarily from two sources: (a) feedback about one's personal worth and competence, and (b) from cultural feedback about the *legitimacy* of a person's primary reference group (Zimbardo, 1979). The negative stereotypes about Chicanas, in particular, convey "illegitimate" messages about our primary reference group. It is not surprising, then, that actual expectations for Chicanas may be lower and that the development of expectations to attend college occurs later. Clearly, it is crucial that Mexican American women with potential to succeed in college receive strong doses of encouragement from parents as well as other significant people in their lives, such as teachers, in order to deter the negative messages from society about their primary reference group. Overt as well as covert, subtle patterns of prejudice and discrimination often result in negative internalized messages about one's general worth as a woman, as a member of an ethnic minority group, and, in most cases, as a member of the low economic group in this country.

First-generation Chicana college students in particular must innoculate themselves against the crippling effects of being a "triple minority" by establishing a sense of pride in their origins, history, and group identity as well as in their abilities. Parents and teachers have been found to be influential. In a study evaluating the effects of school desegregation by court-ordered busing on the subsequent dropout rate of majority and minority students, for example, Felice and Richardson (Note 10) found that the more favorable expectations of teachers at higher socioeconomic-climate schools produced lower minority dropout rates. The National

Academy of Sciences (1977) conducted a study of retention of
minority students in engineering and reported that the amount of
personal contact among students, faculty, and staff was an important variable in a retention program. Using a discriminant analysis
to determine the variables that best discriminated between the
"successful" and "nonsuccessful" groups of Chicana university students, Vasquez (1978) found that "mother encouragement to do
well in school" was one of the most important. Given the oppression that Mexican American women experience as a "triple
minority," self-expectations and self-esteem may be relatively low,
or at best develop more positively at a later time than most non-
Chicana students. These negative effects can be mediated by positive contact, support, and encouragement from parents, teachers,
and other significant individuals in their lives.

In conclusion, several barriers to the participation of Chicanas
in higher education have been identified. Sex-role socialization as
well as negative messages in society about the Mexican American
culture result in conflicts and low self-expectations. Some of the
literature (Heller, 1968; Madsen, 1964; Schwartz, 1971) implied
that identification with the Chicano culture is a liability to educational achievement. The reports of other studies (Henderson &
Merritt, 1969; Ramirez, 1971; Ramirez & Castañeda, 1974; Cordova, Note 4; Long & Padilla, Note 3) challenged the view that
identification with one's culture is damaging. It seems, in fact, that
identification with one's ethnic group is a necessary ingredient of
academic success as well as psychological adjustment.

Low socioeconomic factors result in social and economic disadvantages and oppressions. Many Chicanas thus experience severe
limitations in the development of predispositions, habits, knowl-
edges, and experiences that promote academic achievement. Yet,
many Chicanas from those backgrounds persevere despite those
disadvantages (Hernandez, 1973). Achievement motivation seems
to mediate the otherwise deleterious effects of low socioeconomic
status (Anderson & Johnson, Note 7). Cope and Hannah (1975)
expressed belief that personal commitment either to an academic
or occupational goal was one of the single most important determinants of persistence in college.

Mexican American parents often cannot afford to finance education, and difficulty with financial sources for education is also a
barrier that often results in the inability to continue or delay in
acquisition of a college education. Scholarships, grants, and workstudy were described as the sources of support that enhance stu-

dent persistence; but loans often decrease students' chances of finishing college, possibly because of stresses that students may experience at the thought of continuing to acquire debts.

Because the all-white environment of a university institution may be so different and oppressive compared to that of the Chicana, the lack of "fit" may result in the "culture shock" phenomenon which results in isolation and alienation. Establishment of effective student services, cultural programs, and organizations can help offset the deleterious effects that Chicanas otherwise experience.

Admissions criteria, such as standardized test scores and high school achievement, are not as predictive for Chicanas and other ethnic minority groups as they are for nonminorities. Thus, admissions offices that continue to use the traditional criteria prevent many potentially successful Chicana students from entering the university.

Many barriers thus account for the relatively low participation of Mexican American women in higher education. Support for women and strong identification with the positive aspects of one's culture seem particularly important for Mexican American women who must struggle with sex-role conflicts as well as innoculate themselves against the patterns of prejudice and discrimination that often otherwise result in negatively internalized messages about one's worth as a woman, as a member of an ethnic minority group, and, in many cases, as a member of the low economic group in this country.

Mexican American women are often first-generation college students. The development of expectations to attend college occurs later for Mexican American students than for nonminority students (Munoz & Garcia-Bahne, Note 2). It is thus crucial that Mexican American women with potential to suceed in college be strongly encouraged by parents, teachers, and other significant people in their lives. Vasquez (1978), in an attempt to identify variables that best discriminated between "successful" and "nonsuccessful" groups of Chicana university women, found that "mother encouragement to do well in school" was one of the most important. Felice and Richardson (Note 10) found that more favorable expectations of teachers at higher socioeconomic climate schools accounted for lower minority dropout rates. Positive expectations and encouragement from significant people clearly effect academic persistence of Mexican American students. More research is needed to determine the relative meaningfulness of encouragement from different sources for different populations. For example, is mother encouragement similarly impactful for Mexican American males, or is sex-role identification an important variable? Is encouragement and affirmation from nonminority teachers differentially effective for Chicana students from different backgrounds?

Confronting the barriers that exist for Mexican American women is a responsibility of all individuals who are in positions to offer support as well as impact the environments in which those barriers occur. Only through those efforts will Mexican American women be able to experience more accessibility to higher education, a right purported to exist for all Americans on an equal basis.

Resumen

El propósito de esta revisión fue el de identificar y examinar aquellos obstáculos que supuestamente limitan la participación de la mujer México-Americana en la educación superior así como las estrategias que se pueden utilizar para contrarrestar estos obstáculos. Se encontró que las restricciones debidas al rol sexual y los efectos opresores del bajo status socio-económico y no la cultura o el idioma explicaban parcialmente la relativa baja participación de las Chicanas en la educación superior. El hecho de que las Chicanas deben generalmente buscar y obtener fuentes de ayuda económica dada la imposibilidad de los padres de proveerla, disminuye aún mas las posibilidades de obtener un grado. La alienación y el aislamiento que las Chicanas frecuentemente experimentan dada la falta de "ajuste" y respaldo en el medio ambiente universitario puede tambien impedir la participación de este grupo. Los criterios tradicionales de admisión tales como las calificaciones en tests y los logros en la educación secundaria se utilizan erroneamente y con frecuencia para limitar la admisión de muchas mujeres México-Americanas quienes de hecho pueden tener el potencial para lograr el éxito. La motivación y expectativas personales positivas se han encontrado como mediadoras de los obstáculos a los que se enfrentan muchas Chicanas. Estas variables resultan del respaldo y estímulo, particularmente del estímulo por parte de la madre, las expectativas de los maestros, y la identificación positiva con la cultura e idioma de la persona. Son deseables entonces programas diseñados para proveer respaldo financiero y emocional así como aquellos que sirvan en el rol de defensores y vindicadores.

Reference Notes

1. Women's Equity Action League Educational and Legal Defense Fund. *Facts about women in higher education,* 1977. Available from author, 733 15th Street, N.W., Suite 200, Washington, D.C. 20005.
2. Munoz, D., & Garcia-Bahne, B. *A study of the Chicano experience in higher education.* Final report for the Center for Minority Group Mental Health Programs, National Institute of Mental Health, Grant No. NN24597-01, University of California, San Diego, 1978.
3. Long, K. K., & Padilla, A. M. *An assessment of successful and unsuccessful college students.* Paper presented at the American Association for the Advancement of Science, Regional Meeting, Colorado Springs, 1969.
4. Cordova, I. R. *The relationship of acculturation, achievement, and alienation among Spanish-American sixth grade students.* Paper presented for the Conference on Teacher Education for Mexican Americans, New Mexico State University, ERIC: CRESS, 1969.
5. Ramirez, M., III, Castañeda, A., & Cox, B. G. *A biculturalism inventory for Mexican American college students.* Unpublished manuscript, University of California, Santa Cruz, 1977.
6. Vasquez, M. J., & Banning, J. H. *Needs assessment service utilization and factors of success for minority students: Research findings.* Paper presented at the National Association of Student Personnel Association, Region IV West Conference, Omaha, Nebraska, 1979.
7. Anderson, J. G., & Johnson, W. H. *Sociocultural determinates of achievements among Mexican American students.* Paper presented at the National Conference of Educational Opportunities for Mexican Americans, ERIC Clearinghouse on Rural Education and Small Schools, New Mexico State University, 1968.
8. Baron, A., Valdez, J., Vasquez, M. J., & Hurst, J. C. *Assessing the concerns of minority students: Process and outcome.* Paper presented at the 60th National Association of Student Personnel Administrators Conference, Kansas City, Missouri, 1978.
9. Ulibarri, H. *Educational needs of the Mexican American.* Paper presented at the National Conference of Educational Opportunities for Mexican Americans, ERIC Clearinghouse on Rural Education and Small Schools, New Mexico State University, 1968.
10. Felice, L. G., & Richardson, R. L. *The effects of busing and school desegregation on majority and minority student dropout rates: An evaluation of school socioeconomic composition and teachers' expectations.* ERIC Dialog File 1, 1976.

References

Astin, A. W. *Predicting academic performance in college: Selectivity data for 2,300 American colleges.* New York: The Free Press, 1971.
Astin, A. W. *Preventing students from dropping out.* San Francisco: Jossey-Bass, 1975.

Astin, A. W. *Four critical years: Effects of college on beliefs, attitudes, and knowledge.* San Francisco: Jossey-Bass, 1977.

Astin, H. S., Astin, A. W., Bisconti, A. S., & Frankel, H. H. *Higher education and the disadvantaged student.* Washington, D.C.: Human Service Press, 1972.

Carter, T. *Mexican-Americans in the school: A history of educational neglect.* Princeton, N.J.: College Entrance Examination Board, 1970.

Chronical of Higher Education. 1975, *11*(7), whole.

Cole, N. S., & Hanson, G. R. *Assessing students on the way to college: Technical report for the American College Testing Assessment Program* (Vol. I). Iowa City: The American College Testing Program, 1973.

Cope, R. G. Are students more likely to drop out of large colleges? *College Student Journal,* 1972, *6*(2), 92–97.

Cope, R. G., & Hannah, W. *Revolving college doors: The causes and consequences of dropping out, stopping out, and transferring.* New York: Wiley-Interscience, 1975.

Cuellar, A., & Moore, J. W. *Mexican-Americans.* New York: Prentice-Hall, 1970.

Dalton, S. Predictive validity of high school rank and SAT scores for minority students. *Educational and Psychological Measurement,* 1974, *34*, 367–370.

Dixon, R. Women's rights and fertility. *Studies in Family Planning,* 1975, *17*, 1–20.

Escobedo, T. H. Are Hispanic women in higher education the nonexistent minority? *Educational Researcher,* October, 1980.

Goldman, R. D., & Hewitt, B. N. Predicting the success of black, Chicano, Oriental, and white college students. *Journal of Educational Measurement,* 1976, *13*(2), 107–117.

Goldman, R. D., & Richards, R. The SAT prediction of grades for Mexican-Americans versus Anglo-American students at the University of California, Riverside. *Journal of Educational Measurement,* 1974, *11*, 129–135.

Hamilton, D. *Vocational education research and development for ethnic minority students.* Washington, D.C.: National Academy of Sciences, National Research Council, 1975.

Heller, C. S. *Mexican-American youth: Forgotten youth at the crossroads.* New York: Random House, 1968.

Henderson, R. W., & Merritt, C. B. Environmental backgrounds of Mexican-American children with different potentials for school success. *Journal of Social Psychology,* 1968, *75*, 101–106.

Hernandez, N. G. Variables affecting achievement of middle school Mexican-American students. *Review of Educational Research,* 1973, *43*(1), 1–41.

Keefe, S. E., Padilla, A. M., & Carlos, M. L. The Mexican American extended family as an emotional support system. In J. M. Casas & S. E. Keefe (Eds.), *Family and mental health in the Mexican American community.* Los Angeles: Spanish Speaking Mental Health Research Center, UCLA, Monograph No. 7, 1978.

Maccoby, E. E., & Jacklin, C. N. *The psychology of sex differences.* Stanford, Cal.: Stanford University Press, 1974.

Madsen, W. *Mexican-Americans of South Texas: Case studies in cultural anthropology.* New York: Holt, Rinehart & Winston, 1964.

Martinez, J. L., Jr. (Ed.). *Chicano psychology.* New York: Academic Press, 1977.

Moerk, E. L. Age and epogenic influences on aspirations of minority and majority group children. *Journal of Counseling Psychology,* 1974, *21*, 294–298.

National Academy of Sciences. *Retention of minority students in engineering.* Washington, D.C.: National Research Council, 1977.

National Board on Graduate Education. *Minority group participation in graduate education.* Washington, D.C.: National Academy of Sciences, 1976.

National Center for Education Statistics. *The educational disadvantage of language-minority persons in the United States.* Washington, D.C.: National Center for Educational Statistics, 1978.

Pantages, T. J., & Creedon, C. F. Studies of college attrition: 1950–1975. *Review of Educational Research,* 1978, *48*(1), 49–102.

Ramirez, M., III. The relationship of acculturation to educational achievement and psychological adjustment in Chicano children and adolescents: A review of the literature. *El Grito,* 1971, *4*(4), 21–28.

Ramirez, M., III, & Castañeda, A. *Cultural democracy, bicognitive development and education.* New York: Academic Press, 1974.

Russo, N. F. The motherhood mandate. *Journal of Social Issues,* 1976, *32*(3), 143–153.

Ryan, W. *Blaming the victim.* New York: Vintage Books, 1971.

Schwartz, A. J. A comparative study of values and achievement: Mexican-American and Anglo youth. *Sociology of Education,* 1971, *44,* 438–462.

Sedlacek, E., & Brooks, G. C., Jr. *Racism in American education: A model for change.* Chicago: Nelson Hall, Inc., 1976.

Summerskill, J. Dropouts from college. In N. Sanford, *College and character: A briefer version of the American college.* New York: John Wiley & Sons, 1974.

Thomas, C. L., & Stanley, J. C. Effectiveness of high school grades for predicting college grades of black students: A review and discussion. *Journal of Educational Measurement,* 1969, *6,* 203–215.

U.S. Bureau of the Census. *Characteristics of the population, 1970* (Vol. I). Washington, D.C.: U.S. Government Printing Office, 1973.

U.S. Commission on Civil Rights. *The unfinished education: Outcomes for minorities in the five southwestern states* (Mexican American Education Study, Report II). Washington, D.C.: U.S. Government Printing Office, 1971.

U.S. Commission on Civil Rights. *Social indicators of equity for minorities and women.* Washington, D.C.: U.S. Government Printing Office, 1978.

Vasquez, M. J. *Chicana and Anglo university women: Factors related to their performance, persistence and attrition.* Unpublished dissertation, University of Texas, Austin, 1978.

Zimbardo, P. G. *Psychology and life* (10th ed.). Glenview, Ill.: Scott, Foresman & Co., 1979.

Received January 20, 1981
Revision received March 26, 1982 □

INDIAN, CHICANO, AND PUERTO RICAN COLLEGES: STATUS AND ISSUES*

Michael A. Olivas

ABSTRACT

The enormous problems facing Indian, Chicano, and Puerto Rican colleges have not been addressed by legislative efforts aimed at redressing historic exclusion nor by educational assistance designed for colleges in general. In the unique case of Indian colleges, specific legislation and program initiatives have not been effective, in part because of the fragile nature of the colleges themselves and in part because of the organizational difficulties Indian people face daily in their relationship with government agencies. Because there are only three historically Hispanic colleges, efforts to improve access for Hispanic students are not likely to be successful through minority institution initiatives.

National debates over racial inequality have historically centered upon slavery, its abolition, and its vestiges. Historical perspectives of educational inequality arise from the same memory, inevitably framing educational debates in terms of access for blacks into white institutions and school systems. Because majority Americans frequently perceive equality solely in terms of increased minority access into white institutions, adequacy of public resources for minority-controlled institutions is not often acknowledged as a corollary dimension of increased minority access. Yet, the litigation in the *Adams v. Califano* case,[1] leading to "desegregation" of black higher education institutions, has caused educators and policymakers to confront this dimension and to consider the role of black colleges in a society that perceives itself to be integrated.[2]

The Status of Historically Black Colleges

Lorenzo Morris has succinctly summarized the risk for black colleges in a search for racial balance:

At a fundamental level of the disagreement over the Adams case(s) is a conceptual difference concerning black colleges: What are their goals, and what has been the role they fill in society? On one side, they are viewed as being just like all other colleges and universities, except for their histories of unique service to blacks under conditions in which black students and faculty have had no other educational choices. On the advocates' side, the historical conditions are similarly emphasized, but there is a rarely articulated view that black colleges are a product of the choice of black Americans and not simply a byproduct of a no-choice situation. Some imply that black institutions are an automatic outgrowth of racial inequality. Advocates, however, maintain that black institutions are the willful creations of a people seeking an opportunity that has been restricted everywhere else. Blacks attend and have attended black institutions under great con-

* The author expresses his appreciation to Imelda Escobar, Roberta Wilson, James Koloditch, Dean Chavers, and Virginia Boylan for their assistance. The Joyce Foundation generously supported this research.

straints, but ultimately have made the choice to do so because these institutions offer them what they want and need. Through that free choice, [black colleges] are understood to have developed a special capacity to serve their communities—a capacity which will constitute an essential part of free choice in the education of blacks for a long time to come.[3]

This disagreement has profound implications for the framing of arguments and policy choices. How will white and black institutions co-exist in proximity with each other? How can both recruit a shrinking pool of qualified students? How can both draw upon state and private funds? How can historical funding patterns favoring white institutions be altered to compensate for historical underdevelopment? While no answers are proposed in this article, the questions are not rhetorical, for desegregation plans have been drafted, institutions have merged (e.g., the University of Tennessee at Nashville merged with Tennessee State University[4]), and legislation has been amended to incorporate *Adams* issues. Southern and northern states have submitted *Adams* plans to the courts for approval[5] and the Higher Education Act of 1965 reauthorized by Congress contains language requiring that federal programs comply with *Adams* mandates.[6]

The future of the 106 black colleges, particularly the 43 public black colleges,[7] remains uncertain, although recent events suggest a belated acknowledgement of federal responsibility for the network of historically black institutions. President Carter was aggressive in supporting these institutions. In January 1979, he signed a memorandum for a "Black College Initiative"; in August 1980 he signed Executive Order 12232, directing federal agencies to target money for black institutions; in September 1980 he signed another memorandum to accompany the Executive Order (see Appendix A).[8] A black college "setaside" has been incorporated into Title III of the Higher Education Act, while the College Housing Program targeted 10% of its 1980 monies for black college facilities.[9] Several federal departments have designated staff to monitor the Executive Order and Initiative and the charter of the National Advisory Committee on Black Higher Education and Black Colleges and Universities has been renewed.[10] These formal structures have increased black colleges' share of federal dollars and have provided visibility, portfolio, and support for the Black College Initiative.

The attention paid these institutions, however, has not led to comparable initiatives for other minority institutions. The memory of slavery and its present-day legacy, as well as the existence of a network of historically black colleges, have served to overshadow the more fledgling network of non-black minority institutions. Further, the larger societal perception of "minority" issues as synonymous with black civil rights derives from the larger black presence in the American minority population. Additionally, although the black colleges enroll a smaller percentage of black students than they have in the past when the colleges were the near-exclusive avenues of access (in 1976, the 106 colleges enrolled only 18% of the black students),[11] many black leaders have graduated from these colleges; this alumni network is widespread in black communities and constitutes an important minority constituency.

Non-black minorities lack such an extensive historical network, for the few Indians, Chicanos, and Puerto Ricans who hold college degrees are graduates of majority institutions. No similar network has developed for Indians, Chicanos, and Puerto Ricans, for reasons that are unclear. Although it is incontestable that these minorities have been denied educational access equal to that of majority citizens, the differences in the groups' histories of oppression may account, in part, for the lack of a college network comparable to that of blacks. Many black colleges have been creations of official governmental segregation policies, precluding blacks from attending white colleges. A recent National Center for Education Statistics study noted of black colleges:

> They were established primarily through the efforts of missionary groups, northern-based philanthropists, and the Freedman's Bureau. More than half . . . were created during the Reconstruction period and prior to 1890. The second Morrill Land Grant Act of 1890 spurred the construction of public [black colleges] with the intention of paralleling the network of land-grant institutions which had already been established for whites, thereby legalizing "separate colleges for whites and coloreds." The remainder . . . were constructed for the most part before the outbreak of World War I, although 10 new [black colleges] emerged in the 2 decades following World War II.[12]

No similar large-scale efforts were mounted or developed for colonized American minorities: Native Americans, the first occupants; Chicanos, *mestizo* descendants of Spaniards and Indians; or Puerto Ricans, whose island was claimed by the United States following the Spanish-American War.[13] Although extensive histories of these groups are beyond the scope of this paper, a brief summary of these histories adds context to the development of non-black minority institutions.

The Development of Indian Colleges

The historical development of higher education for Indians, Chicanos, and Puerto Ricans can be characterized as a record of evangelism, majority dominance, paternalism, and neglect. Although several prestigious colleges founded during colonial times (e.g., Harvard, Dartmouth, Columbia) had missions that included instructing Indians,[14] few Indians were educated in these institutions. Indeed, the founder of Dartmouth perhaps typified the colleges' view of educating Indians when he said of one of his students, "I have taken much Pains to purge all the Indian out of him, but after all a little of it will sometimes appear."[15]

Also typical was the abrogation of education treaties signed between the U.S. government and Indian tribes. While the government issued regulations, created special funds, and sold Indian land to finance Indian education, the most common mechanism to educate Indian children before 1870 was by treaty.[16] Of these treaties, Vine Deloria has noted,

> Treaty records and related correspondence in the nation's archives relate only to a fraction of the nearly 400 treaties negotiated from 1778 to 1871. Many agreements were oral; many records have been lost. Records that do exist show conclusively, however, that Indian nations ceded their lands to the federal government with great reluctance and that they did so in the end largely on the basis of federal promises to educate their children.[17]

Appendix B lists over 100 treaties negotiated between 1804 and 1868 that had educational provisions.

Even though the treaties were patently one-sided, the government did not meet its responsibilities. A recent congressional report noted of education treaties, "Many treaty provisions for education were never effective since Congress failed to appropriate the funds to fulfill those obligations."[18] Moreover, as treaties expired, these sources of income became even less secure. The first treaty provisions for Indian higher education appear to be in a September 1830 treaty with the Choctaw Nation,[19] although the money was not used until 1841 when Indian students were given scholarships to attend white colleges; students also attended Hampton Institute, then a black normal school, under other scholarship provisions.[20]

Sheldon Jackson College was founded for Alaskan Natives in 1878 by the United Presbyterian Church.[21] Indian University was founded by the American Baptist Church in Tahlequah, Creek Nation, in February 1880; it moved in 1885 to Muskogee (later Muskogee, Oklahoma) and became known as Bacone College.[22] In 1887, North Carolina established a normal school for Indian students; it became a college in the 1930s and offered its first degree in 1940; in 1969 it became Pembroke State University, which in 1978 still enrolled over 20% Indian students.[23] No additional efforts were undertaken to establish Indian colleges until the 1960s. What federal efforts were aimed at assisting Indians to attend college consisted of establishing normal schools (including Carlisle and Haskell high schools), providing boarding or reservation schools, arranging special contracts with mission schools or black normal schools (e.g., Hampton Institute), and funding scholarships for the few Indian college students to attend majority institutions.[24]

The hodgepodge nature of support had prompted the federal Superintendent of Indian Schools to report in 1886, "The systematic organization of the educational work of the Indian [is] an impossibility."[25] The federal efforts, meager as they were, were consolidated in the Indian Reorganization Act and Johnson-O'Malley Act of 1934, although Indian affairs continued to be spread over the Bureau of Indian Affairs (BIA) of the Department of the Interior, the Office of Education, and other public agencies and departments whose policies affected Indians. It was not until 1966 that BIA officials began to plan for a federally sponsored Indian college, when studies were begun to extend Haskell Institute's high school program into a junior college, offering the first two years of a college curriculum. This effort took four years, resulting in the accreditation of Haskell Indian Junior College in 1970. Other BIA-administered colleges include the Institute for American Indian Arts, which in 1968 became the postsecondary extension of the Santa Fe Indian School, and the Southwestern Polytechnic Institute, established in Albuquerque in 1973.[26]

In addition to state-established and BIA colleges and religious-affiliated colleges, a fourth category of Indian colleges was established in 1968, when Navajo Nation began Navajo Community College. More than a dozen tribes have since established tribal colleges with Indian community boards of trustees. This has become the most fruitful method of establishing Indian colleges. Although Navajo Community College was begun as an independent tribal institution,[27] the smaller tribes have established a fifth type of institution—affiliating themselves with larger, accredited colleges, either as branch campuses or extension centers of majority institutions.

In this manner, a public institution such as Oglala Sioux Community College evolved from its original affiliated status with Black Hills State College and the Univeristy of South Dakota into a preaccredited candidate for formal accreditation on its own. Sinte Gleska College, a private institution, has also moved from its ties to Black Hills and the University of South Dakota to similar preaccredited status.[28] The Lummi tribe has an arrangement with Whatcom Community College in Bellingham, Washington, to offer a degree in aquaculture (fishery management), with technical courses taught on Lummi Island and the certificate awarded by the mainland campus.[29] Through these creative means, Indians have begun to organize and administer tribal colleges and other Indian institutions. However, these schools' relative recency and their dependency upon majority institutions for demographic and political reasons have stifled the development of Indian colleges. Sadly, the status of many of these institutions is uncertain and the list (see Table 1) is fluid. In particular the

TABLE 1

Indian Colleges

College (State) [Affiliated Institution]	Public/ Private 2 yr/4yr	1979 Accred. Status	BIA/ Tribal Affiliation
Bacone College (OK)	Priv, 2	1	—
Blackfeet Community College (MT)	Publ, 2	4	Blackfeet
[Flathead Valley CC]			
Cheyenne River Community College (SD)	Publ, 2	4	Cheyenne River Sioux
[Northern State C]			
College of Ganado (AZ)	Priv, 2	1	Hopi
Dull Knife Memorial College (MT)	Publ, 2	4	Northern Cheyenne
[Miles C]			
Flaming Rainbow University (OK)	Priv, 2	4†	—
Fort Berthold College Center (ND)	Priv, 2	4	Mandan, Hidatsa, Arikara
[Mary C]			
Fort Peck Community College (MT)	Publ, 2	4	Assiniboine and Sioux
Haskell Indian Junior College (KS)	Publ, 2	1	BIA
Hehaka Sapa College at D-Q University (CA)	Priv, 2	1	Hoopa Valley, Soboba
Institute of American Indian Arts (NM)	Publ, 2	2	BIA
Inupiat University (AK)	Priv, 4	2	Inupiaq Eskimo
Little Bighorn Community College (MT)	Publ, 2	4	Crow
[Miles C]			
Little Hoop Community College (ND)	Publ, 2	4	Devil's Lake Sioux
[Lake Region JC]			
Lummi School of Aquaculture (WA)	Publ, 2	3	Lummi
[Whatcom CC]			
Native American Educational Services (IL)	Priv, 4	2	—
Navajo Community College (AZ)	Publ, 2	1	Navajo
Navajo Community College Branch (NM)	Publ, 2	3	
[Navajo CC]			
Nebraska Indian Community College (NE)	Publ, 2	4	Santee Sioux, Omaha,
[Northeast Technical C]			Winnebago
Nebraska Indian Satellite CC (NE)	Publ, 2	3	
[Nebraska Indian CC]			
Oglala Sioux Community College (SD)	Publ, 2	4†	Oglala Sioux
*Pembroke State University (NC)	Publ, 4	1	—
Salish-Kootenai Community College (MT)	Publ, 2	4	Salish, Kootenai
[Flathead Valley CC]			
Sheldon Jackson College (AK)	Priv, 4	1	—
Sinte Gleska College (SD)	Priv, 4	2	Rosebud Sioux
Sisseton-Wahpeton Community College (SD)	Publ, 2	4	Sisseton-Wahpeton Sioux
Southwestern Indian Polytechnic Institute (NM)	Publ, 2	1	BIA
Standing Rock Community College (ND)	Priv, 2	2	Standing Rock Sioux
Turtle Mountain Community College (ND)	Publ, 2	2	Turtle Mountain Chippewa
[North Dakota State U at Bottineau]			

Accreditation Key: (1) Accredited; (2) Preaccredited; (3) Branch or extension campus; (4) Unaccredited.
* Formerly Pembroke State College for Indians.
† Not listed in *Accredited Postsecondary Institutions* (September 1, 1979), but listed as having preaccredited status in *Education Directory* (May, 1980).

rural isolation, lack of property tax bases, and benign neglect by government have stunted the growth of Indian colleges.[30]

Historically Chicano Institutions

The development of higher education for Chicanos has had a radically different history from that for Native Americans, although the benign neglect accorded Indian education policy was similarly accorded Hispanic groups living in the Southwest and Puerto Rico once these lands became United States territory. One commentator, writing in 1914, likened Mexican American educational conditions to those of blacks:

> Just so surely as Booker T. Washington is right in saying that Tuskegee and similar institutions are the ultimate solution of the Negro problem, so surely is the same kind of education the necessary basis upon which to build a thorough and complete solution of the Mexican problem. Like the Negro, the Mexicans are a child-race without the generations of civilization and culture back of them which support the people of the United States.[31]

Not only was this commentator surely ignorant of black and Mexican history and culture, but the reference to Booker T. Washington and Tuskegee makes precisely the opposite point intended: Although many whites sought only to relegate blacks to black colleges and to prevent them from attending white institutions, blacks took the development of their own colleges seriously and developed black leadership through these institutions.[32] Chicanos, however, were not relegated to their own institutions, since racism, their economic condition, and the rural characteristics of the Southwest precluded them from completing elementary and secondary school, while no governmental or religious groups founded colleges for Mexican Americans.[33] One education historian has noted, "Mexican American children suffered not only the general inadequacies and discrimination of the rural school and caste-like community social structure but also the additional handicap of migrancy."[34]

Concerning the children of migrants in California, Irving Hendrick has summarized: "Responsibility for formal schooling of migrant children was not being assumed by any agency of local, county, or state government until after 1920."[35] Even with a California state plan for migrant education begun in 1920, local school districts ignored truancy laws and failed to serve these students.[36] Complex problems of poverty, increasing urbanization of Chicano families, immigration from Mexico, deportation of Mexican-origin Americans, segregation, and English-only instruction characterized Mexican American education and precluded the development of historically Chicano colleges.[37]

In the 1960s, increasing minority political participation led to the development of Chicano Studies programs in majority colleges, the establishment of "Third World colleges" within majority universities (e.g., Oakes College at the University of California at Santa Cruz), and the establishment of alternative Chicano postsecondary institutions: Juárez-Lincoln Center (Austin, Texas); Colegio Jacinto Treviño (Mercedes, Texas); Universidad de Aztlán (Fresno, California); Escuela y Colegio Tlatelolco (Denver, Colorado); Colegio César Chávez (Mt. Angel, Oregon); and Deganawidah-Quetzalcoatl (D-Q) University (Davis, California), begun as a Chicano-Indian college.[38] Of the alternative institutions—all established in the late 1960s and early 1970s—only Colegio César Chávez and the Indian college of D-Q University (Hehaka Sapa) remain in 1980.[39] D-Q University (see Table 1) is accredited by the Western Association of Schools and Colleges (Accrediting Commission for Community and Junior Colleges), and Colegio César Chávez has preaccredited status with the Northwest Association of Schools and Colleges (Commission on Colleges).[40] Both institutions secured their campuses through struggles with the federal government over the land: the Davis land was a federal military base, while the Colegio campus was formerly a Catholic seminary.[41]

TABLE 2

Chicano and Puerto Rican Colleges

	Accred. status	Publ.	Priv.	2 yr.	4 yr.	UG FT Enrollment 1978	UG Total 1978
Chicano							
Colegio César Chávez Mt. Angel, Oregon	2		X		X	25	25
Puerto Rican							
Boricua College New York, NY	2		X		X	455	455
Hostos Community College New York, NY	1	X		X		2506	2634

(1) Accredited; (2) Preaccreditation status

Even with the acquisition of its campus, the establishment of a research institute (Instituto Colegial César Chávez), and preaccreditation status, Colegio César Chávez has a difficult future until it increases and stabilizes its enrollment, which in 1978-79 stood at a mere 25 full-time undergraduates in the four-year institution. Its struggles to become established and to secure its campus, its focus to serve older students and migrant farmworkers, its rural isolation, and its founding in a time when few institutions are being established all have prevented the Colegio from being recognized and supported by the larger Chicano community. Today it remains virtually unknown outside the Chicano education or alternative college communities.

This is unfortunate, for the Chicano condition in higher education is not good, and, with the exception of Colegio César Chávez, Chicano students are enrolled in historically majority schools, predominantly two-year colleges. Furthermore, in mid-1981 the status of Colegio César Chávez became even more precarious when it was denied accreditation by the Northwest Association of Schools and Colleges.[42] Without a developed, historically Chicano college, Chicano students have a diminished range of institutions from which to choose, although the demographics of some previously majority schools have changed to enroll predominantly Chicano student bodies.[43] A few of these institutions (e.g., New Mexico Highlands University, East Los Angeles College, Northern New Mexico Community College) have significant Chicano administrative leadership, while others (e.g., California State University at Los Angeles or Pan American University) have never had Chicano presidents.[44] The future of Chicanos in higher education appears to be in penetrating majority institutions, convincing policymakers that minority institution programs will not reach enough Chicano students, strengthening the network of Hispanic community-based organizations to supplement the colleges,[45] and in attracting wider community support for Colegio César Chávez.

Historically Puerto Rican Colleges

Within the Hispanic communities, Puerto Ricans in the 50 states and D.C. are the most educationally disadvantaged subgroup. For instance, although the 1976 high school noncompletion rate for all Hispanic students was 25%, the figure for Puerto Ricans was 31%.[46] This appalling figure means that 3 of 10 Puerto Ricans between the ages of 14 and 30 were not in school and had not completed their high school degree. The figure for male Puerto Ricans was 35%.[47] Moreover, even the seeming progress has been illusory: "From 1950 to 1970 the median school attainment for continental Puerto Ricans advanced nearly two years. But this was due primarily to a shift from elementary school attainment to partial high school, and not to an increase in the high school completion rate, which remained proportionately the same."[48]

The colonization of Puerto Rico by the United States as a result of the Spanish-American War replaced the Island's earlier colonization by Spain; in 1899, Puerto Rico came under the jurisdiction of the U.S.[49] A series of laws since that time has not yet given autonomy to Puerto Ricans, who, since 1952, have been residents of the Commonwealth of Puerto Rico.[50] Thus, like Native Americans and Mexican Americans, Puerto Ricans share a colonial heritage. The poor condition of Puerto Rican education is, in part, the legacy of the economic exploitation of Puerto Rico, first by Spain and thereafter by the United States.

While sharing a history of colonialism with other indigenous American minority groups, the demographic and political characteristics of Puerto Ricans have resulted in a different educational history. Migration and reverse migration from the Island to the mainland and back have been major determinants of Puerto Rican educational access, including that to higher education. By 1910, Puerto Ricans in the states and D.C. numbered several thousand; by 1940, the number was approximately 70,000; by 1978, the number had grown to more than 1.8 million.[51] While most Puerto Ricans have settled in the industrial Northeast (notably New York, New Jersey, and Connecticut), large numbers of Puerto Ricans have settled in Hawaii, Florida, and California.[52]

That this massive migration occurred did not mean, however, that Puerto Ricans had increased access to mainland higher education. In 1970, for instance, New York City census data revealed that there were only 3,500 Puerto Rican college graduates in the city, an increase of only 1,000 since the 1960 census.[53] The open admissions policy of the City University of New York (CUNY), begun in 1970, substantially increased Puerto Rican enrollments, although the city's fiscal crisis has since decreased minority access.[54] In 1970, Puerto Ricans comprised 4.8% of CUNY undergraduates; by 1974 this had increased to 7.4%; Puerto Rican first-time freshmen in New York State during the same period went from 7.8% to 13.4%.[55]

It was during this time of drafting plans for an open door policy for the CUNY system that Hostos Community College was established in the South Bronx. Begun in late 1969, Hostos was the first historically Puerto Rican college to be established in the continental United States.[56] Hostos enrolls more than 2,500 students as freshmen or sophmores[57] and is accredited by the Middle States Association of Colleges and Secondary Schools, Commission on Higher Education, making it the only fully accredited Hispanic institution in the continental United States.[58]

Despite its successes, however, Hostos remains a poor relation within the CUNY system. Although it is ten years old, it has no permanent campus. Students attend classes in rooms rented in offices on the Grand Concourse in South Bronx, minutes from the spot where President Carter appeared in a "photo opportunity" to pledge his support for rebuilding the devastated slums. The fiscal crisis in New York City has prevented any construction or substantial long-term support to the college, although the students who attend are drawn from the City's poorest borough.[59] However, the college is expanding its curriculum and its status as a public institution assures a continuing base of government support.

Boricua College, the second historically Puerto Rican college, evolved from Universidad Boricua, which in turn had grown from a community group in Washington, D. C.—the Puerto Rican Research and Resources Center, Inc.[60] Boricua was established in Brooklyn in late 1973 and enrolled its first class in 1974; it opened a second facility in Manhattan in 1976.[61] A distinctive characteristic of Boricua is its network of off-campus classrooms. Its catalog boasts that "lofts, storefronts, and other easily-accessible facilities seem quite as satisfactory as ivy-covered monumental structures."[62]

Boricua's enrollment is 455 freshmen and sophmores. It has attempted to reach an extraordinarily neglected segment of the disadvantaged: older students whose situation in life prevented their having been accorded the access made available to the more traditional college-going population through CUNY's open door policies of the early 1970s. Boricua's bilingual courses and academic credits for life experiences may ameliorate to a small extent the historical exclusion of Puerto Ricans from mainland colleges.[63]

Higher education in Puerto Rico, however, has thrived. Whereas in 1940 there were only 5,000 college students on the Island, by 1970 this number had grown to 257,000.[64] By 1978, colleges in Puerto Rico enrolled one quarter of all full-time undergraduate Hispanic students in the United States and awarded over 30% of all the baccalaureate degrees.[65] [See Appendix C for selected characteristics of colleges in Puerto Rico.] In 1975, four percent (4,547) of the Puerto Rican residents enrolled in college attended school in the 50 states or D.C., while 1,300 students from the mainland enrolled in Puerto Rican colleges.[66]

Legal and Legislative Issues

As the initial sections have indicated, the survival status of Indian, Chicano, and Puerto Rican colleges is the major issue confronting these institutions. While majority institutions have serious concerns of survival in difficult economic times and while black institutions continue to face economic and legal peril, non-black minority colleges face far more serious economic futures. Their attempts at development are occurring in a time of retrenchment throughout higher education and at a time when public support of minority issues is less evident than that shown during the enactment of the 1965 Higher Education Act.[67] Moreover, several fundamental issues of a legal and legislative nature uniquely affect Indian, Chicano, and Puerto Rican colleges. Chief among these issues is identification: What is an Indian college? What is an historically Chicano or Puerto Rican college? Although these questions seem rhetorical, government programs and community support issues make the answers important. Much as black college leaders have coined new designations for institutions that serve black students but do not have "historically" or "traditionally" black missions,[68] Indian and Latino educators have insisted upon certain criteria for designation, affiliation, and program eligibility.[69]

For Indians, these criteria include a record of service to Indians or a historical Indian mission, tribal affiliation, majority Indian control or influence, a predominantly Indian student body, or a combination of these factors. Applied strictly, these criteria would include few institutions, particularly since issues of tribal identification and control fluctuate and corollary Indian legislation alters standards and even removes or restores tribal status.[70] A list of Indian institutions such as that in Table 1 necessitates as many footnotes as entries. Pembroke State University, founded for Indians, today enrolls approximately 20% Indians; in this regard, Pembroke resembles three formerly black, now predominantly white, colleges—Bluefield State College, Lincoln State University, and West Virginia State—that have been considered "traditionally black," with an asterisk.[71]

These definitional issues are not mere ethnic nitpicking, for program eligibility and political identification are important factors in minority self-determination and in educational policymaking for minority access. In the 1979 Title III (Strengthening Developing Institutions) awards, for instance, only 7 of the 25 awards to Indian Programs[72] went to the Indian colleges listed in Table 1; four of the majority institutions are affiliated with the Indian colleges in Table 1, and these arrangements had Indian participation. As Indian testimony in the Title III reauthorization noted, however, the bulk of this money designed to strengthen Indian colleges is being administered by majority institutions.[73]

More fundamental definitional issues underlie all of Indian education (indeed, all Indian affairs), and although they are beyond the scope of this article, they deserve mention to show the dilemma inherent in the need for governmental targeting of Indian programs and Indian self-definition and self-determination. Thus, for Census Bureau purposes in the 1970 questionnaire, persons identified themselves as "Indian (American)" and delineated their tribal membership and race.[74] Education eligibility for Indian programs, however, is more specific and draws upon Department of the Interior recognition and the Alaska Native Claims Settlement Act[75] for identification. In the main, these are overlapping definitions[76] incorporated into the Indian Education Act, which consist of tribal membership or enrollment, blood quantum (Indian descendancy in the first or second degree), status as an Eskimo, Aleut, or other Alaska Native, or other evidence of Indian heritage.[77] Of course, these issues have resulted in litigation, which most frequently results in inaccurate or debilitating results for Indians: confusing the Blackfeet and Sioux Blackfoot,[78] ignoring unanimous expert testimony and interpretation of treaties,[79] and deciding that the Wampanoag (Mashpees) were not a tribe and therefore had no standing in a land claim.[80]

Although it has not yet been litigated, the concept of what constitutes an Indian college is a potential conflict area, particularly if more federal programs emerge to direct assistance to minority initiatives and as more majority institutions receive federal money to serve Indian students.[81] Two examples of the ambiguity over Indian institutions or Indian eligibility will serve to illustrate the potential for conflict or confusion: What is an "Indian college" and what is an "institution of higher education"?

Recently published rules and regulations for the Indian Education Act[82] define an "Indian institution" as a "[postsecondary school] that— (1) Is established for the education of Indians; (2) Is controlled by a governing board, the majority of which is Indian; and (3) If located on an Indian reservation, operates with the sanction or by charter of the governing body of that reservation."[83] Under the terms of the Tribally Controlled Community College Assistance Act of 1978 (PL 95-471)[84] stricter definitions are drawn since only tribally controlled community colleges are targeted, except for Navajo Community College, which has its own federal legislation.[85] Any eligible institution[86] is required to be "formally controlled, or . . . formally sanctioned, or chartered, by the governing body of an Indian tribe or tribes, except that no more than one such institution shall be recognized with respect to any such tribe";[87] further, it "must be one which— (1) is governed by a board of directors or board of trustees a majority of which are Indians; (2) demonstrates adherence to stated goals, a philosophy, or a plan of operation which is directed to meet the needs of Indians; and (3) if in operation for more than a year, has students a majority of whom are Indians."[88]

While there may not need to be any clarification of these two definitions, there are curious scenarios that could occur to vitiate the purpose of either act. Taking into account the demographic characteristics of the colleges noted in Table 1, these scenarios are not far-fetched. Under the Indian Education Act, for instance, a predominantly Indian student body is not required for eligibility. It is conceivable that Indians could win election, be appointed to, or otherwise control a majority institution governing board, and by establishing an Indian mission could create an Indian institution—entitling such a non-reservation college to eligibility for a number of adult education programs under the Act.

Several colleges have altered their governance structure and have become tribal institutions. One such college is the College of Ganado, in Ganado, Arizona, on the Navajo Reservation. Previously a private college affiliated with the United Presbyterian Church,[89] the college has become a tribally controlled community college of the Hopi Tribe and is eligible for money from the Tribally Controlled Community College Assistance Act.[90] D-Q University, established as an Indian-Chicano College, is now chartered by the Hoopa Valley and Soboba tribes.[91] In both instances, institutions with predominantly Indian student enrollments reconstituted themselves and secured tribal charters. In both instances, the rural isolation and college characteristics made such transformations possible and economical.

In future cases, however, policymakers would do well to recall the distribution of resources for Indian institutional development, administered by majority institutions. While the eligibility requirements of Title III are not race-specific, many white institutions have taken Indian program initiatives in order to be eligible for Developing Institutions resources without altering their basic governance structures, which rarely include Indians.[92] Indeed, a 1976 survey of all two-year college trustees noted that fewer than .2 of 1% were Indian.[93]

A more important definitional issue than that of "Indian college" may be the definition, seemingly obvious, of "institution of higher education." The Tribally Controlled Community College Assistance Act (PL 95-471) requires that eligible colleges be "institutions of higher education" in the commonly understood and statutory meaning of the terms.[94] However, as with other provisions of law, when applied to special populations—in this case, Indian colleges—the definition becomes less obvious and may prevent the target population from being effectively served. PL 95-471 breaks down at this threshold point, for few tribally controlled community colleges can meet the definitional tests of "institutions," notably in the requirements for accreditation status. In this case, Indian colleges find themselves in a classic catch-22 situation: They are not eligible for Act money because they are not accredited, but they cannot secure accreditation without the development money and technical assistance promised in the Act.

Accreditation and Indian Colleges

The statutory definiton of "institutions of higher education" incorporates elements of post-high school admission, state authorization, degree credit, public or nonprofit status, and accreditation—all important elements for governmental and institutional quality control mechanisms. The fifth requirement, that institutions be "accredited by a nationally recognized accrediting agency or association," has become a hornets' nest as national political forces tug over accreditation authority and policy.[95] However, it is the exceptions to the accreditation requirements that have proven to be the rub for Indian colleges. The two exceptions to the accreditation requirement allow an unaccredited college to be an "institution of higher education" if it:

> (A) is an institution with respect to which the Commissioner has determined that there is satis-factory assurance, considering the resources available to the institution, the period of time, if any, during which it has operated, the effort it is making to meet accreditation standards, and the purpose for which this determination is being made, that the institution will meet the accreditation standards of such an agency or association within a reasonable time, or (B) is an institution whose credits are accepted, on transfer, by not less than three institutions which are so accredited, for credit on the same basis as if transferred from an institution so accredited . . . For purposes of this subsection, the Commissioner shall publish a list of nationally recognized accrediting agencies or associations which he determines to be reliable authority as to the quality of training offered.[96]

Anticipating that the unaccredited status of most Indian colleges would cause eligibil-ity problems, the drafters of the original Tribally Controlled Community College Act bill (which had been proposed as an amendment to the Indian Self-Determination Act)[97] had incorporated the two exceptions into the bill. The legislation that emerged, however, simply incorporated the definition language, eliminating the redundant exemption references.[98]

This final language should not have been problematic, for the two waiver provisions still enabled the Commissioner (now, since the creation of the Department of Education, the Secretary) to interpret the "satisfactory assurance" generously; no regulations have been promulgated by the new Department to guide the Secretary in this regard, but in the face of larger political battles over accreditation, the Department has not chosen to interpret the colleges' status generously. Nor, inexplicably, have the colleges employed the easily avail-able "3-letter" rule to trigger the other exemption provision. All that would be required is to enlist three accredited institutions in order to have credits accepted for transfer, but this waiver has not been widely adopted by the tribal colleges.[99]

As these issues became evident after the passage of the Tribal Act, another twist on the accreditation provisions came into play: feasibility studies. Under the terms of the Act, feasibility studies were required to "determine whether there is justification to start and main-tain a tribally controlled community college."[100] These studies, to be conducted by the Secre-tary of the Interior, were strictly interpreted by the Office of Management and Budget (OMB) and the Bureau of Indian Affairs to require accreditation or candidacy as a measure of feasibil-ity; the Bureau has added to the circularity of this requirement by noting that this criterion could be waived by the 3-letter rule—the accreditation waiver.[101] Thus, the accreditation requirement has an added requirement of feasibility, although accreditation standards are employed in determining feasibility. Indian educators have argued unsuccessfully that these dual requirements are redundant and that a recognized accreditation status should be prima facie evidence of any college's feasibility.[102]

Despite these difficulties, some of the tribal colleges have begun to receive money from the Act.[103] However, a coherent policy for administering Indian programs could have enabled these struggling institutions to receive the money earlier. The OMB has been inflexible in its review of feasibility criteria and has been unwilling to consider these colleges' characteristics as deserving special attention. Many Indian educators have blamed the BIA for its lukewarm support of the Tribal Act;[104] others blame the new Department of Education for its foot dragging.[105]

Both criticisms are accurate, for the BIA was not required to use accreditation as a feasibility criterion, and the Department of Education could have been more flexible in interpreting the colleges' progress toward accreditation. Indeed, the Department, in the absence of regulations governing eligibility, could have employed the discretion accorded it in Title III, where accreditation requirements for Developing Institutions eligibility can be waived in special circumstances where Indian and Spanish-speaking students will be served.[106] In either case, the bureaucratic delays have frustrated legislative attempts to create and enhance these Indian colleges.

The confusion over the Act has continued to mar its delivery of money to Indian colleges. An amendment to the Act was passed by the Senate on January 25, 1980, and was referred to the House Committee on Education and Labor on January 29; it was referred to the Subcommittee on Postsecondary Education, where it has remained since February 1.[107] The amendment clarifies the Indian eligibility requirement and increases the technical assistance authorization provisions.[108] Curiously, however, it further complicates the accreditation issue, for it restores portions of the redundant accreditation waiver provisions incorporated in the statutory definition of "institution of higher education," but gives the Secretary of the Interior (not the Secretary of Education) the authority to determine the reasonableness of the colleges' efforts toward accreditation.[109] This provision, if it were to be adopted, would further complicate the accreditation provisions, for a memorandum of agreement would have to be drafted between Interior and Education Departments to utilize the eligibility staff of the Department of Education, adding yet another layer of administration. A more reasonable approach would employ the Act's present language. Adopting accreditation or its waivers as evidence of feasibility for existing colleges would not require an amendment and would not require any renegotiation of the February 19, 1980, Memorandum of Agreement.[110] Clarifying the difference between accreditation and feasibility would give administrative guidance.

The Department of Interior has opposed passage of the increases in technical assistance authorizations contained in the amendments, predicting it would be too much money: "If all 21 [colleges] were to participate in $10 million worth of technical assistance funds, each college would average approximately $476,000 in [such] funds per year, an amount far in excess of that which can be utilized effectively."[111] That the Act could provide too much money for technical assistance to these institutions seems a curious claim and a false economy, for the money for technical assistance is prerequisite to any developmental activities necessary for accreditation or feasibility. It is not clear whether the fledgling colleges will be able to survive the legislation enacted and administered on their behalf.

Other Financial Issues

As is evident, these small institutions are plagued by rural isolation, lack of property tax bases, lack of experienced Indian personnel, lack of accreditation, and are subject to multiple jurisdictions not always helpful to the unique needs of Indian colleges. Even with special legislation, Navajo Community College, the first and largest tribal college, is in severe financial difficulty.[112] Further, the "band analysis" means of financing tribal institutions under the Indian Self-Determination Act, whereby tribes set aside their BIA funds for postsecondary programs, is being used by the BIA as a "debit" for money allocated to the tribal colleges under the Tribally Controlled Community College Assistance Act, in apparent disregard for the Tribal Act's prohibition against such substitutions: "Eligibility assistance under this title shall not, by itself, preclude the eligibility of any tribally controlled college to receive Federal financial assistance. . . ."[113] This shell game penalizes the colleges for negotiating the Tribal College Act process and punishes tribes who have assessed themselves for education programs. Analyses of these and other Indian education issues are beyond the scope of this article, but the issues clearly warrant study.

Summary and Conclusions

The enormous problems facing Indian, Chicano, and Puerto Rican colleges have not been addressed by legislative efforts aimed at redressing historic exclusion, nor by educational assistance designed for colleges in general. In the unique case of Indian colleges, specific legislation and program initiatives have not been effective, in part because of the fragile nature of the colleges themselves and in part because of the organizational difficulties Indian people face daily in their relationship with government agencies.

While the great majority of minority students will continue to receive their college education in majority institutions, increasing attention is necessary to ensure minority self-determination, particularly through historically minority colleges. The federal government has only recently recognized and acknowledged its considerable responsibility for assisting black colleges and has moved aggressively to rectify its own exclusionary practices in this regard. The Black College Initiative has given long-overdue notice to these institutions' role in educating Blacks. However, similar "Hispanic Initiatives" and "Indian Initiatives," proposing employment and program emphases for federal agencies, have languished.[114] American higher education, justifiably proud of its diversity, will be denied its most unique institutions if historically minority colleges are allowed to languish.

LULAC NATIONAL EDUCATIONAL
SERVICE CENTERS

Notes

[1]430 F. Supp. 118 (D.D.C. 1977).

[2]Haynes, *A Conceptual Examination of Desegregation in Higher Education* (Washington, DC: Institute for Services to Education, 1978); Fleming, *The Lengthening Shadow of Slavery* (Washington, DC: Howard University Press, 1976).

[3]Morris, *Elusive Equality* (Washington, DC: Howard Univeristy Press, 1979), p. 180.

[4]*Education Directory, Colleges and Universities, 1979-80* (Washington, DC: National Center for Educational Statistics [NCES], 1980), p. 468.

[5]Haynes, supra at note 2.

[6]Title III, Sec. 307 (2) prohibits payments "for an activity that is inconsistent with a State plan for desegregation of higher education applicable to such institution."

[7]Turner and Michaels, *Traditionally Black Institutions of Higher Education: Their Identification and Selected Characteristics* (Washington, DC: NCES, 1978).

[8]*Minority Higher Education Reports*, 1, No. 7 (15 August 1980), pp. 1-3.

[9]Title III, Sec. 347 (e). See also *House Conference Report to Accompany H.R. 5192*, p. 165. Under the Education Department's reorganization (PL 96-88), the College Housing Program has been transferred from Housing and Urban Development (HUD) to ED. Under the appropriations process (PL 96-103), 10% of the $85 million is to be reserved for black colleges. *Federal Register*, 1 August 1980, p. 51510.

[10]*Minority Higher Education Reports*, 1, No. 8 (12 September 1980), p. 5.

[11]Turner and Michaels, note 7, at p. 2.

[12]Turner and Michaels, note 7, at p. 1.

[13]Deloria, *Legislative Analysis of the Federal Role in Indian Education* (Washington, DC: Office of Indian Education, 1975); Thompson, ed., *The Schooling of Native America* (Washington, DC: American Association of Colleges for Teacher Education, 1978); Samora, ed., *La Raza: Forgotten Americans* (Notre Dame: University of Notre Dame Press, 1966); Carter and Segura, *Mexican Americans in School: A Decade of Change* (NY: College Board, 1979); *Puerto Ricans in the Continental United States: An Uncertain Future* (Washington, DC: U.S. Commission on Civil Rights, 1976).

[14]Van Amringe et al., *A History of Columbia University, 1754-1904* (NY: Columbia University Press, 1904), p. 32; Rudolph, *The American College and University, A History* (NY: Vintage, 1962).

[15]Rudolph, note 14, at p. 104.

[16]American Indian Policy Review Commission, *Report on Indian Education* (Washington, DC: GPO, 1976), pp. 61-73.

[17]Deloria, *A Brief History of the Federal Responsibility to the American Indian* (Washington, DC: GPO, 1979), p. 13.

[18]*Report on Indian Education*, note 16, at p. 66.

[19]7 Stat. 210; *Report on Indian Education*, note 16, at p. 268.

[20]*Report on Indian Education*, note 16, at pp. 268-69.

[21]*Education Directory*, note 4, at p. 9.

[22]Chavers, *The Feasibility of an Indian University at Bacone College* (Muskogee, OK: Bacone College, 1979).

[23]*Pembroke State University Catalog*, 1980-1981, pp. 15-16, 26-27.

[24]*Report on Indian Education*, note 16, at pp. 51-60. Chavers, "Indian Education: Failure for the Future," *American Indian Law Review*, 2 (1974), 61-84.

[25]Cited in *Report on Indian Education*, note 16, at p. 57.

[26]See, generally, *Report*, note 16, at pp. 273-75; *Southwestern Indian Polytechnic Institute Bulletin, 1975-1977*.

[27]Navajo Community College Assistance Act of 1978, 25 U.S.C. 640a.

[28]*Education Directory*, note 4 at p. 383; *Report*, note 16, at p. 351.

[29]*Report*, note 16, at p. 352.

[30]Table 1 could have included several more institutions, but adequate information was not available for Tanana Land Claims College, Ojibwa College, United Tribes Educational Technical Center, Gila River Community College.

[31]Cited in Carter and Segura, note 13, at p. 16.

[32]Fleming, note 2, at pp. 59-101.

[33]Pitt, *The Decline of the Californios: A Social History of the Spanish-Speaking Californians, 1846-1890* (Los Angeles: UCLA Press, 1966); Sánchez, *Forgotten People* (Albuquerque: University of New Mexico Press, 1940); Berger, "Education in Texas during the Spanish and Mexican Periods," *Southwestern Historical Quarterly*, 51, No. 1 (July 1947), pp. 41-53; Independent School District v. Salvatierra, 33 S.W. 2d. 790 (1930).

[34]Carter and Segura, note 13, at p. 16.

[35]Hendrick, "Early Schooling for Children of Migrant Farmworkers in California: The 1920's," *Aztlán*, 8 (1977), p. 14.

[36]Hendrick, note 35, at pp. 11-26.

[37]Berger, supra at note 33; Barrera, *Race and Class in the Southwest: A Theory of Inequality* (Notre Dame: University of Notre Dame Press, 1979).

[38]*Chicano Alternative Education* (Hayward, California: Southwest Network, 1974); Macías et al., *Educación Alternativa: On the Development of Chicano Bilingual Schools* (Hayward, CA: Southwest Network, 1975).

[39]*Education Directory*, note 4, at pp. 33, 341. Other Chicano schools do remain, but have chosen not to seek

accreditation or to offer collegiate courses. Schools such as Colegio de la Tierra in California and La Academia de la Nueva Raza in New Mexico have chosen to focus on community development or folklore projects.

[40]*Accredited Postsecondary Institutions and Programs* (Washington, DC: GPO, 1979), pp. 5, 42.

[41]Discussions with officials of D-Q University and Colegio César Chávez, Summer 1980.

[42]Olivas, *The Dilemma of Access* (Washington, DC: Howard University Press, 1979). With reference to the recent denial of accreditation to Colegio César Chávez, see "Coast Hispanic College Fights to Survive," *New York Times*, 15 Nov. 1981, p. 75.

[43]Olivas and Hill, "Hispanic Participation in Postsecondary Education," in *The Condition of Education for Hispanic Americans* (Washington, DC: NCES, 1980), pp. 117-215.

[44]Arce, in Smith, ed., *Advancing Equality of Opportunity: A Matter of Justice* (Washington, DC: Howard University Press, 1978), pp. 165-75.

[45]Olivas, "Hispanics in Higher Education: Federal Barriers," *Educational Evaluation and Policy Analysis* (forthcoming).

[46]*Condition of Education for Hispanic Americans*, note 43, at p. 100.

[47]Ibid.

[48]*Social Factors in Educational Attainment Among Puerto Ricans in U.S. Metropolitan Areas, 1970* (NY: Aspira, 1976), p. 2.

[49]*Puerto Ricans in the Continental United States* (Washington, DC: U.S. Commission on Civil Rights, 1976).

[50]39 Stat. 951 (1917); 64 Stat. 319 (1950); 48 U.S.C. § 731 et seq.; De Lima v. Bidwell, 182 U.S. 1 (1901).

[51]*Puerto Ricans in the Continental United States*, note 49, at Table 7, pp. 19-35; *Condition of Education*, note 43, at Table 1.01; Hernández, "La migración puertorriqueña como factor demográfico: solución y problema," *Revista Interamericana*, 4 (1975), pp. 526-34.

[52]*Condition of Education*, note 43, at Table 1.04; *Puerto Ricans in California* (Washington, DC: U.S. Commission on Civil Rights, 1980).

[53]*Puerto Ricans in the Continental United States*, note 49, at p. 119.

[54]Lavin et al., "Open Admissions and Equal Access: A Study of Ethnic Groups in the City University of New York," *Harvard Educational Review*, 49, No. 1 (February 1979), pp. 53-92; Rossman et al., *Open Admissions at the City University of New York: An Analysis of the First Year* (Englewood Cliffs, NJ: Prentice Hall, 1975).

[55]*Puerto Ricans in the Continental United States*, note 49, at Tables 35, 36.

[56]Castro, "Hostos: Report from a Ghetto College," *Harvard Educational Review*, 44, No. 2 (May 1974), pp. 270-94.

[57]*Fall Enrollment in Higher Education, 1978* (Washington, DC: NCES, 1979), p. 132.

[58]*Accredited Postsecondary Institutions*, note 40, at p. 22.

[59]When CUNY closed early in 1976, the state appropriated a special fund to the system, including $3 million for Hostos. *Puerto Ricans in the Continental United States*, note 49, at p. 119.

[60]*Boricua College Catalog*, pp. 1-2.

[61]*Catalog*, note 60, at p. 19.

[62]Ibid.

[63]*Condition of Education*, note 43, at Table 2.32.

[64]*Puerto Ricans in the Continental United States*, note 49, at Table 3.

[65]Olivas and Hill, note 43, at Tables 3.10 and 3.21.

[66]Olivas and Hill, note 43, at Tables 3.19 and 3.20.

[67]Jones, *The Changing Mood in America* (Washington, DC: Howard University Press, 1977).

[68]*Black College Primer* (Washington, DC: Institute for the Study of Educational Policy, Howard University, 1980); Turner and Michaels, note 7, at p. 1.

[69]Olivas and Hill, note 43, at pp. 118-19; Olivas, "Hispanics in Higher Education," supra at note 45; Nichols, "Testimony in Hearings on Title III of the Higher Education Act," 29 March 1979; Middleton, "Indian Tribal Colleges Accuse U.S. Bureaucrats of Delaying $85 Million Congress Authorized," *Chronicle of Higher Education*, 11 February 1980, pp. 1, 12; Chavers, supra at note 22.

[70]Deloria, "Legislation and Litigation Concerning American Indians," *Annals of the American Academy of Political and Social Science*, Vol. 436 (March 1978), pp. 86-96.

[71]Turner and Michaels, note 7, at p. 2. Another classification problem occurs when institutions mislabel their students. Alice Lloyd College reported its racial data for 1976 as if its enrollment were 90.1% American Indian, although its population is predominantly Appalachian whites (Olivas, note 42, at p. 196). Conversations with school officials, however, revealed that they considered their students "minorities," apparently "Native" Americans.

[72]See Appendix D.

[73]Nichols, note 69; Bad Wound, Testimony before Select Committee on Indian Affairs, U.S. Senate, 10 June 1980.

[74]*American Indians, 1970 Census of Population* (Washington, DC: GPO, 1973), p. ix. For a discussion of minority census issues, including undercounts, see *Conference on Census Undercounts* (Washington, DC: GPO, 1980).

[75]85 Stat. 688.

[76]The recently revised Indian Education Act regulations, for instance, drew several comments and incorporated several changes to clarify Indian eligibility. See, for example, *Federal Register*, 21 May 1980, pp. 34180-34181, 34184-34185.

[77]Indian Education Act, Sec. 453(a); 20 U.S.C. 1221 (h) (a). See, generally, Yinger and Simpson, "The Integration of Americans of Indian Descent", *Annals of the American Academy of Political and Social Science*, Vol. 436 (March 1978), pp. 137-51.

[78]United States *ex rel.* Rollingson v. Blackfeet Tribal Court, 244 F. Supp. 474 (D. Mont. 1965).

[79]United States v. Consolidated Wounded Knee Case, 389 F. Supp. 235 (D. Neb. and W.D.S.D. 1975).

[80]Mashpee Tribe v. New Seabury Corp., 427 F. Supp. 899, *aff'd*, 592 F. 2d 575 (lst Cir. 1979). For a sample of legislative attempts to extinguish Indian claims, see S.J. Res. 86, 95th Cong. 1st Session, 123 *Congressional Record* (1977), p. 16232, concerning Mashpee claims in Massachusetts. See Newton, "At the Whim of the Sovereign: Aboriginal Title Reconsidered," *Hastings Law Journal* 31, No. 6 (1980), pp. 1215-85. See, generally, Brodeur, "The Mashpees," *New Yorker*, 6 November 1978, pp. 62-150; Deloria, "Indian Law and the Reach of History," *Journal of Contemporary Law*, 4 (1977), pp. 1-13.

[81]Although it is beyond the scope of this study, there is a small network of minority institution programs scattered throughout the federal government; many of these are being mobilized by the Executive Order on Black Colleges. They include, for example, the Minority Access into Research Careers (National Institutes of Health), Minority Institution Science Improvement Program (Department of Education, relocated from the National Science Foundation), and the Minority Institutions Research Support Program (Environmental Protection Agency).

[82]86 Stat. 334 (as amended); the regulations will be recodified under 34 C.F.R., replacing the 45 C.F.R. regulations. See *Federal Register*, 21 May 1980, p. 34153.

[83]20 U.S.C. 241 (a) (a).

[84]25 U.S.C. 1801.

[85]Navajo Community College Assistance Act of 1978, 25 U.S.C. 640 (a); Amendments to the Navajo Community College Act [sic], Education Amendments of 1980, Title XIV, Part F, Sec. 1451.

[86]Although the institutions are community colleges, they need not be sub-baccalaureate. Higher Education Act of 1965, Title XII, Sec. 1201 (a) (3).

[87]25 U.S.C. 1801.

[88]25 U.S.C. 1804.

[89]Locke, *A Survey of College and University Programs for American Indians* (Boulder, CO: WICHE, 1978), p. 24.

[90]See Table 1.

[91]Supra, at note 38. See also Table 1.

[92]See Appendix D for the distribution of Title III awards in 1979-1980 to Indian programs; Appendix E is the awards to Hispanic programs.

[93]Grafe, *The Trustee Profile of 1976* (Washington, DC: Association of Community College Trustees, 1976), pp. 4-5. See Olivas; note 42, at pp. 86-90.

[94]25 U.S.C. 1801; 20 U.S.C. 1141.

[95]Higher Education Act of 1965, Title XII, Sec. 1201 (a) (5); 20 U.S.C. 1141. See, generally, Orlans et al., *Private Accreditation and Public Eligibility* (Washington, DC: National Academy of Public Administration, 1974); *Approaches to State Licensing of Private Degree-Granting Institutions* (Washington, DC: Institute for Educational Leadership, 1975); Kaplin, *The Law of Higher Education* (San Francisco: Jossey-Bass, 1978), pp. 439-59; Finkin, "Federal Reliance and Voluntary Accreditation: The Power to Recognize as The Power to Regulate," *Journal of Law and Education*, 2, No. 3 (July 1973), pp. 339-76.

[96]Higher Education Act of 1965, Title XII, Sec. 1201 (a) (5); 20 U.S.C. 1141.

[97]S. 1215, 95th Congress, 1st Session (1 April 1977). See Senate Report 95-582, *Hearing before the United States Senate Select Committee on Indian Affairs* (28 July 1977).

[98]25 U.S.C. 1801. In the Act, the requirement that "institutions" be "legally authorized within such State"

(Higher Education Act of 1965, Title XII, Sec. 1201 (a) (2); 20 U.S.C. 1141) was deleted, recognizing that tribes were independent governmental bodies.

[99]Discussions with BIA and Indian college officials suggested that the 3-letter rule had a stigma and that senior institutions were reluctant to recognize the rule for fear it would jeopardize their own status. This subject deserves further scrutiny.

[100]25 U.S.C. 1806. Section 105 of the Act requires an agreement between the Departments of Interior and Education (then the Office of Education, HEW); this memorandum of agreement was signed on 19 February 1980. The feasibility study form is 73 pages long, not including its required appendices.

[101]25 C.F.R. 32b. See *Federal Register*, 21 November 1979, pp. 67040-67048. In testimony on implementation of the Act, Earl Barlow, BIA Director of Indian Education Programs, said: "One of the criteria for feasibility is that it be an accredited institution or a candidate for accreditation, or its credits must be accepted by three accredited institutions. Each of the 10 schools that have been deemed feasible has either been accredited or has been approved as a candidate for accreditation. . . . Our idea was that [technical assistance] funds would be used to assist colleges that were having some problems with either accreditation or candidacy, but the ruling was made that in order to be eligible for technical assistance grants the institution has to be feasible. It put us in a predicament. The schools that really need technical assistance are not feasible and therefore cannot get technical assistance. That is a major problem." *Hearing Before the Select Committee on Indian Affairs* (10 June 1980), Committee draft, p. 9. See also, *Guidelines for the Tribally Controlled Community Colleges.*

[102]Testimony of Leroy Clifford, American Indian Higher Education Consortium, note 101, at Committee draft, p. 17.

[103]Blackfeet Community College had received its 1979-80 check the week before the June 10, 1980, Senate hearing.

[104]Middleton, note 69, at pp. 1, 12.

[105]*Hearing*, note 101, at Committee draft, pp. 11-34; *Higher Education Daily*, 12 June 1980, pp. 5-6.

[106]Higher Education Act, Title III, Sec. 302 (a) (2). The newly reauthorized Education Amendments of 1980 have widened the waivers to include rural people, low-income individuals, and black students. Title III, Part D, Sec. 342 (b) (1-5); *Conference Report* No. 96-1251, p. 164.

[107]Senate Calendar, 24 September 1980, p. 199 [S. 1855].

[108]S. 1855, 96th Congress, 1st Session. *Senate Report*, No. 96-538, p. 6.

[109]*Senate Report*, note 108, at pp. 2-3. Congressional staffers have suggested that this reassignment was in anticipation of Higher Education Act reauthorization changes in Sec. 1201. These changes were not made in the final version of 1201.

[110]25 U.S.C. 1808; supra, note 100.

[111]Letter from Forrest Gerard, Assistant Secretary, Department of the Interior, to Senator John Melcher, 21 November 1979. *Senate Report*, note 108, at pp. 4-5.

[112]*Hearing*, note 101, at Committee draft, p. 25. The Education Amendments of 1980 include special provisions for Navajo Community College, Title XIV, Part F, Sec. 1451; *Conference Report*, note 106, at p. 209.

[113]25 U.S.C. 189; 20 U.S.C. 1001 *et seq.*

[114]Olivas, supra, note 45. Whereas the Black College Initiative was a Presidential Executive Order, the Hispanic and Indian Initiatives were Secretarial. Additionally, the tribal college reporting requirements of PL 95-471 have not been met by either the Department of the Interior or by NCES, despite their responsibility for an annual report to Congress [Sec. 107 (c) (2); 25 U.S.C. 1808].

Appendix A

Executive Order
Historically Black Colleges and Universities

By the authority vested in me as President by the Constitution of the United States of America, and in order to overcome the effects of discriminatory treatment and to strengthen and expand the capacity of historically Black colleges and universities to provide quality education, it is hereby ordered as follows:

1-101. The Secretary of Education shall implement a Federal initiative designed to achieve a significant increase in the participation by historically Black colleges and universities in Federally sponsored programs. This initiative shall seek to identify, reduce, and eliminate barriers which may have unfairly resulted in reduced participation in, and reduced benefits from, Federally sponsored programs.

1-102. The Secretary of Education shall, in consultation with the Director of the Office of Management and Budget and the heads of the other Executive agencies, establish annual goals for each agency. The purpose of these goals shall be to increase the ability of historically Black colleges and universities to participate in Federally sponsored programs.

1-103. Executive agencies shall review their programs to determine the extent to which historically Black colleges and universities are unfairly precluded from participation in Federally sponsored programs.

1-104. Executive agencies shall identify the statutory authorities under which they can provide relief from specific inequities and disadvantages identified and documented in the agency programs.

1-105. Each Executive agency shall review its current programs and practices and initiate new efforts to increase the participation of historically Black colleges and universities in the programs of the agency. Particular attention should be given to identifying and eliminating unintended regulatory barriers. Procedural barriers, including those which result in such colleges and universities not receiving notice of the availability of Federally sponsored programs, should also be eliminated.

1-106. The head of each Executive agency shall designate an immediate subordinate who will be responsible for implementing the agency responsibilities set forth in this Order. In each Executive agency there shall be an agency liaison to the Secretary of Education for implementing this Order.

1-107. (a) The Secretary of Education shall ensure that an immediate subordinate is responsible for implementing the provisions of this Order.

(b) The Secretary shall ensure that each President of a historically Black college or university is given the opportunity to comment on the implementation of the initiative established by this Order.

1-108. The Secretary of Education shall submit an annual report to the President. The report shall include the levels of participation by historically Black colleges and universities in the programs of each Executive agency. The report will also include any appropriate recommendations for improving the Federal response directed by this Order.

Source: *Minority Higher Education Reports* (15 August 1980), p. 9.

Appendix B

Treaties Dealing With
Indian Education

Treaty of August 18, 1804, with Delaware Tribe, 7 Stat. 81; treaty of August 29, 1821, with Ottawa, Chippewa, and Pottawatamie, 7 Stat. 218; treaty of February 12, 1825, with Creek Nation, 7 Stat. 237; treaty of February 8, 1831, with the Menominee Indians, 7 Stat. 342; treaty of September 21, 1833, with the Otoes and Missourias, 7 Stat. 429; treaty of March 2, 1836, with the Ottawa and Chippewa, 7 Stat. 491; treaty of September 17, 1836, with the Sacs and Foxes, etc., 7 Stat. 511; treaty of October 15, 1836, with the Otoes, etc., 7 Stat. 524; treaty of January 4, 1845, with the Creeks and Seminoles, 9 Stat. 821, 822; treaty of October 13, 1846, with the Winnebago Indians, 9 Stat. 878; treaty of August 2, 1847, with the Chippewas, 9 Stat. 904; treaty of October 18, 1848, with the Menominee Tribe, 9 Stat. 952; treaty of July 23, 1851, with the Sioux, 10 Stat. 949; treaty of August 5, 1851, with the Sioux Indians, 10 Stat. 954; treaty of May 12, 1854, with the Menominee, 10 Stat. 1064; treaty of December 26, 1854, with the Nisqually, etc., Indians, 10 Stat. 1132; treaty of October 17, 1855, with the Blackfoot Indians, 11 Stat. 657; treaty of September 24, 1857, with the Pawnees, 11 Stat. 729; treaty of January 22, 1855, with The Dwamish, etc., 12 Stat. 927; treaty of January 26, 1855, with the S'Klallams, 12 Stat. 933; treaty of January 31, 1855, with Makah Tribe, 12 Stat. 939; treaty of July 1, 1855, with the Qui-nai-elt, etc., Indians, 12 Stat. 971; treaty of July 16, 1855, with the Flathead, etc., Indians, 12 Stat. 975; treaty of December 21, 1855, with the Molels, 12 Stat. 981; treaty of October 18, 1864, with the Chippewa Indians, 14 Stat. 657; treaty of June 14, 1866, with the Creek Nation, 14 Stat. 785; treaty of February 18, 1867, with the Sac and Fox Indians, 15 Stat. 495; treaty of February 19, 1867, with the Sissiton, etc., Sioux, 15 Stat. 505.

Treaty of May 6, 1828, with the Cherokee Nation, 7 Stat; treaty of New Echota, December 29, 1835, with the Cherokee, 7 Stat. 748 (provides for common schools and "*a literacy institution of a higher order***"); treaty of June 5 and 17, 1846, with the Pottowautomie Nation, 9 Stat. 853; treaty of September 30, 1854, with the Chippewa Indians, 10 Stat. 1109; treaty of November 18, 1854, with the Chastas, etc., Indians, 10 Stat. 1122; treaty of April 19, 1858, with the Yancton Sioux, 11 Stat. 743; treaty of June 9, 1855, with the Walla-Wallas, etc., tribes, 12 Stat. 945; treaty of June 11, 1855, with the Nez Perce, 12 Stat. 957; treaty of March 12, 1858, with the Poncas, 12 Stat. 997; treaty of October 14, 1865, with the Lower Brule Sioux, 14 Stat. 699; treaty of February 23, 1867, with the Senecas, etc., 15 Stat. 513; treaty of October 21, 1867, with the Kiowa and Comanche Indians, 15 Stat. 581; treaty of October 21, 1867, with the Kiowa, Comanche, and Apache Indians, 15 Stat. 589; treaty of October 28, 1867, with the Cheyenne and Arapahoe Indians, 15 Stat. 593; treaty of March 2, 1868, with the Ute Indians, 15 Stat. 619; treaty of April 29 et seq., 1868, with the Sioux Nation, 15 Stat. 635; treaty of May 7, 1868, with the Crow Indians, 15 Stat. 649; treaty of May 10, 1868, with the Northern Cheyenne and Northern Arapahoe Indians, 15 Stat. 655; treaty of June 1, 1868, with the Navajo Tribe, 15 Stat. 667; treaty of July 3, 1868, with the Eastern Band Shoshones and Bannock Tribe of Indians, 15 Stat. 673.

Treaty of November 15, 1827, with the Creek Nation, 7 Stat. 307; treaty of September 15, 1832, with the Winnebago Nation, 7 Stat. 370; treaty of May 24, 1834, with the Chickasaw Indians, 7 Stat. 450; treaty of June 9, 1863, with the Nez Perce Tribe, 14 Stat. 647; treaty of March 19, 1867, with the Chippewa of Mississippi, 16 Stat. 719.

Treaty of October 18, 1820, with the Choctaw Nation, 7 Stat. 210; treaty of June 3, 1825, with the Kansas Nation, 7 Stat. 244; treaty of August 5, 1926, with the Chippewa Tribe, 7 Stat. 290; treaty of October 21, 1837, with the Sac and Fox Indians, 7 Stat. 543; treaty of March 17, 1842, with the Wyandott Nation, 11 Stat. 581; treaty of May 15, 1846, with the Comanche, etc., Indians, 9 Stat. 844; treaty of June 5, 1854, with the Miami Indians, 10 Stat. 1093; treaty of November 15, 1854, with the Rogue Rivers, 10 Stat. 1119; treaty of November 29, 1854, with the Umpqua, etc., Indians, 10 Stat. 1125; treaty of July 31, 1855, with the Ottowas and Chippewas, 11 Stat. 621; treaty of February 5, 1856, with the Stockbridge and Munsee Tribes, 11 Stat. 663; treaty of June 9, 1855, with the Yakima Indians, 12 Stat. 951; treaty of June 25, 1855, with the Oregon Indians, 12 Stat. 963; treaty of June 19, 1858, with the Sioux bands, 12 Stat. 1031; treaty of July 16, 1859, with the Chippewa bands, 12 Stat. 1105; treaty of February 18, 1861, with the Arapahoes and Cheyenne Indians, 12 Stat. 1163; treaty of March 6, 1861, with the Sacs, Foxes and Iowas, 12 Stat. 1171; treaty of June 24, 1862, with the Ottawa Indians, 12 Stat. 1237; treaty of May 7, 1864, with the Chippewas, 13 Stat. 693; treaty of August 12, 1865, with the Snake Indians, 14 Stat. 683; treaty of March 21, 1866, with the Seminole Indians, 14 Stat. 755; treaty of April 28, 1866, with the Choctaw and Chickasaw Nation, 14 Stat. 769; treaty of August 13, 1868, with the Nez Perce Tribe, 15 Stat. 693.

Treaty of October 16, 1826, with the Potawatomie Tribe, 7 Stat. 295; treaty of September 20, 1828, Potawatamie Indians, 7 Stat. 317; treaty of July 15, 1830, with the Sacs and Foxes, etc., 7 Stat. 328; treaty of September 27, 1830, with the Choctaw Nation, 7 Stat. 333; treaty of March 24, 1832, with the Creek Tribe, 7 Stat. 366; treaty of February 14, 1833, with the Creek Nation, 7 Stat. 417; treaty of January 14, 1846, with the Kansas Indians, 9 Stat. 842; treaty of April 1, 1850, with the Wyandot Tribe, 9 Stat. 987; treaty of March 15, 1854, with the Delaware Tribe, 10 Stat. 1048; treaty of May 10, 1854, with the Shawnees, 10 Stat. 1053; treaty of May 17, 1854, with the Ioway Tribe, 10 Stat. 1165; treaty of June 22, 1855, with the Choctaw and Chickasaw Indians, 11 Stat. 611; treaty of August 2, 1855, with Williamette Bands, 10 Stat. 1143; treaty of February 22, 1855, with the Chippewa Indians of Mississippi, 10 Stat. 1165; treaty of June 22, 1855, with the Choctaw and Chicasaw Indians, 11 Stat. 611; treaty of August 2, 1855, with the Chippewa Indians of Saginaw, 11 Stat. 633; treaty of August 7, 1856, with the Creeks and Seminoles, 11 Stat. 699; treaty of June 28, 1862, with the Kickapoo Tribe, 13 Stat. 623; treaty of October 2, 1863, with the Chippewa Indians (Red Lake and Pembina Bands), 13 Stat. 667; treaty of September 29, 1865, with the Osage Indians, 14 Stat. 687.

Source: Thompson, ed., *The Schooling of Native America* (Washington, DC: American Association of Colleges for Teacher Education, 1978), pp. 183-85.

Appendix C

Selected Characteristics of Institutions of Higher Education
in Puerto Rico: Fall 1978

Institution	Control		Level		Hispanic[1]
	Public	Private	2-year	4-year	enrollment
Total	10	24	16	18	123,329
American College of Puerto Rico		X	X		1,141
Antillian College		X		X	749
Bayamón Central University		X		X	2,911
Caguas City College		X	X		651
Caribbean Center for Adv. Studies		X		X	0
Caribbean University College		X		X	1,204
Catholic University of P.R.		X		X	11,380
Conservatory of Music of P.R.	X			X	249
Electronic Data Processing College	X		X		1,226
Fundación Educativa Ana E. Méndez/					
Colegio Universitario del Turabo		X		X	5,401
Puerto Rico Junior College		X	X		7,686
Instituto Comercial de P.R. Jr. College		X	X		1,800
Instituto Técnico Comercial Jr. College		X	X		1,256
Inter American University of P.R./					
Hato Rey Campus		X		X	8,067
San Germán Campus		X		X	6,337
7 branches[2]		X	X		13,038
Ramírez College of Business & Tech.		X	X		609
San Juan Tech. Community College	X		X		919
Universidad Politécnica de P.R.		X		X	143
Universidad de Ponce	X			X	347
University of Puerto Rico/					
Río Piedras Campus	X			X	23,535
Mayaguez Campus	X			X	8,871
Medical Sciences Campus	X			X	2,583
Cayey University College	X			X	2,601
Humacao University College	X			X	3,282
Regional Colleges Administration	X		X		7,016
University of the Sacred Heart		X		X	5,929
World University		X		X	4,398

---

[1]Hispanics comprised between 95 and 100 percent of total enrollment in virtually all institutions in Puerto Rico.
[2]All branches could not be listed due to space limitations.
Source: Olivas and Hill, "Hispanic Participation in Postsecondary Education," *The Condition of Education for Hispanic Americans* (Washington, DC: NCES, 1980), Table 3.17.

Appendix D

Indian Programs Funded in FY-1979

Strengthening Developing Institutions
Title III, HEA of 1965

Institution & State	Control	Amount	Project Duration	Total Multi-year Award
Alaska Pacific University, AK	4 Pvt	$150,000	1	
Bacone College, OK	2 Pvt	190,000	2	$379,000
Baker University, KS	4 Pvt	187,000	1	
Black Hills State College, SD	4 Pub	515,000	1	
Bismarck Junior College, ND	2 Pub	312,000	1	
College of Ganado, AZ	2 Pvt	315,000	2	630,000
Connors State College, OK	2 Pub	192,630	4	770,520
Flaming Rainbow University, OK	4 Pvt	75,000	1	
Flathead Valley Community College, MT	2 Pub	352,000	1	
Fort Lewis College, CO	4 Pub	144,000	1	
Huron College, SD	4 Pvt	595,000	3	595,000
Lake Region Junior College, ND	2 Pub	140,000	1	
Mary College, ND	4 Pvt	600,000	1	
Mount Senario College, WI	4 Pvt	200,000	1	
Murray State College, OK	2 Pub	100,000	1	
Navajo Community College, AZ—Consortium	2 Pub	547,000	1	
Navajo Community College, AZ—Adv. Funding	2 Pub	50,000		
Navajo Community College, AZ—Bilateral	2 Pub	147,000	1	
Northern State College, SD—Consortium	4 Pub	380,000	1	
Northland College, WI	4 Pvt	689,000	3	689,000
Pembroke State University, NC	4 Pub	800,000	4	800,000
San Juan College, NM	2 Pub	193,000	2	386,000
Seminole Junior College, OK	2 Pub	92,000	1	
Sheldon Jackson College, AK	2 Pvt	185,000	1	
Southwestern Technical Institute, NC	2 Pub	170,000	1	
Turtle Mountain Community College, ND	2 Pvt	200,000	1	
Yavapai College, AZ	2 Pub	435,000	3	1,306,000
FY-1979 Total Awards to Indian Programs		$7,955,630		
25 Institutions Funded				

Source: Department of Education, Office for Postsecondary Education.

Appendix E

Hispanic Programs Funded in FY-1979

Strengthening Developing Institutions
Title III, HEA of 1965

Institution & State	Control	Amount	Project Duration	Total Multi-year Award
Arizona Western, AZ	2 Pub	$320,000	2	$640,000
Bayamón Central University, PR	4 Pvt	351,000	1	
Bee County College, TX	2 Pub	100,000	1	
Biscayne College, FL	4 Pvt	200,000	1	
Boricua College, NY	2 Pvt	310,000	1	
Bronx Community College, NY	2 Pub	175,000	1	
Catholic University of Puerto Rico, PR	4 Pvt	220,000	1	
Cayey University College, PR	4 Pub	200,000	1	
Central Arizona College, AZ	2 Pub	209,000	2	417,000
Colegio César Chávez, OR	4 Pvt	216,000	2	216,000
Colegio Univ. del Turabo, PR	4 Pvt	595,547	3	595,547
College of Santa Fe, NM	4 Pvt	450,000	3	450,000
Eastern Arizona College, AZ	2 Pub	125,000	1	
Eastern New Mexico University—Portales	4 Pub	1,067,000	3	1,067,000
El Paso Community College, TX—Consortium	2 Pub	276,000	1	
Fresno City College, CA	2 Pub	95,000	1	
Humacao University College, PR	4 Pub	200,000	1	
Imperial Valley College, CA	2 Pub	227,000	2	454,000
Incarnate Word College, TX	4 Pvt	900,000	3	900,000
Inter American Univ., San Juan, PR	4 Pvt	465,500	2	465,500
LaGuardia Community College, NY	2 Pub	175,000	2	350,000
Laredo Junior College, TX	2 Pub	289,000	3	866,000
Miami-Dade Community College, FL	2 Pub	300,000	3	900,000
New Mexico Highlands University, NM	4 Pub	755,000	3	755,000
Oxnard College, CA	2 Pub	69,766	1	
Puerto Rico Junior College, PR	2 Pvt	130,000	2	260,000
Saint Philips College, TX	2 Pub	97,983	2	195,966
San Juan Tech. Community College, PR	2 Pub	175,000	1	
Southwestern College, CA	2 Pub	100,000	1	
Texas Southmost College, TX	2 Pub	200,000	2	400,000
Trinidad State Junior College, CO	2 Pub	140,000	2	280,000
University of Albuquerque, NM	4 Pvt	275,000	1	
University of the Sacred Heart, PR	4 Pvt	222,000	1	
Western New Mexico University, NM	4 Pub	390,000	2	390,000
World University, PR	4 Pvt	232,000	1	
FY-1979 Total Awards to Hispanic Programs		$10,252,796		
35 Institutions Funded				

Source: Department of Education, Office for Postsecondary Education.

THE LEGAL EDUCATION OF CHICANO STUDENTS: A STUDY IN MUTUAL ACCOMMODATION AND CULTURAL CONFLICT

LEO M. ROMERO*, RICHARD DELGADO**, and CRUZ REYNOSO***

INTRODUCTION

Before the advent of minority programs, the world of law schools, law students, and law teachers was in a state of relatively stable, if uneasy, equilibrium.[1] Several well-qualified applicants vied for each place in an entering class.[2] Once admitted, students were expected to apply themselves diligently to the study of the standard subjects of the legal curriculum and to respond with intelligent versions of the conventional answers when called upon to recite in class.[3] Those

*Associate Professor of Law, University of New Mexico.
**Assistant Professor of Law; Program in Law, Science and Medicine, Yale Law School.
***Professor of Law, University of New Mexico.

1. For example, the Presidential Address delivered at the General Meeting of the Association of American Law schools, in Chicago, Illinois, on December 28, 1965 (Miller, *Law Schools in the Great Society*, 18 J. Legal Ed. 247 (1965)) declared:

> Many people have tried to assess the implication of the student riots. . . . As far as I know, nothing like them has occurred in law schools. . . . I do not detect any kind of political unrest among our law students. . . . In most of our schools the classroom relations between students and faculty are good. Perhaps our students recognize also that there are overriding professional interests outside the school.

Id. at 253. The address centered around such problems as the high cost of legal education, *id.* at 248, faculty teaching load, *id.* at 252, and faculty salaries and the cost of living, *id.* at 254. The speaker observed that "[t]he principal areas of faculty interest in law school government are curriculum and faculty personnel. On a lesser level is admissions." *Id.* at 255.

The speech concludes:

> Fortunately for us our problems exist within a narrow compass. We can patch up, and we can do a lot as individuals. . . . The times have been good to us. Many recruits are coming to us as law students and teachers. Other men in the profession are seeking our guidance. A law teacher can build a good life for himself. . . . Legal education never had it so good. Let us not spoil it.

Id. at 256.

2. *See, e.g.,* Hughes, McKay, & Winograd, *The Disadvantaged Student and Preparation for Legal Education: The NYU Experience*, 1970 U. Tol. L. Rev. 701, 708; *compare* the growth in law school enrollment figure cited in Hervey, *Law School Registration, 1964*, 17 J. Legal Ed. 209 (1964) *with* Hervey, *Law School Registration, 1966* 19 J. Legal Ed. 200 (1966). In recent years, of course, the press of applicants has even increased, and top schools may receive ten or even twenty applicants for each available slot. *E.g.,* Ass'n of Am. L. Schools & L. School Admission Council, Prelaw Handbook: Official Law School Guide, 1973-1974, 17-18 (1973). As early as 1967, the press of applicants was increasing greatly, *see* Miller, *Personality Differences and Student Survival in Law Schools*, 19 J. Legal Ed. 460, 460 (1967); but the rate of attrition was still high. *Id.*

3. *E.g.,* Gellhorn, *The Second and Third Years of Law Study*, 17 J. Legal Ed. 1, 1-2

who could not, or would not, conform to their prescribed roles dropped out, flunked out, or were encouraged to think about alternative careers.[4] The rate of change and innovation was slow and orderly. Little, if any, radical restructuring of the legal curriculum had been made since Langdell had introduced the case method a century earlier.[5]

The rate of change began to quicken in the mid-1960's. The national political drama of blacks in the South who, during the civil rights movement of the 1960's, could find few local black lawyers to represent them against physical and economic abuse focused attention on the failure of law schools to educate sufficient numbers of minority attorneys. The fruitless initial efforts of the federally funded legal services programs to find Chicano, Puerto Rican, and other minority lawyers increased the sense of anger and frustration in these communities. Identifiable minority groups, such as Chicanos, demanded lawyers belonging to their groups to whom they could turn in their struggles for equal justice and equal economic opportunity.[6] The failure of law schools to train minority lawyers thus gained national attention.[7] This concern served as a catalyst for reform movements that had been slowly building,[8] and in the space of a few years, law schools were experimenting with flexible admissions standards, summer programs, and new courses tailored to the special needs and interests of minority students.

By 1973, however, only seven percent of the total law school enrollment of 106,102 consisted of minority students. Chicanos numbered 1,259 or approximately one percent.[9] Minority communities have seen these low percentages as a token beginning. at best.

(1964). For a brief description of legal education stressing its traditional nature and links with the past, see K. Redden, So You Want to Become a Lawyer 79-82 (1951).

4. E.g., Bell, *Black Students in White Law Schools: The Ordeal and the Opportunity*, 1970 Tol. L. Rev. 539, points out that:
> [A]t some of the most highly regarded law schools the number of applicants exceed the number of admissions by so substantial a margin that the quality of students accepted is so high many of them could learn the law if the school merely provided them with the books.

Id. at 555. But such an approach to education would be inappropriate for minority students, Bell suggests, *id.* at 554-55, and should not be used as "an excuse for reluctantly admitting . . . students in September and then ruthlessly flunking them out the following May. . . ." *Id.* at 555.

5. E.g., Gellhorn, *supra* note 3, at 1-2. Langdell's theory of the "case" method is set out in C. Langdell, A Selection of Cases on the Law of Contracts vii (2d ed. 1879).

6. See note 44 *infra.*

7. O'Neil, *Preferential Admissions: Equalizing Access to Legal Education,* 1970 U. Tol. L. Rev. 281, 300.

8. *Id.* at 333-34.

9. Rudd & White, *Legal Education and Professional Statistics 1973-74,* 26 J. Legal Ed. 342-43 (1974).

But in the last year or two the very programs which have permitted a modest degree of progress in minority enrollment figures have come under sharp attack.[10] Already, the rate of increase of minorities enrolling in law schools is slowing.[11]

This seems an appropriate time, therefore, to review and reflect upon the effect such programs have had on minority legal education. This Article focuses on students from one ethnic group—Chicanos or Mexican-Americans—and of the impact this group has had on schools of law. After a brief review of the development of special admissions programs, the Article examines the Chicano law student, his background, and his adaptation to law school. The article will conclude with the responses law schools have made to Chicano and other minority students, ranging from curricular changes to the adoption of special educational programs. Throughout this article, the focus will be on the need for mutual accommodation if law schools are to succeed in training Chicano lawyers.

ADMISSIONS

Most faculties cannot agree whether law schools, as institutions, have an obligation to train Chicano and other minority lawyers.[12] Nevertheless, while that basic question has gone unresolved, most law schools have voluntarily chosen to implement changes which have permitted increased minority enrollment.[13] In this section we examine those changes and review their impact.

A. Recruitment

By the late 1960's, virtually all vestiges of overt discrimination in the law school admissions process had been removed.[14] The admis-

10. *See, e.g.,* the legal challenge to the University of Washington School of Law's minority admissions program in DeFunis v. Odegaard, 82 Wash.2d 11, 507 P.2d 1169 (1973), *vacated and remanded,* 416 U.S. 312 (1974); *Symposium: Defunis: The Road Not Taken,* 60 Va. L. Rev. 917-1012 (1974); Comment, *But Some Animals Are More Equal Than Others: A Look at the Equal Protection Argument Against Minority Preferences,* 12 Duq. L. Rev. 580 (1974); Ely, *The Constitutionality of Reverse Racial Discrimination,* 41 U. Chi. L. Rev. 723 (1974); Symposium, 3 Black L.J. 222-278 (1973); Totenberg, *Discrminating to End Discrimination,* N.Y. Times, Apr. 14, 1974 (magazine), at 8; Address by William R. Anderson, Law School Admission Council Annual Meeting, June 6, 1974; H. Breland, *DeFunis Revisited: A Psychometric View* (Educ. Testing Serv. Mimeo 1974).

11. Am. Ass'n of Law Schools (AALS) Section on Minority Groups Newsletter, Number 74-1, May, 1974, at 4.

12. *See generally, Symposium: Disadvantaged Students and Legal Education—Programs for Affirmative Action,* 1970 Tol. L. Rev. 277-986. *Cf.* n. 56, *infra.*

13. *See, e.g.,* Reiss, *The Minority Student Program at the University of Southern California Law Center,* 44 S. Cal. L. Rev. 714 (1971).

14. Sweatt v. Painter, 339 U.S. 629, 70 S.Ct. 848, 94 L.Ed. 1114 (1949); AALS Section on Minority Groups Newsletter, No. 74, May 1974.

sion criteria most commonly used—scores on the Law School Admission Test (LSAT) and undergraduate grade point average (GPA)—purported to be racially and ethnically neutral. Yet those criteria produced students who were nearly all Anglo and middle or upper class.[15]

The initial efforts of the law schools to alleviate this imbalance focused on recruitment. The expectations were not grand in scale—after all, the "feeders," the undergraduate colleges and universities, were not graduating great numbers of Chicanos. Nonetheless, since the problem was the absence of minorities, the answer seemed to be to recruit more minority undergraduate applicants.

One of the initial recruitment programs dispelled any notion that Chicanos were not interested in attending law school or that those interested could not be located. In 1968 the Council on Legal Education Opportunity (CLEO) launched an intensive two-month recruitment program in preparation for its planned summer institutes in Los Angeles. The sponsoring Los Angeles law schools—the University of California at Los Angeles, the University of Southern California, and Loyola—undertook the task of recruitment. Publicity in college newspapers and in newspapers of general circulation stressed (1) the institutes' willingness to overlook traditional admissions criteria, (2) the streamlining of application procedures, and (3) the administering of the LSAT free of charge. Over 300 applicants, including 93 Chicanos, applied for the 42 positions. Fourteen Chicanos were admitted.[17]

Recent CLEO figures indicate that the interest of minorities in attending law school has not waned. In 1973, for example, the national office of CLEO received 2,097 applications for 232 positions, a ratio of nearly ten applications for every position. Of the total number of applicants, 373, or 17.8 percent, were Chicanos.[18]

Continued effort to increase the number of Chicanos in law school has produced an increasing, yet small, number of Chicanos: from 180 in 1968,[19] when many such efforts began, to 881 in 1971[20] and to

    15. In 1969-1970, of a total of 82,041 students enrolled in American Bar Association accredited law schools, only 2,933 were minorities. The minority count included traditionally Black schools. See ABA Law Schools and Bar Admission Requirements (1971), at 44. For a description of minority enrollment in a private law school before the institution of special programs, see Reiss, supra note 13, at 716.
    17. Letwin, Some Perspectives on Minority Access to Legal Education, 2 Experiment & Innovation 1 (1969).
    18. Letter from Michael J. Moorehead, Executive Director, CLEO, to Trinidad Gonzales, Puerto Rican Legal Defense and Education Fund, Oct. 3, 1973, on file at CLEO Nat'l Office, 818 18th St. N.W., Suite 940. Wash., D.C.
    19. Letwin, supra note 17, at 10.
    20. AALS, 1971 Survey of Minority Group Students in Legal Education, 24 J. Legal Ed. 487, 488 (1972).

1,259 in 1973,[21] the last year for which figures are available. Still, Chicanos in 1973 represented scarcely more than one percent of the 106,102[22] law students enrolled in accredited law schools.

Those schools that have increased the enrollment of Chicanos substantially have done so as a result of well-planned recruitment programs such as those sponsored and coordinated by CLEO.[23] Many schools do little planning and even less financing of such programs, however.[24] A law school need only examine the undergraduate athletic recruitment program to be convinced that the issue is one of priorities. If minority applicants were sought with the same enthusiasm and attention devoted to place-kickers or halfbacks, much of the problem would disappear in short order.

The best efforts at recruiting will falter, however, if schools fail to recognize that recruitment is only the first of several steps which must be taken. Financial assistance for those who need it must be provided.[25] Chicano families are often poor,[26] and the Chicano who

---

21. Rudd & White, *supra* note 9, at 342-44.

22. *Id.* at 342. At that time more than three per cent of the total population of the United States was Chicano, according to a press release from the U.S. Dept. of Comm. News, Social and Economic Statistical Admin. (May 10, 1974).

23. While no law school will have athletic department type financing, it can plan and execute recruitment plans with the same care as an athletic department. What are the ingredients? (1) assigning of recruitment responsibility to specific individuals. Such individuals should include administrators (dean, assistant dean, etc.), professors, and students. However, one individual should be appointed as over-all coordinator; (2) setting of goals and priorities respecting the number and types of students to be recruited. The goals must be realistically based on past experience and present resources; (3) coordination and information sharing by all the individuals and groups involved in the recruitment effort; (4) financing of telephone, stationery, and travel for students, faculty, or alumni utilized in the recruitment; (5) utilization of minority students and faculty as well as nonminority recruiters; recruitment should not be carried out exclusively by minority personnel; and (6) periodic review of progress.

24. Student-initiated recruitment programs partially fill the void. At the University of New Mexico, the students and the law school administration work cooperatively. The recruitment activities of students are like those found in many law schools. The Mexican American Law Student Association (MALSA) sponsors an annual Chicano recruitment day to reach as many applicants as possible. Posters and all news media are utilized. At the recruitment day and throughout the year, MALSA distributes information and counsels students on the LSAT sources for financial assistance, and admissions problems. MALSA makes recommendations to the admissions committee respecting those applicants who have been interviewed or are otherwise known to the MALSA membership.

More recently, the national La Raza Law Students Association designated its New Mexico chapter (MALSA) to establish the National Clearinghouse for Law School Applicants (hereinafter Clearinghouse). The Clearinghouse will attempt to share applications by Chicanos with all law schools. Nat'l Clearing House for Law School Applicants, Final Report to ABA-LSD, April 20, 1975, on file at University of New Mexico School of Law. Most Chicano applications are made to a few law schools. Other schools have no Chicano applicants. In 1975 118 of 217 applicants in the program were Chicano or Puerto Rican. *Id.*

25. After the 1968 Los Angeles CLEO Institute, the Director recommended that the annual stipend should be $2,500 per student, rather than the $1,500 then awarded. Letwin, *supra* note 17, at 19. Yet, despite extensive efforts to increase funding, CLEO has only been

manages to graduate from college often has acquired substantial educational debts.[27] Second, a substantial number of those recruited must be admitted, trained, graduated, and equipped for the bar exam. Recruitment will be viewed as a hoax if it does not result in increased numbers of Chicano law graduates and attorneys. Successful recruitment, therefore, must be followed by successful education of Chicanos after the students enroll.[28] Those being recruited hear and read about how other Chicanos are doing in school. The reputation of the law school regarding minorities spreads throughout that segment of the minority communities which is concerned about enrolling in law school. If a law school has a reputation for failing minority students, whether deservedly or not, it will receive few minority applicants regardless of its recruitment efforts.

B. Special Admissions Program

Although active recruiting quickly confirmed the attractiveness of the legal profession to racial and ethnic groups, a second obstacle to enrolling minority students appeared: the numerical admission criteria applied by most law schools. Relatively fewer Chicanos than Anglos were achieving the requisite Law School Admission Test score and undergraduate grade point average to gain admission to law school on a competitive basis.[29]

This obstacle, however, need never have appeared.[30] The Law School Admission Council, recognizing that the LSAT cannot measure many qualities that are essential to a good lawyer, such as motivation, intelligence, industriousness, and a sense of justice, had urged law schools "to make intelligent and flexible, rather than slavish, use of numerical predictors."[31] Broadening the base of admissions criteria to include nonnumerical factors has the additional

---

able to award an annual stipend of $1,000 for the last several years. Many schools have approached the financial needs of the students in an ad hoc and unstructured manner often leaving those needs unmet.

26. See United States Comm'n on Civil Rights, The Mexican-American 2-5 (1968).

27. Sander, Financial Aid, 1970 U. Tol. L. Rev. 919, 920-21.

28. See notes 142-275 infra, and accompanying text for a discussion of various programs.

29. Rosen, Equalizing Access to Legal Education: Special Programs for Law Students Who Are Not Admissible by Traditional Criteria, 1970 Tol. L. Rev. 321, 325.

30. Raushenbush, Broadening the Base of Persons Entering the Legal Profession: Recruitment and Admission to Law School, AALS Section on Minority Groups Newsletter, Number 74-1, May, 1974, at 1.

31. Id. at 3. At New Mexico, for example, no student today would be admitted routinely who has an LSAT score of 529 or 549, the average score for incoming students in 1968 and 1969, respectively. For a list of LSAT scores from 1964 to 1972, see Prepared Statement of Frederick M. Hart, offered to the University Study Committee of the New Mexico Legislature, July 20, 1973, p. 3 on file in the office of the Dean, University of New Mexico School of Law.

value of assuring the law school that its student body will have the variety and depth that the legal profession needs. But even if Chicanos in special programs have lower numerical predictors than others, it is important to realize that a few years ago, most such students would have been admitted without special programs.[32] It is the recent, extraordinary increase in law school applicants[33] and the concurrent upward spiral of numerical predictors that necessitates reevaluation of special admissions programs.

Thus, the need for more broad-based criteria is evident. There is also a need to experiment with innovative ways to afford minorities an opportunity to demonstrate competence for school and for practice. The following sections review several programs, and the concluding section of this part proposes a theory of admission which meets the objections that can be leveled at today's procedures.

1. The University of Denver College of Law Program

The population of the Rocky Mountain area of the United States contains a high proportion of Chicanos. Nonetheless, few Chicano attorneys practice in that region. For example, while 40 percent of the population in New Mexico is Chicano,[34] only seven percent of the attorneys have Spanish surnames.[35] In response to such disparities, the University of Denver College of Law established in 1967 the first special admissions program for Chicanos.[36]

The program planners assumed the need for more Chicano lawyers and recognized that numerical admissions criteria severely limited the

---

32. Most of the Chicano students admitted through special programs are qualified for the study of law according to the predictive indexes used by most law schools. For example, the University of New Mexico School of Law uses a formula based on the Law School Admission Test (LSAT) score, Writing Ability score, and undergraduate grade point average to predict the first year grade point average in law school. Any applicant whose predicted first year average (PFYA) exceeds 2.0 (C average) has a better than 50% chance of fully completing the first year at the University of New Mexico School of Law. The validity of this formula has been annually tested against the actual grades earned by the students at UNM to ensure its statistical accuracy. The Chicano law students accepted for the 1977 class by the University of New Mexico, with one or two exceptions, have a PFYA above 2.0, and, thus, are qualified for the study of law. The one or two exceptions had successfully completed a summer pre-law program (CLEO). The experience of New Mexico is that successful completion of such a program is an additional basis for predicting success in law school.

33. *See generally* Ruud, *That Burgeoning Law School-Enrollment is Portia*, 60 A.B.A. J. 182 (1974).

34. U.S. Dept. of Commerce, Bureau of the Census, General Social and Economic Characteristics of New Mexico, PC(11)-C33.

35. A poll of the 1974 N.M. Bar list indicated the number of Spanish-surnamed lawyers.

36. In 1967, only .005 percent of the lawyers in Denver were Chicano, although Chicanos constituted 8 to 9 percent of the population. Sykes & Martinez, *Some Lessons of CLEO*, 1970 U. Tol. L. Rev. 679, at 680-81. The personal experience of the authors has shown that such figures are hard to come by because bar associations refuse to gather such data.

opportunity for a legal education.[37] Accordingly, the program was designed with components now familiar. First, students were admitted to the program on the basis of criteria different from those applied to other first year students.[38] Students were selected who, while strong academically, lacked the requisite LSAT score to be otherwise admitted. Their backgrounds indicated a desire to do well in school, the probability that they would succeed, and a willingness to use the law as a means of protecting the legal rights of minorities. Approximately three times more students applied than could be accepted.[39]

Second, a nine-week summer program was attended by all special admittees. The faculty assumed that each student had the intelligence to perform well in law school.[40] Consequently, instruction centered on a realistic simulation of law school modified to the needs of these students. Special emphasis was placed on contact with professors, small classes, written assignments, and frequent practice examinations.[41]

Ten Chicanos enrolled in the program. What was the result of that experiment? All ten successfully completed law school, two on an accelerated 2½ year program, eight in the normal three years. Two are now private practitioners. Two are legal aid attorneys, one the executive director of a large rural legal services program and the other a staff attorney in an urban program. Two are with the Equal Employment Opportunity Commission, one an assistant to a Commissioner and the other a staff attorney in an EEOC litigation center. One is a deputy clerk of the United States Supreme Court, and one is a law professor and assistant dean.[42] Each of these Chicanos would not have attended law school under established numerical predictive criteria. Each had strong motivation to succeed, each continues to better the life of the Chicano community professionally, and each is making a distinct contribution to society.

Interviews with Chicano students attending the second Denver program suggest that similar results are likely. Most of these students identify strongly with their ethnic group and appear determined to work to make existing social institutions more responsive to the needs of the Chicano community.[43]

---

37. *Id.* at 680-81.
38. Huff, *The Propriety of Preparatory Programs for Minority Students,* 1970 U. Tol. L. Rev. 747, 752.
39. Sykes & Martinez, *supra* note 36.
40. *Id.* at 750.
41. *Id.* at 749-752.
42. Interview with Jess Manzanares, Asst. Dean, University of Denver College of Law, June, 1974, Denver, Colo.
43. Sykes & Martinez, *supra* note 36, at 681-87.

2. Council on Legal Education Opportunity (CLEO)

Success of a nature similar to that of the Denver program, but on a larger scale, has been achieved by CLEO since it was established in January 1968. One example of what CLEO has done may suffice. California Rural Legal Assistance (CRLA), a 40-attorney legal services program serving the rural poor, represents predominantly farm worker clients, approximately 60 percent of whom are Spanish speaking. To properly serve its clients, CRLA must have attorneys who speak Spanish and with whom that portion of the clientele can identify. In 1968, the year CLEO began, only three attorneys in the program were Chicano despite extensive recruitment efforts. By 1973, fully one-half of the attorneys were Chicano. Most of the new attorneys had gone through CLEO or other special admissions programs.[44]

The basic aim of CLEO has been to facilitate a substantial increase in the number of lawyers from minority backgrounds. Since its inception, the program has emphasized summer institutes and financial stipends.

The impact of CLEO has been remarkable. By 1973, approximately 1,300 students had gained admission to law school after attending CLEO regional institutes. Of the CLEO graduates, over 400 had graduated from law school by 1973.[45] In addition, CLEO has continually urged law schools to admit minority applicants who were not admitted to CLEO institutes either because the positions were filled or because some applicants were overqualified financially or educationally for the CLEO program.

The effect of CLEO on the admission of Chicanos to law school goes beyond the numerical impact of its graduates, however. First, the success of CLEO-graduated Chicanos in law school has encouraged other Chicanos to apply to law school. With a larger pool of Chicano applicants, a greater number of Chicanos qualify for admission under the traditional predictive criteria today than in 1968. Second, and more important, while some law schools initially viewed CLEO applicants as poor risks for success in law school, the vast majority have succeeded. As a result, law schools have become more willing to admit Chicanos whose credentials exceed the CLEO

---

44. Advisory client groups consulted with and advised the attorneys in each of the nine offices found throughout rural California. These client groups had, since CRLA was established in 1966, demanded Chicano lawyers at every opportunity. The need had always been there. The legal profession had failed to meet that need. To those clients, the special admissions program, like CLEO, had the special quality of fulfilling the needs and, importantly, dreams.

45. Raushenbush, *supra* note 30, at 2.

standard but are not high enough for them to be admitted on a regular basis.

3. Other Programs

Many law schools have devised other admissions programs that do not rely principally on CLEO. The three examples discussed below are illustrative of a combination of approaches that have been built on the CLEO experience but which have gone beyond that approach. They have been successful efforts, but in view of the small percentage of Chicano law students and lawyers, more must be done in order to meet the need.

The *DeFunis*[46] case has focused attention on the issue of admissions at the University of Washington, a public institution. The admissions process involved separation of the applicants into two groups: minority and nonminority.[47] Each group of applicants was considered separately; the minority applicants competed only against other minority applicants. For minority applicants, both the traditional criteria, LSAT and GPA, and the "soft" criteria such as recommendations, community activity, and employment were considered. While not setting an absolute percentage of minority students to be admitted, the University of Washington selected those minority applicants the admissions committee felt had a good chance of succeeding in law school even though there were some Anglo applicants, like DeFunis, who had better numerical credentials. The University did succeed in increasing the number of minority students despite the problems inherent in the process. The basic rationale for the program was the need for a greater number of minority lawyers, including Chicanos. This position was accepted by the Supreme Court of the State of Washington, and in view of the lack of a decision by the Supreme Court of the United States, the Washington Supreme Court decision stands as the most authoritative court opinion on the issue.[48]

The efforts of a private institution, the University of Southern California (USC), to increase the number of minority students, including Chicanos, are detailed in a 1971 article by Associate Professor Michael Reiss.[49] Despite pressures on the law school to integrate its nearly all-Anglo student body, few steps had been taken in that

---

46. DeFunis v. Odegaard, 82 Wash. 2d 11, 507 P.2d 1169 (1973); *vacated and remanded* 416 U.S. 312 (1974).

47. The admissions process is described in the Washington Supreme Court opinion. 82 Wash. 2d 11, 507 P.2d 1169 (1973).

48. The U.S. Supreme Court vacated and remanded the case as moot without reaching the merits. 416 U.S. 312 (1974).

49. Reiss, *supra* note 13.

direction until 1968 when CLEO provided the impetus.[50] The University of Southern California, as part of a consortium, helped sponsor CLEO institutes in 1968 and 1969. In 1970, however, CLEO did not sponsor an institute in the Los Angeles area, and USC had to devise its own program of admissions.[51] A special committee that worked with and sometimes against the normal admissions committee was established. During the tug of war that ensued, the special committee became more respectful of normal predictive factors, and the regular admissions committee became more impressed with the need for diversity in the student body. There was a gradual increase in the number of minorities from 1968. Although many of the students initially admitted did comparatively poorer academically, by 1971 the minority students were competing favorably with other students at the law school.[52] Moreover, the difference in treatment, other than in admissions, had practically disappeared. There were no special tutorial programs. More importantly, the number of minority students in the incoming class had risen from none in 1968 to near population parity by 1971.[53]

The affirmative efforts to recruit Chicanos into the University of New Mexico Law School date from 1967, when New Mexico accepted several graduates of the Denver program. Since 1967, the University of New Mexico School of Law has accepted an increasing number of Chicanos who have attended CLEO institutes. These students were admitted to the law school provisionally, subject to successful completion of the CLEO institute. More recently, a substantial percentage of Chicanos have been admitted without the benefit of a special summer program. This has been due in part to the adoption of an admissions policy that considers the traditional predictive factors such as the LSAT score to be only part, although an important part, of the admissions criteria. In applying such a policy to all applicants, the admissions committee looks for evidence of social commitment, leadership ability, and participation in extracurricular activities. By this method, the University of New Mexico has been able to admit increasing numbers of Chicanos who do not attend pre-law summer programs, but who might not be accepted on a strictly numerical basis.

These experiences suggest approaches that could be successfully applied by law schools that seek to admit larger numbers of minorities, including Chicanos; some of these are detailed in the next sec-

50. *Id.* at 716-719.
51. *Id.* at 732.
52. *Id.* at 730.
53. *Id.* at 722.

tion. Law schools can no longer depend on CLEO to increase their minority enrollment.[54] The number of CLEO positions has stabilized around 200. Thus. it is unrealistic for law schools to tie their minority admissions system to CLEO. Additional programs must supplement CLEO if minority enrollment is to increase sufficiently to meet the need for minority lawyers.

C. Toward a Unitary Theory of Admissions

Special admissions programs have succeeded in increasing the number of minority law students. but at some cost. The use of different admissions standards suggests to both the special and regular admittee that the minority students are enrolled at the sufferance of the law school. Moreover, some Anglo students may feel that the Chicano student admitted under a special program deprived a friend or relative of a position in the entering class.[55]

Stigma is a high cost. but it can be avoided if different standards for minority applicants are abandoned. To abandon different standards for a minority admissions program will necessitate a change in traditional admissions policy, however. The notion of competitive admissions on the basis of numerical predictors can no longer be accepted as the touchstone of an admissions policy. Other factors deserve and demand consideration in the admissions process. One such factor is the responsibility of law schools to train students who belong to different ethnic and racial groups.[56] Another factor that

54. CLEO has embarked upon a pilot program to assist law schools in recruiting minority students through the Application-Sharing Project. Over fourteen schools that receive comparatively large numbers of minority and Appalachian applicants have agreed to direct applications of qualified students who have not been admitted. Other schools, that do not have large numbers of such applicants, have indicated through a confidential questionnaire the type of applications they would like to receive. By pairing responses, schools may find students not admitted elsewhere. Interested schools contact the applicant directly. AALS Section on Minority Groups Newsletter. Number 74-1, May, 1974, at 1.

55. In 1970-71, the Chicano law students at the University of California at Berkeley focused on a series of demands with respect to the Chicano. One of the demands was that the law school institute what the students called a "unitary admissions system." The Chicano law students were concerned that an environment of distrust and suspicion was being created by a system of admission that brought into the law schools most of the Chicanos as "special admittees." These students more often than not, had lower LSAT scores than their Anglo counterparts. The Chicano students rejected what they felt was the law school position, i.e., that the student was there, not because of merit, but because of the pressures to admit minority students. The Chicano students further sensed that some majority member students felt that the increasing number of brown faces in the student body was the cause of the inability of some of their friends and relatives to get into law school. The Chicano students did not want to continue to be stigmatized in this manner. This account is based upon the personal experience of one of the authors who was asked to attend the negotiations.

56. In the view of the authors, this responsibility lies not so much in terms of fairness to the individual applicants, as in the responsibility of the law school to society as a whole and to the ethnic and racial groups in particular.

deserves consideration is the need for diversity in the educational environment. More fundamentally, law schools must accept that numerical predictive factors only predict probable success in law school and not probable success as a lawyer.[57]

Does a unitary admissions policy mean the abandonment of CLEO and other similar programs? Certainly not for the immediate future. Each school must examine its progress with respect to its responsibility to provide equal educational opportunity to identifiable minorities including Chicanos. Its policies must be evaluated and its resources expended to fill any gap that exists between its present attainment and its future responsibility.

If law schools are willing to accept the limitations inherent in the use of numerical predictors, it is possible to establish a unitary admissions system that will permit the admission of minority applicants on the same basis as nonminority students. Such a system must proceed on the assumption that the relative probability of success in law school is not the sole criterion of admission. Rather, all who are predicted to succeed in law school would be considered qualified.[58] In selecting from among the qualified students, the law schools would consider such policies as geographic and social diversity and the need for minority lawyers, as well as the need for some students with the highest predictions for success in law school. That the LSAT score or GPA differs among the incoming students should be no more important than the fact that they come from different geographic areas. All students must be admitted on the same basis— probability of success in law school and the contribution they can make to the legal profession and society.

Implementation of the unitary admissions system imposes at least two costs, one financial and the other administrative. The financial cost results from the increased time required in reviewing applicant files. It is, of course, easier to look at one number for each applicant. The administrative cost is not so easily measured. The admissions dean or committee will agonize over decisions when more factors than numerical predictors are considered because there is less certainty in the system.

But the benefits argue for the system. The legal profession will be enhanced. Admissions personnel, once freed of complete dependence on numerical predictors, can take a broader view of the needs of the legal profession. If most applicants who would be admitted on

---

57. Law School Admission Council, LSAT Handbook, 5-6 (1964).

58. Care must be exercised in the use of numerical predictors for this purpose. The "cut off" must be set at a level that takes into account the experience of CLEO and other programs.

numerical criteria come from one geographic area, or racial or ethnic group, or one sex, the admissions personnel can consider other factors as criteria for admission. In time, when the students become lawyers, all segments of society will be represented in the bench and bar.

THE CHICANO LAW STUDENT

This section seeks to make some tentative generalizations about the responses of Chicano students to the study of law. It assumes the existence of a core of cultural values which most Chicanos share to some degree[59] and which many Chicano young people bring with them to law school. These shared values and attitudes affect their adaptation to law school in ways that are, to a large extent, a function of their culture.[60] In making this assumption, we by no means are suggesting that all Chicano law students' responses to the study of law are exactly alike. As social scientists have discovered, generalizations about numerically large, widely dispersed groups are notoriously difficult and inexact.[61] Chicanos, as individuals,[62] vary widely in their make-up, personality, and aptitude for the study of law. Some are highly Anglicized and scarcely differentiable in their law school experience from the rest of the law school population.[63]

---

59. Although Chicanos are a heterogeneous, widely dispersed group, nevertheless they possess a common bond of cultural identity. United States Comm'n on Civil Rights, The Mexican-American 1-2, 66 (1968); Reynoso, Alvarez, Moreno, Olmos, Quintero, & Soria, La Raza, The Law, and the Law Schools, 1970 U. Tol. L. Rev. 809, 810 [hereinafter cited as Reynoso]; see Ramirez, Identity Crisis in the Barrios, in Pain & Promise: The Chicano Today 57 (E. Simmen, ed. 1972); see generally Spanish-Speaking People in the United States, in Proceedings of the 1968 Annual Spring Meeting, American Ethnographical Society (J. Helm, ed. 1968) [hereinafter cited as Proceedings].
60. See notes 68-81 infra, and accompanying text.
61. See Weaver, Sampling and Generalization in Anthropological Research on Spanish-Speaking Groups, in Proceedings, supra note 59, at 1.
62. The tendency of some schools to see minority students as representatives of their race, and thus always "on stage" can be a major cause of friction. See Graglia, Special Admissions of the "Culturally Deprived" to Law School, 119 U. Pa. L. Rev. 351 (1970). Other schools consider all minority students, even those with excellent credentials, as potential failures, and require their participation in compulsory remedial programs, tutorials, etc., that may be neither needed nor desired. See notes 258-63 infra, and accompanying text. For a study of the deleterious effects on the morale of Black students of this practice, see Leonard, Foreward, Symposium on The Black Lawyer in America Today, 22 Harv. Law School Bull., Feb. 1971, at 7; Bell, The Black Lawyer in Legal Education, id. at 26. Although there is a voluminous literature on the problems of Black law students in white schools, the entire literature on Chicano law students comprises fewer than a half dozen articles. Despite marked differences between the backgrounds and experiences of Black and Chicano students it will occasionally be useful to compare various features of their interactions with schools of law.
63. See Weaver, supra note 61, at 10; notes 105-110 infra, and accompanying text.

Others retain strong ties with their native language and culture.[64] Moreover, there may be wide differences between Chicanos raised in migrant camps[65] and those who have grown up in city barrios.[66] And differences may be geographical or generational; the experience of the Chicano student from Houston may differ significantly from that of the Chicano from Los Angeles or Denver, and the cultural experience of the fourth-generation Chicano may be different from that of the Chicano whose parents have recently arrived from Mexico.[67] Nevertheless, within broad limits it appears that some generalizations can be made. This section and the next strive to set out some of these in the belief that an understanding of some of the attitudes and qualities shared by many Chicano law students can be of assistance to those who are concerned with the success of minority student programs in schools of law. Following this, a rough typology of Chicano law students is offered. Then, a narrative account is given describing some of the typical experiences Chicano students have in law schools, and, in the final part a number of suggestions are made for ways in which schools and students may meet each other's legitimate expectations more fully than at present.

A. Cultural Values

Chicano students come from many backgrounds. Of central importance, both numerically and for the purposes of this analysis, are those who have been born and raised in predominantly Chicano neighborhoods, or barrios. Barrio residents perceive "the law" differently from the way it is perceived by most Anglo Americans.[68] This perception enables the Chicano law student to contribute unique insights into the way the law operates in present-day society. Indeed, the hope that minority students will contribute new dimensions to the classroom dialogue is one of the more frequently suggested justifications for minority admissions programs.[69]

---

64. Weaver, *supra* note 61 at 1-12; Reynoso, *supra* note 59, at 809, 817-18; Sykes and Martinez, *supra* note 36, at 682. *See generally* Ramirez, *supra* note 59.

65. For an ethnological description of Chicano migrant farm worker families, see Shannon, *The Study of Migrants as Members of Social Systems*, in Proceedings, *supra* note 59, at 34.

66. For an ethnological description of Chicano families in big-city barrios, see Goodman, *Child's Eye View of Life in an Urban Barrio*, in Proceedings, *supra* note 59, at 84.

67. Penalosa, *The Changing Mexican-American in Southern California*, in Pain & Promise: The Chicano Today 61, 61-62 (E. Simmen, ed. 1972); *see generally* Proceedings, *supra* note 59.

68. *See* notes 70-81 *infra*, and accompanying text.

69. Pinderhughes, *Increasing Minority Group Students in Law Schools: The Rationale and the Critical Issues*, 20 Buff. L. Rev. 447 (1971); *cf.* Burns, *Racism and American Law: A New Course in Legal History*, 1970 U. Tol. L. Rev. 903, 905; O'Neil, *Preferential Admis-*

Chicano society prefers to obtain compliance with behavioral norms not primarily by written laws enforced by police power, but by family and community pressure and a shared respect for such values as old age and authority.[70] In Spanish-American culture, a man's word is as good as law;[71] only a person "sin verguenza"[72] would refuse to carry out a promise or to honor an obligation.[73] Such cases, when they arise, are ordinarily dealt with by social ostracism, rather than by resort to formal legal processes.[74]

When the legal processes operate in the barrio, "the law" is often identified with some of the least attractive aspects of its enforcement function.[75] In the barrio resident's mind, "the law" is frequently personified by the towering Anglo policeman who treats him contemptuously because of his foreign manner and appearance, and his halting English.[76] "The law" also means the bail bondsman, the sheriff, and the process server. Unlike the image of the helpful policeman that many Anglo children carry,[77] Chicano children learn to fear the policeman as a representative of an alien and hurtful system.

The Chicano community's perception of the law has influenced its perception of the lawyer. Thus, the Anglo attorney, along with the Anglo merchant, judge, process server, and policeman, has come to be associated with evictions, repossessions, incarcerations, and other personal misfortunes. In some areas of the Southwest, this impression is strengthened by memories of connivance by Anglo attorneys

---

sions: Equalizing the Access of Minority Groups to Higher Education, 80 Yale L.J. 699, 762 (1971). *See also* Leleiko, *Legal Education—Some Crucial Frontiers,* 23 J. Legal Ed. 502, 519-20 (1971).

70. Kritsche, *The Anglo Side of Acculturation,* in Proceedings, *supra* note 59, at 178, 187; United States Comm'n on Civil Rights, Stranger in One's Land 7 (1970). *See generally* A. Rendon, Chicano Manifesto 32 (1971).

71. Kritsche, *supra* note 70, at 187; S. Steiner, La Raza: The Mexican-Americans 59 (1970); A. Rendon, *supra* note 70, at 27-32.

72. Literally, "man without shame." The concept of shame plays a more central role in Chicano than Anglo culture. An accusation of shamelessness is one of the most serious charges that can be leveled at the character or motivation of another person.

73. Kritsche, *supra* note 70, at 187; *cf.* United States Comm'n on Civil Rights, Stranger in One's Land, *supra* note 70, at 7, 26; A. Rendon, *supra* note 70, at 27-32.

74. Kritsche, *supra* note 70, at 187; *cf.* United States Comm'n on Civil Rights, Stranger in One's Land, *supra* note 70, at 15, 21.

75. A. Rendon, *supra* note 70, at 217-40 (1971); *see* United States Comm'n on Civil Rights, Stranger in One's Land, *supra* note 70, at 38; United States Comm'n on Civil Rights, The Mexican-American, *supra* note 59, at 15-18; Reynoso, *supra* note 59, at 818-22; *see generally,* Swett, *Cultural Bias in the American Legal System,* 4 L. & Soc. Rev. 79, 89-93 (1969); *cf.* Carl & Callahan, *Negroes and the Law,* 17 J. Legal Ed. 250 (1964).

76. United States Comm'n on Civil Rights, Stranger in One's Land, *supra* note 70, at 41-42; United States Comm'n on Civil Rights, The Mexican-American, *supra* note 59, at 15-18; *see* S. Steiner, *supra* note 71, at 161-72 (1972).

77. A. Coffey, E. Eldefonso & W. Hartinger, Human Relations: Law Enforcement in a Changing Community 166-67 (1971).

with government officials in the plundering of land-grant property.[78] Nor do Chicanos, in contrast to Blacks, have many lawyer-heroes such as Justice Thurgood Marshall; the crusading attorneys who made such an impact on behalf of the civil rights of Negroes have barely begun to make their appearance in the barrio.[79] It is no surprise, then, that, until recently, few Chicano students perceived the law as a means of advancing the interests of their people.

The Chicano law student may subconsciously fear that his cultural values are threatened by the law school experience. Law schools appear to weed out a disproportionate percentage of those who are concerned with people and who value harmonious human contact.[80] The Chicano places great value on those traits and the Chicano law student may fear that the sacrifice of these traits is the price for success in law school, that law school will somehow make him "less Chicano."[81]

B. Educational Background

The Chicano who comes to law school has typically attended high schools that are academically inferior,[82] underfinanced,[83] and often ethnically segregated.[84] Perhaps even more important is the nature of the education received by Chicano youth in many public schools. Chicanos are generally subjected to curricula, textbooks, and

---

78. Petition of Antonio Maria Pico, et al., to the Senate and House of Representatives of the United States, reprinted in Foreigners in their Native Land; Historical Roots of the Mexican Americans 195, 196-97 (D. Weber, ed. 1973); S. Steiner, *supra* note 71, at 58-59 (1969).

79. Reynoso, *supra* note 59, at 809, 815-16. For example, although the United States Attorney General has intervened in a number of cases involving Negroes, until recently there have been few such interventions on behalf of Chicanos. United States Comm'n on Civil Rights, Stranger in One's Land *supra* note 70, at 42. In the past few years, organizations such as MALDEF (Mexican American Legal Defense and Educational Fund) and CRLA (California Rural Legal Assistance) have made a modest beginning toward remedying the worst of this deficiency.

80. *See* Miller, *supra* note 2 for the view that law school weeds out aspiring lawyers who are concerned with people, who value harmonious human contacts, who are friendly and tactful, and instead rewards students who are agressively cerebral. For a view contrasting Anglo-American and Mexican-American concepts of law and lawyers, see S. Steiner, *supra* note 71, at 59-60.

81. *See* Sykes & Martinez, *supra* note 36, at 683-84; *cf.* Bell, *supra* note 4, at 547-49.

82. Penalosa, *supra* note 67, at 68; Note, 1 N.M. L. Rev. 335 (1974); *see* A. Rendon, *supra* note 70, at 191-215; Montoya, *Bilingual-Bicultural Education: Making Educational Opportunities Available to National Origin Minority Students,* 61 Geo. L. J. 991, 992-94 (1973); O'Neil, *supra* note 69, at 728-37; *see also* United States Comm'n on Civil Rights, Stranger in One's Land, *supra* note 70, at 23-29.

83. *See e.g.,* San Antonio Independent School Dist. v. Rodriguez, 411 U.S. 1 (1973); A. Rendon, *supra* note 70, at 210.

84. United States Comm'n on Civil Rights, The Mexican-American, *supra* note 59, at 5, 9, 33; *see* O'Neil, *supra* note 69, at 728-37.

teachers that are not attuned to the Chicano culture.[85] The subjects taught reflect the dominant Anglo culture and frequently are not relevant to the experience, culture, or interests of the Chicano student. These subjects are often taught by Anglo teachers who cannot present the material in a way that the Chicano students can easily comprehend.[86] These difficulties are compounded when the Chicano students' primary language is Spanish. The lack of ability and resources on the part of schools to educate the Chicanos accounts for the low educational achievement of Chicanos[87] and suggests that Chicanos have not had equal educational opportunity.[88] In fact, such failures on the part of public schools were considered to be a denial of equal protection under the United States Constitution in *Serna v. Portales Municipal Schools.*[89] To remedy these deficiencies in the school system, bilingual education, hiring of Mexican-American teachers, and the introduction of subject matter relevant to Chicanos were required.[90]

Because Chicanos are frequently educated in a system that is not sympathetic to their needs, many drop out before completing high school;[91] those who remain have often been advised by counselors to "learn something practical," such as mechanics or carpentry.[92] Those Chicanos who graduate from high school and attend college frequently enroll in local institutions[93] where they select courses of instruction leading to careers such as teaching and social work. Those who opt for law generally present paper credentials, including grade

---

85. Note, *supra* note 82, at 337.
86. *Id.*
87. *Id.* at 335; U.S. Comm'n on Civil Rights, Stranger in One's Land, *supra* note 70, at 23.
88. *Id.* at 348-49. *See also* United States v. Jefferson County Bd. of Education, 372 F.2d 836 (5th Cir. 1966), *aff'd en banc*, 380 F.2d 385 (5th Cir. 1967), *cert. denied sub nom.*, Bd. of Education of The City of Bessemer v. United States, 389 U.S. 840 (1967); Hobson v. Hansen, 269 F.Supp. 401 (D.D.C. 1967), *aff'd sub nom.* Smuck v. Hobson, 408 F.2d 175 (D.C. Cir. 1969).
89. 351 F.Supp. 1279 (D. N.M. 1972), *aff'd on other grounds*, 499 F.2d 1147 (10th Cir. 1974).
90. Order (unreported), Serna v. Portales Municipal Schools (1974). 351 F.Supp. 1279 (D.N.M. 1972), *aff'd* 499 F.2d 1147 (1974).
91. United States Comm'n on Civil Rights, Stranger in One's Land, *supra* note 70, at 23 (1970).
92. *Id.* at 24-25; United States Comm'n on Civil Rights, The Mexican-American 34 (1968); Macias, *The Chicano Movement*, in Pain & Promise: The Chicano Today 137, 141 (E. Simmen, ed. 1972).
93. *Cf.* United States Comm'n on Civil Rights, Stranger in One's Land, *supra* note 70, at 23-29; O'Neil, *supra* note 69, at 728-37.

point averages[94] and LSAT scores,[95] that do not compete favorably with those of the top Anglo students.

There are exceptions, of course. Just as the Blacks have their outstanding jurists and legal scholars, the Chicano community occasionally produces the kind of student Derrick Bell has so ably described[96] and that professors love: intensely competitive, intellectually able, and determined to beat the Anglo at his own game. The ranks of Chicano lawyers boast several such men, and their numbers are increasing. But the occasional appearance of such an exceptional creature should not be permitted to conceal that he is indeed a rarity, as he is in all minority groups.[97]

C. A Rough Typology

Despire the formidable effect of the screening factors mentioned above, a modest but increasing number of Chicano students are finding their way into our schools of law.[98] As one might expect, these tend to be rather exceptional young people. A substantial number of these have been "community leaders," young men and women who have been active in their barrios and towns and who have experience at political organizing.[99] Intensely involved with the cause of social justice, these students tend to see law school pragmatically, as a brief interlude from which they will emerge with new tools to apply to the

---

94. *Cf.* sources and pages cited in note 93, *supra.*

95. Swineford, *Law School Admission Test: Comparison of Black Candidates and Chicano Candidates with White Candidates,* in Summary of LSAT Research (Mar. 1972).

The existence of such a "credentials gap" by no means implies that Chicano students are unqualified for the study of law. Many, if not most, of the Chicano students are qualified for the study of law according to the predictive indexes used by most law schools. For example, the University of New Mexico School of Law uses a formula based on the Law School Admission Test (LSAT) score, Writing Ability score, and undergraduate grade point average to predict the first year grade point average in law school. Any applicant whose predictive first year average (PFYA) exceeds 2.0 (C average) has a better than 50 percent chance of success at the University of New Mexico School of Law. The validity of this formula has been annually tested against the actual grades earned by the students at UNM to ensure its statistical accuracy. Most of the Chicano law students accepted for the 1977 class by the University of New Mexico have a PFYA above 2.0, and, thus, are qualified for the study of law.

According to the Admissions Committee of the University of New Mexico School of Law, many of the Chicano applicants accepted for the fall of 1974 would have been admitted on a competitive basis five years earlier.

96. Bell, *supra* note 4, at 545.

97. *See* Carl & Callahan, *supra* note 75, at 250.

98. Rudd, *supra* note 33, at 183, reporting that from 1972 to 1973, enrollment of Chicanos in law schools increased by 17.7 percent. In the fall of 1973, 1259 Chicanos were enrolled in accredited schools. Rudd & White, *supra* note 9, at 344.

99. *See* sources cited note 64 *supra.*

struggle. This type of student often, but not always, aspires to an eventual career in politics.[100]

A second and growing group of Chicano law students is composed of those who have grown up in homes that are bicultural.[101] They may have lived in poor-to-middle-class integrated neighborhoods or, if from the barrio, have been exposed to both Chicano and Anglo cultures. In essence, their culture is a blend of both. As a consequence, most of the students in this group do not bring with them to law school a serious cultural conflict. Rather, they seem at ease with, and close to, their Chicano culture while at the same time they are no more intimidated by the uniqueness of the law school experience than most first-year students.

A third substantial group of Chicano law students consists of upwardly mobile, industrious, somewhat Anglicized individuals who see in a legal career a means of acquiring prestige, status, and a respectable income.[102] Often the product of hard-working middle- or lower-middle-class families[103] who place great emphasis on "getting ahead" through education,[104] these students have often achieved good records at the undergraduate level. Their industriousness has won them the favor of their teachers throughout their years in school; the teachers see in them the personification of the American dream of social advancement through education and hard work.[105] These more "assimilated" students may experience an

---

100. *See* Sykes & Martinez, *supra* note 36, at 684.

101. This typology is based upon the collective experiences of the authors both as teachers in law schools with a significant number of Chicano law students and as teachers and administrators in CLEO institutes with substantial numbers of Chicano participants.

102. A desire for a high income is frequently associated with low identification with La Raza issues. Sykes & Martinez, *supra* note 36, at 685. *See also* Rendon, *supra* note 70, at 46-47.

Governmental and institutional employers are often attracted to such individuals, whom they see as "safe" candidates. *See* Braithwaite, *The Black Lawyer in Government*, 22 Harv. L. School Bull. 49 (Feb. 1971). At least one observer has warned that law schools interested in attracting minority students who will return to their communities after graduation, see notes 131-32 *infra*, and accompanying text, should scrutinize carefully the motivations of the applicant from an extremely impoverished background, since such a candidate may see in a legal career only a way of escaping financial destitution and show little concern for his community. Pinderhughes, *supra* note 69, at 449.

103. *See* Ladinsky, *The Impact of Social Background of Lawyers on Law Practice and the Law*, 16 J. Legal Ed. 127, 130-31 (1963).

104. *See, e.g.,* Rodriguez, *Speak Up, Chicano*, in Pain & Promise: The Chicano Today 214, 216 (E. Simmen, ed. 1972); *Tío Taco is Dead*, in *id.* 122, 125-26. Unfortunately, such hopes are in many cases doomed to disappointment. Because of demands from within their own group as well as constraints imposed by discriminatory attitudes in the larger society, success-oriented Chicanos are frequently limited in the extent to which they are able to take advantage of educational and occupational opportunities. An investment in education simply doesn't pay off as well for the Chicano as for the Anglo. Shannon, *supra* note 65, at 34, 52.

internal conflict when exposed to the missionary zeal and intense ethnic loyalty of the "community leader" type[106] or the pride that the bicultural student has in the Chicano culture. Half-forgotten ties and memories are reawakened. Several reactions may occur. The most common reaction is to seek to reestablish ties to the Chicano community; this often includes a reevaluation of career plans. A second reaction, less common today, is to reject involvement in the Chicano community. Some may react by wholeheartedly immersing themselves in everything Chicano, idealizing things that are Chicano and rejecting that which is perceived as Anglo.

A smaller group (at most law schools) is composed of persons of Spanish surname but upper-middle-class background, often having an Anglo parent, who, though Chicano for purposes of admission to law school, are virtually indistinguishable in their attitudes and goals from the mass of Anglo students.[107] These students frequently have superior academic records, often close to the range of applicants who are regularly admitted. Their motivations differ little from those of their Anglo counterparts; some may wish to enter corporate practice, others may aspire to a career in teaching or government. Relatively few members of this group have any deep attachment to the Chicano community or experience divided loyalties while in law school. Those who plan to devote themselves to working with the poor after graduation, as in a legal services office, generally do so out of a commitment that is more intellectual than based on longstanding ties.

Other typologies than the above could, of course, be delineated. Chicano students can be compared with respect to a number of other variables, such as geographical origin and economic or generational status.[108] But, for understanding the student's struggle to adjust to

---

105. S. Persons, American Minds: A History of Ideas 40-43 (1958).

106. *See* Leonard, *Placement and the Minority Student: New Pressures and Old Hang-ups,* 1970 U. Tol. L. Rev. 583, 585. *See generally* Moore, *Social Class, Assimilation and Acculturation,* in Proceedings, *supra* note 59, at 19, 20-21; note 81 *supra* and accompanying text; Ramirez, *supra* note 59, at 57.

107. For the view that law schools often prefer to admit minority individuals in this category in order to avoid facing the necessity of radically reforming their curriculum and teaching approach, see Reynoso, *supra* note 59, at 840-41. *See also* Bailey, *Trying to Make it Real Compared to What?,* 1970 U. Tol. L. Rev. 615. Schools who follow this practice, however, rarely find that the individuals recruited are able to bring to their classes the infusion of fresh insights that is one of the principal objectives of affirmative admissions programs. To the extent the school succeeds in recruiting Chicanos who are at ease with the Anglo world and likely to require few radical changes on the part of the institution, it denies itself an important avenue for cross-cultural enrichment. *See also* Rendon, *supra* note 70, at 46-48.

108. *See* notes 62-67 *supra,* and accompanying text. *See also Tío Taco is Dead,* in Pain & Promise, *supra* note 104, at 122-24.

law school, an approach that focuses on ethnic background and degree of assimilation has considerable explanatory power. It is useful for this purpose because one of the prime determinants of the Chicano student's success or failure at law study, we believe, is the ease or difficulty with which he learns to function in a system dominated by Anglo-American values and thought patterns. The law school must be sensitive to these differences and recognize its responsibilities to make those institutional changes that will enhance the possibility of success in law school of students with non-Anglo cultural backgrounds.

D. The Law School Experience

1. The First Semester

When the Chicano student arrives at law school, upperclassmen, and perhaps pre-law advisors, have forewarned the student that law study is highly demanding and will require great amounts of time.[109] But the feature that causes the greatest anxiety is one about which he has not been fully alerted—the Socratic method.[110] From the first day, the Chicano sees his classmates required to recite in class, notices their discomfiture and the professor's continued probing, and wonders how he will perform when his name is called, as it eventually is. Little in his experience has prepared the Chicano student for the demands the Socratic dialogue places on him. The abstract level of discourse,[111] the conceptual traps,[112] and the pro-

109. The grapevine is very effective at conveying such messages. Students who have attended a CLEO institute during the summer preceding admission to law school of course have first-hand knowledge of this aspect of law school.

110. Devised by Dean Langdell of Harvard Law School almost a century ago, the Socratic method as practiced by most schools of law involves a formalized dialectic in which the student is required to recite cases, distinguish holdings, and apply legal rules to borderline situations. See C. Langdell, supra note 5, at vii. Today, the designation refers to a whole spectrum of instructional approaches, ranging from a very "pure" question-and-answer approach to more eclectic mixtures of lecturing, recitation, and problem-solving.

111. See, e.g., Note, Anxiety and the First Semester of Law School, 1968 Wis. L. Rev. 1201, 1206.

112. For a sharply critical, and perhaps somewhat exaggerated discussion of the traps Socratic law professors spring on unwary students see Savoy, Toward a New Politics of Legal Education, 79 Yale L.J. 444, 457 (1970). Chicanos are easy prey, for most have little experience with the type of precise communication that is called for in the Socratic dialogue. See Huff, supra note 38, at 750. The "community leader" has had a good deal of experience at public speaking and political advocacy, but typically his experience with presenting an unadorned defense of a purely analytical position is slight.

It should be borne in mind that the generalizations about the Chicano experience made herein represent only a rough average, or composite, of the experience of many individuals, and that individual cases may vary widely from the scenarios offered here. Concerning the inherent difficulty of making accurate statements about ethnic groups, individual members of which may differ in many significant respects, see notes 61-67 supra, and accompanying text.

fessor's deliberate refusal to give feedback[113] are difficult enough. But the Anglo student experiences these uncertainties, too. What makes the Socratic experience such a painful one for the Chicano is not so much the intellectual demands it places on him, as the symbolic and emotional quality of the performance. Verbal aggression is discouraged in Chicano culture. Young people are taught to be conciliatory, even deferential, in the face of authority.[114] The professor's probing may be seen as an attack, and his continued questioning as relentless pursuit from which there is no escape.[115] The student's careful preparation, his meticulous briefing of the cases the night before, seem useless in the fact of the professor's parade of hypotheticals.

The shock of being called on to recite and the lack of positive reinforcement in the Socratic method inspires a variety of escape maneuvers.[116] The student learns to duck questions, to say he is "unprepared" when called on (which may not be true), or to volunteer with a trivial, off-the-point insight in hopes the professor will remember that he volunteered and choose not to call on him when his turn comes. In the absence of positive feedback, the Chicano student may begin to doubt his ability or suitability for law.[117] He

---

113. The lack of feedback, which has been decried by many commentators, *e.g.,* Watson, *The Quest for Professional Competence: Psychological Aspects of Legal Education,* 37 U. Cin. L. Rev. 93, 123, 161 (1968); Note, *supra* note 111, at 1201, is especially unsettling for minority students, who are by virtue of their "special" status in school unsure of where they stand. *See* O'Neil, *supra* note 69, at 762.

114. Goodman, *supra* note 66, at 84, 91, 95-96; *see* United States Comm'n on Civil Rights, *supra* note 26, at 61. In the barrio, this reluctance to respond to attacks from authority figures often takes the form of intentional relinquishment of legal rights, rather than "making a fuss," *id.* at 15. Growing numbers of Chicano students have learned to surmount their early conditioning, particularly in instances where the authority figure is viewed as illegitimate or antagonistic to the interests of their people. The "community leader" in particular can be a very articulate spokesman in meetings and public forums. Still, his public speaking ability is likely to be at its best in delivering speeches with a socio-political cast; when pressed on a purely abstract level on points of law, he is much less sure of himself, and is more likely to revert to a more cautious, or defensive, posture.

115. One commentator has described the Socratic approach at its best as, "forceful, scathing, and aggressive," Stone, *Legal Education on the Couch,* 85 Harv. L. Rev. 392 (1971). Another has detailed the psychological destruction of a student whose inner resources were inadequate to cope with the attack of one of his teachers, Watson, *supra* note 113, at 119-20. The rationale that those who cannot tolerate the rigors of this classroom approach do not have what it takes to be a lawyer has been criticized as inappropriate for minority students. *See* Carl & Callahan, *supra* note 75, at 261.

116. For a discussion of the various maladaptive devices students adopt, see Watson, *supra* note 113, at 129-30; Note, *supra* note 111, at 1207.

117. As was mentioned earlier, *see* notes 45-46 *supra,* and accompanying text. Minority students are especially prone to such self-deprecation since their very presence at the law school marks them as "special." A low LSAT score can also perform such a harmful "labeling" function. Abuse of the Socratic method can also contribute to undermining of the student's ego strength and self-esteem. Stone, *supra* note 115, at 411-13.

may begin spending inordinate numbers of hours in the library, poring over hornbooks, commercially prepared outlines, and other study aids, in the hope that rote learning of black-letter rules will ease his dilemma.[118] Other students may respond by withdrawing from the stressful stimulus. They may begin attending classes sporadically, or stop attending at all.[119] Others may turn to community activities,[120] where they experience a sense of accomplishment that is generally unavailable in the classroom. The desire and evident need of the community for their legal services makes such a decision even easier.

Adding to the Chicano student's doubt about his ability to succeed in law school is his presence in a special educational program for minority students. If the program is mandatory and remedial in nature, the Chicano student may feel that he and the other program participants have been set apart in a special caste composed of the most lowly.[121] If the special program is supplemental in nature, however, and if the program has been successful in the past, participation in such a program may provide the Chicano student with the assurance he seeks.

By the latter part of the first semester the Chicano student will have heard of the poor record of previous Chicano graduates on the bar examination.[122] He wonders whether, in the end, his law degree will be worth nothing. Coupled with these uncertainties is the growing realization that law study simply is not as interesting and vital as he thought it would be. There are few dramatic civil rights cases in the first-year curriculum; to the student, an undue number of the cases seem to revolve around the problems of giant corporations or

118. Watson, *Reflections on the Teaching of Criminal Law,* 37 U. Det. L.J. 701, 712 (1960); Note, *supra* note 111, at 1207.

119. Summers, *Preferential Admissions: An Unreal Solution to a Real Problem,* 1970 U. Tol. L. Rev. 377, 395 (1970); *see* Note, *supra* note 111, at 1214.

120. Patton, *The Student, The Situation, and Performance During the First Year of Law School,* 21 J. Legal Ed. 10, 50 (1969); Summers, *supra* note 119, at 396; *see* Hughes, McKay & Winograd, *supra* note 2, at 713.

121. Making available special educational resources for the minority student without at the same time making him feel stigmatized or set apart from the rest of the student body is a very delicate matter. It may well be impossible to achieve where relationships have begun to deteriorate and the student body is predisposed to perceive actions by the school as evidence of polarization. If offered a choice between having a particular compensatory program that results in stigma and no program at all, most Chicano students would choose no program. Reiss, *supra* note 13, at 731; *see* Bell, *supra* note 4, at 551; *cf.* Patton, *supra* note 120, at 61.

122. Clark, *The Bar Examination: Hurdle or Help,* in C. Clark, Minority Opportunities in Law for Blacks, Puerto Ricans & Chicanos 175 (1974). For detailed documentation of the differential pass rates of minority and white graduates on the California bar examination, see Memo of Points and Authorities for Plaintiff, Espinoza v. Committee of Bar Examiners, no. S.S. 229298 (Cal. Sup. Ct., filed June 20, 1972).

insurance companies.[123] An entire course seems to center about medieval nobility, fiefs, and pecular things called "estates." Few of his professors take the time to show the connection between the assigned material and the problems of the poor community, and for some classes the Chicano wonders whether the connection can be made at all.[124] When midterm examinations arrive, he is required to demonstrate proficiency not only in written English, often itself a second language, but in the peculiarly ponderous, highly embroidered style that many legal writers affect.[125]

In response to their common dilemma, the Chicano students draw together. The competitive atmosphere is tempered by the formation of study groups and ethnic student organizations.[126] Tutorials are arranged, and outlines and class notes are duplicated and made avail-

---

123. For a criticism of this orientation as excessively narrow and tending to exclude equally important areas of human need, see Reich, *Toward the Humanistic Study of Law,* 74 Yale L.J. 1402, 1402-07 (1964); Summers, *supra* note 119, at 390; Sykes & Martinez, *supra* note 36, at 683-84; *see* Hughes, McKay & Winograd, *supra* note 2, at 710; *see* Diggs, *Communication Skills in Legal Materials: The Howard Law School Program,* 1970 U. Tol. L. Rev. 763, 767.

124. The fear that law will prove "irrelevant" to the concerns of his people, or, worse, that its study will result in his being co-opted into a system that discriminates against the poor is a frequent cause of low morale and half-hearted efforts by minority students, *e.g.,* Sykes & Martinez, *supra* note 36, at 683-84; *see* Bailey, *supra* note 107, at 615-20; Bell, *supra* note 4, at 547-49; Bok, *The Black Lawyer in America Today; Dinner Speaker,* 22 Harv. Law School Bull. 36, 37 (Feb. 1971); Leonard, *supra* note 106, at 583-87. *But see* Jensen, *Selection of Minority Students in Higher Education,* 1970 U. Tol. L. Rev. 403, 449 for the view that minority students complain of the irrelevance of their education simply because they are unable to do the work. A more plausible view, expressed in socio-political terms, is that of Katz, *Black Law Students in White Law Schools: Law in a Changing Society,* 1970 U. Tol. L. Rev. 589, 603. Katz suggests that the minority student's complaint that the law lacks relevance to his goals is simply a reaction against the moral neutrality of most legal education and a manifestation of the student's resistance to the prospect of becoming a mere technician or "hired gun."

125. Diggs, *supra* note 123, at 765. Despite protestations to the contrary, a student's writing style, diction, spelling, and use of rhetorical devices such as transitions correlates highly with grades received on law school essay examinations. Linn, Klein & Hart, *The Nature and Correlates of Law School Essay Grades,* 1972 Educ. & Psych. Measurement 32, 267-79.

126. Initially, the competitive nature of the law school environment inhibits student exchanges, Rickson, *Faculty Control and the Structure of Student Competition: An Analysis of the Law Student Role,* 25 J. Legal Ed. 47 (1973). Students, especially superior students, are reluctant to help other students for fear of giving them an edge. Typically, when a superior student helps another student with some aspect of the class work, he gives the struggling student a "bite" of the correct analysis, but not the whole thing. Patton, *supra* note 120, at 41. Lower-achieving students generally are driven to associate with each other, and their group work is more sporadic and less productive than that of higher achieving students. *Id.* at 41-43. Chicanos and other minority students may have an advantage over the students described in the above-cited studies, however, since their greater group cohesiveness results in greater sharing of ideas and materials and in earlier formation of study groups.

able to the group. Social gatherings provide a release from the academic pressure.

2. After Graduation: The Bar Examination and a Job

During his second and third year the threat of the bar examination hangs over the Chicano's head like a slowly gathering cloud. He has heard of the dismal record of past Chicano graduates[127] and wonders if the bar examiners consciously discriminate against minority test-takers.[128] He worries about his ability to write a written essay under intense time pressure.[129] What if he fails? How will he support himself for a second try? If he cannot pass the exam after a couple of tries, how can he use his legal training in some alternate capacity? How will he explain his failure to his family and community?

Even before registering for the bar exam, however, comes a more immediate trial: applying for his first legal position. Except for the "community leader," who has maintained strong ties with the community and probably has his future well planned, the Chicano student may face a difficult career choice. Often the choice is perceived as "returning to the community" on the one hand (i.e., some form of poverty or public-interest practice) or opting for a commercial or corporate practice on the other.[130] The law school is able to offer him relatively little guidance in this decision, since it, also, is of two minds on the matter. It would like to see him devote himself to the betterment of his community; after all, that is one of the principal objectives of special admissions programs.[131] On the other hand, the

127. See Clark, supra note 122.
128. See Bell, supra note 4, at 547 for a discussion of the tendency of the law school environment to evoke attitudes of suspicion and distrust, verging on racial paranoia. Unfortunately, there appears to be just enough basis to the rumors of intentional discrimination to ensure their perpetuation. See, e.g., Reinstein, Evaluating Bar Admissions Procedures Under Standards of Equal Protection, 44 Temp. L.Q. 248; The Report of the Philadelphia Bar Association Special Committee on Pennsylvania Bar Admissions Procedures—Racial Discrimination in Administration of the Pennsylvania Bar Examination, id. at 141, 227-34.
129. See Evans & Reilly, A Study of Speededness as a Source of Test Bias, in Summary of LSAT Research (1971), suggesting that black candidates may experience "speededness" (i.e., time pressure) as more of a handicap on reading comprehension questions than white candidates. And many minority students do have difficulties with writing standard English. Brand, Minority Writing Problems and Law School Writing Programs, 26 J. Legal Ed. 331 (1974).
130. Leonard, supra note 106, at 583-84; see Bok, supra note 124; Banks, The Black Lawyer and Institutional Employment, 22 Harv. Law School Bull. 40, 44 (Feb. 1971); cf. Bailey, supra note 107, at 615-20.
131. Sykes & Martinez, supra note 36, at 687-88; see Leonard, supra note 106, at 586-87; see also Pinderhughes, supra note 69, at 447, which recommends a social-commitment test for specially admitted students in order to help guarantee they will return to their

faculty are more attuned to the scholastic world and the world of judges and law firms. To them, a minority student who makes his mark there publicizes and vindicates the school's program to critics.[132] Moreover, minority communities do need tax lawyers and corporate counsel. Thus, a Chicano graduate who sharpens his skills in these areas by working a few years in the business world will later be able to bring them home for the benefit of his community.[133]

INSTITUTIONAL RESPONSES

From an educational standpoint the events described above obviously leave much to be desired. Yet, from our combined experience, they are typical of the experiences of many Chicano students in our schools of law. Special admissions programs, when they result in experiences, like those described above, produce disaffection on the part of both student and law school. The law school, which had hoped to gain an infusion of new insights and creative criticism,[134] finds instead that it has on its hands a new kind of silent minority, tense, withdrawn, and obviously unhappy. The minority student, for his part, feels cheated. His legal education, which appeared to offer such promise, has become instead a daily ordeal.

An essential first step in addressing this obviously unhappy state of affairs is to realize that not all law students are cut from the same cloth. Chicano students bring to law study a constellation of traits and aspirations that set them apart from their Anglo, and even Black, classmates.[135] Viewing special admissions programs for Chicanos as simply offering the traditional product[136] to a class of slightly inadequate but promising proto-Anglos whose skin is simply a few shades darker than usual is an invitation to disaster. Without the

communities when they graduate. Two writers believe that only a relatively small portion of the minority graudates of "prestige" law schools return to their communities. Gozansky & DeVito, *An Enlightened Comparison: The Relevant Strengths and Weaknesses of the CLEO Program and the Pre-Start Program of Emory University,* 1970 U. Tol. L. Rev. 719, 720.

132. *See* Watson, *supra* note 113, at 109; Kinoy, *Crisis in Legal Education,* in The Radical Lawyers 271, 275-76 (J. Black, ed. 1971).

133. *See* Panella & McPherson, *Do You See What I See?: Two Writers Look at CLEO,* 1970 U. Tol. L. Rev. 559, 597; Smith, *The Black Lawyer and Business and Industry,* 22 Harv. Law School Bull. 61, 62 (Feb. 1971); Whitehead, *id.* at 63-65. It has been pointed out, though, that minority communities are able to generate relatively little business for the practitioner interested in commercial practice. Summers, *supra* note 119, at 387. Others have questioned the basic wisdom of studying white institutions as models for minority communities. *See* Leonard, *supra* note 62, at 7.

134. *E.g.,* Hughes, McKay & Winograd, *supra* note 2, at 718; Reiss, *supra* note 13, at 733.

135. *See* notes 58-81 *supra,* and accompanying text.

136. This is the so-called "Jensen" view of compensatory education. *See* Jensen, *supra* note 124, at 455-57; Jensen, *How Much Can We Boost IQ and Scholastic Achievement?,* 39 Harv. Ed. Rev. 1 (1969).

initial acknowledgment of cultural and temperamental distinctness, little progress is likely to be made.

The presence of increased numbers of minority students thus poses a dual challenge to law schools. First, can law schools take students with nonstandard educational and cultural backgrounds and provide them with the necessary educational experiences to make them successful attorneys? Second, can they do so without adopting means that rob the schools of the benefits of cultural diversity and the infusion of fresh approaches that the newcomers can bring to their legal educations?[137]

It must not be forgotten, however, that at the same time that minority students pose a challenge to the ingenuity and adaptability of legal educators, they also present a unique opportunity. Many of the reforms that have been instituted in response to the needs of minority students have been ones that have benefited nonminority students as well. Until the mid-1960's, innovation in law teaching had been stunted by a combination of a steady increase in applications[138] resulting in admission only of "super-qualified" applicants and the traditional sink-or-swim attitude of the schools which placed the onus of accommodation on the student, rather than the educator.[139] As a result, many glaring deficiencies in methods, curriculum, and philosophy went unnoticed. The arrival of minority students brought these into sharp relief and provided an occasion for much-needed self-examination.[140] As a result the first half-decade of minority admissions has witnessed a sharp acceleration in the rate of experimentation with new curricular and instructional approaches.[141] This section examines a number of such approaches.

---

137. This loss can come about in two ways. First, law schools, in an attempt to decrease "minority problems" can concentrate on recruiting "super-Chicanos" and "super-Blacks," students whose academic records and other paper credentials approach or exceed those of the student admitted under ordinary standards. With some exceptions, such a policy is likely to result in the acceptance of relatively Anglicized minority students, who are at home in the Anglo world, and less likely to upset the institution's routine. Second, law schools can admit a "mix" of minority students, *see* notes 98-108 *supra*, and accompanying text, but then require them to conform to the ongoing system on penalty of academic sanction. For students in schools that adhere to the latter philosophy, survival is only possible at the expense of their cultural values and ethnic identity; many are unwilling to pay this price. *See* Bell, *supra* note 4, at 547; Leonard, *supra* note 106, at 585.

138. *See* notes 1-4 *supra*, and accompanying text.

139. *See* notes 2-3 *supra*, and accompanying text.

140. In some areas, the impact of minority students on legal education has been direct and unmistakable, for example, in the adoption of special educational programs. In other areas, however, the presence of minority students has been one of a number of forces influencing the development of change. Areas where the effect of minorities has been less direct, but nevertheless significant, are curriculum, clinical programs, and teaching techniques.

141. *See* notes 5-9 *supra*, and accompanying text.

Although primary emphasis is placed on their impact on minority students, their usefulness to the institutions as a whole is manifest.

A. Curriculum

The curriculum that Chicano law students faced at the advent of minority admissions programs in the mid-1960's had remained unchanged for years. In most law schools the curriculum emphasized commercial law and property law.[142] Even in courses dealing with the law of persons, primary attention was placed on the financial interests involved.[143]

For students who come from minority groups that have been excluded from the mainstream of economic life, a curriculum that emphasizes property interests presents a serious obstacle. Few Chicano students have acquired much familiarity with the internal functioning of the world of business. More important, Chicano students do not have the interest in such courses that would motivate them to master the subject matter.[144] Furthermore, the traditional curriculum appeared to minority students, and some nonminority as well, to be largely irrelevant to the actual practice of law.[145]

Faced with a curriculum they regarded as irrelevant, Chicano law students demanded changes. They demanded new courses, new content in presently offered courses, and new emphases in traditional courses. In response to these demands from Chicanos, and other minority students,[146] and in order to facilitate the education of minority students,[147] a number of changes in the curriculum have been made.[148]

Perhaps the most significant change in the curricula of law schools has been the addition of new courses responsive to the interests of minority students. Courses entitled "Civil Rights," "Poverty Law," "Racism in America," and "Law and the Consumer," are indicative

---

142. Burns, *supra* note 69; *see also* Diggs, *supra* note 123. Diggs claims that the traditional law courses are taught from a money perspective. *Id.* at 767.

143. Diggs, *supra* note 123, at 767.

144. Gozansky & DeVito, *supra* note 131, at 732. *See* Reynoso, *supra* note 59, at 843. Reynoso notes a Chicano pattern of improving school work beyond the first year due to the fact that Chicano students elect courses of interest to them. *See also* Diggs, *supra* note 123, at 764.

145. *See, e.g.,* Reynoso, *supra* note 59, at 837.

146. *See, e.g.,* Law School Division of the ABA, Equal Rights Project Report (1972) that calls for reform of the law school curriculum.

147. The primary thrust and justification of curriculum reform has been the need for more relevant courses for minority law students. *See generally,* Bok, *supra* note 124, at 37; Burns, *supra* note 69, at 903; Gozansky & DeVito, *supra* note 131, at 732; Comment, *Current Legal Education of Minorities: A Survey,* 19 Buff. L. Rev. 639, 647, 653 (1969); Panella and McPherson, *supra* note 133, at 573-75. *Contra,* Jensen, *supra* note 124, at 449.

148. *See* note 140, *supra.*

of the new courses.[149] Casebooks have been published to facilitate teaching such courses.[150]

In addition to new courses, traditional courses such as contracts and property have been infused with new content that reflects the interests of minority students.[151] For example, landlord-tenant issues (public housing) as they affect the poor have been incorporated in property courses,[152] and consumer issues have been integrated into contract and commercial law courses.[153] Traditional courses that have not added new content have modified their perspective. Courses in family law, for example, have begun to focus on the status of illegitimacy with respect to government benefits.[154] Similarly, courses on corporations have begun to emphasize corporate responsibility to minority groups, the poor, and the public.[155] Today, almost every course includes a broader perspective and new emphasis.[156]

The most radical of the changes in the law school curriculum has been the addition of clinical courses. Clinical education is not only a major reform in the curriculum, it is a major reform in the method of teaching in law schools. Chicano and other minority students have responded to clinical education and pushed for its acceptance and

---

149. *See, e.g.,* The University of New Mexico Bulletin for the School of Law, 1973-74. *See also* the survey of law school courses on poverty and related social problems in Proceedings of the National Conference on the Teaching of Anti-Poverty Law, Association of American Law Schools 209-21 (1970).

150. *See, e.g.,* G. Cooper, P. Dodyk, C. Berger, M. Paulsen, P. Shrag & M. Sovern, Cases and Materials on Law and Poverty (1973); E. Jarmel, Legal Representation of the Poor (1972); R. Levy, T. Lewis, & P. Martin, Cases on Social Welfare and the Individual (1971); D. Bell, Race, Racism, and American Law (1974); A. Berney, J. Goldberg, J. Dooley & D. Carroll, Law and the Poor: Cases and Materials on Poverty Law (1975).

151. *See Survey of Seminars in Traditional Areas Retooled for Poor,* Proceedings of the National Conference on the Teaching of Anti-Poverty Law, *supra* note 149, at 214-16.

152. *Compare, e.g.,* A. Casner & W. Leach, Cases and Text on Property, Part VII (1st ed. 1950), *with* A. Casner & W. Leach, Cases and Text on Property, Part VI (2d ed. 1969).

153. The change in title for the second edition of R. Speidel, R. Summers, & J. White, Commercial and Consumer Law (2d ed. 1974) reflects the change in content from the original book, Commercial Transactions (1969). Moreover, the authors stated in the preface to the second edition that the difference in editions is the addition of "four new chapters on protecting the consumer, mainly in credit transactions."

154. *E.g.,* M. Paulson, W. Wadlington, & J. Goebel, Domestic Relations: Cases and Materials xvii (2d ed. 1974); *see* C. Foote, R. Levy, & F. Sander, Cases and Materials on Family Law 4-5 (1966).

155. *See, e.g., Preface* to D. Vagts, Basic Corporation Law (1973):
> Finally, the experience (to be gained in a course in corporation law) ought to enable the student to get a firmer grasp of the corporation in the economy and society, interpreting that aspect with his overall views on politics and economics. It is, I believe, deeply important that lawyers be capable of thinking intelligently about the relationship between corporations and the public interest.

Id. at 1.

156. *See* Bell, *supra* note 62, at 30.

expansion in law schools as a credit-worthy subject.[157] Chicano students see clinical education as relevant to their aims in two ways. First, it advances their objectives in attending law school, *i.e.,* the acquisition of skills necessary to perform services of direct benefit to their communities. And, second, it enables them to begin immediately to provide such services to those who need them most desperately.

Clinical courses can have powerful motivational value for minority students.[158] The student achieves satisfaction in helping someone with a serious problem, and in receiving constructive criticism from his supervisor.[159] For the Chicano student, success in clinical work may be the most rewarding feature of his law school career. The traditional plums in law school, such as high grades, law review, and moot court, go to very few students. For the overwhelming majority of each law school class, there are few institutional awards that give a sense of pride or accomplishment.[160] Recognition by one's peers, faculty supervisors, and especially by one's client for work well done is, for most students, the only pat-on-the-back they will receive in law school.

Unfortunately, such reinforcement usually is not available in the first year of law school where attrition among Chicanos is highest. The first-year curriculum has been the least affected by the forces for change. Only a few schools have introduced clinical courses in the first year.[161] Inclusion of a clinical experience in the beginning of a minority student's law school career would undoubtedly spur his motivation in other courses and give him a sense of accomplishment.[162] Although first-year students would, of course, require greater supervision in their work with clients, it would appear that the educational and personal values to be gained by such an experience would override the additional cost and investment of instructional resources.

In addition to their educational value to the law student, clinics located in poverty areas can provide much needed legal services to a segment of the community most in need of legal counseling and representation. Of the early clinical programs, several were developed

157. *See* Gozansky & DeVito, *supra* note 131, at 732; *cf.* Diggs, *supra* note 123, at 764.
158. Reynoso, *supra* note 59, at 837.
159. Romero, *Second Annual Project Report on the Dickinson School of Law Clinical Program,* 5 Council on Legal Education & Professional Responsibility (CLEPR) Newsletter, No. 9, April 1973, at 4.
160. *See* CLEPR, Survey of Clinical Education 1972-1973, at V, and Table 2.
161. Gozansky & DeVito, *supra* note 131, at 732.
162. Cochran, *Some Thoughts on Law Schools, The Legal Profession, and the Role of Students,* 1970 U. Tol. L. Rev. 623, 627-28.

in response to Chicano student demands and serve barrios located near law schools. For example, the Denver University School of Law and the University of New Mexico School of Law have criminal defense programs named "Centro Legal." Both programs were the results of the efforts of the Chicano student organizations and are primarily staffed by Chicano attorneys and Chicano students enrolled in the clinical programs. Under the supervision of the staff attorney, or faculty supervisors, the Chicano students represent clients (mostly Chicano) charged with misdemeanor offenses. These efforts at the University of New Mexico provided at first a service that would otherwise not have been available to these clients. Now in its second year, it contracts with the Public Defender Agency to provide the service.

In clinical programs that serve a largely Chicano clientele, Chicano students are uniquely qualified to perform an important role. The Mexican-American and Indian minorities are unique because of their language differences. Chicano students who can communicate with Chicano clients are frequently the only persons able to translate the client's problem into effective legal action. Trust, of course, is an additional essential element of a successful lawyer-client relationship. Chicano law students are often able to establish an immediate rapport with barrio clients, who might otherwise be reluctant to discuss a legal problem.

B. Teaching Methods

With respect to methods of teaching, law schools have made but few changes in response to the challenge of educating Chicano and other minority students. Even where new courses have been added to the curriculum, traditional teaching methods are often employed. Only in clinical education do we find reform in both curriculum and methodology.[163] Most instruction is still carried on through the case-Socratic method.[164] This method consists of the analysis of appellate decisions in a classroom setting where the teacher engages a student or several students in a Socratic dialogue.[165]

The case-Socratic method has been the subject of an increasing number of complaints and criticisms.[166] Minority students are only

---

163. "Clinical education refers to learning by doing: teaching a student by having him actually perform the tasks of a lawyer." H. Packer & T. Erlich, New Directions in Legal Education 38 (1972).

164. Id. at 29.

165. Id.

166. See generally Note, supra note 111; Watson, supra note 118, at 711-12; Stone, supra note 115, at 407-26; Watson, supra note 113, at 110-23; Savoy, supra note 112, at 457.

one of the many voices of dissatisfaction with this method of teaching law. These complaints have been summarized by Packer and Erlich as follows:

> The class atmosphere is said to be a hostile one, with the hostility directed from the icily distant teacher toward the student on the spot. Law professors as a group tend to be extremely intellectual and extremely verbal, very often to the point of ignoring the emotional and connotative level of communication. In any case, the student may suffer a severe loss in self-respect and possibly even an identity crisis.
>
> . . .
>
> In addition to criticisms of the emotional result of the Socratic method, we now hear claims that the process does damage to the student's intellectual initiative and imagination. The limits of the discussion are totally controlled by the teacher; his assumptions form the discussion; his questions are considered. The student, it is claimed, is conditioned to work in a "given" framework, not to construct his own.[167]

The complaints described above are of special concern to some Chicano law students. Because of their cultural values and educational background they find it difficult to become active participants in the give-and-take of a Socratic classroom. Finding themselves passive spectators in the daily dramas they may begin to question whether they are destined to be lawyers at all. Morale may drop, and the student may be assailed with self-doubts. Studies indicate that one of the main determinants of a law student's performance is his self-regard.[168] Hence, to the extent that the Socratic method tends to weaken the self-esteem of a law student—minority or non-minority—it may increase his chances of failure.

The case-Socratic method has withstood these complaints and criticisms, however, and remains the primary teaching method in law schools. Other methods, such as lecturing, are viewed as heresy among law school professors.[169] Professors who continue to use some variant of the Socratic method should, at the outset, explain its rationale and purpose.[170] Later, when a natural opportunity presents itself, they should discuss with the class the stresses involved in reciting in a formal, adversarial setting, and point out that some anxiety is only natural.[171] Students should be rewarded for good

---

167. H. Packer & T. Erlich, *supra* note 163, at 30.

168. Patton, *supra* note 120, at 17.

169. H. Packer & T. Erlich, *supra* note 163, at 29. "The instructor does not lecture; among law teachers lecture has been a dirty word." *Id.*

170. *See generally* Watson, *supra* note 113, at 160-63.

171. *Id.*

performances,[172] and the varieties of analytical traps or fallacies students fall prone to should periodically be acknowledged, labeled, and discussed.

Consideration might be given to postponing introduction of Socratic techniques until the second or third semester. Apart from helping to ease the adjustment problems of already overburdened students,[173] such an approach would be in accord with sound learning theory.[174] According to most learning theorists, the preferred sequence is from inductive to deductive thinking processes. Yet, the Socratic approach, which stresses application of legal rules to fact situations, is an essentially deductive technique. Reverting to a more natural sequence would involve not only less anxiety for the student but would place legal education in conformity with recent insights in discovery learning and result in a deeper understanding on the part of students.

Classes should be smaller to permit giving greater attention to each student.[175] A small student-faculty ratio makes for better teaching, and Chicano students, especially, can benefit from better teaching. The more attention each student receives, the more reinforcement and feedback he gets. Additional means of providing systematic feedback should be instituted.[176] Instituting midterm examinations that would be returned to the students with comments would be a big step in that direction. Other measures could be the provision of

---

172. *See* note 121 *supra*.

173. Very few Chicanos have had experience, prior to law school, in dealing with the performance exacted of them in a Socratic classroom. *See* notes 110-120 *supra*, and accompanying text. Indeed, one author has suggested that the purpose of the process of dialectic and recitation is to instill self-doubt, an item most first year minority students have in abundance. Woodey, *Why Law Professors Bark*, Student Lawyer, Mar. 1973, at 40.

174. *See* Diggs, *supra* note 123, at 768; Kelso, *Science and Our Teaching Methods: Harmony or Discord?*, 13 J. Legal Ed. 183 (1961).

175. The average size of a first year class exceeds 100 in most law schools. *See* American Bar Association, A Review of Legal Education in the United States—Fall 1973, Law Schools and Bar Admission Requirements, (1974); H. Packer & T. Erlich, *supra* note 113, at 29. The sheer numbers of law students and the high student-faculty ratio do not permit the law teacher to engage each student in a Socratic dialogue to a substantial degree. For the same reasons, little personal contact is possible between the faculty and students outside of class. See Stone, *supra* note 115, at 404.

176. The lack of feedback is one of the major criticisms leveled against law school education. Examinations are administered only at the end of courses, and examination results are usually not available until a substantial time following the administration of the examination. Moreover, examination papers are rarely returned to the student. Thus, the only institutional feedback that a student receives is a grade that is far removed from his performance and that merely informs the student how he did compared with other students. Qualitative feedback is rare. For complaints about the lack of feedback see Note, *supra* note 111; Bell, *supra* note 4, at 551; Folup, *The 1969 CLEO Summer Institute Reports: A Summary*, 1970 U. Tol. L.Rev. 633, 658; Gozansky & DeVito, *supra* note 131, at 730; Diggs, *supra* note 123, at 764; Watson, *supra* note 113, at 123, 129.

model answers for each final examination, the return of examination bluebooks with comments shortly after the examination, a class meeting shortly after the examination devoted to the examination issues, and the willingness of professors to go over each student's examination. Even compliments for a good recitation in class would be valued by the students.

In addition, the grading system could be modified to reduce the competitive atmosphere. General categories of achievement could be utilized rather than differences based on a scale of 55 to 100 where the difference between an 82 and 83 is so slight as to be insignificant. The maintenance of class ranking is unnecessary for most purposes. Even a pass-fail system may be adequate in many cases to serve the law school's interest in measuring competence.[177]

If competitive grading must be retained, consideration should be given to eliminating some of its more anxiety-producing features. Although they may pretend indifference,[178] minority students tend to be extremely anxious about their grades and what they mean. This is so not only because they worry, as all law students do, about their competitive position in the job market, but also because grades are essential to their forming a realistic self-assessment.[179] As behavioral scientists have observed, a combination of circumstances conspires to make it difficult for many minority students to learn the nature of their abilities.[180] Grades can help them in this search, however, only if the grading scale is uniform and represents clearly defined and understood standards. If a law school finds that the minority students are at the bottom of the class, or failing, the solution is not to

---

177. Insistence upon distinguishing levels of excellence beyond a basic level can have serious detrimental effects on many students. Failure to excel in the first year of law school affects students' motivation and performance in the remaining two years. Patton, *supra* note 120, at 50. Unless a student excels, he does not receive the recognition or prizes that the law school bestows, such as law review. Simply passing is usually not rewarded or appreciated. Yet such achievements should be reinforced in order to motivate these students to involve themselves in their classes and in law school activities. For minority students, reinforcement of success in the sense of passing is essential. *See* Hamblin, Buckholdt & Doss, *Compensatory Education: A New Perspective,* 1970 U. Tol. L. Rev. 459.

178. *See* notes 117-30 *supra,* and accompanying text.

179. *See, e.g.,* Bok, *supra* note 62, at 30. Conflicting messages from educational authorities produce some of this uncertainty; the student is uncertain over the extent to which he has been aided in his educational career by the beneficent, invisible hand of "special" programming and grading. *See* Panella & McPherson, *supra* note 133, at 579-89; Bell, *supra* note 4, at 552.

180. Any suggestion that law school is not an "equal race" can be a devastating experience for the minority student; his progress, his performance in courses, all become suspect in his eyes. *See* O'Neil, *supra* note 69, at 763-64; Graglia, *supra* note 62, at 360-61. *See* Bell, *supra* note 4, at 551-52.

lower standards or adopt a dual grading policy,[181] but to put into effect compensatory programs, such as those discussed in the next section,[182] in order that those students in need of help can progress to the point where they can meet regular academic standards. Differential grading inevitably becomes known and, when it does, it results in a loss of self-esteem on the part of the minority student and degrades him in the eyes of his fellow classmates.[183] It also cheats the more able, hard-working Chicano whose legitimate "B" or "C" grade becomes indistinguishable from the easy grade given those who did not meet the regular standard.[184] When a given Chicano student, despite special assistance, cannot come up to the required standard, probation or expulsion may be the only solution. "Carrying" students through three years of law school only to have them discover that they cannot pass the bar examination serves neither their interest nor that of the minority community.[185]

1. Normative vs. Deductive Analysis.

In its purest form, the Socratic method is highly non-normative. The emphasis is on analysis of cases, distinguishing holdings from one another, and applying legal rules to borderline situations—on technique for its own sake.[186] While the acquisition of analytic skills is a legitimate, indeed, essential, goal, it is often sought to the exclusion of equally important matters. Typically, Socratic teachers devote little or no time to the analysis of the social and economic class interests involved in various rules of law or to the manner in which the law can serve to promote, or deter, race or class oppression.[187]

181. A number of law schools concede that they do employ such a practice, and it appears likely that it is more widespread than is admitted. Graglia, *supra* note 62, at 359-60; Hughes, McKay & Winograd, *supra* note 2, at 710; Ijalaye, *Concessional Admission of Underprivileged Students*, 20 Buff. L. Rev. 435, 440 (1971); Bell, *supra* note 4, at 552.

182. *See* text accompanying notes 199-254 *infra*.

183. *See* notes 179-81 *supra*, and accompanying text. Many Anglo students feel slightly jealous of minority students, whom they see as receiving privileges, such as financial aid, they do not "deserve." Cochran, *supra* note 162, at 655; Pinderhughes, *supra* note 69, at 456-57. *See generally* Summers, *supra* note 119.

184. O'Neil, *supra* note 69, at 763; *see* Leonard, *supra* note 62, at 26.

185. Cabranes, *Careers in Law for Minorities: A Puerto Rican's Perspective on Recent Developments in Legal Education*, 25 J. Legal Ed. 447, 455 (1973); *see* Carl & Callahan, *supra* note 75, at 259. 1973 AALS Proceedings, Part I, at 144, cites a newspaper story critical of the University of Michigan's affirmative admissions policy on the grounds that such a policy inevitably means a dual graduation, as well. *But see* Hughes, McKay & Winograd, *supra* note 2, at 710, arguing that many minority students who are in serious academic difficulty would make fine attorneys if only they were able to pass their school and bar examinations. Leonard, *supra* note 62, at 26, believes that Blacks who have been only marginal students in law school often do well after graduation, freed from the constraints and pressures of law school.

186. *See* Katz, *supra* note 124, at 603-04; *see also* Watson, *supra* note 113, at 110.

187. Diggs, *supra* note 123, at 768.

Many instructors pride themselves on their treatment of "policy" factors, but in too many cases policy analysis is conducted in factual contexts or settings that do not readily lend themselves to exploration of the social issues of greatest concern to the minority communities. Yet such social issues are intellectually valid areas of inquiry,[188] and they are, of course, areas of intense interest to the minority student. Indeed, Anglo students have been pressing for their inclusion for some time, not so much because they concern them personally, but because the absence of any socio-ethical dimension to law study leaves them feeling like "hired guns."[189]

The addition of a valuative dimension would do much to ease the minority student's feeling that law is irrelevant to his aspirations and reduce his fear that he is being co-opted into an alien, hostile world.[190] It would also give him an area in which he could excel. As a result of his background and life experiences, the minority student is often capable of very sophisticated analyses of the racial or class dynamics of a legal prescription. Naturally, incorporation of such questions into classroom methodology would require that they be made a part of examinations as well.

2. Attitudes

Perhaps the most critical need for change is in the attitudes of law schools and law teachers toward teaching. Law schools should restore an emphasis on teaching as its central mission. Scholarship and writing, while important, should be viewed in the context of this principal mission.[191] Law faculties should familiarize themselves with the principles of learning and with the literature relating to methods of imparting information and skills.[192] They should experi-

188. *See* Bell, *Black Faith in a Racist Land,* 17 How. L.J. 300, 317 (1972); *cf.* Pinderhughes, *supra* note 69, at 447-48.

189. Savoy, *supra* note 112, at 462, 472; *see also* Katz, *supra* note 124, at 694.

190. *See* notes 68-81, 105-07, 113-16 *supra,* and accompanying text.

191. The criticism that law teachers are much too busy with building up publication credits to devote the time, energy, and imagination required to teach those students who are not in the top ten percent of their class is widespread. *See, e.g.,* Carl & Callahan, *supra* note 75, at 251; Watson, *supra* note 113, at 111. However, teaching performance has been called the great merit of law teachers. H. Parker & T. Erlich, *supra* note 163, at 32.

192. *See, e.g.,* the principles of learning outlined in Kelso, *supra* note 174, at 184. These principles are (1) need for the student to see the relevance of his study to his goals, (2) feedback, and (3) satisfactory personality adjustment to the educational system. *See also* the suggestion that the psychology of education and the findings of behavioral science be emphasized in law teaching. Diggs, *supra* note 123, at 768. The concepts of teaching and learning are generally not known by law teachers. They come into law teaching by reason of outstanding academic credentials. Law schools assume that new professors will be able to teach, but they are rarely given training in teaching. They have had no courses in educational theory, educational psychology, or even practice teaching. They are generally not observed or critiqued by their colleagues. Although law professors apply themselves vigor-

ment with different methods of teaching such as clinical education, audio-visual aids, the use of problems, and lectures. Professors should strive to make their classes interesting and enjoyable. They should give thought to the question of how to motivate the students to become involved in the subject matter they are teaching by means other than the fear or the reward of grades.[193] Examples and questions can be drawn from areas of interest to all students, including minority students.

A change in attitude should reflect a greater concern for the students as individuals. Who are they? What are their backgrounds,[194] their aspirations, their educational needs? The teacher should cultivate a sensitivity to the students' feelings, their anxieties, their frustrations, and their fears.[195] He should be willing to meet with the students outside of class both formally and informally. He should be accessible to the students to discuss either class material or non-academic subjects. In short, the law teacher needs to change his image from one of detachment to one of understanding and concern.

It should be observed that a recent attempt to teach law teachers how to teach has been made. The Association of American Law Schools has sponsored three Law Teaching Clinics, the first in 1969, the second in 1971, and the third in 1973. These clinics were conducted during the summer for law teachers with no more than four years of law teaching experience. The faculty consisted of experienced law professors. The focus and commitment of the clinics was described as follows by the Director, Frank R. Strong, Professor of Law at the University of North Carolina:

> The program focus was . . . on the teaching learning process—learning theories; educative elements in the cognitive learning of law; awareness of emotive factors in the student-teacher relationship and development of coping capacity; appreciation of the presence of similar emotive factors in attorney-client relationships and of the importance of effective as well as cognitive learning; the place of conative learning in law study. Such focus emphasizes attention to attitudinal considerations and classroom methods and skills. Development of substantive *legal* knowledge is involved only as a means to these ends, but there is definite intent to acquaint the law teacher

---

ously in preparing for class, and pride themselves on this, they devote little effort to the art of teaching. Stone, *supra* note 115, at 403.

193. For example, law schools have been criticized for devoting too little attention to motivating students. Diggs, *supra* note 123, at 764.

194. *See* Bell, *supra* note 4, at 553-54.

195. *Id.; see also* Watson, *supra* note 113, at 113, 160-63.

with elementary psychological and psychiatric knowledge pertinent to the learning process.[196]

One hundred and seventy-five law teachers have participated in the three Law Teaching Clinics. Fifty participated in the 1969 Clinic held at the University of North Carolina, fifty-eight in the 1971 Clinic at the University of Wisconsin, and sixty-seven in the 1973 Clinic at the University of Colorado.[197]

Despite the success of the Law Teaching Clinics, their future is in doubt due to funding problems. The Law Teaching Clinic was fully funded by the Office of Education in 1969 and 1971, and about two-thirds funded in 1973. Although the Law Teaching Advisory Committee has recommended the continuation of the Clinic and the search for further funding of the Clinic,[198] no decision regarding a 1975 Clinic has yet been made.

The Law Teaching Clinics have indeed made an important start in legal education—training law teachers in teaching. If the clinics cannot be continued due to funding problems, the work of the clinics should be carried on by the individual law schools. The faculty of the University of New Mexico School of Law, for example, has experimented with the use of video-taped classes by some of its faculty as a means of ascertaining what are the common elements of a "good" class. Other techniques can readily be devised.

C. Special Programs

The most significant responses of law schools to the challenge of educating Chicano and other minority students are in the nature of special programs for these students. To a certain extent, these programs may involve a change in curriculum or in teaching methods,[199] but they are separately categorized because they are not generally available to the entire student body. For the most part, these programs are designed for and limited to the minority students admitted under different admissions standards. To be sure, special programs in some schools are not limited to minority students,[200]

---

196. *Report of the Law Teaching Clinic Advisory Committee* in 1971 Proceedings of the AALS 132, 133.

197. *See Report of Law Teaching Clinic* in 1969 Proceedings of AALS 118; 1971 Proceedings, at 132; 1973 Proceedings, at 95.

198. *See Report of the Law Teaching Clinic Advisory Committee* in 1973 Proceedings of the AALS 95, 98.

199. *See* notes 142-98 *supra,* and accompanying text for a discussion of the changes in curriculum and teaching methods apart from special programs.

200. For example, the Programmed Studies course at the University of New Mexico is designed for students with low admissions credentials. *See* the description of this program *infra,* at notes 248-54.

but since most programs are aimed at the student with low admissions credentials and since most minority students are admitted on a special basis, practically all special programs are associated with "minority programs."

Special programs for minority students have been developed for a number of reasons,[201] and they may serve a number of different but related purposes. For example, some programs are specifically designed to perform an evaluation function, such as summer pre-law programs, but they may also serve other functions such as public relations, orientation, preparation, and supplemental education. The evaluation and public relation functions are directed to the admissions process, and will not be emphasized here; only those special programs that are directed to meeting the challenge of educating minority law students who are admitted will be examined in detail.

1. Pre-Law Programs

Pre-law programs have generally emphasized the evaluation function,[202] that is, they have been used to assess probable performance in law school. As such, they have served as an alternative to the traditional predictors—the Law School Admission Test (LSAT) and undergraduate grade point average (UGPA).[203] Those students who successfully complete the pre-law program are generally admitted to a law school.

The best-known examples of such programs are the summer regional institutes sponsored by the Council on Legal Education Opportunity (CLEO),[204] the University of New Mexico program for American Indians,[205] and the University of Denver programs, open primarily to Chicanos.[206] These programs serve more than an evaluation function. They serve an educational function. One function or

---

201. The reasons that have been advanced for special programs are (1) evaluation for purposes of admission, (2) public relations in order to project a better image with regard to equal opportunity, (3) orientation for the purpose of acclimating minority students to the rigors of law school, and (4) education, either supplementary or compensatory. See, e.g., Rosen, *Equalizing Access To Legal Education: Special Programs For Law Students Who Are Not Admissible By Traditional Criteria*, 1970 U. Tol. L. Rev. 321, 336-40.

202. Cf. Rosen, *supra* note 201, at 344-48.

203. Fulop, *supra* note 176, at 638.

204. For descriptions and evaluations of the CLEO program *see generally* Rosen, *supra* note 201, at 341-48; Fulup, *supra* note 176; Panella & McPherson, *supra* note 133; Gozansky & DeVito, *supra* note 131; Reiss, *supra* note 13.

205. The University of New Mexico program is described in detail in Christopher & Hart, *Indian Law Scholarship Program at the University of New Mexico*, 1970 U. Tol. L. Rev. 691.

206. The Denver program for Chicanos is described in Huff, *supra* note 38.

the other may be emphasized in the particular CLEO regional institute or other program, but they all serve an educational purpose.[207]

What are the educational purposes served by the pre-law programs? First, they have been used to acclimatize the students to the law schools.[208] The programs are designed to closely resemble a typical law school experience. Several courses, usually from the first-year curriculum, are offered. Students are exposed for the first time to case analysis and the Socratic method. Law school-type examinations are administered and graded. Thus, the shock experienced by all new students in the first semester of law school may be substantially reduced.[209]

In addition to acclimatizing the students to law school study, classes, and examinations, many programs have been used to provide the students with the basic skills essential to success in law school. For example, study techniques such as briefing, outlining, and reviewing have been emphasized. Research techniques, library use, and examination-writing techniques have also been emphasized by some programs.[210]

A third purpose served by some pre-law programs is compensatory or remedial education. This purpose assumes that the minority students admitted to law school with lower credentials as measured by the traditional admissions criteria are likely to be deficient in some of the skills tested by the traditional criteria. This purpose further assumes that the verbal and analytical skills tested by the traditional admissions criteria are important to success in law school.[211] Accepting these assumptions, some programs offer remedial courses in English grammar, composition, etc.[212]

In view of the qualifications of the minority students presently being admitted to law school, a compensatory or remedial aspect is generally unnecessary in pre-law programs today. For example, all but one of the Chicano students admitted to the University of New Mexico School of Law in the fall of 1974 who participated in the CLEO institute were predicted to succeed in law school using the

---

207. *Cf.* Rosen, *supra* note 201, at 344.

208. A description of this particular function of pre-law programs is found in Rosen, *supra* note 201, at 338-39.

209. For an account of the difficulties encountered in adjusting to law school, *see generally,* Patton, *supra* note 120; Note, *supra* note 111.

210. A variety of skills emphasized in CLEO institutes and other pre-law programs are summarized in Rosen, *supra* note 201, at 340, 346.

211. These assumptions are summarized in Rosen, *supra* note 201, at 339-40.

212. *See* notes 222-34 *infra:* Rosen, *supra* note 201, at 346, for examples of CLEO institutes that offered remedial or compensatory programs. *See also* Panella & McPherson, *supra* note 133, at 562, 568.

traditional admissions criteria.[213] Very few students attending the 1974 Southwest Regional Institute at the University of New Mexico scored below 400 on the LSAT, and a substantial number scored above 500.[214] Thus, the need for a remedial component is not present for the overwhelming majority of minority students admitted to a pre-law program.[215] For those students who do need remedial instruction in a basic skill, a remedial program should be designed to meet the particular needs of those students without subjecting all of the students to an unnecessary and demeaning exercise.[216]

Several CLEO institutes have generally rejected the notion of compensatory education. The 1973 and 1974 Southwest Regional CLEO Institutes, largely filled by Chicano students, emphasized the skills essential to success in law school. The Director of the 1973 Southwest Institute described the educational purpose as follows:

> The skills that we attempted to teach were not remedial. We did not pay very much attention to students' grammar, sentence structure, or even diction unless such deficiencies inhibited understanding. Instead, we attempted to teach methods of legal analysis and organization that would be helpful in taking law school examinations.[217]

---

213. See L. Romero, *Final Report of the Director: Southwest Legal Education Opportunity Institute,* 1974 (on file at the national headquarters of the Council on Legal Educational Opportunity, Washington, D.C.).

214. *Id.*

215. The students attending CLEO institutes today are much better qualified than the students attending CLEO programs five years ago. This conclusion is supported by the statistical studies in Council on Legal Education Opportunity, Characteristics and Performance of Minority Group Students Who Entered Law School in 1968, 1969, and 1970: Comparison of CLEO Participants with Other Minority Group Students (Unpublished Study on file at the CLEO headquarters in Washington, D.C.). One study revealed that the percentage of CLEO participants with LSAT scores below 450 decreased from 82.7 in 1968 to 73.1 in 1970. For Mexican-American CLEO students the decrease in the percentage of low LSAT scores is even more dramatic. Table 3 indicates that the percentage of Chicanos in CLEO with LSAT scores below 450 dropped from 66.66 in 1968 to 57.9 in 1970. The latest statistics supplied by CLEO for the CLEO class of 1973 show that 52.2 percent of the participants scored below 450.

It can be inferred, quite legitimately, that the number of students in pre-law programs such as CLEO who need remedial programs has likewise decreased. For example, in the 1969 CLEO institute at the University of Iowa, approximately 27% (13 out of 48) of the participants were found to be in need of a remedial writing program. *See* Panella & McPherson, *supra* note 133, at 562. It may be assumed that the percentage is substantially smaller today.

216. The 1969 University of Iowa CLEO institute is one example of a remedial program designed especially for those students with serious writing difficulties. *See* Panella & McPherson, *supra* note 133, at 562, 568. The 1973 and 1974 Southwest CLEO institutes dealt with students in need of special help on an individual basis. *See* Lee, *Final Report of the Director: Southwest Legal Education Opportunity Program,* Summer 1973, at 16 (on file with the national CLEO office headquarters, Washington, D.C.).

217. Lee, *supra* note 216, at 16.

The distinction between the teaching of certain skills for remedial purposes and the teaching of other skills for purposes of succeeding in law school may seem insignificant, but it is an important one.[218] The latter skills are ones that all students must acquire if they are to succeed in law school. Most students, nonminority as well as minority, will not have these skills—for example, case analysis and organization of answers to a law school examination—when they enter law school. Some students may be more adept at mastering these skills, but, essentially, they are skills that all students must acquire.[219] To the extent that a pre-law program focuses on the teaching of such skills, it is not remedial. Rather, it is supplementary or enriching. And it is supplementary education, not remedial education, that can best benefit most Chicano students.[220] Indeed, supplementary education would benefit most nonminority students as well.

The controversy over remedial and supplementary education in pre-law programs arises primarily in the design of the writing programs. CLEO requires a writing program in each of its regional institutes.[221] Some institutes design the writing program as a compensatory program[222] while a few institutes have structured the writing program to provide supplementary education.[223] Those that offer remedial writing instruction normally employ English teachers[224] and emphasize basic writing skills such as grammar, diction, and organization.[225] Although legal materials may be used for the writing assignments, the focus is on communication skills, not examination-writing skills.

The writing programs that are supplementary rather than remedial

---

218. The distinction is also recognized in Rosen, *supra* note 201, at 343.

219. For an excellent description of the special tasks students must master in order to do well at law school exams, *see* Bell, *Law School Exams and Minority Students,* 3 BALSA Reports 39 (Spring 1974).

220. Moveover, supplementary education minimizes the risk that minority students will view the special program as implicitly treating them as inferior. *See* Rosen, *supra* note 201, at 343.

221. Memorandum from Michael J. Moorhead, Executive Director of CLEO to Law School Deans, September 25, 1973, regarding sponsorship of regional summer institutes, at 5 (unpublished memorandum on file with the Nat'l CLEO Office, Washington, D.C.).

222. *See* Rosen, *supra* note 201, at 346 n. 59; Panella & McPherson, *supra* note 133, at 562, 568.

223. In particular, the 1973 Southwest CLEO Institute at Arizona State University and the 1974 Southwest CLEO Institute at the University of New Mexico designed their writing programs to focus on examination-writing skills. *See* Lee, *supra* note 216, at 28.

224. For example, one of the writing instructors at the 1969 University of Iowa CLEO program was an assistant professor of literature. The other writing instructor was not a lawyer. Panella & McPherson, *supra* note 133, at 559. In addition, one writing instructor at three CLEO institutes is a lecturer in English. Brand, *supra* note 129.

225. *Id.* at 332.

in nature proceed from the assumption that most minority students have the requisite language skills to succeed in law school.[226] Therefore, the focus is on the examination-writing skill that is critical to success in law school. Unlike the remedial writing programs, law professors, usually teachers of first-year courses, are used.[227] The written assignments are law school-type questions that call for legal analysis of a fact situation. Analysis of the problem and recognition of the legal issues are emphasized as the first and most important skills in the process of writing an answer.[228] The second related skill is organization. The students are taught how to outline and organize an answer in a way that will apply legal concepts to the facts of the problem and demonstrate the validity of the writer's analysis.[229]

There are several important considerations when comparing the relative values of the remedial writing programs and the supplementary legal writing programs. First, do Chicano law students have a basic deficiency in communication skills? Advocates of the remedial programs maintain that CLEO and minority students do suffer from communication skills difficulties, but they are careful to point out that these problems are not unique to minority students.[230] It must be recognized that Chicano law students, like other students, are not a homogeneous group. As a whole they have the same range of language abilities and difficulties as other students.[231] Some Chicano law students, like some regular students, may need remedial help. And, of course, it might benefit most students, Chicanos and others as well, to participate in a remedial writing course. The reason students have trouble on law school examinations, however, is usually not an inability to communicate in proper English; rather, it is the lack of preparation for the type of exacting writing that will be required of them in law school examina-

---

226. *See* note 215 *supra.* Writing problems are not unique to minority students, and they have the "same range of abilities and difficulties as other students." Brand, *supra* note 129, at 331. *Contra,* Cabranes, *supra* note 185, at 458.

227. For example, the 1973 Southwest Cleo Institute at Arizona State University and the 1974 Southwest CLEO Institute at the University of New Mexico chose to employ law professors to teach in the writing programs. Since the writing program focused on the skills involved in writing law school examinations, law professors with experience in drafting, reading, and grading law school examinations were best suited for the program. *See* Lee, *supra* note 216, at 20.

228. *See* the description of the writing courses offered in the 1973 Southwest CLEO Institute at Arizona State University by Professor Rose and Mr. Farr in Lee, *supra* note 216, at 42-45, 46-56.

229. *Id. See also* the suggestions for writing law school examinations in Bell, *supra* note 219, at 39, 41-42.

230. Brand, *supra* note 129, at 331.

231. *Id.*

tions.[232] To devote the focus of a writing program to the mastery of the examination writing skill is a far better allocation of resources. It has the further advantage that the students can see the relevance between their writing exercises and survival in law school. Finally, a supplementary writing progam avoids the minority students' reaction to a "remedial" program as evidence of their inferiority.[233] To the extent that some minority students, or some nonminority students, need remedial writing programs, they should be provided on an individual and specially designed basis.[234]

2. Pre-Start Program

The distinguishing characteristics of pre-start programs are: (1) The students take prescribed regular law school courses during the summer; (2) Academic credit is received for such courses; and (3) The students who move from such a program into law school are usually light-loaded during the first year.[235] Pre-start programs, like pre-law programs, may serve a number of functions. For most such programs, however, the predominant purpose is evaluation.[236] If the student receives satisfactory grades in the prescribed summer courses, he is then admitted into law school for the fall semester.

Although such programs are successful as an admissions device,[237] the educational value of such programs for minority students is questionable. In some pre-start programs, there is no supplemental or enrichment component.[238] Nor do pre-start programs serve to acclimatize and prepare the students for the first year of law school, since the program in essence is the commencement of their first year in law school. For students who do not do well, failure in the summer courses spells the end of their legal career. Thus, the effect of pre-start programs which lack supplemental or remedial features is to establish another obstacle for minority students to admission to law school. And this obstacle must be overcome without the benefit of

232. *Id.* at 332. The ways in which law school examinations are unique are described in Bell, *supra* note 219, at 39-40.

233. When special programs are viewed as compensatory or remedial, minority students tend to infer that the predominantly white law school is treating them as inferior. Rosen, *supra* note 201, at 343.

234. *See* note 215 *supra.*

235. *See generally* Rosen, *supra* note 201, at 352-56.

236. The major exception is the University of Michigan pre-start program described in Rosen, *supra* note 201, at 353.

237. *See* Murray, *The Tryout System*, 21 J. Legal Ed. 317 (1969); Murray, *The Tryout Program in Retrospect*, 26 J. Legal Ed. 363 (1974) for a description of the University of Georgia School of Law's summer tryout program.

238. For example, neither the Emory Law School nor the University of Michigan pre-start programs incorporate remedial or supplemental education features. Rosen, *supra* note 201, at 352-53.

any educational assistance. In essence, such programs have adopted the "sink or swim" attitude.

Some schools have attempted to include an educational aspect in addition to the evaluation component in their pre-start programs, by incorporating remedial courses.[239] Others have added supplemental education features.[240] One program has even rejected the evaluation functions; the students cannot fail the pre-start program.[241] Thus, those students who do not receive academic credit may still enroll in law school. For them, the pre-start program is essentially a trial run at law school. Its educational value lies in its capacity to acclimatize and prepare these students for "the real thing."

Since most pre-start programs emphasize the evaluation function for admissions purposes, special educational programs should be specifically designed to aid the students who graduate from these programs and enter law school. Law schools cannot consider most pre-start programs as having provided any kind of supplemental or remedial educational assistance. Therefore, once the successful students of these programs enter law school, the challenge of educating them still remains.

3. In-School Programs

Perhaps the best measure of a law school's commitment to meet the challenge of educating Chicano and other minority students is their provision of special programs for minority students who gain admittance to law school. Failure to provide such special programs is an indication of a school's retention of the "sink or swim" attitude and its unwillingness to accept the challenge of educating all its students.

The types of in-school programs are extremely varied. Moreover, they differ in the degree of responsiveness to the needs of students who lack traditional admissions credentials. It is impossible to survey all of the in-school programs designed by the different law schools, but a summary of the kinds of such programs will be attempted. In addition, those programs that are especially innovative or that serve a substantial number of Chicano law students will be described in more detail.

Many law schools with a minority student program offer some

---

239. Both the University of Missouri at Kansas City and the University of Colorado pre-start programs include a remedial education component. Rosen, *supra* note 201, at 354.

240. The Drake Law School's program has a supplemental education feature. Rosen, *supra* note 201, at 355.

241. *See* the description of the University of Michigan pre-start program in Rosen, *supra* note 201, at 353.

kind of tutorial program.[242] The tutorial programs are sometimes highly structured, but many are informal. Structured tutorial programs are of indisputable benefit to specially admitted law students. They usually involve faculty members or paid student assistants, and the tutorial sessions are regularly scheduled. Good tutorial programs can ensure that the students understand, review, and organize the material in preparation for final examinations. Furthermore, tutorials can reinforce the Chicano law student's confidence in himself by providing feedback on his understanding of the substantive course materials.

Some in-school programs are essentially curricular modifications. For example, one school permits specially admitted minority students to elect a seminar on a "relevant" subject in lieu of a regular first-year course.[243] Other schools have designed a four-year law school program for those students with low admissions credentials.[244] The students in such "stretch-out" programs normally take the first-year curriculum in two years. Some schools with four-year programs supplement the first year courses with courses offered in other departments that may help to overcome certain educational deficiencies or to enrich law school education generally.[245] Such stretch-out programs can do much to help alleviate the pressures certain minority students experience, particularly in the first year.

Writing programs are offered by some schools, but they appear to be mostly remedial; that is, they tend to focus on language skills such as reading, grammar, structure, and diction.[246] For the most part, in-school writing programs, like pre-law writing programs, fail to emphasize the skills involved in writing law school examinations.[247]

A particularly innovative, and successful, in-school educational program has been developed by the University of New Mexico. Since most of the students who participate in this program are Mexican-American students, it will be described in some detail.[248] The pro-

---

242. The most common type of special program operated by law schools for disadvantaged students during 1971-72 was a tutorial program. Stevens, Bar Examination Study Project 3-4 (Mem. No. 12, 1974); *cf.* Rosen, *supra* note 201, at 336-63.

243. *See* the description of the Rutgers (Newark) Law School's program in Rosen, *supra* note 201, at 360-61.

244. *See generally* Rosen, *supra* note 201, at 357-58.

245. The Stanford Law School stretch-out program is described in Rosen, *supra* note 01, at 357.

246. Of the thirteen types of special programs listed in Stevens, *supra* note 242, at 4, two were remedial writing programs and one focused on examination techniques.

247. *See* text accompanying notes 221-29, *supra.*

248. The following description is derived primarily from a letter from Professor Ted arnall, University of New Mexico School of Law, to Professor Rodric Schoen, Texas Tech University School of Law, July 31, 1972, and a letter from Professor Jerrold L. Walden,

gram, called "Programmed Studies," is designed for students with a relatively low predicted first-year average, a group that to a large extent encompasses minority students but includes a substantial percentage of nonminority students as well.

Programmed Studies has several important components. The first is the classroom component. The class meets for one hour each week during the fall semester. The materials utilized for the classroom component are Charles D. Kelso's, "A Programmed Introduction to the Study of Law."[249] These materials contain questions about law, the legal process, application of legal rules, and legal analysis that the student must answer himself. A portion of these materials are assigned for class each week, and the instructor reviews the assigned materials in class to ensure that the material has been understood.

The second component of the program is practice examinations. A short examination is administered to the students each week after the second or third week of the semester. The subjects of the short examinations are taken from the substantive courses that the students are taking. The examinations are graded and critiqued by an instructor with the assistance of tutors or teaching assistants. One additional hour per week of classroom time is devoted to this component.

A third part of the program is the tutorial component. Two student tutors are hired by the law school for each substantive course in which the students are enrolled. There is, in addition, a head tutor who oversees the tutorial program. The tutors attend the classes in the substantive course and meet with the Programmed Studies students on a regular basis throughout the semester. In addition, they assist in the preparation of course outlines.

The final component of the program is the pre-examination review. This part consists of a week-long period of intensive study in the nature of a bar review course for each first-year class in which the students are enrolled.

The results of Programmed Studies are worthy of note. Fifteen persons out of a class of 100 participated in the program in the fall of 1970. Ten of the fifteen had LSAT scores below 500 with no score exceeding 580. Eleven of the fifteen subsequently graduated. One withdrew in good standing, one withdrew while on probation, and two were suspended for academic reasons.[250]

In the fall of 1971, twenty students out of a class of 110 par-

University of New Mexico School of Law, to Professor Judith B. Ittig, University of Tennessee College of Law, August 12, 1974.

249. C. Kelso, A Programmed Introduction to the Study of Law (1965).

250. Letter from Professor Ted Parnall, *supra* note 248.

ticipated in the program. Seven had LSAT scores below 500, and four had scores exceeding 580. Five of the twenty placed in the upper half of the class, and only three received less than a 2.0 (passing) average. Fourteen members of the class who did not participate in Programmed Studies received grade point averages below 2.0.[251]

The results of the Programmed Studies classes of 1972 and 1973 have been equally impressive.[252] On the whole, students enrolled in the program have exceeded their predictions as measured by the traditional admissions criteria.[253] On the other hand, those students admitted on a competitive basis, who did not have the benefit of the program, have either barely met or fallen below their predictions.[254]

The success of Programmed Studies is due to several important factors. Perhaps most important is the commitment of the University of New Mexico to meeting the challenge of educating minority, particularly Chicano, lawyers. This commitment is expressed in the substantial resources that are devoted to the program. Two faculty members are assigned to teach Programmed Studies for which they receive teaching credit. In addition, student tutors are hired for the program. Moreover, Programmed Studies is given the status of a regular course in the fall semester of the first-year curriculum.

The Programmed Studies course carries two hours of academic credit on a pass/fail basis, and it replaces one of the required first-semester courses. The tutorial part of the program, without credit, continues in the second semester of the first year.

An equally important reason for the success of Programmed Studies is its educational design. The program is supplementary in nature, rather than remedial. It focuses on those skills that are most critical to success in law school—good study habits and good examination writing techniques. In sum, Programmed Studies provides Chicano students with the educational assistance and guidance that maximizes the students' opportunities for success in law school.

---

251. *Id.*
252. In 1972, 22 persons out of a class of 106 participated in the third year of the program. Twelve had LSAT scores below 500, and two had scores exceeding 580. Twenty-one of the participants achieved passing grades of at least 2.0 in their first year, and four of them achieved averages above 3.0. One student received an average below 2.0.
In 1973, 18 persons out of a class of 106 participated in the program. Fourteen had LSAT scores below 500 and one had a score exceeding 580. Fourteen achieved passing grades of at least 2.0 in their first year, and two achieved averages above 3.0. Two participants withdrew during the first year, and two failed to achieve a passing average. Memorandum by Admissions Committee to Leo M. Romero, University of New Mexico Law School, Sept. 17, 1974.
253. Letter from Professor Jerrold L. Walden, *supra* note 248.
254. *Id.*

4. Evaluation of Special Programs

Any evaluation of special programs for Chicano and other minority law students must consider both the reasons for such programs and the disadvantages encountered in designing and operating them. The reasons for special educational programs are clear and compelling. Many Chicano and other minority students present an educational challenge to law schools, and special educational programs are required to meet this challenge. To the extent that special programs are educational in nature, rather than evaluative, the justification for special programs is strong.

A number of difficulties are involved in the establishment of any special program, however. They involve separation, stigma, paternalism, nonminority backlash, constitutionality,[255] and economics. The most serious difficulty is clearly financial. Special programs must compete with other law school activities for scarce resources. Especially hard for law schools is choosing between allocating funds for minority scholarships and loans, and supporting a special educational program.[256] If law schools are serious about their commitment to educate Chicano and other minority lawyers, however, they should make the effort to find the funds for both financial assistance to the students and special educational programs.[257] The risks involved in a strong minority admissions effort without an accompanying educational program have been dramatically illustrated by the experiences of some law schools, which have suffered wholesale losses among special admission students at the end of the first year.[258]

Providing extra educational resources to the minority students without these being perceived as degrading by the student or as

---

255. For a discussion of the constitutional considerations concerning special educational programs *see* Rosen, *supra* note 201, at 363. Special educational programs may be constitutionally mandated if necessary to provide equal educational opportunity. *See* Serna v. Portales Municipal Schools, 351 F. Supp. 1279 (D.N.M. 1972), *aff'd*, 499 F.2d 1147 (10th Cir. 1974).

256. *See generally* discussion of the cost in establishing and operating special programs in Rosen, *supra* note 201, at 336.

257. The sources of financial assistance for Chicano law students are severely limited. Outside the law schools, the only sources are the CLEO stipends that presently amount ot $1,000.00 per year and the Mexican-American Legal Defense and Education Fund (MALDEF) grants.

258. *See,* for example, the experience of the Temple Law School in 1968 when many of their specially admitted minority students did not successfully complete their first year courses. Fortunately, a special program was designed to assist these students rather than flunking them out. Rosen, *supra* note 201, at 361. Another recent example occurred in 1972 at a large state university where all of the black students in the first year class were placed on academic probation. 1973 Proceedings of AALS, Part I, at 145-46 [hereinafter referred to as 1973 AALS Proceedings].

tending to isolate him from the rest of the student body is a delicate problem. To a large extent, the way the minority student views the school's efforts to provide for his benefit special review sessions, tutorials, classes in remedial writing, and the like, will be a function of the overall atmosphere.[259] Where attitudes are essentially positive, these programs are apt to be received, and used, by minority students with little comment. Where relationships have begun to deteriorate, any measure taken by the school is likely to be seen as further evidence of polarization.

In general, such resources should be made available on a voluntary, rather than a compulsory basis[260] and should be available to all students whose entrance qualifications or first semester grades fall below a certain point—not just minorities.[261] The programs are apt to be better received if the minority student associations have been consulted during their formulation and if minority students have had a voice in determining their final shape and content.[262] Ideally, such programs should be instituted at the initiative of the minority students, but schools may not feel they can wait until a request is received by the minority groups.[263] In this event, the minority associations can at least be brought into the planning and discussion of such programs and can help select the instructors or tutors. One common error seems to be to wait until it is too late. Supplementary programs should be available very early in the student's career, perhaps from the very start, and the cost of such services should be considered an integral part of the operation of any special admissions program.[264]

---

259. *See* note 121 *supra*, and accompanying text.

260. Placing remedial programs on a compulsory basis conveys a message from the law school to minority students that many find doubly offensive: it not only says we have no faith in your ability to succeed without this extra help, it also says we believe you are too foolish, lazy, or proud to do what is in your own best interest without our prodding.

261. Tutorials and other aids that are available (or required) only for minority students are resented as evidence of the school's failure to view them as individuals. *See, e.g.,* Hughes, McKay & Winograd, *supra* note 2, at 712.

262. There has been growing acceptance of student participation in many aspects of law school decisionmaking, including curriculum. *See generally* Howard, *Goodbye Mr. Chips: Student Participation in Law School Decision-Making,* 56 Va. L. Rev. 895 (1970). If student input into the curriculum-setting process is advantageous, it would appear to be especially so where the school is concerned with establishing special courses that will affect only a small segment of the student population.

263. The University of New Mexico Law School, for example, requires that all students who have been admitted with credentials falling below a certain cut-off enroll in a special course of programmed studies. This is a "given;" the student has no choice about it, and the decision whether to operate the program is not reopened every year.

264. *See, e.g.,* Reiss, *supra* note 13, at 719 for a description of the disadvantages that arise from maintaining the minority program on an ad hoc, year-to-year basis.

D. *Counseling*

Counseling services should be made available to the minority student, perhaps even before he gains admission, in order to help him arrive at a realistic assessment of his own capacities as well as the inherent limitations of what the law can do.[265] Chicano lawyers have very few role models.[266] Provision of counseling services can help avoid needless detours and discouragement and help students understand where the various roads lead.[267] It is not enough that a placement office exist and that notices appear periodically on the bulletin board.[268] Many minority students, especially at first, feel overwhelmed and are unlikely to take the initiative in investigating various lines of professional development. At little cost, placement and counseling services can arrange for visiting lecturers of minority background who speak on various kinds of legal work. Faculty panel discussions can help clarify the advantages and disadvantages of different types of careers, and a faculty member or dean should be informally designated to seek out minority students to see how they are progressing in their career planning and adjustment to law school. Where summer jobs are scarce or highly competitive, or where minority students have been unsuccessful at finding summer work of a legal nature, the placement director should canvass local law firms and government agencies in search of jobs for minorities.[269] This effort should occur early in the year so that students and employers can be paired ahead of time and so that the students can begin to acquire the mental set of a person who is going to do genuine legal work during the summer.

---

265. *See* Stone, *supra* note 115, at 426-27; Watson, *supra* note 113, at 160; *see also* Kelso, *supra* note 174, at 184.

266. *See* notes 5-6 *supra*.

267. Chicanos, in common with other minority law students, tend to get less word-of-mouth information from the students of majority race and hence are often in the dark about very elementary facts relating to placement and careers; *see* Pinderhughes, *supra* note 69, at 456-57.

268. *Compare* Law School Division of the ABA Equal Rights Project Report, 75 (1972), urging that recruitment of minority students, to be successful, must be aggressive; the recruiting school or agency must take the initiative.

269. Even big-city law firms located in cosmopolitan cities have proven remarkably resistant to efforts to interest them in employing minority persons in summer positions. Cohan, *San Francisco Law Firms Hire the Disadvantaged: Guidelines to a Successful Summer Hiring Program*, 15 Student Lawyer Journal 9 (March 1970) (inquiry sent to major San Francisco law firms resulted in 13% response; of those contacted, fewer than 5% demonstrated interest). There are indications the climate is changing, however, and that firms are now more receptive to hiring minority students. *See, e.g.,* Haley, *The Black Lawyer in Government*, 22 Harv. Law School Bull. 51 (Feb. 1971); Whitehead, *supra* note 133, at 63-65. *See* Crockett, *Racism in the Courts*, in The Radical Lawyers 111, 121-22 (J. Black ed. 1971).

E. Non-Anglo Personalities

Many Asian, Chicano, and native American students find it constitutionally difficult, if not impossible, to affect the aggressive, confident air that permits a student to shine at the Socratic game.[270] It is not so much that they lack intellectual ability or proficiency in the English language, as it is a result of long-term cultural and family conditioning.[271] This is not to say that Chicanos, Asians, and native Americans cannot be good lawyers; not every trail attorney can be a Clarence Darrow or Charles Garry. Some successful trial lawyers are soft-spoken individuals who command respect and attention not for their fiery delivery or dynamic approach but for the obvious sincerity and honesty with which they present their case.[272]

Outside the courtroom, many areas of legal practice require an ability to listen, to form an accurate intuitive understanding of another person's position, and to work effectively in reconciling parties with conflicting interests.[273] These are qualities in which the soft-spoken Chicano may well have an advantage over his more extroverted classmate; yet the legal curriculum, as presently structured, offers little opportunity to reinforce and reward these other, equally important, abilities. Acceptance of their legitimacy would help reduce the apparent conflict between minority cultural traits and the ideal of the successful lawyer and, like some of the other changes mentioned above, would offer the Chicano a chance to gain recognition and reinforcement.

F. The Marginal Student

The normal sequence for dealing with a student who fails to achieve a passing average is probation, then suspension, and, later, perhaps, readmission. Many schools follow the practice of placing the marginal student on probation one semester on condition that he brings his average up to the requisite passing grade. If he fails to meet this condition, he is suspended. Readmission is a matter within the discretion of the faculty, but usually readmission will not be considered until the student has been out of school one year.

The marginal student presents a difficult problem to law schools, but the marginal Chicano or other minority student who has been admitted on a special basis presents an even more difficult problem. Part—but only part—of the reason for the greater difficulty in dealing

---

270. *See* notes 114-17 *supra.*

271. *See* notes 113-14 *supra* and accompanying text.

272. *E.g.,* A. Ginger, The Relevant Lawyers 41, 55-56 (1972); *see* G. Abrahams, The Legal Mind 1-9, 106-16 (1954).

273. Watson, *supra* note 113, at 109, 160-63. *See generally* Watson, *supra* note 118.

with the marginal minority student is political. A greater percentage of minority students admitted on lower admission credentials tend to present unsatisfactory records at the end of the first year.[274] The result may be a politically volatile situation.[275]

That the marginal Chicano or minority student presents a difficult political problem does not necessarily imply, however, that special consideration is due such students. Still, certain solutions may be devised to ensure that marginal minority students do not flunk out before being given a fair opportunity to make the grade. One solution may be to extend the length of the probationary period.[276] Another is the establishment of special educational programs, either supplementary or remedial, for students on probation.[277] Most important, perhaps, is the need for flexibility in dealing with such students, both minority and nonminority. Law schools should be sensitive to the particular difficulties encountered by the individual student, and whenever possible, devise special programs to assist the student in overcoming his difficulties.

On the whole, however, no distinction should be made between Chicano students and nonminority students on the basis of academic standards. Both should be held to the same standards. Dual grading standards are not acceptable to the Chicano student, his Anglo classmate, or the Chicano community.

The institutional programs suggested above are in no way talismanic, nor does their adoption guarantee that the school will be populated with happy, diligent, multi-hued individuals working to-

---

274. Of the 1,042 students specially admitted to 79 law schools in the fall of 1970, 606 advanced in good standing into the second year and 222 were placed on probation. Thus, a total of 828, or 79 percent, proceeded into the second year. Stevens, *supra* note 242, at 1. Of the 828 disadvantaged students who started their second year in 1971, 587 or 70.9 percent advanced into the third year in good standing and 120 or 14.5 percent advanced into the third year on probation. Thus, 707 or 85.4 percent advanced into the third year. *Id.* at 16. Of the 531 disadvantaged students in good standing that actually enrolled in the third year in the fall of 1972, 50 or 9.4 percent failed to graduate, of the 74 on probation who enrolled, 29 or 39.2 percent failed to graduate. *Id.* at 21. In summary, of 1,042 disadvantaged students who were admitted in the fall of 1970 to 79 law schools, 96 withdrew voluntarily, 39 were dismissed but readmitted, 154 were dismissed and not readmitted, 167 have disappeared from the study, 178 were still enrolled during the 1973-74 school year, and 408 or 39.2 percent graduated in the spring of 1973. *Id.* at 23.

275. *See*, for example, the charges of discrimination that resulted when all of the black students at a large state university were placed on academic probation. 1973 AALS Proceedings, *supra* note 258, at 145-46.

276. The experience of Emory Law School's pre-start program suggests that law schools should avoid a premature judgment of failure. Gozansky & DeVito, *supra* note 131, at 740.

277. The study of the progress of disadvantaged students admitted to law school in the fall of 1970 through their second and third years shows that a number of schools have adopted special educational programs for students in academic difficulty. Stevens, *supra* note 242, at 3-4.

gether in harmony. So long as society is afflicted with racial animosity and economic inequity, the law school will feel the divisive effects of these forces. All the school can offer the student is a sensitivity to diverse cultural viewpoints, a willingness to restructure itself when necessary, and an opportunity to become a lawyer. If it conscientiously applies itself in these directions the school will win the students' acceptance, and, perhaps, in the long run, their respect.

ACKNOWLEDGMENTS

I would like to thank Susan Halci, Sheryl Jimenez, Jonlyn Martinez, Roberta Marquez and Debbie Garcia for their research assistance. Debbie Garcia was funded by the Center for Regional Studies. I appreciate the Center's support for this project.

Piatt, Bill. "Toward Domestic Recognition of a Human Right to Language." *Houston Law Review* 23 (1986): 885–906. Reprinted with the permission of the University of Houston Law Center. Courtesy of *Houston Law Review*.

Hernández-Chávez, Eduardo. "Native Language Loss and Its Implications for Revitalization of Spanish in Chicano Communities." In Barbara Merino, Henry T. Treuba and Fabián A. Samaniego, eds., *Language and Culture in Learning: Teaching Spanish to Native Speakers of Spanish* (Falmer Press, 1993): 58–74. Reprinted with the permission of Falmer Press. Courtesy of Antoinette Sedillo López.

Perea, Juan F. "English-Only Rules and the Right to Speak One's Primary Language in the Workplace." *University of Michigan Journal of Law Reform* 23 (1990): 265–318. Reprinted with the permission of the University of Michigan Law School. Courtesy of Yale University Law Library.

Ortiz, Vilma. "Generational Status, Family Background, and Educational Attainment Among Hispanic Youth and Non-Hispanic White Youth." In Michael A. Olivas, ed., *Latino College Students* (Teachers College Press, 1986): 29–46. Reprinted with the permission of the publisher, Teachers College Press. All rights reserved. Courtesy of Teachers College Press.

Moran, Rachel F. "Bilingual Education as a Status Conflict." *California Law Review* 75 (1987): 321–62. Reprinted with the permission of the University of California Press. Courtesy of Teachers College Press.

Salinas, Guadalupe. "Mexican-Americans and the Desegregation of Schools in the Southwest." *Houston Law Review* 8 (1971):

929–51. Reprinted with the permission of the University of Houston Law Center. Courtesy of *Houston Law Review*.

San Miguel, Guadalupe, Jr. "Mexican American Organizations and the Changing Politics of School Desegregation in Texas, 1945 to 1980." *Social Science Quarterly* 63 (1982): 701–15. Reprinted from *Social Science Quarterly*, by permission of the authors and the University of Texas Press. Courtesy of Yale University Sterling Memorial Library.

Ortega, Joe C., and Peter D. Roos. "Chicanos in the Schools: An Overview of the Problems and the Legal Remedies." *Notre Dame Lawyer* 51 (1975): 79–90. Reprinted with the permission of the *Notre Dame Lawyer*. The publisher bears the responsibility for any errors which have occurred in reprinting or editing. Courtesy of the *Notre Dame Lawyer*.

Rangel, Jorge C., and Carlos M. Alcala. "Project Report: De Jure Segregation of Chicanos in Texas Schools." *Harvard Civil Rights-Civil Liberties Law Review* 7 (1972): 307–91. Permission granted. Copyright 1972 *Harvard Civil Rights-Civil Liberties Law Review,* and by the President and Fellows of Harvard College. Courtesy of Yale University Law Library.

Avila, Joaquin G. "Equal Educational Opportunities for Language Minority Children." *University of Colorado Law Review* 55 (1984): 559–69. Reprinted with the permission of Colorado Law Review, Inc. Courtesy of the *University of Colorado Law Review*.

Cortese, Anthony J. "Academic Achievement in Mexican Americans: Socio-Legal and Cultural Factors." *Latino Studies Journal* 3 (1992): 31–47. Reprinted with the permission of *Latino Studies Journal*. Courtesy of Antoinette Sedillo López.

Vasquez, Melba J.T. "Confronting Barriers to the Participation of Mexican American Women in Higher Education." *Hispanic Journal of Behavior Sciences* 4 (1982): 147–65. Reprinted with the permission of Sage Publications Inc. Courtesy of Sage Publications.

Olivas, Michael A . "Indian, Chicano, and Puerto Rican Colleges: Status and Issues." *Bilingual Review* 9 (1982): 36–58. Reprinted with the permission of the copyright holder, Bilingual Press/Editorial Bilingue, Arizona State University, Tempe, AZ. Courtesy of *Bilingual Review*.

Romero, Leo M., Richard Delgado and Cruz Reynoso. "The Legal Education of Chicano Students: A Study in Mutual Accommodation and Cultural Conflict." *New Mexico Law Review* 5 (1975): 177–231. Reprinted with the permission of the *New Mexico Law Review*. Courtesy of the *New Mexico Law Review*.